International Handbook of Juvenile Justice

International Handbook of Juvenile Justice

Edited by

SCOTT H. DECKER
Arizona State University
USA

and

NEREA MARTEACHE
California State University, San Bernardino
USA

Springer

Editors
Scott H. Decker
School of Criminology & Criminal Justice
Arizona State University
Phoenix, AZ, USA

Nerea Marteache
California State University
San Bernardino, CA, USA

ISBN 978-3-319-83206-7 ISBN 978-3-319-45090-2 (eBook)
DOI 10.1007/978-3-319-45090-2

Softcover reprint of the hardcover 2nd edition 2016

Printed on acid-free paper

This Springer imprint is published by Springer Nature
The registered company is Springer International Publishing AG
The registered company address is: Gewerbestrasse 11, 6330 Cham, Switzerland

Preface

In 2000 a group of European academics decided to form a European Society of Criminology. From the start, the new Society encouraged the creation of working groups on specialized topics. One of the first such working groups was focused on "juvenile justice," launched by Josine Junger-Tas. Josine also was the lead author of the first edition of this book. Tragically, she passed away on January 22, 2011. She was quite a prolific scholar and passionate advocate for the rights of children everywhere. The idea for this book emerged from the juvenile justice working group in the European Society of Criminology. The working group addressed a number of recent developments in juvenile justice in our own countries, developments that were leading toward an ever more punitive, but not necessarily more effective, system in juvenile justice.

The working group grew in membership over time, and Europeans were joined by a number of American and Canadian experts. This added a truly international dimension to our undertaking. The working group raised a number of key questions in its deliberations. In particular, members were interested in how the juvenile justice evolved and emerged in different states during the last 25 years. The similarities and differences across states became a key point of discussion. This discussion was fuelled in part by the emergence of new states in Eastern Europe, as well as the growing impact of globalization. For many of the older western democracies of Europe, the Welfare system that had existed for most of the twentieth century was evolving, often toward a model that placed more responsibility on individual juveniles and included increased punitiveness. The first volume, published in 2006, addressed these issues, largely in the context of European traditions. That volume was organized into four parts: The Anglo-Saxon Orientation, Western Continental Europe, Eastern Europe, and Two "Special" Systems. In all 19 different countries were represented in that volume. All of the countries whose juvenile justice systems were represented in the first volume were European or North American. The current volume (the second edition) takes a more global look at juvenile justice.

The current volume includes 25 chapters, 6 more than the first edition. In addition to covering juvenile justice systems in North America and Europe, systems from Asia, South America, Africa, and the Middle East are included. In this sense, the book is truly international and goes well beyond the countries covered in the first edition. While hardly all-inclusive, this approach is far more global and comprehensive. A book cannot be considered to be truly international if it ignores multiple continents (Africa, Asia, and South America) or the juvenile justice systems of the two most populous countries in the world (China and India). It is a credit to Dr. Junger-Tas that the book has found its way to a second edition and now truly merits the designation as an "International" Handbook.

Perhaps future editions will expand the number of countries. One virtue of this more comprehensive set of nations is that the book provides a foundation for truly comparative work. We hope that it is instrumental in sparking comparisons of the key issue of juvenile justice.

The inclusion of a diverse set of countries allows for consideration of the role of several key issues in juvenile justice. Given the breadth of countries covered in the second edition, we thought it important to include a set of common issues to be covered. Each chapter is organized around ten key issues in the study and understanding of juvenile justice. These include:

1. The legal status of juveniles
2. Age of majority
3. The country's stance toward the UN Committee on the Rights of the Child
4. Trends in juvenile crime over the period 2004–2014
5. Causes of juvenile crime
6. Policing and juveniles
7. Courts and juveniles
8. Custodial rules for juveniles (detention, prison, mixing juveniles with adults)
9. Alternative sanctions for juveniles: home confinement, restorative justice, restitution, etc.
10. Differences in treatment of boys and girls

This common frame makes comparisons across countries more straightforward.

Readers will notice the addition of Dr. Nerea Marteache as a co-editor. Her contributions have been of high quality and were essential to the timeliness and quality of the edited volume. As was the case with the first edition, we were very fortunate in finding a great number of outstanding experts in the field prepared to write a chapter on trends in juvenile justice in their own country. We are grateful to each of them for their contributions to this work. They were patient with our requests to address a common set of issues as well as our cajoling them for their chapters and revisions. Assembling a group of international scholars to produce a volume in a language that is not their native tongue poses many challenges.

Special mention should also be addressed to those of our English-speaking colleagues who helped us with language issues. Dr. John Shjarback and Natasha Khade provided excellent assistant in this regard. John recently earned a Ph.D. in criminology and criminal justice at Arizona State University and Natasha is a first year doctoral student. They provided considerable help in proofreading and editing chapters. Considering the large number of authors for whom English is not their first language, this was by no means a light task and we owe them many thanks!

Finally, we hope that this book, which has collected information on juvenile justice systems in so many nations, will find its way to an international public of academics, policy makers, and practitioners and may open the eyes of many to different solutions for similar problems.

Phoenix, AZ
San Bernardino, CA

Scott H. Decker
Nerea Marteache

Contents

PART IV EUROPE: EASTERN EUROPE, WESTERN EUROPE, SCANDINAVIA

PART V MIDDLE EAST

Contributors

Peter Aebersold Institute for Criminal Law and Criminology, University of Bern, Switzerland

Nicholas Bala Faculty of Law, Queen's University, Kingston, ON, Canada

Tim Bateman Department of Applied Social Studies, University of Bedfordshire, Luton, UK

María José Bernuz Beneitez University of Zaragoza, Zaragoza, Spain

Karin Bruckmüller Johannes Kepler University Linz, Linz, Austria
Ludwig-Maximilians-University Munich, München, Germany

Michele Burman University of Glasgow, Glasgow, UK

Can Çalıcı Division of Social Sciences, Istanbul University Institute of Forensic Sciences, Istanbul, Turkey

Liqun Cao University of Ontario Institute of Technology, Oshawa, ON, Canada

Peter J. Carrington University of Waterloo, Waterloo, ON, Canada

Jenneke Christiaens Faculty of Law & Criminology, Research Group Crime & Society/Youth Justice Studies, Vrije Universiteit Brussel/Free University Brussels, Brussels, Belgium

Jae Joon Chung Shandong University School of Law, Shandong, People's Republic of China

Els Dumortier Faculty of Law & Criminology, Research Group Crime & Society/ Youth Justice Studies, Vrije Universiteit Brussel, Brussels, Belgium

Frieder Dünkel Rechts-und Staatswissenschaftliche Fakultät, Department of Criminology, Ernst-Moritz-Arndt-Universität Greifswald, Greifswald, Germany

Katja Filipčič Faculty of Law, University of Ljubljana, and Institute of Criminology at the Faculty of Law University of Ljubljana, Ljubljana, Slovenia

Raquel Bartolomé Gutiérrez University of Castilla-La Mancha, Albacete, Spain

Wolfgang Heinz Rechts-und Staatswissenschaftliche Fakultät, Department of Criminology, Ernst-Moritz-Arndt-Universität Greifswald, Greifswald, Germany

Sesha Kethineni Department of Justice Studies, Prairie View A&M University, Prairie View, TX, USA

Susan McVie, OBE, FRSE University of Edinburgh, Edinburgh, UK

Henrietta Joy Abena Nyarko Mensa-Bonsu University of Ghana School of Law, Legon, Accra, Ghana

Esther Fernández Molina University of Castilla-La Mancha, Albacete, Spain

An Nuytiens Faculty of Law & Criminology, Research Group Crime & Society/ Youth Justice Studies, Vrije Universiteit Brussel, Brussels, Belgium

Godfrey O. Odongo Wellspring Advisors, New York, NY, USA

Valéria Cristina de Oliveira Center for Metropolitan Studies (CEM), University of São Paulo, São Paulo, Brazil

Mojca M. Plesničar Institute of Criminology at the Faculty of Law University of Ljubljana, Ljubljana, Slovenia

Ineke Pruin Institute for Criminal Law and Criminology, University of Bern, Switzerland

Mutaz M. Qafisheh College of Law and Political Science, Hebron University, Hebron, Palestine

Rafael Lacerda Silveira Rocha Center for the Study of Criminality and Public Safety (CRISP), Federal University of Minas Gerais, Belo Horizonte, Brazil

Corinne Davis Rodrigues Federal University of Minas Gerais, Belo Horizonte, Brazil

Jerzy Sarnecki Stockholm University, Stockholm, Sweden

Gävle University, Gävle, Sweden

Mairead Seymour School of Languages, Law and Social Sciences, Dublin Institute of Technology, Dublin, Ireland

Barbara Stańdo-Kawecka Jagiellonian University in Kraków, Kraków, Poland

Anette Storgaard Department of Law, Business and Social Sciences, University of Aarhus, Aarhus, Denmark

Melanie Taylor Department of Criminal Justice, University of Nevada, Reno, Reno, NV, USA

Carlos J. Vilalta Division of Public Administration, Center for Economic Research and Education (CIDE), Mexico City, Mexico

Jonas Weber Institute for Criminal Law and Criminology, University of Bern, Switzerland

Flavian Zeija High Court of Uganda, Kampala, Uganda

Ruohui Zhao University of Macau, Taipa, Macau

Neylan Ziyalar Division of Social Sciences, Istanbul University Institute of Forensic Sciences, Istanbul, Turkey

PART I

Africa

1

Ghana

Henrietta Joy Abena Nyarko Mensa-Bonsu

THE LEGAL STATUS OF JUVENILES

The justice system for minors who come into conflict with the criminal law[1] has seen tremendous change in normative terms over the last decade and a half. The normative changes that have occurred both locally and internationally over the last two decades have provided the impetus to redesign the system of protection and justice for minors in Ghana. In 1990, Ghana (as the first country to do so) signed and ratified the United Nations Convention on the Rights of the Child (CRC) and also participated in the making of the Organization of African Unity Charter on the Rights and Duties of the African Child. Both of these instruments contain provisions on juvenile justice that required specific kinds of action by state-parties to achieve compliance.[2] Next, and more important still, came the adoption of a liberal democratic national constitution in January 1993, which meant that standards of decent treatment within the criminal justice system set down under the fair trial provisions in Article 19 of the Constitution of Ghana 1992 had to be taken account of in the system.[3]

The normative changes have translated into substantial shifts in philosophy affecting the treatment of children under the laws of Ghana.[4] Legislation on

[1]In 1993–2003, 10,488 juveniles, i.e., children up to the age of 18 years, were processed through the criminal justice system.

[2]ICRC article 40 provides that every child accused of having infringed the penal law should enjoy the usual guarantees of rights for persons accused of crime.

[3]H.J.A.N. Mensa-Bonsu "Human Rights and The Juvenile Justice System—The Ghanaian Experience" 7 *ASICL Proc.* (Proceedings of the Annual Conference of African Society of International and Comparative Law) 1995, p347

[4]Government of Ghana/UNICEF Study, p26. Although there may have been other factors, such as police collusion with juveniles to inflate their ages, the fact remains that an unduly high number of juveniles went to adult prisons when the juvenile courts disappeared as an entity. They have since been restored.

H.J.A.N. Mensa-Bonsu (✉)
University of Ghana School of Law, P.O.Box LG 70, Accra, Ghana
e-mail: hjanmensa-bonsu@ug.edu.gh; profrit@yahoo.co.uk

S.H. Decker, N. Marteache (eds.), *International Handbook of Juvenile Justice*,
DOI 10.1007/978-3-319-45090-2_1

children in general changed entirely, beginning with the amendment of provisions in the Criminal Code 1960 (Act 29) (now Criminal Offences Act, 1960)[5] and continuing with the enactment of the Children's Act, 1998 (Act 560) and the Juvenile Justice Act, 2003 (Act 653), the law of the child. These two pieces of legislation achieved the separation of the regime for children whose circumstances put them in physical and moral danger, thereby coming to the attention of the law, from children in need of care to those engaging in conduct that would otherwise have been criminal. The new legislation also removed the system of juvenile justice from the statute governing criminal procedure, which it had previously been a part of, thereby affirming the difference in treatment of children in conflict with the law, from that of adult lawbreakers.

The downside to all these changes and new approaches is that the heavy financial outlay that all welfare-based systems require for efficiency is making the stated commitments to improve the system lag behind the reality of improvements in the field, on account of Ghana's financial constraints. The gap between stated intentions and reality, notwithstanding the new system, marks an improvement upon the old one, and with time the new mindset has gradually permeated the operations and will continue to shape the future of the sector and its institutions.

Brief History of the Old Juvenile Justice System[6]

The philosophy that underlay the insistence that the penal system ought to lay its emphasis on the reform and rehabilitation of juveniles in conflict with the law, rather than on punishment for their offenses, begun to gain ground in the mid-nineteenth century in the United States of America and then Europe. By the close of that century, some effort had begun to implement the new ideas.[7] The new philosophy was premised upon the fact that children lacked capacity to make appropriate moral choices. Therefore, they needed to be taken in hand and redirected when they lacked such direction on account of their life's circumstances or when they had engaged in a conduct that would have been punishable as a crime if done by an adult. Thus, the most important goal of the system was

[5]This change in name was occasioned by the recommendations of a Statute Law Revision Project which was established to rationalize the law on the statute books of Ghana following the adoption of a new national constitution.

[6]The history seems to be reflective of the models in all the commonwealth countries. See H.J.A.N. Mensa-Bonsu, *Ghana's Juvenile Justice System … Making Progress with Painful Steps and Slow*, Ghana Academy of Arts and Sciences, Accra, 2005; Allison Morris and Loraine Gelsthorpe, "Towards Good Practice in Juvenile Justice Policy in the Commonwealth 32 *Commwealth. Law Bulletin* 27 2006; Hakeem Ijaiya, "Juvenile Justice Administration In Nigeria" 2 NUJS L. Rev. 573 2009; HEINONLINE, accessed on 28 August 2015.

[7]The first juvenile court was reputed to have been established in Cook County, Chicago, Illinois, in 1899. See Caldwell Robert G, "The Juvenile Court: Its Development and Some Major Problems." in *Juvenile Delinquency*, Rose Giallombardo (ed.) p393, John Wiley and Sons, U.S.A., 1976; Thomas F. Geraghty "The Children & Family Justice Center's 20th Anniversary: Splendid Accomplishments and a Wonderful Future" 6 Nw. J. L. & Soc. Pol'y (2011) 402 at p404.

to help give the child in question a fresh start in life, not only by protecting the child from further contamination but also avoiding the stigmatization of the child. The only problem with the system was that children in moral danger (i.e., children at risk of getting into conflict with the law owing to lack of parental guidance or exposure to risky lifestyles) were treated in the same form and manner as children who had engaged in criminal conduct. The use of "delinquent" to describe both groups of children, i.e., the "erring" and the "errant," obscured the difference in their circumstances, though it shielded the errant juveniles from the tag of "criminal," and thus gave them a second chance.

Consistent with the philosophy and goals of the system, the juvenile offender had to be separated from the adult offender and subjected to a different penal regime. While the lawbreaking adult was a threat to society and needed to be taught a lesson through the infliction of suffering, the child had to be reoriented and redirected onto the "straight and narrow path," the focus being the "long-term welfare of the child."[8] This dichotomy in penal philosophy, in turn, demanded specially designed institutions, such as a special court and also special custodial institutions[9] that made it possible for the state, as the ultimate parent, to exercise guardianship over children and young persons and, with the child's best interests in mind, to attempt to achieve their reform and rehabilitation.[10]

In 1908, a provision was made for the establishment of juvenile courts in England under the Children's Act of 1908, and the idea was transplanted into the rest of the common law world via colonial policy. During early 1940s, recruitment into the British war effort in World War II fueled migration to the urban areas and created momentum in the rate of urbanization that produced the usual casualties of rapid social development—neglected children. As people abandoned their traditional homes and family support for life in urban areas, children in need of care grew in such numbers that the establishment of institutions of juvenile justice[11] to deal with the problem became necessary. This historical development created an overhang of emphasis on custody and custodial institutions within the juvenile justice system in Ghana today.[12]

Following the normative shifts and the corresponding statutory changes effected as a consequence, a number of changes occurred to affect the operations of the juvenile justice system. From the age of criminal responsibility, right down

[8]Nicholas Bala and Rebecca Jaremko Bromwich, "Introduction: An International Perspective on Youth Justice" in *Juvenile Justice Systems An International Comparison of Problems and Solutions* Nicholas M.C. Bala, Joseph P. Hornick, Howard N Snyder (eds.) Thompson Educational Publishing Inc, Toronto, p6

[9]Vedder CB: "*Juvenile Offenders*" Charles Thomas, Springfield Illinois, 1963, p146, supra

[10]Caldwell Robert, op. cit. supra, pp399–400

[11]By the middle of 1940s, specific provision had been made for them in the Courts Ordinance of the Gold Coast Colony (now Ghana). See the Courts Ordinance 1935 as amended by Ordinance No.23 of 1944 and No.26 of 1946. Sections 61–73 of Cap. 4.

[12]Robert Kwame Ame, "The Rights of Children in Conflict with the Law in Ghana," (2011) 19 *International Journal of Children's Rights* 27–293 HEINONLINE, accessed on 28 August 2015

to the mechanisms for disposition, through the alteration of a fixed term of detention of a 3-year term, in favor of a variable and graduated term of detention, a lot has changed within the system.

THE AGE OF CRIMINAL RESPONSIBILITY

One of the major changes effected by an amendment of the Criminal Offences Act, 1960,[13] was to fix a new age of criminal responsibility.[14] In the past, the age of criminal responsibility was fixed at 7 years, but between 7 years and under 12, liability was based on a test of maturity. This discriminated between children based upon the level of their maturity and appreciation of right from wrong at the time they engaged in the wrongful conduct, rather than on what they had done. Such an approach to fixing criminal responsibility was criticized by both scholars and practitioners as it appeared to differentiate between children, not on the basis of what they had done but on the basis of how fast they had attained maturity and a sense of right and wrong.[15] In prescribing 12 years as the minimum age of criminal responsibility in place of the old common law standard of 7 years, the objection to the discrimination between children was addressed, and the minimum age also saw a rise to the higher age of 12 years. In that same amendment in Act 554, the age of sexual consent was also raised to 16 years from 14 years. Further, and in consonance with the prescriptions of the CRC, the Children's Act, 1998 (Act 560) raised the upper limit of childhood from 17 years under the existing law[16] to 18 years. These changes had implications for the criminal justice system because it took from the criminal justice system all those children above 7 and under 12 years who had got into the system and changed the age range of those who could be sent to the junior industrial schools as a means of disposition from the juvenile court.

A RIGHTS-BASED JUVENILE JUSTICE SYSTEM

Under the old juvenile justice system, the language of rights was excluded in favor of the application of welfare principles for children in conflict with the law. The enjoyment of rights by persons accused of crime was given a constitutional basis in the 1992 Constitution,[17] and this necessitated the adoption of a more rights-based approach to the handling of juveniles in conflict with the law.

---

[13] This was by the enactment of the Criminal Code (Amendment) Act 1998, Act 554.

[14] Criminal Offences Act, 1960 (Act 29), Section 26

[15] H.J.A.N. Mensa-Bonsu, "The Young Offender and the Criminal Justice System," (1990–92) vol. XVIII University of Ghana Law Journal, 49–71 at 50–51

[16] Criminal Procedure Code, 1960, Act 30

[17] 1992 Constitution, article 19

Between 1998 and 2003, Ghana made great strides with respect to the law of the child by first amending the existing law on the age of criminal responsibility and the age of consent and then a Children's Act, 1998 (Act 560),[18] with its regulations,[19] and a Juvenile Justice Act, 2003 (Act 653) to replace the provisions in the Criminal Procedure Code 1960 (Act 30) (now Criminal and Other Offences (Procedure) Act of Ghana) (Act 30). These pieces of legislation, in particular the Children's Act, were largely based on commitments assumed under the International Convention on the Rights of the Child, and the Organisation of African Unity's (OAU), now the African Union (AU), Charter on the Rights and Duties of the African Child changed the fundamental assumptions underlying the legal system's approach to issues concerning children. Beginning with setting the age of childhood as 0–18 years, it set a national legal framework for promoting the enjoyment of rights by the child, as well as introducing new philosophies and institutions for dealing with problems relating to the child.[20]

The creation of separate legal regimes for the treatment of children in need of care and who come to the notice of the law, from that for those who come into conflict with the law and thus the proper subjects of the juvenile justice regime, marked a philosophical break from old ideas that conceptualized the neglected or abused child as one leaning toward criminality that justified the intervention of the state. Thus distancing children of unfortunate social circumstances from those who had actually committed infractions of the law removed the tag of "delinquency" (which was only a euphemism for "criminality") on children deemed to be in moral danger on account of their own chosen lifestyles or lifestyles imposed upon them by the extreme poverty or even depravity of their parents. It also separated issues of child welfare, from child reform and rehabilitation issues, and achieved a separation of the "unguided" from the "misguided." In addition to altering the philosophy underlying the system of management of children at risk or in moral danger, the Act also made a bold attempt to introduce methods that would enable a child in conflict with the law avoid having to be processed through the main system, by introducing a number of diversionary mechanisms calculated to prevent or delay the juvenile's entry into the formal justice system by providing a forum for victim-offender mediation.

On its part, the Juvenile Justice Act, 2003 (Act 653), provided a statutory basis for separating the treatment of breaches of criminal law by children, from the adult regime governing crimes. Specifically, it altered the juvenile justice system by making the welfare of the juvenile the primary concern of the system rather than the interest of society in punishing criminal conduct[21] and prescribed that in all decisions affecting a juvenile, the best interests of the juvenile should be the

[18] Children's Act, 1998 (Act 560)

[19] Child Rights Regulations 2002, Legislative Instrument 1705

[20] Esmeranda Manful and Patrick McCrystal, "Ghana's Children's Act 560: A Rethink of its Implementation?" 19 *International Journal of. Children's Rights,* 151 (2011)

[21] Except in special circumstances as under section 17

guiding principle and paramount consideration.[22] It set the scene by defining "juvenile" as a child under the age of 18 years in conflict with the law and thus raised the age of "juvenile" from under 17 years as prescribed under the old regime,[23] to under 18 years. [24] It also incorporated the provisions of the international human rights instruments to which Ghana was a state-party, as well as constitutional requirements as prescribed under the fair trial provisions of Article 14 of the 1992 Constitution. These human rights provisions moved the system from an interest-based welfare system to a rights-based one, as in the adult system.

TRENDS IN JUVENILE CRIME 2004–2014

Official statistics on juvenile justice in Ghana are not properly kept, and so even after access had been granted to the author of this chapter, there was not very much available that was current or complete. 2013 seems to be the last year when complete statistics could be made available. The official figures available from the Senior Correctional Centre seem too modest in comparison with anecdotal evidence of child criminality. The Senior Correctional Centre opened in the year 2012 with 74 inmates. In the course of the year 2012 and 2013, 48 and 45, respectively, were admitted as inmates. These were made up as follows:

Age	*2012*	*2013*
12–15	13	15
16–18	35	30

The offenses mainly involved dishonesty, such as stealing. Of the 74 offenses that were included in the statistics, 12 were sex offenders. It is assumed that those admitted in 2012 and 2013 had the same kind of offense profile.

CAUSES OF CHILD CRIMINALITY IN GHANA

The history of the juvenile justice system dictates that there is a relationship between social upheavals, such as rapid urbanization or social catastrophes such as mass unemployment, and juvenile criminality.[25] As history shows, increased child neglect and child criminality were downsides to rapid urbanization, which gave reason for setting up a full-fledged juvenile justice system in the Gold Coast.

[22] Section 2

[23] Act 30, Section 314 now repealed by Act 653

[24] Act 560, Section 1 (1)

[25] Christopher Slobogin & Mark R Fondacaro, "Juvenile Justice: The Fourth Option" 95 *Iowa Law Review* 1, (2009–2010) pp17–21; HEINONLINE, accessed on 28 August 2015

Migration to urban areas breaks the link between an individual and the extended family which, in ordinary times, is a social safety net for the individual.[26] Such weakened links create a gap in the life of an individual, adult, or child who faces adversity. It is thus not a surprise that child neglect and juvenile delinquency are positively correlated with urbanization, for when there are events such as parental divorce, the children may become vulnerable to homelessness and may eventually get into crime.[27] Again, on account of Ghanaian cultural systems which are either matrilineal or patrilineal and based on unilineal descent, only one side of the family is interested enough in the children of a union to take them in upon the demise of a breadwinner. For instance, where a woman from a patrilineal system has a child with a man from a matrilineal system, the resulting progeny have no "real" extended family that would show interest in them, and if the deceased parents did not have siblings willing and able to take them in, upon the demise of the parents or the absence of the breadwinner, life on the street would become an attractive option. Another source of homeless children is procreation outside socially recognized formal unions by young people, usually unemployed and unprepared for such childcare responsibility. Poor parenting skills characterized by a deliberate withholding of love and affection to children, or an overanxiety to display love and affection resulting in overindulgence, have sometimes been cited as the cause of juvenile delinquency. In addition, inappropriate or inadequate moral guidance often exacerbated by distorted images of morality portrayed in the media have resulted in poor child socialization leading to the child seeking acceptance from equally misguided peers or other undesirable adults. In like manner, parents who never say no to their children deny them the opportunity of learning to manage disappointment stemming from thwarted desires and disable them from coping when they step into a world that will not create new standards to accommodate a child who has never learned to manage the frustration of having wishes unmet. Consequently, inability to postpone gratification soon leads to antisocial habits and delinquency.

These factors of vulnerability such as child neglect have increased with time, as was found in a study on vulnerable children in Ghana. The study[28] relied on the 2008 Ghana Demographic and Health Survey (GDHS), which highlighted inadequate protection from parents as a major concern. Identifying lack of parenting due to the absence of one or both parents as a factor of vulnerability,

---

[26]Max Assimeng, *The Social Structure of Ghana, A Study in Change and Persistence*, Ghana Publishing Corporation, Tema, 1999; Chapter III on kinship in Ghana

[27]Stephen Adongo, Alois Kyaakpier,Gianna Da Re, Brother Jos Vandinther, Vida Asomaning Amoako, Irene Engmann, *Census on Street Children in the Greater Accra Region, Ghana*, Dept of Social Welfare, Ricerca e Cooperazione, Catholic Action for Street Children & Street Girls' Aid, Accra, 2011; 61,492 street children were identified and interviewed. Under causes of Streetism migration and parental divorce are listed as prominent causes. See, p33.

[28]Ellen B.D. Aryeetey, Stephen Afranie, Paul Andoh, Daniel, Thomas Antwi-Boasiakoh, Edward Amponsah- Nketia & Mavis Dako-Gyeke, *Telling the Untold Story. A Study of the Situation of Orphans and Vulnerable Children in Ghana*, UNICEF, Accra, 2011, pp18–19

GDHS figures, national trends were somewhat alarming: only 54% of children lived with both parents. The rest of the 46% was made up as follows: 19% with the mother only, 5% with the father only, and as many as 14% who lived with neither parent.[29] Such occurrences leave the child vulnerable and unprotected, and she or he may seek refuge in a life of criminality when the parent is unable or unavailable to provide the requisite guidance and protection.

Inadequate parenting or the absence of parents or other responsible adults in the life of a child has socioeconomic and psychosocial consequences for the child as well. From the lack of positive role models, through lack of educational opportunities to streetism,[30] vulnerable children suffer all kinds of deprivations on account of this. The lack of educational opportunities/termination of schooling, absence of recreational facilities, inadequate programs for out-of-school youth, and absence of skills training by way of vocational training and apprenticeships are all culprits in juvenile criminality.[31] In a 2009 study on Ghanaian children and social protection jointly sponsored by UNICEF and the Ministry of Employment and Social Welfare,[32] it was found that 42.4% of children engaged in child labor were not in school[33], and since child labor itself has been identified as a source of delinquency, not being in school increases a child's vulnerability to delinquency. In the Senior Correctional Centre in Accra, juveniles detained there by juvenile courts in 2012 and 2013 had similar educational profiles. In the 2012 group, 23 had ended their education in primary school, 21 had completed junior high school, 2 had senior high school education, and 2 had none at all. In 2013, 22 had ended their education in primary school, 16 had completed junior high school, 1 had senior high school education, and 6 had none at all. Thus in 2012, of the 48 inmates admitted, 46 had less than the years required for a school leaving certificate, and in the 2013 group of 45, 44 had fewer years of education or even none, than the legal minimum number of years required. These are interesting figures that depict the kind of juveniles in the system and also indicate that criminality appears to fall off with higher attainment in the educational system.

Sexual offending also appears to have a relationship with the absence of positive role models and exposure to inappropriate media images of morality. As some authors observe, "The primacy of the family, both extended and nuclear as an agent of sexual socialization is well documented in Ghana."[34] That primacy

---

[29] Ibid., at pp18–19. These figures appeared to have been supported by another study that put the number of children living with both parents at 60%; 21% with the mother only% 4 with the father only and 15% living with neither.

[30] *Census on Street Children in the Greater Accra Region, Ghana,* supra, p33

[31] *Telling the Untold Story*, supra, p35

[32] Social Protection and Children. Opportunities and Challenges in Ghana, UNICEF/Ministry of Employment and Social Welfare, July 2009

[33] Ibid., p35.

[34] Adobea Yaa Owusu, John Kwasi Anarfi & Eric Yeboah Tengkorang, "The Socio-Cultural Contexts of Sexual Socialization and Sexual Behavior of Young people Within the Family Setting in Ghana," *Ghana Social Science Journal*, (2013) vol 10 Numbers 1&2, pp156–182 at p170

means then that those children who find themselves outside a family unit lose more than economic resources and psychological well-being but also appropriate socialization. Of the 117 inmates of the Senior Correctional Centre in 2013, 14 were on charges on sexual assault. It is well known that sex offending is a recidivist crime, and therefore sex offenders require special handling as a predisposition to sex with violence is not cured easily and certainly not by endless preaching. In a well-researched article, Earl F. Martin and Marsha Kline Pruett demonstrate the scientific basis for appreciating the special requirements of sex offenders and recommend that juvenile sex offenders must be given appropriate treatment early in their lives or they may wreak havoc later.[35] This is a recommendation that Ghana's legal system should take to heart and take active steps to secure the services of professionals to upgrade the avenues for psychosocial counseling of all categories of offenders. This number is significant enough to cause any system to pay attention. Further, some of the inmates have special needs which would further benefit from such changes.

The absence of social counseling, especially counseling for troubled families so as to rescue children of such families before they have cause to break up the home, impacts negatively upon the social fabric, as also does the absence of psychosocial counseling for bereaved or orphaned children. Estimating "orphanhood" as 18.2% in Ghana, the study identified children who suffer the trauma of losing one or both of their parents at an early age and that often receive no counseling as being at an increased risk of delinquency. Culturally, the needs of children are perceived to be only physical, and so upon bereavement, cultural practices focus upon therapy for the bereaved spouse and none for the child. Thus, the grieving child is left on his or her own to try and deal with the loss and move on. However, some children are unable to come to terms with their loss and deal with the trauma, leaving them seeking attention and affection through deviance. The study also re-echoes the call for psychosocial counseling to address feelings of loss and reduce the vulnerability of orphans to antisocial habits.

POLICING AND JUVENILES

Act 653 prescribes the procedures to be followed when a juvenile is arrested, through to when disposition is made and a detention order is executed. Under the Act, the police must inform a parent, a guardian, or a close relative of a juvenile as soon as an arrest has been made. Failing such persons, the police must inform the probation officer responsible for the district, to enable the relatives of the juvenile to be traced. In addition to the right to have persons responsible for the juvenile's welfare to be informed, the juvenile also has a right to access legal advice.[36] A new provision on

[35] "The Juvenile Sex Offender and the Juvenile Justice System" 35 Am. Crim. L. Rev. 279 1997–1998, at p332

[36] Section 11 (1), (2), and (3)

interviewing of juveniles by the police has been introduced so as to offer a juvenile parental protection right from the beginning of his or her contact with the police. The quality of the protection afforded the juvenile, however, is almost completely undermined by a subsequent provision to the effect that when the police consider that it is not in the best interest of the juvenile to have a parent, guardian, lawyer, or close relative of the juvenile present, they should arrange, instead, for a probation officer to be present at the interview.[37] This power to determine the "best interests of the juvenile" by a police officer who has effected an arrest in the course of a busy workday should be watched carefully as it is open to abuse. It is obvious why there would be no incentive for an arresting police officer not to make such a determination when his or her own work could be frustrated by such determination. Perhaps the law should require such determination to be made with the involvement of a social worker in order to reduce anxiety that the power might be abused on the grounds of expediency and the personal convenience of the police. Apart from the fact that this provision does not indicate when this power may be exercised, thus taking away with the left hand what has been given with the right, it also does not seem to appreciate the fact that probation officers are part of the system and, in terms of protecting the interest of the juvenile, are second best in comparison with a lawyer, parent, or guardian. Why give the juvenile the right to access legal advice if, at the critical time when statements are to be taken, the legal advisor may be prevented from ensuring that the advice has an impact on the process?[38]

Where no diversionary measure is contemplated by the police, they may grant bail on the juvenile's own recognizances or those of a parent, guardian, close relative, or other responsible persons where the offense is not a serious one.[39] The snag is where the offense is a serious one, for the law provides in section 14 (2) that where the juvenile is not released on recognizance, the police should seek an order from a juvenile court to place the juvenile in a remand home or any place of safety and that the order shall be made by the juvenile court within 48 h after the arrest of the juvenile. In the past, the juvenile court sat once a week or once in a fortnight, and therefore the temptation to put the juvenile before the district court instead was great.[40] However, since 2008, a juvenile division has been created in the district court in Accra, putting to rest previous objections to delays due to the existing setup of juvenile courts and that sometimes produced collusion between the police and the juvenile to inflate the age in order to escape the "troublesome" rules of the juvenile justice system.[41]

---

[37] Section 13 (3)

[38] See H.J.A.N. Mensa-Bonsu, "The Young Offender and the Criminal Justice System" (1990) vol. XVIII *University of Ghana Law Journal*, pp49–71

[39] Section 14 (1)

[40] An application for bail may be made to a district court in the absence of a juvenile court. See Section 17 (2).

[41] Where a court is unsure as to age, it may seek medical assistance to do so under section 19; however, this may happen only if the child looks too young to be eighteen years and above. Therefore where the suspicions of the court are not aroused in any way, there would be no challenge.

THE JUVENILE COURT

At the heart of the system of juvenile justice is the juvenile court whose form and nature are shaped by the underlying principles of the welfare approach and individualized justice. Unlike the adult system where emphasis is placed on the nature of the offense committed, the juvenile variety emphasizes the nature of the person who committed the offense, and so decision-making in the juvenile court is guided by what is considered best for the juvenile's future development and not what the society's best interests would demand. The system has its own distinct terminology: its court holds "hearings" not "trials," "makes findings of guilt" not "conviction," and "makes disposition orders" not "passes sentence"; its custodial orders are "detention orders" not "imprisonment"; and juveniles in custody are "inmates" not "prisoners." In order to make the basic principles operational, the juvenile court has continued to be given exclusive jurisdiction over all offenses—except very serious ones—involving juveniles. The juvenile court is presided over by a panel chaired by a lawyer or magistrate, with a social worker and a representative of the community as its members. There has always been a requirement that one of these persons must be a woman in order to ensure that both a female and male perspective would be brought to bear upon the proceedings. Its hearings are private, proceedings of the hearings are not allowed to be reported in the news media, and those who appear before it are protected from being identified.

Ensuring that the juvenile is not corrupted by adult criminals has dictated that such juveniles be sent to remand homes upon arrest or upon the juvenile court determining that the child is required to be kept in safe custody during the pendency of a hearing. A lot of emphasis is put on the social background of the child in order to ascertain whether the requisite amount of care and supervision would be available to the child. Where the residential environment of the juvenile is identified as constituting a source of moral danger, e.g., when parents themselves are of doubtful moral character or peer influence is a factor in the child's delinquency, then the child might be placed in a custodial facility. This was essentially the system put in place in 1960 and practiced for the next 40 years until reforms influenced by national and international commitments were initiated.

Hearings

The essence of the juvenile court sitting in private, in separate premises, or on days different from those of the district court and exclusion of the public is to preserve the privacy of the hearing. In addition to the list of persons permitted to be present, the informality of the proceedings is affirmed by the introduction of a new provision prohibiting the wearing of police uniforms by police officers on duty in a juvenile court. A hearing is not expected to last longer than 3 months in an ordinary case or 6 months if it involves murder. A failure to hear and dispose of the case within the statutory period may result in the juvenile being unconditionally discharged. The exclusive jurisdiction of the juvenile court over juveniles in most matters is maintained, but as has always been the case, there are important exceptions.

A juvenile is entitled, ordinarily, to be granted bail unless there is a danger of the juvenile not appearing to answer the charge, or the possibility of committing further offenses or has the potential for interfering in, or hampering the investigations by the police. Such interference may take the form of threatening witnesses or tampering with the evidence. The conditions for bail are, however, not strenuous and may even be on the juvenile's own recognizance. Where bail is not granted, the juvenile may be remanded into the care of a parent, relative, or other fit persons or, as a last resort, to a remand home. Even when remanded into the care of a relative or parent, the juvenile is deemed to be in custody and can be apprehended without a warrant if he or she attempts to escape. The Act, in fact, incorporates the directions on the grant of bail to juveniles handed down by the high court, e.g., in the old case of *Osei* v. *Republic*,[42] where a juvenile court was held to have acted unlawfully, in remanding the juvenile to custody when the final penalty could not have been higher than a fine, and when there were responsible adults ready and willing to take her into their care. Under the current legislation, it would be impossible to commit a juvenile to custody for a minor offense such as the appellant had committed.

The Social Inquiry Report (SER)

The administrative practice has now been put on a statutory footing.[43] The Act requires that in every case, a social inquiry report (SER) be prepared for each juvenile, in a manner that observes the rules of natural justice, to assist the court to know the background of the juvenile and to determine what factors have influenced the juvenile's behavior.[44] This standard of compliance with the rules of natural justice in the preparation of SER[45] was originally set down in judicial guidelines handed down by the high court in *Donkor* v. *The Republic*.[46] In that case, a parent who was incensed by the imposition of a fine upon him by a juvenile court challenged the findings. The fine was imposed as a consequence of the findings presented in a SER that blamed him for laxity in his supervision of his son. The court held that the parent was right to complain because he did not have

[42] [1971] G.L.R.34

[43] Section 24

[44] D.E.J. MacNamara, in *Juvenile Offenders* (supra) foreword, page X; Francis Allan, "The Juvenile Court and the limits of Juvenile Justice" in *Juvenile Delinquency* op. cit. (supra), p414. This was a quotation adapted from Judge Mack's article: "The Juvenile Court" 23 Harvard Law Review (1909).

[45] Act 653, Section 24

[46] [1977] GLR 373, per Osei-Hwere J (as he then was)

had an opportunity to challenge the findings of the social worker and he had no way of knowing and commenting on whatever evidence had been found against him. The guidelines given by the court have now been incorporated into the Act.

Trial by Court of Summary Jurisdiction

There are a few circumstances in which a juvenile would be tried in a court that is not a juvenile court. A district court or circuit court may have jurisdiction over a juvenile under one of three conditions: (1) there is no juvenile court constituted in the area[47]; (2) the juvenile is charged with an adult for an offense[48]; and (3) the juvenile has committed an offense which would have been punishable by death if committed by an adult.[49] Where a juvenile is tried by a non-juvenile court and convicted, the child has to be remitted to a juvenile court for a disposition to be made, and the juvenile court may proceed as if the child had been tried by that juvenile court.[50] The procedure is the same even for an offense such as murder, which is otherwise punishable by death. Ghana's law has changed dramatically with respect to capital crimes and other serious offenses; therefore, no child can be sentenced to death, however heinous the crime.

Cleaning Up the Record

Another of the major innovations made by the Act is the introduction of a right by a juvenile offender, probation officer, or close relative of a juvenile to apply to the juvenile court before which the original proceedings were taken, for the record of conviction and order imposed on a juvenile to be expunged.[51] This means that the records are now to be kept and thus operates as part of a new regime not to destroy such records. This does not appear to be in tune with the philosophy of the system to permit the juvenile to make a clean start; it merely discriminates between those who deserve such assistance to have a clean record and those whose subsequent lifestyle would bring them into conflict with the law again. In the past, the failure to keep the records sometimes created the situation where a hardened youngster finding his way into the adult prison system after a stint at the Correctional Centre would be treated as a first-time offender and be subjected to considerations during sentencing that might be completely unsuitable for that person's state of depravity.[52] This is particularly of important now that various terms may be imposed instead of the old fixed term of a 3-year detention. Records of those involved in serious and violent crimes that would other-

[47] Act 653, Section 17(2)
[48] Act 653, Section 17(3)
[49] Act 653, Section 17(4)
[50] Act 653, Section 18
[51] Section 37(1)
[52] Vedder, supra, p31

wise have been punished as first-degree and even capital crimes must now be kept so that if they come in contact with the system again, they could be dealt with appropriately.[53] Secondly, the old practice made it impossible for the effectiveness of the system to be assessed. With no attempt to create procedures for follow-up of its past inmates, the system is disabled from engaging in effective self-criticism.

CUSTODIAL RULES FOR JUVENILES

Detention in Police Cells

Juveniles are frequently kept in police cells when there is no other facility available.[54] This goes against the 1992 Constitution which prohibits the locking up of juveniles in the same cells as adults.[55] This is understandably because police stations tend to be inadequately housed,[56] making it difficult for the police establishment to designate a part of the police station for such juveniles to avoid detaining them with adults[57] and to keep male and female juveniles apart.[58]

The juvenile is also not permitted to associate with anyone who is not a relative, lawyer, or public officer while in police custody or while being transported to a remand home.[59] However, in the absence of nourishment supplied by the state, this is a major headache for juveniles in police cells and for the officers in the particular police station. Given the absence of their families, they have to survive on the kindness of the adult cellmates or that of individual police officers even though juveniles have the right to adequate food while in police cells. It is in the face of such reality that it might even be seen as an act of kindness to permit anyone who wishes to visit such juvenile to do so, notwithstanding the well-known fact that often it is only fellow gang members who care to visit their arrested colleague and see him through the days in detention. Merely adopting new rules that recognize the right to adequate food and medical treatment during

[53] Section 37(3)

[54] *A Report on the State of Juvenile Justice Administration in Ghana 1993–2003*. A Government of Ghana/UNICEF Study, 2005, established that 10,488 juveniles were kept in police cells within the decade 1993–2003.

[55] Article 15 (4)

[56] The Commission on Human Rights and Administrative Justice (CHRAJ) was established under the 1992 Constitution of Ghana to act as ombudsman and also to exercise jurisdiction in matters involving the violation of human rights of the individual. Since its establishment, the CHRAJ has been conducting annual checks on police cells with a view to improving the lot of suspects in police custody. Despite this effort, most police cells are still in a deplorable state, and their conditions are almost primitive.

[57] Section 15 (1)

[58] Section 15 (5)

[59] Section 15 (3)

detention in police cells,[60] without providing logistic support to operationalize the rule, is not going to change the *status quo*.

The female juveniles sometimes have it better or worse depending upon the availability of a parent or other fit persons to take charge of them. Where there are no such persons, the practice was, and still seems to be, to keep such female juveniles "behind the counter" till they are put before court. Police stations in Ghana have a wooden table-like barrier behind which the police officer stands to receive complaints from the public. The "counter" separates the general reception area to which the public has access, from the other parts of the room where the public has no access. Although the parts of the room where access is restricted are in full public view, no one except police personnel has access to anyone kept there. A person "behind the counter" is essentially in custody, though not yet placed in police cells at the station, as the person cannot leave at will. It is also the place where suspects are initially kept until a determination of whether they should be allowed bail or detained in cells is made. Once the juvenile females are put before court, they might be ordered to be transported to the nearest remand home. However, since this might not be done immediately as transportation is a major problem for the police in Ghana, the stint behind the counter would continue, as few police stations have more than one set of cells.

A related issue is the absence of a sufficient number of remand homes in the country. Currently the remand homes are in the regional capitals only, with the Upper East Region not having one. Further, not all regions that still have the structures have them in functioning order, and therefore for most juveniles, this provision might never be applicable to them. It is admitted that the recognition of this reality has resulted in a new provision that empowers the Department of Social Welfare and district assemblies to designate particular premises as places of safety where juveniles may be kept on remand. It is further admitted that this power to designate has been granted to enable the police to comply with the law. However, since neither the Department of Social Welfare nor any district assembly has designated any such places of safety in their localities, the police have been disabled from complying with the law. The police authorities must take up the issue with the two institutions concerned in order to deflect criticism of abuse of rights of juveniles from themselves, to those whose inaction makes them the real culprits.

Another thorny issue is the problem of who is responsible for the upkeep of juveniles confined there. It is unclear whether it is supposed to be the Department of Social Welfare or the district assembly. It appears that since the district assemblies are expected to take overall responsibility for the welfare of children in the district and to budget for the same, this must include juvenile offenders. However, at the present time, it does not appear as if the district assemblies are able to shoulder that burden, given their own straitened circumstances.

---

[60] Section 15 (6)

Custodial Orders

In the past, justice was individualized as juvenile courts focused on the needs of the particular juvenile rather than on the nature of the offense committed. Under the current law, the only individualized requirement is that the child be above 12 years but under 18 years of age. Beyond this, the court has to concentrate on the offense committed. Where the offense is one for which a sentence of 1-month imprisonment without the option of a fine would ordinarily have been imposed, then a detention order may be made.[61] This change represents a shift in the old paradigm of focusing on the offender to a new one of focusing on the offense as the criminal justice system requires.

The apparent abandonment of individualized justice of juvenile justice philosophy, in favor of the general penal philosophy of the criminal justice system, is a change that is bound to alter the very shape and achievements of the system in the near future. It is conceded that this change may have been motivated by certain realities in the field, but it is uncertain whether it represents progress or otherwise. It is a well-known fact that it was largely on account of the differences in custodial time limits imposed for offenses in the district courts as opposed to what was obtained in the juvenile courts that usually motivated juveniles to inflate or collude with the police to inflate their ages so they could be tried as adults. Once tried as adults, they would receive sentences of imprisonment that had to be served in adult prisons, and it was only then that they would realize that life in an adult prison was not for children, thus creating difficulties for the system and giving it adverse publicity. Fortunately, the Act gives power to the minister to transfer juveniles and young persons in adult prisons to Senior Correctional Centres,[62] so that if such problems occur, they could be dealt with speedily.

Following from the change in philosophy, a new scale of detention orders, graduated according to the age of the juvenile, has been introduced, thus making "detention order" merely a term of imprisonment by a polite name, particularly when the special terminology of "disposition" seems to have been replaced by "sentence" under the Act. The maximum time for a detention order is:

(a) Three months for a juvenile offender under the age of 16 years
(b) Six months for a juvenile offender of or above 16 years but under 18 years
(c) Twenty-four months for a young offender of or above the age of 18 years
(d) Three years for a serious offense[63]

The shortness of the detention orders, however, means that the system has abandoned all pretense of rehabilitation by offering skills training, as no skill can be acquired in less than 6 months, even with intensive training.

---

[61] Section 43 (1)

[62] Section 49

[63] Section 46 (1)

Juveniles and Prison

A major change in custodial sentencing is the prohibition that no juvenile should be sentenced to imprisonment by a juvenile court or court of summary jurisdiction. The old law fixed the minimum age at which a child could be sent to prison as 15 years,[64] but now imprisonment of a juvenile for any offense whatsoever, even murder and rape, is prohibited. The Act also prohibits death sentence being pronounced or recorded against a juvenile offender. However, the alternative methods of disposition provided under the Act appear to be inadequate, for very serious crimes of violence.

The Correctional Centres

1. Renaming of custodial institutions

   The custodial institutions formerly known as the Industrial Schools and Borstal Institute have been renamed Junior and Senior Correctional Centres under the authority of the Department of Social Welfare (now under the Ministry of Gender and Social Protection) and the Ministry for the Interior, respectively.[65]
2. The state of the Correctional Centres:

   (a) The Senior Correctional Centre

   There is only one Senior Correctional Centre and it is for boys only. Established as the Borstal Institute in 1947 in response to the demands created by the establishment of juvenile courts, its stated mission was "…to save the young and careless from a wasted life of crime."[66]

   At the time of its establishment as the Borstal Institute, it operated under the welfare services branch of the government. However, it was transferred to the Prisons Department in 1949 and has been run by the Prisons Service ever since, as a "prison" for juveniles. The prison officers who run the institute do not have special training for this kind of assignment. It is by normal administrative schedules that officers are posted to that establishment. There is little difference in the manner of handling the juveniles committed to the institution, and the officers are given no special in-service training for the supervision of the inmates at the Correctional Centre. It is unlikely that persons trained to handle prisoners in a certain manner can be expected to forget their training as and when they are transferred from a prison to the Correctional Centre, when there is no requirement of specialization in the handling of juveniles for one to qualify to serve at that center.

---

[64] Section 314 Act 30 repealed by Act 653

[65] Sections 39 and 41

[66] This is the inscription on a monument erected at the main entrance to the Senior Correctional Centre.

The center itself has very pleasant surroundings, with dormitory blocks named after famous religious and other personalities, as is the culture of secondary boarding schools in the country. The campus is kept very clean with neat lawns and gardens carefully tended by the boys, and whitewashed stone borders are kept scrupulously white. The presence of armed and uniformed prison personnel is itself not remarkable as the institution has merged with the living quarters of the prison officers and the training school of the Prisons Service. The place thus has an outward appearance of peace and calm, but like the proverbial "whitewashed tomb," the outward appearance gives nothing but the most misleading picture of the internal conditions. There is severe regimentation—almost military-like. With a lot of emphasis on group discipline, there seems to be very little space for the individual attention that these juveniles obviously need. This regimentation is born of outdated penal philosophies of the twentieth century that discipline can be achieved by regimentation. If the nickname "secondary school" among prisoners (because it feeds the pool of inmates of adult prisons also known as "universities" in those circles) is to be abandoned, then more efforts at appropriate rehabilitation must be made to break the link between Senior Correctional Centre and prison. The approach to corrections at the Senior Correctional Centre must be reviewed to accord with modern notions of penology now that it has adopted a modern name and shed its old one.

There is no Senior Correctional Centre for girls, and so however serious the case of a female juvenile, she is kept at a Junior Correctional Centre for girls. This certainly creates a danger of contamination of younger girls as they may be influenced by the older girls. On the side of the older girls, they may be resentful, leading to a rejection of all the reformatory efforts put at their disposal. The nonsecure surroundings also ensure a high degree of escapes from the institution such that a girl who may have committed murder could be out again in a few months

(b) The rehabilitation programs

The vocational programs in all the Correctional Centres have serious problems that threaten the very basis of the program, yet these programs are important not just for their rehabilitation but also their reintegration into normal society. The causes of these problems are many and varied; some are due to the general depressed economic conditions in the country, others due to the lack of enthusiasm on the part of the inmates, and still others due to the noncooperative attitudes of their parents. These problems must be addressed with some innovative ideas as it is unlikely that Ghana's economy would improve dramatically any time soon. For instance, a commendable innovation is the opening up of the vocational programs at the Junior Correctional Centre (formerly Senior Industrial School) at Osu so that the training offered to the inmates could be extended to the girls in the community. This is a positive development and would need time to make its impact felt, but it is hoped that it would achieve its stated aims, particularly if they were encouraged to attain certification from the relevant trade certification authorities.

(c) Security issues

At the Correctional Centres, security arrangements are completely inadequate for the custodial institutions that they are meant to be. Although there is every effort made to keep the children secure in the institution, not very much exists by way of formal security arrangements, particularly at the institutions run by the Department of Social Welfare. Many of those buildings are so dilapidated that it takes very little effort for the inmates to abscond. The institution, often lacking facilities to photograph each inmate at the time of admission as required by law, finds itself handicapped to provide an adequate physical description of the fugitive to the general public. The problem is compounded by the absence of good residential addresses, etc., and so a juvenile who escapes from detention is able to return to his or her former lifestyle with minimum official interference. The situation at the Senior Correctional Centre is only slightly better, even though the Prisons Service has its own security arrangements. Security definitely is a problem that needs to be addressed, especially now that all juveniles, even those of violent propensity, are to be sent there, rather than to prison[67]; the question, however, is how much of it may be provided without prejudicing the nature of that institution?[68]

NONCUSTODIAL MEASURES

Probation

A juvenile court has the power to make a probation order, should it be in the best interest of the juvenile, based on the recommendations of the SER.[69] Such an order would put the juvenile under the supervision of a social worker for the duration of the order which could normally cover any period between 6 months and 18 months,[70] unless the juvenile is still subject to a fit person order after the expiration of the probation period. A probation order may be with or without conditions.[71]

---

[67] Sometime in September 2015, a case was reported in the newspapers of an inmate who followed a prison officer who was going off duty and with whom he had had a disagreement out of the center and stabbed him.

[68] Escapes are common since the residential facilities of the officers have literally encroached on the center's premises, making it easy for an inmate to escape without detection. In 2004, as many as 27 boys escaped from custody.

[69] Section 31 (1) and (2)

[70] Section 31 (5)

[71] Section 31 (3) and (4)

The constant references to "probation officer" in the Act, as well as plans to introduce noncustodial alternatives to adults, indicate the growing importance of the probation system to the new reforms. The Probation Service is currently in use for juveniles only, but its inadequate numbers give cause for concern. A 2009 study indicated that there were only 127 probation officers nationwide.[72] Though very few, they perform important functions such as tracing families of newly arrested juveniles; paying visits to the homes of juveniles, schools, and other locations where information about a juvenile may be collected in order to prepare a social enquiry report; and then following up to ensure that the juvenile gets taken to and from the juvenile court during the hearing as well as post-committal duties. These duties require a large body of trained staff, as they have to criss-cross their districts, ensuring that juveniles under their care receive the necessary attention.

The absence of professional counselors within the Probation Service is also very evident. Since it is widely known that most inmates tend to be from homes broken either by divorce, separation, desertion, or death, it is by no means complimentary of the system that not much effort is made to address the circumstances that have operated to create delinquency in each inmate.[73] There is an undue emphasis on Christian "counseling" (though more in the nature of Christian teaching) in the institution which is somewhat unhealthy. For instance, of the practitioners of the three major religions that are active in Ghana, the representation among the inmates is as follows:

Religion	*2012*	*2013*
Christian	28	30
Muslim	11	7
Traditional Religion	9	8

This means that although the Christian group predominates, at least 20 of the 48 admitted in 2012 and 15 of the 45 admitted in 2013 would not find that form of counseling more as acts of proselytizing rather than counseling that is intended to serve the ends of reform and rehabilitation. There is clearly no reason to over-emphasize Christian religious teaching, which, admittedly, did fill a void in times past, when the Christian groups were the only ones who made visits to prisons and provided material assistance to inmates. This history has therefore become a part of the culture in Ghana's custodial institutions, but it need not go on, now that everyone has a constitutional right to practice their own religion. Fortunately, there are now opportunities for recruiting professional counselors, and this must be actively pursued to fill a much needed gap in the effort to reshape the lives of inmates.

[72] *Children in Ghana*, Ministry of Women and Children's Affairs/UNICEF, 2009, p136

[73] Chute, L.C., "Objectives of the Juvenile Courts" in *Juvenile Offenders*, Charles Thomas, Springfield, Illinois, 1963, p191

Fit Person Order

A fit person order is an order committing a child with a troubled background to the care of a respectable adult who is deemed fit for that responsibility until the child attains 18 years of age. A fit person order is usually made where there was evidence that the parent or guardian has lost control over such juvenile, the parent or guardian consents to the making of such an order, and there is a relative or other person willing to assume the responsibility of taking care of such juvenile. The juvenile also has to give a reciprocal undertaking to remain with the fit person, while an accompanying probation order ensures that a probation officer would be available to keep an eye on the juvenile. This very important institution has not been appreciated for its value in not only providing the juvenile with a chance to live a happy life but also in the provision of alternate role models and alternate lifestyles to the juvenile. Consequently it has not seen the level of support that would guarantee its continued survival, leading to its virtual collapse as fewer and fewer people have been willing to assume the role of fit persons. It must be appreciated that the state must take the blame for this state of affairs even though the system is one that, of necessity, depends upon the availability of volunteers. It is the state that can do what is required to maintain the interest, or even assure the recruitment, of fresh volunteers, and it must do so now, by resuming its responsibility for the provision of financial support and assistance required by persons volunteering to take custody of troubled children, as well as establishing proper mechanisms for the enforcement of maintenance orders against the parents of such children. As a matter of urgency, the minister must exercise the power granted by the Act for the making of regulations that cover such issues.[74]

Apart from probation and fit person orders, the system includes other diversionary measures.

Diversionary Measures

Principal among these diversionary measures are child panels, police cautions, and restitution through community service:

(a) Child panels

A new system of child panels was introduced under the Children's Act in 1998. These panels were to be formed at the community level under the authority of the district assembly.[75] The essence of this eight member committees was to ensure that it would mediate between victims and child offenders within the community and also promote reconciliation between victims and child perpetrators of minor offenses.[76] This body was also empowered to

[74] Section 38 (5)

[75] Act 560, Section 29

[76] Act 560, Section 28. The minor offenses are defined under section 62 of LI 1705 as "petty theft, petty assault or on a threatening offense."

administer a verbal caution to a juvenile to the effect that future repetition of the offense would result in proper proceedings within the system. The panel also had the power to make a community guidance order and, to this end, may appoint a person of good standing in the community to supervise the juvenile for 6 months, subject to the consent of the parties.[77] This initiative is well intended and enlightened in its approach to providing extra protection from contamination by invocation of the criminal proceeding machinery for minor infractions. However, nearly two decades on, few firm steps have been taken to actualize the legislative intent: first, it took nearly 4 years to enact regulations to actualize the provisions of the Act; second, the legislative instrument is unavailable to the general public, except by diligent research; third the financial burden of sustaining the system has been placed on the normally impecunious district assemblies. Little wonder that only three such panels were ever reputed to have been set up in three districts, but even those were so short-lived that they did not do any work before their demise. Therefore, the much-lauded new system of child panels remains nonfunctional, and the responsibilities confided to them have not been taken up.

There are many reasons why the system never took off. First were the inherent structural defects legislated into the Act, and that created a bottleneck that proved insurmountable. For instance, although it was provided that there could be as many child panels as possible in a district, to enable communities to deal with their own problems, there could, in reality, not be more than one panel, as only two officials in the district, and based in the district capital, could act in the capacity of chairman and secretary, respectively. This unnecessary structure also ensured that the child panels could not be really community based but had to be based at the district capital if transportation difficulties were not to become a stumbling block to the officials servicing the various panels. In addition, provision of administrative personnel to service the panels has been imposed on the district assembly.[78] The inescapable consequence of officials having to go on circuit to the various communities undermined the main attraction of such a system—its ability to give immediate attention to a problem that has occurred. Allied to the membership was the statutory requirement that it meet once in 3 months. This “quarterly meeting” requirement meant that the system’s usefulness as a quick, community-based mediation mechanism could not function as such, as no one would sit around waiting for 3 months to have a child panel mediate in a matter when the police station, which is a tried and tested avenue for dealing with offenders, is open for business 24 h a day.

Again, designed in operational terms as the means by which the district assembly, as the representative of the state, would assume full responsibility

[77] Act 560, Section 32

[78] LI 1705 supra, Section 9 (2). This legislative instrument is intended to actualize the Children’s Act, 1998, Act 560.

for the children in the district, no special provision was made by the central government to empower local government system financially to make the discharge of the responsibility possible. Consequently, the district assemblies, already overwhelmed by their many other responsibilities, have failed to take ownership of the system and expend the resources needed to operationalize its many aspects. Perhaps the legislature did not envisage that the system would cost money to operate, or else it believed that in a spirit of voluntarism, members of the community would take on such duties gratis. The fact that the legislature believed that the district assemblies would fund this initiative that was not even their own is even surprising, considering the fact that it is common knowledge that district assemblies cannot even pay their own staff salaries and members of the legislature are also members of these district assemblies in which their constituencies are located. Again, to the knowledge of members of the legislature, district assemblies have been unable to provide financial support to school management committees within their districts, introduced as part of educational reforms in the early 1990s, to enable them function properly, yet they put on them the burden to support child panels and to designate and maintain places of safety for juveniles in their localities. Little wonder that no district assembly has implemented the concept of community child panels as a primary diversionary measure since the idea was introduced into the juvenile justice system.

(b) Cautions

The Juvenile Justice Act has also introduced a new diversionary measure in the form of cautions at the level of the police. Again this measure is intended to save children accused of nonserious offenses from being processed through the formal criminal justice system. This measure is in the form of informal and formal cautions. An informal caution may be administered verbally and in private by any police officer at a police station, but a formal caution may be administered only by a senior police officer on the recommendation of a probation officer, public prosecutor, or magistrate.[79] There does not seem to be any record of any such cautions ever having been administered, so even if used, the informal and verbal variety may have been the preferred mechanism.

(c) Restitution through service

A further attempt to divert the juvenile from the main justice system is incorporated into the proceedings of the juvenile court if the offense is not a very serious one. Such measures may be imposed upon the recommendations of a probation officer in the social inquiry report, to permit the juvenile to make good any damage that the conduct may have caused. This thus operates as a mechanism for restorative justice and is intended to make the juvenile appreciate the cost of his or her behavior to the victim and to the community at large, by being made to "pay" for what has been lost to the community. The

[79] Section 12 (1)

Act does not specify what such measures might be except that any such measure should not include work that is intended to degrade or dehumanize the juvenile but must be designed to help the juvenile learn the importance of respecting societal rules.[80] In short, the decision to teach the juvenile a lesson should not be motivated by a desire to punish the juvenile with humiliating work but to make the occasion a positive learning experience for such juvenile while ensuring that the community would also derive some benefit.

There are, however, pertinent issues raised by this very enlightened diversionary program as no framework for the institutionalization of this policy has been developed. There is no evidence that any program has been developed so far, whether anyone has ever participated in any of them, and whether any evaluation has been done to ascertain both the utility and cost-effectiveness of any such programs.

Orders Against Parents

When a juvenile court assumes jurisdiction over a juvenile, it inevitably assumes jurisdiction over the conduct of the parents of the juvenile as their parenting skills come under scrutiny. A juvenile court is empowered to refrain from making findings of guilt against a juvenile, even after the charge is proved, but "may instead make an order against the parent, guardian or close relative for the payment of damages or costs or require the person to give security for good behavior."[81] The opportunity for conviction may arise on one of two fronts: when such parent, guardian, or close relative who has been asked to attend court but has failed to do so and when evidence suggests that the parent or guardian has been negligent in the exercise of supervision over the juvenile as what happened in *Donkor* v. *The Republic*.[82] The real importance of this order is that when the child's delinquency has been traced to the lack of effective parental supervision, the parent is shown to be a bad parent. Such failure to live up to proper parental standards becomes punishable conduct, for which the state requires a fine to be paid. There is an issue of fairness here when a parent who has not been given any opportunity to acquire proper parenting skills gets fined for failing to meet standards for which he or she has not been prepared or supported to acquire. Is good parenting a necessary skill with which one is naturally endowed upon becoming a parent? This provision is tantamount to criminalizing bad parenting and punishing a person for not having measured up to a parenting standard for which no help has been provided.

---

[80] Section 26 (1)

[81] Section 28 (2)

[82] Section 30 (1)

DIFFERENCES IN TREATMENT OF BOYS AND GIRLS

In the main, the differences between the treatment of boys and girls as already stated, the product of the nonavailability of remand homes in every locality, and the absence of a Senior Correctional Centre for girls have resulted in:

1. Detention behind the police counter for girls while boys in similar circumstances would be kept in cells with adults
2. The absence of a Senior Correctional Centre leading to inadequate custodial arrangements for girls and custodial supervision done by welfare officers
3. Detention of boys in Senior Correctional Centre under the supervision of prison officers—thus leading to harsher treatment of boys than of girls

CONCLUSION

The system of juvenile justice has been subjected to scrutiny here. To this end, some effort has been made to look at the workings of the system from the moment the processes of the juvenile justice system were activated right until the final disposition is made. The institutions have been looked at, with a view to discovering how much their operations conform to the statutory regime. In particular, the diversionary measures such as cautions and child panels must be used more. District assemblies must be made to assume responsibility for the welfare of the children in the communities and provide funding for the child panels to operate properly. They must also be tasked to designate and maintain places of safety for juveniles in their localities to prevent juveniles having to spend time in police cells with adult criminals, some of whom subject them to sexual abuse in return for protection from the other remanded. To achieve proper results, there should be more interaction among the three Ministries of the Interior, Gender and Social Protection, and Local Government to ensure better enforcement of statutory prescriptions.

Urbanization produces many dysfunctional families, and the absence of avenues for counseling in a period of rapid urbanization is a situation that must not continue. The state must step in and provide the necessary facilities for counseling to the general populace, many of whom have lost their traditional means of support as a result of their migration to urban centers. The religious bodies must strengthen their counseling and other social support programs to assist distressed persons belonging to their community. However, counseling must not be left to them as not all the inmates subscribe to particular religions or even denominations of the same religion.

Trauma counseling for bereaved children should be included in these programs as the churches and other religious institutions are best placed to know which family within their community has suffered bereavement. They must also take up issues of child-rearing norms and parenting as poor parenting eventually has an impact on the integrity of the household. Bereaved children should not be tossed from relative to relative and moved from place to place, since dealing with the loss of a parent, as well as having to adjust to social circumstances that keep changing from relative to relative, can have deleterious effects on their mental health and push them toward seeking solace in the wrong kind of friends, experimentation with substance abuse, or other antisocial habits.

It is generally acknowledged that it is cheaper to build schools than prisons. Therefore, preventive measures that keep children out of the juvenile justice system should also receive attention. Healthy recreational opportunities and avenues for decent entertainment must be provided to occupy the leisure hours of the youth and help them burn off energy. School curricula should be made more interesting and fulfilling so that children stay in school as long as they are required to do so. Religious bodies, which remain the most important operatives of civil society, should strengthen their youth programs so as to give meaning to the lives of young people. Above all, the state must acknowledge that welfare institutions and programs are expensive to support, but in terms of eventual cost on human lives and social dislocation, such investments are cheaper in the long run. Such acknowledgment would enable it to provide better funding for welfare programs and institutions. Institutions such as the Probation Service and fit person programs must be properly supported as they help to stave off future problems with maladjusted youth. The system needs to be supported and equipped to rescue the young from themselves or their social circumstances.

Acknowledgments I am indebted to my research assistant Cletus Alengah for the many hours of research he has invested in this project.

Henrietta J.A.N. Mensa-Bonsu Professor Henrietta Joy Abena Nyarko Mensa-Bonsu LL.B (Ghana) LL.M (Yale) Barrister-at-Law is a Professor of Law, at the School of Law, University of Ghana. She is currently the Director of the Legon Center for International Affairs and Diplomacy at the University of Ghana and a Fellow of the Ghana Academy of Arts and Sciences.

2

Kenya

Godfrey O. Odongo

INTRODUCTION

The history of juvenile justice systems in Africa is more recent compared to other contexts such as Europe and the USA. The development of juvenile justice systems in Africa was shaped by a colonial legacy under which the legal framework in most of the countries mirrored laws received from the colonizing country—Britain in the case of Kenya and most of Anglophone sub-Saharan Africa. This meant that a law received from the British, the Children and Young Persons Act of 1969, was the legal framework for dealing with issues affecting children, including juvenile crime, for over four decades after Kenya's independence in 1963. It was only in 2001 that Parliament enacted a new law—the Children's Act. The new law and subsequent constitutional reform processes motivated the inclusion of a comprehensive children's rights clause in Kenya's Constitution in 2010. Child law reform was impacted by normative legal standards regarding children's rights (e.g., UN Convention on the Rights of the Child ("the CRC")) and the African Charter on the Rights and Welfare of the Child (African Children's Charter), which Kenya has ratified.

This chapter discusses the extent to which children's rights norms have shaped the legal framework governing the Kenyan juvenile justice system across an array of issues such as age and the legal status of children, pretrial diversion, the requirement for separate courts, institutions and procedures specific to children accused of committing crimes, and sentencing practice that could be distinguished from the regular criminal justice system. The author argues that following a trajectory that mirrored competing ideals of welfarist, just deserts, and other philosophies that underpinned Western juvenile justice systems, Kenya is

G.O. Odongo (✉)
Wellspring Advisors, New York, USA
e-mail: godongo22@yahoo.com; godongo@wellspringadvisors.com

S.H. Decker, N. Marteache (eds.), *International Handbook of Juvenile Justice*,
DOI 10.1007/978-3-319-45090-2_2

an example of a country whose ongoing quest for a full-fledged juvenile justice system is impacted by children's rights norms contained in international treaties to which Kenya is legally bound.

THE HISTORICAL CONTEXT OF KENYA'S JUVENILE JUSTICE

From the 1960s until the 1990s, most African juvenile justice systems mirrored the juvenile justice philosophies that informed the legal systems of their colonizing countries (Alemika and Chukwuma 2001). Juvenile justice systems in most of Africa in the period before the CRC in 1990 reflected debates about the influence of "welfarist," "back to justice/just deserts," or "crime control" theories. Thus, examples from Kenya (South Consulting 1999), Nigeria (Owasanoye and Wernham 2004), Uganda (Parry Williams 1993), and Zimbabwe (Kaseke 1998) (all former British colonies) reveal that colonially inherited juvenile justice laws tended to mirror the philosophy of their British counterpart with a strong emphasis on welfarist-oriented provisions. Welfarist-oriented juvenile justice laws were not the norm in all African countries. In the context of countries such as Namibia, juvenile justice law encompassed the major features of what may be described as a "justice model" informed by a theory of "just deserts" (Schulz and Hamutenya 2004).

For Kenya and other former British colonies, the legal architecture that anchored juvenile justice remained "welfarist" on paper despite changes in British juvenile justice, including the end of the dual child care and crime jurisdiction of the family proceedings court and the ushering in of a just deserts approach allied with crime control through the Crime and Disorder Act adopted at the end of the twentieth century. For Kenya, the perceived benign and "rehabilitative" notions of the juvenile justice system mirrored what was recorded in the 1940s in the US context or earlier in the UK. One study discusses:

> ... [T]he Kenyan conceptualization of the criminal justice process for children is generally a benign one, focusing on 'rehabilitation' and 'education' rather than on punishment. This is seen in the fact that even the current law [Children and Young Persons Act, 1969] does not use the terms 'conviction' and 'sentence'. Imprisonment is rarely used and children do not get criminal records. These features indicate a leaning toward welfarism in the criminal justice system for children. The danger in this is that in reality the system may be far less benign than it seems on paper. Children are not sent to prisons but alternatives to imprisonment may also be damaging.... (South Consulting 1999)

The fact that the earlier laws applying in countries such as Kenya were enacted before the recognition of children's rights under international law meant that children's rights ideology was not part of the juvenile justice theoretical debate in Africa before the CRC was adopted in 1989. Since the CRC's adoption, the concept of children's rights has developed to usher in a significant prism in which children are viewed to have "rights" of their own. This counters the concept of "welfarism" in which children could be viewed or treated as objects of intervention. Under the CRC the concept of children's rights impacts all issues concerning children including juvenile justice (Van Bueren 1995). The convention's provisions in Article 37 and Article 40 specifically speak to the subject of juvenile justice. In the African context the influence of children's rights is furthered through the African Children's Charter, whose provisions on juvenile justice (under Article 17) applies to all persons under the age of 18. It is a subject of debate whether the CRC, the African Children's Charter, and other related international instruments can be viewed as providing a new philosophical frame for juvenile justice with an emphasis on children's rights (beyond welfarism or justice theories).

With an entirely novel emphasis on children's autonomy, these normative frameworks provide, at the very least, a standard within which to examine whether children's rights have had an impact on juvenile justice systems across countries around the world that are parties to these treaties and legally bound to implement their provisions (Doek 2002). Six features can be discerned from the CRC which usher in a new normative standard for juvenile justice (Sloth Nielsen 2001):

(a) The establishment of separate laws, institutions, and procedures applicable to children accused or alleged of committing crimes
(b) The setting of a minimum age of criminal capacity
(c) The principle of detention as a last resort and for the shortest period of time
(d) The desirability of diversion as a binding obligation on State Parties to the CRC
(e) The extent to which procedural guarantees under the CRC and related international instruments, such as the UN Beijing Rules on the Administration of Juvenile Justice, are accommodated in a juvenile justice framework
(f) The limitation of certain sentences and need for alternative dispositions at the sentencing stage

Article 40 (1) of the CRC also refers to reintegration as the primary objective of the juvenile justice system and the need for the child to assume a constructive role in the society. These have been said to hint at a more restorative justice approach (Skelton 1996). Thus, State Parties should consider the need for community-based approaches to crime that offer opportunities for the juvenile justice system to communicate denunciation of wrongdoing while establishing in a young offender a sense of empathy with the victim and connectedness to the family and community.

LEGAL STATUS OF CHILDREN AND ISSUES OF AGE OF MAJORITY AND MINORITY

Article 260 of the Kenyan Constitution and section 2 of the Children's Act, drawing from the CRC's and the African Children's Charter's definitions of children, provide that a "child" is any person under the age of 18 years. This definition is an advancement in Kenyan law. Although the law is now explicitly clear in the definition of children, there are still issues about conceptions of childhood including societal and cultural frames (e.g., marriage) to defining who a child is. In the juvenile justice sphere, however, there is no doubt as to the age of majority under Kenyan law in light of the definition in the constitution and the Act that envisages that any persons below the age of 18 should, when accused of crimes, be subjected to separate child-specific procedures and processes. The CRC and the African Children's Charter do not explicitly specify an age below which children are deemed not to have capacity to commit crime or be deemed to bear responsibility for criminal conduct (i.e., a minimum age of criminal capacity or responsibility). The UN Committee on the Rights of the Child, the body charged with monitoring implementation of the CRC, has recommended that State Parties should, at the very minimum, set this age at 12. The Kenyan Children's Act leaves this question to an old legal order—the general penal code—in which the minimum age of criminal capacity is set at 8 years. Children between the ages of 8 and 12 years are legally presumed to lack criminal capacity unless the prosecution provides evidence to prove (or rebut) this presumption. However, the code appears to enact a minimum age of capacity of 12 years for boys in the case of sexual offenses. The UN Committee has twice been unequivocal that these provisions fail to meet the CRC standards. It has urged Kenya to increase the minimum age of criminal responsibility from 8 to "at least the age of 12 years, and consider increasing it" (UN Committee on the Rights of the Child 2007).

A review of the Law Reform Commission's report that led to the enactment of the Children's Act reveals that the commission did not consider the issue of minimum age as a distinct stand-alone legal obligation subject under the CRC. While expressing support for the retention of the current minimum age of 8 years (with a presumption against capacity for children between the ages of 8 and 12 years), the commission appeared to downplay the need to increase the minimum age. Rather, the commission sought to emphasize the need for distinct (exclusive) juvenile courts and procedures for children in direct response to the issue of a low age of criminal responsibility (Kenya Law Reform Commission 1993). With the benefit of hindsight, this position appears contrarian to that of the UN Committee. In 2007, during an examination of the country's record by the UN Committee, the Kenyan government expressed a commitment that it would embark on a review of this issue. As of the time of writing, such a review remains pending. In the absence of detailed disaggregated statistics on children arrested and charged with crimes (including with reference to age), the extent to which very young children are caught up in the criminal justice system because of the low minimum age of criminal responsibility is not fully clear.

KENYA'S STANCE TOWARD THE UN COMMITTEE ON THE RIGHTS OF THE CHILD

Kenya ratified the CRC in July of 1990 and became a party to the African Children's Charter a decade later in July 2000. The UN Committee has stated:

> ... A comprehensive review of all domestic legislation and related administrative guidance to ensure full compliance with the Convention is an obligation...The review needs to consider the Convention not only article by article, but also holistically, recognizing the interdependence and indivisibility of human rights. The review needs to be continuous rather than one-off, reviewing proposed as well as existing legislation. (UN Committee on the Rights of the Child 2003)

In keeping with this obligation, soon after ratifying the CRC, Kenya embarked on a law reform process. The final product was the Children's Act. The law's child care protection and juvenile justice issues are captured in the preamble, which also explicitly speaks of Parliament's intention to domesticate children's rights provisions under international law. The child rights ideology were to subsequently impact discussions about the content of legal provisions in various iterations of draft constitutions, eventually leading to the inclusion of a comprehensive children's rights clause in Kenya's Constitution in 2010. Article 53 provides for the "rights of every child." Article 53(2) provides that "a child's best interests are of paramount importance in every matter concerning the child." In relation to juvenile justice, the Kenyan Constitution provides for the child's "right not to be detained, except as a matter of last resort, and when detained, to be held for the shortest appropriate period of time; separate from adults and in conditions that take into account the child's sex and age."

Kenya has thrice, in 2001, 2007 and 2016 had its progress reports examined by the UN Committee on the Rights of the Child as part of its reporting obligations under the CRC. In its 2007 observations, the Committee appreciated the enactment of legislation aimed at promoting and protecting children's rights, among other areas of positive practical and legal reforms. The Committee, however, pointed to a litany of gaps regarding juvenile justice where it noted that the system fell short of being fully in line with the CRC.

DEMOGRAPHIC, GENERAL, AND JUVENILE CRIME TRENDS IN KENYA

As of 2015, Kenya's population was estimated at 46 million people (United Nations et al. 2015). The country's population, as with most of Africa, is especially young. Kenya's population median age as of 2015 was 18.9 years (compared to a median age of over 40 years in some of the European countries, for example, France and Germany). The age group 0–14 years comprised 41.9% of the population. Persons aged 18 years and below constituted well over half of the population. The number of crimes reported by the public to the police was on the rise in the period 2010–2014 but stayed steady in 2013 and 2014 at an approximate 70,000 cases in each of the 2 years (Kenya National Bureau of Statistics 2015). Cases of homicide, 67.5% of which are murder cases, constituted a small percentage of the overall reported cases (3.8% in 2013, 4% in 2015), as with sexual and related offenses "against morality" (6.6% in 2013; 7% in 2014). A majority of reported cases were characterized as "other offenses against persons" including assault, affray (scuffle) (26.9% of such cases in 2013, 28.7% in 2014). Cases of stealing, theft (of property, livestock, property), robbery, and break-ins collectively comprised 38.6% of all reported cases in 2013 and 34.7% in 2014.

A total of 109,629 people were sentenced to prison in 2014—a 41.6% increase between 2010 and 2014. Prison inmates aged 26 years and above constituted about half of the total prison population. The number of inmates below 18 years was recorded at 2570 in 2013 and 3455 in 2014 (1.1% of the total prison population in 2013; 1.4% in 2014). The government has previously stated that the majority of children formally found guilty of crimes that would warrant a prison term (if committed by adults) are in the 16–17 year age bracket. This is borne out by the data in the 2014 government survey which indicates that compared to the low numbers of children aged 16 and below in prison, thousands of 16–17 year olds were convicted and given prison sentences in the years 2009–2014. The numbers for prison term for children hold despite the prohibition under the Children's Act of imprisonment as a punishment measure for children (as discussed later in this chapter). Even with the low numbers of very young children (aged 16 years and below) in prison, Kenya's overall prison inmate population is young. As of 2014, 52.3% of the total prison population was composed of youth aged 25 years and below.

Causes of Juvenile Crime (Pretty Short)

The situation in Kenya is characterized by high rates of poverty, unemployment, and an increasing number of family and kinship structures under severe socio-economic difficulties. Hence, poverty is a major factor accounting for the vulnerability of the Kenyan youth to commit crimes. In addition, there are questions of the effectiveness of Kenya's criminal justice system in achieving its broad goals of deterrence and the rehabilitation of offenders. A previous government survey has attributed a 76.9% general increase in the number of recidivist offenders between 2012 and 2013 to the fact of "inadequate facilities and rehabilitation programs in prisons, coupled with social stigma that ex-convicts experience from their communities upon release" (Kenya National Bureau of Statistics 2015: 252).

POLICING AND JUVENILES

Under the Kenyan Children's Act children arrested for committing crimes must be brought by the police before a children's court. The act also provides that in general and non-capital offences, before a plea is taken, and pending trial, children should be released on police bail or on the basis of recognizance of their parents and guardians. Further, statutory provisions appear to restrict the use of pretrial detention. The constitution's Article 53 (1) (f) prohibits detention for children, except as a last resort, to be restricted for the shortest period of time. It also provides that in the event of detention, children should be held separate from adults and in conditions that take the child's sex and age into account. However, in the absence of system-wide pretrial diversion programs and procedures, these provisions have remained more theoretical than reality.

There is no specialized police force dedicated to deal with juvenile crime in Kenya. Spurred in part by the child rights ethos of the Children's Act of 2001, the government established child-friendly child protection units staffed by dedicated and specially trained officers equipped with child-friendly holding facilities in a few police stations. However, because of inadequate public resources allocated for the police and the criminal justice system, these units are few and far between, thus limiting their impact. As of 2013 there were only 14 such units in police stations countrywide, constituting less than 10% of the total number of police stations. With limited child-specific dedicated facilities, the risk of mixing children with adults in pretrial detention is high.

A major issue in Kenya is that most children arrested are usually in need of care and protection; they are usually living on the streets (Ennew 1994). Previous studies have indicated that up to 80–85% of the children arrested and placed in pretrial detention in Kenya are children in need of care and protection rather than children accused or suspected of committing crimes (Odongo 2004). An overwhelming number of street children are usually arrested by the police for no reason other than that they are in "need of care and protection"—a term used in past and current Kenyan law dealing with child care and protection. This is exacerbated by the reality that until 1997 (when parliament repealed the Vagrancy Act which had criminalized "vagrancy" or homelessness), street children were deemed to be criminals merely by the fact of their status: that they were on the streets. Detailing the types of abuses and harassment of street children by Kenyan police, Human Rights Human Rights Watch (1997: 52–53) has previously observed that "street children are apprehended and beaten by police, held in lock ups usually with adult criminal offenders, and processed in regular courts."

The culture and attitude of law enforcement authorities in which street children are harshly treated and considered criminals has endured because of a number of factors, including the entrenched nature of this practice. In its consideration of Kenya's record in implementing the CRC in 2007, the UN Committee acknowledged the vulnerability of street children to arbitrary arrest and treatment and urged Kenya to "make sure that street children are not systematically treated as children in conflict with the law." It further called on Kenya to "identify and address the root causes of children living in the streets and develop a comprehensive strategy to address the large number of street children, with the aims of reducing and preventing this situation."

The Kenyan government's broad response has involved an emphasis on economic growth in addition to experimental welfare programs aimed at addressing the vulnerability of families and children to poverty. Broader socioeconomic changes in Kenya have impacted the socioeconomic welfare of families. These include rapid urbanization and the continued deterioration of the family because of deaths from the pandemic of HIV/AIDS among other factors. Due to high levels of poverty (with nearly half of the population considered to be living below the poverty line according to agencies such as the World Bank), thousands of children live, work, and fend for themselves begging for food and money in urban streets. One of the key government programs, implemented since 2004, involves the granting of limited forms of social cash transfers to targeted households considered poor with orphans or vulnerable children—explicitly defined as persons under the age of 18 and not receiving benefits from another program (Odongo 2012). Another program, implemented since 2005, is the Street Family Rehabilitation Trust Fund, which seeks to rehabilitate children working and living on the streets by providing affected children with special protection, education, health care, and psychosocial support. The government estimates that 8820 children, out of which over 800 were reintegrated into their families, benefited from the program between 2005 and 2010. The success of these kinds of programs is qualified to the extent that there remain thousands of children living in and off the streets in part because of the deep-rooted impact of rampant poverty and other factors impacting the socioeconomic welfare of families.

PRETRIAL DIVERSION

Kenya's legal framework, including the Children's Act, is silent on the extent of the applicability of pre- and on-trial diversion programs. The act does not explicitly recognize the possibility of a formal referral of children away from criminal justice processes before trial. In the period since 2001, the government has implemented a "pilot diversion" program with support from some of the development partners. The main aim of the project, which has involved the police since 2005, is to assist in the removal of children who have not committed criminal offenses from the juvenile justice administration into community-based alternatives. Its overall aim is to filter social welfare and child care and protection cases out of Kenya's criminal (juvenile) justice system.

Kenya's criminal procedural law provides the Director of Public Prosecutions with wide powers of discretion over any criminal charges against any person: children or adult at any stage of a criminal trial process (before or during trial). This may be interpreted to provide some room for the state or the prosecution to conduct pretrial diversion of children accused of crimes. To date, however, there is little or no evidence that Kenyan prosecutors view their authority to include pretrial diversion processes. This is largely attributable to the lack of direct statutory provisions and the reality that pretrial diversions of any kind are generally alien to Kenya's general criminal justice system. Hence, the pilot diversion project has had some success in aiding the process of removing children who may be caught in the formal justice system but have not committed any crimes.

COURTS AND JUVENILES

The emphasis on separate courts and procedures for children is central to the provisions of the CRC, the African Children's Charter, and Kenya's Children's Act. Kenya's previous children's law (section 3(1) of the Children and Young Persons Act in 1969) provided for the jurisdiction of "juvenile courts" to try children accused of crimes (with the exception of when they were tried with adults) in addition to civil jurisdiction over care and protection, adoption, maintenance, and other issues. Under the Children's Act of 2001, the provision requiring specialized courts and procedures has not only been maintained but also enhanced. Part VI of the act provides for the establishment of children's courts. In relation to criminal matters concerning children, these courts are exclusively vested with jurisdiction to try children for all and any criminal offenses—serious or otherwise—except where children are charged with murder and where they are jointly accused of committing crimes with adult(s). Under section 76, the act requires that any court order or decision regarding children should take into account "the ascertainable feelings and wishes of the child concerned with reference to the child's age and understanding."

Because of inadequate public allocation and spending in the criminal justice system in general and the juvenile justice system in particular, the law's requirement for separate courts and procedures remains elusive in practice. Officials and courts have often defaulted to conducting and hearing cases involving children in open regular courts (Human Rights Watch 1997). In its 2007 review, the UN Committee expressed its concern regarding the continuing lack of separate courts and procedures:

> …in certain instances children are treated as adults and… only limited progress has been achieved in establishing a functioning juvenile justice system outside the capital….

When reporting to the UN Committee in 2006, the government stated that the number of children tried and sentenced as adults has gradually been decreasing (from 626 in 2003 to 180 in 2006). It attributed this decrease to the implementation of the Children's Act and increased awareness of children's rights.

On the one hand, the failure to establish full-fledged children's courts and separate procedures may be attributed to a question of availability and/or the allocation of public resources to support the operationalization of the Children's Act. On the other hand, this failure reveals a tension inherent in the attempt of Kenya's legal framework to live up to the ideals of a purely rights-based oriented juvenile justice system that is subject to competing goals or ideals.

DUE PROCESS SAFEGUARDS AND AN EMPHASIS ON PROMPTNESS (SUBSECTION OF "COURTS AND JUVENILES")

Part XIII of the Children's Act details provisions guaranteeing the application of fair trial and due process rights for children accused of committing crimes. These provisions straddle a balance of "protection" on the one hand and "autonomy of the child" on the other. The children's courts are required to consider a child's welfare in a manner that a regular court may not be required to do for adults; there is reference to the "best interests of the child." In addition, the court is obligated to have a setting that is friendly to the child offender. Children accused of crimes are guaranteed a number of rights, including the right to prompt notification of the charges and the right to have the matter determined without undue delay.

Subsidiary rules and regulations made under the Children's Act provide specific limits within which Kenyan courts should consider criminal cases involving children. Under Kenyan law, there are no corollary rules applicable to adults. According to the UN Committee, the CRC's provisions restricting the use of detention of children (Article 37) and emphasizing promptness when dealing with alleged child offenders (Article 40(2)) are meant to guard against the practice of keeping children for long periods of time in the justice system—thereby limiting the pedagogical impact of the system and potentially increasing the chances of stigma for the child. Viewed in this light, the time limits made under Kenyan law may be considered to be premised on the understanding that both a prolonged interaction with the formal justice system and detention are harmful for the welfare of children. Hence, detention and delays must be limited.

According to Rule 12 of the Child Offender Rules under Kenya's Children's Act:

1. *Every case involving a child shall be handled expeditiously and without unnecessary delay.*
2. *Where the case of a child appearing before a Children's Court is not completed within 3 months after his plea has been taken the case shall be dismissed and the child shall not be liable to any further proceedings for the same offence.*
3. *Where, owing to its seriousness, a case is heard by a court superior to the Children's Court the maximum period of remand for a child shall be 6 months, after which the child shall be released on bail.*
4. *Where a case to which paragraph (3) of this rule applies is not completed within 12 months after the plea has been taken the case shall be dismissed and the child shall be discharged and shall not be liable to any further proceedings for the same offence.*

Rule 10 deals with situations where a child is refused bail. It provides that in instances of pretrial detention, children should be held in specialized or child-specific remand homes. Any pretrial custody shall not exceed 6 months in the case of capital offenses or 3 months in the case of other offenses.

An examination of court practices reveals that Kenyan courts have yet to fully embrace the time limits and the UN Committee's explanation of the desired pedagogic value of limiting pretrial detention and delayed hearing of cases involving children. In a number of court cases decided in the immediate aftermath of the Children's Act and decided between 2003 and 2006, the High Court seemed intent to uphold the time limits. A second subsequent set of decisions by the High Court, however, held that the act and the rules should not have the effect of imposing time limits within which to "complete trials" per se but provide a basis for encouraging an expeditious handling of criminal cases involving children. In 2006 the Court of Appeal of Kenya (Kenya's highest court at the time, and now second highest court) decided in the case *Kazungu Mkunzo and another versus Republic* to declare that the imposition of time limits for cases involving children was unlawful. The court held that Rules 10(4) and 12 were unconstitutional. It reasoned that the rules purported to set time limits within which to complete the criminal trial of alleged child offenders in a context where Kenya's Constitution (applicable at the time) and the Children's Act did not make corresponding express provisions setting time limits for the completion of trials involving children or adults. The Court of Appeal further examined the provision regarding bail (section 72) under the provisions of the old constitution and noted that any person, child or adult, charged with a capital offense was not entitled to a right to bail.

This decision was not surprising in light of the absence of the corresponding provisions under Kenya's Constitution applicable at the time or the failure by parliament to include the Child Offender Rules as a part of the main body of the Children's Act (rather than their status as subsidiary legislation promulgated by the minister in charge). However, the court's failure to engage with Kenya's obligation to put into effect provisions in compliance with the CRC, which would give effect to the restriction on detention and ensure promptness of criminal procedures involving children, is surprising albeit attributable to a historical reluctance by Kenyan courts in general to engage with international legal norms.

Following the Court of Appeal decision, the status of the rules remains unclear because the government (e.g., minister in charge or the attorney general) has not moved to clarify the status of the Child Offender Rules. Courts have continued to apply the rules, albeit with differing interpretations as to whether they are legally binding or subject to interpretation. Moreover, in many instances where this issue has recently come up (e.g., *C.J. W Guardian ad litem for D. W v Republic*), the Kenyan High Court did not reference the child rights clause under Kenya's Constitution, Article 53, which restricts the use of detention for children (as a last resort and for the shortest period of time) in keeping with the provisions of Article 37 of the CRC. In this case, a 16-year-old boy charged with defilement whose case had been pending before the trial court for over 12 months had petitioned the High Court to consider whether the 12-month lapse from the time of plea was in violation of Rule 12(2) of the Child Offender Rules (which requires criminal trials of non-capital offenses to be disposed of within 3 months from the date of the child taking a plea). The Court dismissed the child's request for a dismissal of the case on the basis of the delay, asserting that the rule in question was instructive rather than mandatory. It discussed that case delays are usually caused by various reasons, including heavy court schedules and requests for adjournments by lawyers defending accused children. Ultimately, a judicial or administrative review is required to harmonize the Children's Act and the Child Offender Rules made under it in light of the implications of the child rights clause under Kenya's Constitution which expressly limit detention, including pretrial detention, as last resort and for the shortest period of time.

CUSTODIAL RULES, SENTENCING, AND ALTERNATIVE SENTENCING REGIME

Part XIII (sections 189–193) of the Children's Act provides courts with an array of alternative sentences for a trial court to impose for children found to have committed a crime. These include orders committing children to the care of parents, families, or charitable institutions; a discharge with or without sureties; a term served in rehabilitation schools (for children between the ages of 10 and 15 years); specialized children's institutions, termed "borstal" institutions (for children over 16 years); educational and vocational schools; probation; community service; and the payment of monetary fines. In keeping with the prohibition under the CRC and the African Children's Charter, the Children's Act prohibits the use of the death penalty for children; Kenyan law also prohibits the use of corporal punishment. The act outlaws any form of detention in a prison or "detention camp." The prohibition of any form of imprisonment goes further than the provisions of the CRC (Article 37) and the African Children's Charter (Article 17), both of which restrict the use of imprisonment while providing for the absolute prohibition of the most extreme form of imprisonment—life imprisonment without parole.

Yet in practice, Kenyan courts have tended to lean in favor of imposing the death penalty and prison sentences on child offenders for capital and other offenses (Ongoya 2007). Relatively high numbers of children can be found among the country's prison population: the number of prison inmates below 18 years of age (with a majority aged 16–17 years) increased from 2570 in 2013 to 3455 (about 1.3% of the total inmate population) in 2014 (Kenya National Bureau of Statistics 2015). In part, the use of imprisonment for children in cases deemed as serious offending (and which are punishable by terms in prison for adults), despite the prohibition in law, reflects a crime control attitude and a retributive goal of the penal system. The tendency by courts to resort to prison custodial sentences also owes to the lack of alternative child-friendly facilities. Even in the wake of the new legal regime, which allows for the imposition of custodial sentences to be served by children in rehabilitation and other facilities (such as "borstal" institutions), the country's facilities for these purposes remain few and far between. There are 11 rehabilitation schools (hosting an average of 70 children each) and four probation hostels in the country—all of which predate the new legislation. The full extent to which the conditions and programs that children undergo within these institutions comply with their legal rights is not clear due to the absence of dedicated research on this issue.

DIFFERENCES IN THE TREATMENT OF BOYS AND GIRLS

The Kenyan criminal justice system mainly focuses on male offenders largely because of the disproportionate representation of males in arrest, trial, and post-trial procedures. According to official data from 2010 to 2014, 79.4% of cases reported to the police in 2014 concerned male offenders (Kenya National Bureau of Statistics 2015). Female offenders constituted only 6.4% (2085) of the total number (32,686) of persons convicted of crimes in 2014. Most police and prison facilities in the country are designed to accommodate male offenders. More specifically related to juvenile justice, only two of 11 rehabilitation schools and only one of the four probation hostels in the country are dedicated to house or cater to girls in the juvenile justice system. Although there are gender desks, which are staffed by specially trained officers at a limited number of police stations in the country, there are no special provisions for female offenders. The only relevant provision is included in the Constitution Article 53(1) (f) (ii) to the effect that in the event of children's detention they should be separated from adults and that such detention should be with regard to their age and sex. This would require the separate detention of girls from boys or males.

In 2013 about 13% (4852) of police officers were female (of the total number of 37,293) (Kenya National Bureau of Statistics 2015). With the limited number and capacity of female-specific facilities, there is a real risk of female offenders being mixed with adults, including males, when deprived of their liberty. This enhances the risk of girls being victims of sexual or gender-based violations and abuses during arrest and detention.

CONCLUSION

Children's rights norms encapsulated in the CRC and the African Children's Charter have had a significant effect on the domestic laws and practices of many African States that are parties to these treaties. In keeping with its treaty obligations to review and reform laws relating to children's issues, Kenya enacted the Children's Act in 2001. This law includes provisions pertaining to juvenile justice.

The child rights-oriented philosophy of the law is very different compared to the previously inherited legal framework. The resulting situation is a legal framework motivated by children's rights norms. The legal framework that anchors the juvenile justice system in Kenya will have to be the subject of further reform if the country wishes to usher in some of the discrete aspects of a rights-based system, envisaged in treaties such as the CRC. Beyond such law reform, the Kenyan example proves that the achievement of a truly separate and rights-based system will also require considerable practical administrative changes, investment in new facilities and an improvement of the capacity and knowledge of judges, the police, and other players within the criminal justice system.

REFERENCES

Alemika, E. O., & Chukwuma, I. C. (2001). *Juvenile justice administration in Nigeria: Philosophy and practice*. Lagos: Centre for Law Enforcement Education.

Doek, J. (2002). Modern juvenile justice in Europe. In M. Rosenheim (Ed.), *A century of juvenile justice*. Chicago: The University of Chicago Press.

Ennew, J. (1994). *Street and working children: A guide to planning*. London: Save the Children.

Human Rights Watch. (1997). *Juvenile injustice: Police abuse and detention of street children in Kenya*. New York: Human Rights Watch.

Kaseke, E. (1998). Juvenile justice in Zimbabwe: The need for reform. *Journal of Social Development in Africa, 8*(1), 11–17.

Kenya Law Reform Commission. (1993). *A new law on children*. Unpublished report.

Kenya National Bureau of Statistics. (2015). *Economic survey*. Nairobi: KNBS, p247, Table 16.1: Number of Crimes Reported to the Police, 2010–2014. Retrieved October 8, 2015, from http://www.knbs.or.ke/.

Odongo, G. O. (2004). The juvenile justice system in Kenya and challenges to law, policy and practice in regard to diversion. *The Chronicle, 13*(2), 6–11.

Odongo, G. (2012). Caught between progress, stagnation and a reversal of some gains: Reflections on Kenya's record in implementing children's rights norms. *African Human Rights Law Journal, 1*, 112–141.

Ongoya, E. Z. (2007). The emerging jurisprudence on the provisions of Act No. 8 of 2001, Laws of Kenya—The Children's Act. *Kenya Law Review, 214*, 221–224.

Owasanoye, B., & Wernham, M. (2004). *Street children and the juvenile justice system in Lagos State*. London: Consortium for Street children.

Parry Williams, J. (1993). *A case study of legal reform in Uganda as part of a strategy for promoting community based care*. Unpublished paper.

Schulz, S., & Hamutenya, M. (2004). *Juvenile justice in Namibia: Law reform towards reconciliation and restorative justice?* Unpublished paper.

Skelton, A. (1996). Developing a juvenile justice system for South Africa: International instruments and restorative justice. In R. Keightley (Ed.), *Children's rights*. Kenwyn: Juta & Co.

Sloth Nielsen, J. (2001). The role of international law in the development of South Africa's legislation on juvenile justice. *Law, Democracy and Development, 59*, 63.

South Consulting. (1999). *Juvenile justice in Kenya: Project identification mission*. Unpublished report commissioned, Royal Netherlands Embassy.

UN Committee on the Rights of the Child. (2003) *General measures of implementation of the Convention on the Rights of the Child*.

UN Committee on the Rights of the Child. (2007). Concluding observations on Kenya's second periodic report, CRC/C/KEN/CO/2, 19 June 2007, para 68 (a).
United Nations, Department of Economic and Social Affairs, Population Division. (2015). *World population prospects: The 2015 revision, key findings and advance tables.*
Van Bueren, G. (1995). *The international law on the rights of the child.* Boston: Martinus Nijhoff.

Godfrey O. Odongo A senior program officer with Wellspring Advisors—a New York-based private philanthropic advisory firm. He has previously served as research expert with Amnesty International's International Secretariat and in a program advisory role with Save the Children, Sweden. An advocate of the High Court of Kenya, he holds a postgraduate diploma in law from the Kenya School of Law, a bachelor's degree in law (LLB) from Moi University, Kenya; master's in law (LLM) in human rights, from the University of Pretoria, South Africa; and a doctorate in law (LLD) from the University of the Western Cape, South Africa. His doctoral research focused on a comprehensive analysis of the extent to which recent African juvenile justice law reform processes comply with international children's rights law. He is author of several journal articles, book chapters, and reports on a range of human rights issues.

3

Uganda

Flavian Zeija

INTRODUCTION

Africa is no stranger to injustices meted out on children. Child sacrifice, albino murders and child soldiers are common occurrences in sub-Saharan Africa. Children are a common sight in stone quarries, mines and commercial agricultural plantations despite the existence of legislation forbidding this. Africa's civil and criminal justice systems are characterized by delays in delivering justice and hence denying justice to many. Children particularly suffer within such a system. As witnesses, they sometimes do not receive the protection they deserve. As accused, they are sometimes held in solitary confinement instead of rehabilitation centers. Poverty and rebel groups have further exacerbated the problem. The Lord's Resistance Army, for example, has abducted many children into their ranks and forced them to become killers against their will. Though defeated from Northern Uganda, the rebel group has moved to Central African Republic where they continue to wreak havoc on children.

F. Zeija (✉)
High Court of Uganda, Kampala, Uganda
e-mail: fzeija@yahoo.co.uk

S.H. Decker, N. Marteache (eds.), *International Handbook of Juvenile Justice*,
DOI 10.1007/978-3-319-45090-2_3

An example of poor children in Uganda. Such children can hardly access justice

This chapter will provide an overview of justice from the perspective of when children get into the realm of the law either as transgressors or victims. This perspective includes both administrative and informal mechanisms of administration of justice in Uganda. Administrative aspects include instances of children getting into trouble with authorities in schools, foster homes and orphanages and may involve corporal punishments. Information was obtained from interactions with the police, children under detention and rehabilitation, officials in charge of a detention centre and rehabilitation home and officials from the Ministry of Education.

LEGAL FRAMEWORK (STATUS) FOR CHILDREN JUSTICE IN UGANDA

The Constitution of the Republic of Uganda 1995

The constitution of the Republic of Uganda is the grand norm. This means that all laws in the country must be consistent with it. Article 34 of the constitution, in particular, is concerned with the rights of children. While the constitution has clearly laid down laws to protect the rights of children, the country has been slow to implement these laws. The Constitution provides:

34. Rights of Children

1. *Subject to laws enacted in their best interests, children shall have the right to know and be cared for by their parents or those entitled by law to bring them up.*
2. *A child is entitled to basic education which shall be the responsibility of the State and the parents of the child.*
3. *No child shall be deprived by any person of medical treatment, education or any other social or economic benefit by reason of religious or other beliefs.*
4. *Children are entitled to be protected from social or economic exploitation and shall not be employed in or required to perform work that is likely to be hazardous or to interfere with their education or to be harmful to their health or physical, mental, spiritual, moral or social development.*
5. *For the purposes of clause (4) of this article, children shall be persons under the age of 16 years.*
6. *A child offender who is kept in lawful custody or detention shall be kept separately from adult offenders.*
7. *The law shall accord special protection to orphans and other vulnerable children.*

The Children Act, 1997 (Cap. 59), Laws of Uganda

The short title to the Act states that the Act consolidates all the laws relating to children and provides for the care, protection and maintenance of children. It establishes a family court for children and makes special provisions for children charged with offences. It also provides for local authorities to have a role in the protection and welfare of children. Courts in Uganda have used the welfare of the child as the guiding principle. In the case of *Wafula Vs Wanyoto and Anor, 2014*, the applicant abandoned his children and disappeared for 3 years. The respondent successfully applied for a maintenance order. The first respondent (mother) applied for a garnishee order and attached 150,000,000 million on the account of the applicant in Equity Bank. The applicant brought this application for a revision order to free his money from attachment.

The Judge stated:

> …It is not necessary for this Court to make any revision order, as the execution was to protect the welfare of the children. I wish to add that the decision of the lower Court was also in conformity with **Article 4 of the African Charter on the rights and welfare of a child**, Article 3 of the United Nations convention on the rights of a child, Section 3 and Principle 1 of the first schedule to the children Act, Cap 59, all stipulate that in all decisions concerning children undertaken by any person or authority, the best interests of the child shall be the primary consideration.

The Prevention of Trafficking in Persons Act No. 7 of 2009

In Africa, children are among the most trafficked group. In response to this, the government, in 2009, enacted the Prevention of Trafficking in Persons Act. Based on this Act, trafficking is an offence and it provides for the prosecution and punishment of offenders. It also has a provision for protection of victims of trafficking and other related matters. An example of the implementation of this Act can be seen in the cases of *Uganda vs Mudeega Ali 2011 and Uganda V Umutoni Annette, 2014*. In the former, the accused kidnapped a child aged 9 years from his grandmother with the intent to sell him in Kenya for a ritual sacrifice. The police were able to rescue the child and arrested the accused. The court sentenced the accused to 7 years in prison, given that the child was rescued and unharmed. In the latter case, the accused trafficked two girls aged 14 years and 16 years from the Republic of Rwanda on the pretext that she was a born-again Christian who would help the girls receive scholarships in Uganda. She ultimately sold the girls to two men who repeatedly had sex with them. The accused was sentenced to 15 years in prison by the court.

The Domestic Violence Act of 2010

The Domestic Violence Act bill was passed in 2010 due to the increasing problem of domestic violence in Uganda. The Act provides for the protection of victims of domestic violence. According to the Act, children who live in a household experiencing domestic violence can be removed from their homes by the local leaders in the community. Further, any person can apply for an interim domestic violence protection order to protect a child, and such children can be taken into custody of another person/institution. The greatest challenge to the implementation of this Act is the lack of resources available to take care of such children.

The Prohibition of Female Genital Mutilation Act No. 5 of 2010

This Act was enacted in response to the judgement of the constitution court that declared female genital mutilation unconstitutional in the case of *Law and Advocacy for Women in Uganda Vs Attorney General, 2007*. Female genital mutilation is practised by three tribes in Uganda on children. The Act prohibits female genital mutilation and other offences related to it. The Act also provides rules and regulations for the prosecution and punishment of offenders and the protection of victims and potential victims. A perpetrator of genital mutilation is liable to imprisonment not exceeding 10 years. The Act creates extraterritorial jurisdiction for offences done out of the country. It is also an offence not to report an act of mutilation. Despite this, however, the practice has persisted. Currently, the government has decided to use persuasion rather than legal means to tackle this problem.

The Employment Act 2006

Section 32 of the Employment Act prohibits the employment of children below the age of 12. Further, based on this Act children under the age of 14 years are allowed to be employed for light work under the supervision of adults. No child can be employed in hazardous work and be employed between 7 pm and 7 am. Nevertheless, the law is silent about children above the age of 14 years and the circumstances under which they can be employed.

The Education (Pre-primary, Primary and Post-primary) Act, 2008

This Act orders the state to ensure the safety of children while at school. Parents are responsible for providing children with parental guidance, food, clothing and medical care. The Act makes education a right for everybody, and parents are required to ensure that their children go to school. However, statistics from Uganda Bureau of Statistics (2014) show that there is a significant problem regarding the education of children. The data show that by the time children reach the age of primary seven, more than half of them drop out of school. The table below provides an overview of the dropout rates for 2011–2013:

No. of Children in Primary Education Schools

Class	*2011*	*2012*	*2013*
P1	1,839,714	1,877,801	1,883,803
P2	1,272,510	1,284,122	1,307,745
P3	1,266,117	1,291,268	1,312,592
P4	1,276,386	1,299,994	1,317,315
P5	1,068,776	1,118,900	1,138,789
P6	842,043	892,338	920,045
P7	532,631	564,217	579,431
Total	8,098,177	8,328,640	8,459,720

Source: Uganda Bureau of Statistics 2014

The trend can be as shown on the Bar graph below:

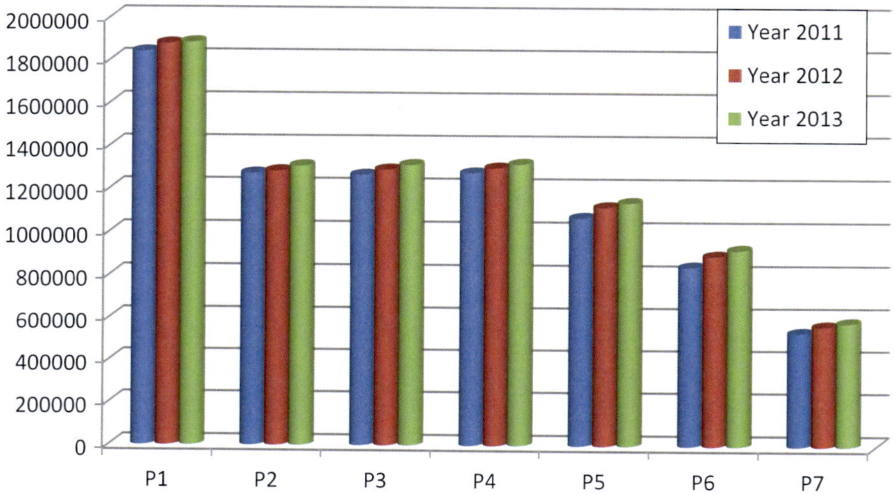

Source: *Generated by Author from the Data above*

An interview with an official from the Ministry of Education reveals that many children drop out of school due to the lack of supplies in the schools, such as food and sanitary pads for girls, and social practices such as early marriages. Currently, there seems to be no immediate government action to address this problem.

The Penal Code Act (Cap 120)

The Penal Code Act in Uganda specifies all offences and penalties that a person can be charged with. It covers offences relating to abduction of children, indecent assault of children, defilement, child-to-child sex, desertion of children, neglecting to provide food for children and child stealing.

The National Council for Children Act of 1996

As the long title suggests, the Act was put in place to create a structure for proper coordination of children affairs in the country. The Council is expected to develop and monitor policies relating to the welfare and protection of children.

The Prisons Act of 2006

Under Section 59 of the Prisons Act, a mother can be admitted into prison with an infant. If a female is either pregnant or breastfeeding, special facilities should be provided to her. The prison authorities are required to provide clothing and other necessities for the child. If a child attains the age of 18 months, the prison authorities can hand over the child to a relative of the prisoner if they are satisfied that the child will be taken care of effectively. If there is no relative who is willing to take care of the child, the Commissioner General of Prisons takes the child to the probation and welfare officer. It should be noted that under section 58(7), a juvenile is not supposed to be admitted in any prison with adults.

The Uganda People's Defence Forces Act 2005

During the bush war from 1981 to 1985, the Uganda People's Defence Forces (UPDF) used infants in their ranks. These infants continued to serve as soldiers even after the war but were given education in the army schools until they were 18 years. Based on the Act, however, the use of children below the age of 18 years as soldiers is prohibited. Section 52(2) specifically states that no person shall be enrolled in the defence forces unless he/she is 18 years old and above.

Local Government Act, 1997 (Cap. 243)

According to the Act, every local government is required to have a secretary for the affairs of children. Local governments are supposed to consider the welfare of children as paramount and are required to pay particular attention to children with disabilities. The district councils or urban councils are further enjoined under the Second Schedule to protect properties of children and not to distribute them.

CRIMINAL RESPONSIBILITY

The age of criminal responsibility is determined by the Children Act. According to section 88 of the Act, a child below the age of 12 years is incapable of understanding his/her criminal responsibility. Further, Section 101(3) of the Magistrates Court Act requires that a *voir dire* be conducted, if a child of tender years is involved in any court proceedings as a witness. If a child understands the importance of speaking the truth, he/she can provide unsworn evidence. Otherwise, the evidence is not admitted, as was seen in the case of *Kibangeny Arap Kolil V R, 1959*. If a juvenile is above 14 years, his/her evidence can be admitted without the need for corroboration. For children below the age of 14 years, however, corroboration is necessary. Nevertheless, the biggest challenge in such cases is establishing the age of the child as 70% of the births are not registered in Uganda.

UGANDA'S STANCE TOWARDS THE UN COMMITTEE ON THE RIGHTS OF THE CHILD

Article 123 of the Constitution of Uganda (1995) allows for the president to execute international treaties, conventions and agreements on behalf of the country. Under the Ratification of Treaties Act (Cap 2004), the cabinet has the power to ratify treaties. The cabinet, however, is required to bring such treaties before the parliament "as soon as possible" after ratification. There is confusion whether the parliament can reverse the ratification of the cabinet or if putting forward the treaty is just to ensure that the parliament is informed.

Uganda respects many of the international agreements it signs. However, there have been instances when Uganda has openly criticised some of the agreements it is signatory to, like the Rome Statute of the International Criminal Court of 1998. While Uganda is signatory to many human rights conventions/treaties, Uganda's human rights record has not always been the best as Human Rights Watch has observed (Human Rights Watch 2015). The implementation of international conventions relating to children can, therefore, be considered in that light.

The United Nations Convention on the Rights of the Child (1989)

Uganda signed and ratified the convention on the 17th day of August 1990. Since then, Uganda has been making periodic reports to the Committee on the Rights of the Child established under this convention. The last report submitted to the committee was on the 16th of August 2007. This report was considered by the committee at its 1369th meeting held on 3 October 2008. The committee noted the following positive aspects on Uganda:

(a) Putting in place the child orphans and other vulnerable children's policy and action plan of 2004
(b) The establishment of Child Labour Unit in the Department of Labour at the Ministry of Gender Labour and Social affairs to address the worst forms of child labour
(c) The establishment of Children and Family Protection Units (CFPU) in police stations
(d) The collaboration with the Office of the United Nations High Commissioner for Human Rights through the agreement, which established a national country office in Uganda in 2006

Nevertheless, the committee noted the lack of "a central database for registering violations of child rights". It recommended that Uganda should "ensure that data relating to offences covered by the Protocol, are systematically collected and disaggregated *inter alia* by age, sex, minority group and geographic location and analysed, as they provide essential tools for measuring policy implementation" (UN 2008).

In addition, the committee also noted inadequate funding to the National Council for Children and the lack of a clear mandate. There was lack of "National Plan of Action in place to combat the violations of the Optional Protocol, in view of the high incidence of sale of children, child prostitution and child pornography" (UN 2008). The Committee noted the lack of resources for criminal investigations, legal assistance and physical and psychological recovery measures for juvenile victims. The Committee recommended the allocation of resources "for coordination, prevention, promotion, protection, care, investigation and suppression of acts covered by the Optional Protocol, including by earmarking human and financial resources for the implementation of programmes relating to its provisions, and in particular for criminal investigations, legal assistance and physical and psychological recovery of victims to relevant authorities and civil society organisations" (UN 2008). The social reintegration and physical and psychosocial recovery measures for child victims are not mentioned. As noted ahead, these issues are still prevalent in Uganda. The next report was to be submitted in 2011, but there is no record to show that Uganda submitted a report. It is unclear if this reflects contempt of the committee.

Uganda has ratified other international/regional instruments that are essential for the rights of the child. These include the United Nations Rules for the Protection of Juveniles Deprived of their Liberty (1990); the United Nations Guidelines for Action on Children in the Criminal Justice System (1997); the United Nations Guidelines on Justice in Matters involving Child Victims and Witnesses of Crime (2005); the African Charter on the Rights and Welfare of the African Child, OAU DOC. CAB/LEG/24. 9/49 (1990); and the Protocol to the African Charter on Human and People's Rights on the Rights of Women in Africa (Maputo Protocol).

TRENDS IN JUVENILE JUSTICE IN UGANDA

The trends in juvenile justice in Uganda lack sufficient data. The police only began to compile such statistics in the year 2008.

Children as Victims of Crime

Crime statistics prior to the year 2008 are scanty due to the lack of computerisation by police. Further, at the time this chapter was being compiled, statistics for the year 2012 were not available. Thus, crime statistics for the years 2008–2014 were acquired and are presented below (Uganda Police, 2008, 2009, 2010, 2011, 2013, 2014)

Children as victims of crime. Number of victimisations by crime type

Crime	*2008*	*2009*	*2010*	*2011*	*2012*	*2013*	*2014*
Child neglect	2628	3126	9293	8075		11,519	11,791
Abuse and torture	660	552	1315	1775		1332	1205
Abduction	188	615				729	771
Child stealing	157	206	301	261		295	216
Abortion	48	72	23	66		555	2578
Child sacrifice/ ritual murder	25	15	14			9	
Child desertion		754	1732	1973		3541	3335
Infanticide		46	46	66		82	55
Child trafficking		16		69		187	220
Child kidnap		49		125		1061	1146

Source: Uganda Police Statistics Reports

A bar graph showing the trends of child victimisation from the year 2008–2014 is presented below.

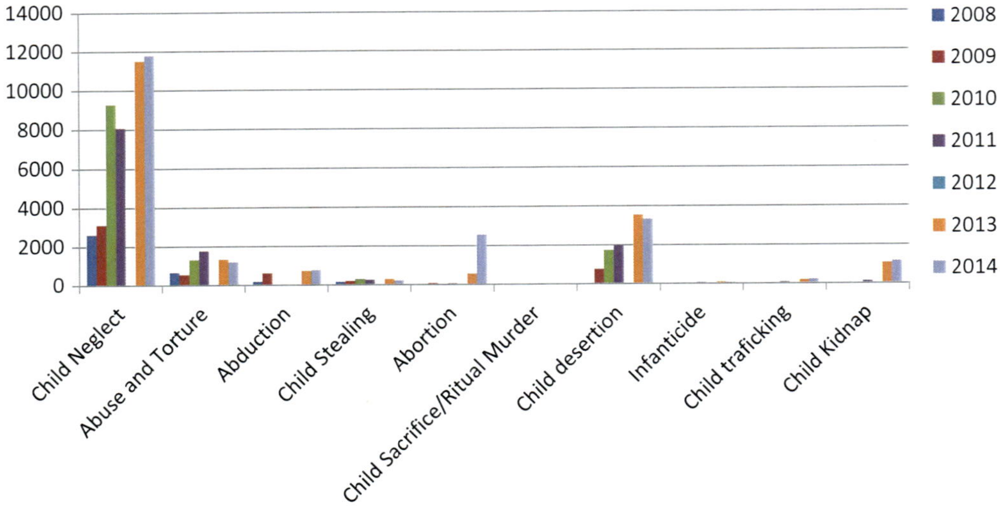

From the graph above, it can be seen that child neglect constitutes the largest proportion of crimes committed against children. According to the police, such a trend is a reflection of widespread poverty as well as society that no longer views children as belonging to the community. From the graph, it can also be seen that child abuse and torture occur at a high frequency. Finally, in 2013, the police noted an increase in child trafficking in the country. A total of 435 Ugandan nationals were trafficked to different countries. Of these, 44 were male juveniles and 36 were female juveniles. The rest were adults.

Kidnapping refers to where a child is taken out of the parent/guardian's control without the authority of the parent/guardian (S.239 Penal Code Act). Abduction on the other hand refers to where a child is taken out of the control of the parent/guardian by compulsion or deceit with the aim of doing something wrong to the child, e.g. marriage (S 241, Penal Code Act). Child stealing occurs where a child is below the age of 14 years and is taken out of the custody of the parent (S.159, Penal Code Act).

There are children who are injured in accidents which translate into criminal negligence. For example, in 2010, a total of 417 male and 217 female juveniles died in accidents. 968 male and 761 female juveniles were seriously injured in accidents including losing limbs or becoming disabled. 142 males and 111 females were slightly injured. In 2011, 365 male and 265 female juveniles died in accidents. 981 male and 703 female juveniles were seriously injured. 179 male and 141 female juveniles were slightly injured.

Children as Offenders

The statistics below show that juvenile crime in Uganda is increasing in some crime categories. There are some statistics missing especially on drug abuse, but the explanation from police is that many of the drug abusers are usually returned to their parents and may not be prosecuted by police. Some may not be entered in the criminal register. The other aspect is on robbery which is sometimes recorded as housebreaking or murder if it resulted in death. The crime prevalence is shown below:

Children as offenders. Number of offenders by crime type

Crime	*2008*	*2009*	*2010*	*2011*	*2012*	*3013*	*2014*
Defilement	680	785	466	534		545	418
Thefts	291	441	268	318		424	323
Assaults	344	305	163	306		216	208
Killings	36						
Breaking		199	147	201		234	13
Drug abuse	57		13				
Robberies		113	62	35		56	66

Source: *Uganda Police Statistics*

The graphic representation is as shown below.

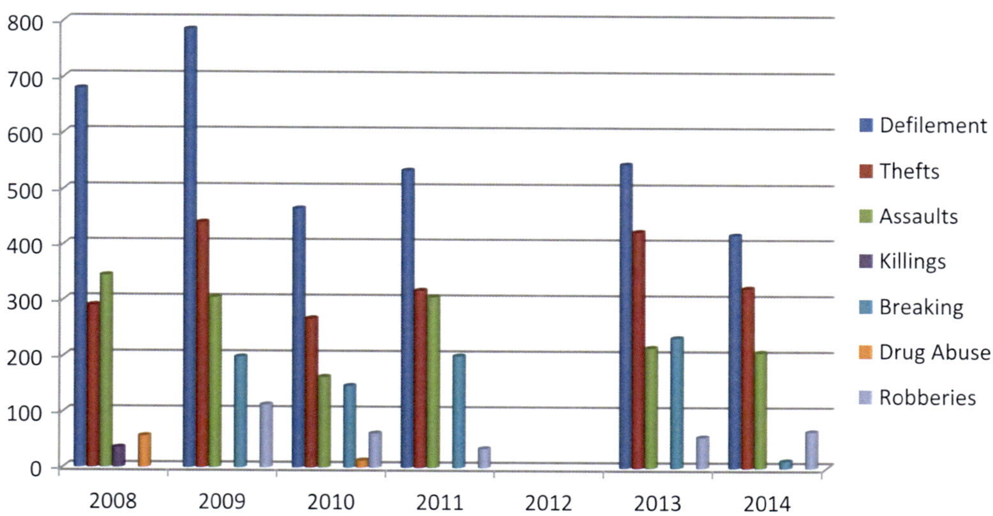

The graph above shows that defilement has the highest crime rate in Uganda, followed by theft.

Corporal Punishment in Schools

A recent study in 2008 by the Ministry of Education showed that corporal punishment is still rampant in schools. (Ministry of Education and Sports, 2008) Below are the statistics provided by the Ministry of Education.

Survey on corporal punishment

	Percentage males	*Percentage females*
Canning	90	88
Slapping	84	86
Pinching	61	63
Overwork	56	58
Denying food	40	36
Burning	22	20
Locking up	20	18
Tying up	10	16
Others	10	12

Source: Ministry of Education: Creating Safer Schools Series Vol. I, 2008

A graphic representation of this data is provided below.

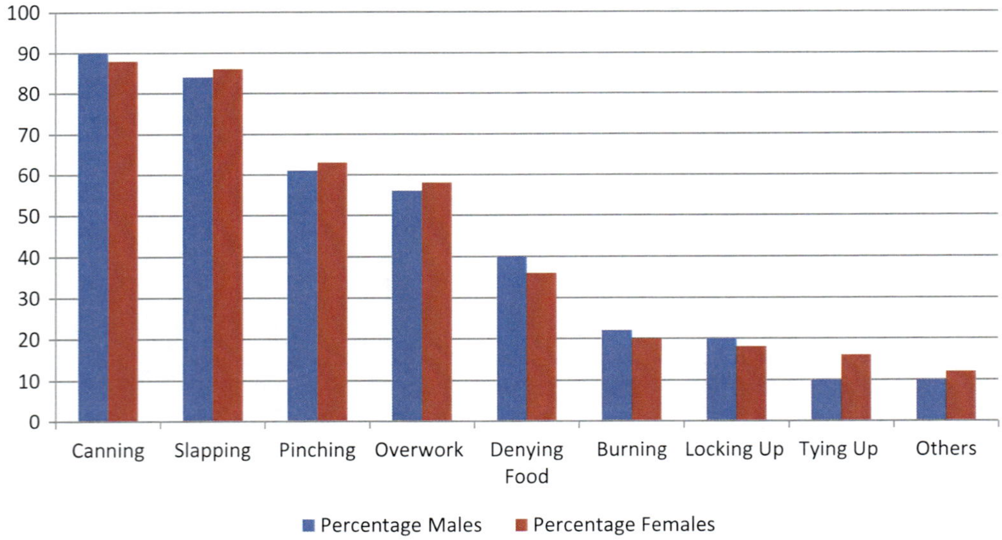

From the graph above, it can be seen that corporal punishment is still rampant in the country. Males tend to receive the most painful punishments like canning and slapping. To further understand the seriousness of the situation, findings from a 2013 US Department of State report shows that 29 of the 30 schools surveyed in Kampala engaged in corporal punishment. Deaths due to corporal punishment in school were also reported (US Department of State Report 2013).

CAUSES OF JUVENILE CRIME

I was able to interview 110 juveniles who were remanded at Nagulu detention centre to understand the main causes of delinquency in Uganda. The Nagulu detention centre is located in the city centre of Kampala. There were only six girls and 134 boys. Based on the interviews, the following issues were identified as being the main causes of juvenile crime.

Theft Due to Adult Influence and Necessity

Some of the juveniles were in the centre for stealing. The thefts ranged from minor thefts to more major ones. For example, some juveniles interviewed were involved in housebreaking but were working with adult criminals. The adults used the children to gain access to the houses by making them pass through narrow openings where more mature people could not pass. The adults gave them part of the earnings from the theft. Other juveniles were involved in pickpocketing on the streets. One of the juveniles interviewed seems to have stolen out of necessity. He stated:

> I was staying with my grandmother. She fell sick and yet she was the one who was fending for me. Subsequently, I had to go to the neighbour who is rich, to beg for food. Our neighbour ignored me but I spotted some food in some store near the garage. When I saw him driving out and the maid also moved out, I climbed the gate and picked a basket full of various food stuffs. I opened the gate from inside but as I was getting out, another neighbour saw me. He informed the maid who in turn called her boss. The boss returned with police and I was arrested with the food. I had started cooking part of the food. My grandmother eventually died.

Necessity is not a defence in a crime of theft in Uganda.

Broken Homes

One of the juveniles indicated that he left his home and began living on the street when his mother died and his father married another woman. The step mother started torturing him. In order to cope with the cold nights, he started taking drugs, upon the advice of a more seasoned street child and juvenile. Yet another juvenile claimed that when his parents divorced, his father, who was an alcoholic, took custody of him. His mother got married to another man who did not allow her to bring her children from her previous marriage to her new home. The juvenile ran away from home and went to a town called Masaka where he was introduced to crime. This cause fits in with Gorman-Smith et al.'s (1998) theory that families that are divorced are more prone to child delinquency than those that are not divorced (p26). Further, Rutter and Smith (1995) observe that a family as a source of delinquency has four paradigms: the neglect paradigm, conflict paradigm, divergent behaviour and value paradigm and disruption paradigm (p450).

Drug Abuse

Drug abuse has become a common phenomenon among juveniles in Uganda. School-going juveniles are introduced to drugs by delinquent peers. Once addicted, the desire to acquire more drugs causes them to commit other crimes like theft to maintain this habit. Ten of the juveniles at Nagulu remand home had committed drug-related offences. Some of these juveniles were charged with capital offences such as rape, murder, robbery and child-to-child sex.

False Accusations

One of the girls who was in custody at Nagulu remand home had been working as a maid and was accused by her boss of stealing. The girl claimed that her boss owed her money. When she asked for the money that was owed to her as she was quitting the job, the boss accused her of stealing so as to avoid paying her salary. It is surprising that the police were not bothered by the fact that her boss was employing a juvenile as a baby sitter.

HIV and Aids

This disease has resulted in a large number of orphans with no relatives to care for them. These children are not only left without parental guidance but also with little means of survival. In order to survive, some of these children get involved in criminal activities like stealing. This cause is intertwined with poverty which forces the poor children to fend for themselves by engaging in criminal activity.

Domestic Violence

Some of the children claimed that domestic violence was one of the key factors that led them to desert their homes and join criminal gangs. Some children were repeatedly abused by their parents/maids. This is in agreement with Albert Bandura's (Bandura, 1975) social learning theory. Bandura believes that an environment characterised by conflicts, decay and insufficient social organisation is a major determinant of delinquency among juveniles.

Inherited Traits

Some children inherit factors from their parents that are criminal in nature. If their parents were thieves, they are likely to be thieves as well. This is learning by observation as expounded by Bandura in his social leaning theory. The probation officer in Nagulu indicated that they had some juveniles accused of theft whose parents were also thieves.

Uncontrolled Media

While there is some level of control in the West on what children can watch on television and print media, in Uganda, such control is left to the parents at home. Public television shows action films where murder and war are glorified. This is in agreement with Centerwall's views on the effect of Television (Centerwall, 1993). After viewing these films, children ask for toy guns as gifts for their birthdays. In Uganda, there are places called "bibanda" (rudimentary local movie theatres) where there is no control on the content that can be viewed. The proprietors do not check the age of children before they enter. In *Uganda Vs Kidyel Henry Komakec, 2014*, the accused was a 12-year-old boy who was left at home with a 4-year-old child. He defiled the girl, allegedly due to watching pornography. He was charged with aggravated defilement and was convicted accordingly.

Influence of Adults Who Mentor Juveniles

One of the juveniles I interviewed who was a street kid indicated that he was lured into criminal activity by adult criminals on the street who became his mentors. This is in agreement with Kyeyune's findings on street kids (Kyeyune, 1999). Cases of juveniles working with adults to commit crimes are common in Uganda. For example, in the case of *Uganda vs Businge Kugonza & 2 others, 2012*, the accused with two juveniles murdered a person in the process of robbing a mobile phone. The juveniles pleaded guilty and were sentenced separately from the accused. Their mentor was sentenced to 20 years in prison.

In some instances however, juveniles have committed offences of murder on their own. In the case of *Uganda Vs the Juvenile (O.R)*, 2014, the accused was a primary school pupils aged 11 years. He killed a fellow pupil. When the deceased was grazing goats, he strangled him and tied his body with a rope on a tree. He was found guilty of murder. What is surprising is the thought and planning that went behind the execution of the murder by this juvenile.

POLICING AND JUVENILES

The interaction of police with juveniles once they get on the wrong side of the law is founded in the Children Act. Under the Act, once police arrest a child, they should caution the child and immediately release the child (Section 89(1)). This section empowers the police to handle and dispose of the matter without referring it to any formal courts for hearing. Upon arrest of the child, the child's parents/guardians are supposed to be informed as soon as possible. The secretary for children's affairs at the local government council of the area in which the child resides is also supposed to be informed immediately. In the event that parents or guardians of the child cannot be contacted, the child should be interviewed in the presence of the probation and social welfare officer. Under Article 34(6) of the Constitution of Uganda, a child offender who is kept in lawful custody or detention shall be kept separately from adult offenders. Further, a child is not allowed to be in police custody for more than 24 h. It is prohibited to detain a child with adults, and if a child is female, she should be in the custody of female police officers.

Emergency Protection of Children by Police

The Children Act mandates the police to protect children in situations of emergency (Section 37). Once the child is put under emergency protection, the police should make provisions for the child until the child is produced in court for further orders on his/her welfare or until the child is returned to his/her parents or guardians. The parents or guardians of the child should be informed as soon as possible.

Action by Police to Protect the Rights of the Child

Police in Uganda pursuant to the provisions of the Children Act set up a Child and Family Protection Unit in 1998. All cases involving children are handled by this unit. It is staffed with professional officers who are trained in childcare and counselling. A substantial number of these officers are elderly females with experience in childcare. One of them I interviewed indicated that when she receives children who are abandoned, she gives them temporary shelter at her home until a decision is made about their next destination. Many police stations have child detention centres. Police emphasise the system of referring minor offences to local council courts/school administration to handle such cases so that children are not inconvenienced. The unit handles cases involving the violation of the rights of woman as well. Specifically, the unit is focused on domestic violence, rape, defilement, sexual harassment, child abuse and neglect, child labour, indecent assault, child desertion, children offenders and trafficking of women and children. Other than investigating these offences, the unit creates awareness on the rights of women and children and counsel child victims of abuse. This is done through visiting schools and talking to children and teachers on child abuse. Nevertheless, a visit to various police units revealed the following:

Understaffing of the Units

Many of the units were found to be understaffed. Some of them had two officers to receive complaints, carry out investigations and take care of children. This makes it difficult for the units to run efficiently. Sometimes, the same unit investigates cases of domestic violence as well as family conflicts. While the police guidelines require that cases involving juveniles should be investigated and completed within 1 month, this has not been achieved in many of the cases due to understaffing. Some units especially those in the upcountry remain closed when officers are in the field investigating cases.

Lack of Facilities for Witness Protection
Perhaps the biggest challenge facing the various units is how to protect witnesses to the crimes against juveniles. One of the heads of the unit who preferred anonymity mentioned that in cases of defilement, once victims return to their parents, there is an attempt by the perpetrators to negotiate with the parents of the victim and pay them off. This makes it difficult for the prosecution to pursue the case if the witnesses become complacent and fail to testify. Another problem that was identified is the possibility of victims disappearing or being killed by the perpetrators of the crime. This has happened in some instances in Fort Portal where a victim of defilement was eventually murdered. When the police attempt to withdraw the witness/victim from the community for fear of reprisal, they are constrained by the limited resources available to them. The police depend heavily on NGOs for placement of children, but NGOs tend to have strict rules on who they can admit.

Lack of Resources
When children are abandoned, the police budget is so small that there is little left for taking care of children. One police woman intimated that she often takes such children to her home in the interim and feeds them using her own scarce resources. It is worse when children are very young and require supplies like baby food. When the police cannot pass on these children immediately to foster homes, the burden falls on the police officers manning the unit. There are some instances where the police receive battered mother and children. In such situations, the battered mother has nowhere to go but the police cannot take care of the mother either. If police cannot provide basic necessaries like food, shelter and medical care, it compromises the purpose for which the units were created. Some victims escape from police protection due to poor living conditions. One police officer complained that they are not given transport while investigating cases and they rely on the victim's relatives to do the medical reports and other tests.

Corruption

One of the probation officers in Kampala complained that police officers handling children matters are sometimes prone to corruption. They are bribed by child offenders to turn a blind eye to some of their transgressions. Many victims of defilement end up being accused of lying and chased away from the units. The rich are in most cases protected. Some police officers connive with traffickers and release some unclaimed kids to them. Cases where children are victims are sometimes "messed up" by police and investigations are not completed or inconclusive. Police demand for "facilitation" from the victim's relatives, to enable them to carry out the investigations. Money for buying supplies for kids is sometimes embezzled by police.

COURTS AND JUVENILES

There are essentially three courts that handle child-related matters. These are the local council courts (Local Council Judicial Powers Act, 1988) as courts of first instance, the children and family court/magistrate courts (Children Act, 1997) and the High Court (Judicature Act, 1996) which handles capital offences. Cases involving children are supposed to be handled expeditiously. However, the officer in charge of Nagulu detention centre informed me that some cases take long. Due to a shortage of judicial officers in Uganda, many cases involving children can take more than 3 years, contrary to the provisions of the Children Act. Indeed, she had children in her custody that have been there for more than 2 years on remand. It is even worse where the child is indicted jointly with an adult person.

The principles governing litigation involving children are enshrined in the Children Act. A right to a speedy trial is the cornerstone of the administration of justice to children. The Act provides:

99. Duration of Cases

1. *Every case shall be handled expeditiously and without unnecessary delay.*
2. *Where the case of a child appearing before a family and children court is not completed within 3 months after the child's plea has been taken, the case shall be dismissed, and the child shall not be liable to any further proceedings for the same offence.*
3. *Where, owing to its seriousness, a case is heard by a court superior to the family and children court, the maximum period of remand for a child shall be 6 months, after which the child shall be released on bail.*
4. *Where a case to which subsection (3) applies is not completed within 12 months after the plea has been taken, the case shall be dismissed and the child shall be discharged and shall not be liable to any further proceedings for the same offence.*

Upon the child being found guilty, the family and children court can order any of the following where the charges are successfully proven against the child:

(a) Absolute discharge.
(b) Caution.
(c) Conditional discharge for not more than 12 months.
(d) Binding the child over to be of good behaviour for a maximum of 12 months.
(e) Compensation, restitution or fine, taking into consideration the means of the child so far as they are known to the court; but an order of detention shall not be made in default of payment of a fine.
(f) A probation order in accordance with the Probation Act for not more than 12 months, with such conditions as may be included as recommended by the probation and social welfare officer; but a probation order shall not require a child to reside in a remand home.
(g) Detention for a maximum of 3 months for a child under 16 years of age and a maximum of 12 months for a child above 16 years of age and in the case of

an offence punishable by death, 3 years in respect of any child. Detention connotes placement in a centre designated for that purpose by the minister in such circumstances and with such conditions as may be recommended to the court by the probation and social welfare officer.

CUSTODIAL CONDITIONS OF JUVENILES IN UGANDA

Uganda has four functioning detention centres in the whole country serving a population of 36 million. These centres house juveniles awaiting trial. There is only one rehabilitation centre in the whole country called Kampiringisa Rehabilitation Centre. This houses juveniles who are already convicted and sentenced.

When I visited Nagulu detention centre, I was impressed by the conditions under which the children were sleeping. The buildings were painted and they had good bedding. Girls were separated from boys, and juveniles indicted of serious crimes were separated from the rest. Children were dressed in clean uniforms, courtesy of a NGO.

The detention centre had a computer room but did not have any computers. There was a health centre without equipment and had only one nurse. The only equipment she had was a thermometer, no gloves, no stethoscope and no blood pressure machine. There was a small garden and some carpentry/craft workshops for training juveniles.

For police cells, the conditions can be described as pathetic. They ease themselves in the bucket at night, and inmates take turns to power the excrete in the morning.

Nevertheless, a visit to Kampiringisa where they send juveniles for rehabilitation showed a different story. The place was dilapidated and looked miserable. The children looked miserable as well. It was over congested. The place is in the middle of nowhere, perhaps intended to ensure that children do not escape from detention. There were no mental health or drug rehabilitation services. There were no educational programmes for juveniles, thus resulting in a discontinuity in education for these children. The only training available was geared towards skill development. Some children complained of torture, beatings, isolation, restraints and humiliation when they committed certain transgressions like fighting with their fellow inmates. These findings rime with Moore's findings in 2010 (Moore, 2010). The US Department of State report for 2013 on Uganda indicates that as of August 2013 the Kampala remand home, designed for 45 children, held 1374, while the Nagulu detention centre, designed for 30 children, held 116 (US Department of State 2013).

The Law of Juveniles in Practice

While various laws guarantee the rights of a child and provide for the protection of children, in practice this does not seem to be the case. One of the guiding principles in the implementation of the Children Act is time being of the essence. The

Act provides that all matters relating to a child should be handled expeditiously. Nevertheless, I established that many children spend more than a year on remand before a trial especially in capital offence cases. Due to the lack of capacity in magistrate courts, as well as the office of the Director of Public Prosecutions, the timelines as provided for in the law are not adhered to. This was evident in Nagulu detention centre where many juveniles had gone past their due date of trial.

The Human Rights Commission report of 2014 (Published in 2015) established that suspects could be detained for periods ranging from 10 to 30 days in police custody for reasons such as delays by the resident state attorney to sanction a file, incomplete investigations, corruption, lack of resources and lack of skills in investigations (UHRC Annual Report, 2015).

While children below 12 years are precluded from criminal responsibility, some children below this age have found themselves on trial within various courts in the country. In fact, an official at the remand home in Nagulu put the figure between 3 and 5. The Nagulu detention centre had only one old omnibus to transport juveniles to various courts in Uganda, but it is often out of fuel and when it breaks down, children cannot go to court.

Resettling the children after they have left the home is another big challenge. The officer in charge of Nagulu detention centre indicated that once children are released, they are passed on to their relatives, and no follow-up is done due to the lack of resources. Some of these children turn out to be worse criminals than they were before they left the homes. In essence, there is practically no known system to track juvenile offenders from the time they come into the homes up to the time they are released. No one knows what happens to these juveniles when they leave the homes. It is a sad state of affairs.

While the law prohibits corporal punishments, some juveniles in Kampiringisa confided in me that this method is sometimes used to punish them. It is mainly used against those who become violent against their fellow inmates. Isolation is also used as one of the tools for punishing children.

Detaining juveniles with adults at the police station is still rampant. While the law prohibits this, all the police stations in Kampala admitted that they detain adults with juveniles due to the lack of facilities. Each police post has one cell, and once juveniles are arrested, they do not have special treatment. Although they are supposed to have detention centres, juveniles are taken there within 2 days of their arrest. It is worse when they are arrested over the weekend. They spend the entire weekend in police cells before they are taken to detention centres on Monday. There is also evidence that once in these police cells, they are tortured by adult detainees. In 2014, the Uganda Human Rights Commission found 91 juveniles incarcerated with adults compared to 26 in 2013 (UHRC Annual Report, 2014). Some were found in prisons while others were found in police stations detained. Three government prisons were found to have these juveniles.

Nevertheless, some prisons have constructed juvenile facilities for detention. The Human Rights Commission in 2014 established that seven prisons and one military detention centre have constructed these facilities (UHRC Annual Report,

2014). They have also found that 10.3% of police stations have constructed detention facilities for children. This is a drop in the ocean compared to the number of police stations in the country. What this means is that many children are still detained with adults in police stations before they are passed on to juvenile detention facilities.

ALTERNATIVE SANCTIONS FOR JUVENILES

The Children Act provides for alternative sanctions for juveniles rather than remand/detention. It provides:

> **91 Remand**
>
> Whenever possible, the court shall consider alternatives to remand such as close supervision or placement with a fit person determined by the court, on the recommendation of a probation and social welfare officer.

Nevertheless, I established that while police try to use diversion methods, they encounter difficulties in some instances. One police officer explained that in most cases, some of the juveniles they detain are brought in by their parents. This makes it difficult to convince their parents to take them back. This is usually the case when juveniles have stolen from their parents or are violent as a result of drug abuse. This is in agreement with the Uganda Human Rights Commission report, 2014, that established that families of the juveniles do not visit them in detention and that children's families rejected them when they were taken back to resettle in the community. This is compounded by lack of psychologists in the remand homes to counsel the children. Their transformation therefore becomes difficult and could result in detained children committing more crimes in the future.

DIFFERENCES IN TREATMENT OF BOYS AND GIRLS

At the time when I visited Nagulu detention centre home, there were only six girls in the home. While the girls have their separate dormitory, they attended the same assembly where I met them for a brief interaction. Given that girls have special requirements and needs and given the prevalence of defilement in the country, there is need to build a separate home for girls. This is not the case however as all the homes are mixed. There is no preferential treatment for girls, apart from giving them supplies during menstruation. This was the same situation at Kampiringisa rehabilitation centre. The number of girls was very small compared to the number of boys.

CONCLUSION

There is a fundamental gap between what is provided in the laws and what happens in practice in Uganda. It is not clear why boys are more prone to crime than girls. In the detention centres and the rehabilitation centre, the number of boys compared to girls is overwhelming. This calls for a critical study of this phenomenon. It is not clear why defilement is on the increase. I intend to study these phenomena.

Upon critical investigations and like Penal International established (Penal Reform International 2012), there is missing data on the following: the time spent in detention before sentence, time spent in detention after sentence, number of child deaths in detention, percentage of children not wholly separated from adults during detention, percentage of children visited by family member, percentage of children who enter a pre-trial or pre-sentence diversion scheme, percentage of children in detention who are victims of self-harm, percentage of children who become victims of sexual abuse during detention and percentage of children in detention who have experienced closed or solitary confinement as a punishment during detention. Efforts should be made towards establishing these numbers.

Acknowledgements PhD in Law and Governance (University of Dar es salaam), LLM (Makerere University), LLB (Makerere University) ICSA (Institute of Chartered Secretaries and Administrators-London) Diploma in Legal Practice (Law Development Centre).

REFERENCES

Bandura, A. (1975). *Social learning and personality development*. New York: Holt, Rinehart and Winston, Inc.

Centerwall, B. S. (1993). *Television and violent crime*. New York: The Public Interest.

Gorman-Smith, D., & Tolan, P. (1998). The role of exposure to community violence and developmental problems among inner-city youth. *Development and Psychopathology, 10*(1), 101–116.

Gorman-Smith, D., Tolan, P. H., Loeber, R., & Henry, D. (1998). The relation of family problems to patterns of delinquent involvement among urban youth. *Journal of Abnormal Child Psychology, 26*, 319–333.

Kyeyune, G. S. (1999). *Uganda book on rehabilitation of street children*. Kampala: Christian Graphics.

Ministry of Education and Sports. (2008). *An introductory handbook for promoting positive discipline in schools for quality education: Alternatives to corporal punishment, creating safer schools series* (Vol. 1). Kampala: UNICEF.

Moore, M. (2010). *Juvenile detention in Uganda: A review of remand homes and national rehabilitation centres, African prisons project*. Retrieved from http://resourcecentre.savethechildren.se/sites/default/files/documents/3994.pdf.

Rutter, M., & Smith, D. J. (1995). *Psychological disorders in young people: Time trends and their causes*. New York: John Wily and Sons Ltd.

Human Rights Watch. (2015). World Report 2015: Uganda. Retrieved 20 April, 2016, from www.hrw.org/world-report/2015/country-chapters/uganda.

Uganda Bureau of Statistics. (2014). *Statistics abstract 2014*. Kampala: Ministry of Finance, Planning and Economic Development.
Uganda Human Rights Commission. (2015). *Uganda Human Rights Commission Annual Report, 2014*. Entebbe: Uganda Printing and Publishing Corporation.
Uganda Police. (2008). *Uganda police annual crime and traffic road safety report*. Entebbe: Uganda Printing and Publishing Corporation.
Uganda Police. (2009). *Uganda police annual crime and traffic road safety report*. Entebbe: Uganda Printing and Publishing Corporation.
Uganda Police. (2010). *Uganda police annual crime and traffic road safety report*. Entebbe: Uganda Printing and Publishing Corporation.
Uganda Police. (2011). *Uganda police annual crime and traffic road safety report*. Entebbe: Uganda Printing and Publishing Corporation.
Uganda Police. (2013). *Uganda police annual crime and traffic road safety report*. Entebbe: Uganda Printing and Publishing Corporation.
Uganda Police. (2014). *Uganda police annual crime and traffic road safety report*. Entebbe: Uganda Printing and Publishing Corporation.
UN. (2008). Committee on the Rights of the Child, Forty-ninth session consideration of reports submitted by states parties under article 12(1) of the Optional Protocol to the Convention on the Rights of the Child on the sale of children, child prostitution and child pornography, 16 October 2008.
US Department of State. (2013). *Country Reports on Human Rights Practices for 2013, Uganda*. Retrieved September 20, 2015, from http://www.state.gov/j/drl/rls/hrrpt/2013humanrightsreport/index.htm?dlid=220173&year=2013#wrapper

CASES REFERRED TO

Kibangeny Arap Kolil V R, (1959) E.A 92.
Law and Advocacy for Women in Uganda Vs Attorney General, Constitutional Petition No. 08 of 2007
Uganda vs Businge Kugonza & 2 others, CRIMINAL CASE NO. 0162 OF 2012
Uganda Vs Kidyel Henry Komakech, CRIMINAL SESSION NO. 0009 OF 2014
Uganda Vs Mudeega Ali, CRIMINAL SESSION CASE NO. 166 OF 2011
Uganda Vs the Juvenile (O.R), HCT – 02 – CR – SC – 0377 OF 2014
Uganda Vs Umutoni Annette, HCT- 00- ICD-CR -SC- NO. 003 OF 2014 (International Crimes division)
Wafula Vs Wanyoto and Anor, CIVIL REVISION NO. 17 OF 2014

LEGISLATION

Local Governments Act, Cap. 243
The Children Act, Cap 59
The Constitution of the republic of Uganda, 1995
The Domestic Violence Act, No. 12 of 2010
The Employment Act, 2006
The National Council for Children Act Cap. 60
The Penal Code Act, Cap. 120
The Prevention of trafficking in Persons Act No. 7 of 2009
The Prisons Act, 2006

The Prohibition of Female Genital Mutilation Act, No. 5 of 2010
The Uganda People's Defence Forces Act, 2005

INTERNATIONAL INSTRUMENTS

Protocol to the African Charter on Human and People's Rights on the Rights of Women in Africa (Maputo Protocol).
The African charter on the rights and welfare of the African child, OAU DOC. CAB/LEG/24. 9/49 (1990).
The United Nations Convention on the Rights of the Child. (1989).
The United Nations Guidelines for the appropriate use and conditions of alternative care for children. (2009).
The United Nations Guidelines on Justice in Matters involving Child Victims and Witnesses of Crime. (2005).
United Nations Guidelines for Action on Children in the Criminal Justice System. (1997).
United Nations Rules for the Protection of Juveniles Deprived of their Liberty. (1990).

Flavian Zeija Flavian's experience in juvenile justice dates back to 1998. He was a private legal practitioner under the leading law firm of Kwesigabo, Bamwine and Walubiri Advocates, 1998–2001, where he represented juveniles in courts of law and handled child maintenance cases as well as divorce cases involving children rights. In 2003, he founded a law firm called Zeija, Mukasa and Co. Advocates. He has been part of this law firm as a partner from 2003 until March 2016 when he was appointed by the Judicial Service Commission and the President of Uganda as a judge of the High Court. He was approved by parliament of Uganda in May 2016.

Flavian was at the same time a lecturer and later a senior lecturer in Makerere University Business School from 1998 to 2016. He was due for promotion to the rank of associate professor when he was appointed as a judge of the High Court. He was the head of the Department of Business Law at Makerere University Business School before he was appointed as a judge. He was also a member of the university council, the top policymaking body of the university for 8 years where he represented academic staff as their elected representative. Makerere University is the only university in sub-Saharan Africa in the global ranking of the best 1000 universities in the world. It was part of the University of London from 1923 until 1962 when Uganda gained independence from Britain. He is an author of a book entitled *Employment Law in Uganda*, where the problem of child labour was amplified. He has written a series of journal articles and book chapters.

PART II

America: North America, South America

4

Brazil

Corinne Davis Rodrigues, Valéria Cristina de Oliveira,
and Rafael Lacerda Silveira Rocha

THE LEGAL STATUS OF JUVENILES: HISTORICAL BACKGROUND

The development of juvenile justice in Brazil follows many of the same patterns experienced by the rest of Latin America during the nineteenth and twentieth centuries, that is, a process of gradual specialization and differentiation from a penal system oriented for adults heavily influenced by the experiences of mainly European countries (Méndez 2006).

Until the mid-nineteenth century, the juvenile justice system was an undeveloped legal field, and the treatment of children and adolescents who engaged in crime was equivalent to that provided to adults. This phase, known as the undifferentiated criminal character, lasted from the Colonial period (sixteenth century to the early nineteenth century) through Royal Portuguese Ordinances (Ordenações Reais Portuguesas). It provided that only those younger than 7 years of age could be treated differently from adults in the case of deviant conduct (Arruda, Jalusa Silva de 2011).

The independence of Brazil from Portugal resulted in significant changes in its political structure. The legal framework related to children and adolescents (or "minors," being more consistent with the terminology used at the time), however, made little progress. The Penal Code approved in the imperial period (1822–1899) and the first Republican Penal Code (1890) did not break with the undifferentiated

C.D. Rodrigues (✉)
Federal University of Minas Gerais, Belo Horizonte, Brazil
e-mail: cdrodrigues@ufmg.br

V.C. de Oliveira
Center for Metropolitan Studies (CEM), University of São Paulo, São Paulo, Brazil
e-mail: valeria@crisp.ufmg.br; rochaunit02@gmail.com

R.L.S. Rocha
Center for the Study of Criminality and Public Safety (CRISP),
Federal University of Minas Gerais, Belo Horizonte, Brazil
e-mail: valeria@crisp.ufmg.br; rochaunit02@gmail.com

S.H. Decker, N. Marteache (eds.), *International Handbook of Juvenile Justice*,
DOI 10.1007/978-3-319-45090-2_4

model. Only specific changes such as mitigating penalties for adolescents and the creation of specific institutions for interning minors separate from adults were suggested (Arruda, Jalusa Silva de 2011).[1]

In the nineteenth century, in the wake of the juvenile reform movement in the United States and the influence of reforms in Western Europe, the new republic became more sensitive to the particularities linked to the treatment of juveniles and the idea of a separate juvenile justice system. At that time, the proposed reforms moved the country closer to a social juridical guardianship or "social welfare" model (Marinho 2012; Méndez 2006).

Generally speaking, this guardianship model was based on an approximation between the social and criminal dimensions of the offense. Thus, the legal instruments reflect a tendency to consider the child or adolescent who commits a deviant act not as an individual responsible for his or her actions and as such is exempt from punishment. The deviant act is considered the result of a process of social exclusion that makes the accused a victim of the process. There is therefore a greater approximation between social assistance and criminal law, so that the focus is much more on protecting the juvenile than in the application of classic principles of criminal law as due process and the right to a full defense (Arruda, Jalusa Silva de 2011; Marinho 2012).

The vague definition of the norms and punishments made the application of juvenile justice in the protection model very subjective and open to abuse given that there was no difference in the treatment between an abandoned or abused child and a juvenile. The judges took on a paternalistic role in responding to children and adolescents, especially those in socially vulnerable situations, whose motivation for the crime mostly had structural roots (Marinho 2012).

Through the adoption of the Juvenile Code, in 1927, Brazil was the first country in Latin America to approve specific legislation for measures of "assistance and protection" dedicated to the "minors of either sex, abandoned or delinquent under 18 years of age" (Brasil 1927). The Code made children and adolescents unpunishable via criminal law, given that children under 14 who committed offenses would be punished on the basis of special code. Those aged between 14 and 18 could be accepted in reform schools, while those aged between 16 and 18, with high degree of dangerousness, could be housed in common (adult) units of detention. Regulatory instruments adopted between 1927 and the 1940s were based on the definition of a so-called irregular situation like the one involving the commission of an offense which, according to Marinho (2012), reinforced the criminalization bias of poverty and legalization issues by making equivalent

[1] In the Imperial Penal Code (1830), persons of age 14 (fourteen) to 18 (eighteen) were considered criminally responsible with mitigation of penalty, being that confinements took place in the so-called houses of corrections. The Penal Code of 1890 stipulated that persons under 9 years of age were not legally considered criminally responsible, while those from 9 years of age to 14 years of age were not criminally liable only in cases where the acts was committed without understanding. Finally, confinements took place in industrial disciplinary establishments rather than the houses of corrections (Arruda, Jalusa Silva de 2011).

social phenomena such as abandonment, crime, and vagrancy (Arruda, Jalusa Silva de 2011; Marinho 2012).

It was only with the approval of the Penal Code in 1940 that the legal age and the consequent liability for commission of offense were mandated at 18 years of age (Brazil 1940). This wording of the Code was amended in 1984 and remains in effect to this day. This amendment kept the age of legal majority at 18 years of age, characterizing minors as "criminally incompetent" and therefore "subject to the rules laid down in special legislation," i.e., the Juvenile Code.

At that time, in the mid-twentieth century, the first institutions in the executive branch emerged to organize the services of social assistance and the application of correctional measures for juveniles. The Assistance Service for Minors (Serviço de Assistência ao Menor—SAM), created in 1941, was linked to the Ministry of Justice and dedicated to the implementation of the Juvenile Code. In compliance with the Juvenile Code, dedicated detention centers were created to house abandoned children and juveniles involved in illegal acts. Over time, such centers became spaces characterized by the expansion of the duties of the SAM, encompassing instruction, social assistance, and control, reinforcing its repressive character. This made it the subject of numerous allegations of ill treatment and torture of the juveniles it served.

This scenario and the publication of the Declaration of the United Nations Rights of the Child in 1959 motivated the creation of a new project for the care and assistance of children and adolescents. Progressive for its time, the legislation was guided by humanitarian principles, such as the need to keep children and adolescents with their families, treating internment as an exceptional and secondary measure, applied only in cases of extreme need (Brasil 1964; Marinho 2012).

In a way unprecedented until that time, the federal government proposed a national policy of social assistance to minors with the creation of the National Foundation for Welfare of Minors (Fundação Nacional do Bem Estar do Menor—FUNABEM; Brasil 1964). The FUNABEM replaced the SAM as the agency responsible for the implementation of the Juvenile Code. Its main purpose was the formulation and implementation of national policy for the welfare of minors. This was accomplished at the state level through the administration of the State Foundations for the Welfare of Minors (Fundações Estaduais do Bem Estar do Menor—FEBEM). Compared to the previous model, under the FUNABEM, the child or adolescent who committed an infraction was treated as a social service case, but not in the strict sense of the previous protection model. Under the system implemented by FUNABEM, it was the responsibility of individual states to provide care and assistance to juveniles and to ensure that institutional care was provided when necessary, while respecting the principles laid out in the Declaration of the Rights of the Child.

However, it should be noted that 1964 is also the same year of the establishment of military dictatorship in Brazil (1964–1986). This period was marked by a paradigm of National Security, with policies and practices designed to protect Brazil from external and internal threats (particularly communist ideology).

Therefore, even with the progress represented by FUNABEM (whose reflection is prior to the outbreak of regime in 1964), the dynamics observed in juvenile correctional institutions were based on building an image of juveniles as a source of social danger, thus maintaining the repressive model. As such, FEBEM, especially in states such as Rio de Janeiro and São Paulo, did not represent a progressive model of social service and protection but rather centers rife with reports of mistreatment and coercive practices (Silva 1997).[2]

The beginning of the gradual democratic opening in 1979 promulgated the creation of a new Juvenile Code. The 1940 Juvenile Code was replaced definitely in 1990 by the Children and Adolescents Statute (Estatuto da Criança e Adolescente—ECA; Brasil 1990) that transforms FUNABEM into the Brazilian Center for Childhood and Adolescence (Centro Brasileiro de Infância e Adolescência—CBIA). Before 1990, however, the end of military rule and the promulgation of the democratic Federal Constitution (FC) of 1988 already alluded to changes in the country's juvenile justice system. The FC reaffirmed the age of legal majority at 18 years of age and stated that juveniles were subject to specific legislation (in this case the ECA).

AGE OF MAJORITY

As discussed in the previous section, until the passage of the Penal Code in 1940, minors as young as 8 years (in the colonial period) and 9 years (during the Brazilian Empire) could be held responsible for illicit actions, even though the Imperial Penal Code of 1890 specified that criminal liability was reserved for those over 14 years. With the passage of the Penal Code of 1940, the legal age of majority was established at 18, and it remains so to this day. Article 228 of the 1988 Constitution reaffirmed that persons under the age of 18 are not criminally liable.

The notable changes of current legislation, the Statute of the Child and Adolescent, make one additional distinction regarding criminal responsibility. Those under 12 years of age are classified legally as "children" and are considered completely exempt, not capable of understanding the consequences of their actions. Those between the ages of 13–18 years are classified as "adolescents" and are presumed to understand the implications of their actions. While they are criminally responsible, they are not liable for punishment under the adult Penal Code.

In recent years, there has been much debate among the public and the national legislature regarding lowering the age of legal majority. The discussions reached an apex in 2015 with the passage of a bill in the Chamber of Representatives (Câmara de Deputados) proposing a constitutional amendment that would lower

[2] For a good representation of the popular images of FEBEM at the end of the military dictatorship, see the Brazilian film "Pixote," released in 1980.

the age of majority to 16 years. The proposed bill was authored in 1993, but did not gain enough traction in the legislature for passage. At the time this chapter was being written, the bill was in the Senate committee process. However, its passage there is unlikely due to the lack of support. In addition, the current president, Dilma Rousseff, is against the legislation and has affirmed her intention to veto, if passed by the legislature.

THE COUNTRY'S STANCE TOWARD THE UN COMMITTEE ON THE RIGHTS OF THE CHILD

The approval of the ECA in 1990 is a milestone for the country. It represents the start of the so-called third phase in the development of juvenile justice in Brazil. Substantiated by the contents of the Convention on the Rights of the Child of 1989, this third phase according to Méndez (2006) is characterized by the separation of social problems from those linked to conflict with the law. This guarantees the right of children and adolescents to express their desires and *ultimately the accountability of children and adolescents, including in the criminal sense* (Méndez 2006).

Prior to the passage of the ECA, articles 227 and 228 of the 1988 Constitution laid out a number of rights and guarantees for children. This brought national Brazilian law in accordance with the international laws and doctrines regarding children of the United Nations. For the first time, children and adolescents were recognized as full legal subjects and were given specific rights separate from those laid out as family rights, which could only be exercised by adults in the family unit (mothers and fathers). In addition, it made a distinction between youth in situations of risk or abandonment and those who committed an illegal act. Thus ending the guardianship model of juvenile justice that often treated socially vulnerable youth as criminals (Marinho 2012). In addition, both article 227 of the 1988 Constitution and the ECA call for the full protection of children and adolescents, to be provided by the family, the State, and civil society. As such, these actors are responsible for the survival, development, and protection of all children and adolescents and not just those in "irregular situations," i.e., at risk, delinquent, or abandoned (Arruda, Jalusa Silva de 2011).

The ECA distinguishes between a child, any individual under 12 years of age, and an adolescent, all persons aged between 12 and 18 years. A child is not criminally liable, while adolescents are seen as criminally liable, but this liability is not punishable by the adult Penal Code. For adolescents who have committed illegal acts, the ECA provides the guarantee of the same rights of due process found in the adult legal system (Brasil 1990).

The ECA laid out three systems of guarantees for the protection of children. The first is in regard to the creation and maintenance of public policies serving children and adolescents. The second system of guarantees is in regard to protective measures for socially vulnerable or abandoned children and adolescents.

The third system is in regard to socio-educational measures, the nomenclature for sanctions levied against adolescents who have committed illegal acts. With this distinction between protective and socio-educational measures, the ECA laid out a separate set of procedures, actions, and institutions for at-risk or socially vulnerable youth than those for juvenile offenders.

For juvenile offenders, article 12 of the ECA stipulates a plurality of sanctions, following the UN Riyadh Guideline Directives for juvenile offenders. These options range from giving a warning to incarceration, thus providing judges more options for sentencing.

JUVENILE CRIME TRENDS IN BRAZIL

In the first two decades of the twenty-first century, Brazil witnessed the intensification of the public debate about the possibilities of lowering the age of legal responsibility. Although they still contain passionate defenses both in favor and opposed to change the age of criminal responsibility in the country, the discourse of both sides lacks a basis in concrete data regarding the participation of adolescents in crime, especially violent crime. This comes about for two main reasons: first, the discourse is heavy with previously adopted defensive positions of an ideological nature without room for middle ground or the building of consensus points and, second, the difficulty of getting official data on the profile of criminal offenders in Brazil. For these reasons, Brazil has seen a long debate about the possibility of reducing the legal age without, in most cases, minimally reliable data incorporated in the discussion.

If access to official data on the profile of criminal offenders in Brazil is already considered difficult, with regard to juveniles who have committed crimes, this difficulty is redoubled. The information about juveniles "in conflict with the law" (the terminology used in the ECA) is even more scarce. Ironically, the intensification of the debate about the project on reducing the legal age in recent years has highlighted the need for information on juvenile crime rates, resulting in the production of more consistent data by some of the states of the federation and its compilation in a systematic way.

According to data from the 9th Brazilian Yearbook of Public Security, Brazil went from a total of 4245 adolescents completing a sentence in the juvenile justice system in 1996 to 23,066 teenagers in 2013, an increase of 443.36% in less than two decades. Of the 23,066 adolescents completing a sentence in 2015, 15,221 juveniles were serving a sentence of imprisonment. *This explosive increase in the number of young people sentenced points not only to the increased participation of juvenile offenders but also to the expansion of the application by the juvenile justice system of social control mechanisms of imprisonment provided for by the Statute of the Child and Adolescent (ECA) over this period* (Graph 4.1).

The rate of juveniles between 12 and 17 years under sentencing by ECA increased from 97.7 per 100,000 in 2012 to 111.3 in 2013, a variation of 13.3%

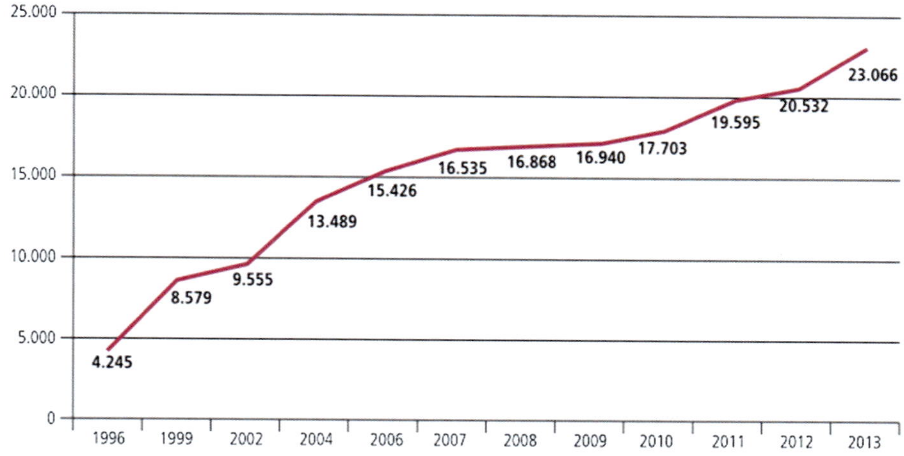

GRAPH 4.1. Juveniles under ECA sentencing in Brazil—1996–2013. **Fonte**: Secretaria Especial dos Direitos Humanos da Presidência da República (SEDH/PR)/Subsecretaria de Promoão dos Direitos da Criana e do Adolescente (SPDCA). Levantamento nacional do atendimento socioeducativo ao adolescente em conflito com a lei; Instituto Brasileiro de Geografia e Estatística (IBGE); Fórum Brasileiro de Segurana Pública.

in the period. However, in 2013 some states registered juvenile sentencing rates up to four times higher than the national average, as is the case of Acre (396.9 per 100,000), the Federal District of Brasília (294.5 per 100,000), Espírito Santo (236.4 per 100,000), and São Paulo (226.4 per 100 thousand). This indicates that both juvenile crime and the implementation of sentencing are disproportionately distributed throughout the country (Fórum Brasileiro de Segurança Pública 2015).

Of the total number of illegal acts committed by adolescents in Brazil in 2013, theft constituted the largest percentage with 42% followed by drug trafficking, with 24.8%. Homicides committed by teenagers, usually presented as the main argument for the defense of the reduction of legal age, represented 9.2% of the illegal acts committed by adolescents sentenced in Brazil that year.

Another way to measure the participation of adolescents in the murders committed in the country is to compare the total number of homicide cases either cleared or under investigation with the share of such cases reportedly committed by teenagers aged 12–17 years. According to the data of the 9th Brazilian Yearbook of Public Security, in 2014, there were 17,854 murders either cleared or under investigation, and of these 1915 were committed by teenagers between the ages of 12 and 17 years, making the percentage of juveniles reported and/or charged as suspects for homicides 10.7% of the total homicide cases in Brazil that year. Whether using this measure or examining the percentage of juveniles sentenced for ECA infractions with definitions similar to homicide, one can say with some confidence that teenagers account for 9–10% of all murders in Brazil in the last 2 years.

However, it is important to point out that these data, although aggregated by the Brazilian Forum on Public Security, are provided primarily through the State Departments of Public Safety and Social Defense and the State Civil Police, who are not obliged to publish data on juveniles. Additionally, the data available includes information from only 15 of the 27 states in Brazil, making it difficult to have accurate estimates of national juvenile crime rates.

Despite its incompleteness, it is possible to detect, with these data, a close resemblance between the profile of juveniles and adult offenders. In the case of adult offenders, those sentenced for committing theft and drug trafficking predominate among the percentage of those incarcerated (Fórum Brasileiro de Segurança Pública 2015).

It is also crucial to point out that juveniles, especially non-whites, make up a significant portion of all murder victims in the country, either as a murder victim or a victim of police lethality. The annual homicide rate of children and adolescents between 0 and 19 years increased from 3.1 per 100,000 in 1980 to 16.3 per 100,000 in 2013, a cumulative increase of 426.9% in these three decades (Waiselfisz 2015). When analyzing only juveniles aged 16 and 17 years, the segment of the population that will be most affected by the proposed reduction of the legal age in Brazil to 16 years of age, the homicide rate in 2013 was 54.1 per 100,000 inhabitants. This rate is about 2.5 times higher than the already high homicide rate of 20.4 murders per 100,000 registered in the country in the same year. Although the discussion about the effects of crime on a possible reduction of the age of majority from 18 to 16 years is still open, it is certain that teens in this age group are most vulnerable to the murders in Brazil.

CAUSES OF JUVENILE CRIME IN BRAZIL

The study of juvenile delinquency in Brazil is intertwined with the study of general crime. Given the similarities between the types of crimes committed by juveniles and adults, it is useful to examine the general trends in academic research on crime causation. Current research on crime causation and crime trends has its origins in two specific debates regarding the initial rise in violent urban crime in the mid-1980s. The first of these debates is centered on debunking common sense perceptions of poverty as the primary cause of crime.

Unlike in the United States, where academic research has found support for theories that link poverty to crime, such as anomie theory and subculture theories of violence, the academic research in Brazil have focused on countering the link between poverty and crime. This was done in response to public opinion about the causes of crime. Public perceptions of crime in urban Brazil depicted (and still depict) criminals as poor youth from the shantytowns or *favelas*. Thus, some of this research is aimed at demonstrating the bias of the criminal justice system toward repressing crime committed by such youth, even though crime is present in all social groups (Zaluar 1994). Other research has sought to dispel this public perception through the analysis of official data, demonstrating the spuriousness of the relationship between poverty and crime (Beato et al. 1998).

The second debate focuses on the role of the criminal justice system in contributing to the rise in crime. Some authors have pointed out to the relationship between the rise of crime and the lack of the deterrent capacity of the criminal justice system. They argue that reforms and improvements in the criminal justice system rather than social policies will have greater impacts on crime rates (Coelho 1978; Beato Filho et al. 2004). Others have explained rising crime rates as a consequence of the arbitrary action of the police and its impact on the legitimacy of the State, both as an entity with the monopoly over the use of force and as a mediator of conflicts. They specifically examined the role of the legacy of Brazil's 20-year dictatorship and its return to democracy in the 1980s as part of the explanation for the arbitrary nature of police behavior and practices (Adorno 1999; Cardia 2008; Caldeira 2000).

Current research on crime causation builds upon each of these original debates. Emerging out of the original discussion of poverty and crime is a body of current research reexamining the role of inequality (specifically income inequality) in the growth of urban crime. Rather than exclusively associating poverty with crime, these scholars examine the impact of inequalities of opportunities in the commission of crime (Beato Filho et al. 2004), as well as explanations for the spatial distribution of violent crime (especially homicide) in poor neighborhoods (Beato et al. 2001; Cardia 2008). Included here is the work of Brazilian economists, especially in collaboration with the World Bank (Fajnzylber et al. 1998) who examine the links between inequality and crime, as well as others (Andrade and Peixoto 2008) who have begun to examine the economic costs of crime, both in terms of state expenditures and loss of property and lives.

Emerging out of the original discussions of the role of the State and the criminal justice system is a body of work that examines the links between crime, citizenship, and human rights. Much of this work focuses specifically on the criminal justice system and will be covered more extensively in the next section. The research relating to crime causation following this perspective focuses on the impacts of criminal justice practices (especially authoritarian and arbitrary police practices) on crime causation. Also considered in these explanations is the level of impunity (crimes not prosecuted) of the criminal justice system and the implications of Brazil's democratic transition and the impact on the level of crime (Adorno 1998; Caldeira and Holston 1999).

However, these two central explanations for the causes of crime do not specifically examine one important feature of youth crime, the intersection of juvenile crime (especially theft, drug trafficking, and homicide) with participation in territorialized youth groups. Drug trafficking can take many forms according to the type of substances sold, sales volume, and distribution strategies, among other features. However, based on the profile of juveniles serving sentences for drug trafficking in Brazil—black or brown, with low education and residents of the urban periphery and slums—it can be inferred that a significant proportion of juveniles arrested for drug trafficking participate in street-level retail sales that are highly territorialized through the divisions of slums and peripheral urban areas into competitive drug sale points, often with hierarchical organization and the intensive use of young people as labor. In this specific model of drug trafficking, criminal practice emerges as a stable and high source of income if we take into account the low level of education of these young people. As an occupation, drug trafficking, in this format, resembles to some extent formal employment, with fixed income expectations, clearly defined responsibilities, and even the ability to climb the hierarchy of the local organization, shifting to jobs that are more profitable and less exposed to police surveillance (Teixeira 2013).

However, this model of drug trafficking present in the slums and other poor urban neighborhoods in Brazil produces a number of other consequences. Each drug sale point, as well as their operators, is part of the larger community, but also makes up a micro-territory to be defended from drug gangs from other territories, as well as from police raids. This territorial control exercised by the drug trade in some neighborhoods makes it necessary for traffickers to arm themselves openly and engage in violent clashes with rivals for control of these territories and their points of sale (Zaluar 1994; Zilli 2011).

Research that has examined the social organization of drug trafficking (Zaluar 2004; Alvito 2001; Dowdney 2003; Mingardi 1998) attempts to understand the patterns of drug trafficking and the reasons for juvenile participation in drug trafficking gangs. This research draws heavily from theorists examining patterns of social interactions and civility such as Norbert Elias (1994), rather than classic gang research from the United States.

Beyond drug trafficking, another phenomenon that may account for the involvement of adolescents in crime in Brazil is armed youth groups, whether they be called gangs, bands, or crews. Much like juvenile gangs described in the classical sociological literature, these groups stand out for their territorialization, the strong identification of its members with the group, and their violent clashes with similar groups from other regions. These juvenile groups may be associated with the practice of drug trafficking and theft and usually commit such offenses, but they can also be structured through disputes involving graffiti, the funk or rave dance, and party circuit (Abramovay 2010; Andrade 2007; Diógenes 2008) or a dynamic of intra-community retribution and revenge against other gangs' attacks, which are linked to local rivalries that span years or even decades (Rocha 2015; Zilli 2011).

In some Brazilian cities, the rivalries between these juvenile groups, and the armed clashes resulting from them, are responsible for a significant proportion of homicides involving teenagers and young adults, either as perpetrators or as victims. For example, in Belo Horizonte and in the cities that make up the metropolitan region, a significant proportion of registered homicides committed by juveniles stem from territorialized armed conflict between gangs operating in the slums of the capital and the cities around it (Zilli 2011). These atomized clashes involving numerous groups and their relations of enmity and alliances appear as a major cause of homicides committed by adolescents in several other Brazilian cities as well, such as Fortaleza (Diógenes 2008), Brasilia and its satellite cities (Abramovay 2004; Andrade 2007), and São Paulo especially in the decades of 1990 and 2000. Apart from drug trafficking or other criminal practices, the rivalries between these groups and gangs organize and structure the relations of the members with the group itself, making up essential dynamics to the process of gang membership and membership maintenance, since it is by participating in violent clashes with rivals that solidarity among members and group identity are reinforced.

POLICING AND JUVENILES

In any discussion of the role of the police in the juvenile justice system, it is necessary to briefly describe the organization of policing in Brazil. Brazil is a federation with 26 states, and policing is primarily organized on the state level, although there is a Federal Police charged with the duties of border security and acting as the national judicial police. At the state level, policing is divided into two autonomous organizations, the Military Police (Polícia Militar) and the Civil Police (Polícia Civil), both part of the state executive branch. The Military Police operate as the preventive and repressive arm of the police, responsible for maintaining public order. The Civil Police are the investigative arm of the police, responsible for investigating crimes.

In relation to juvenile offenders, there is no special branch of the Military Police tasked with supervision or control of juveniles. The regular precincts of the Military Police will detain a juvenile if he or she is caught committing an illegal act or in the course of fulfilling a judicial order of apprehension (similar to a warrant). If the youth is under 12 years of age, he or she will be brought to the municipal Guardianship Council (Conselho Tutelar) or the judge of the acting state Childhood and Juvenile Court. If the youth is an adolescent (12–17), a police report will be filed and the minor turned over to a specialized branch of the Civil Police, the Juvenile Police Station (in the case of apprehension during commission of an illegal act). If the Military Police detain a minor to fulfilling a judicial order, the adolescent will be taken to the juvenile judge who issued the order.

The Civil Police, charged with investigating crimes, have a specialized department, the Juvenile Police Station, to investigate juveniles suspected of committing illegal acts. The police are required to follow procedures designed to protect the rights of the juvenile being investigated, such as dispensing the use of handcuffs, identifying by name and badge number the detaining officer, and informing the judge or family of the minor's detention as per his or her request (Art. 107 ECA, Brasil 1990).

Regardless of such procedural guarantees, the police, especially the Military Police, have constantly come under attack from academics, nongovernmental organizations, and the media for their violent and often lethal treatment of juveniles suspected of crimes, citing evidence of profiling and discriminatory treatment of poor, non-white youth (Adorno 2002). Some explain this bias as part of the legacy of "criminalization of poverty" that has shaped juvenile justice for much of Brazil's history (Misse 2009; Marinho 2012).

COURTS AND JUVENILES

The ECA stipulates the creation of specialized juvenile courts at the state level to not only handle juvenile offenders but also make decisions on matters such as adoption, juvenile emancipation, and travel authorizations. In terms of juvenile offenders, the specialized courts, known as Childhood and Juvenile Courts (Vara da Infância e Juventude), only handle cases of adolescents (12–18), given that juveniles under 12 years of age are not criminally responsible. Cases involving children under 12 years are handled by the Guardianship Council established in each city.

When the police detain a juvenile offender, the case is turned over to the state attorney's office. Once with the state attorney's office, this branch is responsible for interrogating the suspected juvenile, his or her parents, and any victims or witnesses available. It is the responsibility of the state attorney's office to decide how the case should proceed. Within the ECA, there are three possible trajectories: (1) the case can be shelved (arquivado); (2) the state's attorney can concede remission-forgiveness of the offense; or (3) it can be presented to the judge with a recommendation of sanctioning. The second option, remission-forgiveness, is analogous to the situation of plea bargaining in North American courts and is an option only available in juvenile cases. This procedure, initiated prior to taking the case to court, acts as a form of dismissal of the case. However, remission does not imply necessarily the absence of recognition of criminal responsibility nor does it exclude the juvenile from the application of sanctions, with the exception of semi-liberty and confinement. A case where remission has been applied can be reviewed judicially upon request of either the juvenile or the state attorney's office (Brasil 1990).

There is no recent national data available to examine the distribution of custodial and noncustodial sanctions given in the context of the use of remission. Data from the state of Minas Gerais for 2010 provides a picture of the use of these measures, however. In 2010, a total of 7929 first-time offenders passed through the juvenile state court. Of this total, in the preliminary hearings, 3.8% were shelved and 44.9% were given remission, either completely or with the addition of a noncustodial sanction (the highest application of these was a warning, at 23.8%). This data demonstrates that almost half of the cases in juvenile court are resolved in the first instance and with noncustodial sanctions (Tribunal de Justiça do Estado de Minas Gerais 2011).

JUVENILE SANCTIONS

The ECA introduced a plurality of sanctions for juvenile offenders, as well as separating the responses of the system to socially vulnerable or abandoned juveniles from its responses to juvenile offenders. ECA provides for custodial as well as noncustodial sanctions.

Custodial Rules for Juveniles

The custodial sanctions for juveniles include confinement in an educational facility and "semi-liberty," in which the juvenile attends work or school during the day and returns to an educational facility at night. According to ECA, the sanction of confinement is to be used "when an infraction is committed using grave threat or violence to another" and "under no circumstance will internment be applied when there is another applicable sanction available" (Art. 122, ECA, 1990).[3] There are no set limits for confinement based on the type of offense. Rather, the continuance of a sanction of confinement is to be reevaluated at least every 6 months. The ECA stipulates that no period of confinement shall exceed a period of 3 years. After such a period, the juvenile should be placed in semi-liberty or a noncustodial sanction. Release from custody is also compulsory when the juvenile reaches 21 years of age.

The sanction of semi-liberty can be applied either as an initial measure or a transitional one from a custodial to a noncustodial sanction. Such a sanction requires that the juvenile be engaged actively in employment or schooling. Juveniles in semi-liberty return to the same facilities as those in traditional confinement, and the length and nature of the sanction follow the same guidelines as confinement (no prescribed length, minimum 6 months review, and maximum 3 year sanction). In addition to the sanctions of confinement and semi-liberty, some juveniles are held in provisional confinement, when, after initial detention by police, their release poses an immediate threat to themselves or the community. Such confinement is limited to a maximum of 45 days.

The facilities for confinement, described as educational facilities in the ECA, are establishments for the exclusive purpose of housing juvenile offenders, with separation of offenders by age and type of offense. The ECA also stipulates that while in confinement, juveniles must have access to weekly visits; correspondence with family and friends; schooling and job training; cultural, sporting, and leisure activities; and religious guidance, if desired. These facilities are run by each of the individual states, under a branch of the executive. In 2013, the most recent data was made available by the SENASE (the National System of Socio-Educational Services). The data show that there were a total of 23,066

[3]ECA, article 122, section I, "tratar-se de ato infracional cometido mediante grave ameaça ou violência a pessoa" and ECA, article 122, paragraph 2, "Em nenhuma hipótese será aplicada a internação, havendo outra medida adequada," author's translation.

juveniles in custody in Brazil, either in confinement (64%), semi-liberty (10%), or provisional confinement (23%), equivalent to 0.08% of the total juvenile population. These juveniles were housed in 466 juvenile custodial facilities in Brazil, with 46% of these concentrated in the more populous southeast region of the country. Of this total, 377 were dedicated to housing only male juvenile offenders, 52 housed both female and male offenders, and 37 housed only female offenders. The administration of most juvenile facilities falls under the secretaries of social defense and citizenship (13 states). In some states, however, the administration is part of the secretaries of justice (7 states), labor (4 states), specific secretaries for juvenile welfare (2 states), or even under the secretary of education (1 state) (Secretaria de Direitos Humanos da Presidência da República 2013).

Alternative Sanctions for Juvenile

There are four noncustodial sanctions for juveniles stipulated in the ECA: warnings, reparation of harm, community service, and supervised probation. Unlike the custodial sanctions for juveniles, which are carried out by state agencies, the noncustodial sanctions are under the jurisdiction of the municipal authorities. The warning is a verbal admonition, formalized in writing. The reparation of harm consists of compensation, restitution, or replacement of the property of the victim. This sanction is limited to infractions committed against property. Community service consists of performing works free of compensation and in the general interest for a period of no more than 6 months. These works are performed in social service entities, hospitals, schools, and other similar agencies as well as community and government programs. Community service activities are designed by taking into account the aptitudes of the juvenile and do not exceed more than 8 h of service weekly. They are carried out on the weekends, holidays, or weekdays in such a manner as not to interfere with school or employment activities.

Supervised probation, according to the ECA, should be applied in cases where the intention is to "accompany, aid, and advise" the juvenile. In practice, it consists of the designation of a supervisor to accompany the juvenile for a period of 6 months. This period can be extended, suspended, or substituted by another sanction, based on the recommendation of the supervisor, the state's attorney's office, or the public defender (or juvenile's defense attorney). The supervisor has the responsibility to (1) socially advance the juvenile and his or her family, providing them advice and enrolling them, if necessary, in official or community programs and social aid and assistance; (2) supervise the frequency of school attendance; and (3) aid the juvenile in his or her further professionalization and insertion into the job market. These activities are carried out within the parameters of specific municipal programs, designed to support and oversee the responsibilities of the supervisor. The exact form of this program and their specific activities or structure vary by municipality.

In the case of the municipality of Belo Horizonte, the third largest city in Brazil, for example, the Assisted Liberty Program (Programa Liberdade Assistida) is implemented by the Municipal Secretary of Social Assistance in partnership with the Catholic Church and the juvenile court. It consists of a program center in the nine administrative units of the city where juveniles meet on a weekly basis with an interdisciplinary team (social service, psychology, and psychoanalysis). This team articulates necessary actions and referrals. The supervisors are volunteers from the community, referred to as social advisors, whose duties are more mentorship than that of traditional case supervisor.

Regardless of the plurality of sanctions and the stipulation in the ECA that confinement is to be used sparingly, confinement continues to be the sanction of choice in the juvenile courts for cases of homicide, drug trafficking, and robbery (Marinho 2012). In addition, extrajudicial factors such as years of schooling, family structure, and family income appear to be significant factors in the determination of sanctions, especially the choice between noncustodial and custodial options. Juveniles enrolled in school or with more schooling, living with both parents and in families with higher incomes, are more likely to receive noncustodial sanctions than juveniles who are not in school or who come from low-income families, for similar infractions (Silva 2011; Marinho 2012).

DIFFERENCES IN TREATMENT OF BOYS AND GIRLS

The paradigm of full protection that guided the creation of the ECA brought the issue of citizenship to the center of legislation and public policies for juvenile offenders. However, the ECA makes no specific mention to issues related to gender and race. The only mention of gender is in regard to the procedures for the punishment and combating of violence and sexual exploitation of children and adolescents, which is an unquestionable achievement brought about by the Statute (Brasil 1990). However, in addition to a specific agenda toward combating sex crimes, it would be expected that the document contemplates the positive expression of rights related to sex, gender, and sexuality, especially for the implementation of educational measures.

Specific language regarding gender, however, was included in later legislation amending the ECA. The National System of Socio-Educational Services (SINASE) was approved in 2006 by the National Council for the Rights of Children and Adolescents (CONANDA) (Brasil 2006) and was established by Federal Law No. 12,594, of January 18, 2012. The SINASE regulates the execution of socio-educational measures throughout the national territory (Brasil 2012). In order to determine the norms and standards SINASE would follow, the federal government prepared and published the National Plan for Socio-Educational Services in 2013. Included in its guidelines is the guarantee of the "right to sexuality and reproductive health, respecting gender identity and sexual orientation."

In the resolution creating the CONANDA (Brasil 2006), there are more specific guidelines on the issue of differential treatment for men and women in fulfillment of socio-educational measures. In that document, the socio-educational measures are defined by parameters organized by a series of strategic axis, among which is the axis of "ethno-racial diversity, gender, and sexual orientation." With respect to educational management within the juvenile justice system, the document states that it is the responsibility of all institutions and/or programs that perform educational measures "to ensure equity in the socio-educational measures provided to adolescents of both sexes, especially with regard to the quality and supply of services and activities" (Brasil 2006: 58).

With regard to architectural parameters, SINASE guarantees physical separation between male and female dormitories for detainment as well as special housing to accommodate adolescent mothers and their newborns and babies up to 6 months of age (Brasil 2006: 70). Law 12,594/2012 specifically states that "to ensure the exercise of sexual and reproductive rights, through deliberations over juveniles with children in detainment units and visitation of children to their mothers and teenage parents; as well as access to conjugal visits" is a goal to be fully met by the Secretariat on Human Rights (SDH) and State/District systems by the end of the year 2023.

However, for now, the annual survey conducted by SINASE compiling data on detainment and supervision of juveniles indicates that in 2015, the female adolescents accounted for 4% (984) of the total 23,913 adolescents detained or under supervision in the country. These teens were distributed between 37 (7.93%) exclusively female units and another 52 (11.15%) mixed institutions, with five (05) Federal States responding that they had no units solely dedicated to female adolescents.

CONCLUSIONS

The Statue of the Child and Adolescent (ECA) passed in 1990 was a major advancement in juvenile justice in Brazil. In the first place, it solidified into national law the international treaties on the rights of children and adolescents of its day. Secondly, it moved juvenile justice in Brazil away from a guardianship model to a full protection model that conceived of children as full legal subjects. This resulted in the decoupling of practices and services for at-risk and abandoned youth from those for juvenile offenders. However, in practice, the legacy of the guardianship model has been hard to break. The police and juvenile courts continue to equate juvenile offenders with poor, non-white youths residing in the slums or peripheral neighborhoods of urban centers, thus continuing what some have referred to as the "criminalization of poverty" (Marinho 2012). While the expansion of the use of noncustodial sanctions, such as supervised probation, has been on the rise, the racial and economic biases present in the juvenile justice system echo the same biases present in the adult criminal justice system.

Countering these biases in the juvenile justice system needs to be done in conjunction with countering these same biases in the general criminal justice system, a task made all the more difficult with the rising crime rates, both for juveniles and adults in Brazil.

REFERENCES

Abramovay, M. (2004). *Gangues, galeras, chegados e rappers: Juventude, violência e cidadania nas cidades da periferia de Brasília*. Brasília: Editora Garamond.

Abramovay, M. (2010). *Gangues, gênero e juventudes: Donas de rocha e sujeitos cabulosos*. Brasília: Secretaria de Direitos Humanos.

Adorno, S. (1998). *Violence, security and public perceptions in Brazil*. Paper presented at 1998 Meeting of the Latin American Studies Association, Chicago, September.

Adorno, S. (1999). Racial discrimination and criminal justice in São Paulo. In R. Reichmann (Ed.), *Race in contemporary Brazil. From indifference to equality* (pp. 123–137). Pennsylvania: The Pennsylvania University Press.

Adorno, S. (2002). Youth crime in São Paulo: Myths, images and facts. In S. Rotker (Ed.), *Citizens of fear—Urban violence in Latin America* (pp. 102–116). New York: Rutgers, The State University of New Jersey Press.

Alvito, M. (2001). *As cores de Acari: Uma favela carioca*. Rio de Janeiro: Editora Fundação Getúlio Vargas.

Andrade, C. C. (2007). *Entre gangues e galeras: Juventude, violência e sociabilidade na periferia do Distrito Federal*. Tese de Doutorado defendida junto ao Instituto de Ciências Sociais do Departamento de Antropologia da Universidade de Brasília. Brasília, Distrito Federal.

Andrade, M. V., & Peixoto, B. T. (2008). Avaliação econômica de programas de prevenção e controle da criminalidade no Brasil. In C. Beato (Ed.), *Compreendendo e Avaliando projetos de segurança pública*. Belo Horizonte: UFMG.

Arruda, Jalusa Silva de. (2011). *Para ver as meninas: Um estudo sobre as adolescentes em cumprimento de medida socioeducativa de internação na CASE/Salvador*. Dissertação de Mestrado—Universidade Federal da Bahia. Faculdade de Filosofia e Ciências Humanas, Salvador.

Beato Filho, C. C., Assunção, R., Santos, M. A. C, Santo, L. E. E., Sapori, L. F. & Batitucci, E. (1998). Evolução da Criminalidade Violenta em Minas Gerais 1985–1997. In: *XXII Reunião da ANPOCS, 1997, Caxambu*. Sessão Violência Justiça e Direitos. São Paulo: ANPOCS.

Beato Filho, C. C., Marinho, F. C., & Silva, B. F. A. (2001) Conglomerados de homicídios e o tráfico de drogas em Belo Horizonte, Minas Gerais, Brasil, de 1995 a 1999. *Cadernos de Saúde Pública, n. 17*. Rio de Janeiro.

Beato Filho, C. C., Viegas, M., & Peixoto, B. T. (2004). Crime, oportunidade e vitimização. *Revista Brasileira de Ciências Sociais, 19*(55), 73–89.

Brasil. (1927). Consolida as leis de assistência e proteção a menores. Lei 17.943 de 12 de outubro de 1927. Diário Oficial da União.

Brasil. (1940). Código Penal. Decreto-Lei 2.848 de 7 de dezembro de 1940 Diário Oficial da União.

Brasil. (1964). Lei que Autoriza o Poder Executivo a criar a Fundação Nacional do Bem-Estar do Menor, a ela incorporando o patrimônio e as atribuições do Serviço de Assistência a Menores, e dá outras providências. Lei 4.513 de 1° de dezembro de 1964. Diário Oficial da União.

Brasil. (1990). *Estatuto da Criança e do Adolescente. Lei Complementar 8.069 de 13 de julho de 1990*. Diário Oficial da União.

Brasil. (2006). Conselho Nacional dos Direitos da Criança e do Adolescente. Sistema Nacional de Atendimento Socioeducativo. Resolução n. 119, de 11 de dezembro de 2006. Diário Oficial da União.

Brasil. (2012). Institui o Sistema Nacional de Atendimento Socioeducativo (Sinase). Lei 12.594 de 18 de janeiro de 2012. Diário Oficial da União.

Caldeira, T. P. R. (2000). *City without walls: Crime, segregation and citizenship*. California: University of California Press.

Caldeira, T. P. R., & Holston, J. (1999). Democracy and violence in Brazil. *Comparative Studies in Society and History, 41*(4), 691–729.

Cardia, N. G. (2008). Risco de ocorrencias de homicidios dolosos em São Paulo. In Secretaria Municipal de Planejamento; Departamento de Estatísticas e Produção de Informações. (Org.). *Olhar São Paulo—Violência e Criminalidade*. São Paulo: Secretaria Municipal de Planejamento.

Coelho, C. E. (1978). *A criminalização da marginalidade e a marginalização da criminalidade* (Revista Brasileira de Administração Pública). Rio de Janeiro: Fundação Getúlio Vargas.

Diógenes, G. (2008). *Cartografias da cultura e da violência: gangues, galeras e o movimento hip hop*. São Paulo: Annablume.

Dowdney, L. (2003). *As crianças do tráfico: Um estudo de caso de crianças em violência armada organizada em Rio de Janeiro*. Rio de Janeiro: 7 Letras.

Elias, N. (1994). *The civilizing process*. Oxford: Blackwell.

Fajnzylber, P., Lederman, D., & Loayza, N. (1998). *Determinants of crime rates in Latin America and the world: An empirical assessment*. Washington, DC: World Bank Latin American and Caribbean Studies.

Fórum Brasileiro de Segurança Pública. (2015). *Anuário do Fórum Brasileiro de Segurança Pública—2015*. Ano 9.

Marinho, F. C. (2012). *Mudanças, resistências e mediações no campo sociojudiciário da gestão da delinquência juvenil: uma abordagem comparativa entre França e Brasil*. p326. Tese de Doutorado. Belo Horizonte: Faculdade de Filosofia e Ciências Humanas (FAFICH).

Méndez, E. G. (2006). Evolución histórica del derecho de la infância: ¿Por que uma historia de los derechos de la infância? ILANUD, ABMP, SEDH, UNFPA (Orgs.). *Justiça, adolescente e ato infracional: socioeducação e responsabilização*. São Paulo: Ilanud.

Mingardi, G. (1998). *O que é crime organizado: Uma definição das ciências sociais* (Revista do Ilanud). São Paulo: Ilanud.

Misse, M. (2009). Sobre a acumulação social da violência no Rio de Janeiro. *Civitas—Revista de Ciências Sociais, 8*(3), 371–385.

Rocha, R. L. S. (2015). A guerra como forma de relação: Uma análise das rivalidades violentas entre gangues em um aglomerado de Belo Horizonte. *Dilemas: Revista de Estudos de Conflito e Controle Social, 8*(2), 277–301.

Secretaria de Direitos Humanos da Presidência da República. (2013). *Levantamento Anual do SINASE*.

Silva, R. (1997). *Os filhos do Governo. A formação da identidade criminal em crianças órfãs e abandonadas*. São Paulo: Ática.

Silva, G. M. (2011). Justiça juvenil no Brasil: Breve revisão da literatura. *Revista Brasileira de Adolescência e Conflitualidade, 5*, 160–182.

Teixeira, A. (2013). *O lugar dos adolescentes na dinâmica do crime e sua gestão na cidade de São Paulo*. XVI Congresso Brasileiro de Sociologia.

Tribunal de Justiça do Estado de Minas Gerais. (2011). *Relatório Estatístico*. Setor de Pesquisa Infracional. CIA/BH—Centro Integrado de Atendimento ao Adolescente Autor de Ato Infracional. Vara Infracional da Infância e da Juventude.

Waiselfisz, J. J. (2015). *Mapa da violência 2015: Adolescentes de 16 e 17 anos no Brasil*. Brasília: Flacso Brasil.

Zaluar, A. (1994). *Condomínio do diabo*. Rio de Janeiro: Editora Revan.

Zaluar, A. (2004). *Integração perversa: Pobreza e tráfico de drogas*. Rio de Janeiro: FGV Editora.

Zilli, L. F. (2011). *O bonde tá formado: gangues, ambiente urbano e criminalidade violenta*. Tese de Doutorado defendida junto ao Departamento de Sociologia da Universidade Federal de Minas Gerais.

Corinne Davis Rodrigues Associate professor in the Department of Sociology and director of the Center for Urban Studies (CEURB) at the Federal University of Minas Gerais. Her main areas of research are urban crime and perceptions of safety in Brazil, with publications in *Latin American Politics and Society*, *the Annals of the American Academy of Political and Social Science*, and *Estudios Sociológicos*. Her current research is focused on understanding the causes of interurban variations in crime in Brazil.

Valéria Cristina de Oliveira Post-doctoral fellow at the Center for Metropolitan Studies (CEM) at the University of São Paulo. She earned her Ph.D. in sociology from the Federal University of Minas Gerais in 2016, during which she completed a year of training in the Department of Criminology and Criminal Justice at the Florida State University (2014/2015). She also has a master's degree in sociology (2009) and an undergraduate degree in social science (2006), also from the Federal University of Minas Gerais. Her academic publications are focused on understanding the causes and correlates of criminal victimization, especially the effect of neighborhood characteristics and fear on criminal victimization.

Rafael Lacerda Silveira Rocha Researcher at the Center for the Study of Criminality and Public Safety (CRISP) at the Federal University of Minas Gerais. He is a doctoral candidate in the Graduate Program in Sociology at the Federal University of Minas Gerais, where he also received his master's degree in sociology and undergraduate degree in social science. His academic publications are in the area of youth and violence, especially focusing on gangs and homicide.

5

Canada

Nicholas Bala and Peter J. Carrington

INTRODUCTION: THE CONTEXT FOR JUVENILE JUSTICE IN CANADA

In Canada the federal parliament has jurisdiction to enact criminal law, including juvenile justice legislation, while responsibility for the establishment of youth courts and the provision of services for young offenders, as well as jurisdiction over child welfare, rests with the provincial governments.

Prior to the coming into force of the *Youth Criminal Justice Act* (*YCJA*) in 2003, Canada had a discretionary approach to youth justice and one of the highest rates in the world for juvenile court referrals and imposing custody in matters involving adolescent offenders (Doob & Cesaroni 2010). The *YCJA* significantly structured the discretion of police, prosecutors, and judges, resulting in substantial reductions in court referral and youth detention rates; more cases involving youth are being diverted from the courts and more use being made of community-based sentencing options—with no increase in youth crime rates.

This chapter reviews key provisions of the *YCJA* and leading precedents on juvenile justice in Canada, considers Canadian empirical research on juvenile offending, and analyzes the most recent Canadian statistical data on juvenile offending and the use of youth court.

N. Bala (✉)
Faculty of Law, Queen's University, Kingston, ON K7L 3N6, Canada
e-mail: bala@queensu.ca

P.J. Carrington
University of Waterloo, Waterloo, ON N2L 3G1, Canada
e-mail: pjc@uwaterloo.ca

S.H. Decker, N. Marteache (eds.), *International Handbook of Juvenile Justice*,
DOI 10.1007/978-3-319-45090-2_5

THE LEGAL STATUS OF JUVENILES

In Canada, those charged with offenses that are alleged to have occurred between their twelfth and eighteenth birthdays are referred to as "young persons" and dealt with under the *Youth Criminal Justice Act.* Children under the age of 12 who engage in offending behaviors are typically dealt with by voluntary measures arranged by their parents, though child welfare authorities may also become involved, and in very serious cases a child might be removed from parental care under a court process and placed in a foster home or mental health facility under child welfare legislation.

AGE OF MAJORITY

For the purposes of criminal liability, adulthood in Canada commences on the 18th birthday, though those who commit offenses prior to that date will be dealt with as youth offenders. In exceptional cases involving very serious offenses, there is the possibility of a young person receiving an adult length sentence, though no one under the age of 18 may be detained in an adult correctional facility, and young persons' receiving an adult sentence of life imprisonment for murder are eligible for parole earlier than adult offenders who have committed the same offense.

For most civil law purposes in Canada, adulthood also commences at 18, though in British Columbia the age of majority for some civil purposes is 19.

CANADA AND THE CONVENTION ON THE RIGHTS OF THE CHILD

Canada ratified the United Nations *Convention on the Rights of the Child.* The Preamble to the *Youth Criminal Justice Act* makes specific reference to the *Convention* and respect for the rights of youth.

The *Convention* has been cited by the Supreme Court in a number of cases and has been influential in the interpretation of the *YCJA.* The most significant decision to rely on the *Convention* was the 2008 decision in *R v. D.B.* where Court quoted Art 40(1) of the Convention and held that the principle of the "*limited* accountability" for youthful offenders has a constitutional dimension. The Supreme Court concluded that Section 7 of the *Canadian Charter of Rights and Freedoms* and the "principles of fundamental justice" require that youths are to be afforded a "*presumption* of diminished moral blameworthiness." Accordingly, the Court ruled unconstittuional a provision of the *YCJA* that created a presumption that adult sentences should be imposed on youth who committed the most serious offenses, including murder and manslaughter; that provision has been repealed as a result of the decision.

In 2012, Parliament amended the *YCJA* to reflect *R v. D.B.* by adding a statement to the Declaration of Principle that criminal justice for young persons "must be based on the principle of diminished moral blameworthiness or culpability". Furtther the Act was amended to provide a process for imposition of adult sentences that in all cases imposes an obligation on the prosecution to justify this most serious sanction. *R. v D.B.* has in effect "constitutionalized" adolescence in terms of criminal law in Canada. At some points in the past, conservative politicians criticizing youth justice law argued that the age of adult criminal responsibility in Canada should be reduced to 16 years of age, as it was prior to 1984. However, based on the *Convention on the Rights of the Child* and the *Canadian Charter* the Supreme Court in *D.B.* has established that it would be unconstitutional not to recognize all youths under 18 years as being subject to special legal treatment, and that age cannot be reduced.

In other cases the Supreme Court has invoked *Convention* to hold that the provisions of the *YCJA* that allow for imposition of custodial sentences should be "narrowly construed," so as to restrict the use of custody for adolescents (*R v C.D.* 2005b) and to exclude general deterrence as a principle for youth sentencing (*R. v. B.W.P.* 2006). The Court has also cited the *Convention* as the basis for a ruling that the a judge should take account of the "heightened vulnerability of youth" in determining whether to require a youth found guilty of offense to provide a DNA sample for the permanent police records (*R v C.D.* 2005a).

In 2012, in response to the concerns raised in the Report of the United Nations Committee (2012) on the Rights of the Child (para 17) about inconsistency with the *Convention*, Parliament amended the *YCJA* to ensure that youths who receive adult sentences cannot be placed in an adult correctional facility until after their 18 birthdays.

TRENDS IN JUVENILE CRIME OVER THE PERIOD 2004–2014

There are two sources of data on trends over time in youth crime in Canada. The Uniform Crime Reporting (UCR) Survey is an annual census of police-reported crime and apprehended (alleged) offenders of all ages (Statistics Canada 2015a). The General Social Survey on Victimization is a module of Statistics Canada's General Social Survey that captures data on Canadians' personal and household victimization experiences. It is administered every 5–6 years to a representative sample of Canadians aged 15 or older (Perrault 2015).

Figure 5.1 shows the recent trend in the per capita rates of police-reported chargeable youth in Canada.[1] The annual youth crime rate fluctuated around 7500–8000 per 100,000 youth during 2004–2007 and then decreased substantially

[1] In the UCR Survey, a "chargeable" person is defined as "person who has been identified as an accused person in an incident and against whom a charge may be laid in connection with that incident" (Canadian Centre for Justice Statistics 2013: 14)—whether or not that person was actually arrested or charged.

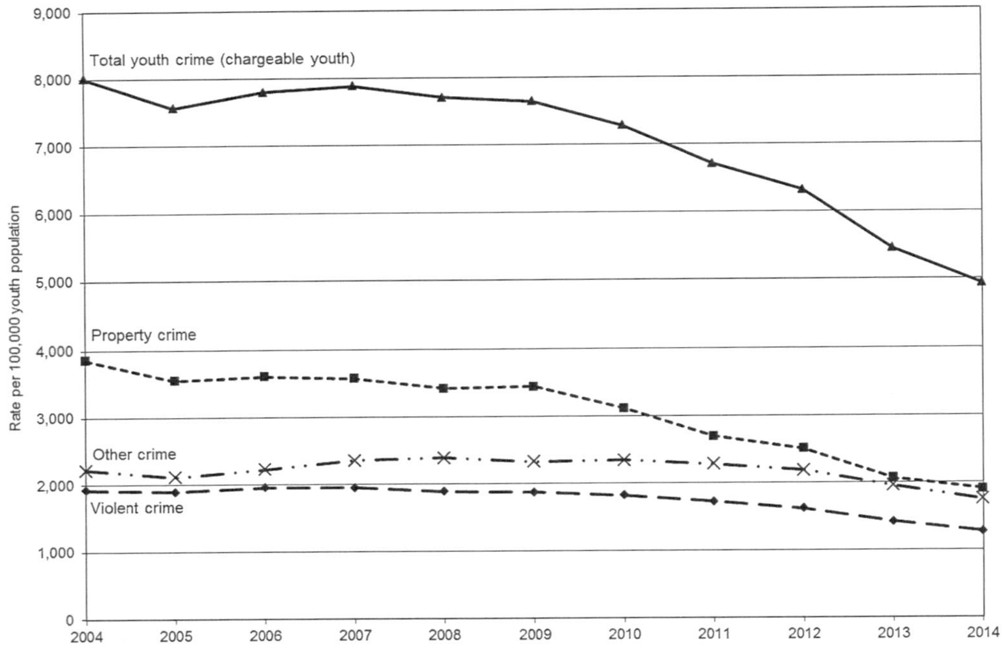

FIGURE 5.1. Trends in police-reported youth crime rates in Canada, 2004–2014. Note: Prepared by the authors using data from CANSIM Table 252–0051 (Statistics Canada 2015b).

through 2014. The youth crime rate in 2014 was 4934 per 100,000, which is 62% of the rate in 2004 (8006). The rates of violent, property, and other[2] youth crime all decreased over the period but to differing degrees. The property crime rate in 2014 (1904 per 100,000) was 49% of the rate in 2004 (3858). The violent and other youth crime rates in 2014 were, respectively, 66% and 79% of the rates in 2004. In 2004, property crime constituted approximately 50% of all police-reported youth crime; by 2014, this proportion had declined to 39% (Fig. 5.2). Meanwhile, other crimes (principally drug offenses) increased from 28% to 36% of police-reported youth crime. The proportion of violent crime increased slightly from 24% in 2004 to 26% in 2014. More detailed analyses have found that the overall seriousness of police-reported youth crime decreased from 1986 to 2011 (Carrington 2013, 2015a) and has continued to decrease since then.

According to Perrault (2015: 5), the overall rate of violent victimizations in Canada in 2014, by perpetrators of all ages, was 72% of the 2004 rate. The proportion of violent victimizations in which the perpetrator was identified as a young person decreased slightly from 13% in 2004 (Gannon & Mihorean 2005: 10) to 12% in 2014 (Perrault 2015: 37): that is, the proportion in 2014 was 92%

[2]"Other" crime in the UCR Survey includes weapons possession and storage, prostitution, gambling, other public orders, administration of justice, serious traffic, drug-related, and miscellaneous offenses.

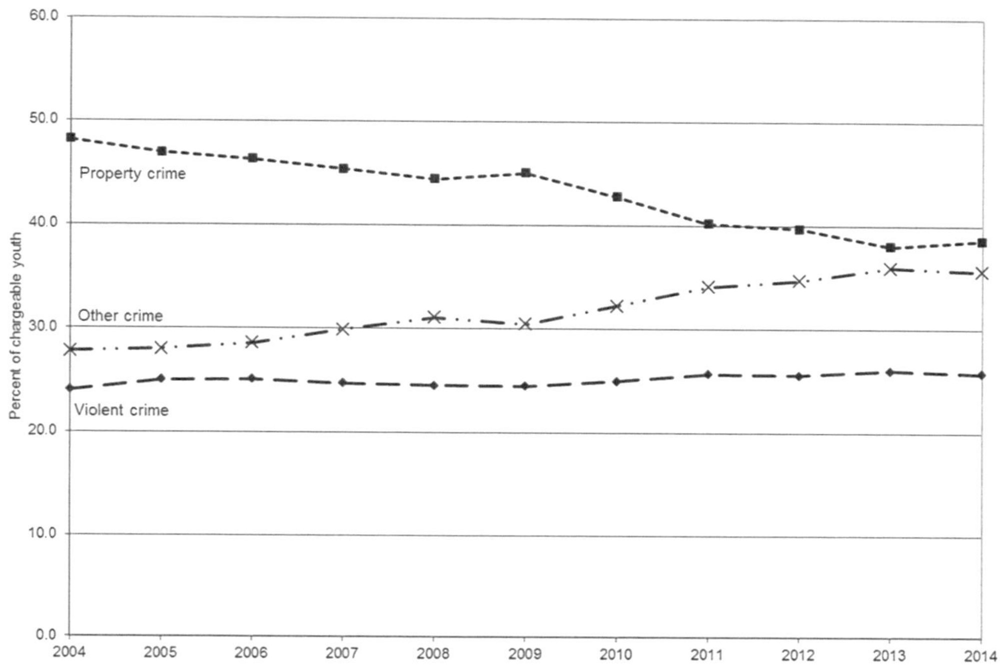

FIGURE 5.2. Trends in the nature of police-reported youth crime in Canada, 2004–2014. Note: Prepared by the authors using data from CANSIM Table 252–0051 (Statistics Canada 2015b).

(12/13) of that in 2004. Thus, the rate of violent victimizations perpetrated by young persons in 2014 was approximately 66% (72%×92%) of the rate in 2004. The analysis of UCR data (above) also concluded that the 2014 per capita rate of violent youth crime was 66% of the 2004 rate. It is not possible to use the victimization data to corroborate the findings for property and other crimes committed specifically by youth, but Perrault (2015: 7) does note that the rate of property-related victimizations by perpetrators of all ages reported in the Victimization Survey decreased from 2004 to 2014 by approximately the same amount as the rate of police-reported property crime. These findings based on victimization data provide some corroboration of the findings on the decline in police-reported youth property crime.

CAUSES OF JUVENILE CRIME

Canadian research on the causes of youth crime has been mainly empirical, based largely on existing theories developed in other countries, mainly the United States. However, a few Canadian criminologists have made major contributions to new theories of youth crime. Notable examples include the major contributions of Le Blanc and his colleagues who formulated and tested developmental criminology (e.g., Le Blanc & Fréchette 1989; Le Blanc & Loeber 1998), the work of Tremblay on the development of violence in early childhood (e.g., Broidy et al. 2003; Nagin & Tremblay 1999; Tremblay 2000; Tremblay et al. 2004), and the power-control theory of Hagan and his colleagues (e.g., Hagan et al. 1985, 1987, 1988).

The bulk of Canadian research on the causes of youth crime is situated within one of the following theories: social control, differential association and peer influence, life course and developmental theory, feminist theories, and social disorganization theory. This necessarily brief review of research is organized under those headings.

Social control theory: Canadian research on the relationship between poor parental attachment and delinquency (reviewed in Bell 2015: 208–222) includes studies of the impact of parenting styles and family violence on childhood aggression or other behavioral problems. Family problems can lead to running away from home, thence to street life and involvement in violence, drugs, and prostitution (Bell 2015: 218–219). Studies of the relationship between school attachment and delinquency (reviewed in Bell 2015: 223–233) include demonstrations that a bad school climate and failure at school are associated with delinquency and that good school attachment can be protective against delinquency.

Differential association and peer influence: Friendships with peers who have delinquent attitudes (Zeman & Bressan 2008) or who engage in delinquent activities (Statistics Canada 2001; Wong 1999) have been shown to be criminogenic for Canadian youth, as elsewhere. Research has also been done on membership in youth gangs (Gordon 1995, 2001; Mathews 1993; Smith-Moncrieffe 2013; Tanner & Wortley 2002; Totten 2000) and on youth committing crimes in groups ("co-offending") (Carrington 2002, 2009, 2015b, c; Carrington et al. 2013; Carrington & van Mastrigt 2013).

Developmental and life-course theory: Le Blanc and his colleagues have made notable empirical as well as theoretical contributions to this school of criminological theory in their studies of the "psychosocial" development and delinquency of young males in the province of Quebec (e.g., Le Blanc 2003, 2005a, b; Le Blanc & Fréchette 1989). Tremblay has made major contributions to the study of the development of violence in children (e.g., Broidy et al. 2003; Nagin & Tremblay 1999; Tremblay et al. 2004). Corrado and his colleagues have also made major contributions to the relationship between psychological development and delinquency (e.g., Corrado & McCuish 2015; Corrado et al. 2004; McCuish et al. 2015; Vincent et al. 2003), including a recent theoretical scheme for a set of models of pathways to delinquency (Corrado & Freedman 2011). Corrado and Lussier (2011) have edited a special journal issue incorporating Canadian research on early developmental prevention of antisocial behavior. Jacob (2010) replicated and extended Sampson and Laub's (1993) life-course theory of delinquency, using Canadian data. Further, MacRae and her colleagues have studied developmental risk factors and reoffending in the province of Alberta (MacRae et al. 2009, 2011). Finally, Studies of criminal careers in Canada include Carrington et al. 2005, Carrington 2007, Day et al. 2007, Day et al. 2012, Kazemian et al. 2007, Lee 1999, Ward et al. 2010, and Yessine and Bonta 2009.

Feminist theories: The power-control theory of Hagan and his colleagues (Hagan et al. 1985) combines elements of Marxist conflict theory, social control theory, and feminist gender role theory. It posits differences in child-rearing practices in patriarchal and egalitarian households that explain both the genesis of delinquency and differences in boys' and girls' delinquency. It has motivated a substantial body of empirical research, in Canada and elsewhere (e.g., Blackwell et al. 2002; Browning & Erickson 2012; Jacob 2006; Jensen & Thompson 1990; Morash & Chesney-Lind 1991; Nakhaie et al. 2000a, b). Other Canadian feminist research includes Landry's (2008) study of female aggression and studies of girls' roles in gangs (Dorais & Corriveau 2009; Totten 2000).

Social disorganization theory: One of the major contributions of Canadian criminology to the understanding of the causes of youth (and adult) crime is the adaptation of social disorganization theory to explain the high incidence of reported crime by Aboriginal Canadians. Classic social disorganization theory explained high crime in terms of "socially disorganized" neighborhoods (Shaw & McKay 1931; Shaw et al. 1942), characterized by poverty, unemployment, poor housing, and other social and physical pathologies.

The high crime rate of Aboriginal Canadian youth and adults has been explained by the social disorganization—or attempted destruction—of an entire racial community, which has recently been described by a commission appointed by the Canadian government as "cultural genocide": the "destruction of those structures and practices that allow the group to continue as a group" in order to "cause the Aboriginal peoples to cease to exist as distinct legal, social, cultural, religious, and racial entities in Canada" (Truth and Reconciliation Commission of Canada 2015: 1). Numerous Canadian researchers and government commissions have documented the socially disorganized living conditions of Aboriginal Canadians, both on- and off-reserve, and linked them to elevated Aboriginal crime rates (e.g., Fitzgerald & Carrington 2008; Hamilton & Sinclair 1991; La Prairie 1994, 1995, 2002; Ratner 1996; Yessine & Bonta 2009; York 1990).

POLICING AND JUVENILES

The *YCJA* has provisions that are intended to encourage police to consider diverting juveniles to a range of "extrajudicial measures," including simply warning a youth not to reoffend through to referral to a community-based program that may require compensation to a victim or counseling, but does not result in a youth record. The impact of the *YCJA* on the use by police of charges is indicated by trends in the percentage of youth who were charged (Fig. 5.3). Prior to 2003, this indicator declined slowly from a high of 69% in 1990 to 57% in 2002. In 2003, when the *YCJA* came into force, this indictor fell by approximately one-fifth to 45%, with the result that the number of youth dealt with by extrajudicial measures exceeded the number charged for the first time since youth justice statistics were collected in Canada. Since 2003, it has been relatively constant and

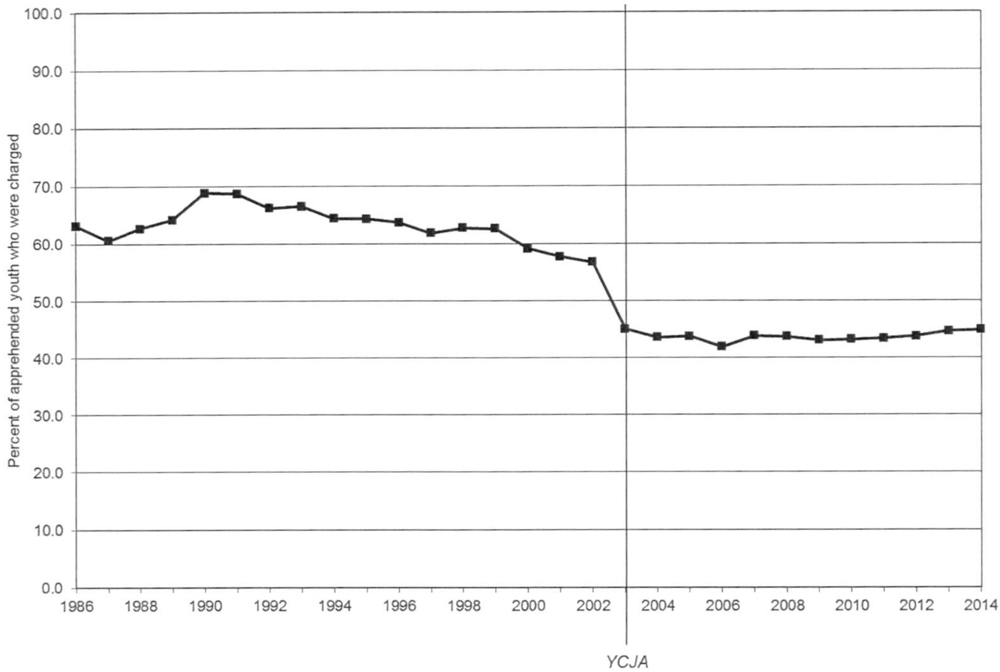

FIGURE 5.3. Trends in police charging of apprehended youth in Canada, 2004–2014. Note: Prepared by the authors using data from CANSIM Table 252–0051 (Statistics Canada 2015b).

remained at 45% in 2014. A more detailed analysis up to 2007 is in Bala et al. (2009).

The *YCJA* constrains questioning by the police of young persons suspected of offenses. Section 146 of the *YCJA* provides that a statement made by a youth being questioned by the police is admissible only if the youth has received an explanation "in language appropriate to his or her age and understanding." Further, a youth is not obliged to make a statement and has right to have a lawyer or parent present while a statement is made; any waiver of these rights must be in a signed statement or video-recorded waiver. The Supreme Court has made clear that it is not sufficient for a police officer to merely "read a youth his rights" from a form, but rather the police must provide an explanation that takes account of the youth's age and cognitive conditions, including learning disabilities. In its 2008 decision in *R. v. L.T.H.*, the Supreme Court of Canada emphasized the importance of the protection against improper questioning of youth suspects by police (*R v L.T.H.* 2008, at para 21–24):

> Young persons, even more than adults, are inclined to feel vulnerable when questioned by police officers who suspect them of crime and can influence their fate. Parliament has for that reason provided them by statute with a complementary set of enhanced procedural safeguards… procedural and evidentiary safeguards available to adults

do not adequately protect young persons, who are presumed on account of their age and relative unsophistication to be more vulnerable than adults to suggestion, pressure and influence in the hands of police interrogators.

Despite these protections, in practice, youth interrogated by police often fail to appreciate the significance of their legal rights and make statements that implicate them in the offense, almost always waiving the right to advice from counsel or parents.

COURTS AND JUVENILES

In recognition of the vulnerability of youth and the challenges that they face in understanding and participating in the youth court process, the *YCJA* has special provisions to facilitate access to legal representation. In proceedings under the *YCJA*, if a youth wants to have legal assistance and is unable to afford a lawyer, Section 25 requires the judge to order that representation be provided; parents' financial means are not to be taken into account when determining whether a youth is able to afford representation, though parents may choose to pay for counsel for their child. Lawyers for youth may provide assistance at the time of questioning by the police, at a pretrial bail hearing, at trial, and at a sentencing or review hearing. Youth in Canada have the right to legal representation, but there are continuing concerns about access to justice and the quality of legal representation for adolescents. Not infrequently there are delays in securing access to counsel, and some youths, especially those in detention, may plead guilty "to get things over" without having proper legal advice and representation (Bala 2015).

In each jurisdiction one court is designated as the "youth court." In most provinces, judges who deal with youth cases also deal with less serious adult criminal cases, and in some provinces judges dealing with youth cases also have jurisdiction over child welfare matters. Youth court trials are almost always resolved by a judge sitting without a jury. Youths have the right to a jury trial only in a murder charge or if an adult sentence is being considered. The public and media may attend youth court and are only excluded under limited circumstances, but reporting of youth court proceedings cannot identify the youth, unless an adult sentence is imposed.

The impact of the *YCJA* on the caseload of the youth court is shown in Fig. 5.4. Trends in the per capita rate of young persons' brought to court reflect trends in police charging. During the 11 years from 1991/1992 to 2002/2003, the rate of court cases declined on average by 2.5% per year, to 3015 per 100,000. In 2003/2004, the first year of the YCJA, the rate dropped by 17% to 2505. During the following 10 years, it dropped by an average of 3.3% per year to 1668 per 100,000 in 2013/2014. The per capita rate of cases heard in youth court in 2013/2014 was only 40% of the rate in 1991/1992. In practice, in many cases involving less serious charges, the prosecutor may decide, often after discussion

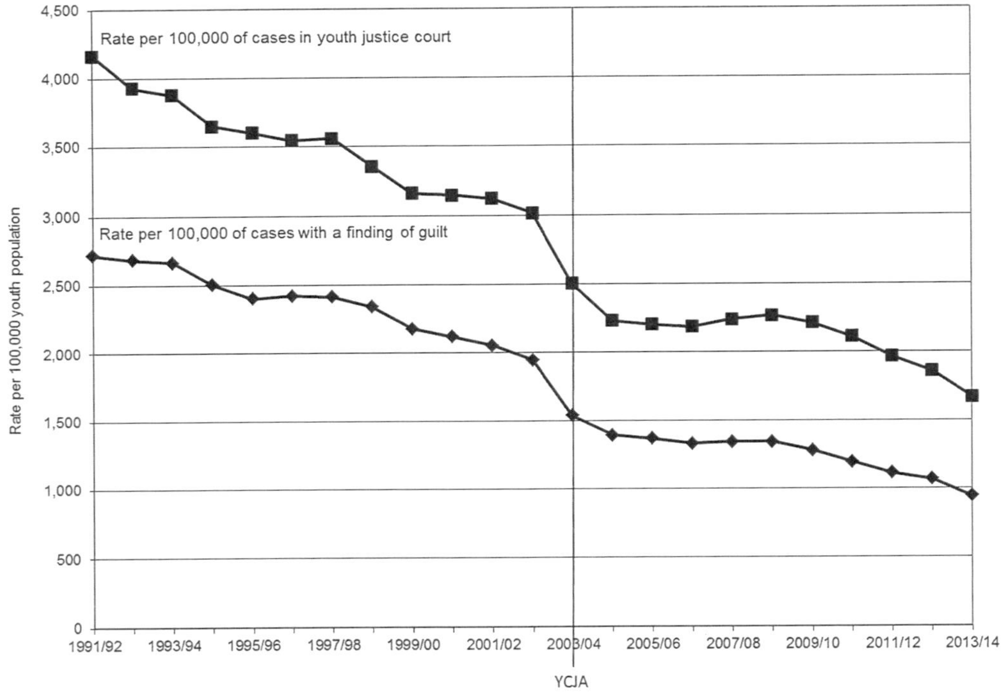

FIGURE 5.4. Trends in youth brought to court and found guilty, Canada, 1991/1992–2013/2014. Note: Prepared by the authors using data from CANSIM Table 252–0064 (Statistics Canada 2015b).

with youth and defence counsel, that the case should be diverted from court with charges dropped and a referral made for some type of extrajudicial measures. Largely as a result of increased use of diversion, cases in which youths were found guilty on at least one charge dropped by 21% from 1946 in 1991–1992 to 1538 in 2003/2004 and by a further 39% to 942 per 100,000 in 2013/2014 and only 35% of the rate in 1991/1992. If a case proceeds, most youths decide to plead guilty, sometimes in the context of a plea bargain arranged by their counsel with the Crown Prosecutor, and a relatively small portion of all youth court cases result in a trial.

SENTENCING

The *YCJA* establishes a process to provide the youth court judge with information to allow an appropriate sentence to be imposed as well affording the youth, parents, the victim, and other interested parties an opportunity to engage in the sentencing process. It is generally mandatory for a pre-sentence report to be prepared by a youth probation officer before a custodial sentence can be imposed. In some more serious cases, a medical or psychological assessment may also be prepared to provide the court with a fuller understanding of the needs of the youth.

Judges have a range of sentencing options under the YCJA, from a "verbal reprimand" to a 3-year sentence of custody. For murder, there is a longer maximum youth sentence, up to 10 years in custody for first-degree murder. Adult sanctions (i.e., up to life imprisonment) are also possible for the most serious cases.

The *YCJA* establishes the purpose of sentencing in youth court and sets out specific principles to guide courts in sentencing youth. Section 38(1) states that "[t]he purpose of [youth court] sentencing ... is to hold a young person accountable for an offense through the imposition of just sanctions that have meaningful consequences for the young person and that promote his or her rehabilitation and reintegration." The Supreme Court of Canada in *R. v. B.W.P.* (2006) upheld a trial decision that emphasized the importance of rehabilitation in sentencing a youth found guilty of manslaughter. The court discussed the role of deterrence in sentencing, observing that for adults "general deterrence is factored in the determination of the sentence, the offender is punished more severely, not because he or she deserves it, but because the court decides to send a message to others who may be inclined to engage in similar criminal activity." The Supreme Court also recognized that while deterrence of that specific young person should not be an objective of sentencing in youth court, the fact that a youth is to be held accountable in youth court undoubtedly has "the effect of deterring the young person and others from committing crimes." In 2012, the *YCJA* was amended so that denunciation and specific deterrence were added as principles of youth sentencing. General deterrence, however, is still not a factor in youth sentencing.

The Act significantly structures judicial discretion in youth sentencing, limiting the situations in which custody can be used and encouraging use of community-based approaches to youth crime. Sections 38(2) (e) requires that, subject to the requirement that sentences are to be proportionate to the offense, "the sentence must be the least restrictive sentence that is capable of achieving the purpose [of sentencing]." Under section 39(1), a custodial sentence can only be imposed for cases involving violence, repeat offending, breaches of noncustodial sentences, or "exceptional circumstances." Thus, custody may not be an option for the least serious cases. For example, youth without a prior record appearing on a first or even second minor property offense cannot receive a custodial sentence. In its first sentencing decision under the *YCJA*, *R. v. C.D.* (2005b), the Supreme Court held that section 39(1) should be "narrowly construed," emphasizing that this provision should be interpreted in a manner consistent with the intent of the act, as set out in the Preamble, in a way that restricts the use of youth custody.

Further, the YCJA prohibits the use of custody sentences for "social purposes." Section 39(5) explicitly states that a youth court "shall not" use custody as a substitute for a child protection, mental health, or other social measures.

The sentences available in youth court, and their frequency of use in 2013/2014, are shown in Table 5.1. More than half (58%) of sentenced cases received probation, followed by community service orders (25%) and sentences of custody (15%). Other types of sentences were used infrequently.

TABLE 5.1. Distribution of sentences handed down in youth justice court, Canada, 2013/2014

Type of sentence	*Number*	*Percent*
Total sentenced cases	22,524	
Custody and supervision	3361	14.9
Deferred custody and supervision	1062	4.7
Intensive support and supervision	285	1.3
Probation	12,992	57.7
Community service order	5601	24.9
Attend a nonresidential program	226	1.0
Fine	719	3.2
Reprimand	625	2.8
Other sentences[a]	8347	37.1

Note: Percentages add to more than 100% because multiple sentences may be given in a case. Prepared by the authors using data from CANSIM Table 252–0067 (Statistics Canada 2015b)
[a]"Other sentences" include absolute discharge, restitution, prohibition, seizure, forfeiture, compensation, pay purchaser, essays, apologies, counseling programs, and conditional discharge. This category also includes deferred custody and supervision, intensive support and supervision, attendance at nonresidential program, and reprimand for jurisdictions and years for which these types of sentence are combined

The *YCJA* had a large effect on the use of custodial sentences for youth (Fig. 5.5). The percent of cases with a finding of guilt in which a custodial sentence was handed down increased between 1991/1992 and 2002/2003, from 24% to 27%. In 2003–2004, the first year that the *YCJA* was in force, custody dropped from 27% to 22% of sentences and then to 21% in the following year and continued to fall until it leveled off at 15% in 2009/2010. With the drop in per capita rates of cases coming to court and resulting in a finding of guilt (Fig. 5.4) and the decline in the percent of guilty cases receiving a custodial sentence, the resulting per capita rate of cases receiving a custodial sentence fell dramatically: from 660 per 100,000 youth in 1991/1992 to 524 in 2002/2003, then to 337 with the coming into force of the YCJA in 2003/2004, and to 141 in 2013/2014. In 2013/2014, the per capita rate of custodial sentences was approximately one-fifth (21%) of the rate in 1991/1992. The actual number of young persons receiving a custodial sentence in 2013/2014 was 3361 compared with 15,016 in 1991/1992.

The reduction in youth court cases and in the use of custodial sentences resulted in a very substantial decrease in the numbers and per capita rates of youth in sentenced custody (Fig. 5.6). From 1997/1998 to 2003/2004, the average daily per capita rate of youth held in sentenced custody[3] decreased by approximately 7% per year. In 2003/2004, the first year that the *YCJA* was in effect, it dropped from 127 to 68 per 100,000 youth: a drop of 46% in 1 year. From 2003/2004 to 2013/2014, it fell further by an average of 8% per year. The per

[3]In Canada, excluding Quebec and Alberta, due to unavailability of data for some years for those provinces

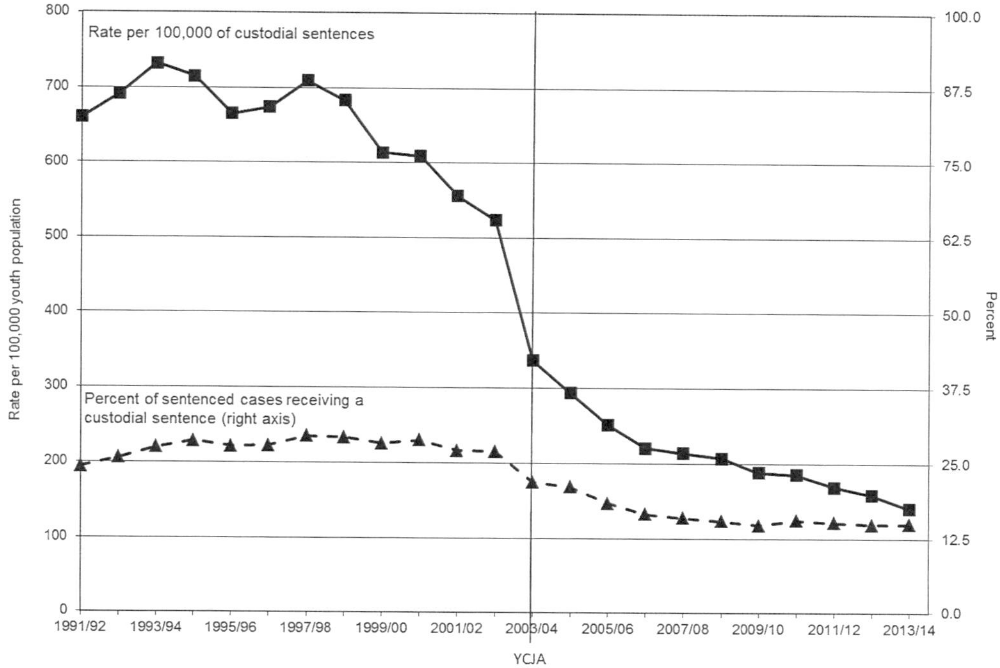

FIGURE 5.5. Trends in youth receiving custodial sentences, Canada, 1991/1992–2013/2014. Note: Prepared by the authors using data from CANSIM Table 252–0067 (Statistics Canada 2015b).

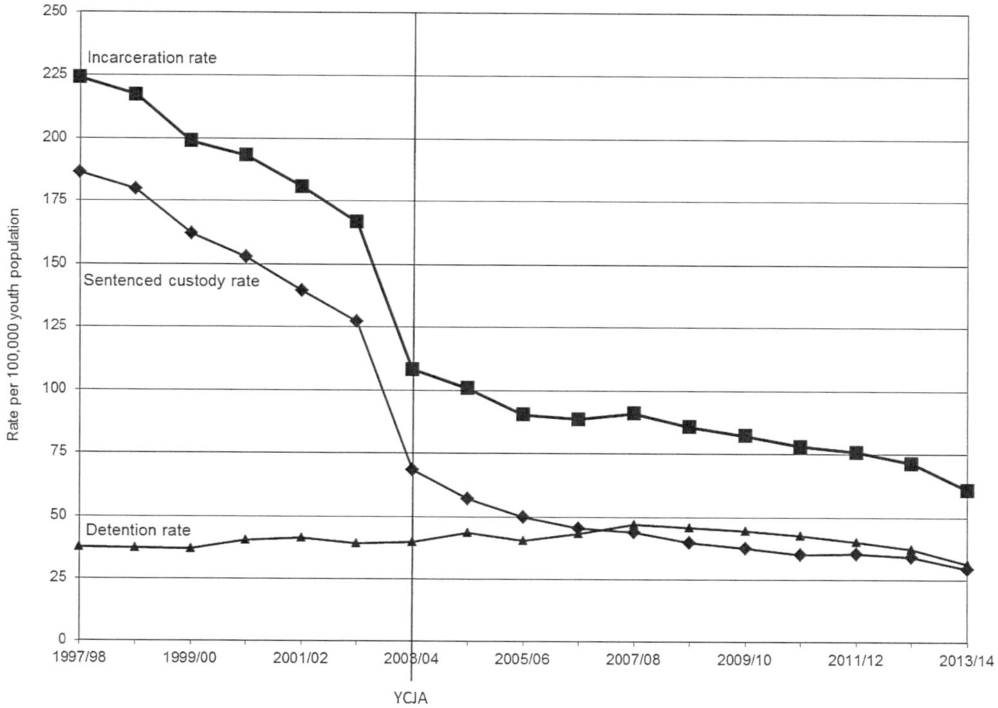

FIGURE 5.6. Trends in average daily rates of incarcerated youth, Canada, 1997/1998–2013/2014. Note: Quebec and Alberta are excluded due to the unavailability of data for some years. Prepared by the authors using data from CANSIM Table 252–0008 (Statistics Canada 2015b).

capita rate of youth in sentenced custody in 2013/2014 was 30 per 100,000 or 16% of the rate in 1997/1998 (186). The average daily number of youth held in sentenced custody in Canada, in 2013/2014, was about 475, which is roughly 16% of the number (approximately 3000) in 1997/1998.[4]

INCARCERATION OF YOUTH: CUSTODY AND REMAND DETENTION

While the *YCJA* emphasizes community-based responses for the majority of youth who commit less serious offenses, violent or persistent offenders may receive youth sentences of up to 3 years in custody (and up to 10 years for murder). The most serious adolescent offenders face the possibility of having an adult length of sentence, albeit with earlier parole eligibility than for adults if a life sentence is imposed.

For youths who receive a custody sentence, the court must divide the sentence between a period in custody and a period of community supervision: normally the sentence is two-thirds in custody and one-third under supervision. This is intended to ensure that youths who receive a custody sentence have supervision for their transition back into the community. Further, judges imposing a youth custody sentence must determine whether the sentence will be in a secure custody facility or an open community-based facility like a group home.

As discussed above, the *YCJA* resulted in a significant decline in the rate of youth custody. However, the coming into force of the *YCJA* in 2003 did not result in a reduction in the rate of pretrial detention (known as "remand custody"). Crown Prosecutors may seek the detention of youth awaiting trial who have a history of involvement in the justice system or are charged with more serious offenses or who may not attend court. While the *YCJA* established a presumption against detention if charges did not involve a "custody gateway" situation, the act had little effect on levels pretrial detention. A number of explanations were offered for this difference, and it is likely that there are several factors involved (Canada 2007). One explanation was that the provisions restricting the use of custody were significantly clearer and more detailed and in some situations absolutely precluded the use of custody, while the provisions concerning the use of remand custody gave more discretion to judges. The high rate of pretrial remand custody was concerning for a number of reasons. There are generally less recreational, educational, and rehabilitative programming available for youth on remand. Further, the sudden and unplanned removal of a youth from their communities and families that resulted from remand makes this experience disruptive for youth and possibly increases their likelihood of reoffending by exposing them to negative peer influences. The 2012 amendments provided more specific restrictions against the use of remand custody. The per capita rate of

[4] The excluded provinces, Quebec and Alberta, accounted for approximately 35% of the population of Canada in 2014 (Statistics Canada 2015c).

youth in remand detention in Canada changed very little from 1997/1998 to 2005/2006, fluctuating around an average of 40 per 100,000 youth population, but has notably declined since the 2012 reforms came into effect (Fig. 5.6). Since 2007/2008, the rate of youth in detention has decreased by approximately one-third, reaching 31 per 100,000 in 2013/2014.

The youth incarceration rate is the sum of the rates of youth in sentenced custody and in detention. As Fig. 5.6 shows, the trend in the incarceration rate in Canada followed the decline in the rate of sentenced custody. From a high of 224 in 1997/1998, the incarceration rate fell by an average of 6% until 2002/2003 and then by 35% in 2003/2004, the year that the *YCJA* came into force. It then fell by an average of 4% until 2012/2013, with a pronounced drop of 14% in 2013/2014. The youth incarceration rate in 2013/2014 was 61 per 100,000, which is 27% of the rate (224) in 1997/1998.

ALTERNATIVE SANCTIONS FOR JUVENILES

To encourage judges to place fewer youths in custody, the *YCJA* provides a number of community-based sanctions at the youth court level in addition to such traditional noncustodial sentences as probation, community service, or a fine. Some of these sentences, such as requiring involvement at an "attendance center" or "intensive supervision and support," are intended to provide youth with more support in the community and address the circumstances leading to the youth's offending.

The most significant community-based sentence added by the YCJA was the "deferred custody and supervision order" (DCSO), which can be imposed by a youth court judge. This sentence allows the court to permit the youth to remain in the community for the duration of the order, subject to supervision by probation officers and with other supports. In the event of a breach or apprehended breach of the terms of release, the youth may be placed immediately in custody for the balance of the sentence without the need for another court hearing. This sanction represents a "last chance" provided by the court to spare a youthful offender's committal to custody. This sanction has been used quite frequently, also contributing to the decline in the use of youth custody (Carrington et al. 2011).

DIFFERENCES IN TREATMENT OF BOYS AND GIRLS

The police decision to charge: Canadian research on the charging of apprehended youth under the *Young Offenders Act* (1984) and the *Youth Criminal Justice Act* (2003) found only minimal differences by gender and no substantial evidence of gender discrimination. Multiple regression analysis of charge data for 1992 and 1993 from the Uniform Crime Reporting (UCR) Survey found that when the type of crime and other factors were controlled, boys who were apprehended

TABLE 5.2. Police disposition of apprehended youth, by gender and "morals" offense, Canada (parts), 1992–1993

	Morals offenses			*Other offenses*		
	Male	*Female*	*Total*	*Male*	*Female*	*Total*
Charged	59.0% (62)	99.4% (155)	83.1% (217)	58.8% (46,832)	59.9% (8544)	58.9% (55,376)
Dealt with informally	41.0% (43)	0.6% (1)	16.9% (44)	41.2% (32,853)	40.1% (5731)	41.1% (38,584)
Total	100.0% (105)	100.0% (156)	100% (261)	100.0% (79,685)	100.0% (14,275)	100.0% (93,960)

Note: Prepared by the authors using custom tabulations provided by Statistics Canada for Carrington (1998)

were slightly (4%) more likely to be charged (Carrington 1998: 16–17). This difference was not necessarily due to gender per se: it could have been due to factors omitted from the analyses, such as the youth's prior record or demeanor (Carrington 1998: 18), both of which have been found to have significant effects, in Canada, on the police decision to charge (Carrington & Schulenberg 2003).

Follow-up studies by Carrington and Schulenberg (2003, 2004) supplemented statistical analysis of 2001 UCR Survey data for six provinces with interviews with a nationally representative sample of more than 200 Canadian police officers. Only 1% of police respondents said they considered the youth's gender when deciding whether to lay a charge (Carrington & Schulenberg 2003: 240). This was corroborated by the statistical analysis, which found that although apprehended male youths were 9% more likely to be charged, this difference was reduced to 2% when other factors such as the type of offense and age of the youth were controlled. This 2% difference "could well be due to other factors" that were not statistically controlled, such as the youth's "demeanor" (Carrington & Schulenberg 2003: 231–232).

Several writers have noted that girls are disproportionately likely to be charged with certain offenses, such as "soliciting for the purposes of prostitution" and assaulting a police officer (Bell 2015: 397), and have taken this as evidence of paternalistic differential treatment of girls by Canadian police. Reanalysis of Carrington's (1998; see above) UCR data for 1992–1993 is illuminating. Table 5.2 shows the proportions of apprehended boys and girls who were charged, broken down by whether or not they were accused of a "morals" offense. As noted above, boys and girls implicated in offenses other than morals offenses were charged in practically equal proportions: 59% of boys and 60% of girls. Among boys who were implicated in morals offenses, the same proportion was charged (59%); however, every girl but one—99%—of the girls implicated in morals offenses was charged. This is strong *prima facie* evidence of differential treatment by gender. Whether such charging practices exist in the rest of Canada, and whether they have persisted under the YCJA, is not known.

Pretrial detention and release: Youths who are charged may be arrested and then released by police, or they may be held for the court to decide upon release or continued detention before and during the processing of their charges. Release by the police or the court is usually accompanied by conditions.

There is very little data available on police decision-making with respect to detention and release in Canada: it is largely a "hidden" decision. Carrington, Moyer, and Kopelman (1988), and Moyer et al. (1986a, 1986b) performed multivariate statistical analyses of the decision to detain at arrest in five large Canadian cities, when the JDA was in force. They found that gender was a factor in the decision in four of the five cities but was an independent factor ("main effect") in only one city (Toronto), where "females were detained more than males regardless of other factors" (Carrington et al. 1988: 471). In the other three cities, the roles of other factors varied according to the youth's gender. None of the police officers interviewed by Carrington and Schulenberg (2003) in 2002 cited the youth's gender as a factor considered when deciding to detain or release a youth. A very small number (3%) said they would detain in order to remove the youth from prostitution—which would presumably mean in most cases the youth was a female.

Concerning the decisions by the court to release from detention ("bail decisions"), Carrington et al. (1988) found that—unlike the police decision to detain—the juvenile court's bail decisions were not affected either directly or indirectly by the youth's gender and were "quite legalistic" (1988: 474). Recent research by Sprott and Doob (2009) has found that bail conditions are used paternalistically by youth courts to impose social control on girls and their sexual behavior in particular: in effect, as a substitute for the status offenses of "immorality" and "incorrigibility" that are no longer available and that girls disproportionately receive the rehabilitative condition to "attend a treatment program" (Sprott & Doob 2010).

Sentencing: Several writers (reviewed in Bala & Anand 2012: 76) have pointed out that the sentencing of female young offenders in Canada tends to be more lenient than that of males, when the seriousness of the offense and the prior record are taken into account. However, girls tend to receive more severe sentences for certain offenses, such as administration of justice offenses (like breach of terms of bail), mischief, and disturbing the peace, suggesting a paternalistic sentencing orientation (Bell 2015: 331, 397). Sprott and Doob (2009), Sprott and Doob (2010), and Sprott (2012) have pointed out that the apparently excessive use of conditions of bail and probation with girls "sets them up" for breaches, which in turn result in custodial sentences. Thus, the greater leniency—in practice, the greater use of probation rather than prison—of the sentencing of girls found guilty of crimes against property or the person may eventually result in greater severity, as they are sentenced to prison for breaching conditions of probation (Sprott & Doob 2009: 91).

Analysis of the most recent national statistics of sentencing in youth justice court in fiscal 2013/2014 (Table 5.3) confirms some, but not all, of the previously

TABLE 5.3. Custodial sentences by gender and selected offenses, Canada, 2013/2014

	Male		*Female*		*Total*			
	Total cases sentenced	*Percent receiving a custodial sentence*	*Total cases sentenced*	*Percent receiving a custodial sentence*	*Total cases sentenced*	*Percent receiving a custodial sentence*	*Male to female ratio: proportions of custodial sentences*	*Percent of cases with a male accused*
Total offenses	15,767	16.3	3882	10.9	19,649	15.2	1.49	24.6
Offenses against the person	4581	18.7	1195	9.2	5776	16.7	2.03	26.1
Offenses against property	4706	13.1	992	7.1	5698	12.0	1.85	21.1
Mischief	795	7.8	154	7.8	949	7.8	1.00	19.4
Prostitution	2	50.0	1	0.0	3	33.3	n/a	50.0
Disturb the peace	27	3.7	8	0.0	35	2.9	n/a	29.6
Administration of justice	3516	22.9	1255	18.2	4771	21.7	1.26	35.7
Bail violations	1069	18.9	397	15.1	1466	17.9	1.25	37.1
YCJA[a]	1852	21.7	642	18.8	2494	21.0	1.15	34.7

Note: Prepared by the authors using data from CANSIM Table 252–0067 (Statistics Canada 2015b)

[a]The great majority of charges under the Youth Criminal Justice Act are for failing to comply with a community disposition, i.e., breaching the conditions of a probation order

reported findings on gender differentials.[5] Overall, boys received a considerably higher proportion of custodial sentences: 16.3% versus 10.9% for girls: the "sex ratio" is 1.5 (16.3%/10.9%). However, this difference may be partly explained by boys' greater prior records, which were not available in the published sentencing statistics. The greater severity of sentences received by boys is even more evident in both offenses against the person ("violent" offenses, with a sex ratio of 2.0) and against property (with a sex ratio of 1.9). In striking contrast, girls found guilty of mischief (property damage) received custodial sentences in the same proportions as boys—7.8%. Breakdowns by age group showed that younger female mischief offenders were treated slightly more severely than their male peers: 6.8% of 12–15-year-old female mischief offenders, versus 5.3% of 12–15-year-old boys, received a custodial sentence. There were so few youth found guilty of prostitution-related offenses (two boys and one girl) that no conclusion can be drawn about differential sentencing for this offense. However, the trivial numbers of girls and boys found guilty of these offenses, and the fact that there were more boys than girls, suggest that if there is any differential treatment in the youth justice system related to prostitution, it is confined to the areas of charging and pretrial detention. Numbers of boys and girls found guilty of disturbing the peace were also very small and show no evidence of harsher treatment of girls: on the contrary, no girls found guilty of this offense were sentenced to custody.

CONCLUSION

There has been significant change in Canada's youth justice since the start of the millennium, with marked declines in rates of charging, youth custody, and more recently youth remand, while consistent with trends in other countries, the youth crime rate is slowly falling. The declines in rates of charging and incarceration are at least partially attributable to the enactment of new legislation, which has both restricted use of charging and incarceration. This also contributed to a change in the professional culture of police, prosecutors, and judges. While the increased use of diversion and community responses to youth offending in Canada are encouraging, there remain significant issues, including the high rate of involvement of Aboriginal and racialized youth in the justice system and lack of community-based resources for youth offenders in many communities.

Acknowledgments This chapter reports analyses of data provided by Statistics Canada. The views expressed are those of the authors and do not represent the views of Statistics Canada. Preparation

---

[5]The statistics reported in Table 5.3 are for all ages from 12 to 17. As female offenders tend to be younger than males (Carrington 2007), their more lenient treatment might be due to the age difference. However, breakdowns by age group (12–15 and 16–17) (not shown in Table 5.3) replicated the gender differences show in Table 5.3, with rare exceptions that are noted in the text.

of this chapter was supported by a research grant to the second author from the Social Sciences and Humanities Research Council of Canada.

REFERENCES

Bala, N. (2015). Reducing use of courts & custody for youth offenders despite 'get tough' on crime talk: The Youth Criminal Justice Act and Bill C-10. *Saskatchewan Law Review, 78*(1), 127–160.

Bala, N., & Anand, S. (2012). *Youth Criminal Justice Law* (3rd ed.). Toronto: Irwin Law.

Bala, N., Carrington, P. J., & Roberts, J. V. (2009). Evaluating the Youth Criminal Justice Act after five years: A qualified success. *Canadian Journal of Criminology and Criminal Justice, 51*(2), 131–167.

Bell, S. J. (2015). *Young offenders and youth justice* (5th ed.). Toronto: Nelson Education.

Blackwell, B. S., Sellers, C. S., & Schlaupitz, S. M. (2002). A power-control theory of vulnerability to crime and adolescent role exits—Revisited. *Canadian Review of Sociology and Anthropology, 39*(2), 199–218.

Broidy, L. M., Nagin, D. S., Tremblay, R. E., Bates, J. E., Brame, B., Dodge, K. A., et al. (2003). Developmental trajectories of childhood disruptive behaviors and adolescent delinquency: A six-site, cross-national study. *Developmental Psychology, 39*(2), 222.

Browning, S., & Erickson, P. (2012). Neighbourhood variation in the link between alcohol use and violence among Canadian adolescents. *Canadian Journal of Criminology and Criminal Justice, 54*(2), 169–201. doi:10.3138/cjccj.2009.E.37.

Canada. (2007). *Pre-trial detention under the Youth Criminal Justice Act: A consultation paper*. Ottawa: Department of Justice Canada.

Canadian Centre for Justice Statistics. (2013). *Uniform crime reporting incident-based survey*. Unpublished manual.

Carrington, P. J. (1998). *Factors affecting police diversion of young offenders: A statistical analysis*. Ottawa: Solicitor General Canada.

Carrington, P. J. (2002). Group crime in Canada. *Canadian Journal of Criminology, 44*(3), 277–315.

Carrington, P. J. (2007). *The development of police-reported delinquency among Canadian youth born in 1987 and 1990.* Crime and Justice Research Paper Series. Ottawa: Canadian Centre for Justice Statistics, Statistics Canada.

Carrington, P. J. (2009). Co-offending and the development of the delinquent career. *Criminology, 47*(4), 1295–1329.

Carrington, P. J. (2013). Trends in the seriousness of youth crime in Canada, 1984–2011. *Canadian Journal of Criminology and Criminal Justice, 55*(2), 293–314.

Carrington, P. J. (2015a). Trends in serious and violent youth crime in Canada, 1986–2011. In R. R. Corrado, A. Leschied, P. Lussier, & J. Whatley (Eds.), *Serious and violent young offenders and youth criminal justice: A Canadian perspective* (pp. 29–44). Burnaby, BC: SFU Publications.

Carrington, P. J. (2015b). The structure of age homophily in co-offending groups. *Journal of Contemporary Criminal Justice, 31*(3), 337–353.

Carrington, P. J. (2015c). Gender and age segregation and stratification in criminal collaborations. *Journal of Quantitative Criminology, 31*, 1–37.

Carrington, P. J., Brennan, S., Matarazzo, A., & Radulescu, M. (2013). *Co-offending in Canada, 2011*. St. Louis: Juristat.

Carrington, P. J., Matarazzo, A., & de Souza, P. (2005). *Court careers of a Canadian birth cohort.* Crime and Justice Research Paper Series. Ottawa: Canadian Centre for Justice Statistics, Statistics Canada.

Carrington, P. J., Moyer, S., & Kopelman, F. (1988). Factors affecting pre-dispositional detention and release under the Juvenile Delinquents Act. *Journal of Criminal Justice, 16*, 463–476.

Carrington, P. J., Roberts, J. V., & Davis-Barron, S. (2011). The last chance sanction in youth court: Exploring the deferred custody and supervision order. *Canadian Criminal Law Review, 15*, 299–336.
Carrington, P. J., & Schulenberg, J. L. (2003). *Police discretion with young offenders*. Ottawa: Department of Justice Canada.
Carrington, P. J., & Schulenberg, J. L. (2004). *Prior police contacts and police discretion with apprehended youth*. Crime and Justice Research Paper Series. Ottawa: Canadian Centre for Justice Statistics, Statistics Canada.
Carrington, P. J., & van Mastrigt, S. B. (2013). Co-offending in Canada, England and the United States: A cross-national comparison. *Global Crime, 14*(2–3), 123–140.
Corrado, R., & Freedman, L. (2011). Risk profiles, trajectories, and intervention points for serious and chronic young offenders. *International Journal of Child, Youth and Family Studies, 2*(2.1), 197–232.
Corrado, R. R., & Lussier, P. (2011). Early developmental prevention of antisocial behaviour. *International Journal of Child, Youth & Family Studies, 2*(1–2), 1–11.
Corrado, R. R., & McCuish, E. C. (2015). The development of early onset, chronic, and versatile offending: The role of fetal alcohol spectrum disorder and mediating factors. *International Journal of Child and Adolescent Health, 8*(2), 241.
Corrado, R. R., Vincent, G. M., Hart, S. D., & Cohen, I. M. (2004). Predictive validity of the psychopathy checklist: Youth version for general and violent recidivism. *Behavioral Sciences & the Law, 22*(1), 5–22.
Day, D. M., Bevc, I., Duchesne, T., Rosenthal, J. S., Rossman, L., & Theodor, F. (2007). Comparison of adult offense prediction methods based on juvenile offense trajectories using cross-validation. *Advances and Applications in Statistics, 7*, 1–46.
Day, D. M., Nielsen, J. D., Ward, A. K., Sun, Y., Rosenthal, J. S., Duchesne, T., et al. (2012). Long-term follow-up of criminal activity with adjudicated youth in Ontario: Identifying offence trajectories and predictors/correlates of trajectory group membership. *Canadian Journal of Criminology and Criminal Justice, 54*(4), 377–413.
Doob, A., & Cesaroni, C. (2010). *Responding to youth crime in Canada*. Toronto: University of Toronto Press.
Dorais, M., & Corriveau, P. (2009). *Gangs and girls: Understanding juvenile prostitution*. Montreal: McGill-Queen's Press.
Fitzgerald, R. T., & Carrington, P. J. (2008). The neighbourhood context of urban aboriginal crime 1. *Canadian Journal of Criminology and Criminal Justice, 50*(5), 523–557.
Gannon, M., & Mihorean, K. (2005). *Criminal victimization in Canada, 2004*. Ottawa: Canadian Centre for Justice Statistics.
Gordon, R. (1995). Street gangs in vancouver. In J. Creechan & R. A. Silverman (Eds.), *Canadian delinquency*. Toronto: Prentice Hall.
Gordon, R. (2001). Street gangs and criminal business organizations: A Canadian perspective. In R. C. Smandych (Ed.), *Youth crime: Varieties, theories, and prevention* (pp. 248–265). Toronto: Harcourt Canada.
Hagan, J., Gillis, A. R., & Simpson, J. (1985). The class structure of gender and delinquency: Toward a power-control theory of common delinquent behavior. *American Journal of Sociology, 90*(6), 1151–1178.
Hagan, J., Simpson, J., & Gillis, A. R. (1987). Class in the household: A power-control theory of gender and delinquency. *American Journal of Sociology, 92*(4), 788–816.
Hagan, J., Simpson, J., & Gillis, A. R. (1988). Feminist scholarship, relational and instrumental control, and a power-control theory of gender and delinquency. *British Journal of Sociology, 39*(3), 301–336.
Hamilton, A., & Sinclair, C. (1991). *Report of the aboriginal justice inquiry of Manitoba. Vol. 1. The justice system and aboriginal people*. Winnipeg: Queen's Publisher.

Jacob, J. C. (2006). Male and female youth crime in Canadian communities: Assessing the applicability of social disorganization theory. *Canadian Journal of Criminology and Criminal Justice, 48*(1), 31–60.

Jacob, J. C. (2010). *Pathways of crime and delinquency: A life-course analysis of informal social control of antisocial behaviour*. Waterloo, ON: University of Waterloo.

Jensen, G. F., & Thompson, K. (1990). What's class got to do with it? A further examination of power-control theory. *American Journal of Sociology, 95*(4), 1009–1023.

Kazemian, L., LeBlanc, M., Farrington, D. P., & Pease, K. (2007). Patterns of residual criminal careers among a sample of adjudicated French-Canadian males. *Canadian Journal of Criminology and Criminal Justice, 49*(3), 307–340.

La Prairie, C. (1994). *Seen but not heard: Native people in the inner city*. Ottawa: Department of Justice Canada.

La Prairie, C. (1995). Seen but not heard: Native people in four Canadian inner cities. *The Journal of Human Justice, 6*(2), 30–45.

La Prairie, C. (2002). Aboriginal over-representation in the criminal justice system: A tale of nine cities. *Canadian Journal of Criminology, 44*, 181–208.

Landry, N. E. (2008). *The mean girl motive: Negotiating power and femininity*. Halifax: Brunswick Books.

Le Blanc, M. (2003). Évolution de la délinquance cachée et officielle chez les adolescents au Québec entre les années 1930 et 2000. In M. Le Blanc, M. Ouimet, & D. Szabo (Eds.), *Traité de criminologie empirique*. Montréal: Presses de l'Université de Montréal.

Le Blanc, M. (2005a). Self-control and social control of deviant behavior in context: Development and interactions along the life course. In P. O. Wikström & R. Sampson (Eds.), *The social contexts of pathways in crime: Development, context, and mechanisms*. Cambridge: Cambridge University Press.

Le Blanc, M. (2005b). An integrative personal control theory of deviant behavior answers to contemporary empirical and theoretical developmental criminology issues. In D. P. Farrington (Ed.), *Integrated developmental and life course theories of offending* (pp. 125–164). Piscataway, NJ: Transaction.

Le Blanc, M., & Fréchette, M. (1989). *Male criminal activity from childhood through youth: Multilevel and developmental perspectives*. New York: Springer.

Le Blanc, M., & Loeber, R. (1998). Developmental criminology updated. *Crime and Justice, 23*, 115–198.

Lee, N. (1999). Youth crime trends in British Columbia. *Forum on Corrections Research, 11*(2), 3–6.

MacRae, L. D., Bertrand, L. D., Paetsch, J. J., Hornick, J. P., & DeGusti, B. (2009). *A study of youth reoffending in Calgary*. Calgary, AL: Canadian Research Institute for Law and the Family.

MacRae, L. D., Bertrand, L. D., Paetsch, J. J., & Hornick, J. P. (2011). Relating risk and protective factors to youth reoffending: A two-year follow-up. *International Journal of Child, Youth and Family Studies, 2*(2.1), 172–196.

Mathews, F. (1993). *Youth gangs on youth gangs*. Ottawa: Solicitor General Canada.

McCuish, E. C., Corrado, R. R., Hart, S. D., & DeLisi, M. (2015). The role of symptoms of psychopathy in persistent violence over the criminal career into full adulthood. *Journal of Criminal Justice, 43*(4), 345–356.

Morash, M., & Chesney-Lind, M. (1991). A reformulation and partial test of the power control theory of delinquency. *Justice Quarterly, 8*(3), 347–377.

Moyer, S., Kopelman, F., & Carrington, P. J. (1986a). *Correlates of the pre-dispositional detention of juveniles in five Canadian cities*. Report to the Solicitor General of Canada.

Moyer, S., Kopelman, F., & Carrington, P. J. (1986b). *The conformity of juvenile court judicial interim release practices to the provisions of the criminal code*. Report to the Solicitor General of Canada.

Nagin, D., & Tremblay, R. E. (1999). Trajectories of boys' physical aggression, opposition, and hyperactivity on the path to physically violent and nonviolent juvenile delinquency. *Child Development, 70*(5), 1181–1196.
Nakhaie, M. R., Silverman, R. A., & LaGrange, T. C. (2000a). Self-control and resistance to school. *Canadian Review of Sociology and Anthropology, 37*(4), 443–460.
Nakhaie, M. R., Silverman, R. A., & LaGrange, T. C. (2000b). Self-control and social control: An examination of gender, ethnicity, class and delinquency. *Canadian Journal of Sociology, 25*(1), 35–59.
Perrault, S. (2015). *Criminal victimization in Canada, 2014*. St. Louis: Juristat.
Ratner, R. (1996). In cultural limbo: Adolescent aboriginals in the urban life-world. In G. M. O'Bireck (Ed.), *Not a kid anymore: Canadian youth, crime and subcultures* (pp. 185–202). Toronto: Nelson Canada.
Sampson, R., & Laub, J. (1993). *Crime in the making: Pathways and turning points through life*. Cambridge, MA: Harvard University Press.
Shaw, C. R., & McKay, H. D. (1931). Social factors in juvenile delinquency. *Report on the Causes of Crime* (Vol. II). Washington, DC.
Shaw, C. R., McKay, H. D., & Hayner, N. S. (1942). *Juvenile delinquency and urban areas*. Chicago: University of Chicago Press.
Smith-Moncrieffe, D. (2013). *Youth gang prevention fund projects: What did we learn about what works in preventing gang involvement?* Ottawa: Public Safety Canada.
Sprott, J. B. (2012). The persistence of status offences in the youth justice system. *Canadian Journal of Criminology and Criminal Justice, 54*(3), 309–332.
Sprott, J. B., & Doob, A. N. (2009). *Justice for girls?* Chicago: University of Chicago Press.
Sprott, J. B., & Doob, A. N. (2010). Gendered treatment: Girls and treatment orders in bail court. *Canadian Journal of Criminology and Criminal Justice, 52*(4), 427–441.
Statistics Canada. (2001). *Children and youth in Canada* (Canadian Centre for Justice Statistics Profile Series). Ottawa: Statistics Canada.
Statistics Canada. (2015a). *Uniform crime reporting survey*. Retrieved from http://www23.statcan.gc.ca/imdb/p2SV.pl?Function=getSurvey&Id=243837.
Statistics Canada. (2015b). *CANSIM*. Retrieved from http://www5.statcan.gc.ca/cansim/a01?lang=eng.
Tanner, J., & Wortley, S. (2002). *The Toronto youth leisure and victimization survey: Final report*. Toronto, ON: University of Toronto.
Totten, M. D. (2000). *Guys, gangs, and girlfriend abuse*. Toronto: Broadview Press.
Tremblay, R. E. (2000). The development of aggressive behaviour during childhood: What have we learned in the past century? *International Journal of Behavioral Development, 24*(2), 129–141.
Tremblay, R. E., Nagin, D. S., Seguin, J. R., Zoccolillo, M., Zelazo, P. D., Boivin, M., et al. (2004). Physical aggression during early childhood: Trajectories and predictors. *Pediatrics, 114*(1), e43–e50.
Truth and Reconciliation Commission of Canada. (2015). *Honouring the truth, reconciling for the future: Summary of the final report of the truth and reconciliation commission of Canada.* Retrieved from http://www.trc.ca/websites/trcinstitution/File/2015/Findings/Exec_Summary_2015_05_31_web_o.pdf
United Nations Committee on the Rights of the Child, Canada. (January 4, 2012). CRC/C/CAN/3-4.
Vincent, G. M., Vitacco, M. J., Grisso, T., & Corrado, R. R. (2003). Subtypes of adolescent offenders: Affective traits and antisocial behavior patterns. *Behavioral Sciences & the Law, 21*(6), 695–712.
Ward, A. K., Day, D. M., Bevc, I., Sun, Y., Rosenthal, J. S., & Duchesne, T. (2010). Criminal trajectories and risk factors in a Canadian sample of offenders. *Criminal Justice and Behavior, 37*(11), 1278–1300.

Wong, S. K. (1999). Acculturation, peer relations, and delinquent behavior of Chinese-Canadian youth. *Adolescence, 34*(133), 107.

Yessine, A. K., & Bonta, J. (2009). The offending trajectories of youthful aboriginal offenders. *Canadian Journal of Criminology and Criminal Justice, 51*(4), 435–472.

York, G. (1990). *The dispossessed: Life and death in native Canada*. London: Vintage UK.

Zeman, K., & Bressan, A. (2008). *Factors associated with youth delinquency and victimization in Toronto, 2006*. Crime and Justice Research Paper Series No. 14. Ottawa: Statistics Canada.

STATUTES AND TREATIES

Canadian Charter of Rights and Freedoms, Part 1 of the *Constitution Act,* enacted as Schedule B to the *Canada Act 1982*, 1982, c. 11 (U.K.).

Safe Streets and Communities Act, S.C. 2012, c.1.

Convention on the Rights of the Child, Can. T.S. 1992 No. 3.

Juvenile Delinquents Act, R.S.C. 1970, Chap. J-3

Young Offenders Act, **S.C.** 1980-81-82-83, c. 110.

Youth Criminal Justice Act, S.C. 2002, c.1

CASE LAW

R v C.D., 2005 SCC 61 (2005a)

R v D.B., 2008 SCC 25

R. v. B.W.P., [2006] 1 S.C.R. 941

R. v. C.D., 2005 SCC 78 (2005b)

R. v. L.T.H., 2008 SCC 49

N. Bala Professor, Faculty of Law, Queen's University, Kingston, Canada. He has law degrees from Queen's University in Kingston, Canada (J.D. 77), and Harvard (LL.M. 80). His research focuses on issues related to families, children, and youth in the justice system. Much of his work is interdisciplinary in approach, dealing with such issues as youth offenders, children as victims and witnesses, economic and parenting obligations after separation, family violence, and high conflict separations. He has published extensively, and his work is frequently cited by Canadian courts and occasionally by courts in the USA and the UK.

P.J. Carrington Professor of Sociology and Legal Studies at the University of Waterloo, Canada. His current research project, the Canadian Criminal Careers and Criminal Networks Study, combines his long-standing interests in social network analysis and in the development of crime and delinquency. His articles have appeared in various journals, including Criminology, Journal of Quantitative Criminology, Journal of Mathematical Sociology, Social Networks, American Journal of Psychiatry, and Archives of Suicide Research. He was editor from 2004 to 2014 of *Canadian Journal of Criminology and Criminal Justice* and was editor or co-editor of the books *Applications of Social Network Analysis* (Sage, 2014), *The SAGE Handbook of Social Network Analysis* (Sage, 2011), and *Models and Methods in Social Network Analysis* (Cambridge University Press, 2005).

6

Mexico

Carlos J. Vilalta

INTRODUCTION

A long time has passed in Mexico since the time of the Aztecs, when minors under 15 could be sentenced to death if found drunk or for having homosexual relations (Soto 2007). There are factual records in the Mendocino Code (1541) of harsh punishment of children between the ages of 7 and 10, such as being tied up naked for a whole day inhaling the fumes of burned peppers (Rodriguez 1987). Today, Mexico is a totally different place. In spite of the foreign stereotyping and its own problems and limitations, the Mexican criminal justice system, including juvenile justice, is a modern and progressive system, and above all, improving rapidly.

Several factors can explain the progress recently made in the juvenile criminal justice system. One main factor has been the legal reforms of the last 10 years. These reforms cannot be understood in a historical vacuum. For this reason, this chapter explains what the Mexican juvenile justice system is from a historical perspective. As such, most sections in this chapter provide a historical account of the topic in hand. But history is *empirics* in practice. For this reason, most sections contain data sources and references when possible. Criminal statistics is another major improvement in recent years. Thus, even though juvenile criminal and judicial data is still limited and far from what we would like it to be, sufficient statistical evidence is available to learn from the Mexican experience and to produce a satisfactory understanding of it.

This chapter provides a succinct historical and empirically based summary of the Mexican juvenile justice system. It summarizes the main aspects as it aims to serve as a comprehensive yet concise introduction to the facts and state of affairs of the Mexican juvenile justice system.

C.J. Vilalta (✉)
Division of Public Administration, Center for Economic Research and Education (CIDE), Carretera Mexico-Toluca 3655, Alvaro Obregon, Mexico City CP 01210, Mexico
e-mail: carlos.vilalta@cide.edu

S.H. Decker, N. Marteache (eds.), *International Handbook of Juvenile Justice*,
DOI 10.1007/978-3-319-45090-2_6

THE LEGAL STATUS OF JUVENILES

In Mexico today, a juvenile is any minor between the ages of 12 and 18 years old. This is not only the current legal definition, but it is also a modern definition. Many things over a number of years have had to happen to reach this point of modernity.

In my opinion, five historical periods can be seen regarding the legal status of juveniles in Mexico. These periods are neither found in previous texts nor are they fine-grained, but it is conceptually valid as it delineates the major historical moments and changes regarding the legal status of juveniles in this country.

Even though we have no record of an established criminal justice system in Mexico's pre-Hispanic times, we do know of two codes of rules which included guidelines for juveniles. They even included definitions of age of majority. These were the *Nezahualcoyotl* Code and the *Mendocino* Code (also named the Mendoza Codex after the first Viceroy of New Spain). The former was created by the emperor *Nezahualcoyotl* (1427–1472) with the aim to regulate a variety of behaviors regarding civil law, criminal law, music, sciences, war, and even the public budget (Salcedo 2010). It is also known by the name of the *Texcoco* Ordinances. The latter was written in 1541, some years after the Spanish conquest, and it is a historical document that contains the history of the Aztec empire as well as a description of the lives and ways of these peoples, including matters of justice (Fig. 6.1).[1]

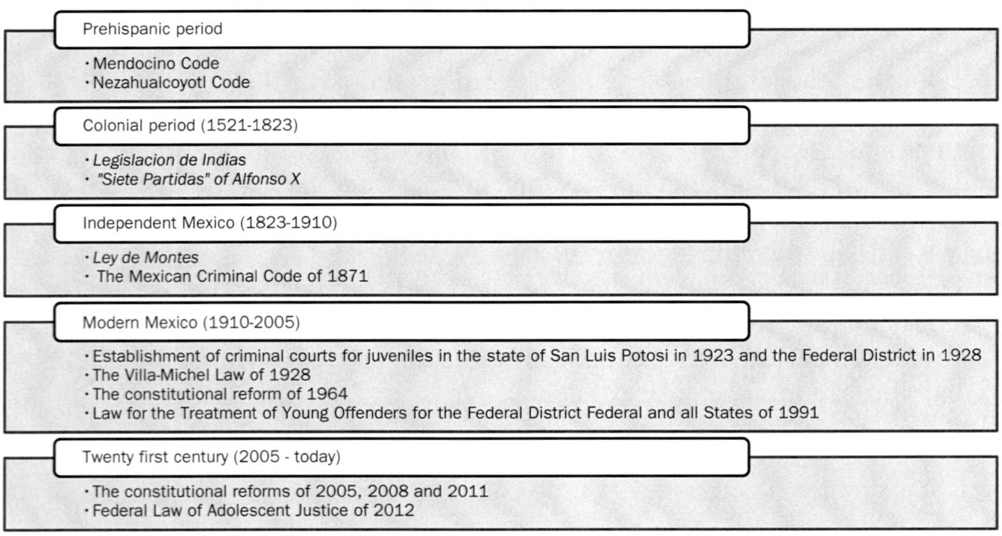

FIGURE 6.1. Mexico: The legal status of juveniles through time. *Source*: *Own elaboration*.

[1] The references to juveniles can be found in pages (*folios*) 60 and 61.

During the colonial period, the legal status of juveniles was included in the *Legislacion de Indias* of 1680 established by the *Real Consejo de Indias*. The legal age of majority (18) and terms of punishment and rules for imprisonment for juveniles and adults were established in this code.

Mexico's war of independence occurred between 1810 and 1821. In spite of the promise of social justice, modernity, and equality that the independent movement made to the general population, in reality, the juvenile justice system and the criminal system, overall, evolved very slowly during this period. For a good number of years after independence, the colonial legislation remained in function for all matters. The first change regarding juveniles happened with the so-called Ley de Montes of 1841. This law defined the age of majority, but it really did not bring major changes in comparison to the previous *Legislacion de Indias*. In any event, this was the first Mexican law regarding the legal status of juveniles.

The first true legal reform regarding the status of juveniles came into being just a few years before the *Porfiriato* (1876–1911)[2] in 1871, when the first Mexican criminal code was promulgated. Some important changes were made regarding the age of majority and the rules for punishment, particularly regarding minors under 9 years old. Still, during this historical period, juveniles were judged in the same courts as adults, and, in practice, they were also punished as adults (Blanco 2006).

Even though some important legal discussions occurred between 1908 and 1912 regarding the need for a specific criminal justice system for juveniles, the Mexican revolution of 1910–1920 put a stop to all discussions concerning the criminal justice system as a whole (Blanco 2006).

Still, these discussions were quickly restarted and followed by action. In 1923 the first juvenile court was established in the state of San Luis Potosi, followed in 1928 by the Federal District (Mexico City) with the promulgation of the Law for the Social Prevention of Child Delinquency in the Federal District and the Territories, also called the *Villa-Michel* law. This law was a breakthrough in the sense that it emphasized rehabilitation, in opposition to punishment, the main goal behind the juvenile justice system. As such, it established different types of penalties varying from school arrest and probation to reclusion in correctional institutions, agricultural colonies, or service in school (Cruz 2007). In fact, the next federal criminal codes of 1929 and 1931 included these principles regarding the legal status of juveniles.

The next major advancement came in 1964 when the Federal Congress imposed the establishment of juvenile courts in all states. This can be considered a major reform since it included a reform of article 18 in the Constitution.

[2]The *Porfiriato* is a period of Mexican history during which General Porfirio Diaz was president. It is characterized by a wave of political centralization, economic modernization, and social inequality. It ended with the Mexican revolution of 1910.

Later on, in 1991, the Law for the Treatment of Young Offenders for the Federal District and all States was enacted. It conceived of juvenile crime as a crime prevention problem. As such, it considered a variety of legal principles such as the principle of legality, the presumption of innocence and orality in the process, and the establishment of a child advocate called *Consejo de Menores*. Two criticisms of this law were that it basically replicated the inquisitorial criminal justice system of adults and that the Consejo de Menores was both an administrative and judicial institution, thus violating article 37 of the Convention of the Rights of Children of 1989 in the sense that children have the right to "... challenge the legality of the deprivation of his or her liberty before a court or other competent, independent and impartial authority, and to a prompt decision on any such action" (Castillo & Zuñiga 2010).

Interestingly enough though, the major conceptual changes and improvements have occurred during the last 10 years. Today, the juvenile justice system in Mexico benefits from three constitutional reforms that have happened during this century. These were the constitutional reforms of 2005, 2008, and 2011. They can be considered major reforms because they involved constitutional changes and, in fairness, a major advance in the treatment of juveniles and adults in the criminal justice system. The reform of 2005 (again) changed article 18 of the Constitution by introducing the legal basis for an integral juvenile system of justice nationwide, from a perspective of Children's Rights as they are considered nowadays by the United Nations. The reform of 2008 changed article 20 of the Constitution by introducing the oral adversarial system in the criminal justice system as a whole, including the juvenile criminal system. As a result of this reform, the previous inquisitorial system of justice will be eliminated. In June of 2016, the new system must be operating in all states. Finally the reform of 2011 changed article 1 (and title of Chap. 1) of the Constitution to include human rights, this meaning that from now on (1) all human rights international agreements made by Mexico have the same status as constitutional law and (2) all legal processes must guarantee the human rights of every person, including juveniles, as safeguards against abuses of power.

Finally, in 2012 the Federal Law for Adolescent Justice was enacted.[3] All of the recent constitutional reforms were considered and imprinted in this piece of legislation. This law also considers other important measures as the existence of different alternatives to the trial of the juvenile, such as the conciliation and mediation alternatives between the offender and the victim, and measures of restorative justice. This law is the most modern and probably the best legislation ever enacted in this country. This law will be abrogated in 2016 in order for the Federation and all States to begin operating with the National Code of Criminal Process which makes the adversarial system the only criminal system in the country. As such, in

[3] It can be downloaded here: http://www.diputados.gob.mx/LeyesBiblio/ref/lfja.htm.

2016 a new federal law and 32 State laws on juvenile justice will have to be enacted. These new laws must not be too different from the 2012 federal law.

These reforms for the benefit of juveniles are not without limitations. Among them are the following (IJPP 2013): Juvenile programs are scarce, criminal justice institutions are not responding fast enough to reduce exclusion and labeling, and there is a lack of data regarding juvenile delinquency. While I agree that not much progress can be made without better institutions for juveniles, I partially disagree with the last criticism. A lot of progress has been made recently, but indeed much more than legal changes are needed for the betterment of the Mexican criminal justice institutions.

AGE OF MAJORITY

As said in the introduction, we can go far into the past to see the progress made regarding the concept of age of majority. The age of majority is conceptually defined as the age when one becomes an adult. Age of majority may vary between countries, but legal implications are equally important: the capacity to contract, to exercise political rights, to become subject of adult criminal punishment, etc.

Let me start by saying that the age of majority is not a Western-only concept. In Mexico, the code of *Nezahualcoyotl* (1427–1472) stated that children under the age of 10 could not be held responsible for a crime (Soto 2007). The majority of age in Aztec times was 15 years old. For today's standards, penalties under the Aztec rule were extremely severe, including for minors. Minors between the ages of 10 and 14 could be held responsible for a crime and punished by death, slavery, confiscation of property, and/or exile (Gutierrez 2008). However, it is said that punishment for minors was more lenient in comparison to adults, with two exceptions: crimes of insults against parents or parricide, where the penalty was death, irrespective of age (Gutierrez 2008). This clearly shows that family as an institution was more important than the concept of childhood for the Aztec. Later on, at the age of 15, youngsters would become adults and had to leave home for the *Calmecac*[4] or the *Tepuchcalli* in order to receive religious, military, and civil instruction (Soto 2007). It must be said that these schools had a court of their own with a judge and its own procedures to assure justice among their students.

During colonial times, the *Legislacion de Indias* of 1680 fixed the age of majority at 18. It stated that those under the age of 10 could not be punished for a crime as they could not be held responsible for their behaviors. Between the ages of 10 and 17, minors could be held responsible. But the death penalty could not be applied to them in any case. These legal terms were based on the *Siete Partidas* of *Alfonso X*, which also stated that children under 10 could not be found guilty

[4]The first type of school was for the Nobility, while the second was for the rest.

of any crime, yet those between the ages of 10 and 17 could be punished to some degree for most crimes, although not for all (e.g., minors under 14 could not be found guilty of sexual crimes).

The year 1841 marks the date of the first true Mexican criminal justice legislation with references to minors. It was called *Ley de Montes*. It established the age of majority at 18 years old. It also stated that minors below the age of 10 could not be held responsible for a crime and that those between the ages of 10 and 17 could be prosecuted and sanctioned. It did not bring major changes, but it was the first Mexican legal document referring to the legal status and age of majority of juveniles.

The criminal code of 1871 was an example of modernity and progress. It established that children under 9 years old would be exempt of criminal responsibility (Cruz 2007). The responsibility of those between 9 and under 14 would be decided upon expert opinion, while those between 14 and under 18 could be held responsible for a crime (Cruz 2007). In all cases, convicted juveniles would have to be held in a correctional center for the time of their sentence and until they had finished their primary education.

The 1928 Law for the Social Prevention of Child Delinquency in the Federal District and the Territories, also called the *Villa-Michel* law, established that minors under 15 could not be judged according to the criminal code. The age of majority remained at 18, but minors under 15 years were not to be prosecuted nor convicted by police and courts for adults. They were sent to specialized courts for juveniles. In 1929, the institution of Court Judge for Minors was created.[5]

Today, the 2005 constitutional reform of article 18 homologated across all Mexican states (32) the age of majority as 18 years old. Only minors between the ages of 12 and 17 can be held responsible for a crime. No minor under the age of 12 can be held responsible for a crime in Mexico; however if they committed a crime, they will have to be rehabilitated and provided with guidance. Internment can only be applied to minors over 14 and only for violent crimes.

THE COUNTRY'S STANCE TOWARD THE UN COMMITTEE ON THE RIGHTS OF THE CHILD

Mexico subscribed to the United Nations (UN) Convention on the Rights of the Child in 1989. In 2014, the Committee on the Rights of the Child examined the 2012 report of Mexico and concluded that more effort is needed with regard to the prevention of bullying and how to reinforce child development in a context of violence, poverty, and poor distribution of wealth. The report also emphasized the need to focus on children under the age of 5.[6] It also mentioned that the

[5] In Spanish *Juez del Tribunal para Menores.*

[6] The full report can be downloaded here: http://tbinternet.ohchr.org/_layouts/treatybodyexternal/Download.aspx?symbolno=CRC/C/MEX/4-5&Lang=en. The news media summary can be downloaded here: http://www.ohchr.org/en/NewsEvents/Pages/DisplayNews.aspx?NewsID=15986&LangID=E.

new law on juvenile justice was not fully in line with the provisions of the convention in terms of the definition and length of pretrial detention of juveniles.

Mexico's UN delegation responded to these criticisms assuring that the Senate was working on adopting a uniform law on juvenile justice to ensure a comprehensive justice system applicable to children aged 12–18 years of age. Likewise, that the new justice of juveniles would be oral and adversarial, involving hearings and aiming to rehabilitate and reintegrate the offenders to society.

TRENDS IN JUVENILE CRIME

Mexico started to systematically collect data on juveniles in 2010. There are several important trends that will be particularly pertinent to those interested in juvenile crime policy.

First, between 2009 and 2014, the total number of juveniles charged with crimes nationwide decreased by 28%. Overall, this is a very positive trend. At this pace, the total number of juveniles charged with a crime may be reduced to half before the year 2020 (Fig. 6.2).

This trend may be attributed to a decrease in the number of repeat offenders in the same period (−27%), but also the total number of first-time offenders has

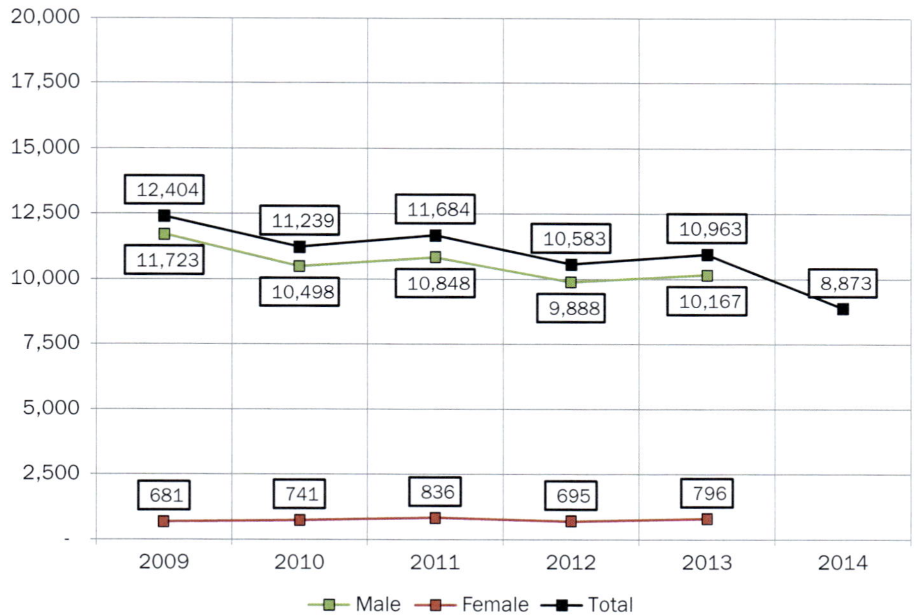

FIGURE 6.2. Total number of juveniles charged with a crime per gender, 2009–2014. Source: Author's own based on INEGI data. Data on gender for 2014 has not yet been released.

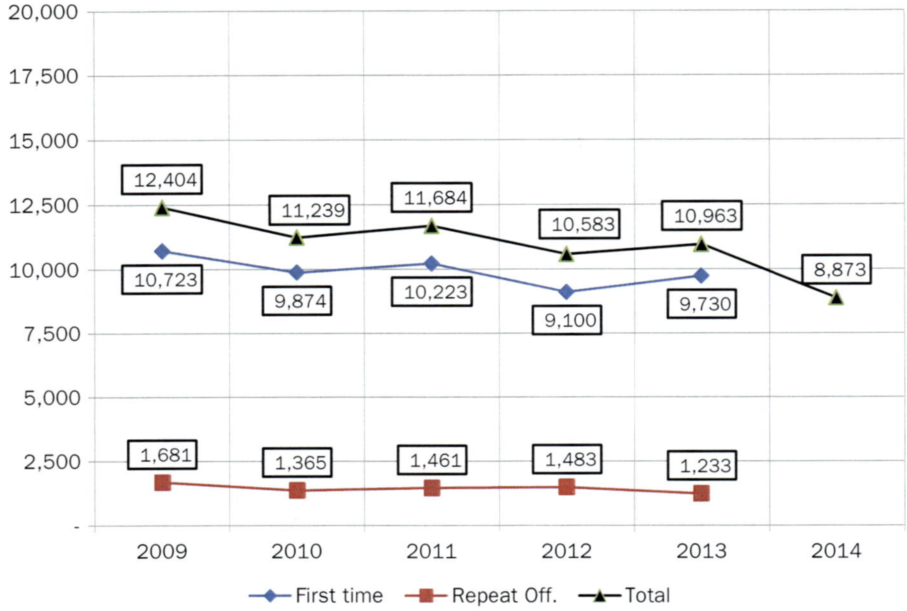

FIGURE 6.3. Total number of juveniles charged with crimes as first timers or repeat offenders, 2009–2014. Source: Author's own based on INEGI data. Other data for 2014 has not yet been released.

experienced a significant reduction (−9%).[7] The percent of repeat offenders in the total number of juveniles charged with a crime has varied around 11% and 14% of the total (Fig. 6.3).

In fact, Table 6.1 shows that the trends between adults and juveniles charged with a crime seem to differ considerably between 2009 and 2014. The rate of juveniles charged with a crime per 100 thousand has decreased by almost a third in only 6 years. On the other hand, the rate of adults has increased by a fifth in the same period.

Regarding the type of crime, most juveniles are charged with theft or robbery. However, there has been a noticeable increase recently in the proportion of juveniles charged with drug crimes and assault. The proportion of juveniles charged with homicide is not small: around 5% every year. This statistic is not different from the adult population charged with a homicide crime. In 2013, 6% of adults charged with a crime have been charged with a homicide.[8] Of course, there are major differences in terms of magnitude between these two populations. In the same year, 174 thousand adults were charged in comparison to (almost) 11 thousand minors (Table 6.2).[9]

[7] At the moment of writing, not all data on juveniles had been released from the latest 2015 National Census of Government, Public Security and State Prison System (with data from 2014).

[8] *Source*: National Census of Government, Public Security and State Prison System of 2014

[9] Of these, 10,503 were charged with a homicide.

TABLE 6.1. Mexico: Juveniles charged with crimes per type of crime, 2011–2014

	Total number		*Rates per 100 thousand*	
	Juveniles	*Adults*	*Juveniles*	*Adults*
2009	12,404	142,111	99.0	233.3
2010	11,239	150,731	88.9	240.3
2011	11,684	151,820	91.7	235.2
2012	10,583	170,017	82.3	256.2
2013	10,963	197,046	84.6	289.0
2014	8873	199,563	67.9	285.1
Relative change	−28.5%	40.4%	−31.4%	22.2%

Source: Author's own based on INEGI data and population estimates of minors aged 12—17 and adults respectively. Data does not include federal crimes

TABLE 6.2. Mexico: Juveniles charged per type of crime, 2011–2013

	2011	*2012*	*2013*
Juveniles charged	11,684	10,583	10,963
Theft/robbery	67.5%	65.8%	59.4%
Drug dealing	3.5%	3.6%	5.3%
Homicide	5.1%	5.1%	5.0%
Assault	2.7%	3.1%	3.6%
Sexual crimes	5.1%	4.2%	3.6%
Other crimes	16.1%	18.2%	23.1%
Total	100.0%	100.0%	100.0%

Source: Author's own based on INEGI data

TABLE 6.3. Mexico: Juveniles charged with a crime per gender, 2006–2013

	Total	*Male (%)*	*Female (%)*
2006	33,665	90.2	9.8
2007	22,969	91.1	8.9
2008	17,878	93.9	6.1
2009	12,404	94.5	5.5
2010	11,239	93.4	6.6
2011	11,684	92.8	7.2
2012	10,583	93.4	6.6
2013	10,963	92.7	7.3
Total change	−22,702	2.6	−2.6
Relative change	−67.4%	2.9	−26.2

Source: Author's own based on INEGI data

As expected, there are less female juveniles than males. Their proportion in the total population of juveniles charged with a crime in 2013 was 26% less than in 2006 (see Table 6.3).

Gender surely plays a role in criminal behavior. In 2013, female juveniles were more likely to be associated or charged with drug dealing, an assault, or a

Table 6.4. Mexico: Juveniles charged with crimes by gender and type of crime, 2013

	Male	*Female*
Juveniles charged	10,167	796
Theft/robbery	60.4%	47.1%
Drug dealing	5.0%	9.4%
Homicide	5.1%	3.9%
Assault	3.3%	7.7%
Sexual crimes	3.9%	0.0%
Kidnapping[a]	1.4%	3.6%
Other crimes	20.9%	28.3%
Total	100.0%	100.0%

Source: Author's own based on INEGI data

[a]This crime is not reported in previous table as it is a very low-frequency crime overall

kidnapping, whereas males were much more likely to be associated or charged with theft/robbery or a homicide. It is very notable that females are two times more likely to be charged with a drug-dealing crime (i.e., *narcomenudeo*). This type of crime is loosely defined in current legislation as the possession, trading, supply, or any other conduct related to the narcotics expressly forbidden in the Mexican public health legislation[10] and only when the quantity in question is less than 1 thousand times the amount established by the law for personal and immediate consumption (Table 6.4).[11]

The reasons for these differences between juvenile males and females are not known, but some hypotheses are not hard to present as an invitation for future research: One is that Mexican organized crime in cities is beginning to use girls to sell drugs in small amounts (i.e., *narcomenudeo*) as they are less likely to be stopped and searched by the local police.[12] With regard to kidnapping crimes, it might be the case that more females are charged because they are more likely to be found and arrested in police raids of kidnapping houses, as their role in the gang is normally to feed and watch the victim rather than to participate in the actual kidnap.

CAUSES OF JUVENILE CRIME

The National Crime and Violence Prevention Program (PRONAPRED) of 2014–2018 identifies the adolescent population as a high crime-risk population. The main causes identified are not different from what is being reported in the

[10]Ley General de Salud

[11]Each type of substance has specific amounts established as for personal consumption.

[12]I want to thank my colleague Alejandro Hope for this insight.

Latin American specialized literature, among them teen pregnancy, drug use, family disruption, school desertion, unemployment, lack of social capital, lack of public spaces, a culture of illegality, and social exclusion (PRONAPRED, 2014).

These risk factors or causes of juvenile crime have been investigated in a small number of studies. Not that many studies and empirical evidence can be found regarding the causes or correlates of juvenile crime in Mexico, but some good accounts exist. In fact, the same risk factors, particularly family disruption and poor parenting, are repeated time and again in the specialized literature (see Table 6.5).

TABLE 6.5. Mexico: Summary of selected studies on the causes of juvenile delinquency

Year	*Author(s)*	*Method*	*Major finding/argument*
1946	Hayner	Statistical	School dropout, extreme poverty, weakening of parental controls, early exposure to criminal adults
2003	Frias et al.	Statistical	Negative environments facilitate antisocial behaviors
2004	Castillo	Subjective assessment	Poverty, lack of socialization, recreation and employment opportunities, labeling, family breakdown, marginalization and exclusion, school dropout, and organized crime
2005	Jimenez	Subjective assessment	Social exclusion, discrimination, drugs, family disruption, lack of employment, health and education opportunities, and lack of cultural activities and sports
2007	Cisneros	Statistical	Social exclusion, alcohol and drug misuse, media labeling, and the failure of the family and education institutions among others
2007	Quiroz et al.	Statistical	Family hostility and rejection, lack of communication with parents, and the use of severe discipline from parents
2008	Herrera et al.	Statistical	Alcohol, amphetamine, and/or cocaine use prior to crime
2010	Castillo	Statistical	Gangs, unemployment, lack of education opportunity, overcrowding, lack of proper housing, and urban expansion toward the periphery
2012	Estrada and Cano	Qualitative	Lack of public spaces and sports, family disruption, lack of parental supervision as both parents work, lack of police in streets, neighborhood social decay, and vigilante justice

Source: Author's own based on previous studies

One recent argument advanced by Jiménez (2005) is that contemporary Mexican youth, particularly the poor, are socially excluded and discriminated, this resulting in juvenile violence and crime. Other reasons are access to drugs, family disruption, lack of employment opportunities, health, education, and access to culture and sports (Jiménez 2005). Also in Mexico, Frias-Armenta et al. (2003) found that negative environments or ecological factors around adolescents (e.g., poor parenting, child abuse, alcohol misuse by parents, school and neighborhood signs of social disorder, etc.) could explain more than half of the variation in their self-reporting of antisocial behaviors. Some of these findings were later verified by Cisneros (2007) based on demographic and risk factors data of juveniles and young adults aged 18–21 that were serving their sentences in correctional institutions and prisons in the State of Mexico in 2000. He found high proportions of juveniles convicted and young adult prison inmates that had suffered from social exclusion as well as having problems of alcohol and drug misuse. Also, a good number of them were raised in low-income households with a history of child abuse.

One last comment before we continue to the next section is that the National Survey of Victimization and Perception of Public Safety (ENVIPE) allows to know the total number and proportion of offenders under 18 years. This is of course based on the perception and memory of the victims surveyed. In this respect, it is important to know that in 2014, only 2.8% of the victims surveyed were able to identify the age of their attacker as being someone under 18 years old. In 2010, this proportion was 3.0%, that is, a difference within the margin of error.[13] As such, considering that the total population under 18 years old nationwide was around 39 million or 32% of the total population in 2015, it is clear that the number of crimes committed by minors is well below their percentage in the total population. These figures give us a reference point from which we can assess the real magnitude of the juvenile crime problem in Mexico.

POLICING AND JUVENILES

The juvenile justice system begins with the preventive police or the investigative judicial police either receiving a report of a crime or arresting a suspect. Criminal cases begin with criminal investigations initiated by the investigative judicial police.[14] Criminal investigations can only be initiated by state or federal prosecutors. Prosecutors, or *Ministerios Publicos* in Spanish, are not police officers themselves nor do they work for the judicial branch as their name would suggest, but they are prosecuting attorneys working for the investigative police in the executive branch.

[13] In fact, the age group in the ENVIPE with the highest percent of offenders as identified by the victims is those between 26 and 35 years old with around 30% of all offenders.

[14] In Spanish *averiguaciones previas*.

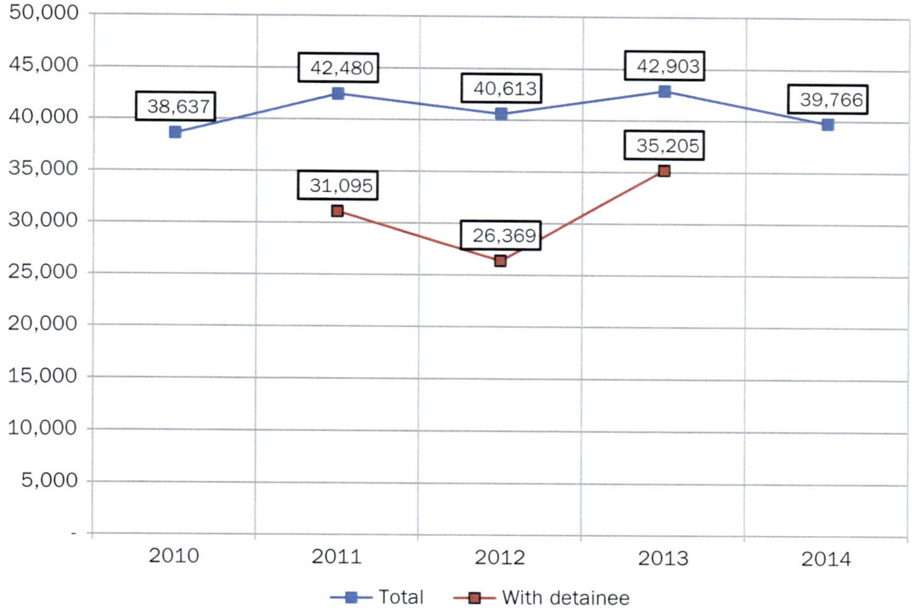

FIGURE 6.4. Total number of criminal investigations for juvenile crimes initiated and in process per year and with detainee, 2010—2014. Source: Author's own based on INEGI data.

In the case of juveniles, there are specialized prosecutors for minors in every state. Naturally, criminal investigations may be initiated with or without an arrestee or suspect. The graph below shows that the number of criminal investigations of juvenile related crimes has remained about the same between 2010 and 2014. What varies across time is the number of criminal investigations with detainees. They represent between 70% and 80% of criminal investigations (Fig. 6.4).

It is important to know that the number of criminal investigations is a function of the number of crimes committed and the number of crimes reported to the police. In this respect, Mexico suffers from a major problem of underreporting of crime. According to INEGI's National Survey of Victimization and Perception of Public Safety (ENVIPE), between 2010 and 2014, fewer than 12% of all crimes reported in the survey were actually reported to the police. In addition, not all crimes reported to the police resulted in a criminal investigation. According to the same survey, less than 8% of all crimes resulted in a criminal investigation. The main reason of this underreporting is that crime victims view the reporting of a crime as a waste of time.

It is also interesting to know the opinion of youth on policing. The Social Cohesion Survey for the Prevention of Violence and Crime (ECOPRED)[15] of 2014 shows that the population between 12 and 29 years old neither trust in their

[15]Designed by the National Institute of Statistics and Geography (INEGI) and the Secretary of the Interior (SEGOB)

local police nor do they think that the police is capable to arrest a criminal. To be specific, 63.4% either do not trust or have a low level of trust in the police and 73.2% think the police would not catch the criminal ().

COURTS AND JUVENILES

The judicial activity of minors is not small scale. Between 2011 and 2013, around 15 thousand juveniles were processed in Mexican specialized courts for minors. Also, around 6 thousand sentences were given each year of which approximately 83% were guilty verdicts. Still, the conviction rate for juveniles was slightly lower than those for adults, which in 2013 was of 87% (INEGI) (Table 6.6).

Juvenile justice is not quick either. Most juvenile processes take more than a year. This comes in line with the concerns argued by the Committee on the Rights of the Child in 2014. In fact, data suggests that between 2011 and 2013, there was a considerable increase in the length of the legal process. In fact, several states have made changes in their procedural codes to increase the minimum duration of the process for juveniles (Vasconcelos 2011). However, this deduction must be considered with precaution, as in 2011, the duration of the criminal process was not specified in almost half of the cases. More complete time series are needed to be conclusive in this respect. In any event, recent data from 2013 show juvenile justice as slow and in need for further reform (Table 6.7).

Table 6.6. Mexico: Total number of juveniles in court, 2011–2013

	2011	*2012*	*2013*
Juveniles in court	15,137	15,713	15,292
Sentences given in court	n.a.	6144	6710
Found guilty	n.a.	5141 (83.7%)	5650 (84.2%)

Source: Author's own based on INEGI data. These data do not include appeals to previous sentences

Table 6.7. Mexico: Duration of the criminal process, 2011 and 2013

	2011		*2013*	
	Sentences given in court	*Percent (%)*	*Sentences given in court*	*Percent (%)*
Less than 3 months	240	8.0	676	14.3
Between 3 and 6 months	238	8.0	193	4.1
Between 6 months and 1 year	1585	53.0	1480	31.4
More than 1 year	930	31.1	2370	50.2
Total	2993	100.0	4719	100.0

Source: Author's own based on INEGI data. The mismatch between tables is because the duration of some cases was not specified in the data source. For 2011, in almost half of the cases, the duration of the criminal process was not specified

CUSTODIAL RULES AND INFRASTRUCTURE FOR JUVENILES

Juveniles cannot be mixed with adult populations, neither during a trial nor as convicts. They are always separated from the moment of detention to the moment of conviction. There are five main types of treatment facilities for juveniles in Mexico: treatment centers (previously known as correctionals), schools of social rehabilitation, community shelters, specialized centers, and other types of centers which fall under a different statistical category from the previous (INEGI 2015). It must be noted that around half of the juveniles in 2014 were in treatment centers, while the other half were being rehabilitated in other facilities, that is, in external treatment or assisted liberty. Also, around a third of those in treatment centers were on trial, while the other two thirds had already been convicted of a crime. This proportion has remained the same since 2010 when such data was first made available (Table 6.8).

In 2014 there were 57 treatment centers across the country with different levels of infrastructure. All centers were equipped with dormitories, and most had medical service facilities, workshops, and classrooms. The ratio of juveniles per employee was 1:7. Of course, not all personnel in internment centers are in charge of custody (Table 6.9).

Overall, the infrastructure has remained about the same since 2009 although the number of juveniles in these treatment centers has increased. It must be noted that there are reports of mistreatment of minors in some of these centers. In

Table 6.8. Mexico: Juveniles in treatment centers convicted and awaiting trial, 2010–2014

	2010		*2014*	
	Number	*Percent (%)*	*Number*	*Percent (%)*
Convicted	4237	64.3	5134	65.4
Awaiting trial	2348	35.7	2715	34.6
Total	6585	100.0	7849	100.0

Source: Author's own based on INEGI data. The not specified were not included

Table 6.9. Mexico: Internment centers, personnel, and juveniles, 2009–2014

	2009	*2010*	*2011*	*2012*	*2013*	*2014*
Centers	58	61	59	60	57	57
Personnel	4605	5154	5180	5741	4374	4748
Juveniles	6563	7634	7303	8261	8256	8024
Ratio J/C	113	125	124	138	145	141
Ratio J/P	1.4	1.5	1.4	1.4	1.9	1.7

Source: Author's own based on INEGI data

2014, a study of the Mexican National Commission for Human Rights (CNDH) reported that approximately 66% of minors had been mistreated either physically or verbally.[16]

ALTERNATIVE SANCTIONS FOR JUVENILES: HOME CONFINEMENT, RESTORATIVE JUSTICE, RESTITUTION, ETC.

Not all juveniles convicted of a crime are sent to treatment facilities. In 2014, almost 5 thousand convicted juveniles were treated outside a treatment facility of some kind. More than half of the total population of juvenile convicts were treated outside treatment centers. This proportion has never been under 55% since 2009, that is, after the two constitutional reforms of 2005 and 2008. Prior to these reforms, we do not know how many juveniles were convicted of a crime nor what proportion of them were being treated inside or outside a treatment facility. It is also important to know that only those juveniles are 14 years or older and only those convicted of violent crimes can be treated in a treatment center (previously known as correctional).

According to the Federal Justice Law for Adolescents, there are 15 different types of sanctions for juveniles (see Table 6.10).

Looking at the trends in the number of juvenile convicts in connection to the number of juveniles charged with a crime (see Sect. 4) and juveniles in trial (see Sect. 7), we cannot claim that the observable swing between 2009 and 2014 in the number of juvenile convicts (see graph below) is due to these constitutional reforms. As observed, the total number of juvenile convicts in treatment centers has remained about the same in this time period, while the number of juvenile convicts in external treatment first increased between 2009 and 2012 and then decreased in 2013 and 2014 (Fig. 6.5).

It must be noted that conviction rates (i.e., the number of juveniles convicted divided by the number of juveniles on trial) can be a function only of the number of (1) arrests, (2) criminal investigations, (3) criminal charges made, and/or (4) the severity of judges. Even though we do not have evidence of the number of arrests, we do have evidence that (1) criminal investigations have remained about the same, (2) the conviction rate by judges remained about the same as well, and (3) the number of juveniles charged with a crime decreased by a 28% between 2009 and 2014. As such, it would be difficult to make the claim that the number of convicts is a function of the reforms affecting the dynamics of the steps prior to conviction in the juvenile criminal justice system. In fact, based on available data, it looks like the number of juvenile convicts will continue to decrease, at least in the short run.

---

[16] *Source*: Newspaper *La Jornada*, March 3, 2015. See: http://www.jornada.unam.mx/ultimas/2015/03/03/en-centros-para-recluir-jovenes-se-comenten-torturas-reporta-cndh-7024.html.

TABLE 6.10. Mexico: Sanctions and their duration in the Federal Law for Adolescents

Attention call	*No duration established*
Assisted liberty	No less than 3 days and up to 4 years
Community service	No less than 3 days and up to 4 years
Restorative justice	No duration established
Limitation or prohibition of residence	Up to 4 years
Prohibition relating to certain people	No less than 6 months and up to 4 years
Prohibition to attend certain places	No less than 6 months and up to 4 years
Prohibition to drive	No less than 6 months and up to 4 years
Obligation to attend certain institutions to receive educational or technical training or guidance	No less than 3 days and up to 4 years
Obligation to get a job	No less than 1 month and up to 4 years
Obligation to abstain from alcohol or drug consumption	No less than 6 months and up to 4 years
Confinement in a treatment facility different from a treatment center	Depends on the crime committed
Home confinement	No less than 1 month and up to 4 years
Confinement in leisure time	No less than 1 month and up to 4 years
Confinement in a treatment center	If juvenile is between 14 and 15 years old, no less than 1 year and up to 5 years; if juvenile is between 16 and 17 years old, no less than 2 year and up to 7 years

Source: Author's own based on the Federal Law for Adolescents of 2012

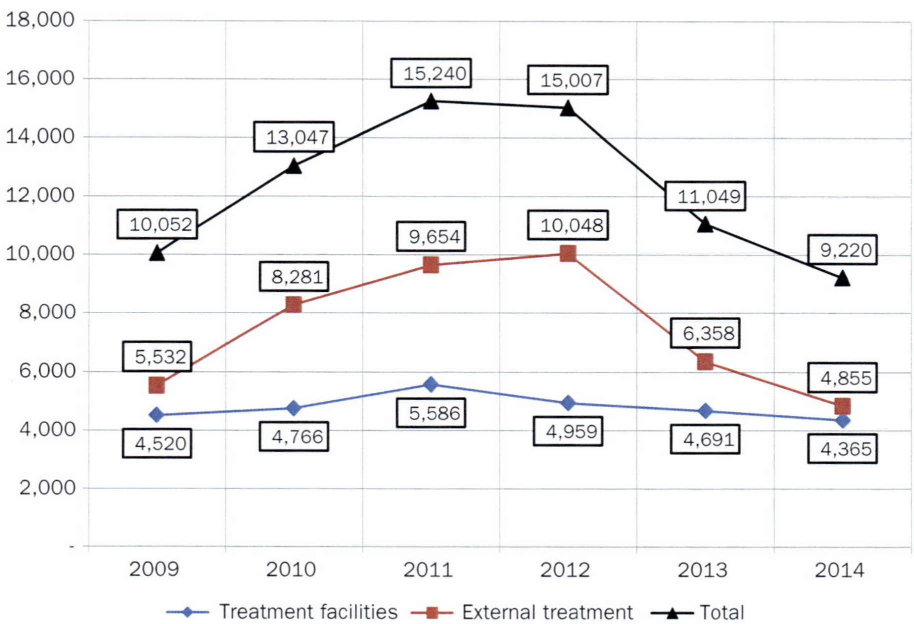

FIGURE 6.5. Juvenile convicts in treatment facilities and in external treatment, 2009–2014. Source: Author's own based on INEGI data.

DIFFERENCES IN TREATMENT OF BOYS AND GIRLS

Juveniles are separated by gender from the moment of detention to the moment of conviction. If convicted in a treatment center, they are also physically separated in dormitories for each gender. In federal treatment centers, dormitories must not hold more than four minors per room irrespective of their gender. The only obligation regarding the treatment of female convicts that is established in the federal law for Adolescent Justice of 2012 is that female inmates in treatment centers must be taken care of by female personnel only. Both genders are allowed to have intimate time with visitors in treatment centers.

REFERENCES

Blanco, C. (2006). Estudio historico y comparado de la legislación de menores infractores. In N. Gonzalez (Coord.), *Estudios jurídicos en homenaje a Marta Morineau: Sistemas jurídicos contemporáneos*. Mexico: UNAM.et Retrieved from http://biblio.juridicas.unam.mx/libros/4/1968/7.pdf.

Castillo, J., & Zuñiga, J. (2010). La Ley para adolescentes para el Distrito Federal. *Alegatos, 76*, 749–786. Retrieved from http://biblioteca.cide.edu/.

Cisneros, J. (2007). Cultura, juventud y delincuencia en el Estado de México. *Papeles de Población, 13*(52), 255–280. Retrieved from http://www.redalyc.org/pdf/112/11205210.pdf.

Cruz, E. (2007). El concepto de menores infractores. *Revista del Posgrado en Derecho de la UNAM, 3*(5), 335–355. Retrieved from http://www.juridicas.unam.mx/publica/librev/rev/posder/cont/5/cnt/cnt17.pdf.

Frias-Armenta, M., Lopez, A., & Diaz, S. (2003). Predictores de la conducta antisocial juvenil: Un modelo ecológico. *Estudos de Psicologia (Natal), 8*(1), 15–24. doi:10.1590/s1413-294x2003000100003.

Gutierrez, A. (2008). El delincuente infantil: El nacimiento de su tutelaje en San Luis Potosi, Siglos XIX-XX. *Epikeia: Revista de Derecho y Politica, 9*, 1–27. Retrieved from http://epikeia.leon.uia.mx/old/numeros/09/epikeia09-el_delincuente_infantil.pdf.

Instituto de Justicia Procesal Penal. (2013). *Informe sobre la justicia para adolescentes en conflicto con la ley penal en México: Estado actual después de las reformas constitucionales de 2005, 2008 y 2011*. Mexico: Mexico D.F. Retrieved from http://setecc.egobierno.gob.mx/files/2013/03/Informe-sobre-la-Justicia-para-Adolescentes.pdf.

Instituto Nacional de Estadistica y Geografia. (2011a). *Censo Nacional de Gobierno, Seguridad Publica y Sistema Penitenciario Estatales*. Mexico: Inegi. Retrieved from http://www.inegi.org.mx/est/contenidos/proyectos/censosgobierno/.

Instituto Nacional de Estadistica y Geografia. (2011b). *Censo Nacional de Procuracion de Justicia Estatal*. Mexico: Inegi. Retrieved from http://www.inegi.org.mx/est/contenidos/proyectos/censosgobierno/.

Instituto Nacional de Estadistica y Geografia. (2011c). *Censo Nacional de Imparticion de Justicia Estatal*. Mexico: Inegi. Retrieved from http://www.inegi.org.mx/est/contenidos/proyectos/censosgobierno/.

Instituto Nacional de Estadistica y Geografia. (2012a). *Censo Nacional de Gobierno, Seguridad Publica y Sistema Penitenciario Estatales*. Mexico: Inegi. Retrieved from http://www.inegi.org.mx/est/contenidos/proyectos/censosgobierno/.

Instituto Nacional de Estadistica y Geografia. (2012b). *Censo Nacional de Procuracion de Justicia Estatal*. Mexico: Inegi. Retrieved from http://www.inegi.org.mx/est/contenidos/proyectos/censosgobierno/.
Instituto Nacional de Estadistica y Geografia. (2012c). *Censo Nacional de Imparticion de Justicia Estatal*. Mexico: INEGI. Retrieved from http://www.inegi.org.mx/est/contenidos/proyectos/censosgobierno/.
Instituto Nacional de Estadistica y Geografia. (2013a). *Censo Nacional de Gobierno, Seguridad Publica y Sistema Penitenciario Estatales*. Mexico: Inegi. Retrieved from http://www.inegi.org.mx/est/contenidos/proyectos/censosgobierno/.
Instituto Nacional de Estadistica y Geografia. (2013b). *Censo Nacional de Procuracion de Justicia Estatal*. Mexico: Inegi. Retrieved from http://www.inegi.org.mx/est/contenidos/proyectos/censosgobierno/.
Instituto Nacional de Estadistica y Geografia. (2013c). *Censo Nacional de Imparticion de Justicia Estatal*. Mexico: INEGI. Retrieved from http://www.inegi.org.mx/est/contenidos/proyectos/censosgobierno/.
Instituto Nacional de Estadistica y Geografia. (2014a). *Censo Nacional de Gobierno, Seguridad Publica y Sistema Penitenciario Estatales*. Mexico: Inegi. Retrieved from http://www.inegi.org.mx/est/contenidos/proyectos/censosgobierno/.
Instituto Nacional de Estadistica y Geografia. (2014b). *Censo Nacional de Procuracion de Justicia Estatal*. Mexico: Inegi. Retrieved from http://www.inegi.org.mx/est/contenidos/proyectos/censosgobierno/.
Instituto Nacional de Estadistica y Geografia. (2014c). *Censo Nacional de Imparticion de Justicia Estatal*. Mexico: INEGI. Retrieved from http://www.inegi.org.mx/est/contenidos/proyectos/censosgobierno/.
Instituto Nacional de Estadística y Geografía. (2015). *Censo Nacional de Gobierno, Seguridad Pública y Sistema Penitenciario Estatales*. México: Aguascalientes.
Instituto Nacional de Estadistica y Geografia. (2015a). *Censo Nacional de Gobierno, Seguridad Publica y Sistema Penitenciario Estatales*. Mexico: Inegi. Retrieved from http://www.inegi.org.mx/est/contenidos/proyectos/censosgobierno/.
Instituto Nacional de Estadistica y Geografia. (2015b). *Censo Nacional de Procuracion de Justicia Estatal*. Mexico: Inegi. Retrieved from http://www.inegi.org.mx/est/contenidos/proyectos/censosgobierno/.
Instituto Nacional de Estadistica y Geografia. (2015c). *Censo Nacional de Imparticion de Justicia Estatal*. Mexico: INEGI. Retrieved from http://www.inegi.org.mx/est/contenidos/proyectos/censosgobierno/.
Jiménez, R. A. (2005). La delincuencia juvenil: Fenomeno de la sociedad actual. *Papeles de Población, 11*(43), 215–261. Retrieved from http://148.215.2.10/articulo.oa?id=11204310.
Rodriguez, L. (1987). *Criminalidad de menores*. Mexico: Porrua.
Salcedo, A. (2010). El universo sociojuridico de los culhuas o antiguos texcocanos: Un acercamiento a partir de la imagen codificada. *Alegatos, 76*, 837–858. Retrieved from http://www.azc.uam.mx/publicaciones/alegatos/pdfs/69/76-09.pdf.
Secretaría de Gobernación. (2014). *Programa Nacional para la Prevención de la Violencia y la Delincuencia (PRONAPRED)*. México D.F.
Soto, F. (2007). Historia de la justicia de menores (adolescentes) en Mexico. *Epikeia: Revista de Derecho y Politica, 4*, 1–18. Retrieved from http://epikeia.leon.uia.mx/old/numeros/04/epikeia04-justicia_de_menores.pdf.
Vasconcelos, R. (2011). Avances y retrocesos de la justicia para adolescents en Mexico a cuatro años de su establecimiento. *Boletin Mexicano de Derecho Comparado, 130*, 309–350. Retrieved from http://biblio.juridicas.unam.mx/revista/pdf/DerechoComparado/130/art/art10.pdf.

Carlos J. Vilalta Professor of research methods at the Center for Economic Research and Education (CIDE) in Mexico City and Visiting Fellow at the Center for Latin American Studies at the University of Florida. He studies the spatial and temporal elements of crime, crime prevention policies, and prison populations in Latin America. He is member of the Mexican National System of Researchers (SNI-Conacyt) and has been a visiting researcher at the University of Cambridge, McGill University, University of California in San Diego (UCSD), Washington University in St. Louis, University of Missouri in St. Louis, University of North Carolina in Chapel Hill, and University of Houston.

7

USA

Melanie Taylor

A separate justice system for juveniles has existed in the United States for over 100 years. It was originally intended to function as a social welfare system with dual aims: to shield young delinquents from the corrupting influence of seasoned adult offenders and to provide delinquents and status offenders with the guidance and treatment necessary to make the often difficult transition through adolescence to become law-abiding adults. Over the last century, and most especially since the 1960s, juvenile justice policy has shifted dramatically, undergoing a series of reforms that have reshaped the system and challenged the principles on which it was founded.

This chapter examines trends in juvenile justice policy and practice in the United States, with a focus on changes that have occurred over the last 10 years. The first section provides a background of the juvenile justice system and initial treatment orientation toward juveniles, as this helps inform the understanding of very recent shifts in the system back toward a more rehabilitative nature. The chapter then details issues pertaining to ages of juveniles punished in juvenile and criminal courts, as the United States faced international scrutiny for laws that allowed for the lifetime incarceration and execution of juvenile offenders. The next section details policy and procedural shifts impacting policing, courts, and custodial institutions, as all levels of the juvenile justice system endured significant structural changes that have fluctuated in recent years between a rehabilitative and punitive nature. Finally, the chapter concludes with a brief discussion of the most recent shift of the juvenile justice system back to a treatment orientation where alternatives to detention and appropriate services based upon the specific needs of juveniles are now receiving greater attention.

M. Taylor (✉)
Department of Criminal Justice, University of Nevada, Reno,
1664 N. Virginia St, Reno, NV 89557, USA
e-mail: Melanietaylor@unr.edu

S.H. Decker, N. Marteache (eds.), *International Handbook of Juvenile Justice*,
DOI 10.1007/978-3-319-45090-2_7

THE LEGAL STATUS OF JUVENILES

In the United States, juvenile delinquents are believed to be less responsible than adults for their offenses due to their immaturity, lack of self-control, and inability to rationally weigh the costs and benefits of offending. In response to their diminished responsibility, separate systems for juveniles and adults were first developed in the 1800s, with the first juvenile court being established in Cook County, Illinois, in 1899 and the first juvenile institution being built in New York City in 1825 (Feld 1999). The American juvenile justice system has long been influenced by the legal doctrine of *parens patriae*, which allows states the power to discipline and protect juveniles, thereby assuming a parental role. In contrast to the criminal justice system, which tends to be more punitive and crime control oriented, the juvenile justice system is oriented toward rehabilitation and treatment. In an effort to lessen the impact of juvenile system involvement and better rehabilitate juveniles, the juvenile justice system treats delinquents differently than adult criminals. Most notably, the juvenile justice system is similar to civil proceedings, as juveniles do not develop criminal records, whereas prosecution in criminal courts results in lifelong records. Juveniles have extensive safeguards that prevent their hearings and delinquency records from becoming public, so that they may successfully reenter their communities without a delinquent history harming future outcomes. However, many states have recently been allowing for greater public access to juveniles' delinquency records (Shah et al. 2014).

A main differentiating factor of juvenile and criminal courts is the informal nature of the juvenile system, which provides for individualized treatment. In order to ensure informality, juveniles historically had limited rights, as they were not entitled to counsel, confront witnesses, a trial by jury, an appeal, and hearings prior to being waived into adult courts. In many cases this resulted in juveniles being punished more harshly than adults for minor offenses, leading one Supreme Court justice to argue that their lack of basic rights resulted in juveniles being punished in a "kangaroo court." Landmark cases in the 1960s including *Kent v. United States and 383 U.S. 541 (S. Ct* (1966) and *In re Gault. 387 U.S. 1., 20* (1967) served to grant some of these basic rights to juveniles, although juveniles still do not have the right to a trial by a jury.

Despite the informal nature and treatment orientation of the juvenile system, historically juveniles could be treated punitively if they were transferred into criminal courts. Arguably two of the harshest sentences—capital punishment and life in prison without the possibility of parole (LWOP)—were inflicted upon juveniles until recently. After decades of challenges in the U.S. Supreme Court, the case of *Roper v. Simmons, 543 U.S. 551. (S. Ct* (2005) prohibited juveniles who offended under the age of 18 from being sentenced to death, as it was ruled to be a violation of their Eighth and Fourteenth Amendment rights against cruel and unusual punishment because of their diminished culpability. In the five-to-four decision, Justice Kennedy wrote for the majority that the "United States is the only country in the world that continues to give official sanction to the juvenile death penalty" (p. 5). Later, the case of *Graham v. Florida (2011) v. Florida, 130 S. Ct* (2010) challenged LWOP parole sentences for juveniles. At the age of 17, while Graham was on parole for armed burglary, an offense for which he could have received an LWOP sentence, he was caught leaving the scene of another robbery. The criminal court judge in his case believed Graham was a habitual offender, thereby sentencing him to the original sentence of LWOP. The Supreme Court ruled in Graham's case that LWOP sentences for juveniles who committed offenses other than homicide were unconstitutional as they were cruel and unusual punishment. In the case of *Miller v. Alabama (2012) v. Alabama, 567 U.S., (S. Ct* (2012), the Supreme Court expanded LWOP restrictions for juveniles to also include homicide offenders. Juveniles can no longer be sentenced to death or given LWOP sentences in the United States, but considerable variation in the age of jurisdiction and transfer still exists between states.

AGE OF MAJORITY

There continues to be variation across the states regarding the age of jurisdiction for the juvenile court (Zang 2016). In the United States, states set age limits for the minimum age of responsibility and upper age limit of jurisdiction. The minimum age to consider a case for a delinquency hearing ranges from age 6 in North Carolina to age 10 in 11 states, while 33 states do not specify a minimum age. The maximum age for consideration ranges from 15 (New York and North Carolina) to 17 (41 states and the District of Columbia). The majority of states also have an option to extend jurisdiction well past the maximum court jurisdiction so that those who offended in adolescence continue to receive treatments and punishments well into adulthood. Thirty-six states allow for jurisdiction to be extended until the juvenile is 20 years old, while four states (California, Oregon, Montana, and Wisconsin) allow jurisdiction to extend until the juvenile is 24 years old. The age of jurisdiction policies of American states have attempted to have it both ways, arguing that responsibility begins early but ends late.

In addition to juvenile court jurisdiction, states have also outlined the age at which juveniles may be transferred into the criminal justice system through a variety of mechanisms, including judicial waiver (44 states), prosecutorial discretion (14 states), and statutory exclusions (40 states) (National Center for Juvenile Justice 2016). In states that allow for judicial waivers, many do not specify the minimum age at which juveniles may be transferred (e.g., Arizona and Oklahoma) (Griffin et al. 2011). States with a minimum transferrable age range from 10 to 16 years old depending upon the offense committed (e.g., felony, murder, property offense, drug offense). In states where prosecutors have the discretion to transfer jurisdiction, the minimum age by which transfer can occur ranges from 12 to 16 years old. Finally, juveniles are increasingly being waived due to statutory exclusions, which exclude juveniles from juvenile court jurisdiction based upon the type of offense committed and the age of the defendant. The minimum age of statutory exclusions ranges from 10 to 17 years old. Over time, the trend across most states has been to lower the age at and expand offense types for which juveniles can be placed into the criminal justice system. This treatment of juveniles in the United States has been criticized globally, as countries worldwide have been increasingly recognizing the need to protect young juveniles from harsh punishments.

THE COUNTRY'S STANCE TOWARD THE UN COMMITTEE ON THE RIGHTS OF THE CHILD

In 1989, the United Nations (UN) adopted the Convention on the Rights of the Child (CRC), a treaty that calls for various juvenile rights, including protections from abuse, valuing the opinions of juveniles, and equal treatment (United Nations Human Rights 1989). Additionally, the CRC outlined appropriate treatment of juveniles in the justice system, including prohibiting capital punishment and life imprisonment of individuals who offended prior to the age of 18, requiring that confinement of juveniles "be used only as a measure of last resort and for the shortest appropriate period of time" (article 37, para 2), requiring confined juveniles be separated from adults, and providing juveniles with access to legal counsel (United Nations Treaty Collection 2016).

Although the United States initially provided extensive support in drafting several portions of the CRC and signed it in 1995 (Gainborough & Lean 2008), it is currently the only UN country that has failed to ratify the CRC, as Somalia ratified in 2015 (United Nations Human Rights 2016). Failing to ratify limits the power of the United States to intervene in international children's rights issues (Gainborough & Lean 2008). In 2008, U.S. President Barack Obama criticized the failure to ratify by past presidents stating "it is embarrassing to find ourselves in the company of Somalia… I will review this and other treaties and ensure that the United States resumes its global leadership in Human Rights" (Deen 2008, para 2). Despite the support of President Obama, the CRC has yet to be voted upon in the Senate, as Republicans would reportedly oppose it (S.C. 2013). Critics have argued that the United States should not ratify because it limits the rights of parents and "prevents nations and peoples from sheltering their own unique cultures" (Middleton 2016, para 15). While it appears that the United States will not ratify in the near future, most U.S. laws and practices are already in compliance with the CRC. Following the Supreme Court rulings in 2005 and 2012 that juveniles could no longer be executed or incarcerated for LWOP, respectively, American policies were no longer in direct contention with the CRC (Korkoya 2015).

TRENDS IN JUVENILE CRIME OVER THE PERIOD 2004–2014

Measured in terms of arrests, juvenile crime in the United States has undergone major shifts over the past 20 years. Juvenile arrest rates for violent crimes rose sharply from the early 1980s to the mid-1990s but began decreasing in the mid-1990s. During the period 2004–2012, juvenile arrest rates for violent and property crimes continued their general decreasing trend that began in the mid-1990s (Fig. 7.1) (Puzzanchera & Kang 2014).

The major source of official data on juvenile offending is the Federal Bureau of Investigation's Uniform Crime Report (UCR). In 2012, an estimated 1.3 million juveniles were arrested. Nearly three-quarters of these arrests were for non-index offenses (i.e., 21 generally less serious offenses, including drug abuse violations, simple assaults, and vandalism) (Puzzanchera & Kang 2014). Thus, although a substantial number of juveniles were arrested each year, the vast majority were arrested for minor offenses. Only 5% of juvenile arrests (61,070) were for violent index crimes (i.e., murder/nonnegligent manslaughter, forcible rape, robbery, and aggravated assault), of which 720 were for murder. Twenty-two percent of juvenile arrests were for property index crimes (i.e., burglary, larceny-theft, motor vehicle theft, and arson), 76% of which involved larceny-theft.

Juvenile crime is largely a male phenomenon. In 2012, females contributed 29% of all juvenile arrests and only 19% of those in the violent index category (Puzzanchera 2014). With the exception of prostitution, males committed the majority of every crime in each category in the UCR in 2012, but female arrests did account for a large portion of many nonviolent offenses (e.g., 42% of larceny-thefts

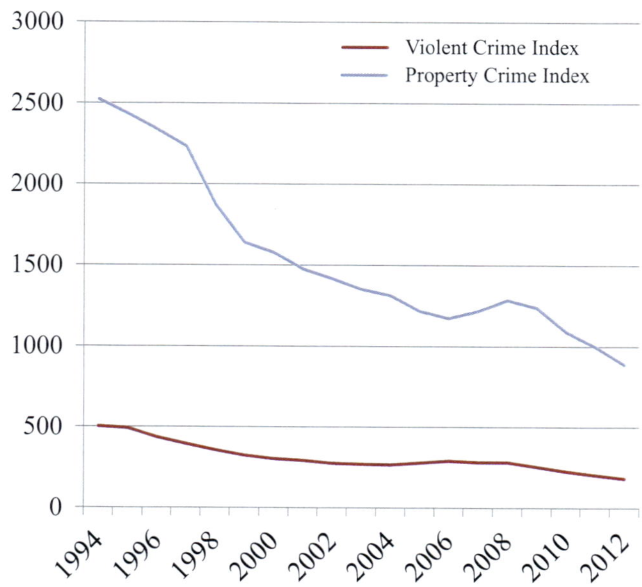

FIGURE 7.1. Juvenile arrest rates (per 100,000) in the United States. *Source*: Puzzanchera and Kang (2014).

and 39% of embezzlement arrests). Over the period from 2003 to 2012, the number of arrests for both males and females decreased for all crimes.

Juvenile arrests were also disproportionately concentrated among racial minorities (Puzzanchera 2014). Although rates of arrest for overall and property offenses followed the same general trend for Blacks and Whites, arrest rates for Blacks are approximately double those for Whites. The gap between Whites and Blacks is much more pronounced for violent crimes. However, in 2000 there was a dramatic shift in offending, as the arrest rate for violent crime among Blacks dropped to its lowest level in decades and the gap in arrest rates of Blacks and Whites narrowed.

CAUSES OF JUVENILE CRIME

Explanations for the causes of juvenile offending are extensive, and most are not unique to the United States. For example, biological theories may explain offending patterns of juveniles across countries and cultural groups. However, some characteristics of the United States may explain nuances of juvenile offending unique to the country. The following section addresses just a few of the notable factors that have shaped juvenile delinquency in the United States, including the changing social structures of cities, shifts in labor markets, and harsh drug sentences.

Some of the earliest research examining the relationship between social structure and delinquency in the United States originated in Chicago and found that social conditions impacted neighborhoods differently, as weak social controls were unable to prevent crime (Shaw & McKay 1942). Shaw and McKay found a uniform pattern of juvenile delinquents residing in the city, with high rates of delinquents living near the center of Chicago and fewer when moving out from the center of the city. They found that delinquents typically resided in inner city neighborhoods characterized by disorganization, racial heterogeneity, high truancy rates, high unemployment rates, and frequent residential mobility. This concentration of disadvantage in inner cities was worsened in many U.S. cities as many labor markets, especially those in the Northeast, shifted from manufacturing to service in the 1970s (Wilson 1987). Less-educated African Americans in these shifting labor markets had difficulties in obtaining employment, while middle-class African Americans left the inner cities behind for more affluent suburbs. The result was that young African American boys lost many positive role models and social ties, further weakening noncriminal social ties.

Another key factor that shaped delinquency in the United States was the response to emerging crack cocaine markets in the 1980s. After the declaration of the "War on Drugs," states quickly began enacting mandatory minimum sentences and sentencing guidelines that treated low-level drug offenders punitively (Walker 2011). Poor African Americans were the typical users of crack cocaine, so the policy responses were primarily inflicted upon this population. Individuals reentering their communities with a felony record found it much more difficult to obtain legal employment, secure housing, and acquire educational loans. As many cities lost legal sources of employment, illicit drug markets filled their void. The high rate of arrests of young African American males in many American cities (e.g., Baltimore, Chicago) resulted in a large segment of residents in cities who were either incarcerated or unemployable, ultimately contributing to a cycle of violence and crime.

Concurrently, juveniles in these neighborhoods encountered increased challenges as many faced parental incarceration. Seven percent of juveniles have a parent with an incarceration history, a factor that places juveniles at risk for future delinquency (Murphey & Cooper 2015; Murray 2005). The impact of parental incarceration disproportionately harms African American juveniles, as 11.5% of African American juveniles have a parent with an incarceration history, but only 6% of Caucasian juveniles are impacted by parental incarceration. While parental incarceration may be beneficial to some juveniles (e.g., removal of abusive parent), others may be negatively impacted as they experience the trauma of separation and loss of parental resources (Johnson 2009). Cumulatively, these issues have impacted juvenile delinquency in the United States, as many juveniles growing up in neighborhoods with limited social capital and economic opportunities may turn to crime and gang membership, placing them in greater contact with police.

POLICING AND JUVENILES

In contrast to courts and detention facilities, which respond to juveniles separately from adults, most law enforcement officers respond to situations involving juveniles and adults. However, officers use much more discretion in policing juveniles, as they are typically engaged in nonserious offenses. Depending upon the seriousness of the offense, officers have a wide range of options in responding to juveniles, including informal counseling, release to parents, and arrest. In recent years, several changes in the juvenile justice system have changed the role of law enforcement officers, resulting in officers responding to very young juveniles for relatively minor offenses, including the policing of juveniles in schools and zero-tolerance policies.

Following the rise in juvenile crime in the 1980s, many schools began partnerships with local law enforcement where officers were embedded within schools (Trump 1998). Schools were previously reliant upon teachers and administrators to provide a security function and respond to disruptive students, but "their presence pose[d] little threat to the more disruptive offenders" (p. 31), thereby necessitating a more authoritative presence. Various models of school policing exist across the country, including school security departments, school police departments, and school resource officers (SRO). School security departments are designed to provide a security function in schools. While staff typically have less training and authority when compared with other models, in some cases they may carry weapons or make arrests. This practice recently came under fire in Florida, as security officers employed at Hillsborough County elementary schools were unsworn officers, yet could carry firearms and engage in defensive tactics (Kourkounis 2014). Other districts retain school police departments where sworn officers are paid by the district to provide services. Finally, the SRO model has gained popularity in recent years, where local law enforcement agencies assign officers to schools. Officers embedded within schools provide a varying array of services, including deterrence, security, program implementation, mentoring, and delinquency prevention. In many schools, officers implement the G.R.E.A.T. program, a program designed to provide younger juveniles with the skills and information to assist them in avoiding gang membership.

Despite their increasing popularity, school officer programs face several challenges and criticisms. One major challenge in implementing SRO programs is that the initial funding tends to be based upon temporary federal grants of 3 years (Weiler & Cray 2011). After this, departments or schools are expected to locate alternate funding sources. This has led some to criticize the sustainability of these programs, as they are likely to draw uncommitted officers who question the longevity of their positions. Officers also frequently regard a school officer assignment as "babysitting" and undesirable, potentially resulting in apathetic officers being placed in these positions. Additionally, many programs fail to effectively train SROs, instead relying upon on the job training while shadowing another SRO (Finn & McDevitt 2005). The training and effectiveness of SROs have come under recent scrutiny, as several cases of punitive treatment of juveniles have been made public. For example, one sheriff's department was sued following the handcuffing of two children under the age of 10, while another was criticized for handcuffing and arresting a 5-year-old (Zalatoris 2015).

A related issue that shapes law enforcement responses to juveniles in schools is the adoption of zero-tolerance policies across the United States. In the 1990s, schools introduced policies of automatic suspension or expulsion and arrest for bringing weapons of any type into schools (Curtis 2014). Implemented in response to public concerns of juveniles engaging in gang activities and abusing drugs, these policies have expanded to include formal punishments for less serious offenses (e.g., cigarettes, fighting) and minimal violations (e.g., swearing, carrying a butter knife for lunch). Because zero-tolerance policies have been implemented disproportionately in inner city schools, they have also had a harsh impact on impoverished minority youths. Recently termed "the school to prison pipeline," juveniles are now receiving formal punishments in the criminal justice system that will impact them in the long term for behaviors that would have previously been responded to informally by school administrators. The increased presence of officers in schools and punishment of juveniles for seemingly minor offenses means that a growing number of juveniles are removed from schools, which coupled with limited resources and opportunities, results in greater criminal justice system involvement well after adolescence (Heitzeg 2009; Price 2009).

COURTS AND JUVENILES

Juvenile courts process a large number of cases annually but still only a fraction of all juvenile arrests. In 2013, over one million cases were handled by the juvenile courts of the United States.

Once a case has been referred to juvenile court, it proceeds through a number of decision steps. During intake, a decision is made to close the case by handling it formally or informally. In 2013, 55% of cases resulted in a formal petition. The detention decision determines whether the youth will be held in detention pending the outcome of the case, with about 21% of youths being held at this stage. If a petition is filed, the case then proceeds to the adjudicatory stage (equivalent to a criminal trial). If a youth is found or pleads guilty, he or she is adjudicated delinquent, representing 55% of formally handled cases. The case then proceeds to disposition (equivalent to sentencing in the criminal justice system). Disposition generally involves a hearing where the judge determines the most appropriate sanction (e.g., probation, residential placement, fine).

Legislatures have not abandoned the rehabilitative mission of juvenile courts. Currently all 50 jurisdictions still maintain provisions that distinguish juvenile courts from criminal courts in ways that are compatible with the juvenile court's traditional mission (Sanborn & Salerno 2005). However, in terms of processing in the juvenile court, there are clear indications that juvenile courts are beginning to converge with the criminal courts in their emphasis on punishment. This shift in orientation is partially attributable to the juvenile "superpredator myth" of the 1990s, an idea that juveniles were becoming more violent, which resulted in more punitive treatment directed toward juveniles (Krisberg 2005). In the past two decades, legislatures in many states have revised their juvenile codes to endorse "punishment," "accountability," and "public safety" as objectives of the juvenile court. Nationally, the trend is moving toward sentencing youth based on notions of punishment and accountability, rather than rehabilitation (National Council of Juvenile and Family Court Judges 2005). The federal government has endorsed a policy of "graduated sanctions" under which youth who have been adjudicated delinquent receive sanctions "proportionate to the offense" to hold them accountable for their actions and to prevent further law violations. The Office of Juvenile Justice and Delinquency Prevention Juvenile Accountability Incentive Block Grants program indicates that although participation in the graduated sanctions approach by individual courts is voluntary, states must encourage courts to participate. This clearly moves federal policy closer to a "pure punishment" approach.

Another development suggesting that a punishment agenda had taken hold was the establishment of boot camps in the 1980s. These short-term (90–120 day) residential programs where juveniles are subjected to military-style basic training include physical labor, regimented activity, and intense verbal degradation. Evaluations of juvenile boot camps have shown inconsistent results, as some research indicates that boot camps decrease recidivism of participants, while other studies indicate that they increase recidivism or have null effects (MacKenzie et al. 2001). Programs shown to reduce recidivism are typically accompanied by intensive aftercare, suggesting that the limited success of boot camps may be attributable to supervision upon reentry (Muscar 2008). Despite their growth in the 1990s, boot camps have largely fallen out of favor, in part due to reports of abuses and one highly publicized death of a juvenile in Florida (Krisberg 2006). While commitment rates of juveniles have been sharply decreasing, due in large part to declines in juvenile offending and changing national sentiments toward confinement, judges are now less likely to commit juveniles to boot camps when compared with other options. From 1997 to 2013, there was a 33% decrease in juveniles in detention and a 64% decrease in juveniles committed to long-term secure detention facilities. In contrast, there was a 91% reduction in juveniles committed to boot camps, as 3,800 juveniles were committed in 1997, but only 320 were committed in 2013 (Sickmund et al. 2015).

Finally, one of the most notable movements that is slowly chipping away at the rehabilitative orientation of juvenile courts is the increasing practice of transferring juveniles into criminal courts. All states offer some mechanism to transfer juveniles, with 44 states allowing for judicial waivers, 14 states allowing for prosecutorial waiver, and 40 states allowing for statutory exclusions (National Center for Juvenile Justice 2016). New "statutory exclusion" (i.e., legislature specifies criteria for transfer) and "prosecutorial waiver" (i.e., prosecutor makes transfer decision) statutes have increasingly shifted the responsibility of transfer away from judges. These new transfer methods accomplished three things: they expedited the transfer process, restricted the powers of a judiciary that was perceived as "too soft on crime," and removed the offender focus that had the hallmark of the transfer decision. Unlike judicial waiver, the new transfer methods are purely offense driven. Many states have also instituted blended sentencing, permitting (and sometimes requiring) judges to impose lengthy sentences—served initially in the juvenile system and then in the adult system—for specified offenses.

Over time, states have lowered the age and increased the types of offenses for which juveniles may be transferred. In some states, these reforms have greatly increased the numbers of youths entering the criminal courts. From 1985 to the mid-1990s, the number of judicial waivers increased 90%, with over 13,000 waivers occurring in 1994 (Sickmund et al. 2015). In 2013 the number of juveniles waived to adult court had dropped to under 4,000. Unfortunately, inconsistent data are reported for prosecutorial transfers and statutory exclusions; however, the decline in judicial transfers can be partially attributed to a growing number of juveniles who are removed from the system before they ever come into contact with a judge. Additionally, it was estimated that in 2010 nearly 140,000 juveniles were placed in the criminal justice system via a jurisdictional age law (Sickmund & Puzzanchera 2014).

Transfer reforms have a tremendous impact on the types of juveniles who are entering adult corrections systems. Because exclusion statutes most often target serious and violent offenders regardless of their age or offense histories, the proportions of young adolescents, racial minorities, and first-time offenders entering the adult system have increased. Finally, youth who enter the criminal justice system frequently have not had the opportunity to benefit from any sort of rehabilitative intervention they would have received in the juvenile system (Lanza-Kaduce et al. 2002; Sridharan et al. 2004). Transferred juveniles also reportedly have worse outcomes, as they are sentenced more punitively than young adults who committed similar types of offenses (Kurlychek & Johnson 2004) and they are more likely to recidivate than juveniles who were retained in the juvenile system (Lanza-Kaduce et al. 2002).

CUSTODIAL RULES FOR JUVENILES

In the United States, juveniles may be confined to a variety of nonsecure (e.g., group homes, halfway houses, camps) and secure (e.g., boot camps, industrial schools, jails) institutions, although judges are encouraged to use the least restrictive option possible in confining the juvenile. Since the mid-1990s, the youth confinement rate has significantly dropped, as 381 youths per 100,000 were confined in 1995, but by 2010 the rate had dropped to 173 youths per 100,000 (Sickmund et al. 2015). In 2013, only 55,000 juvenile offenders were held in residential placement facilities. Of juveniles in residential placement, 37% were held for person offenses, 24% were held for property offenses, and 7% were held for drug offenses, while the remaining juveniles were held for public order offenses, technical violations, and status offenses. Roughly 70% of these juveniles were held in public facilities, with the remainder in private facilities. Similar to the arrest and petitioning stages of the juvenile justice system, minority youth were overrepresented in custody in 2013. Only 32% of juveniles in residential placement were White, 40% were Black, and 23% were Hispanic. On the other hand, females comprised 14% of juveniles in custody, presenting challenges for management in residential facilities. They tended to be younger than males in custody, as 37% of females were under the age of 16 and 30% of males were under 16.

By the 1970s, growing recognition that juveniles are different from adults in their degree of culpability, maturity, and self-control and that confinement within the system actually worsens long-term outcomes for juvenile delinquents resulted in the passage of the Juvenile Justice and Delinquency Prevention Act (JJDPA) in 1974 (Hughes 2011). The passage of the act led to two major changes for confined juveniles—the elimination of confinement for status offenders and the requirement that confined juveniles be sight and sound separated from adults.

Status offenses continue to be an important avenue for referral to the juvenile court. Status offenses are acts that if committed by an adult would not be considered violations of the law (e.g., curfew violation, incorrigibility, truancy). Some states have moved to handle status offenses in a manner similar to neglect or dependency cases as indicators of social problems rather than delinquency. Following the passage of the JJDPA, states receiving federal funding for juvenile justice institutions were required to deinstitutionalize status offenders (DSO).

Status offenders continue to be among the most difficult challenges for most juvenile court jurisdictions.

While it was recognized that juvenile detention worsened reentry outcomes, the director of the National Center for Juvenile Justice reported that many judges were critical of the DSO, as judges claimed, "we have kids who have not followed rules set for them. What else do you want us to do?" (Gately 2015, para 13). The result was the passage of the Valid Court Order (VCO) exception, an amendment of the JJDPA in 1980. Twenty-seven states and the District of Columbia currently allow for exceptions to be made when confining a juvenile status offender, as long as the juvenile violated the terms of probation (Smoot 2015). For example, a juvenile who is adjudicated delinquent for a status offense may be placed on probation with the condition to attend school. The juvenile may subsequently fail to attend school and be rearrested. The juvenile may then be adjudicated delinquent for the probation violation, even though the probation initially stemmed from a status offense. While the prevalence of status offenders committed to juvenile institutions has decreased in recent years, in 2013 nearly 2000 juveniles were reportedly committed to institutions for the commission of a status offense (Sickmund et al. 2015). This issue presents challenges in juvenile institutions, as status offenders are then housed with more serious and violent offenders (Levin & Cohen 2014). This means that juveniles who have committed relatively minor offenses will be exposed to a criminogenic environment that may hinder their desistance from crime.

The JJDPA also required that confined juveniles be sight and sound separated from adults. One loophole remains where juveniles who have been charged as adults can be housed with adults, even prior to a conviction in criminal court (Arya 2007). Juveniles detained in jails pretrial experience dire conditions when compared with juveniles retained in the juvenile system. Juveniles in jails are frequently the victims of physical and sexual abuse by adult inmates. The solution that many jails resort to is solitary confinement of juveniles, which frequently contributes to mental illness and in many cases results in juveniles committing suicide. The irony of confining juveniles in jails is that a large number of juveniles are not convicted in the adult system. For example, only 45% of juveniles placed in the criminal court through a statutory exclusion were convicted (Juszkiewicz 2007). Several attempts have been made in recent years to reauthorize the JJDPA to remedy these issues, including ending confinement of all status offenders and maintaining sight and sound separation of all juvenile delinquents from adult offenders, but these changes have yet to take place (Smoot 2016).

ALTERNATIVE SANCTIONS FOR JUVENILES

It has been well documented that placing juveniles in detention facilities increases their likelihood of future offending; therefore detention is commonly used as a last resort for delinquents who are habitual offenders or have committed serious crimes. Following the Great Recession beginning in 2007, many states began to reconsider juvenile confinement practices and sought less expensive alternatives. Due to the exorbitantly high cost of incapacitating juveniles and the recognition that placement in the community is more effective in reducing recidivism, states increasingly turned to alternative options that allowed juveniles to remain in their communities, while still being supervised and provided with rehabilitative services (Butts & Evans 2011). These alternatives include nonresidential treatment-oriented programs, changes in detention practices prior to adjudication, and home confinement of juveniles.

In the last 15 years, there have been major advances in evaluation research, and both private foundations and the federal government have invested significant funding in assessing the effectiveness of various forms of treatment. This research has produced fairly consistent evidence that treatment-oriented programs, especially those that focus on interpersonal skill development and parent/family interventions, are considerably more effective than punishment-oriented ones (Lipsey & Wilson 1998; Lipsey et al. 2000). Research has identified effective nonresidential treatment programs for minor and first-time offenders as well as effective residential interventions for serious and chronic offenders. In addition to Lipsey's research, the Center for the Study and Prevention of Violence has identified a number of "Blueprint Programs" that have produced reductions in recidivism (e.g., multisystemic therapy, life skills training, and multidimensional treatment foster care).

Likely the most notable effort in the United States to reform pre-adjudication detention practices and retain juveniles in their communities is the Juvenile Detention Alternatives Initiative (JDAI) (Mendel 2014). Started by the Annie E. Casey Foundation (AECF) in the 1990s, over 40 sites have implemented the JDAI model. While a brief pretrial detention may appear trivial, this practice has a serious impact on the long-term outcomes of juveniles. For example, juveniles who are detained prior to adjudication are treated more punitively during the adjudication and placement phases when compared with juveniles who are allowed to remain at home prior to adjudication; these findings occur even after controlling for factors that would be expected to impact adjudication outcomes (e.g., delinquency history, seriousness of the offense) (Jordan 2012). Additionally, incapacitated juveniles fare worse in several important long-term outcomes, including employment, education, and mental health, when compared with juveniles not exposed to detention. Recommendations made by the AECF under the JDAI include detaining only juveniles who are at risk or dangerous, developing community alternatives to detention, and developing alternative solutions to detention for low-risk juveniles who have violated probation (The Annie E. Casey Foundation 2013). One of the main goals of the AECF is to prevent juveniles from unnecessarily moving deeper into the juvenile justice system. While all states nationwide have recently experienced decreases in detention populations as juvenile offending rates have been falling, jurisdictions that have implemented the JDAI model have had even greater reductions in detention rates (Mendel 2014).

Home confinement has also become an increasingly popular alternative to confinement for judges, especially now that it is coupled with electronic monitoring (EM) in many agencies (Development Services Group and Inc 2014). EM allows for probation and parole departments to maintain a degree of control and supervision over juveniles but at a much lower cost than secure confinement. While these benefits are compelling, concerns have been raised that EM is harmful to the reentry and rehabilitation of juveniles, potentially drawing them further into the juvenile justice system (Weisburd 2015). Additionally, EM results in net widening, where juveniles who would have received little or no supervision are now monitored. As juveniles are increasingly placed on EMs, it is more likely that they will be rearrested and adjudicated for technical violations. Research on the effectiveness of EM programs in reducing recidivism of juveniles tends to be mixed, suggesting that EMs may not be the most effective solution in responding to juvenile delinquency. Despite the questions over the effectiveness of EMs, they represent just one of the changes that have been made in recent years as the juvenile justice system begins to shift back toward a rehabilitative orientation and becomes less reliant upon detention.

DIFFERENCES IN TREATMENT OF BOYS AND GIRLS

As the orientation of the juvenile justice system moved toward a punitive nature in the 1980s, females increasingly become ensnared in the system. Girls now represent a greater share of juveniles processed in court, as they were less than 20% of those brought into the juvenile system in the 1980s, but by 2010 they had grown to 28% (Sickmund et al. 2015). While both boys and girls have experienced declines in juvenile court involvement from the 1990s to 2013, females only experienced a 36% decrease in court involvement compared with the 47% decrease experienced by males. In fact, males are now brought into court less than they were in the 1980s, whereas females have yet to reach those levels. While girls were increasingly punished during the 1990s and early 2000s, their offending patterns based upon self-reports actually suggested stability or a decline in offending (Goodkind et al. 2009). Perceptions of girls as violent and criminal were partially shaped by media portrayals of girls that showed them engaging in delinquent acts, drug selling, and gang activities, as well as crime statistics indicating that girls were offending more, both of which contributed to the punitive responses toward girls (Chesney-Lind & Pasko 2013). One additional alternative explanation for the rise in female offending is that following the deinstitutionalization of status offenders, some status offenses were merely "relabeled" as more serious offenses, in order to impose harsher punishments (Feld 2009).

The juvenile justice system has long struggled in developing adequate responses in treating delinquent girls entering the system, as they have many unique differences from boys (Bender 2010). For example, delinquent girls are more likely to be abuse victims, and they frequently engage in criminal activities (e.g., prostitution, joining gangs) in order to escape from abusive and neglectful homes. Girls entering the system are more likely than boys to have mental illnesses and abuse drugs or alcohol. They also have high rates of risky sexual behaviors and pregnancy, with one study reporting that 37% of detained girls were either currently or previously pregnant (Williams & Hollis 1999). Once they enter the juvenile justice system, there are several notable differences in the treatment and responses to girls and boys. Most notably, institutional programs for girls tend to be gender specific, as they were designed for boys and then applied to girls (Garcia & Lane 2013). As girls historically have represented a smaller portion of detained juveniles, they have been largely neglected in programming and treatment. As girls now represent a growing share of detained juveniles, states are increasingly devoting resources to programs that take into account the unique needs of girls (Wiltz 2015).

CONCLUSION

It is still too early to tell, but the punitive tide may be turning. Over the past 10 years, fewer juveniles were arrested, processed through the juvenile justice system, and transferred to the adult system. Opinion polls show that the public continues to support treatment for juvenile offenders. In addition, public officials have begun to express real worry about how they are going to manage the financial costs of America's "imprisonment binge" (Irwin & Austin 2011). In combination with the research evidence showing the substantial advantages of rehabilitative programs over punitive ones, these considerations may support a revival of interest in returning to traditional core principles of rehabilitation and treatment in juvenile justice.

REFERENCES

Arya, N. (2007). Jailing juveniles: The dangers of incarcerating youth in adult jails in America. *A campaign for youth justice report*. Retrieved from http://ssrn.com/abstract=1697706.

Bender, K. (2010). Why do some maltreated youth become juvenile offenders?: A call for further investigation and adaptation of youth services. *Children and Youth Services Review, 32*(3), 466–473.

Butts, J. A., & Evans, D. N. (2011). *Resolution, reinvestment, and realignment: Three strategies for changing juvenile justice*. New York: Research and Evaluation Center, John Jay College of Criminal Justice, City University of New York.

Chesney-Lind, M., & Pasko, L. (2013). *The female offender: Girls, women, and crime*. Los Angeles: Sage.

Curtis, A. J. (2014). Tracing the school-to-prison pipeline from zero-tolerance policies to juvenile justice dispositions. *Georgetown Law Journal, 102*(4), 1251.

Deen, T. (2008, November 13). U.S. and Somalia still opt out of children's treaty. *Inter Press Service*. Retrieved from http://www.ipsnews.net/2009/11/rights-us-somalia-still-opt-out-of-childrens-treaty/.

Development Services Group, Inc. (2014). *Home confinement and electronic monitoring.* Washington, DC: Office of Juvenile Justice and Delinquency Prevention. Retrieved from http://www.ojjdp.gov/mpg/litreviews/Home_Confinement_EM.pdf.
Feld, B. (1999). *Bad kids: Race and the transformation of the juvenile court*. New York: Oxford University Press.
Feld, B. C. (2009). Violent girls or relabeled status offenders? An alternative interpretation of the data. *Crime & Delinquency, 55*(2), 241–265.
Finn, P., & McDevitt, J. (2005). *National assessment of school resource officer programs*. (Document Number 209273). Washington, DC: U.S. Department of Justice.
Gainborough, J., & Lean, E. (2008). Convention on the rights of the child and juvenile justice. *The Link, 7*(1), 1–5.
Garcia, C. A., & Lane, J. (2013). What a girl wants, what a girl needs findings from a gender-specific focus group study. *Crime & Delinquency, 59*(4), 536–561.
Gately, G. (2015, April 10). *New report finds incarceration for status offenses still widespread.* Washington, DC: National Council on Crime and Delinquency. Retrieved from http://jjie.org/new-report-finds-incarceration-for-status-offenses-still-widespread/108565/.
Goodkind, S., Wallace, J. M., Shook, J. J., Bachman, J., & O'Malley, P. (2009). Are girls really becoming more delinquent? Testing the gender convergence hypothesis by race and ethnicity, 1976–2005. *Children and Youth Services Review, 31*(8), 885–895.
Graham v. Florida, 130 S. Ct. 2011, 560 U.S. 48, 176 L. Ed. 2d 825 (2010).
Griffin, P., Addie, S., Adams, B., & Firestine, K. (2011). *Trying juveniles as adults: An analysis of state transfer laws and reporting*. Washington, DC: U.S. Department of Justice, Office of Juvenile Justice and Delinquency Prevention.
Heitzeg, N. A. (2009). Education or incarceration: Zero tolerance policies and the school to prison pipeline. *Forum On Public Policy Online, 2*, 1–21.
Hughes, D. (2011). An overview of the Juvenile Justice and Delinquency Prevention Act and the valid court order exception. *Arkansas Law Notes, 642*, 29–37.
In re Gault. 387 U.S. 1., 20 (1967)
Irwin, J., & Austin, J. (2011). *It's about time: America's imprisonment binge*. Belmont: Wadsworth Publishing.
Johnson, R. C. (2009). Ever-increasing levels of parental incarceration and the consequences for children. In S. Raphael & M. Stoll (Eds.), *Do prisons make us safer? The benefits and costs of the prison boom* (pp. 177–206). New York: Russell Sage.
Jordan, K. L. (2012). Preventive detention and out-of-home placement: A propensity score matching and multilevel modeling approach. *Journal of Juvenile Justice, 2*(1), 41–53.
Juszkiewicz, J. (2007). *To punish a few: Too many youth caught in the net of adult prosecution.* Washington, DC: Campaign For Youth Justice.
Kent v. United States, 383 U.S. 541 (S. Ct. 1966).
Korkoya, E. (2015). Convention on the Rights of the Child: Would ratification impact American kids? *North Carolina Journal of International Law*. Retrieved from http://blogs.law.unc.edu/ncilj/2015/11/03/convention-on-the-rights-of-the-child-would-ratification-impact-american-kids/.
Kourkounis, E. (2014, September 1). Security officers settle into Hillsborough elementary schools. *Tampa Bay Times*. Retrieved from http://www.tbo.com/news/education/hillsborough-school-security-now-elementary-20140901/.
Krisberg, B. (2005). *Juvenile justice: Redeeming our children*. Thousand Oaks, CA: Sage.
Krisberg, B. (2006). Rediscovering the juvenile justice ideal in the United States. In J. Muncie & B. Goldon (Eds.), *Comparative youth justice* (pp. 6–18). London: Sage.
Kurlychek, M. C., & Johnson, B. D. (2004). The juvenile penalty: A comparison of juvenile and young adult sentencing outcomes in criminal court. *Criminology, 42*(2), 485–515.
Lanza-Kaduce, L., Frazier, C. E., Lane, J., & Bishop, D. M. (2002). *Juvenile transfer to criminal court study: Final report*. Tallahassee, FL: Florida Department of Juvenile Justice. Retrieved from http://nicic.org/Library/017540.

Levin, M., & Cohen, D. (2014). *Kids doing time for what's not a crime: The over-incarceration of status offenders*. Austin, TX: Texas Public Policy Foundation. Retrieved from http://www.modelsforchange.net/publications/521.
Lipsey, M., & Wilson, D. (1998). Effective intervention for serious juvenile offenders: A synthesis of research. In R. Loeber & D. Farrington (Eds.), *Serious and violent juvenile offenders: Risk factors and successful interventions* (pp. 313–345). Thousand Oaks: Sage.
Lipsey, M. W., Wilson, D., & Cothern, L. (2000). *Effective interventions for serious juvenile offenders*. Washington, DC: Office of Juvenile Justice and Delinquency Prevention. Retrieved from http://www.ncjrs.gov/App/publications/abstract.aspx?ID=181201.
MacKenzie, D., Wilson, D., & Kider, S. (2001). Effects of correctional boot camps on offending. *The ANNALS of the American Academy of Political and Social Science, 578*, 126–143.
Mendel, R. A. (2014). *Juvenile detention alternatives initiative: Progress report*. Baltimore, MD: The Annie E. Casey Foundation.
Middleton, M. (2016, March 1). ABA adds its voice to calls for the U.S. to ratify the Convention on the Rights of the Child. *ABA Journal*. Retrieved from http://www.abajournal.com/magazine/article/aba_adds_its_voice_to_calls_for_the_us_to_ratify_the_convention_on_the_righ.
Miller v. Alabama, 567 U.S., (S. Ct. 2012).
Murphey, D., & Cooper, P. M. (2015). *Parents behind bars: What happens to their children? Child Trends*. Bethesda, MD: Child Trends.
Murray, J. (2005). The effects of imprisonment on the families and children of prisoners. In A. Liebling & S. Maruna (Eds.), *The effects of imprisonment* (pp. 442–492). Cullompton, England: Willan.
Muscar, J. E. (2008). Advocating the end of juvenile boot camps: Why the military model does not belong in the juvenile justice system. *Juvenile Justice Law & Policy, 12*, 1–50.
National Center for Juvenile Justice. (2016). *Jurisdictional boundaries*. Retrieved from http://www.jjgps.org/jurisdictional-boundaries#transfer-trends?&state=52.
National Council of Juvenile and Family Court Judges. (2005). *Graduated sanctions for juvenile offenders*. Retrieved from http://www.ncjfcj.org/sites/default/files/vol.2planningguidejsc18_0.pdf
Price, P. (2009). When is a police officer an officer of the law?: The status of police officers in schools. *The Journal of Criminal Law and Criminology, 99*(2), 541–570.
Puzzanchera, C. (2014). *Juvenile Arrests, 2012*. Washington, DC: Office of Juvenile Justice and Delinquency Prevention.
Puzzanchera, C., & Kang, W. (2014). Easy access to FBI arrest statistics 1994–2012. *National Center for Juvenile Justice, U.S. Department of Justice*. Retrieved from: http://www.ojjdp.gov/ojstatbb/ezaucr/.
Roper v. Simmons, 543 U.S. 551. (S. Ct. 2005).
S.C. (2013, October). Why won't America ratify the UN convention on children's rights? *The Economist*. Retrieved from http://www.economist.com/blogs/economist-explains/2013/10/economist-explains-2.
Sanborn, J. B., & Salerno, A. W. (2005). *The juvenile justice system: Law and process*. Los Angeles: Roxbury Publishing Company.
Shah, R. S., Fine, L., & Gullen, J. (2014). Juvenile records: A national review of state laws on confidentiality, sealing, and expungement. *Juvenile Law Center*. Retrieved from http://juvenilerecords.jlc.org/juvenilerecords/documents/publications/national-review.pdf.
Shaw, C., & McKay, H. (1942). *Juvenile delinquency and urban areas*. Chicago: The University of Chicago.
Sickmund, M., & Puzzanchera, C. (2014). *Juvenile offenders and victims: 2014 national report*. Pittsburgh, PA: National Center for Juvenile Justice.
Sickmund, M., Sladky, A., & Kang, W. (2015). Easy access to juvenile court statistics: 1985-2013. *Office of Juvenile Justice and Delinquency Prevention*. Retrieved from http://www.ojjdp.gov/ojstatbb/ezajcs/.

Smoot, N. (2015). *Status offenses: A national survey*. Washington, DC: Coalition for Juvenile Justice.

Smoot, N. (2016, May 19) Cotton out of step on justice reform, out of line in blocking JJDPA. *Juvenile Justice Information Exchange.* Retrieved from http://jjie.org/cotton-out-of-step-on-justice-reform-out-of-line-in-blocking-jjdpa/248190/.

Sridharan, S., Greenfield, L., & Blakley, B. (2004). A study of prosecutorial certification practice in Virginia. *Criminology and Public Policy, 3*(4), 605–632.

The Annie E. Casey Foundation. (2013). *Reducing Youth Incarceration in the United States*. http://www.aecf.org/m/resourcedoc/AECF-DataSnapshotYouthIncarceration-2013.pdf.

Trump, K. (1998). Keeping the peace. *The American School Board Journal.* Retrieved from http://www.schoolsecurity.org/resources/KeepingThePeace.pdf.

United Nations Human Rights. (1989). *Convention on the Rights of the Child*. Retrieved from http://www.ohchr.org/EN/ProfessionalInterest/Pages/CRC.aspx.

United Nations Human Rights. (2016). *Ratification of 18 international human rights treaties*. Retrieved from http://indicators.ohchr.org/.

United Nations Treaty Collection. (2016). *Convention on the Rights of the Child*. Retrieved from https://treaties.un.org/Pages/ViewDetails.aspx?src=TREATY&mtdsg_no=IV-11&chapter=4&lang=en.

Walker, S. (2011). *Sense and non-sense about crime, drugs, and communities*. Belmont, CA: Wadsworth Publishing.

Weiler, S. C., & Cray, M. (2011). Police at school: A brief history and current status of school resource officers. *The Clearing House: A Journal of Educational Strategies, Issues and Ideas, 84*(4), 160–163.

Weisburd, K. (2015). Monitoring youth: The collision of rights and rehabilitation. *Iowa Law Review, 101*, 297–341.

Williams, R. A., & Hollis, H. (1999). Health beliefs and reported symptoms among a sample of incarcerated adolescent females. *Journal of Adolescent Health, 24*(1), 21–27.

Wilson, W. (1987). *The truly disadvantaged: The inner city, the underclass, and public policy*. Chicago: University of Chicago Press.

Wiltz, T. (2015). States grapple with girls in the juvenile justice system. *The Pew Charitable Trusts.* Retrieved from http://www.pewtrusts.org/en/research-and-analysis/blogs/stateline/2015/11/25/states-grapple-with-girls-in-the-juvenile-justice-system.

Zalatoris, J. (2015). Helpful or harmful: The role of school resource officers. *New America Ed Central.* Retrieved from http://www.edcentral.org/school-resource-officers/.

Zang, A. (2016). U.S. age boundaries of delinquency 2015. *Juvenile Justice Geography, Policy, Practice, and Statistics*. Retrieved from http://www.ncjj.org/pdf/JJGPS%20StateScan/JJGPS_U.S._age_boundaries_of_delinquency_2015_8.pdf.

Melanie Taylor Assistant professor in the Department of Criminal Justice at the University of Nevada, Reno. She received a doctorate in Criminology and Criminal Justice from Arizona State University. She previously was employed as a deputy juvenile correctional officer with the Orange County Probation Department. Her current research interests are abuses in correctional facilities, civil rights of inmates, juvenile detention, juvenile delinquency, and the long-term outcomes of system-involved youth.

PART III

Asia

8

China

Ruohui Zhao and Liqun Cao

China leads the world in its population for years. Youth are the future of a nation and their problems are a national concern. Available statistics shows that in 2012, China had a population of 1.354 billion, among which 20.39% (0.18 billion) were juveniles under the age of 18. Adolescents under the age of 14 accounted for 15.32%; those between 14 (including 14) and 16 years old accounted for 2.33%; and adolescents between 16 (including 16) and 18 accounted for 2.74% of the overall population (China Statistical Bureau of Population and Employment, National Bureau of Statistics 2013). For a juvenile population of this size, it becomes imperative to build a solid legal basis for the protection of juveniles and the prevention of juvenile crime. This chapter introduces and discusses the following issues on juvenile justice in China: the legal status of juveniles, the age of majority according to Chinese laws, China's stance toward the UN committee on the rights of the child, trends in juvenile crime using both official and scholarly research statistics, causes of juvenile crime, and the juvenile justice system in China.

One caveat is in order: China is the second largest country in the world, and there are huge differences between urban and rural areas, between coastal and inland regions, and between laws on the book and laws in action. What we describe below is largely laws in book rather than laws in action, and it is more accurate for cities than for rural areas and for the coastal regions than for the inland regions owing to the greater formality in such places.

R. Zhao
University of Macau, Taipa, Macau
e-mail: rzhao@umac.mo

L. Cao (✉)
University of Ontario Institute of Technology, Oshawa, ON, Canada, L1H 7K4
e-mail: Liqun.cao@uoit.ca

S.H. Decker, N. Marteache (eds.), *International Handbook of Juvenile Justice*,
DOI 10.1007/978-3-319-45090-2_8

THE LEGAL STATUS OF JUVENILES

With modernization and recent legal reconstruction, China has developed many unique features of its legal system with three sources of influence: its traditional culture, its socialist values, and its structure similar to that of Romano-Germanic legal family. Its laws are national in nature. Several laws indirectly or directly concern youth and juvenile delinquency: the Constitution, the Public Security Administration Punishment Law, the Criminal Law, the Criminal Procedure Law, the Law on the Protection of Minors, and the Law on Prevention of Juvenile Delinquency. The Constitution is concerned with children's rights in general and does not have specific provisions on how to deal with delinquent youths. As the country's basic law, the Constitution has several provisions on the rights of youth including the right to receive education (Article 46), parents' responsibility to raise and educate children (Article 49), and the state's responsibility to protect children from maltreatment (Article 49). For example, Article 46 of the Constitution stipulates that the state promotes the all-round development of children and young people, morally, intellectually, and physically.

Three laws deal with crime and offending behavior in general: the Public Security Administration Punishment Law, the Criminal Law, and the Criminal Procedure Law (Zhang 2015). In China, crime is defined as law-violating behavior that reaches a certain level of severity. Minor law violations, such as gang fights (Article 26), theft of public property (Article 33, 34, and 35), and possession of firearms or dangerous substances (Article 31 and 32), are not defined as crime. They are handled by the police instead of judges according to the Public Security Administration Punishments Law which was adopted at the seventeenth session of the Standing Committee of the Tenth National People's Congress of the People's Republic of China in 2005. More serious offending is defined as crime and regulated by the Criminal Law and handled by the people's courts at various levels. Although the laws are set out to provide specific provisions on the punishment of offending behavior, they both stress protection of juveniles and stipulate mitigated or none punishment on juvenile delinquents. In addition, the Criminal Procedure Law contains several provisions on how to handle juvenile criminal cases. For example, Article 152 provides that cases of first instance in a people's court shall be heard in public. However, no cases involving crimes committed by minors who have reached the age of 14 but not the age of 16 shall be heard in public; cases involving crimes committed by minors who have reached the age of 16 but not the age of 18 shall not be heard in public either. In spite of the fact that the Criminal Procedure Law aims to protect delinquent youth from being stigmatized, it provides only limited procedural rights, in the eyes of Western experts, instead of full procedural rights to juvenile offenders (Zhang 2015), reflecting the collective and patriarchal values of the society.

The other two laws are specific to juveniles and focus on the protection of youth and prevention of delinquency. In order to protect both the physical and mental health of minors, the Law on the Protection of Minors generally stipulates four types of protection measures, implemented by different parties including the family, the school, the society, and the judicial system. Specifically with respect to adolescent offenders, the law states that if minors commit crime, the policy of education, persuasion, and redemption shall be implemented; education shall be upheld as the main method and punishment as the subsidiary strategy. In addition, alleviated or mitigated punishment shall be applied (Article 54). The Law on Prevention of Juvenile Delinquency composes of eight chapters in regard to various delinquency prevention strategies including, but not limited to the following: education for prevention of delinquency, prevention of juvenile misbehaviors, ratification and treatment of serious juvenile misbehaviors, juvenile self-protection against crimes, prevention of juvenile recidivism, and legal responsibilities of guardians of children and other parties. Consistent with other laws, the Law on Prevention of Juvenile Delinquency stresses the importance of protecting both mental health and physical health of juveniles. Article 2 of the law stipulates that the prevention of juvenile delinquency shall be based on education and protection; the work shall be started with school children, and efforts shall be made to prevent, rectify, and treat juvenile misbehavior before it manifests itself.

Strictly speaking, there is no corresponding word for "delinquency" in Chinese. The word "delinquency" should be roughly translated into "weichengnianren fanzui," which is a legal term, but it has not avoided the word "criminal" in Chinese. From the view of labeling theory, this Chinese corresponding term has not eliminated stigma label. In addition, the popular Chinese usage tends to lump "youth" and "juvenile" together as if they were interchangeable. The best journal for the topic is called *Issues on Juvenile Crimes and Delinquency* (in Chinese), which piles up the two separable concepts together. In the statistical yearbooks and in all police documents, there is a separate listing for crime committed by youth under the age of 25 (Zhang 2013a).

AGE OF MAJORITY AND AGE OF CRIMINAL RESPONSIBILITY

The age of majority in China is 18 years. The Law on the Protection of Minors (Article 2) defines minors as persons under the age of 18. The age of majority, however, is different from *the age of criminal responsibility*. According to the Criminal Law of China, the minimum criminal responsibility age is 14 years old. Chapter 2, Article 17 of the Criminal Law defines criminal responsibility age into the following four scenarios: (1) in general, criminal offenders who have reached the age of 16 shall bear criminal responsibility; (2) if he/she has reached the age of 14 but not the age of 16 and commits one of the eight serious offenses (e.g., intentional homicide, intentional hurting of another person so as to cause serious injury or death of the person, or commits rape, robbery, drug trafficking, arson, explosion, and poisoning), the offender shall bear criminal responsibility; (3) an offender who has reached the age of 14 but not the age of 18 shall be given a lighter or mitigated punishment; (4) if an offender is not given criminal punishment because he/she has not reached the age of 16, the head of his/her family or his/her guardian shall be ordered to discipline him/her. When necessary, he/she may be taken in by the government for mandatory rehabilitation. Finally, the Law stipulates that no death penalty could be carried out on young offenders under the age of 18 (Chap. 3, Article 49).

In addition, since minor offenses are regulated by the Public Security Administration Punishment Law (PSAPL), age is also a concern. PSAPL stipulates that youth who violate the law should be dealt with leniency. Specifically, Article 12 stipulates that offenders under 14 years at the time of an offense are immune from punishment, but his/her guardian shall be ordered to strictly discipline him/her; for offenders who attain to the age of 14 but are younger than 18, a lighter or mitigated punishment should be given. Article 21 further stipulates that the punishment of administrative detention shall not be executed when an offender has reached the age of 14 but younger than the age of 16 or he/she has attained the age of 16 but younger than the age of 18 and violated public administration law for the first time. Interrogation of offenders under the age of 16 requires the presence of parents or guardians of the violator (Article 84).

A comparison on responsibility according to different ages between the Public Security Administration Law and the Criminal Law is summarized in Table 8.1.

TABLE 8.1. A comparison between the PSAPL and the Criminal Law

	Public Security Administration Punishment Law as revised in 2012	*Criminal Law as revised in 2011 (defines age of criminal responsibility)*
Severity of offense	Minor	Serious
Handling party	Police	Official criminal justice authorities (e.g., prosecutors and judges)
Younger than 14	Immune from any administrative punishment, but with strict discipline by legal guardian	No criminal responsibility, but with strict discipline by legal guardian or taking in by government when necessary
Age of 14–less than 16	Mitigated administrative punishment No administrative detention as punishment under all circumstances	Criminal responsibility for commission of eight major types of crime, but with mitigated criminal punishment No criminal responsibility for commission of other crimes, but with strict discipline by legal guardian or taking in by government when necessary
Age of 16–less than 18	Mitigated administrative punishment No administrative detention as punishment for first-time violators	Full criminal responsibility, but with mitigated criminal punishment
Age of 18 and above	Administrative punishments	Full criminal responsibility

CHINA'S STANCE TOWARD THE UN COMMITTEE ON THE RIGHT OF THE CHILD

China is among the nations that have ratified the UN Convention on the Rights of the Child ("Convention" hereafter). Both the Law on Protection of Minors and the Law on Prevention of Juvenile Delinquency were enacted in consistency with the UN Convention. The Convention stresses that "the best interest of children" shall be the primary consideration in handling all juvenile-related matters (Article 3.1). Although Chinese laws do not specifically use the term "the best interest of children," the principles behind juvenile laws are in consistency with it. For example, the very first article of the Law on the Protection of Minors stipulates that:

> This Law is enacted in accordance with the Constitution for the purpose of protecting the physical and mental health of minors, safeguarding their lawful rights and interests, promoting their all-round development—morally, intellectually and physically, and training them into successors to the socialist cause with lofty ideals, sound morality, better education and a good sense of discipline.

Article 4 of the Law articulates that the protection of minors shall follow four principles: (1) safeguarding the lawful rights and interests of minors, (2) respecting the personal dignity of minors, (3) fitting in with the characteristics of minors' physical and mental development, and (4) combining education with protection. In reading these laws, we should bear in mind that China is one of the East Asian nations where there is a tendency to downgrade law (David and Brierley 1978). This has not fundamentally changed after more than 1 hundred years' efforts in its modernization and in its legal reconstruction.

TRENDS IN JUVENILE CRIME

Juvenile crime was not seen as a separate social problem because of the total system of control created by Mao (Cao 2007). It was only after the end of the Cultural Revolution (1966–1976) when the new leaders, under Deng Xiaoping, changed the course of China's development and opened its door to the outside world (i.e., the "open-door" policy; Cao and Cullen 2001). The period from early 1980s to the present is believed to be a period with relatively high juvenile crime rates (Liu 2007). Although official crime statistics have been criticized for having many shortcomings (see He and Marshall 1997; He 2014), they are the most systematic source of data available in China (Liu 2008). The China Statistical Yearbook and the Law Yearbook are the major sources of statistics on crime including juvenile crime (Zhao et al. 2014). They report mainly the number of juvenile offenders tried by the court, the percentage of juvenile offenders among all offenders tried by the courts, and the number of young offenders incarcerated

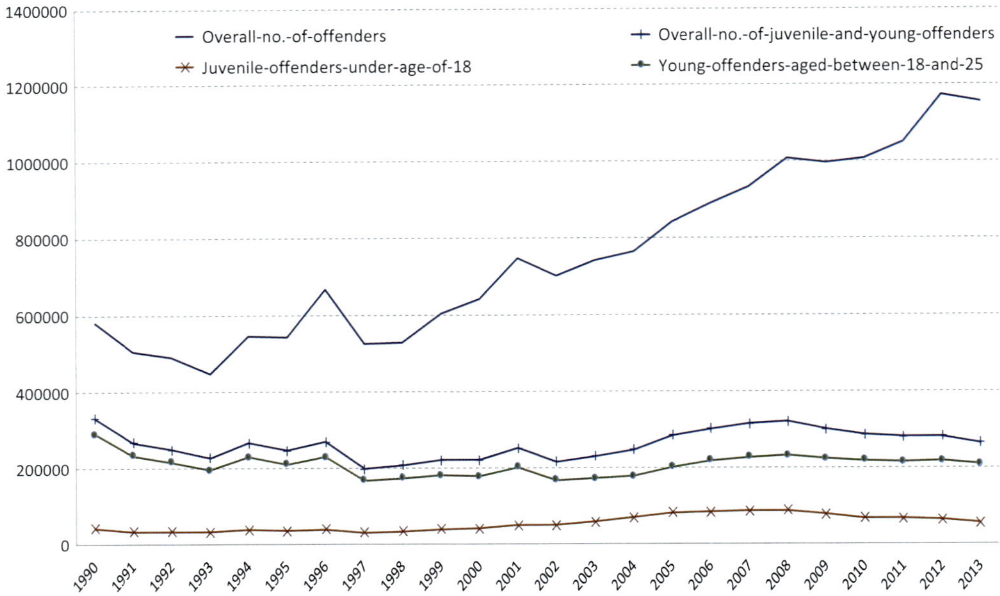

FIGURE 8.1. Number of offenders reported by the courts. Data source: China Statistical Bureau (1991–2014), China Statistical Yearbook.

in prisons and juvenile reformatories. This means that only serious adolescent offenders are included in the two statistical sources. It is possible that a large number of juvenile offenders who committed minor offenses were dealt with by the police according to the Public Security Administration Punishment Law and they were not included. In addition, juvenile crime rates were not calculated or reported by the official crime statistics. Therefore, the juvenile crime trend reported as the number of offenders tried by the courts below needs to be interpreted with caution.

Figure 8.1 shows that from 1990 to 2013, the overall number of crimes tried by the courts dramatically increased. The sharp increase largely comes from adult offenders above the age of 25. The number of juvenile offenders and young offenders fluctuated and shows some increase over the same period. For example, in 1990 the number of juvenile offenders under the age of 18 was 42,033; this number increased to 55,817 in 2013, showing an increase of over 20%.

Although the overall number of juvenile offenders increased, it does not necessary mean that juvenile crime became more serious because the size of the juvenile population increased as well. Because the China Population and Employment Statistics Yearbooks include census statistics for every 10 years and statistics from selected samples for other years, it makes it unlikely to calculate the juvenile crime rate. One way to explore this issue is to compare the percentage of juvenile offenders among all offenders and the percentage of juvenile population among overall population of China.

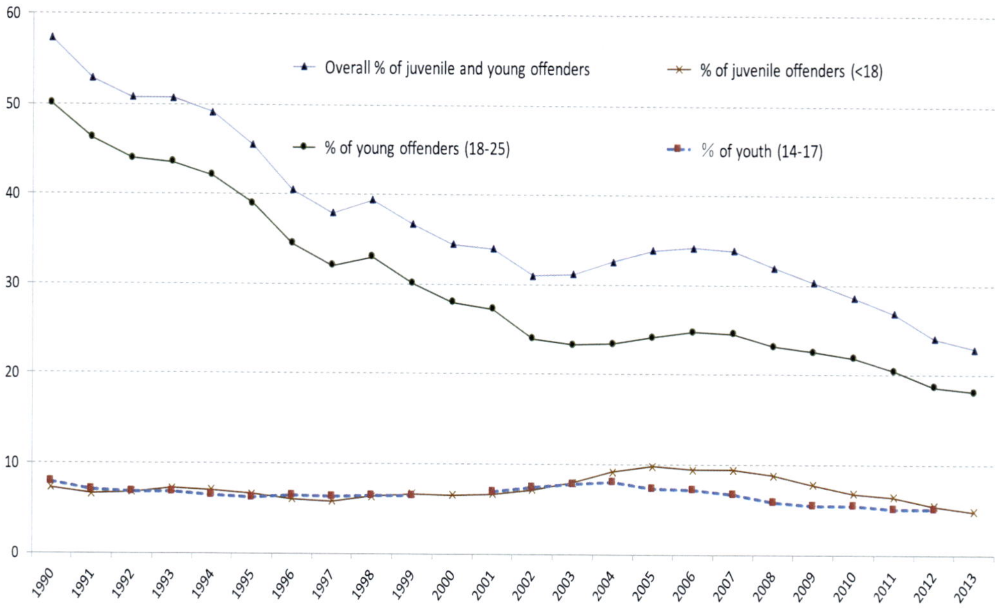

FIGURE 8.2. Percent of offenders reported by the courts. Note: (*1*) Due to the fact that the population size for youth at the age between 14 and 17 (inclusive) was not provided by the China Population and Employment Statistics Yearbook in 2000, the percentage of youth at the age between 14 and 17 was not calculated for the same year. (*2*) The most recent statistics reported by the China Population and Employment Statistics Yearbook was for the year of 2012. Data source: China Statistical Bureau (1991–2014), China Statistical Yearbook; China Statistical Bureau and Employment Section (1991–2013), China Population and Employment Statistics Yearbook.

Figure 8.2 shows that the overall percentage of juvenile and young offenders actually demonstrates a decreasing trend in the past 20 years. This might be partially explained as the result of continuous implementation of "one-child policy" (newly revised to "two-children policy" in 2015) and low birth rates in China. The percentages of juvenile offenders under the age of 18 roughly overlap with the percentage of juvenile population, except during the period from 2003 to 2012. During this period, the percentages of serious juvenile offenders are higher than the percentages of juveniles in the population. This means that juvenile offenders are overrepresented in the court statistics. In other words, juvenile crimes became more serious during that time period. The peak was in 2008 when the juvenile population accounted for 5.87% of the overall population, while the juvenile offender population accounted for 8.82% of the overall offender population.

It is worth noting that the statistics in the figures include only serious juvenile offenders, i.e., those tried by the courts at the various levels. It is likely that non-serious offenses have been increasing accompanying with the rapid social and economic changes in China.

Scholarly research using either official data or self-report delinquency data found that (1) juvenile deviance and delinquency had been on the rise and (2) the delinquency rate in China is lower than those in many Western societies. Bakken (1993) using official data found that, during the 1950s and 1960s, juvenile delinquency among those at ages 14–18 years old accounted for 0.2–0.3% of overall crimes and it increased to close to 20% in 1989. Wei et al. (2004) compared self-reported offending in school students and apprehended juvenile offenders in Brisbane, Australia, and Shanghai, China. They found that the rate of participation in most categories of offending in the Brisbane sample was higher than that in the Shanghai sample; Brisbane school students were much more likely than Shanghai students to report at least one type of offense (85.8% vs. 28.8%); co-offending was found to peak at an older age and was more common among the Shanghai school students than the Brisbane students. Using data collected from a birth cohort study in the city of Wuhan, Friday et al. (2005) found that only 81 of the 5341 respondents had official records of delinquency/crime. Comparatively, the rate of crime was over 30% in the Philadelphia cohort. Webb et al. (2011) collected data from 1043 junior high school students in China using the International Self-Report Delinquency Survey and found similar results: the US sample has higher prevalence of self-nominated gang membership than the Chinese sample. In addition, the lifetime and last year participation rates in various criminal acts among the gang members in the Chinese sample (2%) were much lower than those in the US sample (4%). Pyrooz and Decker (2013) reported a level of gang involvement of 11% among 2163 school students in Changzhi City of China, but made no comparison between the Chinese sample and Western samples. The higher level of gang involvement by Pyrooz and Decker (as compared with Webb et al. 2011) may probably be explained by the fact that Pyrooz and Decker (2013) employed a sample which was older including both high school students and college students and that delinquency was measured as involvement in 15 types of offenses ranging from minor deviant behavior (skipping classes) to relatively serious offense (attacking someone with a weapon).

In terms of minor deviant behavior, such as smoking and drinking, the rates seem to be higher. Using data collected from 1040 students in sixth, eighth, and tenth grades from five public schools in Beijing, Li et al. (1996) found that 70% of the students reported prior experience of alcohol consumption and that there was a likely link between drinking and other problem behavior. A high level of involvement in delinquency among children of migrant adolescents, as a result of rapid social and economic changes in China, was reported. Chen (2015) collected data among 485 migrant students and 836 native urban students from 32 junior high schools in 10 districts of Guangzhou City and found that migrant adolescents have higher propensity for delinquency than their native urban counterparts.

Overall, scholarly research has found evidence in support of relatively low levels of juvenile delinquency in China. It should be noted, however, that these studies have limitations. First, Chinese studies on juvenile delinquency are largely descriptive and rudimentary without much conceptualization and theorizing (Liu 2007). Second, although a number of empirical studies made use of quantitative data, many contain methodological problems. For example, data were collected from convenience samples with limited number of measures. Third, unique Chinese characteristics of juvenile delinquency were not identified.

CAUSES OF JUVENILE CRIME

Research conducted in Western societies has identified various causes of juvenile crime ranging from micro-individual factors to macrostructural factors (Lanier and Henry 2014). The dominant traditional view of human nature in China has been that all human beings are born with equal potential for being good (Cao and Cullen 2001; Troyer et al. 1989; Wu and Cao 2014). Therefore, crime and delinquency are largely considered the result of nurture. What should be blamed is the negative influence from the environment instead of a person's inherent nature. Chinese media reported a number of sources of delinquency in recent years including but not limited to the following: uncensored Internet materials and Internet games (Ni 2003; Liu 2007), one-child policy (Liu 2007), unpleasant experience at school (Ying 2004), social inequality and poor social management of the migrant population for causing increased delinquency among children of migrant workers (Chen and Zhong 2012; Li 2010), negative social environment in general (Wang 2000), and "idle juveniles" who are "high-risk groups" because they are not bonded into social organizations, such as school and/or work units.

Previous scholarly research published in English, however, is not limited to studying environmental factors only. At the individual level, Agnew's general strain theory was used to assess the relationship between interpersonal strain and delinquency (e.g., Bao et al. 2007). At the group level, peer association and gang involvement were studied for their impact on delinquency (Zhang and Messner 1995). Friday et al. (2005) confirmed the impact of peer influence on delinquency. At the institutional level, families and schools have become the focus of relevant research. A number of studies have found that family attachment, family opportunities for conventional activities, and parental supervision/monitoring are significantly associated with delinquency (e.g., Wang et al. 2002; Deng and Roosa 2007; Liu 2015). Attachment and bonds to other conventional institutions, such as schools and work units, are also significant predictors of delinquency (e.g., Wang et al. 2002; Ngai et al. 2007; Zhang et al. 2014). These findings from China are largely consistent with those found in Western societies. However, most of these studies are cross-sectional, and the causal relationship between the influences of the aforementioned factors on delinquency cannot be firmly established.

JUVENILE JUSTICE SYSTEM

The contemporary juvenile justice system is believed to begin with the establishment of the first juvenile tribunal in Changning District, Shanghai, in November 1984 (Yao 2001). Between 1949 and 1983, all special tribunals for juveniles and youth were abolished. Supported by the supreme court, these juvenile and youth courts spread rapidly in China. Since then, the concept of juvenile delinquency was reintroduced and a subsystem of juvenile justice has emerged.

Currently, two types of cases are handled by the juvenile tribunals, protection cases for children's welfare or property rights and criminal cases involving juvenile offenders between the ages of 14 and 18 years. Unlike its Western counterparts, especially the USA, where juvenile courts conduct civil proceedings exclusively designed for juveniles, Chinese juvenile court proceedings are considered largely as criminal proceedings (Zhao et al. 2014). Although the juvenile proceedings demonstrate the protection of the juvenile and focus on their interests, the divergence between the juvenile justice proceedings and the adult criminal justice proceedings is not remarkable. The subsystem of juvenile justice can be summarized as follows: round-table trial, social enquiry investigation, appearance with eligible adults, conditional non-prosecution, suspended judgment, mitigation and standardization of penalties, psychological correction and treatment, various forms of relief and education, and sealed criminal records for minors. All these might be categorized into different stages of the juvenile justice proceedings and involve various parties in the system, including the police, the prosecutors, the judges, and the correctional staff. There is no national unifying system and many of these are experiments that are local initiatives.

POLICING AND JUVENILES

As discussed previously, crime in China is defined as offending behavior that reaches a certain level of severity. Minor offenses are often handled by the police according to the PSAPL, and only serious offenses are required to go through the official criminal justice proceedings, i.e., from police arrest to prosecution, to court trial and sentencing, and to correctional punishment/rehabilitation. The police have tremendous discretionary power over juveniles, including warning, arrests, detention, and administrative punishment.

There are no specialized police officers for dealing with juveniles, but police officers work closely with the neighborhood committees and schools. Much of the police work with juveniles involves either order maintenance or service activities. When there is a sign for juvenile delinquency, the police often work with the parents, schoolteachers, and neighborhood committees as a coalition to provide assistance and counseling to the problem kids. Chinese police devote most of their time and resources to provide services for various community work and to resolve community conflicts, by using counseling, mediation, negotiation, or conciliation. Because the majority of the cases are handled at the community, school, or family level, arrest of juvenile offenders is considered a last resort (Zhao et al. 2014).

For serious offenses, if a juvenile delinquent cannot be held responsible because of his/her age, the police may decide to issue an order to their parents or legal guardians asking them to strictly discipline the child. According to the PSAPL, adolescents younger than the age of 14 are immune from any administrative punishment. They do not carry any criminal responsibility either. When it comes to the more serious crimes (e.g., the eight major types of crime committed by youth between the age of 14 and 16 years) and other major crimes by older adolescents (at the age of 16 or older as described by the Criminal Law), the police will then need to take the juvenile into custody and conduct a criminal investigation. In recent years, there has been a decreasing trend of police arrests in China. The Chinese Criminal Procedure Law requires that arrests of juvenile criminal suspects be rigorously restricted (Article 269). Statistics show that in 2011 the approval rate for arrests of juvenile suspects by the prosecution's offices at various levels decreased by 5% compared with the previous year (Huang 2012).

After a juvenile is arrested, he/she is locked up in a secure facility while waiting for a court trial or a decision not to prosecute. Before 1996 juvenile offenders were housed with adult offenders, which caused serious "cross-contamination" problems. After 1996 juvenile offenders were separated from adult offenders whenever possible; *despite this however, they* continued to be subjected to the reeducation through labor *system* which did not differ much from that for adult offenders (Zhang 2013b).

In some circumstances, a juvenile can be placed under house detention or be granted bail. The practice of granting juvenile bail has been rare in many jurisdictions in China. However, its use has been steadily increasing in more economically developed jurisdictions (Zhang 2007; Zhao et al. 2014). For detained juveniles, Article 269 of the Criminal Law requires that juveniles who are detained, are arrested, or are being punished for a crime should be locked up, supervised, and educated separately from adults.

In 2013, the controversial program of "Re-education Through Labor System" (RTLS thereafter) was finally abolished. RTLS was an administrative incarceration for both adults and juveniles, which targeted minor offenders, and was administered by the police as an expedient tool. The police had great discretionary power as to who to incarcerate and the length of incarceration (Zhang 2013b). RTLS was criticized for the lack of legal basis. Offenders were deprived of their freedom without going through the judicial procedures. This led to the abuse of power by the police due to the lack of supervision mechanisms. The abolition of RTLS has restricted police discretionary power and represents a step forward toward "rule by law."

The police are also responsible for interrogating juvenile offenders in the presence of the juvenile's parents or other legal guardians. Article 56 of the Law on Protection of Minors stipulates that to interrogate minors suspected of crime or question victims or witnesses who are minors, public security organs or people's procuratorates shall notify the guardians of the minor to be present. If the legal representatives cannot attend the interrogation or trial, or are accomplices of the juvenile suspect, other parties, such as the juvenile's close relatives, representatives of his/her schools, work units, and neighborhood committees, might be informed to attend the interrogation and trial (Zhao et al. 2014).

The Law on Protection of Minors further provides that in dealing with cases involving crimes committed by minors and cases that involve preserving the rights and interests of minors, public security organs, people's procuratorates, and people's courts shall take the characteristics of juvenile's physical and mental development into consideration, respect their personal dignity, and safeguard their lawful rights and interests and may, where necessary, set up special agencies or designate special persons to handle such cases (Article 55).

PUBLIC PROSECUTION, COURTS, AND JUVENILES

Serious juvenile crime cases are handed over to the public prosecutors for their decision on whether to prosecute (Yue 2002). A recent development in the public prosecution has been the practice of conditional non-prosecution, which is modeled on the Western practice that allows juvenile delinquents to stay outside jails by successfully completing a certain period of time under supervision (Zhao et al. 2014). It may be considered as a form of pretrial diversion (Zhao et al. 2014). According to the Criminal Procedure Law of 2012, conditional non-prosecution may apply to juvenile offenders whose possible criminal punishment is not more than a year of prison term and have demonstrated repentance (Article 271). Statistics of some pilot programs show that the use of conditional non-prosecution has not been frequent. For example, the prosecution office of Nansha District of Guangzhou City reported only eight cases of conditional non-prosecution in 2013 and early 2014 (The Research Team of the Prosecution's Office of Nansha District, Guangzhou 2014).

Serious juvenile crime cases are brought to the courts. Similar to adult criminal cases, the juvenile criminal procedure is a two-tier system. The decisions from the court of second instance are final. Normally, at the court of first instance (e.g., county court or city district court), a juvenile criminal trial can be heard either by a bench or a single judge. However, if the court of first instance is the intermediate court, the case could only be heard by a bench (Zhao et al. 2014). Because a juvenile tribunal is largely seen as part of a criminal court, the court proceedings are formal and adversarial. On November 2012, the Supreme People's Court published its interpretation on the Criminal Procedure Law ("Interpretation" hereafter), and the Proceedings on Handling Juvenile Criminal Cases are included in the Interpretation. Special standards were established for handling juvenile criminal cases in the trail stage. Article 459 of the Interpretation provides that during the trial stage, in order to strengthen special protection of youth, education should be upheld as the main strategy and punishment as subsidiary method. Recently, some courts require mandatory education for juvenile offenders with noncustodial sentences (Zhao et al. 2014). The Interpretation further stipulates that the courts at various levels could form juvenile tribunals to handle juvenile-related cases (Article 462). There are two types of tribunals: the ones which are independent from criminal tribunals and the ones under the criminal tribunals with dedicated staff specializing in juvenile cases.

The juvenile tribunals handle criminal cases committed by adolescents under the age of 18 at the time of crime commission. At the trial stage, the juvenile defendant's legal guardians need to be informed to be present. If the legal guardians cannot attend the court trial due to various reasons, representatives from the juvenile defendant's school, work unit, or neighborhood committees need to be informed of their presence (Article 465). Those present at the court trial, with approval by the court, could participate in court education on the juvenile defendant. Despite this, juvenile court proceedings are closed to the public since juvenile matters are confidential. Both the Criminal Procedure Law and the Interpretation prohibit public trial of juvenile criminal cases. Nor should the court reveal personal information of the juvenile defendant, such as name, residence address, and photos to the public.

Another advancement of juvenile tribunals experimented in the southern coastal cities focuses on psychological correction and treatment. Many juvenile tribunals request psychological evaluation of juvenile offenders in order to serve as an objective basis for sentencing and treatment. Seats are arranged in the courtroom for counselors, who may provide psychological counseling and treatment to juvenile offenders. In addition, their professional evaluation might be considered by the judge while making a sentencing decision (Su 2014).

CUSTODIAL RULES FOR JUVENILES

Historically, Chinese juvenile justice policy has stressed the importance of reform and reeducation as the main method supplemented by punishment (Cao and Cullen 2001). Both the Criminal Law (Article 17) and the Law on the Protection of Minors (Article 54) state that the policy of education, persuasion, and redemption shall be implemented on juvenile offenders; reeducation shall be upheld as the main method and punishment as the subsidiary strategy. In addition, the laws both require alleviated or mitigated punishment on juvenile offenders. In reality, re-enforcement of these laws depends on the local criminal justice agents, and they are frequently ignored or bypassed for convenience.

The Criminal Law of China categorizes punishments into five principal punishments and three supplementary punishments (Article 33 and 34). The five principal punishments include public surveillance, criminal detention, fix-term imprisonment, life imprisonment, and the death penalty. The three supplementary punishments are fine, deprivation of political rights, and confiscation of

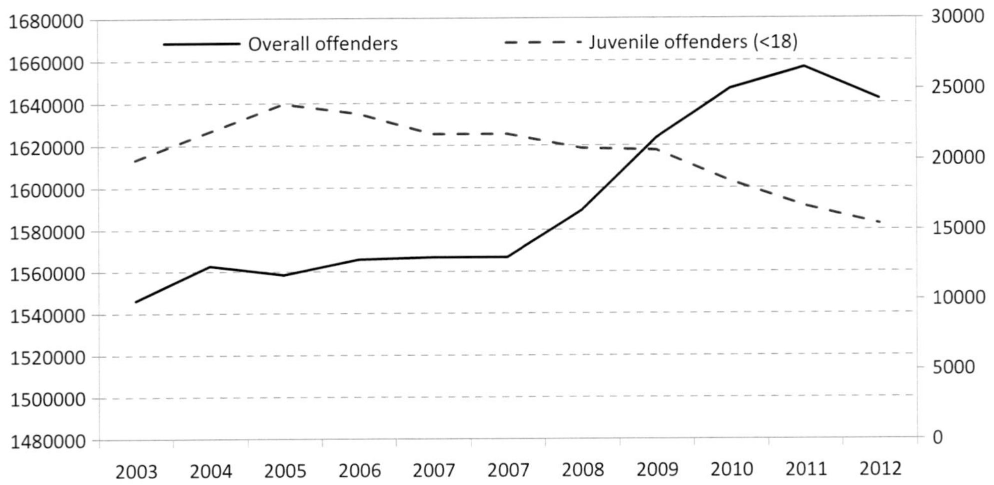

FIGURE 8.3. Number of juvenile offenders incarcerated. Data source: China Law Society (2004–2013), Law Yearbook of China.

property. Among the principal punishments, both public surveillance and criminal detention might be used on juvenile offenders who commit relatively serious crimes. Both are carried out by the police instead of correctional institutions (Article 38 and 43). The Criminal Law, however, does not strictly prohibit the use of a life sentence on serious juvenile offenders. The Supreme People's Court's Interpretation on Proceedings on Handling Juvenile Criminal Cases provides that life sentence can only be used on juvenile offenders who committed extremely serious crime.

Fix-term imprisonment is carefully implemented. Official crime statistics show that although the overall number of serious juvenile offenders increased in the past 10 years, the use of prison incarceration has been declining. Figure 8.3 shows that from 2003 to 2012, the number of overall offenders being incarcerated steadily increased from 1.55 million in 2003 to 1.64 million in 2012; the number of juvenile offenders (under the age of 18) being incarcerated, however, decreased from 19,990 in 2003 to 15,429 in 2012. The decline is consistent with the recent changes in juvenile-related policies which highlights the importance of reform and reeducation which place rigorous restriction of incarceration of juvenile offenders. These policies are in line with the international treaties including UN Standard Minimum Rules for the Treatment of Prisoners and UN Standard Minimum Rules for the Administration of Juvenile Justice.

The Law on Protection of Minors requires that minors who are under custody or serving sentences shall be detained or imprisoned separately from adults (Article 57). This means that juvenile offenders should be separated from adult offenders in order to avoid "crime contamination." The implementation of such laws, however, largely depends on the availability of the facility at a given jurisdiction. In many jurisdictions, juvenile suspects still run the risk of being detained with adult suspects (Yue 2002).

ALTERNATIVE SANCTIONS FOR JUVENILES

The Criminal Law of China provides that for offenders who commit relatively minor offenses and do not need criminal punishment, noncriminal punishments/sanctions can be imposed. These alternative sanctions include the following: reprimand or order the offender to make a statement of repentance, order the offender to offer an apology or pay compensation for the losses, impose administrative penalty or administrative sanctions by the competent department, order the juvenile's parents or legal guardian(s) to strictly discipline him/her, or put the juvenile under government custody for reform and reeducation (Gao and Zhang 2008). These sanctions, however, are not all juvenile-specific sanctions. The Criminal Law does not provide specific explanation on how these sanctions should be carried out. In addition, many sanctions such as community services and participation in collective counseling, as described in the UN Standard Minimum Rules for the Administration of Juvenile Justice, are not covered. It is believed that the Chinese Criminal Law lacks a chapter to systematically address alternative sanctions on juvenile offenders (Gao and Zhang 2008).

DIFFERENCES IN TREATMENT OF BOYS AND GIRLS

Traditional Chinese culture emphasizes the dominant role of males (Wu and Cao 2014). Females are often considered subordinate to males. Article 33 of the Constitution of PRC provides that all citizens of the People's Republic of China are equal before the law. In reality, the patriarchal culture remains strong, and actual gender inequality exists in every aspect of social life, including the juvenile justice system.

The official crime statistics do not provide information regarding female juvenile crimes nationwide. It is believed that the overall number of female juvenile offenders has been growing in the recent years (Bing 2010; Shao 2010). For example, a judicial report by Henan Provincial High Court reveals that the percentage of female juvenile offenders increased from 1.91% in 2007 to 3.04% in 2011 (Henan Provincial Higher Court 2012). The UN Standard Minimum Rules for the Administration of Juvenile Justice calls for fair treatment of female offenders at every stage of the criminal justice process and for special attention to the particular problems and needs they face while in custody. Article 26.4 stipulates that young female offenders placed in an institution deserve special attention as to their personal needs and problems. They shall by no means receive less care, protection, assistance, treatment, and training than young male offenders. Their fair treatment shall be ensured (Article 26.4). The special treatment needs of female juvenile offenders, however, have not been articulated in any Chinese laws concerning juvenile offenders.

CONCLUSION

China has changed dramatically since the beginning of its economic reform in the late 1970s. With an enlarged stratification system (Cao and Dai 2001), juvenile and youth crime, as part of the ever-increasing crime trend, has become a prominent social issue. It is an indicator of the deeper tension within a society that has rapidly modernized certain parts while leaving other parts untouched. Despite the legal and procedural improvement, the juvenile justice system still appears to offer less protection of juvenile rights and few effective programs for rehabilitation (Wong 2004). For example, Chinese laws are largely silent on special needs or treatment of female juvenile offenders. Furthermore, since the Chinese juvenile justice system remains a part of criminal justice system, it is not an independent system, and thus the proceedings of juvenile cases are formal and adversarial (Su 2014; Zhao et al. 2014). Juvenile courts are marginalized and do not have separate funding. Protection of children's rights remains inseparable with the divide by the urban and rural registration system (Su 2014). Migrant children's rights are totally ignored in all big cities. The nicety of laws is frequently sacrificed for convenience.

On the positive side, an acknowledgment has been expressed on juvenile protection and juvenile crime prevention. Many local initiatives are being experimented within different locations and some have showed desired effects. In addition, the Chinese government has adopted a total-society approach to delinquency prevention, and Chinese laws prescribe behavior rules not only to guide juvenile behaviors but also to regulate institutional behaviors that are alleged to constitute the nurturing environment for juveniles. The long arm of the government has strengthened the networks to prevent juvenile crime at the same time, however, have disregarded juveniles' rights in due process. Their comparability with the desires of modernity and in being consistent with prevailing international standards is in question.

REFERENCES

Bakken, B. (1993). Crime, juvenile delinquency and deterrence policy in China. *The Australian Journal of Chinese Affairs, 30*(1), 29–58.

Bao, W., Hass, A., & Pi, Y. (2007). Life Strain, negative emotions, and delinquency: An empirical test of general strain theory in the People's Republic of China. *International Journal of Offender Therapy and Comparative Criminology, 48*(3), 281–297.

Bing, X. (2010). The current status, characteristics, and prevention measures of juvenile delinquency—The case of Xinjiang Uygur Autonomous Region. *Journal of Hunan Financial and Economic College, 26*, 136–138 (in Chinese).

Cao, L. (2007). Returning to normality: Anomie and crime in China. *International Journal of Offender Therapy and Comparative Criminology, 51*(1), 40–51.

Cao, L., & Cullen, F. T. (2001). Thinking about crime and control: A comparative study of Chinese and American ideology. *International Criminal Justice Review, 11*, 58–81.

Cao, L., & Dai, Y. (2001). Inequality and crime in China. In J. Liu, L. Zhang, & S. E. Messner (Eds.), *Crime and social control in a changing China* (pp. 73–85). Westport, CT: Greenwood Press.

Chen, X. (2015). *Strain, family socioeconomic status, and delinquency among migrant adolescents in China: A multilevel model of general strain theory*. The Chinese University of Hong Kong (Hong Kong), ProQuest Dissertations Publishing.
Chen, X., & Zhong, H. (2012). Pressure, negative emotion and deviant behavior among migrant children. *Issues on Juvenile and Youth Crime, 5*, 22–33 (in Chinese).
China Law Society. (2004–2013). *Law Yearbook of China*. Beijing: Press of Law Yearbook of China.
China Statistical Bureau. (1991–2014). *China Statistical Yearbook*. Beijing: China Statistics Press.
China Statistical Bureau of Population and Employment, National Bureau of Statistics. (2013). *China Population Yearbook*. Beijing: China Statistics Press.
China Statistical Bureau and Employment Section. (1991–2013). *China Population and Employment Statistics Yearbook*. Beijing: China Statistics Press.
David, R., & Brierley, J. E. C. (1978). *Major legal systems in the world*. New York: The Free Press.
Deng, S., & Roosa, M. (2007). Family influences on adolescent delinquent behaviors: Applying the social development model to a Chinese sample. *American Journal of Community Psychology, 40*, 333–344.
Friday, P. C., Ren, X., Weitekamp, E., Kerner, H., & Tailor, T. (2005). A Chinese birth cohort: Theoretical implications. *Journal of Research in Crime and Delinquency, 42*(2), 123–146.
Gao, M., & Zhang, J. (2008). On sanction's improvement for juvenile crime in Chinese criminal code—Inspected from the angle of international human rights law. *Legal Forum, 23*, 12–17.
He, N. (2014). The politics of numbers: Crime statistics in China. In L. Cao, I. Sun, & B. Hebenton (Eds.), *The Routledge handbook of Chinese criminology* (pp. 147–159). London: Routledge.
He, N., & Marshall, I. (1997). Social production of crime data: A critical examination of Chinese crime statistics. *International Criminal Justice Review, 7*, 46–63.
Henan Provincial Higher Court. (2012). *Judicial report on juvenile crime prevention in Henan province (2007–2011)*. Retrieved December 10, 2015, from http://www.hncourt.org/public/detail.php?id=137219 (in Chinese).
Huang, H. (2012). The modifications of criminal procedure law and construction of juvenile criminal prosecution. *Juvenile Delinquency Prevention Research, 5*, 16–19 (in Chinese).
Lanier, M. M., & Henry, S. (2014). *Essential criminology* (4th ed.). Boulder, CO: Westview Press.
Li, J. (2010, December 7). Juvenile delinquency among Chinese migrants on the rise. *McClatchy-Tribune Business News*.
Li, X., Fang, X., Stanton, B., Feigelman, S., & Dong, Q. (1996). The rate and pattern of alcohol consumption among Chinese adolescents. *Journal of Adolescent Health, 19*(5), 353–361.
Liu, J. (2007, December 5). China riding wave of juvenile crime: Internet, one-child policy blamed. *Edmonton Journal*, A4.
Liu, J. (2008). Data sources in Chinese crime and criminal justice research. *Crime, Law and Social Change, 50*, 131–147.
Liu, R. X. (2015). The effects of gender and bonds with parents and grandparents on delinquency among Chinese adolescents. *Sociological Focus, 48*(1), 68–87.
Ngai, N., Cheung, C., & Ngai, S. S. (2007). Cognitive and social influences on gang involvement among delinquents in three Chinese cities. *Adolescence, 42*, 381–403.
Ni, S. (2003, August 25). Chinese lawmaker claims internet causes juvenile delinquency. *Xinhua News Agency-CEIS*.
Pyrooz, D., & Decker, S. (2013). Delinquent behavior, violence, and gang involvement in China. *Journal of Quantitative Criminology, 29*(2), 251–272.
Shao, J. (2010). Study on juvenile crime prevention and correction mechanism in Tianjin. *Tianjin Legal Science, 103*, 83–89 (in Chinese).
Su, K. (2014). On improvement of juvenile justice in China. *People's Justice*, 17. Retrieved from http://article.chinalawinfo.com/ArticleFullText.aspx?ArticleId=87787 (in Chinese).
The Research Team of the Prosecution's Office of Nansha District, Guangzhou. (2014). Research on conditional non-prosecution by prosecution's office: The case of Nansha district prosecution's office. *Legal System and Society, 5*, 59–61 (in Chinese).

Troyer, R. J., Clark, J. P., & Rojek, D. G. (1989). *Social control in the People's Republic of China*. New York: Praeger.
Wang, S. (2000, August 23). Good social environment crucial for preventing juvenile delinquency. *Xinhua News Agency—CEIS*, 1.
Wang, G. T., Qiao, H., Hong, S., & Zhang, J. (2002). Adolescent social bond, self-control, and deviant behavior in China. *International Journal of Contemporary Sociology, 39*(1), 53–68.
Webb, J. V., Ren, L., Zhao, J. S., He, N., & Marshall, I. H. (2011). A comparative study on youth gangs in China and the United States: Definition, offending and victimization. *International Criminal Justice Review, 21*, 243–262.
Wei, Z., Homel, R., Prichard, J., & Xu, J. (2004). Patterns of juvenile offending in Shanghai and Brisbane. *The Australian and New Zealand Journal of Criminology, 37*, 32–51.
Wong, D. S. (2004). Juvenile protection and delinquency prevention policies in China. *The Australian and New Zealand Journal of Criminology, 37*, 52–66.
Wu, Z., & Cao, L. (2014). Historical themes of crime causation in China. In L. Cao, I. Sun, & B. Hebenton (Eds.), *The Routledge handbook of Chinese criminology* (pp. 3–15). London: Routledge.
Yao, J. (2001). The creation of juvenile courts and issues related to its developments. *Youth Studies*. Retrieved from http://www.law-lib.com/lw/lw_view.asp?no=1050 (in Chinese).
Ying, G. (2004, May 20). Juvenile delinquency often starts with unpleasant experience at school. *Xinhua News Agency—CEIS*, 1.
Yue, L. (2002). Youth justice in China. In J. Winterdyk (Ed.), *Juvenile justice system: International perspective* (pp. 103–126). Ontario: Canadian Scholars' Press Inc.
Zhang, Y. (2007). *A study on juvenile bail*. Retrieved December 10, 2015, from http://old.chinacourt.org/html/article/200711/16/274929.shtml (in Chinese).
Zhang, H. (2013a). *Essentials of juvenile justice*. Beijing: People's Publishing House (in Chinese).
Zhang, Y. (2013b). Juvenile re-education through labor and community corrections. *Issues on Juvenile and Youth Crimes, 5*, 77–81 (in Chinese).
Zhang, H. (2015). *On juvenile justice*. Beijing: People's Publishing House (in Chinese).
Zhang, L., & Messner, S. F. (1995). Family deviance and delinquency in China. *Criminology, 33*(3), 359–387.
Zhang, H., Zhao, R., Ren, L., & Zhao, J. (2014). Social attachment and juvenile attitudes toward the police in China: Bridging eastern and western wisdom. *Journal of Research in Crime and Delinquency, 51*(6), 703–734.
Zhao, R., Zhang, H., & Liu, J. (2014). Juvenile justice system in China: A system in transition. In J. Winterdyk (Ed.), *Juvenile justice: International perspectives, models and trends* (pp. 137–162). Boca Raton, FL: CRC Press, Taylor and Francis Group.

Ruohui Zhao Associate professor in the Department of Sociology at the University of Macau, China. She earned her Ph.D. from the University of Nebraska at Omaha in 2007. Her research interests include juvenile delinquency, corrections, and crime and social control in Greater China. Her essays have appeared in many national and international journals, including top journals like *Social Forces*.

Liqun Cao Professor of sociology and criminology at the University of Ontario Institute of Technology, Canada. He is also an adjunct professor at Queensland University of Technology, Australia. His research interests include comparative sociology, criminological theory, gun ownership, police integrity, public attitudes toward ascetic deviance, race and ethnicity in criminal justice, etc. His research essays have appeared in *Criminology*, *International Journal of Offender Therapy and Comparative Criminology*, *Journal of Criminal Justice*, *Justice Quarterly*, *Social Forces*, *Social Problems*, etc. He is the author of *Major Criminological Theories: Concepts and Measurement* (2004) and the lead author of *Policing in Taiwan: From Authoritarianism to Democracy* (2014). He is also the lead editor of *The Routledge Handbook of Chinese Criminology* (2014) and coeditor of *Lessons from International/Comparative Criminology* (2004).

9

India

Sesha Kethineni

INTRODUCTION

According to the 2011 Census of India, adolescents (10–19 years of age) represented 19.6% of 1.21 billion people in the country. Compared to 2001 Census data where the literacy rate for adolescent females was 75.1% and for adolescent males was 85.5%, the 2011 Census data show higher rates of literacy among the adolescent population. For example, the literacy rate for adolescent females in 2011 is 88.2%, and the rate for adolescent males is 91.7%, showing a narrowing gender gap. The 2011 adolescent sex ratio is 898 females to 1000 males, indicating a continued preference for boys over girls (Census of India 2011). Young people are also exposed to child labor, trafficking, and sexual exploitation (Sharma 2014). UNICEF (2011a) estimates that children in the age group of 5–14 are engaged in some form of work. The National Child Labour (Prohibition and Regulation) Act of 1986 only bans child labor in hazardous occupations. The Right of Children to Free and Compulsory Education Act of 2009 made free and compulsory education for children a right. Although the Act does not ban child labor, there is an implicit recognition that children should not work at a young age (UNICEF 2011a).

The data on missing children presented by the Ministry of Home Affairs (2015) show that over 325,000 children went missing between 2011 and June 2014, which amounts to an average of nearly 100,000 children going missing every year. About 55% of the missing children are girls and about 45% of all missing children are untraceable (Tiwary 2014; Sharma, n.d.). Many of these juveniles are trafficked for child prostitution, bonded labor, begging, and organ trade. According to Bhattacharya and Bhattacharya (2015), poverty creates a

S. Kethineni (✉)
Department of Justice Studies, Prairie View A&M University, Prairie View, TX 77446, USA
e-mail: srkethineni@pvamu.edu

S.H. Decker, N. Marteache (eds.), *International Handbook of Juvenile Justice*,
DOI 10.1007/978-3-319-45090-2_9

vicious cycle. For example, poverty drives low-income families to push their children into the labor market, which affects the children's emotional and intellectual growth. These children are exploited by traffickers, who turn them into child prostitutes, beggars, or bonded laborers. These victimized and neglected children often show behavioral problems, including engaging in delinquent acts such as theft, assaults, drug peddling, etc.

Traditional social practices such as child marriages deny children their fundamental rights, such as proper health, nutrition, education, and freedom from violence and exploitation, and deprive them of their childhood. Although the Prohibition of Child Marriage Act (2006) was passed requiring states and union territories (are directly under the central government rule) to develop standards and strategies to implement the Act, some states have yet to implement a plan. Also, India has passed the Juvenile Justice Act (JJA 1986), the Juvenile Justice (Care and Protection of Children) Act (JJCPA 2000), and an amendment of this legislation in 2006, 2011, and 2015. This chapter will discuss the nature and extent of juvenile crime, the juvenile justice law, the role of police, the incorporation of the principles of the UN Convention on the Rights of the Child (CRC), and the status of juvenile justice in India.

AGE OF CRIMINAL RESPONSIBILITY

The Indian Penal Code (IPC) sets the age of criminality at 7 years and considers children between 8 and 12 years as not criminally responsible if the juvenile has not attained sufficient maturity to understand the nature and consequences of her or his conduct. There is no such immunity for children above age 12. The JJA, on the other hand, sets the juvenile court jurisdiction differently for boys and girls—18 for girls and 16 for boys. The assumption was that girls in India needed extended protection due to differences in the socialization of boys and girls; boys are given more freedom and opportunities to venture into the real world, whereas similar opportunities are limited for girls (Bhattacharya and Bhattacharya 2015). The age disparity has been rectified in later legislation.

THE STATUS OF CHILDREN IN CONFLICT WITH LAW IN INDIA IN THE CONTEXT OF CRC

In 1923, the Declaration of the Rights of the Child was adopted by the Save the Children International Union and was endorsed by the League of Nations General Assembly in 1924 as the World Child Welfare Charter. The Declaration established the rights of children to the means for material, mental, social, moral, and spiritual development. The Declaration also recognized the right to adequate nutrition, housing, recreation, and medical care; free education at least at the elementary school level; freedom from all forms of exploitation; and an upbringing that instills a sense of social responsibility (UNICEF 2004).

In 1948, the United Nations (UN), which had replaced the League of Nations, adopted the Universal Declaration of Human Rights (UDHR). In the Declaration, the nations of the world acknowledged that children were entitled to special care and assistance. After 1948, the UN took other initiatives to protect the rights of children, such as the 1959 Declaration of the Rights of the Child and the UN Educational, Scientific, and Cultural Organization's (UNESCO) proclamation of 1979 as International Year of the Child. The goal of the declaration was to draw attention to the problem of children throughout the world as well as prevent malnutrition and improve access to education (UNICEF 1979). These efforts resulted in the CRC in 1989. The following year, the UN World Summit for Children convened to consider how to guarantee children a better life. The CRC was ratified by the required quorum of 20 countries. As of 2015, the United States is the only country that has not ratified CRC.

Other guidelines that work in close conjunction with the CRC in the area of juvenile justice are (1) the UN Standard Minimum Rules for the Administration of Juvenile Justice (i.e., the Beijing Rules) of 1985, (2) the UN Rules for the Protection of Juveniles Deprived of Their Liberty (i.e., the JDL Rules) of 1990 (Office of the United Nations High Commissioner for Human Rights 1990), and (3) the UN Guidelines for the Prevention of Juvenile Delinquency (i.e., the Riyadh Guidelines) of 1990. The Beijing Rules provide a framework for operations of national juvenile justice systems and offer states guidelines for the investigation and prosecution of juveniles, the adjudication and disposition of juveniles, and the treatment of juveniles in both institutional and noninstitutional settings (Office of the United Nations High Commissioner for Human Rights 1985; Van Bueren and Tootell 2007). The Rules operate within the framework of the Riyadh Guidelines and the UN Rules for the Protection of Juveniles Deprived of their Liberty (i.e., the JDL Rules; Office of the United Nations High Commissioner for Human Rights 1990). These three sets of rules provide guidelines for juvenile justice processes. First, the Riyadh Guidelines recommend states to develop proactive policies to prevent and protect young people from offending. Second, the Beijing Rules provide guidelines for establishing a separate and specialized juvenile justice system. Third, the JDL rules establish measures for the social reintegration of young people deprived of their liberty, whether in prison or other institutions (Van Bueren and Tootell 2007; UNICEF 2011b).

For all practical purposes, the criminal justice personnel should first look to the CRC and then to the Riyadh Guidelines for preventing children from coming into conflict with the law. Second, they should look to the CRC and the Beijing Rules when dealing with the kids accused of having come into conflict with the law. Third, the personnel of the criminal justice system should look to the CRC and the JDL Rules for dealing with children found to be in breach of criminal law (Srinivasan 2010).

Many of the rights provided in the CRC had already existed, in a different form, in the Constitutional Law of India that came into force on January 26, 1950. For example, Article 14 guarantees equal protection before the law. Article 15 prohibits discrimination of any citizen and allows states to develop special protections for women and children. Article 23 prohibits trafficking in human beings and beggar[1] and other forms of forced labor. Article 24 prohibits employment of children under 14 in hazardous occupations.

The right to participation accords children the freedom of thought and expression, conscience, and religion and the right to participate in decision-making. States that are party to the CRC are obliged to develop and undertake all necessary actions and policies to promote the best interests of children (Bullis 1991). India ratified the CRC in 1992, along with 193 other countries (United Nations Treaty Collection 2011). By ratifying the CRC, India is obligated both morally and legally to uphold the principles enumerated in the CRC. The participatory rights of children are discussed below.

The participatory rights of children are defined in the CRC's Article 5 (parental accountability), Article 9 (nonseparation of children from families), Article 12 (participation in judicial or administrative proceedings), Article 13 (freedom of expression), Article 14 (freedom of conscience, thought, and religion), Article 15 (freedom of association), Article 16 (right to privacy), Article 17 (right to information), and Article 29 (right to education). Though all the above articles spell out the participatory rights of children, Article 12 deals specifically with the right to be heard in any judicial and administrative proceedings relating to children violating criminal laws, children as victims of crime, and children as witnesses in criminal offenses committed by adults/juveniles (Office of the United Nations High Commissioner for Human Rights 2011; Srinivasan 2010).

The lack of enforcement of many of the provisions of the JJA, coupled with the government of India's ratification of the CRC, prompted India to enact the JJCPA in 2000 (Kethineni and Braithwaite 2014). The Act was intended to provide proper care, protection, and treatment by catering to children's development needs as well as adopting a child-friendly approach in the adjudication and disposition of juveniles (Srinivasan 2010). Some of the provisions of the JJCPA were challenged in the High Court of Delhi through public-interest litigation. The Court proposed amendments to the Act. Although the initial bill with these changes lapsed, a revised amendment (i.e., the Juvenile Justice (Care and Protection of Children) Amendment Act 2006) was passed.

A 2010 study of the participatory rights of juveniles revealed that a significant percentage of the police said that when they apprehended children, they did not inform them of the reasons for the arrest (Srinivasan 2010). Also, they did not tell the children of the offense for which they were apprehended. In this context, it is worth mentioning certain provisions of the CRC. Article 40[2][a][ii], one of the essential rights of children, states that children have the right to be informed promptly and directly of the charges against her or him. However, in reality, a majority of law enforcement personnel, particularly the police, have not fulfilled this right. Plausible explanations include ignorance on the part of the police or

[1] Beggar was a form of forced labor practiced during the British rule by government officers and landowners compelling laborers to carry their goods from one place to another without any remuneration.

the police's apathetic attitude toward children in conflict with the law. The findings also revealed that a considerable percentage of police officers admitted that children in conflict with the law were kept at the police station after their apprehension. This practice was in contravention of Section 10(1) of JJA (2000): When the police apprehend a juvenile, the officer-in-charge of the special juvenile police unit or the designated police officer should produce the juvenile before the Juvenile Justice Board (JJB) without any loss of time. It was also noted that in no case should a juvenile be placed in police lockup. Thus, the practice of keeping juveniles in police stations should be viewed seriously (Srinivasan 2010).

According to Article 18(a) of UN Rules for the Protection of Juveniles Deprived of their Liberty (i.e., the JDL Rules), children in conflict with the law should have the right to legal counsel and be able to apply for free legal aid. Such a provision also appears in Article 40(2)(a)(ii) of the CRC. The findings of the 2010 study by Srinivasan show that a vast majority of respondents reported that if children were not in a position to engage their legal counsel, the Board arranged for legal counsel. The findings also revealed that children were allowed to speak with their legal counsel confidentially. This practice followed Article 16 of the CRC and Article 18(a) of the JDL Rules. It should also be noted that, as reported by members and chairpersons of Juvenile Justice Boards, children were given the opportunity to express their opinion. Also, children were allowed to cross-examine their witness/witnesses. Although it appeared right that the children were released on bail, the time it took to release them on bail was a matter of concern, because the period of detention for a child should be for the shortest period. This rule was clearly enunciated in the CRC (Article 37[b]).

TRENDS IN JUVENILE CRIME, 2004–2014

In India, the National Crime Records Bureau (NCRB) compiles an annual juvenile crime report, *Crime in India*, for the entire country. The data do not reflect the actual extent of juvenile delinquency because many of these crimes are not reported to the police (Chakraborty, n.d.). However, the data show the trends in reported crimes, including incidents of juvenile crimes under the Indian Penal Code (IPC) 1860 and under Special and Local Laws (SLL) by age groups and gender. Offenses under IPC include: Murder; Attempted murder; Culpable homicide (i.e., manslaughter); Rape (including gang rape and other forms of rapes); Kidnapping (with intent to murder for ransom, and compel women for marriage); Dacoity (i.e., gang robbery with murder and robbery); Burglary and criminal trespass; Theft (including auto theft); Riots, including participation in communal, industrial, political, caste, or student conflicts; Criminal breach of trust, cheating, forgery, and offenses related to counterfeit coins, stamps, currency, bank notes, or documents; Arson; Grievous hurt (aggravated assault, acid attack, or attempted acid attack); Dowry death; Assault on women with intent to outrage her modesty such as sexual harassment, voyeurism, and stalking; Insult

TABLE 9.1. Incidence and rate of delinquency under Indian Penal Code, 2004–2014

Year	*Incidence of juvenile IPC crimes*	*Total IPC crimes*	*% Juvenile IPC crimes to total IPC crimes*	*Mid-year projected population (in 100,000)*	*Rate of IPC crime by juveniles*
2004	19,229	1,832,015	1.0	10,856	1.8
2005	18,939	1,822,602	1.0	11,028	1.7
2006	21,088	1,878,293	1.1	11,198	1.9
2007	22,865	1,989,673	1.1	11,366	2.0
2008	24,535	2,093,379	1.2	11,531	2.1
2009	23,926	2,121,345	1.1	11,694	2.0
2010	22,740	2,224,831	1.0	11,858	1.9
2011	25,125	2,325,575	1.1	11,202	2.1
2012	27,936	2,387,188	1.2	12,134	2.3
2013	31,725	2,647,722	1.2	12,288	2.6
2014	33,526	2,851,563	1.2	12,440	2.7

Source: NCRB (2014), *Crime in India*. New Delhi: Government of India

the modesty of women (in public places, office premises, or other places related to work)' Cruelty by husband or relatives; Importation of girls from foreign country; Causing death by negligence (e.g., death due to negligent driving); Offenses against state; Extortion; Reckless driving; and Human trafficking (National Crime Records Bureau (NCRB) 2014).

Crimes under SLL include violations of Arms Act, Narcotic Drugs and Psychotropic Substances Act, Gambling Act, Prohibition Act, Explosives and Explosive Substance Act, Immoral Traffic Act, Indian Railways Act, Registration of Foreigners Act, Protection of Civil Rights Act, Indian Passport Act, Essential Commodities Act, Terrorists and Disruptive Activities (Prevention) Act, Antiquities and Art Treasures Act, Dowry Prohibition Act, Child Marriage Restraint Act, Indecent Representation of Marriage Act, Copyright Act, *Sati*[2] (Prevention) Act, Scheduled Caste and Scheduled Tribes (Prevention of Atrocities) Act, and Forest Act. Tables 9.1 and 9.2 provide juvenile crime under IPC and SLL from 2004 through 2014. Juvenile crimes under IPC accounted for 1–1.2%, whereas juvenile crimes under SLL represented less than 1% of all SLL crimes (National Crime Records Bureau (NCRB) 2014).

SPECIFIC JUVENILE CRIMES IN 2014

In 2014, a total of 33,526 IPC crimes and 5039 SLL crimes involving 48,230 juveniles were reported to the police. Of this, 46,638 (96.7%) were boys and 1592 (3.3%) were girls; 80.2% were living with parents, and 2.4% were considered

[2] *Sati* is the self-immolation of a woman.

TABLE 9.2. Incidence and rate of delinquency under Special and Local Laws, 2004–2014

Year	*Incidents of juvenile SLL crimes*	*Total SLL crimes*	*% Juvenile SLL crimes to total SLL crimes*	*Mid-year projected population (in 100,000)*	*Rate of SLL crimes by juveniles*
2004	5756	4,196,766	0.14	10,856	0.53
2005	6662	3,203,735	0.20	11,028	0.60
2006	4163	3,224,167	0.13	11,198	0.37
2007	4163	3,743,734	0.11	11,366	0.36
2008	3156	3,844,725	0.20	11,531	0.27
2009	4321	4,553,872	0.09	11,694	0.37
2010	2558	4,525,917	0.05	11,858	0.21
2011	2837	3,927,154	0.07	11,202	0.25
2012	4037	3,654,371	0.11	12,134	0.33
2013	4136	3,992,656	0.10	12,288	0.33
2014	5039	4,377,630	0.11	12,440	0.40

Source: NCRB (2014), *Crime in India*. New Delhi, India: Government of India

homeless. The ratio of boys to girls apprehended for IPC crimes in 2014 was 97:3 and for SLL crimes was 95:5. The majority of juveniles apprehended for IPC offenses (73.7%) were in the age range of 16 to 17 years, and a quarter of juveniles (24.7%) ranged in age from 12 to 15 years. Fewer than 2% (1.6%) were in the age group of 7–11 years (see Tables 9.3 and 9.4). The highest share of IPC offenses involving boys were theft ($n=8820$), burglary ($n=3802$), rape ($n=2144$), rioting ($n=2074$), and grievous hurt ($n=1972$). These five offenses made up 44% of all IPC crimes committed by juveniles. In addition to these crimes, juveniles were involved in serious criminal activities such as murder or attempted murder, attempted rape, kidnapping and abduction, and other forms of violence against women. Girls, although in small number, were primarily involved in the theft-related offenses. They also committed serious offenses such as murder ($n=55$), grievous hurt ($n=51$), and rioting ($n=48$).

Over half (55.6%) of the juveniles came from families with an income of up to 25,000 (US$380), about one-fifth (22.4%) were from households with an income of 25,000–50,000, another one-fifth hailed from families whose income levels ranged from 50,000 to 200,000. Regarding the education of apprehended juveniles, 21.8% were illiterate, 31.1% had a primary-level education, and 36.6% had above a primary-level education but below high-school education (NCRB 2014).

The most common crimes registered under SLL were for violating specific Acts (in particular, the Prohibition Act, the Juvenile Justice Act, the Gambling Act, and the Exercise Act) as well as all other SLL crimes. The majority (90.8%) of these offenses were committed by males, while females were involved in fewer than 10% of SLL crimes. Also, the majority of them were in the 16–18-year age group for both genders (see Table 9.4).

TABLE 9.3. Juveniles apprehended under IPC by age group and gender during 2014

Crime head IPC crimes	*Below 12 years boys/girls*	*12 and below 16 years boys/ girls*	*16 and below 18 years boys/ girls*	*Total for all ages boys*	*Total for all ages girls*	*Total for all age groups boys and girls*
Murder	14/5	291/9	803/41	1108	55	1163
Attempt to commit murder	6/0	213/4	793/13	1012	17	1029
C.H. not amount to murder*	1/0	18/1	43/4	62	5	67
Attempt to commit C.H.	1/0	15/1	61/0	77	1	78
Rape	23/0	632/1	1484/4	2139	5	2144
Attempt to commit rape	0/0	25/0	72/0	97	0	97
Kidnapping	7/0	283/7	1626/9	1916	16	1932
*Dacoity***	4/0	47/1	227/0	278	1	279
Preparation of dacoity	0/0	21/0	105/0	126	0	126
Robbery	7/0	339/0	1052/3	1398	3	1401
Burglary/ trespass	83/0	1254/14	2436/15	3773	29	3802
Theft (including auto)	237/12	2505/52	6012/45	8754	109	8863
Unlawful assembly	2/1	24/2	102/7	128	10	138
Riots	6/2	318/15	1702/31	2076	48	2074
Criminal breach of trust	0/0	5/0	62/1	67	1	68
Cheating	0/1	35/1	711/6	746	8	754
Forgery	0/0	1/0	20/0	21	0	21
Counterfeiting	1/0	10/0	25/0	36	0	36
Arson	1/0	13/0	58/2	72	2	74
Grievous hurt	28/3	404/12	1489/150	1921	51	1969
Dowry death	0/0	7/5	31/4	38	9	47
Assault on women outrage her modesty	20/0	360/0	1389/3	1769	3	1772
Insult to the modesty of women (sexual harassment)	0/0	27/0	117/0	144	0	144

(continued)

TABLE 9.3. (continued)

Crime head IPC crimes	*Below 12 years boys/girls*	*12 and below 16 years boys/ girls*	*16 and below 18 years boys/ girls*	*Total for all ages boys*	*Total for all ages girls*	*Total for all age groups boys and girls*
Cruelty by husband or relative	3/0	24/2	188/4	215	6	221
Causing death by negligence	0/0	50/0	512/3	562	3	565
Promoting enmity	0/0	1/0	0/0	1	0	1
Extortion	1/0	10/0	103/1	114	1	115
Reckless driving	5/0	149/5	1312/17	1466	22	1488
Human trafficking	0/0	1/2	4/3	5	5	10
Unnatural offenses	10/0	67/0	100/0	177	0	177
Other IPC crimes	159/25	3109/142	7979/494	11,427	661	11,908
Total cognizable crimes under IPC	619/49	10,258/276	30,618/746	41,495	1071	42,566

NB: * *C.H.*, culpable homicide; ** *Dacoity*, gang robbery
Source: NCRB (2014), *Crime in India*. New Delhi: Government of India

TABLE 9.4. Juveniles apprehended under SLL by age groups and gender during 2014

Crime head SLL crimes	*7–12 years boys/girls*	*12–16 years boys/girls*	*16–18 years boys/girls*	*Total for all ages boys*	*Total for all ages girls*	*Total age groups boys and girls*
Arms Act	2/0	41/0	134/0	177	0	177
Narcotic Drugs and Psychotropic Substances Act	2/0	28/2	114/1	144	3	147
Gambling Act	1/0	44/0	448/1	493	1	494
Excise Act	1/0	22/1	380/2	403	3	406
Prohibition Act	0/0	13/0	1655/420	1668	420	2088
Explosives and Explosive Substances Act	0/0	2/0	46/0	48	0	48

(continued)

Table 9.3. (continued)

Crime head SLL crimes	*7–12 years boys/girls*	*12–16 years boys/girls*	*16–18 years boys/girls*	*Total for all ages boys*	*Total for all ages girls*	*Total age groups boys and girls*
Immoral Traffic Act	0/0	2/1	15/2	17	3	20
Indian Railways Act	4/0	2/0	0/0	6	0	6
Registration of Foreigners Act	0/0	0/0	1/1	1	1	2
Indian Passport Act	0/0	1/1	2/1	3	2	5
Essential Commodities Act	0/0	0/0	127/0	127	0	127
Dowry Prohibition Act	0/0	2/0	15/0	17	0	17
Copyright Act	0/0	0/0	7/0	7	0	7
SC/ST (Prevention of Atrocities) Act	0/1	20/1	69/0	89	2	91
Forest Act	0/0	0/0	4/0	4	0	4
Prohibition of Child Marriage Act	0/0	1/0	6/0	7	0	7
Information Technology Act	2/0	7/0	21/0	30	0	30
Electricity Act, 2003	0/0	5/0	41/0	46	0	46
Wildlife Protection Act	0/0	0/0	2/0	2	0	2
Environmental Protection Act	0/0	0/0	5/0	5	0	5
Air (Pollution and Control) Act	0/0	0/0	2/0	2	0	2
Unlawful Activities Act	1/0	2/0	1/0	4	0	4
Prevention of Damage to Public Property Act	0/0	4/0	13/0	17	0	18
Foreigners Act	4/3	17/1	8/3	29	7	36
Juvenile Justice Act	147/28	279/27	35/5	461	60	521
Representation of People Act	0/0	0/0	1/0	1	0	1
Other SLL crimes	8/0	156/4	1170/14	1334	18	1352
Maritime Zones Act	0/0	0/0	1/0	1	0	1
Total cognizable SLL crimes	172/32	648/38	4323/451	5143	521	5664

Source: NCRB (2014), *Crime in India*. New Delhi, India: Government of India

CAUSES OF JUVENILE CRIME

Compared to many developed and developing counties, delinquency and youth crime in India are relatively small (Hartjen and Kethineni 1996). Although children make up over 400 million of the billion plus population in India, they represent less than 4% of the total crimes reported to the police. Family factors, peer influence, and individual factors were found to be contributing factors for delinquency. Sahmey (2013) found that 90% of juveniles involved with the juvenile justice system came from families where parents were illiterates with an average monthly income of 4000–5000 (US$60). The study also reported the influence of the peer group as a salient factor for delinquency. Similar to youth in the United States, Indian youth heavily involved with peers tend to engage in delinquency behaviors (Hartjen and Kethineni 1996). Others have reported a lack of family control, neglect, poverty, and exposure to media violence as contributing factors for delinquency (Haveripet 2013).

THE JUVENILE JUSTICE SYSTEM IN INDIA

Before India's independence, a few states had enacted legislation applicable to children. Three states—Madras (now Chennai), Bengal, and Bombay (now Mumbai)—passed the children's acts in the form of Madras Children's Act (1920), Bengal Children's Act (1922), and Bombay Children's Act (1924). These acts lacked uniformity regarding court jurisdiction, procedure, or sanctioning of juveniles. After India's independence in 1947, the central government enacted the Children's Act (1960) for the protection and care of children in union territories that were directly under the central government rule. By 1980, many states had enacted juvenile laws, yet procedures and treatment of juveniles varied from state to state. Although national-level discussions for uniformity in juvenile legislation was occurring, a public-interest suit filed in the Supreme Court of India by a social worker and freelance journalist, Sheela Barse, changed the face of juvenile justice in India. In *Sheela Barse v. Union of India* (1986), the petitioner challenged the detention of 1400 physically and mentally challenged children as well as children who were abandoned or destitute in adult jails. The Court noted delays in prosecution and directed state governments to take necessary steps to set up a sufficient number of courts and trained judges to expedite the process. The Court further ordered the establishment of necessary remand and observation homes (i.e., pretrial detention centers for those accused of committing a crime) and created a uniform application of laws by enacting a national legislation (Kumari 2004).

In 1986, the Juvenile Justice Bill was introduced in Parliament in conformity with "the United Nations Standard Minimum Rules for the Administration of Juvenile Justice, an international obligation that India had agreed to abide by" (Kethineni and Braithwaite 2014: 309). The same year, the Juvenile Justice Act

(JJA) was passed for the care, protection, treatment, development, and rehabilitation of neglected and dependent children as well as those accused of committing delinquent acts. Child-friendly terminology, similar to the 1960 Children's Act, was introduced. The JJA also established separate structures, procedures, and institutions to handle neglected and dependent children as one group and delinquents as another. Juvenile courts were set up for those accused of committing crimes, and welfare boards have been established to deal with neglected and dependent children (Kethineni and Klosky 2000).

THE JUVENILE JUSTICE (CARE AND PROTECTION OF CHILDREN) ACT OF 2000

The Juvenile Justice (Care and Protection of Children) Act (JJCPA) was passed in 2000, and it continues to emphasize the welfare model, focusing on protecting children and providing care, rehabilitation, education, and vocational training. Additional features included replacing the word "delinquent juvenile" with the term "juvenile in conflict with law" and "neglected juvenile" with the term "child in need of care and protection." The term "arrest" was replaced with "apprehension" (Gupta 2015) to avoid any stigma attached to those words. Further, the term "juvenile courts" was replaced with "Juvenile Justice Boards" (JJBs) and "juvenile welfare boards" (JWBs) was replaced with "Child Welfare Committees" (CWCs). The Act also included a provision for adoption based on the child's consent, removed gender and age discrimination regarding court jurisdiction (below 18 years for both boys and girls), emphasized rehabilitation and resocialization of children in conflict with the law, and recommended minimal formal intervention by the police and correctional authorities.

The JJCPA allowed greater involvement of voluntary organizations in the juvenile justice process by enabling them to compile social investigation reports and run observation homes, juvenile homes, children's homes, and shelter homes (Srinivasan 2010). For the first time, the JJCPA recognized the need to create a special home (for children in conflict with the law) for different age groups—girls above age 10 and boys 11–15 and 16–18 years—for the purpose of keeping younger juveniles separate from more mature juveniles (Kethineni and Braithwaite 2014: 314). Furthermore, special homes that house adjudicated juveniles have to meet the UN Standard Minimum Rules for the Administration of Juvenile Justice (Chakraborty, n.d.).

Amendments to JJCPA. The JJCPA has been amended in 2006, 2011, and 2015. The 2006 amendment clarified the definitions of "adoption," "adoptive parents," and "child in need of care and protection." For example, a child in need of care and protection includes children who are begging, street children, or working children without a home or any other means of support. It also clearly stipulates that each state government may constitute a JJB in each district within one year from the date of the commencement of the Amendment Act. Also, the bill mandated the creation of state and district-level child protection units. These units are obligated to monitor the implementation of the Act.

The 2011 amendment was specifically geared toward juveniles or children who are mentally ill or addicted to alcohol or drugs held in special homes, observation homes, children's homes, or shelters. If children show behavioral changes due to their addiction or illness, such children may be sent to a psychiatric hospital or psychiatric nursing home in accordance with the Mental Health Act (1987). Furthermore, after the children were discharged from these facilities, the state government may send these children to an integrated rehabilitation center for addicts or an inpatient treatment center (for mentally ill children only; Bhasin 2011).

The 2015 amendment, which came into force in January 2016, incorporated significant changes to the existing legislation. The provisions include providing proper training for police assigned to the juvenile unit; trying older juveniles (16–18 years old) as adults for committing heinous offenses; creating JJBs and CWCs in every district (i.e., county); expanding aftercare services; instituting guidelines for adoption and adoptive parents; and introducing foster care for children who are abandoned, orphaned, or in conflict with the law. Also, the Act has emphasized fundamental principles such as presumption of innocence, best interest of the child, equality and nondiscrimination, procedural justice, right to dignity and worth, right to be heard and to participate in all proceedings, right to privacy and confidentiality, promoting well-being of the child, and use of institutionalizating as a last resort (The Gazette of India 2016).

POLICING AND THE JJCPA

The JJCPA mandated that each state was to set up Special Juvenile Police Units (SJPU) in every district and city to coordinate various aspects of the police–juvenile interface. In every police station, at least one police officer should be designated as "juvenile" or "child welfare" officer. These officers are members of SJPU. Each unit must have two paid social workers. The central government provides financial assistance to state governments to set up these units (Chakraborty, n.d.).

If the juvenile was brought before the JJB by persons or agencies other than SJPU, they must inform the concerned police station or SJPU. The apprehended juvenile must be brought before JJB within 24 h. If the Board was not in session, the juvenile could be presented before a single member of the Board. At that time, the SJPU or the police must provide details about the case, including what were the reasons for the arrest, whether the juvenile was kept in police lockup or jail, and whether parents or guardians were notified about the juvenile's arrest. If a juvenile was not released on bail, he or she should be kept in an observation home until he or she can be brought before the Board (Adenwalla 2006). With the best interest of the child as its priority, the JJB ensures that the SJPU also "promote[s] the well-being of the juvenile and avoid harm to her or him" ("the Beijing Rules") (United Nations General Assembly 1985: 64).

As stated above, more than 65% of the children detained were apprehended for "theft" in 2014. (The commission of theft by such a large percentage of children is obviously due to poor economic conditions.) Such underprivileged children have to undergo many hardships at the hands of the agencies of the juvenile justice system, including the police. Despite what the JJCPA establishes, the findings of a study conducted by Srinivasan (2010) determined that the police physically and verbally abused more than 60% of the children after their apprehension. It should also be noted that a vast majority of children were kept in a police station between 1 and 5 days. Moreover, none of the children was allowed to meet with probation officers or lawyers at the police station. As stated earlier, practices such as detaining the children in a police station, physically or verbally abusing them, or not allowing them to meet with probation officers or lawyers at the police station are a violation of procedures established by law. The practices adopted by the police are also in contravention of international standards and procedures.

Regarding the provision of bail for children in conflict with the law, more than 85% of the children said that they were not released on bail. According to Section 18(1) of JJA (1986):

> When any person accused of a bailable or non-bailable offense, and apparently a juvenile is arrested or detained or appears or is brought before a Board, such person shall, notwithstanding anything contained in the Code of Criminal Procedure, 1973 (2 of 1974) or in any other law for the time being in force, be released on bail with or without surety....

Given that this is the legal position, it is puzzling why children, particularly given that the majority was charged for the offense of theft, were not released on bail. It is a matter of concern.

To prevent police abuse of power, the 2015 JJCPA included provisions that allow the JJB to conduct an inquiry concerning any ill-treatment of the children by the police, or any other individuals dealing with children such as a lawyer or probation officer.

COURTS AND JUVENILES

Courts and Juveniles Under the JJA

Under the Juvenile Justice Act, each state was authorized to establish one or more juvenile courts represented by judicial or metropolitan magistrates to handle children in conflict with the law; one of the magistrates would serve as a principal magistrate. In addition to magistrates, each court had a panel with two social workers, one of whom had to be a woman (Kethineni and Klosky 2000). Magistrates were required to be knowledgeable in child psychology or child welfare.

Juvenile welfare boards (JWBs) were made up of a chairperson and other appointed members. Like the juvenile court, at least one of the board members was required to be a woman. Each member of the board has the powers of a metropolitan or judicial magistrate. Appeals from juvenile courts or Juvenile Justice Boards could be filed either in the Sessions Court[3] or the High Court.[4] Juveniles who were arrested or detained by the police were needed to be released on bail unless such a release was considered detrimental to the juvenile. Denial of bail could be appealed to the High Court.

Courts and Juveniles Under the JJCPA

A juvenile in conflict with law may be brought before any member of the JJB when the Board is not in session, provided at least two members, including the principal magistrate, are present at the final disposition of the case. Juveniles are entitled to procedural rights (e.g., bail), irrespective of the nature of the offense, and fair trials. If release on bail is likely to expose the juvenile to criminal elements or defeat the purpose of justice, the juvenile must be brought to the observation home or place of safety during the inquiry phase. Other rights include representation by an attorney of their choice, and, if the juvenile cannot afford one, access to free legal aid service is available. Also, information regarding juvenile arrest has to be sent to parents directing them to be present before the JJB. A probation officer compiles the social history information and assists the Board in conducting an inquiry. The investigation must be completed within 4 months unless exceptional circumstances warrant an extension, in which case reasons have to be documented.

According to the 2015 JJCPA, "a child in conflict with laws" is any child who is alleged or has committed an offense and who has not reached the age of 18 years at the time of the offense (The Gazette of India 2016). The Act expands the definition of "a child in need to care and protection." It includes children who are homeless, destitute, abused, victimized, neglected, runaways, mentally or physically challenged, and those suffering from terminal or incurable diseases and no one to take care of them (The Gazette of India 2016). The Act classifies offense into "petty offenses" (maximum imprisonment is up to 3 years), "serious offenses" (incarceration from 3 to 7 years), and "heinous offenses" (incarceration 7 or more years). When a child in conflict with the law is brought before the Board, the Board conducts the preliminary inquiry. If it is a petty offense, the Board uses summary procedures. If a child under the age of 18 years commits a

[3]The Sessions Court deals with criminal cases at the district (county) level.

[4]The High Court is the highest court at the state level and it has both original and appellate jurisdiction.

serious offense or a child under the age of 16 years commits a heinous crime, the Board uses the summons proceedings where the Board issues summons for the accused to attend. For a child above the age of 16 years and commits a heinous crime, the Board has the option to transfer the case to be tried as an adult in the Children's Court, which has the jurisdiction over such cases.

With a few exceptions, any aggrieved party may appeal the orders passed by the CWC or the Board to the Children's Court; however, if the appeal is against the order of the Board involving a heinous offense, it can be filed with the Court of Session. An order of the Children's Court involving a heinous case may be appealed to the High Court. The High Court may order the CWC or the Board to amend the order.

Concerning a "child in need of care and protection," the state government may appoint a Child Welfare Committee (CWC). The Committee is made up of a chairperson and four members, of which at least one member shall be a woman and another must be an expert on child welfare. Both public and private agencies (e.g., law enforcement, social services, or any registered volunteer organizations) may bring a child before the Committee. A child by him- or herself may appear before the Committee. Like the JJB, the CWC must complete the inquiry within 4 months unless special circumstances require an extension. Upon completion of the investigation, if the Committee finds that the child has no family or means of support, they refer the child to the children's home or shelter facility until proper rehabilitation is available or the child reaches the age of majority (i.e., 18 years).

CUSTODIAL SANCTIONS FOR JUVENILES

Custodial Sanctions for Juveniles Under the JJA

Given the welfare approach to the treatment of juveniles, separate types of institutions were created: *observation homes* (pretrial detention centers), *special homes* (facilities for adjudicated delinquents), and *juvenile homes* (residences for neglected children). If juveniles were not released on bail, the arresting officer or the juvenile court would refer them to an observation home (Menon 1990). The observation homes were also used to house neglected and dependent children before a final determination by the JWB.

Upon being adjudicated as delinquent, the juvenile court could send the boys over 14 and girls over 16 to special homes for up to 3 years. The courts could not impose the capital punishment or a prison sentence. The courts, however, could commit older juveniles (14 years of age and above) who had committed serious offenses to be kept in safe custody (JJA 1986, Section 22[1]). Concerning neglected juveniles, a JWB could send a neglected child to a juvenile home until the child reached the age of majority. Aftercare services were available to those who were not under any court or formal supervision, such as accommodation and skill training for possible employment (Janeksela 1991).

Rehabilitation and reintegration for all children shall begin during the length of stay in either the special home or the children's home. Reintegration is carried out through adoption, foster care, or sponsorship (i.e., supplemental support for families) or through aftercare organizations (The Gazette of India 2000).

Custodial Sanctions for Juveniles Under the JJCPA

Sanctions under JJCPA (2000) are similar to JJA, although there are a few exceptions. The Board may send a juvenile to a special home. If a juvenile is above 17 years of age but less than 18, the length of his or her stay in the special home should not be less than 2 years. In other cases, the stay continues until the juvenile ceases to be a juvenile (The Gazette of India 2000). However, if a juvenile is 16 years old or older and had committed a serious offense, the Board may place the juvenile in safe custody in a manner that it thinks fit. Juveniles cannot be given solitary confinement, corporal punishment, incarceration, or a death sentence.

The JJCPA (2015) has added additional custodial provisions for children transferred to adult court for committing heinous offenses. The Children's Court, with jurisdiction over such cases, orders the child to serve his/her sentence in a "place of safety" until the age of 21 years. The reminder of the sentence is served in a jail. However, the Children's Court may release the child on conditions after assessing the evaluations provided by the probation officer or the District Child Protection Unit or a social worker (The Gazette of India 2016).

Under the JJCPA (2015), the CWC may place the child in need of care and protection in a children's home until the child reaches the age of majority or foster care or adoption agency. Aftercare services are available to those who are not under any court or formal supervision, such as temporary accommodation and skill training for possible employment (Janeksela 1991). Rehabilitation and reintegration for all children shall begin during the length of stay in either the special home or the children's home. Reintegration is carried out through adoption, foster care, or sponsorship (i.e., supplemental support for families) or through aftercare organizations (The Gazette of India 2000). Children receive medical care, psychiatric and psychological support and counseling, occupational therapy, skill training, legal aid, educational services, etc. (The Gazette of India 2016).

ALTERNATIVE SANCTIONS FOR JUVENILES UNDER THE JJA AND JJCPA

Under the JJA, the JJB may allow the juvenile in conflict with the law to go home after he or she was admonished, or it may order payment of a fine if the juvenile was 14 years of age and earns money. Otherwise, his or her parents or guardians will be ordered to pay the fine. Less punitive sanctions include participation in group counseling and community service.

The 2015 JJCPA has allowed the Board to pass the following orders:

(1) Release the child after admonition after advice of the child and his/her parents.
(2) Direct the child and his/her parents to participate group in counseling.
(3) Order the child or parents to pay fine.
(4) Order the child to perform community service.
(5) Order the child to be released on probation and under the care and supervision of a parent or guardian or a "fit" facility.
(6) Order the child to attend school, vocational training, and therapy.
(7) Order the child to attend de-addiction program (The Gazette of India 2016).

DIFFERENCES IN TREATMENT OF BOYS AND GIRLS

Comparison of official statistics from 2004–2014 clearly indicates that boys were arrested more frequently than girls at all age categories (see Table 9.3). Violent crimes such as murder, rape, and robbery were within the purview of boys at every age group. Older boys were also involved in riots due to their increased political activism (Hartjen and Kethineni 1996; National Crime Records Bureau (NCRB) 2014). Similar to boys, girls were arrested in higher numbers for theft and prohibition offenses, although the figures were not substantial for girls. Despite their low levels of criminal activity, the JJA extended the juvenile court jurisdiction to girls until the age of 18, while limiting the jurisdiction to boys until the age of 16. Girls were often given fewer resources than boys. Also, families prefer boys to girls: "investment in boys might have larger returns…; boys might be seen as needing more resources…" (Barcellos et al. 2010: 4). Due to cultural discrimination of girls, both governmental and nongovernmental programs were developed to empower girls from rural and economically and socially deprived families. These programs focus on "creating social-awareness, building positive self-esteem, learning life skills, and developing academic skills" for girls (Saraswathi and Larson 2002: 354). Also, child activists campaigned to increase the age of boys under the juvenile court jurisdiction in par with the girls. In conformity with CRC, the government of India passed the JJCPA 2000 prescribing a uniform age of 18 for both boys and girls.

DISCUSSION

Compared to many Western countries, juvenile justice reforms in India have been slow. However, significant strides have been made in enacting various child-friendly laws. Most importantly, the JJA (1986) and JJCPA (2000) have developed child-friendly policies, judicial infrastructure, and institutions to house children in need of care and protection as well as juveniles in conflict with the law. In 2000, the JJA was replaced with the JJCPA due to criticisms that the JJA lacked many of the provisions enumerated in the CRC. Also, the JJA failed to incorporate the standard definition of "juvenile" (boys under age 16; girls under 18 years old) and did not make procedural rights (e.g., appellate review of juveniles placed in observation homes and right to an attorney in neglected cases) available (Van Bueren 1999).

Both the JJA and the JJCPA represent a modified justice model; they contain elements of welfare and justice principles (Chakraborty, n.d.). Also, any violations of the provisions of the CRC can be invoked before the courts or entities with judicial powers (Srivastava 2004). More important, children's activists, nongovernmental organizations, and the Indian Supreme Court have played significant roles in upholding children's rights. The JJCPA brought children who faced social and economic deprivation within its protective jurisdiction (Kumari 2004). Despite these developments, access to justice for many poor children remains problematic. The National Human Rights Commission in India documented various forms of violations of child rights, including inadequate enforcement of child labor laws, child trafficking, and various forms of violence against children (National Human Rights Commission 2006). Although some states have successfully implemented laws protecting the rights of children, others have either ignored children or do not have the infrastructure, funds, or the necessary training.

Changing public opinion also shapes the future of the juvenile justice system. For example, a case in 2012 prompted public outcry over the lenient treatment of juveniles who commit heinous crimes. The involvement of a 17-year-old juvenile in the brutal rape of a 23-year-old college student, Jyoti Singh, in New Delhi turned public opinion against the JJCPA (2000). The young woman was brutally gang-raped and left to die by six men, including the 17-year-old adolescent. The 17-year-old was tried as a juvenile and received a three-year sentence, which was to be served in the special home. Following this incident, a new bill—the Juvenile Justice (Care and Protection of Children) Bill (2014)—was introduced in the Parliament which lowered the age of juveniles who can be tried as adults from 18 to 16 years if charged with heinous crimes such as murder, rape, and dacoity. The Bill also stipulates that 16–18-year-olds can be tried as adults for committing serious offenses if they are apprehended after they reach the age of 21 years.

Opponents of this bill argue that such a law violates the CRC's prohibition of trying a juvenile under the age of 18 as an adult. Further, treating juveniles who commit serious crimes as adults based on the date of apprehension violates Article 14 (right to equality) and Article 21 (requiring fair and reasonable procedures) of the Indian Constitution (PRS Legislative Research 2015). They further argue "that the 16–18 years is a tender and critical age requiring greater protection" (p. 2). Proponents of this bill, however, argue that there are several safeguards in place, such as allowing the Board to decide whether a juvenile over 16 years should be tried as an adult. If the court convicts the juvenile, the order must contain a rehabilitation plan. Once the juvenile is found to be in conflict with the law, he or she will stay in the special home until the age of 21, at which point he or she will be transferred to an adult jail. The bill was passed into law [the Juvenile Justice (Care and Protection of Children) Act 2015] and will be enforceable starting from January 15, 2016. Time will tell if the punitive nature of this legislation will affect how the public, police, and the judiciary perceive juveniles.

REFERENCES

Adenwalla, M. (2006). *Child protection and juvenile justice system for juvenile in conflict with law*. Mumbai: Childline India Foundation.

Barcellos, S. H., Carvalho, L., & Lleras-muney, A. (2010). *Working paper: Child gender and investments in India*. Rand Labor and Population. Retrieved May 18, 2016, from https://www.rand.org/content/dam/rand/pubs/working_papers/2010/RAND_WR756.pdf.

Bhasin, V. K. (2011, September). *The Juvenile Justice (Care and Protection of Children) Amendment Act, 2011*. Retrieved from http://megpolice.gov.in/acts/central/juvenile_justice_care-protection_children_amendment_act_2011.pdf.

Bhattacharya, S., & Bhattacharya, S. (2015). Human rights violations of children in India: An overview. *International Journal of Child Adolescent Heath, 8*(1), 51–70.

Bullis, R. K. (1991). The conventions on the rights of the child: A young legal regime for the world's youngest citizens. *Child & Adolescent Social Work Journal, 8*(3), 239–251.

Census of India. (2011). *The Government of India, Ministry of Home Affairs*. Retrieved December 1, 2015, from http://www.censusindia.gov.in/pca/Searchdata.aspx.

Chakraborty, T. (n.d.). *Juvenile justice in India*. New Delhi, India: Institute of Social Sciences.

Gupta, N. K. (2015). The guardian state and the child: Juvenile justice system in India. *International Journal of Advanced Research in Management and Social Sciences, 4*(4), 261–270.

Hartjen, C., & Kethineni, S. (1996). *Comparative delinquency in India and the United States*. New York: Garland.

Haveripet, P. (2013). Causes and consequences of juvenile delinquency in India. *Recent Research in Science and Technology, 5*(3), 29–31.

Janeksela, G. (1991). Descriptive analysis of five juvenile justice systems: United States, Scotland, England, India, and South Africa. *International Review of Modern Sociology, 21*, 1–19.

Juvenile Justice (Care and Protection of Children) Act. (2000). Retrieved February 15, 2011, from http://www.law.yale.edu/rcw/rcw/jurisdictions/assc/india/India_Juv_Just.pdf.

Juvenile Justice (Care and Protection of Children) Amendment Act, 2006 (No. 33 of 2006). Retrieved December 10, 2015, from https://www.childlineindia.org.in/CP-CR-Downloads/JJAct2006.pdf.

Juvenile Justice (Care and Protection of Children) Act. (2015). Ministry of Women & Child Development. Retrieved December 5, 2016, from http://wcd.nic.in/acts/juvenile-justice-care-and-protection-children-act-2015.

Juvenile Justice Act (JJA). (1986). *Introduction*. Retrieved October 21, 2010, from http://www.vakilno1.com/bareacts/juvenilejusticeact/juvenilejusticeact.htm.

Kethineni, S., & Braithwaite, J. (2014). Toward a compliance model: The Indian Supreme Court and the attempted revolution in child rights. In N. P. Unnithan (Ed.), *Crime and justice in India* (pp. 300–325). Thousand Oaks, CA: Sage.

Kethineni, S., & Klosky, T. (2000). The impact of juvenile justice reforms in India. *International Journal of Offender Therapy and Comparative Criminology, 44*(3), 312–325.

Kumari, V. (2004). *The juvenile justice system in India: From welfare to rights*. New Delhi: Oxford University Press.

Menon, M. N. R. (1990). *The rights of the child: Law, policy and enforcement*. A background paper prepared for the National Law School of India University, Bangalore, India.

Ministry of Home Affairs. (2015, July 22). *Children missing from Delhi*. Retrieved from http://mha1.nic.in/par2013/par2015-pdfs/rs-220715/202.pdf.

National Crime Records Bureau (NCRB). (2014). *Crime in 2014*. The Government of India, Ministry of Home Affairs. Retrieved from http://www.ncrb.gov.in/.

National Human Rights Commission. (2006, July). *Annual report 2004–2005*. New Delhi, India. Retrieved from http://nhrc.nic.in/Documents/AR/AR04-05ENG.pdf.

Office of the United Nations High Commissioner for Human Rights. (1985). *United Nations standard minimum rules for the administration of juvenile justice ("The Beijing Rules") (1985)*. Retrieved February 15, 2011, from http://www2.ohchr.org/english/law/pdf/beijingrules.pdf.

Office of the United Nations High Commissioner for Human Rights. (1990). *United Nations Rules for the protection of juveniles deprived of their liberty (1990)*. Retrieved December 15, 2015, from http://www.un.org/documents/ga/res/45/a45r113.htm.

Office of the United Nations High Commissioner for Human Rights. (2011). *Convention on the Rights of the Child*. Retrieved February 20, 2011, from http://www2.ohchr.org/english/law/crc.htm.

Prohibition of Child Marriage Act. (2006). NO. 6 of 2007 [10th January 2007]. Retrieved December 5, 2015, from http://www.hsph.harvard.edu/population/trafficking/india.childmar.07.pdf.

PRS Legislative Research. (2015).

Sahmey, K. (2013). *A study on factors underlying juvenile delinquency and positive youth development programs*. Odisha, India: Department of Humanities and Social Sciences, National Institute of Technology Rourkela. Retrieved June 1, 2016, from http://ethesis.nitrkl.ac.in/4634/1/411HS1010.pdf.

Saraswathi, T. S., & Larson, R. W. (2002). Adolescence in global perspective: An agenda for social policy. In B. B. Brown, R. W. Reed, & T. S. Saraswathi (Eds.), *The World's youth: Adolescents in eight regions of the globe* (pp. 344–362). New York: Cambridge University Press.

Sharma, D. (2014). The Juvenile Justice (Care and Protection of Children) Act, 2000: Protection, rehabilitation, and reform. In N. P. Unnithan (Ed.), *Crime and justice in India* (pp. 389–403). Thousand Oaks, CA: Sage.

Sharma, P. C. (n.d.). *Report of the NHRC Committee on missing children*. Retrieved December 5, 2015, from https://childlineindia.org.in/CP-CR-Downloads/Missing%20Child%20report%20NHRC.pdf.

Sheela Barse v. *Union of India,* (1986) 3 SCC (Cri) 352; 1986 Cri LJ 1736 (SC).

Srinivasan, M. (2010). *Existing mechanisms to ensure child participation: An assessment in the State of Tamil Nadu*. Chennai: United Nations Children's Fund.

Srivastava, N. (2004). The status of the child in India in the context of the Convention on the Rights of the Child. *Social Change, 34*(3), 113–124.

The Child Labor (Prohibition and Regulation) Act. (1986). Retrieved December 20, 2015, from http://bba.org.in/sites/default/files/Child%20Labour%20_Prohibition%20_%20Regulation_%20Act,%201986.pdf.

The Gazette of India. (2000, December 30). *The Juvenile Justice (Care and Protection of Children) Act, 2000 (Act No.56 of 2000)*. Ministry of Law, Justice and Company Affairs. Retrieved December 10, 2015, from http://khoyapaya.gov.in/mpp/resources/Juvenile%20Justice%20Act%202000.pdf.

The Gazette of India. (2016, January 16). *The Juvenile Justice (Care and Protection of Children) Act, 2015 (Act No.2 of 2016)*. Ministry of Law, Justice. Retrieved June 5, 2016, from http://wcd.nic.in/sites/default/files/JJ%20Act%2C%202015%20_0.pdf.

Tiwary, D. (2014, August 7). One lakh children go missing in India every year: Home ministry. *Times of India*. Retrieved December 2, 2015, from http://timesofindia.indiatimes.com/india/One-lakh-children-go-missing-in-India-every-year-Home-ministry/articleshow/39779841.cms.

UNICEF. (1979). *The year of the child.* Retrieved May 10, 2016, from http://www.unicef.org/about/history/files/Child-Nation-M-Black-Ch15-p353-377-year-or-child.pdf.

UNICEF. (2004). *The state of the world's children—2005*. New York: UNICEF House.

UNICEF. (2011a, May). *The situation of children in India: A profile*. New Delhi, India. United Nations Children's Fund. Retrieved December 5, 2015, from http://unicef.in/Uploads/Publications/Resources/pub_doc36.pdf.
UNICEF. (2011b). *Convention on the Rights of the Child.* Retrieved February 19, 2011, from http://www.unicef.org/crc/index_30229.html.
United Nations General Assembly (1985). *United Nations standard minimum rules for the administration of juvenile justice ("The Beijing Rules") resolution.* A/RES/40/33, Retrieved October 14, 2010, http://www.unhcr.org/refworld/docid/3b00f2203c.html
United Nations Treaty Collection. (2011). *Chapter IV: Human rights, Convention on the Rights of the Child.* Retrieved February 19, 2011, from http://treaties.un.org/Pages/ViewDetails.aspx?src=TREATY&mtdsg_no=IV-11&chapter=4&lang=en.
Van Bueren, G. (1999). *Childhood abused: Protecting children against torture, cruel, inhuman, and degrading treatment and punishment*. London: Ashgate.
Van Bueren, G., & Tootell, A. M. (2007). *United Nations standard minimum rules for the administration of juvenile justice (Beijing Rules)*. Retrieved February 15, 2001, from http://www.child.abuse.com/childhouse/children_rights/dci_be29.html.

Sesha Kethineni Department of Justice Studies at Prairie View A&M University in fall 2015 and currently serving as the department head. She comes from Illinois State University (ISU) after serving for over 25 years; she received her M.A. from the University of Madras, India; M.C.J. from the University of South Carolina; Ph.D. from Rutgers, The State University of New Jersey, in 1991; and LL.M. from the University of Illinois in 2005. She was promoted to full professor in 2001 and received the College of Applied Science and Technology's (ISU) Outstanding Researcher Award (2002) and the University (ISU) Outstanding Researcher of the Year Award (2010). Her professional contributions are as follows: consultant of McLean County Court Services, Vermilion County Probation and Court Services, and other criminal justice agencies and publication in professional journals (23), books (2), book chapters (10), and conference presentations (over 40). Her recent works include evaluation of the Redeploy Illinois program (funded $110,000), comparative juvenile justice, domestic violence, international criminal justice, and human rights. She served as the chair of the International Division of the American Society of Criminology (2013–2015).

10

Japan

Jae Joon Chung

INTRODUCTION

Japan has one of the lowest crime rates in the world, with a stable criminal index, including incarceration rates. The total number of reported Penal Code cases has been stable for the last three decades, with recent declines. However, the number of arrested juveniles per 100,000 is at least 2.5 times (and a maximum of 5 times) of the number of the arrested adults per 100,000. To further elaborate, the proportion of the crime rate attributable to juveniles is relatively higher (20–45% of the all arrested offenders) than in neighboring countries (South Korea and China), where this proportion is under 10%. For this reason, Japanese juvenile justice (and the subject of juvenile criminality) is of considerable interest to juvenile justice experts. This chapter focuses on the peculiar characteristics of Japanese juvenile crimes by analyzing the historical context of Japanese juvenile crime, juvenile crime statistics for in recent years, the institutional juvenile justice system, and recent juvenile justice trends.

CONTEXT FOR UNDERSTANDING POLICY

Historical Context

Japan first wrote articles about juvenile justice in the "OmiRyoWoo (Ancient Law Books)" in 1668, and the first juvenile reformatory was formed by the private sector in Osaka in 1884 with the stated purpose of protecting juvenile offenders. The reformatory movements in Europe and the United States affected the way in which the Japanese reformatory establishment instituted this reform. Juvenile reformatories had been formed in each Japanese administrative district

J.J. Chung (✉)
Shandong University School of Law, 5 Hongjialo street, Jinan,
Shandong 250100, People's Republic of China
e-mail: heisjjj@sdu.edu.cn

S.H. Decker, N. Marteache (eds.), *International Handbook of Juvenile Justice*,
DOI 10.1007/978-3-319-45090-2_10

by 1911; however, these facilities did not adequately protect juvenile offenders and had many defects with regard to the methods of protection. During the world economic crises that ensued after World War I, the number of juvenile offenders rapidly increased. Under these circumstances, the laws related to juvenile justice being applied in the United States and other foreign countries were introduced in Japan. The Law Inspection Committee accepted the responsibility of making special laws for juveniles after 1911. Considerable debate occurred concerning the content of these laws, but the committee persisted, preparing a draft entitled "Juvenile Law." The Juvenile Law and the Juvenile Reformatory Law were finally formed in 1922. The first juvenile training school was established in 1923; the first juvenile classification home, designed to work with families to help diagnose the issues that juveniles who broke the law faced and form a corrective course of action, was established in 1949.

The original Juvenile Law of Japan announced in 1922 already included articles to protect juvenile offenders in the spirit of education (Morita 2002). Nevertheless, the *Parens Patriae* doctrine was not completely assumed as the model for Japanese Juvenile Law. In the early twentieth century, Japanese legislators, while sympathetic toward the American doctrine of protection, were also critical of its views. In Japan's eyes, the notion behind the *Parens Patriae*, that no child younger than 18 could be held criminally accountable, was too simplistic. Practitioners of this system at the time characterized its spirit as "the strict-father, tender-mother approach." It is fair to say that it achieved its dual aim. The American occupation of Japan after World War II by the General Headquarters (GHQ)/Supreme Commander of the Allied Powers displayed a bold initiative in the legal and political reform of postwar Japan. The *Parens Patriae* doctrine was reaching its culmination in American juvenile courts at this time. A GHQ document from the same period, supporting the proposals of Burdett G. Lewis (chief administrator of the Supreme Commander of the Allied Powers), declared, "It is established that the Juvenile court is a chancery court with jurisdiction based on the doctrine of the *Parens Patriae*" (Morita 2002: 367).

After Japan was defeated in World War II, all Japanese laws and systems, including Constitutional Law, needed to be reconsidered and revised; the Juvenile Law of 1922 was no exception. The new draft of the Juvenile Law, which revised the Juvenile Law of 1922, was drawn up by the Protection Department in the Ministry of Justice. Burdett G. Lewis sent a four-point guideline to Japan's Ministry of Justice. He ordered a total revision of its Juvenile Law based on the Standard Juvenile Court Act. The changes would require the setting up of the Juvenile Court and rejected the prosecutor's prior-decision right that was codified in the juvenile justice system of the Juvenile Law of 1922 and was also in the current draft of the Juvenile Law that would supersede the 1922 original. Eventually, the new Japanese Juvenile Law was influenced by the ideology of US law, adopting into the juvenile justice system the judge's "prior decision right." However, the new Japanese Juvenile Law revised the Juvenile Law of 1922 and elected the Juvenile division of the Family Court instead of separate Juvenile

Court. Broadly speaking, juvenile justice systems had already been in place in the United States for half a century, and the Family Court and juvenile justice system of Japan were American initiatives during the occupation (Ryan 2005). Accordingly, the new Juvenile Law (passed in 1948) contained the purpose and overall ideals of the juvenile justice system of the United States.

This Juvenile Law had, by and large, four characteristics that differentiated it from the Juvenile Law of 1922. First, the definition of a juvenile was broadened to include those younger than 20 years old. Secondly, the ability of prosecutors to decide whether to refer juveniles to the Juvenile Court or Family Court was abolished. Prosecutors are now required to transfer all juvenile suspects to Family Court, even when detention is necessary. Third, a juvenile suspect could be referred back to prosecutors if a Family Court judge concludes that the juvenile committed a serious crime and if the juvenile was at least 16 years old at the time of the trial; those younger than 16 years had to remain in Family Court. Lastly, during this period it was possible to detain the juvenile for 2 weeks, with a possible 2-week extension. During these detentions, juveniles were primarily kept in a Juvenile Detention and Classification Home (*shônenkanbetsusho*). The hearing was closed and informal (Ryan 2005). Thus, the philosophy and implementation of the original Juvenile Act were characterized by an emphasis on rehabilitation and on directing juveniles away from the criminal justice system.

The Legal Status of Juveniles

According to the Japanese Penal Code (article 41), 14 years is the minimum age for which one can be criminally responsible (Takahashi 2010a, b). This does not necessarily mean that those under 14 years of age do not have enough capacity to appreciate the nature and quality of (or wrongfulness of) their acts. Rather, 14 years of age is considered the minimum age at which a decision concerning the purpose of a criminal activity can be made according to criminal justice policy. Pursuant to this, no criminal responsibility can be attributed to those under the age of 14 years. Cases involving those aged 14–19 years are considered juvenile offenders. Prior to 2000, as a general rule, the Family Court refers cases to the public prosecutor when a juvenile over 16 years old has caused death by an act committed with criminal intent at the time of the offense. The revised Juvenile Law in 2000 lowered the minimum age of suspects for reverse referral from 16 to 14 years of age. In cases in which a person under 18 years old commits an offense, those crimes which could carry the death penalty or life imprisonment will be punished via lesser sentences (i.e., mitigated).

According to the Juvenile Law (article 2), persons younger than 20 years of age are legally considered juveniles; these juvenile cases go to Family Court (Article 41–42) (Nakayama 2011). The court subsequently determines the need to subject the juveniles in question to protective measures. The Juvenile Law states that juvenile cases should be, in principle, separated from adult cases in order to benefit the future development of juvenile offenders. Although there are exceptions, juveniles are criminally prosecuted when the case involves a certain punishment in response to a very serious offense.

Age of Majority (seems a little off track talking about voting rights, sexual/marriage rights)

Article 3 of Japanese Civil Law states that the age of majority is 20 years old. Other articles provide some reference points for what might be considered the age of majority by the law. Articles 731 and 737 of Civil Law state that the age of consent for marriage is eighteen (18) years for men and sixteen (16) years for women. Article 177 of the Penal Code places the age of consent for sexual activity at thirteen (13) years. Article 4 of the Child Welfare Act defines "child" as "anyone below eighteen (18) years of age." Measures for promoting child welfare have been implemented in accordance with the fundamental policy of the Act. Recent movements have advocated for lowering the ages for adulthood and for voting in Japan (Sato et al. 2008). On June 17, 2015, Japanese parliament passed a bill to lower the voting age from 20 to 18 years—the biggest reform of the nation's electoral laws in 70 years. The legislation will come into effect in time for next year's upper house election. The passage of the bill follows a law passed last year lowering the voting age to 18 years in 2018 for national referendums on the Constitution. In terms of passing a bill to lower the voting age from 20 to 18 years, the juvenile's age of the Juvenile Law has been recently considered again (Edit Committee for Children & Laws 2015). In Japan, the legal age for drinking alcohol and smoking is 20 years and the minimum driving age is 18 years.

Category of Juvenile Offenders as Subjects of the Jurisdiction

There are three categories of juvenile offenders in Japanese Family Court jurisdiction: "juvenile criminals" (*Hanzai Syounen*) who are juveniles 14 years old but younger than 20 years old who have committed a crime for which they can be arrested; "child offenders" (*Syokuhou Syounen*) who are under 14 years old and have violated laws and regulations in a criminal fashion; and "juveniles liable to commit a crime" (*Guhan Syounen*) identified as those who might be vulnerable to committing crimes in the future.

For the first category, *Hanzai Syounen*, Article 41 of the Penal Code stipulates that persons 14 years old and older are criminally accountable (Toshihiro 2015). It may be noted that Japan's Penal Code was established at the end of the nineteenth century using the model of Germany, which included a fixed age for criminal accountability. All juvenile criminals are referred to the Family Court by the police or public prosecutors. The Family Court judge implements the preventive and protective measures available to a juvenile criminal, yet the juvenile will be prosecuted at the ordinary criminal court if sent back by the Family Court. Punishment at the Criminal Court for juveniles under 18 years of age at the time of commission of an offense shall mitigate in the following two circumstances: (1) in case a juvenile is to be punished with the death penalty, life imprisonment shall be imposed; (2) in case a juvenile is to be punished with life imprisonment, imprisonment with or without work for a definite term may be imposed. In this case, the term of imprisonment imposed shall be neither less than 10 years nor more than 15 years. Furthermore, in case a juvenile is to be punished with imprisonment with or without work for a definite term with a maximum term of 3 years or more, the juvenile shall be given a sentence that prescribes the maximum and minimum imprisonment terms determined within the limit of said penalty; provided, however, that in case the juvenile is to be punished with imprisonment with the minimum term exceeding 5 years, the minimum term shall be reduced to 5 years.

The second category (*Syokuhou Syounen*) comprises all juveniles under 14 years of age who commit an act that would constitute a crime under the Penal Code for a person 14 or older. In this group, Criminal Procedure Law is not applicable during the evidence-gathering process on the part of the police and investigators, as committing a crime when under the age of 14 years does not constitute being able to engage in "the formation of the crime" (Takahashi 2010a, b). According to the Penal Code (Article 41), the minimum age of criminal responsibility is 14 years of age. Furthermore, the Juvenile Law does not contain any related codes. For this reason, the police may investigate child offenders on the basis of Article 2 of the Police Act and Article 1(1) of the Police Duties Execution Act, which are stipulated in duties that protect the lives, bodies, and property of individuals, prevent crime, and maintain public safety. Juveniles in this second category are initially placed in the custody of a Child Guidance Center provided for by the Child Welfare Act and set up by local governments. Child guidance centers employ casework methods. As a rule, compulsory placement of the child by a center is not allowed without parental consent. The center refers juveniles to the Family Court only when it concludes that they require protective measures by the court.

The third category includes juveniles who run away, incorrigible youth, and others for whom discipline in the home has failed. "Juveniles liable to commit a crime" (*Guhan Syounen*) have committed a minor offense that usually results in protective measures. A child is considered to be "liable" or inclined to commit a crime when any of the following reasons exist; these reasons reflect the personality and environment of the juvenile and increase the likelihood that the juvenile will commit a crime or violate laws and regulations of criminal nature in the future: (1) has a propensity not to submit to legitimate supervision by the custodian; (2) stays away from home without a justifiable reason; (3) associates with persons with a criminal nature or with immoral persons; frequents places of "ill repute"; and (4) has a propensity to engage in activities that hurt his or her own morals or the morals of others. There are three kinds of procedures for "the juveniles" after police investigation according to Article 2 of the Police Law. First, the juveniles under 14 years of age in this category shall be referred to the director of the Child Consultation Center (Toshihiro 2015). The Family Court may only subject a juvenile who is under 14 years of age to a hearing and decision when a prefectural governor or a child consultation center's director refers the juvenile to the Family Court. Second, the juveniles 14 years old and above (up to under 18 years of age) in this category shall be referred to the Family Court. However, the police or the Custodian of a juvenile in this case may directly notify the Child

Consultation Center of the juvenile if it is found to be appropriate to subject the juvenile to the measures under the Child Welfare Act in preference to direct referral or notification to the Family Court. Third, juveniles over 18 years old in this category, as a rule, shall be referred to the Family Court (Toshihiro 2015).

Even though "status offenders" (*Huryoukoui Syounen*) do not belong to the aforementioned categories of juvenile offenders, they remain subjects to juvenile justice. According to Article 2(6) of the Juvenile Police Acting Rule (National Safety Committee No. 20, 2002), the police, for the purpose of juveniles' sound development and preventing crimes, shall act in the capacities of "warning," "measuring," and "giving advice" to the status offenders. The status offenders handled by police officers numbered 731,174 juveniles in 2014. Status offenders have committed an act that would not be a crime if committed by an adult. Juvenile delinquency refers to antisocial or criminal acts performed by juveniles. Status offenses may include underage consumption of alcohol or tobacco, truancy, running away from home, or the general inability to be controlled by adults.

JAPAN'S STANCE TOWARD THE UN COMMITTEE ON THE RIGHTS OF THE CHILD

The Convention on the Rights of the Child is the most widely accepted human rights treaty; Japan signed it in 1990 and ratified it in 1994 (Toshio 2015). Even though the Ministry pointed out that it did not need to amend the related Japanese laws because the ideology of the UN Committee on the Rights of the Child would already coincide with the Japanese Constitutional Law and Fundamental Law on Education, the Japanese government practically amended the Child Abuse Prevention Law in 2004 and 2008, the Child Welfare Act in 2004 and 2008, the Penal Code in 2005, the Fundamental Law on Education in 2010, and promulgated the Act on Promotion of Development and Support for Children and Young People in 2010. The Japanese government submitted the third periodic report of Japan to the Committee on the Rights of the Child (UN Committee on the Rights of the Child 2010). Alternatively, the Japanese government revised the Juvenile Law in 2000 to strongly reinforce penalties in juvenile criminal cases (Ryan 2005). The second revision to the Juvenile Law shows that the "get tough" policy is gaining more support after the previous amendment in 2000 lowered the minimum age of suspects for reverse referral from 16 to 14 years old. The second revised Juvenile Law contains more "get-tough" content than ever. Hereinafter, the Juvenile Law constitutes an obstacle to the treatment of child offenders by a specialized juvenile court.

The "Recommendations of the Justice System Reform Council for a Justice System to Support Japan in the twenty-first century" report pointed out the need to promote juveniles' rights in the process of trial (Ikenaga 2005). Furthermore, the Committee on the Rights of the Child also pointed out the problems in juvenile justice in the Japanese second report (CRC/C/104/Add.2) in 2004 and the third report (CRC/C/JPN/3) in 2010; in particular, the area of juvenile justice would be still inconsistent with the principles and provisions of the Convention.

Japanese Juvenile Law has adopted a rather punitive approach and has restricted the rights and judicial guarantees of child offenders. Japan's stance toward the overall rights of the child strengthens efforts to promote for it, but it has a different stance toward child offenders. In Japan currently, the protection of society and victims of crime is considered more of a priority than are the rights of child offenders, particularly in light of the Juvenile Law.

CRIME TRENDS IN JUVENILE CRIME

Trends in Juvenile Crime during the Period 2004–2014

Japan has one of the lowest crime rates in the world. The total number of reported (non-traffic) Penal Code cases and the overall clearance rate of cases have been stable for the last three decades, with recent declines. The proportion of juvenile offenders arrested relative to all offenders, however, has interestingly been very high. As you can see Fig. 10.1a, even though the proportion of arrested juvenile offenders is just approximately 25%, the number of arrested juveniles per 100,000 is at least 250% (and a maximum of 500%) of the number of the arrested adults

Year	Arrested Juveniles	Rate per Population of Juveniles	Arrested Adults	Rate per Population of Adults
2004	155,051	1,209.3	254,437	246.6
2005	144,255	1,146.4	263,498	255.3
2006	131,623	1,058.8	271,794	261.6
2007	121,165	987.9	262,741	252.2
2008	108,592	894.5	249,076	238.7
2009	108,358	900.9	242,876	232.6
2010	103,627	864.7	237,056	227.5
2011	94,369	787.2	228,198	217.3
2012	79,430	666.5	221,901	211.5
2013	69,113	583.9	206,302	196.7
2014	60,251	514.2	203,200	193.8

Source: 1. Criminal Statistics of the National Police Agency (2005-2015).

2. The Statistics Bureau, Ministry of Internal Affairs and Communications (population data).

FIGURE 10.1. (**a**) The number of arrested juvenile offenders and rate per population (100,000) for non-traffic Penal Code offenses (2004–2014). (**b**) The number of arrested male and female juvenile offenders and the rate per population (100,000) for non-traffic Penal Code offenses (2004–2014). (**c**) The number of all types of arrested juvenile offenders for non-traffic Penal Code in Japan (2004–2014).

Year / Crime	2004	2005	2006	2007	2008	2009	2010	2011	2012	2013	2014
Total	155,051	144,255	131,623	121,825	109,088	108,920	104,175	94,859	79,965	69,545	60,733
Homicide	62	73	73	67	56	55	47	60	48	56	57
Robbery	1,301	1,172	912	814	752	739	591	625	643	573	490
Injury	6,996	6.927	6,683	6,372	5,902	5,551	5,671	5,553	5,714	5,343	4,670
Violent Crime	1,962	1,969	1,887	1,977	1,975	1,728	1,770	1,646	2,046	2,128	1,969
Larceny	90,347	91,409	74,582	69,611	64,141	67,073	64,751	59,382	47,740	41,390	36,147
Fraud	1,106	1,062	1,224	1,144	1,104	1,133	962	947	919	842	908
Threat embezzlement	3,542	3,141	2,569	2,077	1,900	1,564	1,634	1,403	1,281	1,022	809
embezzlement	40,442	35,767	33,687	29,617	23,399	21,424	19,445	16,421	13,178	10,314	8,706
Rape	158	153	113	139	140	143	142	82	147	147	147
Compulsion	597	472	443	394	402	438	490	455	524	557	501
Arson	282	245	297	233	141	192	135	141	174	137	127
House breaking	3,234	3,260	3,554	3,369	3,345	3,304	3,256	2,992	2,812	2,413	2,238
Destruction	1,972	2,308	2,354	2,596	2,702	2,457	2,142	2,187	1,911	1,909	1,576
Anything else	3,050	3,703	5,761	3,415	3,129	3,119	3,139	2,965	2,828	2,714	2,388

Source: *White Paper on Crime*, Ministry of Justice, 2005-2015, Tokyo in Japan.

FIGURE 10.1. (continued).

per 100,000. This means that juveniles commit crimes at rates at least 2.5 times those of adults in Japan. As previously mentioned, the Japanese crime rate has been very low historically. Thinking about this phenomenon, the extremely low crime rate would indicate that the Japanese government has been effectively able to control crime from the vantage of preventing juvenile crime from evolving into adults committing crimes in later years.

As can be seen in Fig. 10.1a, the number of arrested juvenile offenders who committed non-traffic Penal Code offenses has decreased for the last 10 years (2004–2014). The number of arrested adult offenders has been decreasing slightly during the same time period, but the rate for juveniles rapidly decreased in comparison.

Year	Arrested Male Juveniles	Rate per Population of Male Juveniles	Arrested Female Juveniles	Proportion of the Rate for the all Arrested Juvenile Offenders	Rate per Population of Female Juveniles
2004	102,587	2,501.5	33,231	24.5	852.0
2005	94,758	2,373.6	29,785	23.9	787.1
2006	87,415	2,231.1	26,155	23.0	703.3
2007	79,611	2,078.4	24,310	23.4	667.4
2008	71,460	1,894.8	20,060	21.9	558.5
2009	72,301	1,938.4	18,590	20.5	522.9
2010	69,200	1,862.6	17,248	20.0	488.5
2011	63,257	1,697.0	14,986	19.2	423.2
2012	54,345	1,463.2	11,675	17.7	330.4
2013	47,524	1,283.8	9,429	16.6	267.5
2014	41,823	1,136.5	7,064	14.7	201.6

Source: 1. Criminal Statistics of the National Police Agency (2005-2015).

2. The Statistics Bureau, Ministry of Internal Affairs and Communications (population data).

FIGURE 10.1. (continued).

According to the Fig. 10.1b, the number of arrested male juvenile offenders decreased from 102,587 in 2004 to 41,823 in 2014 by 59.2%; for female offenders, the parallel number decreased from 33,231 in 2004 to 7064 in 2014 by 78.7%. In other words, even though all groups have seen a decreased crime rate, the crime rate among female juveniles has declined more drastically and to a greater degree than it has among the other groups in Japan.

The following figure shows the number of arrested juvenile offenders who committed non-traffic Penal Code offenses alongside all of the types of juvenile offenses, including felonies. The number of crimes related to body and life (such as homicide, injury, and rape) has remained stable. However, the number of crimes related to property and theft has decreased (robbery, larceny, embezzlement). Considering that the most frequently committed major types of crime are larceny and embezzlement, consisting of about 74% of all the crime types, and the number of crimes are decreasing, these two crime types take the lead with respect to the decreases in juvenile crime rates.

Causes of Juvenile Crime

Moriyama (2011) points out that the culture and traditions of Japan play the most important roles in maintaining the low crime rate in modern Japan. The following characteristics are salient in Japanese culture and help account for the low crime rate: (1) certain types of cultural impacts from other countries do not take hold in Japan because it is an isolated, island country; (2) Japan is a country that is overwhelmingly composed of one race, and people's values are very similar; (3) there are traditionally strong bonds in each district; (4) people accept the existence of informal controls; (5) the government strictly controls weapons; and (6) the criminal justice system is efficient in suppressing crime. Japanese society emphasizes solidarity rather than liberty, cooperation rather than competition, collectivism over individualism, process over results, stability over change, dependence over independence, and harmony over difference. This set of societal preferences has a crucial impact on the juvenile crime phenomena in Japan. Contingency, the holding of grudges, greed, and excessive consumption of alcohol are representative causes of crimes for juvenile offenders. These cultural and traditional factors might account for the relatively strong control of crime that Japanese society exhibits.

In Japan, the most frequently committed crime is larceny, accounting for about 60% of the total number of crimes in 2014; embezzlement, the second most-frequent crime, accounted for 14% of crimes. Juveniles have been found to mainly steal abandoned bicycles. For this reason, about 74% of juvenile crime might not be serious crime, and people do not strongly fear juvenile crime in Japan (Ayukawa 2011).

The Task Force for Juvenile Justice (under the Office of the Prime Minister) surveys "Overall Research on the Cause of Juvenile Offenders" every 10 years, with the last survey(the 4th Report) being conducted in 2009. Juvenile offenders are influenced by elements related to seven categories: (1) family relationships; (2) friend relationships; (3) everyday lives; (4) schooling and study; (5) experience of offenders; (6) juveniles' characters; and (7) local activities. This survey examined the differences between normal juveniles and juvenile offenders in detail. It is difficult to explain the reasons for juvenile crime because these reasons are an intricate mix of economic, social, and personal factors. Even though many scholars and law enforcement authorities point out that the most important cause of juvenile offending is the juvenile's relationship with his or her family, the rate was highest at 53.0% for juveniles who consider that their delinquency was "their own fault," followed by those who consider that their delinquency was caused by "their friends and peers (32.7%)," and those who consider that their delinquency was caused by "their family or parents (8.4%)." The juvenile offenders' parents also have a similar stance on this question.

THE INSTITUTIONAL STRUCTURE OF THE JUVENILE JUSTICE

Persons younger than 20 years of age are legally considered juveniles. According to the Juvenile Law, juvenile cases go to Family Court. The court subsequently determines the need to subject the juvenile in question to protective measures and the most beneficial treatment for the juvenile. Possible measures include placement under the supervision of probation officers, commitment to juvenile education, or placement in a training home or a house for defendant children. Another option is commitment to a juvenile training school.

When the police clear a juvenile case, the case is referred directly to Family Court for offenses that may be punished with fines or a lighter punishment. Either that or they are sent to a public prosecutor for offenses that may be punished with imprisonment, capital punishment, and so forth. After the referral, if any crime is suspected the public prosecutor must complete an investigation of the case and then refer the case to a Family Court. When a public prosecutor refers the case to the Family Court, the prosecutor can offer a request for the treatment of the juvenile. The public prosecutor may request detention only in juvenile cases where it is deemed necessary. When detention is required, a judge may order the juvenile to be detained in a juvenile classification home based on the decision by the judge (Article 17 of the Juvenile Law) (Fig. 10.2).

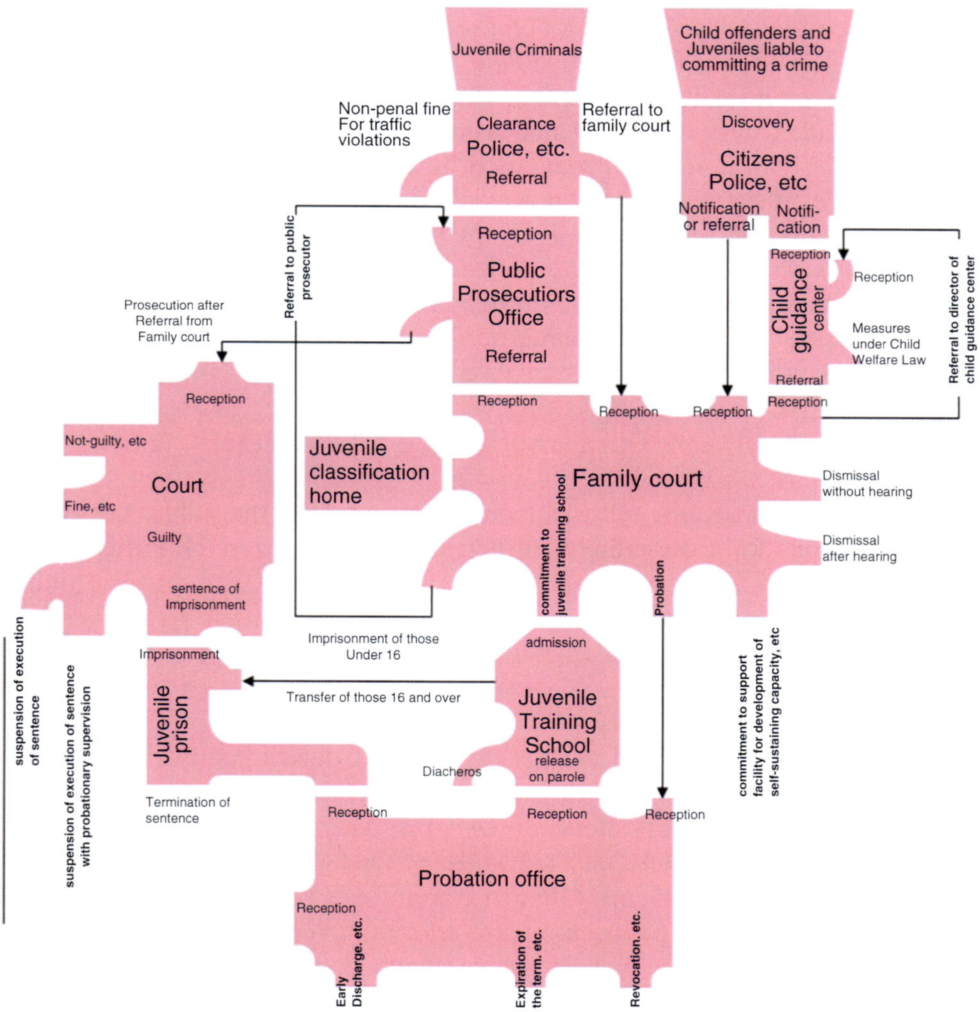

FIGURE 10.2. Flowchart of treatment procedure for juvenile offenders and offenders in Japan. *Source*: White Paper on Crime Tokyo in Japan (2005).

Policing and Juveniles

A judicial police officer shall refer to a Family Court a case involving a juvenile who is, as a result of the investigation of the case, suspected of committing a crime punishable by fine or lighter punishment. The same applies even when the juvenile is not suspected of committing a crime if grounds exist for which the juvenile should be subject to a hearing and the decision of the Family Court. In practice, this means that the police refer minor cases of juvenile offenders directly to the Family Court and other cases to the public prosecutors. But the public prosecutors also refer all cases to the Family Court after completing their investigations. Therefore, in the end all cases are sent to the family court (Hiroyuki 2004). At this point, the police begin their initial investigations of a juvenile offender. This is accomplished through the specialized departments of the prefecture police (headquarters of *Todofuken*) and through specialized groups in police stations who take full responsibility for juvenile offenders. As a rule, juvenile criminals are investigated under the Criminal Procedure Law. The documentation and evidence related to juvenile crimes are transferred to the prosecutors without delay, even if it is not mandated by laws. With a warrant issued by a judge, a police officer may arrest the suspected juvenile. The maximum period for the detention of an arrested juvenile by the police before the referral of cases to prosecutors is 48 h; otherwise, the police are required to release the juvenile. If the punishment for an accused crime demands more than a fine, the police may transfer the case to the public prosecutor. During the pre-referral detention, the police and the public prosecutors may interview the juvenile (Hiroyuki 2004).

The Juvenile Offenders Process at the Prosecutor

Unless a public prosecutor releases a suspected juvenile, the public prosecutor must ask a judge for a pre-indictment detention order within 24 h after receiving the juvenile. The pre-indictment detention period is 10 days. The public prosecutor may ask a judge for an extension of the detention for up to 10 days, if necessary. A suspected juvenile's maximum term of detention before being referred to the Family Court is 23 days (including the detention on the part of the police). A prosecutor should transfer a suspected juvenile to a Family Court even when a detention is more necessary. The Family Court judge has the right to suspend an indictment in lieu of the prosecutor, which is an important exception for the "principle of appropriateness" (*Opportunitatsprinzip*). However, the suspected juvenile can be reverse referred to the prosecutor when the Family Court judge concludes that the juvenile offender committed a serious crime (Cho 2004). The prosecutor who investigates a reverse-referred juvenile offender can file the case in a district criminal court or in a summary court according to the adult criminal procedure. The prosecutor can also drop the reverse-referred case when he or she cannot prove the juvenile offender guilty. The Criminal Court should transfer the juvenile to Family Court when protection and treatment are required as a result of the classification of the case.

The Process in Court for Juvenile Offenders

Process in the Family Court

Investigation and Hearing

The Family Court places priority on the protection and correction in the treatment of all juvenile offenders referred to it. The 1500 Family Court probation officers stationed throughout the country play a substantial role in the treatment of juveniles. From the time a juvenile enters the system until a hearing is conducted, the probation officer makes an in-depth investigation into the child's character, life history, family background, and environment. Juvenile Law, Article 22, Section 1 stipulates that "hearings shall be conducted softly and mildly with warm consideration"; the hearings shall not be open to the public. Although findings of fact must be established beyond a reasonable doubt, hearings do not employ the rule of evidence stipulated by the Criminal Procedure Law. In Japan, the processes of adjudication and disposition (in adult as well as juvenile cases) are not separated but rather conducted in an integrated fashion (Morita 2002).

Jurisdiction at the Family Court

All juvenile trials are held in the Family Court except for reverse-referred cases and dropped cases. Juvenile offenders are categorized into three classes ("juvenile criminals," "child offenders," and "juveniles liable to commit a crime"). The Family Court proceedings involving juveniles generally commence when: (1) a judicial police officer or public prosecutor sends a juvenile case to the court; (2) a prefectural governor or chief of the Child Guidance Center refers a juvenile case to the court; (3) a Family Court probation officer who has found a juvenile offender reports the case to the court; or (4) someone who is in charge of the protection of a juvenile (e.g., school teacher) informs the court of the case. The juvenile offender is committed to his own home or a juvenile classification home after the case is referred to a Family Court. The Family Court judge takes the investigation report and the classification report from the juvenile classification home into consideration in the decision of protection for the juvenile offender (Toshio 2015). The judge's determination may take one of several forms. It is made on the basis of the Family Court probation officer's report, the judge's own research and inquiry, and the results of the hearing. The possible forms are as follows: (1) a decision to refer the case to the competent prefectural governor or the chief of the Child guidance center (this action is taken when it is deemed that the juvenile should be dealt with under the Child Welfare Act rather than be placed under protective measures); (2) a decision to dismiss the case (in cases where the court finds it unnecessary to recommend any particular disposition of the juvenile); (3) a decision to refer the case to the public prosecutor; or (4) a decision to place the juvenile under protective measures. According to Article 24(1) of the Juvenile Law, there are three kinds of protective measures: (1) the juvenile is placed on probation under the purview of the probation office; (2) the juvenile is placed in a support facility to develop skills related to self-care and self-sustaining (*Jidojiritsushien-shisetsu*) or in a home for defendant children (*Jidoyogo-shisetsu*) (both of these institutions are provided for under the Child Welfare Act); and (3) the juvenile is placed in a juvenile training school (*Shonen-in*).

Adults who have committed special acts injurious to the welfare of juveniles are subject to the Family Court jurisdiction as well. The specific offenses are set out in the Child Welfare Act, the Labor Standards Act, the School Education Act, among other places. The purpose of the jurisdiction over these crimes is the protection of juveniles and the maintenance of juveniles' basic human rights.

Process at the Criminal Court

A juvenile offender will be prosecuted at the ordinary Criminal Court if he/she is sent back by the Family Court. A decision refers the case to the public prosecutor. The basis of this decision is the view that the juvenile should be subjected to normal Criminal Court proceedings due to the serious nature of the crime or the circumstances of the case, on the condition that a juvenile is 14 years old or over when he/she committed the crime. Juvenile criminal cases shall be governed by the same rules as non-juvenile criminal cases, except for what is provided for the Juvenile Law. The Family Court also refers the case to the public prosecutor when it ascertains that the person is 20 years of age or over. A public prosecutor must act in this case. The Criminal Court proceedings for juvenile offenders are the same as those for adult offenders. In other words, juveniles 14 years or older can be transferred to the adult Criminal Court and face regular criminal prosecution as if they were adult criminals (Daniel 2007). The Criminal Court judge chooses the kind of punishment and determines its term or degree with broad discretion. The juvenile found culpable is incarcerated in a juvenile prison if sentenced by a Criminal court judge.

Custodial Rules for Juveniles

According to the Criminal Procedure Law, the police shall detain arrested juvenile criminals for 48 h and the public prosecutor shall detain them for 24 h. As previously noted, prosecutors may apply for the detention within 10 days and be able to extend it for another 10 days. This process is the same as that of arrested adult criminals.

The Juvenile Law serves as the foundation of the most important custodial rules at each stop along the justice system, including at the juvenile classification home, the detention house, the juvenile training school or prison, the children's self-reliance support facility, or a foster home. Additional guidance on custodial rules also appears in criminal procedure law, Rule of Disposition Juvenile, the Act of Revised Juvenile Training School of 2015 (or, the revised Act related to juvenile training schools), and the Act of juvenile classification homes. As of October 2015, there are 52 juvenile classification homes, 52 juvenile training schools, and 7 juvenile prisons in Japan.

Year	Juveniles in Detention[2]	Juveniles in Custody[3]	Juvenile Prisoners[4]	Total Number of Confined Juveniles[5]	Juvenile Incarceration, Custody & Detention Rate (Per: 100,000 Juveniles)
2004	21,031	5,300	86	26,419	206.2
2005	19,626	4,878	86	24,590	194.7
2006	18,171	4,482	52	22,705	182.6
2007	15,800	4,074	42	19,916	162.4
2008	15,098	3,971	63	19,132	196.1
2009	14,559	3,962	54	18,575	192.3
2010	13,639	3,619	29	17,287	178.8
2011	13,189	3,486	49	16,724	173.7
2012	12,547	3,489	39	16,075	167.4
2013	11,491	3,193	31	14,715	153.8
2014	10,194	2,872	39	13,105	111.8

Source : 1. *White Paper on Crime* (Ministry of Justice, 2005–2015).
2. This table is constructed by the author, using data from the Ministry of Justice.
3. Branch facilities are included in these numbers

FIGURE 10.3. Number of juveniles confined (detention, custody, and incarceration) at juvenile facilities run by the Ministry of Justice in Japan (2004–2014).

The juvenile classification home serves as a place of detention for a temporary period (usually less than 2 weeks) until a formal decision is made by the Family Court. Therefore, an important statistic in the discussion of juveniles in detention is the number of confined juveniles at a given time. According to Fig. 10.3a, the number of juveniles in custody at juvenile training schools has decreased by 45.8%, from 5300 in 2004 to 2872 in 2014. The number of confined foreign juveniles at juvenile training schools was around 90 in 2008 (Ayukawa 2011). Of the total number of confined juveniles, about 2.5% are from other countries.

Juvenile Classification Home

Juvenile classification homes house those juveniles who have been there from the Family Court when the court orders "protective detention" pending court proceedings. Professionals at the juvenile classification home assess the juveniles under their care using medical science, psychology, and pedagogy. This evaluation provides relevant information for the investigation and hearing by the Family Court. In the event that measures prescribed in the referral of a juvenile to a juvenile classification home are implemented, the period for which the juvenile is committed to the juvenile classification home shall not exceed 2 weeks; however, the period may be renewed by the court's ruling if continued commitment is particularly needed. The renewal pursuant to the provision of the preceding paragraph shall not take place more than once; however, the renewal may take place up to two additional times in certain situations. According to Article 4 of the Act related to juvenile classification homes, boys and girls shall be segregated. Fifty-two juvenile classification homes (including one branch school) are currently in place nationwide.

Juvenile Training School

Juvenile training schools house juveniles who have been referred by the Family Court as a means of enforcing the court's order of "protective measures." They essentially provide juveniles with correctional education. The school classifies each juvenile by the nature of the problems causing the delinquency and the individual strengths to be developed in the future. According to Article 4 of the Act of that revised how juvenile training schools operated in 2015, a juvenile training school shall be able to assume custody of juveniles from the age of 12 years up and could apply to those up to the age of 23 years. In certain circumstances (*DaiSanshu* juvenile training schools), the juvenile training schools could provide custody for juveniles under 26 years old. They are separately confined by these categories as outlined in the revised Article 4 related to juvenile training schools. A juvenile training school is also able to confine a juvenile who was originally confined at a juvenile classification home. A juvenile training school is required to refer prisoners who attain the age of 16 years to a correctional facility. According to the revised Article 5 related to juvenile training schools, juveniles in custody should be segregated according to gender. Any necessary examinations of a female body should be conducted by female officers working at the juvenile training school. However, in cases where female juvenile training school officers are unable to conduct the examination, a male juvenile training school officer conducts the examination by directing female staff members who serve as the warden of the penal institution or juvenile training school. Of the 52 juvenile training schools in Japan, there are 9 for girls (including 4 branch schools) nationwide.

Detention House

A *detention house* is an institution where juvenile offenders can be held temporarily, usually while they are under the supervision of a Family Court. In a general criminal adult case, the accused shall be confined in a detention center by means of a prosecutor's file and a judge's decision under certain legal conditions. In a case involving juveniles, the public prosecutor shall not file a request for general detention except in cases where this is unavoidable. In this case, a public prosecutor may file with a request for the measures of observation and protection in lieu of a request for detention by Article 17(1) of the Juvenile Law; however, the request for measures shall be filed with a judge of the Family Court. Therefore, measures for the observation and protection of juveniles (*Kanho*) are different from general detention (Ministry of Justice Rehabilitation Bureau 2014). Nevertheless, a juvenile who would be disposed of in the case of general detention may be detained in a juvenile classification home. With regard to the place for detention of the measure (*Kanho*), there are special codes in the Rule for the Disposition of Juveniles. Under the judge's agreement, a prosecutor can put a juvenile who would otherwise assigned to a detention measure for observation and protection (*Kanho*) to a juvenile classification or a correctional facility.

Juvenile Prison
The Correctional Bureau of the Ministry of Justice administers the adult correctional system as well as the juvenile correctional system. The Bureau directs and supervises the correctional institutions to ensure the proper treatment of inmates with regard to their security, prison work, education, classification, medical treatment, and hygiene. The Bureau is currently conducting research and studies on new treatment techniques. The penal institutions consist of prisons that house inmates sentenced to imprisonment with or without work. As a matter of fact, when a Family Court decides to refer a juvenile to a prosecutor, the detention location usually changes from a juvenile classification home to a correctional detention house (center) (Ministry of Justice Rehabilitation Bureau 2014). In case a juvenile is to be punished with imprisonment with or without work for a definite term with the maximum term of 3 years or more, the juvenile shall be given a sentence that prescribes the maximum and minimum imprisonment terms determined within the limit of said penalty; however, in case the juvenile is to be punished with imprisonment with the minimum term exceeding 5 years, the minimum term shall be reduced to 5 years. Regarding a juvenile sentenced to imprisonment with or without work, the punishment shall be executed in a specially established penal institution or a specially partitioned area within a penal institution or detention facility. A punishment for a juvenile under 16 years of age who is sentenced to imprisonment with or without work may be executed at a juvenile training school until he or she reaches 16 years of age. Female juvenile prisoners shall be referred to women's prisons; there are 9 women's prisons and no female juvenile prisons in Japan. There are 7 prisons for male juveniles.

CHARACTERISTICS OF THE JUVENILE JUSTICE SYSTEM

Alternative Sanctions for Juveniles

Incarceration in juvenile training schools, juvenile prisons, and juvenile classification homes has been the traditional response to juveniles convicted of crimes. *Alternative sanctions* utilize nontraditional sentences in lieu of imprisonment and fines. Alternative sanctions include probation service, community service, in-home detention (electronic monitoring), and victim-offender programming (restorative justice). The main alternative sanction for juveniles is probation, which is a noncustodial sentence of conditional liberty. According to the Article 24 of the Juvenile Law, the Family Court shall subject a juvenile to protective measures as listed in the following items: (1) placing the juvenile under probation by the probation office; (2) referral to a children's self-reliance support facility or a foster home; (3) referral to a juvenile training school. Nevertheless, the Family Court shall make decisions to alternative sanctions indirectly. While taking measures prescribed in the provisions of the Child Welfare Act is found to be appropriate as a result of the investigation of the Family Court, the Family Court shall refer the case to a prefectural governor or to the director of a child consultation center, each of which have authority over the case. There are no formal systems of restorative justice in Japan because the rules related to this type of system do not have support; however, "the victim's feeling conveyance system (VFC)" and "the meeting for conversation between juvenile offenders and victims (MCJ)" are actively applied as practical restorative justice (Ota, 2010: 129).

Probation Service

A Family Court shall subject a juvenile under protective measures, such as the placement of the juvenile under probation by the probation office. Offenders Rehabilitation Act (Act No. 88 of 2007) reviews probation services in detail. According to Article 48 of this Act, probation should be initiated for the following individuals: (i) persons under the protective measures specified in Article 24 of the Juvenile Law, (ii) persons for whom release on parole from the juvenile training school is permitted and who are under probation pursuant to the provision of Article 40, (iii) persons for whom release on parole is permitted and who are under probation pursuant to the provision of Article 40, and (iv) persons under probation pursuant to the provision of paragraph (1) of Article 25-2 of the Penal Code.

The probationers and parolees shall comply with the "general conditions" and the "special conditions." Additionally, the director of the probation office may, if deemed necessary in conducting the instruction and supervision of the probation suitably for the probationers and parolees, establish guidelines for life and conduct that contributes to the improvement and rehabilitation of such probationers and parolees. Except for the public probation officers, there are volunteer probation officers (VPOs), in the spirit of volunteer social service, to assist juvenile offenders in their efforts to improve and rehabilitate themselves. Other duties of these VPOs include enlightening the public on crime prevention, thereby enhancing the local community and contributing to the welfare of both individuals and the public (Imafuku 2015a, b).

When there is a request pursuant to the provisions of Article 67, paragraph (2) of the Offenders Rehabilitation Act, the Family Court shall subject a person with regard to whom a ruling determines that grounds exist indicating that the person failed to comply with compliance rules. Furthermore, the person must have failed to adhere to these rules despite warnings as prescribed in Article 67, paragraph (1) of the Offenders Rehabilitation Act, that the failure is so serious, and that the educational and supervisory measures in place are not sufficient to improve or rehabilitate the person.

Referral to a Children's Self-Reliance Support Facility or a Foster Home

When a juvenile who committed a minor crime needs to be strongly protected from his/her environment (e.g., parents not involved), a Family Court judge makes discussion concerning whether to refer the juvenile to a children's self-reliance support facility or a foster home (Toshio 2015). As subjects to the Child Welfare Act, juveniles are defined as a person under 18 years of age. The director of the child guidance center shall take a measure set forth in Article 26 of the Child Welfare Act when he or she finds this to be necessary for a child. The report is primarily developed by the child's guardian or an expectant and nursing mother for whom consultation is provided. According to Article 27 of the Child Welfare Act, a prefectural government shall take a measure set forth in any of the following items of Article 27 with regard to a child for whom a report pursuant to the paragraph. The following items include the entrusting of the child to a foster parent, or admission of the child into an infant home, a foster home, an institution for mentally retarded children, a daycare institution for mentally retarded children, an institution for blind or deaf children, an institution for periodically impaired children, an institution for severely retarded children, a short-term therapeutic institution for emotionally disturbed children, or a children's self-reliance support facility. When it is necessary to take a compulsory measure that may unintentionally be conducive to restrictions on a child's liberty of action or deprivation of his or her liberty, the prefectural government shall refer that case to the Family Court.

Restorative Justice

Restorative justice programs have not yet been institutionalized in community supervision (mainly probationary and parole supervision) or in other stages of criminal proceedings. However, a type of victim impact statement called the "victim's feelings conveyance system (VFC)" was established in community supervision by amending the Offenders Rehabilitation Act in 2007 (Ota 2012). The Act provides that a head of a probation or parole office shall listen to the victim's expressions of feelings and of the overall impact of the crime in question as well as the victim's opinion on the probationer's or parolee's case. These emotions and thoughts should be conveyed to the probationer or parolee when the perpetrator of a criminal act applies for parole. The first 3 years after implementation, the application of VFC was limited, especially for the community supervision of serious offenders like murderers and robbers. Instead, VFC has been applied in property offense cases like theft, fraud, and embezzlement. Another important form of restorative justice, undertaken since 2005 by the National Police Agency (NPA), is "the meeting for conversation between juvenile offenders and victims (MCJ)" on "the simple referral case." All juvenile cases shall be referred to the Family Court, but the police shall exceptionally dispose a case as a simple referral (diversion) when the case is trivial. The police may send the simple referral cases en masse to Family Court or the prosecution office in every month by special referral. The Family Court shall make a ruling of non-commencement of hearing or decide to render a ruling not to subject the juvenile to protective measures. In the meantime, the police are able to send the simple referral case to the Juvenile support center after arbitration between juvenile offenders and victims. The Juvenile support center organizes the meeting and promotes reconciliation between them (Ota 2010). In addition, "the solution of conflict centers" as an Alternative Dispute Resolution (ADR) has been put forth by the lawyers' association; every district has additional programs related to accepting victims' status in criminal facilities and juvenile training schools.

CONCLUSION

Juvenile crime rates of all categories have been stable or have slightly decreased for several decades in Japan. More recently, the number of juvenile offenders who committed non-traffic Penal Code offenses has decreased for the last 10 years (2004–2014). This can be attributed to Japan's unique cultural and traditional characteristics (e.g., racial homogeneity, strong societal bonds, strict weapons control, and an efficient juvenile justice system). Even though the collective responsibility and solidarity in Japanese society are able to suppress crimes, other side effects such as the high rate of suicide and school violence (*Ijime*) offset the mythology of that Japan is a completely safe society.

Nevertheless, the Japanese juvenile justice system has reinforced the advantages of the society at large, and all juvenile cases shall be sent to the Family Court first, which specializes in the disposition of juvenile offenders. Different from the adult criminal justice system, the public prosecutor has no "power to screen cases for prosecution" in the juvenile justice system. The Family Court has a right to prior consideration in juvenile disposal procedures, and the court's right to prior consideration is based on welfare-protective dispositions. In the Japanese juvenile justice system, there is the double-track system: the protective procedure track versus the punishment procedure track. The two tracks attempt to secure a balance between protection and accountability. The Family Court is following the Anglo-Saxon model in the pursuit of harmony between a welfare and penal function, referred to as the "specialization of juvenile justice."

The Juvenile Law is the primary stipulation that influences and guides the functioning of the juvenile justice system in Japan. Even though the minimum criminal responsible age is 14 years or old, individuals under 20 years of age when they commit a crime are considered juveniles. There are three categories of the juvenile offenders as the jurisdiction of the Japanese Family Court: "juvenile criminals" (14 years old or over to under 20), "child offenders" (under 14), and "juveniles liable to commit a crime" (under 20). Judges and investigators of Family Court investigate and hold hearings with the aid of the juvenile classification home. The court subsequently determines the need to subject the juvenile in question to protective measures and the most beneficial treatment for the juveniles. Possible measures include placement under the supervision of probation officers, commitment to juvenile education, or placement in a training home or a house for defendant children. Another option is commitment to a juvenile training school. The Japanese juvenile justice system has recently been challenged to observe the UN Committee on the Rights of the Child and to institutionalize restorative justice.

Acknowledgments I wish to express my deep appreciation to Professor Zimring at U.C Berkeley School of Law, he led me pursue the field of political philosophy about criminal justice. My thanks also go to the Shandong University School of Law. Owing to the law school's support I could have finished this research.

REFERENCES

Ayukawa, J. (2011). "Juvenile Delinquency in Japan," Understanding Low crime rate in modern Japan, *Japanese Criminology Society*. The 8th Report of Research Foundation for Social Safety.

Cho, D.-H. (2004). *Comparison study of juvenile justice—USA, Japan and Korea*. Seoul: Myunggi University.

Daniel, H. (2007). *Law in Japan—A turning point*. Seattle: University of Washington Press.

Edit Committee for Children & Laws. (2015). *Children's Law 21C communication*. Retrieved from http://www.kodomo-hou21.net/.

Hiroyuki, K. (2004). Juvenile diversion and the get-tough movement in Japan. In *Annual Conference Proceedings of the American Society of Criminology* (Nashville, Tennessee, November 17–20, 2004).

Homepage of *Tobacco Reporter*. Retrieved from http://www.tobaccoreporter.com/2015/09/.

Ikenaga, T. (2005). *Reconsideration of Japan's revised Juvenile Law, and considerations regarding juvenile justice reform*. Berketey, CA: Center for the Study of Law and Society Jurisprudence and Social Policy Programs.

Imafuku, S. (2015). The significant contribution of volunteer probation officers and other citizens towards the rehabilitation of offenders and a crime-free society in Japan. In *Workshop 4, the Thirteenth United Nations Congress on Crime Prevention and Criminal Justice* (Doha, Qatar, April 12–19, 2015).

Imafuku, S. (2015). The significant contribution of volunteer probation officers and other citizens towards the rehabilitation of offenders and a crime-free society in Japan. In *Workshop 4, the Thirteenth United Nations Congress on Crime Prevention and Criminal Justice* (Doha, Qatar, 12–19 April 2015), p5.

Japan Federation of Bar Associations, JFBA, (2015), *Opinion on lowering the adult age in Juvenile Law*, from http://www.nichibenren.or.jp/en/..

Ministry of Justice Rehabilitation Bureau. (2014). *The New Act of Juvenile Training Schools and the Act of Juvenile Classification Homes*. Tokyo: Japanese Correctional Association.

Morita, A. (2002). Juvenile justice in Japan: A historical and cross-cultural perspective. In M. Rosenheim, F. Zimring, D. Tanenhaus, & B. Dohrn (Eds.), *A Century of Juvenile Justice*. Chicago: The University of Chicago Press.

Moriyama, T. (2011). "Analyzing a low crime rate in Japan," *Understanding the low crime rate in modern Japan*, Japanese Criminology Society. The 8th Report of Research Foundation for Social Safety.
Nakayama, K. (2011). *New edition of Penal Code I*. Tokyo: Seibundoh.
Ota, T. (2010). Restorative justice in Japan, *Law Journal*, 15(1), 1229-179X KCI, Research Law Center at Ewha Women's University.
Ota, T. (2012). Community-based offender treatment and restorative justice in Japan: Victim impact statement in probation and parole supervision, *Law Journal*, 16(1), 1229-179X KCI, Research Law Center at Ewha Women's University.
Ryan, T. (2005). Creating 'Problem Kids': Juvenile Crime in Japan and Revisions to the Juvenile Law. *Journal of Japanese Law, 19*, 155.
Sato, R., Oochuki, A., Ochi, A., & Sawamura, M. (2008). *The statutory age in major countries: Lowering for voting age & adult age*. Republic of Korea: National Library Survey & the National Assembly Research Service.
Takahashi, N. (2010). *Penal Code*. Tokyo: Seibundoh.
Toshihiro, K. (2015). *Juvenile Law*. Tokyo: Yuhikaku.
Toshio, S. (2015). *Introduction of Juvenile Act* (6th ed.). Tokyo: Yuhikaku.
UN Convention on the Rights of the Child. (2010). *Fifty-fourth session of Committee on the Rights of the Child* (25 May–11 June 2010). GE.10-43132.

Jae Joon Chung Professor of Law, Shandong University School of Law, Jinan-city, Shandong, P.R. China, J.S.D & LL.M. at U.C Berkeley School of Law in the U.S., Ph.D. course in law at Korea University School of Law (Seoul).

PART IV

Europe: Eastern Europe, Western Europe, Scandinavia

11

Austria

Karin Bruckmüller

INTRODUCTION

Austria is a small country in the middle of Europe with a population of about 8.6 million people (2.4 million live in Vienna, the capital). Approximately 1.1 million are children aged under 14 years old, 0.370 million are minors aged from 14 but under 18, and 0.303 million are so-called young adults aged from 18 up to 21 years old. About 20% of the population has a migration background, 1.2 million are migrants of first generation, additionally 0.4 million are migrants of second generation, so born in Austria as children of migrants. The official language is German. The predominant religion is the Catholicism.

Austria is a federal democratic parliamentarian republic. Since 1995 it is a member state of the European Union and therefore part of the EU police and judicial cooperation in criminal matters. The human rights are characterized by the European Convention on Human Rights and Fundamental Freedoms and the jurisprudence of European Court of Human Rights.

THE LEGAL STATUS OF JUVENILES

In Austria juveniles, who come in conflict with criminal law, have a "special" legal status, because the reactions possible under Austrian criminal law to cases of juvenile and young adult delinquency behaviour are covered by the so-called Juvenile Court Act (*Jugendgerichtsgesetz* 1988—JGG), which is adapted to the needs of young offenders and take the difficulties associated with the adjustment to adulthood into account.[1]

[1] See also Ministry of Justice (2012); Bruckmüller and Schumann (2014); Bruckmüller et al. (2011b).

K. Bruckmüller (✉)
Johannes Kepler University Linz, Linz, Austria

Ludwig-Maximilians-University Munich, Munich, Germany
e-mail: karin.bruckmueller@jku.at; karin.bruckmueller@jura.uni-muenchen.de

S.H. Decker, N. Marteache (eds.), *International Handbook of Juvenile Justice*,
DOI 10.1007/978-3-319-45090-2_11

This Federal Act contains substantive and procedural regulations, including regulations on the enforcement of imprisonment. The focus of the Juvenile Court Act is decriminalization (Jesionek and Edwards 2010; Bogensberger 1992). Emphasis has been put on special deterrence (*Spezialprävention*), as opposed to general deterrence (*Generalprävention*), which can be taken into consideration only in exceptional cases, and on resocialization of the young offender.

Therefore, the conventional punishments, both fines and imprisonment, should only be used as last resort when juvenile delinquency is involved. To achieve this aim, the substantive rules of the Juvenile Court Act provide a wider range of possibilities to sanction the offence. The potential for non-intervention and diversion was expanded significantly and efforts were made to replace traditional convictions and sentences imposed by a criminal court. The implementation of diversionary measures was based on a successful practical experiment at some courts and offices of prosecution (Jesionek 2013). In addition, a new form of immunity from punishment was introduced for misdemeanours committed by the youngest. For cases in which conventional criminal penalties prove unavoidable, legislation made sentencing more flexible by the removal of minimum sentences.

The aim of the procedural rules in the Juvenile Court Act is to support und protect the juvenile during the proceeding in a better way, because of the young age the suspects and accused are unaware of the judicial consequences of their actions. Special regulations with regard to custody were introduced. Release of information pertaining to criminal records was restricted to avoid the stigmatization of offenders as much as possible.

Moreover the Criminal Code and the Code of Criminal Procedure are applicable if the Juvenile Court Act does not provide specific rules.

AGE OF MAJORITY

The Juvenile Court Act defines "juveniles" as persons from 14 to 18 years of age. The relevant date is the time the alleged offender committed the crime.

Children not yet 14 years of age are not criminally responsible. Their offences are not sanctioned by criminal reactions. They can only be subject to measures mentioned in the Federal Child- and Youth-Welfare Act 2013 (*Bundes-Kinder- und Jugendhilfegesetz 2013—B-KJHG 2013*), such as institutional care. In this cases the youth welfare authorities, and not criminal courts, are responsible.

When the juveniles turn 14 years old, criminal majority begins and the juvenile will be held culpable under the Juvenile Court Act, whereby the youngest aged 14–15 years are granted immunity from punishment for misdemeanours in cases of delayed maturity (see below p. 234).

Persons between 18 and 21 years of age, the so-called "young adults", are also addressees of the Juvenile Court Act, because most of the special procedures (Schroll 2002), and since late 2015 also some substantive regulations, of the

Juvenile Court Act are applicable to this age group (AG "Jugend im Recht" 2012; see below pp. 228, 231, 234).

In former years the full criminal majority started at the age of 19. An amendment in 2001 changed the age of civil majority from 19 to 18 years in the General Civil Code (*Allgemeines Bürgerliches Gesetzbuch*). For this amendment it was argued that the 1988 reform had granted access to the more flexible and milder juvenile justice system to an age group commonly associated with a great deal of criminality. As limited compensation for this move, certain new regulations of procedure were introduced for "young adults", i.e. persons from 18 to 20 years. This legislation recognized that crime levels in this age group can rise temporarily, due to the difficulties associated with the adjustment to adulthood. Experts' demands for including an extended age group into the group of "young adults" (Miklau 2002; Jesionek 2003), all adults younger than 25 specifically, have not been met by the legislator due to political and public oppositions.

Only some regulations on the enforcement of imprisonment—and only in exceptional cases—are applicable to persons up to the age of 27.

Hence the Austrian juvenile justice system follows a graded concept of criminal responsibility. In every single case the judge, in some constellations also the prosecutor, can decide in the best interest of the child or the young adult.

THE COUNTRY'S STANCE TOWARD THE UN COMMITTEE ON THE RIGHTS OF THE CHILD

The UN Convention on the Rights of the Child was ratified from Austria in 1992, 2 years after its enforcement. Most of the rights laid down in the UN Convention had already been part of the Austrian national law prior to the ratification. It was seen as a rather symbolic act to sign the Convention (Berka et al. 2014). Also the optional protocols are ratified by Austria.[2]

However, three rights, not concerning criminal matters, have not been implemented even after the ratification. Austria made a reservation related to those Articles of the Convention concerning freedom of speech, freedom of association, and freedom to access information (Article 13, 15, 17). It was argued that the Convention Articles do not comply fully with the European Convention on Human Rights (ECHR), which is of constitutional rank in Austria.

In 2011 the core provisions of the UN Convention of the Rights of the Child were stated explicitly in a separate constitutional Act in Austria, in the so-called "Constitution on the Rights of the Child" (*Bundesverfassungsgesetz über die Rechte von Kindern*). The above-mentioned articles with the said reservation had still not been included.

[2] See https://www.bmeia.gv.at/en/european-foreign-policy/human-rights/priorities-of-austrian-human-rights-policy/rights-of-the-child/ (31.1.2016).

After growing criticism that Austria still abides to the above-mentioned reservations, the Federal Ministry for Family Affairs established an independent advisory board on the Rights of the Child (*Kinderrechte-Monitoring-Board*) in 2012 to examine the compatibility of the UN Convention Articles the EHCR and the Austrian Constitution. The members of the advisory board decided that both documents can be conciliated; thereupon, Austria departed from the reservations in 2015.

The core provision concerning delinquent juveniles is Art. 40 of the UN Convention of the Rights of the Child, dealing with the treatment of children in criminal law and criminal procedure. These basic matters are implemented in the constitutional law and more detailed in the federal law of Austria.

In Art. 40 Section 1 of the UN Convention of the Rights of the Child, the signatory states are obliged to conduct criminal proceedings with focus on the rehabilitation and resocialization of the juveniles. This aim is the underlying principle of the Austrian Juvenile Court Act, and it is especially reflected in its specific deterrence approach. Rehabilitation and resocialization is also the objective of the Penal Code (*Strafvollzugsgesetz*).

The principle of *nulla poene sine lege*, which is stipulated in Art. 2a of the UN Convention on the Rights of the Child, is guaranteed by Art. 7 ECHR as well as by Art. 1 of the Austrian Criminal Code. The procedural rights listed in Art. 2b of the UN Convention can be found as minimum standards for a fair trial in Art. 6 ECHR, and they are regulated in even more detail in the Austrian Code of Criminal Procedure (as the principle of presumption of innocence and the right to silent) as well as in the special provisions of the Juvenile Court Act (e.g. that the parents can accompany the young suspect to court).

Equally fundamental is Art. 37 of the UN Convention. The protection of children against torture and the guarantees concerning imprisonment are laid down in Art. 3 and Art. 5 of the ECHR. The Austrian law also complies with Section 2 of Art. 37 of the Convention. According to the Juvenile Court Act, pretrial detention and imprisonment have to be ordered only as ultima ratio sanction and as short as possible. Life imprisonment is precluded for both juveniles and young adults. Additionally, visitation by and correspondence with the parents are allowed also for young offenders during prison time.

Even those articles of the UN Convention safeguarding children against crimes, such as protection from the use of violence, abuse (Art. 19), sexual abuse, abduction, child trafficking or exploitation (Art. 34 et seq.) or abuse of narcotic drugs (Art. 33), can be found in detail in the national law. The corresponding offences are listed in the Criminal Code, most of them with higher threat of punishment if the victims are minors. The protection from use of violence in general is also guaranteed in the Federal Constitution (Bundes-Verfassungsgesetz—Art. 5). Moreover, it falls within the scope of Art. 3 ECHR (prohibition of torture and inhuman and humiliating treatment) (see to the implementation of the other Art. Berka et al. 2014).

The social rehabilitation of child-victims (Art. 39) is pursued in Austria, not only by comprehensive victim rights including psychosocial support, but also by highly committed social workers and child protection centres.

In total, it can be ascertained that Austrian law and in practice does comply with the requirements of the UN Convention of the Right of the Child.

TRENDS IN JUVENILE CRIME OVER THE PERIOD 2004–2014

Registered Juvenile Suspects

In Austria, usually the annual Crime Reports by the Federal Ministry of Interior are used to demonstrate trends in juvenile delinquency. Table 11.1 shows the data of registered juvenile suspects (i.e. persons who have been identified as alleged offenders based on a strong suspicion by police) between 2004 and 2014. In detail, the table provides the data of all police-reported alleged offenders regardless of the offenders' age in Austria per year, as well as the data for juveniles (14 < 18) and young adults (18 < 21).[3]

For all age groups, the absolute figures and the special crime rates (*Besondere Kriminalitätsbelastungszahl—BKBZ*) are included. The BKBZ refers to the number of suspects among 100,000 inhabitants of the same age, in order to see crime trends over years in a better way by eliminating demographic changes.

TABLE 11.1. Juvenile delinquency

	Total		*14<18*		*18<21*	
Year	*No*	*BKBZ*	*No*	*BKBZ*	*No*	*BKBZ*
2004	247,425	3048	28,700	7511	30,962	10,440
2005	243,493	2979	27,678	7159	30,784	10,393
2006	238,111	2892	28,683	7314	28,726	9682
2007	247,021	2983	33,068	8343	30,092	10,119
2008	240,554	2893	35,912	9010	28,261	9445
2009	246,378	2955	33,063	8289	30,571	10,145
2010	239,954	2869	29,306	7441	27,927	9167
2011	259,028	3088	28,045	7251	30,486	9914
2012	259,923	3087	26,549	6988	28,467	9200
2013	270,967	3215	25,935	7004	28,908	9400
2014	255,815	3017	26,809	7403	26,577	8751

Police reported alleged offenders per age group in absolute numbers (No) and per 100,000 inhabitants of the peer group in Austria (BKBZ).
Source: Austrian Ministry of Interior (annual Austrian Crime Reports—Kriminalitätsberichte)

[3]Data to minors, who are not criminal responsible in Austria, see Bruckmüller and Schumann (2014), see also Grafl (2009).

TABLE 11.2. Typical offences committed by juveniles (BKBZ)

Year	*Total*	*Life and limb*	*Property*
2004	7511	1739	4423
2005	7159	1712	3915
2006	7314	1854	4189
2007	8343	2174	4768
2008	9010	2270	5355
2009	8289	2135	4662
2010	7441	1997	4195
2011	7251	1987	3925
2012	6988	1846	3590
2013	6698	1625	3417
2014	7404	1616	3343

Police reported alleged juvenile offenders (all offences; offences against life and limb; property offences) per 100,000 inhabitants of the peer group in Austria (BKBZ)
Source: Austrian Ministry of Interior (Austrian Crime Reports—Kriminalitätsberichte)

From 2004 to 2008 there was an increase from about 7500 to 9000 suspects among 100,000 inhabitants of the same age (BKBZ) and from 2008 to 2014 a decrease to about 7500. The BKBZ of young adults has always been between 9100 and 10,500, only in 2014 the number went below 9000 suspects.

The figures in Table 11.1 show also that the delinquency rate of juveniles is two times as high as the average criminal delinquency rate in Austria, and the delinquency rate of young adults is even twice as high as the juveniles. These numbers underline the understanding of juvenile delinquency as being primarily a temporary phenomenon in the coming of age period, which legitimates specially adapted rules for juveniles.

Research indicates, however, that registered offences in the official statistics of police reports are influenced by internal and external factors that are not directly linked to an increase or decrease in delinquency.

The official police-registered data of juvenile delinquency significantly depends on the public's willingness to report criminal behaviour. However, it is assumed that the increasing trend to report does not correlate to an increasing danger of falling victim to crime (Fuchs and Krucsay 2011).

The typical offences (allegedly) committed by juveniles are offences against life and limb and property-related offences (e.g. property damage and theft). The data can be seen in Table 11.2.

Conviction Rates

Table 11.3 shows the numbers of convictions in Austria between 2004 and 2014 in total as well as the absolute numbers and percentages of juveniles and young adults.

TABLE 11.3. Convictions per age group

	Total		*14<18*		*18<21*	
Year	*No*	*%*	*No*	*%*	*No*	*%*
2004	45,185	100	3336	7.4	5500	12.2
2005	45,691	100	2953	6.5	5999	13.1
2006	43,414	100	2889	6.7	5594	12.9
2007	43,158	100	3084	7.1	5916	13.7
2008	38,226	100	2988	7.8	5259	13.8
2009	37,868	100	3155	8.3	5257	13.9
2010	38,394	100	3063	8	5246	13.7
2011	36,461	100	2747	7.5	5152	14.1
2012	35,541	100	2562	7.2	4903	13.8
2013	51.696	100	2248	6.5	4524	13.1
2014	49.94	100	2086	6.3	3968	12

Convictions per age group (absolute numbers and percentages)
Source: Austrian Ministry of Justice (annual Austrian Criminal Justice Reports, Part 2)

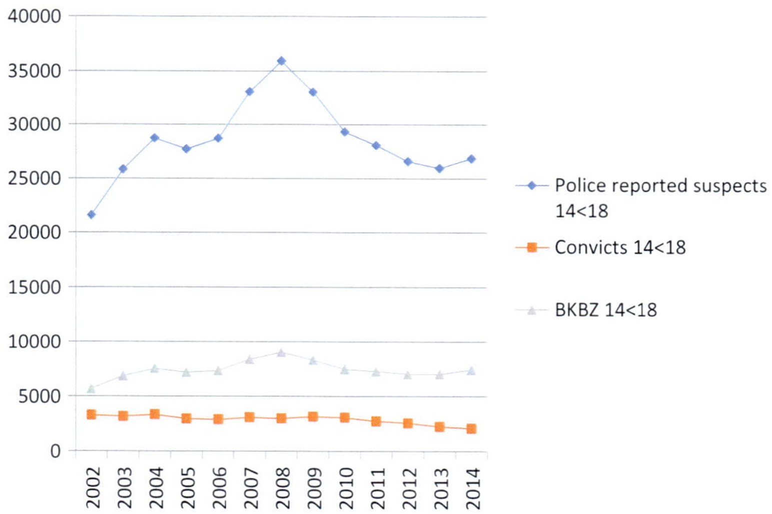

FIGURE 11.1. Development of police-reported juvenile suspects and convicts. Police reported suspects (No and *BKBZ*) and convictions. *Source*: For database, see Tables 11.1 and 11.3.

In general, a slight decrease in the number of convictions can be seen.

In Fig. 11.1—for reasons of comparison—the data on convictions of juveniles as well as the data on registered suspects (see also Table 11.1) are shown together.

It becomes obvious that the conviction rate remains relatively constant (in fact, it even decreased temporarily), whereas, by contrast, the rate of alleged juvenile offences temporarily increased strongly from 2004 to 2008 (see also Table 11.1), probably influenced by the peoples' willingness to report offences by juveniles.

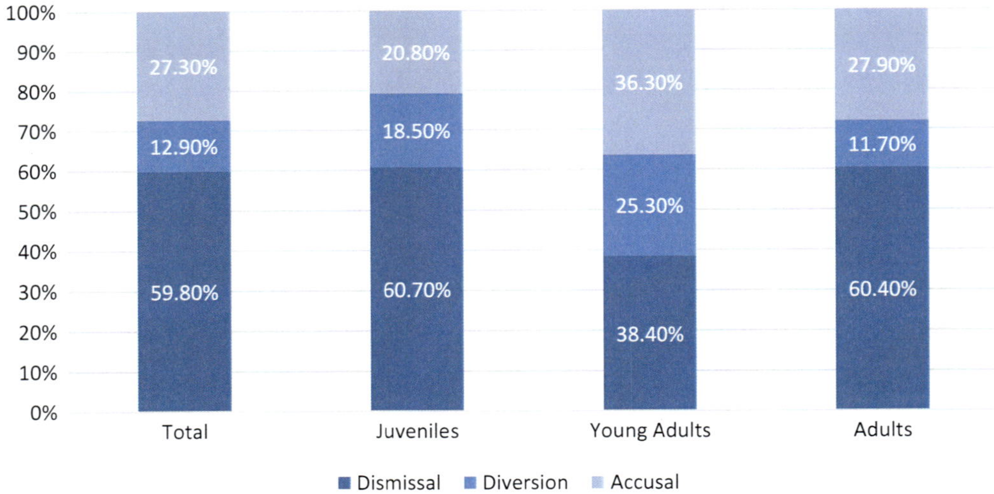

FIGURE 11.2. Decisions by public prosecutor 2014. Decisions by public prosecutor in % (total, juveniles, young adults, adults) in 2014. *Source*: Ministry of Justice (annual Austrian Criminal Justice Reports, Part 2), 2014.

The difference between the suspects' and the convicts' rates can be explained by the high rate of dismissals and the wide variety of sanction possibilities in Austria ordered by the public prosecutor or by court without a conviction (see to the decisions of the prosecutor and the court for the year 2014 the following Figs. 11.2 and 11.3). Such measures of diversion to settle juvenile criminal proceedings—which have been implemented in 2001 (see below the sanction system p. 234)—have effectively been applied.

Public Prosecutors' Decisions in 2014

The sanctioning practices of the public prosecutors during the pretrial phase can be seen in Fig. 11.2. It shows that the proceedings against juveniles in most of the cases—60%—are dismissed; in 18.5% there is a decision for a diversionary measure; in 20.8% the juvenile is accused and has to go to court.

Courts' Decisions in 2014

The cases, which come to court, were decided as follows in 2014 (Fig. 11.3): in about 20% a diversionary measure was ordered, in 60% the juveniles were convicted, and in 13% acquitted.

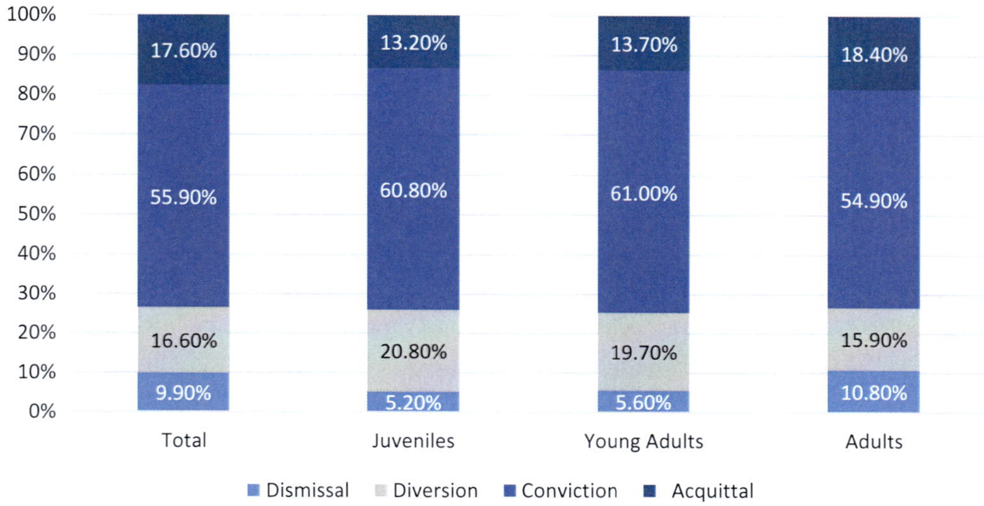

FIGURE 11.3. Decisions by Court 2014. Decisions by court in % (total, juveniles, young adults, adults) in 2014. *Source*: Ministry of Justice (annual Austrian Criminal Justice Reports, Part 2), 2014.

CAUSES OF JUVENILE CRIME

Delinquency of juveniles and also of young adults is seen as a phenomenon during a period in which children are coming of age and are still searching for their own identity.

However, there have been conducted no comprehensive studies on causes of juvenile delinquency in Austria. There is only one Austrian study, specialized in shoplifting, which shows in the first results that in groups, peer pressure has a significant role to play for deviant behaviour (Hirtenlehner 2012; Hirtenlehner and Leitgöb 2012).

Otherwise findings from research in Germany and Switzerland are transferred to the Austrian discussion due to the comparable social, cultural, and also legal situation in these countries. The presumption is that usually there is no prevailing single causal factor for juvenile delinquency. It is generally accepted that juvenile delinquency is rooted in a wide range of circumstances and also risk factors which are at times unique to each single case. Biological factors, especially any disturbances of personal development, social factors, such as problems in the family, with friends, at school, unemployment, difficulties due to different cultural backgrounds, and also issues of migration are seen as typical causes (Bruckmüller and Schumann 2014).

POLICING AND JUVENILES

The police are strongly involved with many crime prevention programmes for juveniles in schools and leisure centres, as well as with seminars for parents.

In criminal matters, the police have a strongly supportive function, particularly for the prosecutor in the pretrial stage; but they do not have the right to make decisions regarding criminal sanctions. They are responsible for the actual enforcement of an arrest or detention as well as for the questioning and interrogation of suspects and potential witnesses. Generally, detention by security officials is dealt with under the general rules of the Criminal Procedure Code (§§ 170 et seq.). Therefore, in most cases an arrest warrant issued by a judge is required. Only when the delay caused by obtaining a warrant, or at least a prosecutor's request, would be prejudicial, police may act autonomously. Grounds for arrest or detention are risks of absconding, danger of recurrence, danger of influencing the procedure of taking evidence, or if the minor has been caught in the act or falls under suspicion within a very limited time after the offence has been committed.

Special evaluation of whether the arrest is suitable to the age of the suspect is required regarding minors and young adults (§§ 35 et seq. Juvenile Court Act; see details p. 230). In addition, there exists the obligation to inform either a legal guardian or relative who lives with the suspect if the suspect is not to be released immediately. If necessary, an already involved parole officer and a youth welfare officer must be informed as well. Minors and young adults have the right to have a trusted adult (including a legal guardian, or representative of parole) present throughout interrogation by organs of the security services and formal hearings of the security authorities. The suspect must be informed of this right in a timely manner. The interrogation or questioning must be delayed until the requested adult arrives, unless this is out of proportion with the punishable act. The principal reason for the presence of a trusted adult is to provide the minor with psychological support (though they may not ask questions or participate in the proceedings), since an arrest can cause considerable shock, particularly among minors. This may even lead to later misbehaviour and the ensuing grave consequences. Another reason for the presence of the trusted adult is that he plays the role of an independent monitor, whose presence leads to transparency of the conditions under which the interrogation takes place.

COURTS AND JUVENILES

All special procedural provisions in the Juvenile Court Act are applicable for juveniles (aged 14–18), and most of them are also applicable for young adults (18–21). With these adaptions to the Code of Criminal Procedure, the accused's legal protection should be strengthened by providing stronger support during the main trial. At the same time, stigmatization during the court proceedings shall be avoided as far as possible, and the personal development of the accused shall be protected in a better way.

The court in charge is determined by the young offender's usual place of residence to not unduly disrupt the young person's life during the trial (§ 29 Juvenile

Court Act). Departments for juvenile cases have been established at the district and regional courts with specialized judges and prosecutors. They must have pedagogical skills and should have a certain expertise in psychology and social work (§ 30 Juvenile Court Act). Where a court of lay judges or a jury is to decide, at least half of the laypersons must be experienced in dealing with juveniles as teachers or social workers in youth welfare. Moreover, at least one lay judge or two jury members, respectively, must be of the same gender as the accused (§ 28 Juvenile Court Act).

The aim to increase the protection of the young offender should be achieved by a confidante being present during the entire proceedings (§ 37 Juvenile Court Act). Some procedural rights can be exercised not only by the young offender himself, but also by the legal guardian. Also the applicability of mandatory defence and the access to free legal aid is extended in cases of young alleged offenders (§§ 39 et seq. Juvenile Court Act).

In Austria, the principle of publicity (*Öffentlichkeitsprinzip*) is stipulated for trials. This can be restricted if in the interest of the juvenile (§ 42 Juvenile Court Act). For example, if public proceedings might reflect negatively on the development of the young accused, the trial will be closed to public and media (Schroll 2010). Furthermore, the young person's identity is particularly protected from being revealed under media law (§ 7a *Mediengesetz*). Therefore, also access to police records on juveniles is restricted (§ 33 Juvenile Court Act) and the data are deleted earlier than in cases of adults (§ 3 *Tilgungsgesetz*).

A Juvenile Court Assistance (*Jugendgerichtshilfe*) is established in Vienna (Essenther 2003) and at some other courts to support the judges. This support should help the court to act in the best interest of the young offender. At the moment, an ongoing project aims at instituting such units at all courts specialized on juvenile decisions. However, where no Juvenile Court Assistance is established at the moment, the tasks have to be carried out by the regional youth welfare organizations. The Juvenile Court Assistance provides the prosecutors and judges with youth inquiry reports. Those reports contain important information on the accused's family, social, educational, and health-related situation, and the background in general (§§ 47 et seq. Juvenile Court Act). In case of doubt, a medical expert or a psychologist should be consulted. The information is intended to support the court especially in choosing the most effective sanction in every single case. But it is left to the judge's discretion which information of the inquiries are necessary and used for the decision.

When the juvenile is already under the supervision of a probation officer, the probation officer can (also) provide important information to the court, because he is entitled to be present and to be heard at the main trial (§ 40 Juvenile Court Act). At the same time, he is also entitled to abstain from any statement in the main trial to sustain the mutual trust between him and his young client (see p. 234).

Although in Austria there are high standards of victims' rights, these are partly restricted in juvenile cases. So-called "private suits" or "subsidiary suits", for example, are inadmissible, as is joining the proceedings as a private party

(§ 44 Juvenile Court Act). Thereby, the aim of the Juvenile Court Act to protect the young offender is persuaded consequently.

At last, the court has to order the sanction. Juvenile law covers a wide range of sanction possibilities in JGG. The court orders a diversionary measure (see more under alternative sanctions for juveniles), or, in cases of a conviction, a fine or a prison sentence, both can be partly or fully suspended. These last two "traditional" sanctions may only be implemented as a last resort (*ultima-ratio* principle). The court, on a case by case basis, must always choose the sanction that causes the least impact on the lifestyle of the minor, yet which at the same time has the best special preventative effect (Jesionek and Edwards 2010; Löschnig-Gspandl 2002).

CUSTODIAL RULES FOR JUVENILES

Pretrial Detention

Pretrial detention (*Untersuchungshaft*) is governed by the Code of Criminal Procedure and has to be imposed by court where there is the risk of absconding, suppressing evidence, or of an imminent criminal act. In addition to the general rules—which require its application to be proportionate to the offence, i.e. to the probable punishment, and as short as possible—detaining minors in pretrial detention should only be a measure of last resort and is strictly limited by the Juvenile Court Act (§§ 35 et seq. Juvenile Court Act).

Not only is the maximum duration shorter than for adults, but the special criteria are also stricter. Pretrial detention is not permitted—even if the legal preconditions exist—if the purpose of detention can be achieved by a family law or welfare measure, albeit with softer methods. This is the case, for example, if the aim can be achieved by the minor undergoing treatment for drug addiction or in a residential care facility.

Moreover, the minor may only be detained if the related disadvantages for the personal development or for the reintegration into society are not out of proportion with the offence. Thus, an evaluation of interests must be made with utmost care but at the same time rapidly. The younger the suspect is (Jesionek and Edwards 2010), the greater is the likelihood of rejecting the detention.

However, the proportionality rule applies not only to the detention in relation to the offence, but also to the probable punishment. In a ruling, the Supreme Court has taken to interpreting this literally and thus exclude any pretrial detention as long as no punishment at all is to be expected (conviction without sentence, conviction with suspended sentence). There has also been a new rule since 2015 stating that pretrial detention is not allowed in cases which fall within the remit of district courts (see § 35 Juvenile Court Act).

To avoid the unnecessary extension of the time in custody and the delays in legal proceedings, the duration of arrest should generally not exceed 48 h.

Remand in custody is reviewed according to the general regulations of the Code of Criminal Procedure. Thus, the first control should take place at a hearing after 14 days, the second after a month, and all further hearings every other 2 months. The maximum period for pretrial detention of minors may not exceed 3 months, in cases within the jurisdiction of mixed courts or juries trials 6 months, in extraordinary cases 1 year.

Recently, the possibility to convene a so-called "Pre-trial Detention Conference" ("*Untersuchungshaftkonferenz*"), headed by a probation officer and with the cooperation of the Juvenile Court Assistance, has been created. It aims at the early release from custody. The accused has to consent to this kind of "Socialnet-Conference"[4].

Altogether pretrial detention should be avoided as far as possible (Ministry of Justice 2013).

If a pretrial detention has to be ordered, the Juvenile Court Act tries to protect the rights of the minors comprehensively. It grants the minor a special right of participation of trusted adults from the first pretrial proceedings onward. The legal guardian must be notified that the juvenile has been arrested, unless there is a plausible reason not to do so. Moreover, a parole officer already appointed to the minor can also act as a trusted adult. The adult also has the right to attend the main trial and to be heard in it. Furthermore, the legal representative is granted all the same legal rights as the accused minor. In addition, the court must appoint a pro bono attorney, if necessary. This must be accomplished by the time of the first legal proceedings in court (first questioning).

Imprisonment After A Conviction

Adopted Sentences

The threatened prison sentences, which are included in the offences in the Criminal Code, are adopted and shortened for juveniles. As of the last amendment, most of these regulations are also applicable for young adults. The maximum sentence is halved, and there are no minimum sentences. However, there are two exceptions. Life, or 10–20 years punishment is replaced by 1–15 years, if the juvenile committed the offence when he or she was 16 or older, and 1–10 years if the offence was committed before the age of 16. The maximum sentence for young adults is also not lifelong but up to 15 years.

If a prison sentence is ordered, the shortest time is 1 day. A prison term can also be suspended in whole or in part.

Regulations For Imprisonment

Generally, young offenders in prison are subject to the provisions of the Penal Code (*Strafvollzugsgesetz*—StVG), but special regulations of the Juvenile Court

[4]See: http://www.neustart.at/at/de/unsere_angebote/nach_haft/sozialnetz_konferenz.php (31.1.2016).

Act have to be considered. These rules make allowances for the needs of young prisoners. The aim of the prison time is to educate the young offender to a social adequate behaviour.

In the special rules of the Juvenile Court Act important issues are mentioned, aiming at supporting the resocialization of the juveniles and avoiding stigmatization, such as the need for schooling, the appropriate nutrition required for their physical development, as well as physical exercise in the fresh air. Furthermore, it is important to note that prisoners are not publicly exposed, in particular during transfer or when working outside the penal institution. In addition, visiting times and the right to receive parcels are expanded, and the regulations regarding house arrest and solitary confinement are softer, both of which are intended to maintain social ties between the juvenile and other relations. Social workers assist the young prisoners and, where necessary, psychotherapeutic support should be provided (Jesionek and Edwards 2010).

As a rule, juveniles serve their sentences in more relaxed conditions. This means that the doors to the common rooms, sometimes even the gates during the day, are not locked. The prisoners are only guarded—if at all—in a limited manner when working outside the premises, and there is the possibility of leaving for work or for educational purposes. The law also allows the offender to undergo therapy as an outpatient (Jesionek and Edwards 2010).

Convicts up to the age of 18 fall under the regulations of the penal system of the Juvenile Court Act. If it can be taken for granted that there will be no negative or other detrimental effects on juvenile convicts, persons who are not yet 22 years of age may begin to serve their sentence in the juvenile penal system. The relevant decision lies within the discretion of the competent court.

If a convict is already in the juvenile penal system, he may remain in it under the aforementioned preconditions until he turns 24. If the person in question has to remain in detention beyond that age, he may remain in the juvenile system if the remainder of the sentence does not exceed 1 year, or if the transfer to the adult system would entail substantial setbacks for the young prisoner. The relevant decision is within the discretion of the head of the penal institution or the Ministry of Justice. Persons 27 years of age have to be transferred to the regular penal system.

Juveniles are to be assigned to the institution where the objectives of the juvenile penal system are met in the best possible manner. Moreover, the special regulations of the Juvenile Court Act are also supposed to prevent "criminal contagion" by eliminating contact with adult inmates. For this reason, young offenders should serve their sentence in special institutions, or at least in a prison section separated from adults. According to the Juvenile Court Act, this separation can only be lifted if a detrimental influence on the juvenile can be discounted. This exception is to be handled extremely restrictively (Schroll 2010). It is to be applied in practice only in special cases, for instance, in order to obviate isolation if there are too few juveniles in an institution (Jesionek and Edwards 2010). According to heads of institutions, exceptions are also made if juveniles need the calming, positive influence of an adult.

Similarly to the judges and public prosecutors who are involved with juvenile cases, all those dealing with minors should have some pedagogical knowledge and an understanding of the basics of psychology and psychiatry. Because no specific training for guards in juvenile institutions exists at present, this requirement is only rarely met. There is, however, a "mentor system" in which a guard is appointed to each prisoner to watch over him or her and in whom he or she can confide. In this way, conflicts and problems should be more easily spotted and countered.

Prisons For Young Offenders

For the time being Austria has only one special institution for male juveniles (Gerasdorf), which is reserved for individuals with sentences of more than 6 months (Schroll 2010; Jesionek 2003). Female convicts with sentences this long are housed in an institution reserved for women (Schwarzau). In all other cases juveniles serve their sentences in special sections of the penal institutions.

For years now, the installation of a so-called "Competence-Center" for juveniles in the capital of Austria, Vienna, has been demanded by experts. This institution should also include a special prison for young offenders (AG "Jugend im Recht" 2012).

"Enforcement commissions", introduced to fulfil the OPCAT obligations, monitor the treatment of prisoners and lawfulness of the enforcement. They fall under the field of duty of the Austrian Ombudsman ("*Volksanwaltschaft*").

Early Release

Early release from serving an unconditional prison term is possible after half of the term if there is a positive prognosis in regard to recidivism. After two-thirds of the term, however, release must be granted, unless there is a high risk of reoffending. There is a minimum of 1 month of prison to be served before any early release. For minors, a further rule excludes any consideration of general prevention. Early release must be combined with the allocation of a parole officer unless there are reasons to believe there will be no relapse.

Since 2016 the leader of the institution has the possibility to consign a probation officer with a "Release-Conference" to prepare an early release for the inmate. This is a kind of Family Group Conference. If the young prisoner agrees, the probation officer will bring together the juvenile with his social attachment figures (the family, but also e.g. teachers, and friends). Thereby the social environment is activated and together they find opportunities to support the prisoner after his release and finally work out strategies for the young to take care for himself in liberty[5].

[5]See http://www.neustart.at/at/_files/pdf/sozialnetz-konferenz2014.pdf (31.1.2016).

In every early release decision a probation time has to be ordered, during which social workers will be at the juvenile's side to aid their return to "normal life". The priority objective of the probation officer is the support of the juveniles, and the aspect of monitoring should be subordinated (see § 20 Act on Probation—*Bewährungshilfegesetz*).

ALTERNATIVE SANCTIONS FOR JUVENILES

Next to the traditional fines and imprisonment sentences (see the special modifications for young adults p. 231), juvenile law covers a wide range of reactions and sanctions (with or without intervention) in the Juvenile Court Act.

Beyond the sanctions in the JGG, it has to be noted that Austrian juvenile criminal law offers special rules in cases of delayed maturity and moderate misdemeanours committed by juveniles under the age of 16.

Next to the minimum age of criminal responsibility—near to the age of 14 years—§ 4 excludes punishment when the juvenile offender, due to certain circumstances, was not capable of distinguishing right and wrong, or of acting accordingly. This so-called "delayed maturity", which must be demonstrated by an unusual level of development retardation, must be examined in relation to the single criminal act. It may be caused, e.g. by social or psychological defects, child neglect, or by illness. As a rule, such cases are settled with the help of experts.

There is another reason for non-punishment for juveniles under 16. There is immunity for members of this privileged group for any moderate misdemeanour. If the juvenile who has committed a misdemeanour without serious fault does not show special reasons which speak for the enforcement of juvenile penal law to prevent the offender from committing further acts, immunity is granted; the threshold of serious guilt (*schweres Verschulden*) is reached when, in a specific case, the guilt and unlawfulness of the act concerned surmounts the typical. In all such cases, the public prosecutor must drop the charge.

Non-intervention ("*Absehen von der Verfolgung*")

According to § 6 Juvenile Court Act, the prosecutor and the judge may drop a juvenile's case if the offence is punishable by a fine or not more than 5 years of imprisonment (which corresponds to a 10-year sentence in adult penal law), unless measures of interventionist diversion appear necessary to prevent the juvenile from re-offending. Non-intervention is not an option if the crime has led to the death of a person.

Non-intervention is recommended in cases of petty misdemeanours by "non-problem" juveniles, for whom a special preventive effect results from the mere fact that the authorities have become involved (*Jesionek* 2007; *Schroll* 2010). The premise of presumed innocence should be noted.

Diversion With Intervention ("*Rücktritt von der Verfolgung*")

Austrian legislation includes the concept of diversion with intervention.

The public prosecutor or the judge decides on diversion as an intervention when it is not possible to simply drop the case and yet there are no grounds of general prevention that make it seem indispensable to institute criminal proceedings including the pronouncement of a sentence (§ 7 Juvenile Court Act) (see details in Schwaighofer 2001). Furthermore, the prosecutor may only use this instrument in the cases of criminal offences that carry the penalty of a fine or not more than 5 years of imprisonment, the circumstances of the case are clarified, and if the remaining general preconditions of a diversion measure are met. Excluded are cases of "severe guilt", a resulting death (with the exceptions that the victim was killed by negligence or that the dead person is a relative of the young alleged offender and he has physiological problems because of his act), or when there are grounds of special preventative nature requiring punishment (Schütz 1999).

The implementation of diversion is independent of the agreement or cooperation of the victim, but is based on the principle of consent of the suspect (Höpfel 2002). The palette of diversion options ranges from suspending prosecution for a probation period, via out-of-court settlement, such as victim–offender mediation known as "*Tatausgleich*" or community service, to a kind of fine (*Geldbuße*).

Compensation or resettlement should be provided by the alleged offender. Whenever possible this should bear a direct relation to the diversion measure, although it must be appropriate to the capabilities of the young person, and not unnecessarily render reintegration into society more difficult.

Diversion measures are recorded in the court register for a period of 5 years. However, no entry in police records is made, hence there is no criminal record.

Diversion After Narcotic Drug Offences

In the field of narcotic drugs, the public prosecution or judge must drop the charge for a probation period of 2 years (Schwaighofer 1997; Bruckmüller et al. 2011a) if a person only possessed or purchased a small amount of narcotic drugs for their own consumption, or committed a criminal act in order to finance the purchasing of drugs (§ 35 Narcotic Act—*Suchtmittelgesetz*). This special form of diversion—which actually is one of the historic roots of the entire system—must be deemed more appropriate on special preventative grounds than to reach a conviction.

Prior to withdrawing the charge, information must be gathered from the Ministry of Employment, Health and Social Welfare and an opinion must be obtained from the local health authority in the case of a small amount of cannabis on whether or not the accused must undergo health-related treatment. Such treatments may include, among others, being monitored by a doctor, taking part in a rehabilitation or substitution programme, or even undergoing psychotherapy.

The preliminary withdrawal of the charge may also take place if the accused agrees to being supervised by a parole officer. In the case of withdrawal symptoms, the Ministry, and in some cases also the local health authorities, must be informed.

Conviction Without Sentence ("*Schuldspruch ohne Strafe*")

After the trial, instead of pronouncing a low sentence (up to 3 months of imprisonment, Schroll 2010), the court may convict the young offender and abstain from passing sentence if it is considered that the official conviction is sufficient to prevent the offender from committing further criminal acts and no exceptional general preventative grounds are found to pre-empt such an approach (§ 12 Juvenile Court Act) (Schroll 1986). Hence, a formal conviction is made, yet no sentence is passed. Thus the offender has received a slap on the wrist, but no further damage has been caused. No sentence may be passed in retrospect. Whether or not a conviction without sentence can be passed is left to the discretion of the court. The conviction has to be recorded in the register but will be expunged after only 3 years.

Conviction With Suspended Sentence
("*Schuldspruch unter Vorbehalt der Strafe*")

Instead of a conviction without sentence the court has the possibility to retrain the right to pass a sentence with a probation period between 1 and 3 years. A prerequisite is that the court considers that a conviction and the mere threat of a sentence, alone or in combination with other measures, sufficiently serve as a deterrent. Here also general preventative concern has to be taken into account. Once again, the implementation of this measure is left to the discretion of the court. A conviction with a suspended sentence can be ordered with a personal directive and/or the appointment of a parole officer if this is deemed necessary or advisable on grounds of special prevention.

The passing of a sentence in retrospect is only possible if the convicted person commits another criminal offence within the probation period and reasons of special prevention speak in favour of such action or if the offender disregards a court directive with bad intent or stops seeing his or her parole officer.

Here, the conviction is also deleted from the criminal record earlier than in cases of adult, after 3 years.

DIFFERENCES IN TREATMENT OF BOYS AND GIRLS

In Austria, boys and girls are imprisoned in different wings of the prison; in Schwarzau prison, there is also one building only for female prisoners (see above p. 233).

Moreover, there are no differences in treatment between boys and girls in court or in prison.

CONCLUSION

The Austrian approach to handle a young person, who came in conflict with criminal law, is more a protective than a punitive one. Therefore prosecutors and judges should predominantly use non-intervention or diversion measures like suspending prosecution for a probation period, training, community service, or victim–offender mediation instead of fines and imprisonment. Rehabilitation has proven more successful if the young offender is not sentenced. Moreover, by using mediation with the victim the juvenile delinquent is encouraged to reflect about his offence. Hence young offenders also have a higher level of suspects' rights than adults.

That the idea of protection is still a key issue in juvenile criminal law can be seen in the last amendment to the Juvenile Court Act in 2015. With the new regulations pretrial detention should be further reduced; instead of the arrest a "social conference" under the supervision of a social worker can be ordered. Additionally the sanction possibilities for young adults were expanded. Now they are nearly equal to juveniles in criminal proceedings.

REFERENCES

AG (Working Group) "Jugend im Recht." (2012). Thesen zu einer Reform des Jugendstrafrechts in Anlehnung an die "Tamsweger Thesen." *Journal für Strafrecht, 221.*

Austrian Ministry of Justice (Bundesministerium für Justiz), Sicherheitsberichte (Security Reports)—Berichte über die Tätigkeit der Strafjustiz (Criminal Justice Reports). Retrieved Jan 31, 2016, from http://www.bmi.gv.at/cms/bmi_service/start.aspx

Berka, W., Grabenwarter, C., & Weber, K. (2014). *Studie zur Kinderrechtskonnvention.* Retrieved Jan 31, 2016, from http://www.kinderrechte.gv.at/wp-content/uploads/2013/01/Studien-zur-Kinderrechtskonvention-und-ihrer-Umsetzung-in-Oesterreich.pdf

Bogensberger, W. (1992). *Jugendstrafrecht und Rechtspolitik: Eine rechts- und sozialwissenschaftliche Studie zur Genese des österreichischen Jugendgerichtsgesetzes.* Graz.

Bruckmüller, K., & Schumann, S. (2014). Of justice and of justice and juveniles in Austria: Achievements and challenges. In J. Winterdyk (Ed.), *Juvenile justice: International perspectives, models and trends.* Boca Raton, London, New York: CRC Press, 24.

Bruckmüller, K., Köchl, B., Fischer, G., Jagsch, R., & Soyer, R. (2011a). Medizinische und juristische Beurteilung substanzabhängiger (mutmaßlicher) Täter. *Journal für Rechtspolitik, 19,* 267.

Bruckmüller, K., Pilgram, A., & Stummvoll, G. (2011b). Juvenile justice system in Austria. In F. Dünkel, et al. (Eds.), *Juvenile justice systems in Europe—Current situation, reform, developments and good practices.* Merching, 41.

de Gobernación, S. (2014). *Programa Nacional para la Prevención de la Violencia y la Delincuencia (PRONAPRED).* México D.F.

Essenther, M. (2003). Pädagogik und Sozialpädagogik in der Jugendgerichtshilfe. In V. Dittmann, K. Beier, & J. M. Jehle (Eds.), *Kriminologie zwischen Grundlagenwissenschaften und Praxis,* 207.

Fuchs, W., & Krucsay, B. (2011). Zählen und Verstehen: Jugenddelinquenz, erfahrungswissenschaftlich betrachtet. In Bundesministerium für Wirtschaft, Familie und Jugend (Ed.), *6. Bericht zur Lage der Jugend in Österreich.* Vienna.

Grafl, C. (2009). Kinderkriminalität in Österreich—Grund zur Sorge? *Journal für Strafrecht,* 192.

Hirtenlehner, H., & Leitgöb, H. (2012). Zum empirischen Status der Power-Control-Theory. Eine Replikationsuntersuchung. *Zeitschrift für Jugendkriminalrecht und Jugendhilfe, 175*

Hirtenlehner, H. (2012). Ladendiebstahlskriminalität von Jungen und Mädchen. Der Erklärungsbeitrag der Power-Control-Theory. *Monatsschrift für Kriminologie und Strafrechtsreform, 325.*

Höpfel, F. (2002). Das Freiwilligkeitselement bei der Diversion. In R. Moos, et al. (Eds.), *Festschrift für Udo Jesionek zum 65. Geburtstag*. Graz & Graz, 329.

Jesionek, U. (2003). 80 Jahre Jugendgerichtsbarkeit in Österreich—Rückblick and Ausblick (Parts I–IV). *Österreichische Richterzeitung*, 66 (Part I); 94 (Part II); 118 (Part III); 142 (Part IV)).

Jesionek, U. (2007). Jugendgerichtsbarkeit in Österreich. *Zeitschrift für Jugendkriminalrecht und Jugendhilfe*, 120.

Jesionek, U. (2013). Modellversuch ATA für Jugendliche. Das Linzer Modell (Oral History—ein sehr persönlicher Bericht). In B. Loderbauer (Ed.), *Kriminalität; Gesellschaft und Recht. 40 Jahre interdisziplinärer Kriminalpolitischer Arbeitskreis*. Linz, 79.

Jesionek, U., & Edwards, C. (2010). *Das österreichische Jugendgerichtsgesetz*. Vienna.

Löschnig-Gspandl, M. (2002). Österreich. In: H.-J. Albrecht & M. Kilchling (Eds.), *Jugendstrafrecht in Europa*, Freiburg i. Br., 269).

Miklau, R. (2002). Junge Menschen und das Strafrecht – Perspektiven eines Heranwachsendenstrafrechts in Österreich. In: Moos R., et al. (Eds.). *Festschrift für Udo Jesionek zum 65*. Geburtstag. Wien/Graz, p. 137

Ministry of Interior (Bundesministerium für Inneres), Sicherheitsberichte (Security Reports)—Kriminalitätsberichte (Crime Reports). Retrieved Jan 31, 2016, from http://www.bmi.gv.at/cms/bmi_service/start.aspx

Ministry of Justice (Bundesministerium für Justiz). (2012). *Responses of Justice to Urban Violence. Urban Violence—Juveniles—New Media Tackling the current challenges in Austria* (Country Report Austria for the 31st Council of Europe Conference of Ministers of Justice). Retrieved Jan 31, 2016, from http://www.coe.int/t/dghl/standardsetting/minjust/mju31/Country-Report-Austria-Final-09-08-2012.pdf

Ministry of Justice (Bundesministerium für Justiz). (2013). *Untersuchungshaft für Jugendliche. Vermeidung, Verkürzung, Vollziehung. Abschlussberichts des Rundes Tisches.* Retrieved Jan 31, 2016, from http://www.justiz.gv.at/web2013/file/2c94848642280636O142c82f9ac124b8.de.0/bericht.pdf

Schroll, H.-V. (2002). Die strafrechtlichen Sanktionen bei jungen Erwachsenen in Österreich. In: R. Moos, et al. (Eds.), *Festschrift für Udo Jesionek zum 65. Geburtstag*. Graz, 189.

Schroll, H.-V. (2010). Kommentierung zum Jugendgerichtsgesetz. In F. Höpfel, E. Ratz (Eds.), *Wiener Kommentar* (2nd ed.). Vienna.

Schroll, H.-V. (1986). Das Linzer Konfliktregelungsmodell. *Richter Zeitung, 100.*

Schütz, H. (1999). Das schwere Verschulden als Diversionsgrenze. In R. Miklau, et al. (Eds.), *Diversion. Ein anderer Umgang mit Straftaten*. Vienna.

Schwaighofer, K. (1997). *Das neue Suchtmittelrecht*. Vienna.

Schwaighofer, K. (2001). Zum Anwendungsbereich der Diversion bei Jugendstraftaten. *Richter Zeitung, 60.*

Karin Bruckmüller is researcher and lecturer at the Johannes Kepler University Linz (Austria) and the Ludwig-Maximilians-University Munich (Germany). Her research fields are criminal law and criminal procedure law, especially juvenile criminal law, suspects' and victims' rights as well as (bio) medical law. On these topics, she wrote numerous articles.

She is a co-founder of an Austrian working group on juvenile delinquency and juvenile justice, which influences the legislation of juvenile law by making recommendations to the Ministry of Justice. Additionally she was an expert for the United Nations and the European Unions in the field of juvenile justice.

12

Belgium

Els Dumortier, Jenneke Christiaens, and An Nuytiens

INTRODUCTION

In comparative studies, the Belgian juvenile justice system has always been mentioned as one of the most welfare oriented in Europe (Put and Walgrave 2006). In the last few decades, several Western European countries have abandoned welfarism and have taken a punitive turn (Bailleau and Cartuyvels 2007; Muncie and Goldson 2006). At first sight, Belgium is not heading in that direction: the age of criminal responsibility remains very high (18 years) and juvenile justice is still underpinned by a mainly protective philosophy. However, it is important to take a closer look at this strong welfare image of the Belgian juvenile justice system. *Law in books* does not (necessary) correspond with *law in action*. In the same way political discourse and policy rarely resemble the views of professionals in the field. Policy documents therefore do not equal street level or daily practices. Moreover, recent reform (2006) of the juvenile justice system has introduced new (penal as well as restorative) elements in the welfare-oriented Belgian model.

Due to a process of federalisation in the 1970s and 1980s, Belgium has been transformed into a federal State consisting of two major[1] communities: the French-speaking and the Dutch-speaking (or Flemish) community. This process

[1]The German community composes the third constitutionally recognised community in Belgium. This is however a quantitatively very small community and will therefor not be discussed in this contibution.

E. Dumortier (✉)
Faculty of Law & Criminology, Research Group Crime & Society/Youth Justice Studies, Vrije Universiteit Brussel, Pleinlaan 2, 1050 Brussels, Belgium
e-mail: Els.Dumortier@vub.ac.be

J. Christiaens
Faculty of Law & Criminology, Research Group Crime & Society/Youth Justice Studies, Vrije Universiteit Brussel/Free University Brussels, Pleinlaan 2, 1050 Brussels, Belgium

A. Nuytiens
Faculty of Law & Criminology, Research Group Crime & Society/Youth Justice Studies, Vrije Universiteit Brussel, Brussels, Belgium
e-mail: an.nuytiens@vub.ac.be

S.H. Decker, N. Marteache (eds.), *International Handbook of Juvenile Justice*,
DOI 10.1007/978-3-319-45090-2_12

had consequences for the organisation of the competencies concerning the juvenile justice system and the societal reaction to juvenile delinquency. The (definition of) judicial reactions to youth delinquency remained a federal matter, while the execution of educational measures imposed (by the juvenile justice judge or court) became a community competence. Recently, due to the sixth State Reform of 2014–2015, it was decided that also this definition of judicial reactions towards young delinquents will become a community competence and that the communities hence have the competence to work out new legislation. Meanwhile the federal (Belgian) Youth Protection Act of 2006 remains in place.

Because of the Belgian state structure and the tension between theory and practice, it is rather difficult to present the Belgian juvenile justice system and its practice in all its complexity. Therefore this report aims to outline the main features of the Belgian juvenile justice system and must be read as an introductory but critical report on the Belgian juvenile justice system today. We start with a historical overview of the major legal evolutions because they help us to understand both the foundations and the complexities of Belgian juvenile justice. We therefore consecutively elaborate on (1) the legal status of juvenile delinquents, (2) the age of majority, (3) the unclear boundaries between "voluntary" and "coercive" welfare measures and between the different federal and non-federal (community) entities competent in juvenile justice matters and (4) the contemporary trend of growing "hybridisation" of Belgian juvenile justice. Afterwards we focus on (5) the country's stance towards the UN Committee on the rights of the child and on (6) trends in juvenile crime and on causes of juvenile crime. In the last part we investigate different (procedural) levels of the Belgian juvenile justice system: (7) the police, (8) the Juvenile Courts, (9) custodial rules and (10) alternative sanctions. We will end our overview with some remarks on (11) differences in treatment of boys and girls and (12) a general conclusion.

THE CHILD PROTECTION ACT OF 1912 AND THE LEGAL STATUS OF JUVENILES

From the beginning of the twentieth century, with the Child Protection Act of 1912, delinquent children and juveniles became separated from their adult counterparts. As contrasted to adults, the Belgian child protection system becomes underpinned by the idea that children should be protected and (re)educated rather than punished. The main purpose of juvenile justice is to reintegrate and to rehabilitate. Within this protection or welfare model, young offenders are not considered to be responsible for their acts; rather the offences they commit are considered to be symptoms of underlying problems. As a consequence, interventions of the Juvenile Court were not grounded on the offences and on the principle of proportionality, but on the young offender's personality and social context. Instead of punishments, protective measures were imposed "in the best interest of the child" (Christiaens 1999).

From the beginning of the twentieth century, young offenders were tried by a special court (*kinderrechtbank*) and a specialised judge (*kinderrechter*). It is important to stress that this early child protection system concerned not only young offenders (under the age of 16) but also minors who were considered to be in danger because of their pre-delinquent or bad behaviour. Different age groups were covered by the Belgium juvenile justice system at the beginning of the twentieth century: under the age of 16 for young offenders and pre-delinquent youngsters, and under the age of 18 for badly behaving children, whose parents could file a complaint to the Juvenile Court, or for children who were found begging or in vagrancy. Consistent with the welfare and protection philosophy, Belgian youngsters were (theoretically) not punished but were re-educated through protection measures or welfare sanctions (Garland, 1981). Until 1965, young offenders over the age of 16 were prosecuted before (adult) penal courts. Protection measures provided by the Child Protection Act of 1912 consisted of (1) admonition (2) placement of the minor in public as well as private facilities and/or placement in a foster family and (3) custody at Her Majesty's pleasure (*terbeschikkingstelling*) until majority, which made detention in public "closed institutions" possible. Finally, every protective measure imposed by the juvenile justice court could be associated with the probationary measure of *liberté surveillé*, an important innovation of the 1912 Child Protection Act. Notwithstanding the new welfare approach, the Belgian Child Protection Act of 1912 did not totally abolish detention in prison for children under 16 years of age. In exceptional cases these children could be placed in adult prisons during the pretrial phase.

Finally, the Belgian Child Protection Act of 1912, based upon the welfare model, introduced a new, specialised and unique judge, and a procedural model that confirmed the "paternal" role of this magistrate. Within the Belgian juvenile justice system the same judge handles the case throughout the procedure (pretrial phase, trial and execution of measures). This can be seen up to the present as one of the key characteristics of the juvenile justice system.

THE YOUTH PROTECTION ACT OF 1965 AND THE AGE OF MAJORITY

In 1965 a reform of the Child Protection Act was passed by the Belgian Parliament, by an almost unanimous vote. The new Youth Protection Act confirmed the welfare and protection model. The 1965 reform resulted in a more elaborated welfare model for the juvenile justice system.

First, the 1965 reform increased the age of criminal responsibility from 16 to 18 years. Since then, Belgium has had one of the highest age limits of *doli incapax* in Europe and the world. However, this rise in age limit was "compensated" by the introduction of a legal waiver mechanism. The possibility of transfer of cases to the adult penal courts concerned young offenders between the ages of 16 and 18. This transfer was not based upon the offence, but rather on the opinion of the Juvenile Court that welfare measures were no longer adequate for the minor involved. Thirdly, the Youth Protection Act of 1965 held the possibility of putting minors in pretrial detention in an adult prison in exceptional cases (Article 53). This possibility was seen as a sort of "in case" escape from overcrowded youth institutions. However, the use of this pretrial "adult" detention pointed at a problematic "short sharp shock" practice that, eventually, would lead to the decision of the European Court of Human Rights in *Bouamar v. Belgium* (1988) (Dumortier et al. 2012). This decision was at the origin of the abolition of Article 53 and the subsequent creation of a *provisional* federal institution (prison) for pretrial detention of minors in Belgium (see below, residential care). At the same time, in *Bouamar v. Belgium* the European Court of Human Rights condemned the lack of legal rights for minors during the pretrial phase, which led to the Act of 1994 that strengthens the legal position of minors (e.g. the right to legal assistance and the right to be heard before any "provisional measure" is taken during the pretrial phase).

THE INTRODUCTION OF SOCIAL WELFARE INTERVENTIONS AND THE BELGIAN STATE REFORM (1970S–1980S)

Besides the augmentation of the age of criminal responsibility, the 1965 Youth Protection Act also introduced the "voluntary" social welfare interventions. Youngsters (and their families) in danger or in need could call upon new local social welfare boards (*jeugdbeschermingscomités*) for social intervention and assistance. This voluntary welfare protection was directly related to the coercive judicial social welfare protection, and families who were unwilling to co-operate "freely" could be forced to do so by the Juvenile Court. Therefore this extension of the juvenile justice system can be (and was) characterised as an extension (and thus net-widening) of the *police des familles* or social control of juveniles and their families (Donzelot 1977; Van de Kerchove 1976).

However, soon after the 1965 Act an intense process of federalisation (1970–1988) transformed Belgium into a federal state consisting of three communities—a French, a Dutch and a German community. This process had important consequences for the reorganisation of competencies concerning the juvenile justice system. The communities became almost exclusively competent concerning legislation and interventions towards "children in danger" (both the "voluntary", social welfare interventions and the judicial coercive interventions). Moreover, and even though the (definition of) judicial responses to "youth delinquency" remained a federal matter, the execution of these welfare measures ordered by the Youth Court became a competence of the communities. This implies, for example, that the federal state is competent to decide whether or not a youngster can be placed in a closed institution and for what time, but the communities are solely competent to create and organise these institutions. However, in 2002, the federal authorities (and not the authorities of the communities as one might have supposed) created and organised a new detention institution (youth prison) for boys from 14 years on. In case there was no place available in the community institutions, boys could be sent to this federal institution (see also further section "Custodial rules for juveniles").

It is clear that this complex division of competences—a real imbroglio—resulted *de facto* in a reform (restructuring) of the intervention possibilities of the Belgian juvenile justice system. On the federal level, the juvenile justice system can prosecute juveniles for "facts described as a penal offence". On the community level, the same juvenile justice system can prosecute juveniles who are considered to be in danger because of their own behaviour or of their problematic educational and/or family context (*verontrustende situatie*, *enfant en danger*) and who do not "freely" co-operate with the social, welfare institutions of the different communities. This category of problematic, non-delinquent youngsters can include youngsters with a wide range of problems, from being a victim of abuse to being the author of bad behaviour. Recently, due to the sixth State Reform of 2014–2015, it was decided that also the definition of judicial reactions towards young delinquents will become a community competence and that the communities hence have the competence to work out new legislation. Meanwhile the federal (Belgian) Youth Protection Act of 2006 remains in place.

THE FEDERAL YOUTH PROTECTION ACT OF 2006 AND THE GROWING "HYBRIDISATION" OF JUVENILE JUSTICE

After almost four decades of discussions on the juvenile justice system and the reform of the Juvenile Protection Act of 1965, a reform was passed through parliament in 2006. This Federal Act of 2006 considers the definition of the measures that Youth Courts can impose on minors who have committed offences (measures on minors "in danger" or who behave badly must be defined by the communities due to the State Reform of the 1970s and 1980s, see above). Key features of this 2006 reform can be synthesised as follows: (1) the model of a welfare system remains the stated characteristic of Belgian juvenile justice; (2) parents should be held responsible for their problematic or delinquent offspring; (3) the practice of alternative sanctioning acquires a formal and legal status within the juvenile justice system; (4) the reinforcement of the waiver or transfer mechanism for serious young offenders; and (5) the implementation of a restorative answer to young delinquents complementary to the classical welfare sanctions of the Juvenile Court.

It is important to stress that this reform took place within the legal framework of the 1965 Youth Protection Act. The basic principles of the welfare model remain at the core of the Belgian juvenile justice system. However, we can notice the infiltration of a penal and a restorative logic within the reformed Belgian welfare model. For example, from now on, juvenile justice judges will have to give full reasons for their decisions in a more objective way. Therefore a list of criteria guiding the decision of the Juvenile Court was introduced (Article 37). It is relevant that the seriousness of the crime is formally recognised as an element in the "sentencing" or decision-making process. Another example is, of course, the formal implementation of restorative justice procedures in the Belgian juvenile justice system. These procedures, mediation and family group conferencing, are introduced as a complementary possibility of societal reaction to an offence committed. As we will elaborate below, we can point out that the actual juvenile justice system in Belgium draws on a hybrid model rather than a "pure" welfare model (Christiaens and Dumortier 2006; Christiaens and Cartuyvels 2007; Cartuyvels et al. 2010; Christiaens et al. 2010).

THE COUNTRY'S STANCE TOWARD THE UN COMMITTEE ON THE RIGHTS OF THE CHILD

There exists a long tradition in Belgium of upholding children's rights, both on a scientific and on a policy level. On a scientific level, for example, there was the creation of the Inter-University Children's Rights Knowledge Centre that advises policymakers and practitioners. Besides, both the Flemish and the French Community instituted a Children's (Rights) Ombudsperson. Also on the federal (Belgian) level mention must be made of the National Commission for Children's Rights. The different authorities are also prepared to write the necessary periodic reports for the UN Committee on the Rights of the Child and answer additional questions.

However, on the basis of the Concluding Observations of the UN Committee on Belgium it becomes clear that certain bottlenecks in juvenile justice practice are recurrent. Specifically the possibility of transferring youngsters (16–18 years old) has been mentioned by the UN Committee at several occasions as problematic (see also further). Other difficulties in Belgian juvenile justice mentioned by the UN Committee concern the lack of a lawyer and a trusted adult at all phases of a proceeding including during questioning by a police officer; the lack of a comprehensive policy of alternative sanctions to make sure that detention should only be used as a measure of last resort; and the possibility to hold children in isolation and/or in facilities far from home and with few or no public transport serving these facilities. Furthermore, the possibility to impose administrative penalties on youngsters for antisocial behaviour, outside the juvenile justice system, and this from the age of 14 years and on, must be critically assessed, according to the UN Committee on the Rights of the Child (UN Concluding Observations 2010). Finally, the Committee remains concerned "about the fragmented approach to data collection" and the fact "that the National Commission for the Rights of the Child has not been provided with the necessary resources to cope with its responsibility to coordinate data collection" (UN Concluding Observations 2010).

JUVENILE CRIME IN BELGIUM: TRENDS AND CAUSES

The consequences of this problematic data collection in Belgium become clear when statements on trends in juvenile crime have to be made. Two kind of sources might be used—official administrative data and self-report studies—but both show fundamental problems.

Official Administrative Data

Since the end of the 1980s, official statistics concerning youngsters prosecuted before the Belgian Youth Courts are simply lacking or non-existing. That is to say, we have no reliable (public) police and judicial data on the phenomenon and on the prosecution of juvenile delinquency. When available, official data remain fragmented (produced by several federal, regional and local authorities). Hence they are neither reliable nor comparable (Goedseels 2002: 30). Officially published police statistics do not specify age as a descriptive parameter. Thus, it is impossible to establish based on police statistics how many youngsters came into contact with the police and for which offences. Only regional data and fragmented figures exist, for example, regarding local phenomena of delinquency.

At the beginning of the twenty-first century a new governmental project on juvenile justice statistics resulted in a first report on (youth) prosecution figures for 2005 (Vanneste et al. 2007). The year 2005 can be considered as a reference year (zero). Although the published figures concern only the number of minors and the (delinquent and non-delinquent) "facts" that were reported to the public prosecution office by the police or by welfare agencies, it is a beginning. Based on these statistics we can draw a rough picture (and trend) of reported youth delinquency and welfare cases to the prosecution office between 2006 and 2014 (latest available: http://www.om-mp.be/stat). These statistics still have many flaws, such as the double counting of youngsters involved in different offenses and different youngsters in one and the same offense. Moreover, we remain without official data on the decisions taken during the juvenile justice procedure in Belgium.

As described above, the Belgian juvenile justice court has jurisdiction over youngsters (1) charged with committing "facts described as a penal offence", (2) who are considered to be in danger. Between 2006 and 2010 cases of delinquency represented more than 50% of all reported cases. Moreover, in the same period reported youth delinquency cases remain more or less stable, around 80,000 cases every year. However, 2011 was clearly a turning point. Since then reported youth delinquency cases are clearly decreasing. In 2014 less than 60,000 judicial cases of delinquency were reported to the public prosecutor, whereas in 2010 still over 80,000 judicial cases were registered. In 2006 about 46,000 (unique) minors were reported to the public prosecutor for offenses. This amount increased up to over and around 50,000 between 2007 and 2009. However, since 2010 the public prosecutors' statistics show a steady decline of delinquent youngsters reported to the prosecutors' office. In 2014 this decline is up to almost 20% compared to 2006, with only 37,494 youngsters reported for delinquent facts.

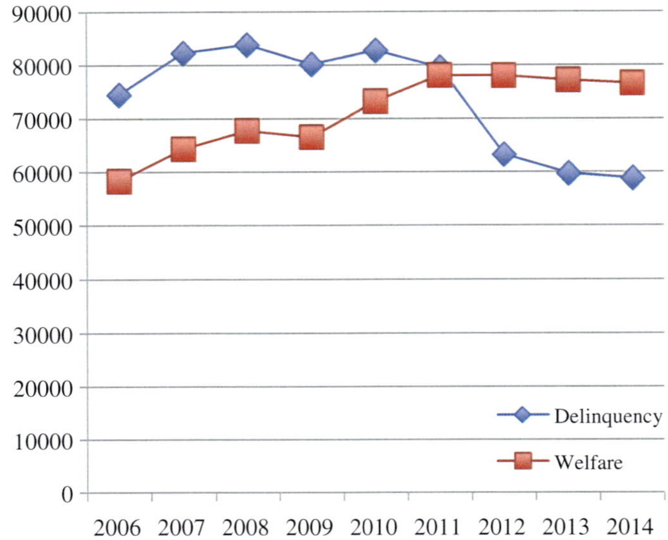

FIGURE 12.1. Yearly statistic reported youth justice cases reported to the public prosecutor office (2006–2014): http://www.om-mp.be/stat.

Hence, and in line with other European countries and with general crime statistics, the major contemporary trend in Belgian reported youth delinquency is its obvious and clear decrease (Fig. 12.1).

However, it remains hazardous and may be even too early to explain this decline in registered youth crime over the last 4–5 years. As criminologists we need to stress that these administrative data tell us more about the activity of the judicial system and its selectivity, instead of the "phenomenon" of youth crime in our society. The Belgian judicial statistics on youth delinquency cases are merely a source in developing hypothesis on how trends can be further investigated. Moreover, it could be that this decline in youth delinquency cases is related to the increase of non-delinquent—welfare cases.

Reported youth delinquency cases are clearly "gendered". In 2006 almost 80% of the cases involved boys, whereas less than 20% of the cases involved girls[2]. However, in 2010, girls were involved in almost 22% of the reported cases (Openbaar Ministerie 2012: De instroom van protectionele zaken op de jeugdparketten (2006–2010); http://www.om-mp.be/stat). In 2014, girls still are involved in 20, 68% of the registered cases (http://www.om-mp.be/stat). If we look at unique minors reported to the prosecutor for delinquent behaviour between 2006 and 2014 we notice a relative increase of girls compared to boys (2006: 21, 83%; 2014: 23, 70%), although both categories diminish in absolute numbers.

The available statistics do not make it possible to calculate the average age of all reported youngsters between 2006 and 2014. However, it is clear that over the

[2]In non-delinquent, so-called welfare, cases (problematic behaviour, predelinquency or victim situations) these gender differences are at a general level non-existent since long: boys represent slightly more than half of the cases, whereas girls are involved in less than 50% of all cases.

same period of time the majority of youngsters reported for offenses to the public prosecutor are aged between 14 and 18. More than 45% of all registered delinquency cases concern adolescents between 16 and 18 years old. In 2014 this age category increased proportionally to 49% of all reported delinquency cases. It would also be an interesting hypothesis to analyse the decline in reported youth delinquency through the "age" looking glass. These statistics suggest that younger minors come (proportionally) less and less in contact with judicial authorities. The available statistics since 2006 confirm, however, the age-linked evolution of reported youth delinquency, showing an increase towards adolescence. They confirm the gender difference in the (registered) age-crime curve. Boys involved in delinquency cases peak more in the category of 16–18 years, whereas girls peak slightly more in the age category of 14–16.

Juvenile delinquency reported to the public prosecutor in 2014 concerns mainly property crimes (43%), followed by offences against persons (20%), drug-related offenses (13%) and offences against public order and authorities (11%). This classical pattern of registered youth delinquency is also reflected in the previous years. However, we can see that the category of property crimes proportionally declined (2006: 49%) and offenses against persons increased slightly (2006: 16%). Probably, the character of delinquent facts for which youngsters are caught and reported is an important line of analysis in understanding the overall decline of registered youth delinquency.

Although girls and boys have a comparable proportional profile concerning these categories of offenses, there are some interesting "gendered" differences throughout the considered period. Girls are more reported to the Public Prosecutor in 2014 for "simple theft" (31%; in 2006: 30%), than boys (17%; in 2006: 16%). Boys are more reported for "aggravated theft" (12%, in 2006: 13%) than girls (5%, in 2006: 7%).

Beyond this general image of reported youth delinquency cases in Belgium, it remains important to take into account local differences between judicial districts, and between the three Belgian communities in relation to the categories of cases (delinquent and non-delinquent) as well as the categories of offences.

Self-Report Studies

Official and administrative data can provide a constructed and misleading image of offending behaviour of youngsters. Self-report studies were invented precisely to escape these limitations and to expose juvenile delinquent behaviour beyond judicial registration. In Belgium (official) systematic national self-report data are not available. Since the 1970s, self-report research has been carried out by different official as well as academic stakeholders (Born 1987; Goedseels et al. 2000; Junger-Tas 1976; Junger-Tas et al. 1994; Spaey 2004; Vercaigne et al. 2000; Vettenburg et al. 2007). For the Flanders region there is the repeated (2005–2006; 2008; 2013) self-report survey of the JOP—Jeugdonderzoeksplatform (Pleysier 2014; Pleysier and Put 2015). Hence, these studies use different survey instruments, target different delinquent or problematic behaviour and different age groups and were used with very different population samples. Therefore, Belgian self-report data are difficult to compare over time and space. However, Belgian researchers participated in the subsequent ISRD 1, 2 and 3 (Gavray and Vettenburg). Although there are some publications for the first and second ISRD survey concerning the Belgian sample, no overview concerning the results of the most recent sample (2012–2016) is available. Some results have been presented at international conferences, but have not been published yet.

It is clear that this lack of (uniform) data collection, a well-known and ongoing problem in Belgium, turns scientific research on trends in, but also on the causes of, youth delinquency into a difficult and hazardous endeavour. Critics might even wonder on the basis of what information the federal and community governments actually shape their juvenile justice policies.

POLICING AND JUVENILES

As mentioned in the historical introduction, due to the complex state structure of Belgium, and hence the need to find political compromises, a fundamental reform of the Youth Protection Act of 1965 has not been achieved (Brolet and Dumortier 2004). This means that the "old" Youth Protection Act and the traditional actors and procedures involved in juvenile justice highly remain the same. In this way, when a juvenile has committed or is alleged to have committed a criminal offence, three levels of interventions remain fundamental: (1) the police, (2) the public prosecutor and (3) the juvenile's judge.

On the level of the police authorities, the new Youth Protection Act of 2006 does not foresee anything new. According to law, the police act under the authority of the public prosecutor, to whom they have to report all crimes. In theory the police cannot decide to withdraw charges, nor do they have any autonomous competence to respond to acts of juvenile delinquency. In practice, however, they often give unofficial warnings (cautions) and may also require juveniles to participate in educational training such as traffic courses or to make restitution for minor damages (Van Dijk et al. 2006) (see also below, section "Diversion and Alternative Sanctions for Juveniles").

Though the new Youth Protection Act of 2006 was not innovative on the level of the police, European case law and, more specifically, the *Salduz v. Turkey* judgment (Eur. Court of Human Rights, 27 November 2008) obliged the federal state to adjust its legislation and foresee the right to legal assistance to all suspects (of crimes of a certain seriousness) from the first police interrogation on ("Wet consultatie- en bijstandsrecht", 2011). For suspects who have not yet reached the age of criminal liability, this Belgian Act of 2011 foresees a mandatory right to legal assistance, which, as contrasted to US legislation, cannot be waived.

COURTS AND JUVENILES

When confronted with an offence committed by a minor, the *public prosecutor* in the Youth Court is always a prosecutor that is specialised in youth cases. This public prosecutor can decide whether or not to dismiss the case. Besides these traditional competences of the Belgian public prosecutor, the new federal Youth Protection Act of 2006 introduces three possibilities for action on juvenile delinquency. From now on, the public prosecutor can accompany the dismissal of the case (1) with "a warning" to the youngster and/or his or her parents. Furthermore the public prosecutor can also launch (2) a "mediation offer" or (3) a "parental internship". These two last measures call for some further specifications.

The introduction of *mediation* in the old welfare system is one of the major innovations of the new Act of 2006. Mediation has been made possible both on the level of the public prosecutor and on the level of the juvenile justice judge. Following the new Act, the participants must be explicit in accepting mediation. A right to legal assistance is foreseen and the law guarantees the confidentiality of the mediation process. Nevertheless one might wonder whether these legal provisions are and can be guaranteed in practice. The offer of mediation, for example, is launched by the public prosecutor, who has the power to prosecute whenever a youngster does not voluntarily agree to participate in a mediation process, or by the juvenile justice judge who can always react more "thoroughly" when there is no co-operation (Eliaerts and Dumortier 2002).

It should also be mentioned that mediation is not introduced as a real alternative or "diversionary" approach for the traditional welfare model. Even when mediation is successful the public prosecutor can still prosecute the youngster and, on the level of the juvenile justice judge, mediation (even in successful cases) can be cumulated with other measures (see below). In this way, mediation seems to become one out of many possibilities in the panoply of welfare measures instead of "real" diversion. Moreover the recent General Comment No. 10 on children's rights in juvenile justice of the UN Committee for the Rights of the Child (2007) clearly states that "the completion of the diversion by the child should result in a definite and final closure of the case" (§27).

The introduction of *the parental internship* is another important innovation of the new Youth Protection Act of 2006. As is the case with mediation, they can be imposed on both the level of the public prosecutor and the level of the juvenile judge. According to the legislature, this new reaction should be seen as a "sanction" aimed at failing parents who "clearly show a lack of interest" for the delinquent behaviour of their offspring. This parental internship consists of 30 h and in general includes individual as well as group counselling. Parents who refuse to follow these parental classes can be punished with a fine or an imprisonment (maximum of 7 days). The new possibility to punish parents for delinquent behaviour of their children, together with the use of vague legal descriptions, was heavily criticised by academics and fieldworkers (Delens-Ravier 2008). The Belgian Constitutional Court saved the Belgian legislature, however, by claiming that the new "sanction" vis-à-vis parents was in fact a "welfare measure" aimed at sustaining these failing parents (Constitutional Court 2008, Arrêt n° 49/2008, B.8.2). Since 2010, neither the Belgian Government nor the governments of the communities foresee any fundings for these kinds of "parental internships" (Put 2015). As a consequence, for the moment, this new measure only exists on paper and not in practice.

Finally, it should be noted that the new Act does not foresee the possibility of imposing community service or intermediate treatment on the level of the public prosecutor. This leads to the supposition that these actions are no longer tolerated under the new Act.

Level of the Juvenile Justice Judge: As mentioned above, since the Children's Act of 1912, the juvenile justice judge is a single-seated and "specialised"[3] judge who follows the youngster throughout the whole judicial process: pretrial phase, trial and execution of the measure (post-trial phase). The new Youth Protection Act of 2006 did not change this old idea of the welfare-oriented juvenile justice judge. Nevertheless the new Act did introduce a new list of criteria to render judicial decisions (whether they are taken during pretrial, trial or execution of measure) more objective. This list refers to criteria, among others, like "the personality of the minor", but also "the seriousness of the offence" and "public safety". At the same time the criteria for the decision to place a minor in public "community institutions" became more stringent. Age limits, as well as criteria concerning the seriousness of the offence, were introduced. These new criteria are applicable for all placements in "community institutions" at every stage of the judicial procedure (pretrial, trial, execution of measure), but will be handled in section "Custodial rules for juveniles" of this article.

During the *pretrial phase*, the juvenile justice judge can take "provisional measures" in order "to investigate the youngster's personality and home situation" and "to guard" him. Within that scope, the juvenile judge can either place the youngster "under supervision" of the social service of the Youth Court (with or without the imposition of additional conditions) or impose a measure of "provisional placement" (with a competent person, in a private institution or, under certain conditions, in a public "community institution").

The new Act states that these provisional measures should only be taken for the shortest time possible and that they should never be taken with the aim to sanction in an immediate way the youngster involved. Nevertheless we notice that the "provisional measures" can also consist of fulfilling 30 h of community service, interdiction on leaving the parental house and placement in a "closed" public "community institution" (see also below, on residential care). Hence the "provisional measures" in practice leave plenty of possibilities to *sanction* a

[3]This specialisation refers to the fact that the juvenile justice judge, even though he or she is an "ordinary" judge of the *Tribunal de Première Instance* (and so definitely a "jurist"), is also used to handle juvenile cases and shows a specific interest in children's matters (e.g. by pursuing further training or conferences on children's matters).

minor immediately during the pretrial phase. At the same time the Act does not foresee real stringent criteria concerning the duration of the measures during the pretrial phase. Moreover, pursuant to the new Act, these provisional measures can also be cumulated.

Besides these traditional "provisional measures", the new Act also allows the juvenile justice judge to launch a "mediation offer" during the pretrial phase, which again may be cumulated with other measures.

As a consequence, one can easily claim that the new Act offers very broad possibilities to intervene during the pretrial phase even though research has identified the growing importance of the pretrial phase as the "decisive phase" and the tensions this brings with the respect of human rights and children's rights, like the right to a fair trial (*before* any measure is taken instead of afterwards) (Dumortier 2006; Van Dijk et al. 2006). As a counterforce, the new Act of 2006 stated that these provisional measures could only be imposed when there are "sufficient serious indices of guilt". However, and quite remarkably, the Belgian Constitutional Court thought this to be unconstitutional, because the judge that has decided whether there are indices of guilt during the pretrial phase cannot be allowed to sit during the trial phase (i.e. the right to an independent judge). Instead of introducing the obligation of a different juvenile justice judge during trial, the Constitutional Court has opted to abolish a new legal guarantee for youngsters during the pretrial phase (Constitutional Court 2008, Arrêt no. 49/2008).

Finally it should be mentioned that a Federal Act of 2002 allows the juvenile justice judge to place a minor in pretrial detention in a Federal Centre, which further enlarges the juvenile judge's possibilities to intervene during the pretrial phase (see below, Sect. "Custodial rules for juveniles").

Once *at trial* the juvenile justice judge has at his or her disposal a panoply of measures. In contrast with the old Act of 1965, the new Act of 2006 foresees, in sentencing guidelines, following the principle of subsidiarity. First of all, the juvenile justice judge has to consider a "mediation or group conferencing offer", then a "written project proposed by the youngster", then the possibility of imposing a measure of "supervision" (with or without further conditions) and only as a last resort the possibility of a custodial sentence (by preference in an "open" institution, otherwise in a "closed" institution). These measures, which can be imposed in a cumulative way, call for some further explanations.

Firstly, we notice again the importance in the new Act for restorative justice initiatives. As contrasted with the level of the public prosecutor, besides victim-offender mediation, the juvenile justice judge can also impose a group conference (*Herstelgericht Groepsoverleg*). This group conference is characterised by the fact that both victim and offender are allowed to invite significant others and that a police officer and social worker can be present.

Secondly, the "written project" proposed by the minor to the juvenile justice judge can be aimed at restoring the damage caused by the offence, apologising, participating in a mediation, following intermediate treatment for a maximum

45 h, etc. This "written project" is an innovation surrounded with more questions than answers. It is not quite clear what exactly the legislature intends from this measure, nor how this "written project" should emerge in practice. We assume that the lawyer of the minor will have to play an important role in informing and encouraging here. Otherwise, if the social services of the Youth Court or the juvenile justice judge should even *whisper* what the minor should propose, this written project can easily become an instrument to "self-inflict" what the Youth Court in fact wants to impose (Christiaens and Dumortier 2006).

Thirdly, a wide range of ambulatory measures are foreseen to keep the minor in freedom instead of placing him or her in custody: admonition, supervision by the social services of the Youth Court (with or without further conditions), intensive educational supervision, community service for a maximum of 150 h, ambulatory treatment by psychological services, etc. It is important here to notice that only the first three measures can be imposed on children under the age of 12 years, excluding as a consequence the possibility of imposing community service on young children.

Fourthly, the new Act introduces a diversification of the possibilities to place a minor. Besides the old possibilities to place a youngster with a (1) "competent private person" (foster family), (2) in a private institution or (3) in an "open" or "closed" community institution, the new Act of 2006 creates the additional possibilities to (4) place a minor with a "(legal) corporate body" in order to fulfil a "positive achievement", or (5) to place the minor in a hospital, in a service that organises withdrawal courses (alcohol, drugs) or in an open or closed juvenile psychiatric institution.

As mentioned above, the Youth Protection Act of 2006 introduced new legal criteria for the placement of minors in community institutions (see Sect. "Custodial rules for juveniles"). Moreover, pursuant to the new Act, the juvenile justice judge has to specify in his or her judgment the duration of the placement, a duration that can only be prolonged in the exceptional case of "continuously bad behaviour" of the youngster or "dangerous behaviour towards himself or others". The new Act also introduces the possibility for juvenile justice judges to adjourn the placement if the minor is prepared to fulfil a community service order of up to 150 h.

To complete this overview of the juvenile justice judge's options at trial, one should not forget that the juvenile justice judge can also transfer juvenile delinquents from the age of 16 to adult courts (see further on transfer) and/or impose a parental internship (see above).

During the *execution of the measure*, the juvenile justice judge can revise the measure at any time, always taking into account, of course, the legal criteria imposed by the new Youth Protection Act (especially concerning placements in community institutions). Finally, all measures imposed by the juvenile justice judge end in principle at the age of majority (18 years). Nevertheless, the juvenile justice judge can extend provisional measures until the age of 20 years. Measures taken at trial can also be prolonged until 20 years when the minor requests this himself or herself or in case of "continuously bad or dangerous behaviour" by the youngster. In cases where a minor committed an offence after the age of 16 or in cases of very serious offences committed by children older than 12 years, the juvenile justice judge can even prolong measures until the age of 23 years.

CUSTODIAL RULES FOR JUVENILES

To explain the custodial rules in depth is quite a complex task. This is due to the complicated division of competences in Belgium and the ongoing state reform processes, but also the mixing of delinquent youth with non-delinquent youth—at least in the Flemish community institutions—the mixing of convicted juveniles with juveniles detained on remand and the existence of the transfer mechanism. Moreover, from a legal point of view, juveniles are according to the Youth Protection Act of 2006 never *imprisoned*, but always *placed in community institutions*, even though in practice certain *institutions* resemble heavily *youth detention centres or prisons*. Therefore we will limit ourselves to some general principles and data concerning custodial rules and capacity for juveniles. First we will explain that, in principle, only welfare-oriented community institutions are allowed to execute the detention of youngsters. Afterwards we will elaborate on custodial rules during pretrial phase and the remarkable existence in Flanders of a penal-oriented community institution. Then the custodial rules after conviction will be explained and finally we will elaborate on the transfer mechanism that exists in Belgium.

Welfare-Oriented Community Institutions: The Basic Custodial Approach in Belgium

In principle, only community institutions are allowed to organise the detention of minors in Belgium. These community institutions can be characterised as *open* or *closed* public institutions. The former, in general, have less rigid discipline and provide more possibilities to exit the institution (for reasons of schooling, visiting parents, etc.). The latter provide a more structured daily regime with less possibility to leave the institution and more attention is paid towards the protection of the public.

Pursuant to the new Youth Protection Act of 2006, certain legal criteria should be fulfilled in order to place a minor in a community institution (whether this happens during the pretrial phase or after sentencing). Minors who have reached the age of 12 and who have committed (or are alleged to have committed) an offence of a certain seriousness (punishable with 3 years of imprisonment or more if the offence was committed by an adult) can be send to "open" community institutions. For "closed" institutions the criteria are even more stringent. The minor has to be at least 14 years old (in exceptional cases the age of 12 is accepted) and should have committed (or is alleged to have committed) an offence punishable with at least 5 years' imprisonment if the offence was committed by an adult. Certain "violent offences" can also lead to a placement in open or closed community institutions. In cases of recidivism the legal criteria concerning the seriousness of the offence become less stringent for both types of institutions (Christiaens and Dumortier 2006). Minors who have not complied with a protection measure imposed by the juvenile justice judge can also be sent, under certain conditions, to an open or closed community institution. In this case a clear maximum duration of 6 months is prescribed, with no possibility of extension.

The community institutions play a double role in Belgian juvenile justice practice. On the one hand they fulfil a mission of observing and guarding the minor during the pretrial phase. This leads to an "observation report" which should guide the juvenile justice judge in imposing the most appropriate measure after conviction. On the other hand the community institutions also have a mission to re-educate minors who have been sent there by the juvenile justice judge after their conviction. However, there is no specialisation at the institutional level in this perspective since all minors are mingled.

Detention on Remand

A placement in a community institution during the pretrial phase is normally ordered for 3 months, a period that can be prolonged by the juvenile justice judge once for 3 months and subsequently on a monthly basis. Even though in principle community institutions are competent for the organisation of juvenile delinquents' detention, a federal centre opened its doors in the beginning of 2002. This was due to the fact that Belgium, after being condemned by the European Court of Human Rights in the *Bouamar v. Belgium case* (1988) for having unlawfully detained a juvenile in an adult prison, decided to abolish the possibility for juvenile judges to detain youngsters on remand in adult prisons. However, this abolition in the beginning of 2002 immediately led to some releases with huge media attention of young delinquents due to a claimed lack of capacity in the community institutions. Only 2 months after the abolition of adult detention during the pretrial phase, the federal "Youth Detention Act" of 2002 was passed and an old military casern was speedily turned into a federal centre to detain delinquent boys in order to "protect public safety" (Christiaens and Dumortier 2002). In the years that followed other federal youth detention centres were created.

According to the "Youth Detention Act" of 2002, these institutions can only play a role during the pretrial phase by offering detention on remand for *boys* over 14 years old, who are alleged to have committed a crime of a certain seriousness (punishable with 5 years' imprisonment or more if committed by an adult) and for whom there is no place available in a community institution. They are initially placed by the juvenile justice judge for a period of 5 days, after which the judge has to reconsider whether to prolong the pretrial detention for 1 month.

After that month the juvenile justice judge again has to reconsider whether a prolongation for 1 month is necessary. After a maximum of 2 months and 5 days the minor can no longer be held at these centres.

Consequently, from 2002 on, there were two kinds of youth detention institutions: (1) the more *welfare-oriented* community institutions where pretrial and convicted youngsters are mingled indiscriminately together, since the main aim of these institutions is the welfare of the child, and (2) federal centres that were emblematic of the emerging *penal-oriented approach* and that functioned solely as a pretrial youth detention centre in order to protect public safety and to be a "backup" for community institutions in case they were full. However due to the recent State Reform of 2014 communities became competent for these federal centres. In Flanders, the federal centre became a Flemish community institution, however still functioning under the realm of the federal more *penal-oriented* Act of 2002 (and this until and if the Flemish parliament decides otherwise). The parliament of the French community however decided to abolish the Federal Act of 2002 and to turn their federal detention centre into a traditional welfare-oriented community institution. Consequently in the French community, as contrasted with the Flemish community, all community institutions are welfare-oriented institutions (at least according to the *law in books* ...).

Custodial Rules After Conviction

Once convicted, juvenile delinquents can only be placed in the traditional welfare-oriented community institutions (the "Flemish" penal-oriented exception only count during pretrial phase). The same legal criteria as mentioned above (regarding the seriousness of the offence, the age of the juvenile, etc.) must be taken into account. Moreover, placing a juvenile in a community institution is prescribed in the Youth Protection Act of 2006 as a measure of last resort (see also art. 40 of the UN CRC). As mentioned above, convicted juvenile delinquents end up in the same community institutions as juveniles awaiting their trial (with the exception of the penal-oriented community institution in Flanders that only functions as a "detention-on-remand" institution for delinquent boys). Moreover, pursuant to Flemish legislation, minors who grow up in a "problematic educational situation" (*verontrustende situtatie*) can also be placed in (Flemish) community institutions. Hence the Flemish community institutions can have a mixed population of delinquent and non-delinquent minors. In practice this situation especially occurs in the community institution for girls at Beernem (Flanders).

When, at trial, the juvenile justice judge wants to order a placement in a community institution, he or she has to specify the duration of the placement. This duration however can, later on, be prolonged by the juvenile justice judge in the exceptional case of "continuously bad behaviour" of the youngster or "dangerous behaviour towards himself or herself or others" (see Table 12.1).

TABLE 12.1. Number of places in institutions, girls-boys, French-Flemish community

	French community			*Flemish community*		
	Boys	*Girls*	*Total*	*Boys*	*Girls*	*Total*
Open places	214	44	258	126	10	136
Closed places	64	5	69	66	46	112
Federal centre[a]	37	0	37	52	0	52
Total	315	49	364	244	56	300

Source: Gilbert et al. 2012: 63

[a]With the recent state reform of 2014 these federal centres became community institutions

Transfer of Juveniles

To end our discussion on custodial rules, the transfer mechanism will be explained. As mentioned in the beginning of this contribution, the age of criminal responsibility was raised from 16 to 18 with the Youth Protection Act (YPA) of 1965. Since 1992 the age of civil majority in Belgium has also been set on 18 years. From that age on youngsters are considered as adults. There are no special provisions for young adults within the Belgian criminal justice system. For example, there is no possibility to keep young adults aged between 18 and 21 in the juvenile justice system, and protective youth measures cannot be applied by the criminal justice system. However, with the recent *sixth state reform* (2014–2015), some exceptions blurring the boundaries between minority and majority were included in the law (e.g. if the offence was committed before the 18th birthday, youth measures can be prolonged until the age of 23) (D'Hondt 2007).

In general, juveniles younger than 18 are presumed to lack penal responsibility and are dealt with separately from adults. Youth offenders are prosecuted within the juvenile justice system. However, *two exceptions* to this rule exist. The first exception is when a juvenile aged 16 years or older commits a *violation of traffic regulations* or related violations. In this case the youngster is automatically prosecuted before the police court (this is the lowest level of penal jurisdiction). However, the police magistrate may still refer the youngster to the juvenile judge when a juvenile measure is assumed to be more adequate. The legislator installed this collective automatic waiver for practical reasons, namely to prevent an overstocking of the juvenile justice system with traffic violations which might impede its core activity of protection and re-education (Van Dijk et al. 2006).

The second exception is *transfer to adult court* (waiver) for young offenders aged 16 or older.[4] This exceptional mechanism was created for young offenders "steeped in antisocial behaviour" (Lox 1966). In other words, transfer was created for the so-called hardcore young offenders or serious offenders. As the

[4]In fact, the Youth Court transfers the case to the public prosecutor, who—theoretically—can still dismiss the case or propose mediation. In practice, this only happens sporadically, because as a rule, it is the public prosecutor who requests the transfer.

transfer mechanism was intended to be exceptional, the judgement to transfer had to be extensively motivated by the Youth Court. Although the criteria for transfer were not specified, the personality of the young offender was decisive in the decision whether or not to transfer the case. In order to obtain relevant information on the personality and the social context of the young offender, two inquiries were (and still are) required; a medical-psychological examination, carried out by a psychiatrist, a psychologist or a multidisciplinary team of experts, and a social inquiry, carried out by social workers.

In 2006, the *transfer regulations were modified*. Surprisingly, although politicians came under heavy pressure and a retributive discourse prevailed, the lower age limit (16 years) for transfer was not altered with the reform of 2006. Before 2006, neither the seriousness of the offence nor previous contacts with the juvenile justice system were legal prerequisites for transfer. The Youth Court could take these elements into account, however, if they provided information on the personality of the young offender (Nuytiens et al. 2005). This changed in 2006, with the introduction of two new *non-cumulative criteria* to decide to transfer. The first one states that the offence(s) of which the young offender is charged has to be a severe one: aggravated violent theft, sexual assault (with threats or violence) and battery resulting in death or severe physical injuries, rape, robbery with murder, torture or homicide/murder. The second criterion stipulates that when the offence is not a serious one, at least one youth protection measure had to be imposed on the youngster.

Before 2006 transferred juveniles were *sent to trial* in the Magistrates Court (*Correctionele Rechtbank*) or in the Crown Court (*Hof van Assisen*), depending on the gravity of the offence(s). With the 2006 YPA a new jurisdiction was put in place: the Extended Youth Court. In each youth court a special chamber was created that takes over the role of the Magistrates Court after the juvenile transfer. This special chamber consists of three judges: one judge from the Magistrates Court and two judges with specific training in juvenile justice matters. Only the most severe offences are still tried in the Crown Court. When a transferred juvenile appears before this court, two of the three judges need to have had this special training.

Since transferred offenders are equated with adults, both the Extended Youth Court and the Crown Court can impose *punishments* from the criminal justice system, including imprisonment. The reform of 2006 abolished the life sentence for transferred offenders, establishing the maximum penalty at 30 years of imprisonment (Christiaens and Nuytiens 2009). Mandatory sentencing in the Crown Court for grave offences, as in England and Wales, was proposed, but was not retained. Before 2006, although international conventions prescribe the separation of children and adults, transferred juveniles who were remanded in custody after the transfer decision ended up in an adult prison (Nuytiens et al. 2006). If the juvenile was eventually sentenced to *prison* by the Magistrates Court or the Crown Court, this too was served in an adult facility and juveniles were not separated from the adult prisoners (Nuytiens et al. 2006). Since 2006 it is no longer possible to detain juveniles in adult prisons. The remand custody as well as the prison sentence are executed in a specialised juvenile detention centre. Both in the Flemish and the French community, 10–20 places are foreseen for these transferred juveniles (in Flanders in a separate "detention" centre that recently—due to the state reform—became a community institution; in the French community in a separate wing of a community institution). However, youngsters who seriously disrupt or disturb life in the juvenile detention centre or endanger the integrity of other youngsters and/or staff members can still end up in adult prisons. Also, when there is no vacancy in the detention centre a youngster can be transported to an adult prison. Above this, girls still end up in adult prisons as the government omitted to create such a centre for transferred girls (Nuytiens et al. 2015).

It appears that transfer of youngsters in Belgium has been and still is a *moderate practice*, but that the application of transfer shows remarkable geographical diversity (Gilbert et al. 2012). Besides, recent research illustrates that the *judicial pathway following transfer* does not end there for the majority of the transferred offenders. A sample of 210 transferred offenders was followed into adulthood (current age between 30 and 40). It appears that more than half of them were convicted recently, and almost a third is currently residing in prison or has left prison recently (Nuytiens et al. 2015).

Finally, keeping the transfer mechanism in place is a *principal and political matter*. It seems as though children's rights are weighed against the perceived necessity of a "harsher" approach to severe juvenile delinquency. At present it appears that juvenile transfer will remain a part of the Belgian legislation (Put and Hespel 2014). Neither the Flemish- nor the French-speaking community authorities, who recently became competent in this matter, are planning to abolish it.

DIVERSION AND ALTERNATIVE SANCTIONS FOR JUVENILES

While *police-level* diversion is not foreseen in the YPA, in practice there are some diversion projects at this level. For example, several Flemish communities have launched a *first-offenders-project* targeting young offenders who commit petty offences (e.g. shoplifting) and who are arrested for the first time (Put 2015). Also, the practice of police mediation is quite common. In this case the police organises a mediation procedure before sending the case to the public prosecutor. Research has shown that large differences exist among these mediation practices (Aertsen and Lemonne 2003).

In 1965, the Belgian legislator also omitted to include regulations on diversionary practices for young offenders at the *level of the public prosecutor*. The rise of "alternative sanctions" in the 1980s in Belgium was clearly a bottom-up movement, setting up all kinds of diversionary and alternative sanction projects in the field. These pilot projects (1980s) were generalised during the 1990s, but with clear differences between the northern, Flemish-speaking community and the southern, French-speaking community. Most notable are the differences in the development of restorative justice mediation practices. Research has made clear that in the 1990s diversionary or informal ways of dealing with young offenders were still very "marginal". Only 4.2% of the prosecutors' decisions concerning young offenders resulted explicitly in an alternative sanction (Vanneste 2003). For example, youngsters who successfully completed community service or a victim-offender mediation would not be prosecuted before the youth court. In about 70% of all cases, the public prosecutor's decision resulted in a dismissal of the case. However, these dismissals may represent the front window for a more informal practice of dealing with young offenders.

The *2006 YPA* formalised practices of diversion and (in)formal dealing with young delinquents at the public prosecutor's level. The *cautioning of young offenders* and their parents was formally introduced as a "low-level" intervention. Indifferent parents of young offenders could also be required to follow a "*parental internship*" (this was however already abolished in practice in 2010). Within the reformed Belgian juvenile justice system, priority must be given to the principle of restoration. Hence, *restorative mediation* on the public prosecutor's level was also formalised in the 2006 YPA. A successful mediation procedure however does not guarantee a dismissal of the case (Put 2015). This contradicts the viewpoint of the Children's Rights Committee that a successful diversionary procedure must result in dismissal (General Comment 10 Children's Rights Committee, 2007).[5]

The 1965 YPA provided the possibility of alternative ways of dealing with young offenders by *the youth court*. It was not until the 1980s that the alternative sanctioning practice was set up through different local pilot projects. In general, the discourse held that these sanctions had to be an alternative to the detention or placement of young offenders in public institutions. However, studies illustrated that these alternative ways of dealing with young offenders functioned more as an alternative to the dismissal of the case, resulting in net widening, rather than in a deinstitutionalisation or a reduction of incarceration of youngsters (Vanderhaegen & Eliaerts 2002).

Since 2006, alternative ways of dealing with young offenders by the youth court include community service, learning projects, mediation and family group conferencing (FGC). In the 2006 YPA is referred to these settlements as "restorative and constructive measures". Youngsters are seen as active agents, held responsible for their acts and expected to take action to restore the damage done (Put et al. 2012). This is remarkable as it contradicts the general principle of youth justice systems, where children are perceived as (partially or fully) irresponsible for their acts (Haines and O'Mahony 2006: 119).

The youth court can impose *community service* on young offenders aged 12 or older. Community service can be imposed autonomously, but also as a condition to keep the youngster in his or her environment. If community service is imposed

[5]http://www2.ohchr.org/english/bodies/crc/docs/CRC.C.GC.10.pdf.

in the preliminary phase (as part of a supervision order), the maximum is 30 h. *Learning projects* can also be imposed by the youth court. These projects consist of training programmes focusing on specific topics (e.g. aggression, drugs). The goals, methods used and structure (individual, in group) are very diverse. Learning projects can be imposed on young offenders in several ways. For example, just as is the case for community service, the youth court can impose a project as condition to keep the youngster in his or her environment. *Victim-offender mediation and FGC* are perceived as "the" restorative justice measures, because—as opposed to community service and learning projects—the victim has a central place. The mediation and FGC practices however have several flaws. For example, success rates of mediation practices are quite low (e.g. stopped prematurely), the involvement of victims remains low and youngsters from ethnic minorities are underrepresented. Furthermore, while the youngster has to participate voluntarily, the concept of voluntariness can be questioned as the youth court is obligated to reckon with the outcome of the mediation procedure. In that sense, the youngster might feel obliged to participate (Cartuyvels et al. 2010).

The application rate of "restorative and constructive measures" is and has always been different depending on the judicial district (Gilbert et al. 2012; Nuytiens and Van Grunderbeeck 2003).

It appears that, today, mediation is the most popular restorative and constructive measures, but it is most often imposed on the level of the public prosecutor. FGC is not imposed that often (60 times imposed in 2014 as opposed to 2955 mediations).[6]

Since the 2006 reform, some *new/innovative alternative measures* were included in the law. We will discuss the most important ones here: the parental internship, the written project, home confinement ("house arrest") and intensive educational guidance. As the *parental internship* was hardly ever imposed, this measure was abolished in practice in 2010. Research shows that the *written project* is also quite unpopular and that it is only imposed by French-speaking judges (Gilbert et al. 2012). *Home confinement* for youngsters originated from practice. It was launched in 2003 by the Antwerp police. The youngster must stay at home and is checked upon by the police. The youth court can decide to impose other restrictions. There are a lot of geographical differences for what concerns the application of this measure (Gilbert et al. 2012). To date, the measure of *intensive educational guidance* is only implemented in Wallonia as "SAMIO"[7], and focuses on serious offenders. Research shows that this measure is especially used as "last resort" to compensate for the lack of space in the institutions. This contradicts the initial goal of the measure, namely to serve as an alternative for placement.

In *2012*, all decisions of the youth court (25 out of 27 judicial districts) concerning young offenders of 2 months were registered and analysed (Gilbert et al. 2012). It appears that measures implicating that the young offender can stay in

[6] www.steunpuntjeugdhulp.be.

[7] Sections d'Accompagnement, de Mobilisation Intensifs et d'Observation.

his or her environment (with or without conditions) are the most popular ones. In *Flanders*, 1 in 3 measures are conditional decisions that keep the youngster at home. The most frequently mentioned conditions imposed are community service (19%), learning project (18%), attending school regularly (15%), home confinement (12%) and complying with pedagogical or medical guidelines (10%). It appears that the distribution of decisions is quite similar in *the French community*. Also 1 in 3 measures are conditional decisions to keep the youngster at home. The most mentioned conditions are attending school (30%), community service (15%), complying with pedagogical or medical guidelines (13%), not attending a specific place/not meeting a specific person (12%) and home confinement (4%). French-speaking juvenile judges impose more placements in a youth offender institution, but this might be explained by the lack of space in Flemish Youth Offender Institutions.

DIFFERENCES IN TREATMENT OF BOYS AND GIRLS

In the previous chapters we already pointed out some differences between boys and girls. As opposed to boys, girls are mostly drawn into the youth justice system due to non-delinquent cases. Also, girls are younger when they are arrested for an offence (average girls: 15 years; average boys: 17 years). While for both girls and boys property offences are the most common offences, it appears that boys are more arrested for serious property offences (e.g. burglary and violent thefts) (Openbaar Ministerie 2012). Another difference is the number and nature of places foreseen in the residential institutions. Furthermore, as mentioned, there is no specific specialised juvenile detention centre for girls transferred to adult court. These girls still end up in adult prisons. For what concerns differences in treatment, it appears that in Flanders, girls are more often placed in a closed section of a residential institutions and less often in an open section. This may be due to the fact that there are less open places for girls. Also, community service is less frequently imposed on girls than on boys (Gilbert et al. 2012).

CONCLUSIONS: CURRENT DEBATES AND CHALLENGES

> In 2006 Belgium saw its "old" Youth Protection Act of 1965 modernised into a hybrid model of welfare, restorative justice and "just desert". Politicians and field workers seemed more or less satisfied that the reform of the old Act of 1965 had finally been achieved without too much damage. After all, the welfare model and the old Youth Protection Act of 1965 remain the basis of the new Youth Justice Act. At the same time, however, proponents of, on the one hand, restorative justice and, on the other hand, tough (penal) approaches can hardly be described as the "losers" of this 2006 reform.

On the contrary, restorative justice approaches, following the new sentencing guidelines in the Youth Justice Act of 2006, receive the "gold medal" for preferable judicial approaches towards juvenile delinquency. And (political) proponents of tough approaches have encouraged a notable enlargement of (often highly secured) youth detention capacity (as a means to detain youngsters on remand and/or for transferred youngsters). Moreover, the "modernisation" of the old Protection Act of 1965 managed to sail around many fundamental questions and critiques on the Belgian youth justice system.

A first fundamental question remains the respect for children's rights. In this sense we specifically want to stress, on the one hand, the continuing importance in law and in practice of the pretrial phase as the "decisive phase" and the tensions this brings with fundamental human and children's rights. On the other hand, the new Act of 2006 did not take any steps either towards improving the legal position of juveniles deprived of their liberty (e.g. lack of right to formally complain). Finally, the continuing (political) support and encouragement for the transfer of minors can hardly be regarded as in concordance with the UN Convention on the Rights of the Child.

Secondly, we notice the continuing policy and practice of mingling delinquent and non-delinquent children in the youth protection system, even in closed (Flemish) community institutions. The reform of 2006 did not even try to go into this question. Moreover, huge societal and scientific attention for punitive trends towards *delinquent* children does not have to divert our attention from the important presence of "problematic" (but non-delinquent) children within the juvenile protection system. Are these children also to be confronted with punitive tendencies? Within this perspective it is noteworthy to mention that in 1999 (and in 2004 and 2013) the federal parliament passed an Act that regulated the possibility for local authorities to sanction in an administrative and speedy way "incivilities" of adults and youngsters. Research is needed to unravel the influence of this new legislation on the sanctioning practice towards (non-delinquent) juveniles and its relation to the youth protection system. After all, pursuant to legislation from the French and the Flemish communities, "problematic behaviour" by youngsters (like "incivilities") should normally be handled by the juvenile protection system on the basis of welfare-oriented principles and in the best interests of the child.

Finally, the governmental authorities in Belgium, and there are many of them, show an obstinate incapacity to collect and centralise statistical data on the phenomena of youth delinquency and on the reactions of the youth protection and the juvenile justice systems. This situation turns any scientific research on the Belgian youth justice system's practice into a hazardous enterprise. Within this context, governmental policy like increasing residential capacity seems anything but evidence based.

However, with the recent state reform, the Flemish and French communities will be able to take a new direction. There might be a new opportunity to create a more coherent and transparent juvenile justice legislation guided and inspired by a children's rights approach. However, on the basis of available governmental documents, such major transformations are not in sight yet.

REFERENCES

Aertsen, I., & Lemonne, A. (2003). *Lokale bemiddeling of schadebemiddeling als 'alternatieve maatregel voor lichte misdrijven in België'*. Eindverslag, Leuven/Brussel: K.U. Leuven/Université Libre de Bruxelles.

Bailleau, F., & Cartuyvels, Y. (Eds.). (2007). *La justice pénale des mineurs en Europe. Entre modèle Welfare et inflexions néo-libérales*. Paris: L'Harmattan.

Born, M. (1987). *Jeunes déviants ou délinquants juvéniles?* Brussels: Mardaga.

Brolet, C., & Dumortier, E. (2004). Où va la protection de la jeunesse ? De la peur de la répression et la réforme du droit de la jeunesse'. In *Les dossiers de la Revue du Droit Pénal et de Criminologie—La réaction sociale à la délinquance juvénile* (pp. 99–115). Brussels/Bruges: La Charte/die Keure.

Cartuyvels, Y., Christiaens, J., De Fraene, D., & Dumortier, E. (2010). Juvenile Justice in Belgium seen through the sanctions looking-glass. In F. Bailleau & Y. Cartuyvels (Eds.), *The criminalisation of youth. Juvenile justice in Europe, Turkey and Canada* (pp. 29–58). Brussel: ASP. (Original work published in 2009 in Déviance et Société).

Christiaens, J. (1999). A history of Belgium's Child Protection Act of 1912: The redefinition of the juvenile offender and his punishment. *European Journal of Crime, Criminal Law and Criminal Justice, 7*(1), 5–21.

Christiaens, J., & Dumortier, E. (2002). Wanneer de nood hoog is, is de gevangenis nabij: Over de afschaffing van art. 53 JBW en de invoering van de jeugdgevangenis. *Tijdschrift voor Jeugdrecht en Kinderrechten, 1*, 53–57.

Christiaens, J., & Dumortier, E. (2006). De hervorming van de jeugdbescherming: Tussen pendel en schijnbeweging? In *Kinderrechtengids* Deel 1, 1.8, 20p.

Christiaens, J., & Nuytiens, A. (2009). Transfer of juvenile offenders to adult court in Belgium: critical reflections on the reform of a moderate practice. *Youth Justice, 9*(2), 131–142.

Christiaens, J., and Y. Cartuyvels. (2007). Le modèle perdu de la justice des mineurs en Belgique? Entre droit et protection, paternalisme et responsabilisation, gestion des risques et idéal de traitement. In F. Bailleau & Y. Cartuyvels (Eds.), *La justice pénale des mineurs en Europe. Entre modèle Welfare et inflexions néolibérales* (pp. 77–98). Paris: L'Harmattan.

Christiaens, J., Dumortier, E. & Nuytiens, A. (2010). Belgium. In F. Dünkel, J. Grzywa, P. Horsfield & I. Pruin (Eds.), Juvenile Justice Systems in Europe. Current situation and reform developments (Vol. 3) (pp. 99–130). Mönchengladbach: Forum Verlag Godesberg GmbH.

Constitutional Court (Belgium). (2008). Arrêt n° 49/2008 & Arrêt n° 50/2008, 13 March 2008.

D'Hondt, S. (2007). Nieuwe en vernieuwde maatregelen: overzicht en algemene kenmerken. In J. Put & M. Rom (Eds.), *Het nieuwe jeugdrecht* (pp. 45–66). Brussel: De Boeck & Larcier.

Delens-Ravier, I. (2008). Les parents : partenaires ou adversaires ? In Th. Moreau, I. Ravier & B. Van Keirsbilck (Eds.) *La réforme de la loi du 8 avril 1965 relative de la protection de la jeunesse: premier bilan et perspectives d'avenir. Actes du colloque des 31 mai et 1er juin 2007* (pp. 285–304). Liège: Editions jeunesse et droit.

Donzelot, J. (1977). *La police des familles. Postface de Gilles Deleuze*. Paris: Minuit.

Dumortier, E. (2006). *De jeugdrechter in twijfel. Een onderzoek naar het ontstaan en de praktijk van de kinderrechter*. Ph.D. thesis, Vrije Universiteit Brussel, Brussels. onuitgegeven.

Dumortier, E., Snacken, S., Gutwirth, S. & De Hert, P. (2012). The rise of the penal state. What can human rights do about it? In S. SNACKEN & E. DUMORTIER (Eds.), *Resisting punitiveness in Europe? Welfare, Human Rights & Democracy* (pp. 107–132). New York: Routledge.

Eliaerts, C., & Dumortier, E. (2002). Restorative justice for children: In need of procedural safeguards and standards. In E. Weitekamp & H.-J. Kerner (Eds.), *Restorative justice. Theoretical foundations* (pp. 204–223). Uffculme, Devon, UK: Willan.

European Court of Human Rights (1988) Bouamar v. Belgium, Date: 29 February 1988.

European Court of Human Rights. (2008). *Salduz v. Turkey* judgment of 27th of November 2008.

Gilbert, E., Mahieu, V., Goedseels, E., & Ravier, I. (2012). *Onderzoek naar de beslissingen van jeugdrechters en jeugdrechtbanken in MOF-zaken*. Brussel: Nationaal Instituut voor Criminalistiek en Criminologie.
Goedseels, E. (2002). Cijfers met betrekking tot jeugddelinquentie. In L. Walgrave & P. Goris (Eds.), *Van kattenkwaad en erger. Actuele thema's uit de jeugdcriminologie* (pp. 29–38). Louvain: Garant.
Goedseels, E., Vettenburg, N., & Walgrave, L. (2000). Delinquentie. In H. de Witte, J. Hooge, & L. Walgrave (Eds.), *Jongeren in Vlaanderen: gemeten en geteld. 12- tot 18-jarigen over hun leefwereld en toekomst* (pp. 253–282). Louvain: Universitaire Pers.
Haines, K., & O'Mahony, D. (2006). Restorative approaches, young people and youth justice. In B. Goldson & J. Muncie (Eds.), *Youth crime and justice* (pp. 110–124). Londen: Sage.
Junger-Tas, J. (1976). *Verborgen jeugddelinquentie en gerechtelijke selectie* (public n°38), Brussels: SCJM.
Junger-Tas, J., Terlous, G.-J., & KLEIN, M. (Eds.) (1994). *Delinquent behavior among young people in the western world*. Amsterdam: Kugler.
Lox, F. (1966). Les mesures à l'égard des mineurs. *Annales de Droit, 37*(1), 165–197
Muncie, J., & Goldson, B. (2006). States of transition: Convergence and diversity in international youth justice. In J. Muncie & B. Goldson (Eds.), *Comparative youth justice* (pp. 196–218). London: Sage.
Nuytiens, A., & Van grunderbeeck, S. (2003). Herstelgerichte afhandelingen van delicten gepleegd door minderjarigen. Leerprojecten, gemeenschapsdienst en herstelbemiddeling. *Panopticon, 24*(6), 573–577
Nuytiens, A., Christiaens, J., & Eliaerts, C. (2005). *Ernstige jeugddelinquenten gestraft? Praktijk van de uithandengeving*. Ghent: Academia.
Nuytiens, A., Christiaens, J., Eliaerts, C., & Brolet, C. (2006). *Trajecten van uithanden gegeven jongeren in het strafrecht. Ernstige jeugddelinquenten gestraft—deel 2*. Ghent: Academia.
Nuytiens, A., Jaspers, Y., & Christiaens, J. (2015). Trajecten van uit handen gegeven jongeren in de volwassenheid. *Panopticon, 36*(3), 248–265.
Openbaar Ministerie. (2012). Retrieved from www.om-mp.be/stat
Pleysier, S. (2014). Ondanks beperkt zicht'. De context van 'jongeren in cijfers en letters. In: L. Bradt, S. Pleysier, J. Put, J. Siongers & B. Spruyt (Eds.). *Jongeren in cijfers en letters. Bevindingen uit de JOP-monitor 3 en de JOP-schoolmonitor 2013* (pp. 19–39). Acco: Leuven.
Pleysier, S., & Put, J. (2015). Watskeburt?! Criminaliteit door de jeugd van tegenwoordig. In: B. Pattyn & P. d'Hoine (Eds.), *Jongeren vandaag en de wereld morgen. Lessen voor de eenentwintigsteeeuw eeuw* (pp. 25–46). Leuven: Leuven University Press
Put, J. (2015). *Handboek jeugdbeschermingsrecht*. Brugge: Die Keure.
Put, J., & Hespel, S. (2014). Het jeugdbeschermingsrecht en de zesde staatshervorming. *Panopticon, 35*(5), 463-467.
Put, J., & Walgrave, L. (2006). Belgium: From protection towards accountability? In J. Muncie & B. Goldson (Eds.), *Comparative youth justice* (pp. 111–126). London: Sage.
Put, J., Vanfraechem, I., & Walgrave, L. (2012). Restorative dimensions in Belgian youth justice. *Youth Justice, 12*(2), 83–100.
Spaey, P. (2004). *Violences urbaines et délinquance juvénile à Bruxelles. Les 12-20 ans témoignent*. Paris: L'Harmattan.
UN Committee on the Rights of the Child (CRC). (2007). *CRC General Comment No. 10. (2007): Children's Rights in Juvenile Justice, 25 April 2007*. CRC/C/GC/10. Online. UNHCR Refworld. Retrieved Dec 17, 2008, from http://www.unhcr.org/refworld/docid/4670fca12.html
UN Committee on the Rights of the Child, Concluding Observations: Belgium (2010). CRC/C/BEL/CO/3-4. Online. Retrieved Oct. 20, 2016, from http//www2.ohchr.org/english/bodies/crc/docs/CRC.C.BEL.CO.3-4.doc.
Van De Kerchove, M. (1976). Des mesures répressives aux mesures de sûreté et de protection. Reflexions sur le pouvoir mystificateur du langage. *Revue de droit pénal, 1976–1977*, 245–279.

Van Dijk, C., Eliaerts, C., & Dumortier, E. (2006). Survival of the protection model? Competing goals in Belgian juvenile justice. In J. Junger-Tas & S. H. Decker (Eds.), *International handbook of juvenile justice* (pp. 187–223). Dordrecht: Springer.

Vanderhaegen, R., & Eliaerts, C. (2002). Drie jaar onderzoek in het arrondissement Brussel-Halle-Vilvoorde. In: C. Eliaerts (Ed.), *Constructief sanctioneren van jeugddelinquenten. Een commentaar bij vijf jaar werking van Bas!* (pp. 182–221). Brussel: VUB Press

Vanneste, C. (2003). Les logiques décisionnelles des magistrats du parquet et des juges de la jeunesse à l'égard des mineurs délinquants. *Revue de Droit pénal et de Criminologie, 2*, 232–263.

Vanneste, C., Goedseels, E., & Detry, L. (2007). *Onderzoek met betrekking tot de productie en wetenschappelijke exploitatie van cijfergegevens aangaande jeugddelinquentie en jeugdbescherming. Eerste onderzoeksrapport. Analyse van instroom op de jeugdparketten voor het jaar 2005*. Brussels: NICC.

Vercaigne, C., Walgrave, L., Mistiaen, P., & Kesteloot, C. (2000). *Verstedelijking, sociale uitsluiting van jongeren en staatcriminaliteit*. Louvain: Onderzoeksrapport, DWTC.

Vettenburg, D., Elchardus, M., & Walgrave, L. (Eds.). (2007). *Jongeren in cijfers en letters, Bevindingen uit de JOP-monitor 1*. Louvain: LannooCampus.

Els Dumortier (1972) holds a master's degree in law (1995, Vrije Universiteit Brussel) and in criminology (1997, VUB). She is a fulltime professor and teaches three bachelor courses (youth justice law, law and criminology and introduction to criminological research methods) and one master course (youth criminology) at the Faculty of Law and Criminology, Vrije Universiteit Brussel (Belgium). She is a member of the European Council for Juvenile Justice and a founding member of the (Flemish) Children's Rights Knowledge Centre in Belgium.

Her research specifically focuses on questions concerning youth justice (practices) and children's rights both in contemporary times and in the past (twentieth century). She participates in several national and international scientific networks in the domain of youth justice (Dutch, English and French speaking), both contemporary focussed and historical. International publications include *Resisting punitiveness in Europe?: welfare, human rights and democracy* (with Sonja Snacken).

Jenneke Christiaens is a fulltime professor at the Vrije Universiteit Brussels. She is a member of the Criminology department and at the present chair of CRiS—Crime and Society research group. Between 2002 and 2008 she was a professor at the University of Genth in the Dept. of Criminology and Penal Law. Jenneke Christiaens has a master degree in educational as well as criminological sciences, and obtained her Ph.D. in criminology in 1998 with a criminological-historical study on the birth of the Belgian juvenile justice system. She teaches *introduction to criminology* (1st Bachelor), juvenile justice and youth criminology (3rd bachelor), and the master courses *Youth criminology* and *Crime and the city*. Her research interests concern juvenile justice practices, youth delinquency as well as (youth) crime, public space and the city.

Current research focuses on judicial trajectories of youngsters into adulthood, desistance and impact of judicial intervention from a life history perspective; detention of young people; gendered youth justice practices; judging juveniles in court; youngsters, their use(s) of public space and criminalisation.

An Nuytiens is a postdoctoral researcher and a research professor at the Crime and Society research group (CriS) of the Vrije Universiteit Brussel (Belgium). She conducted studies on restorative youth justice, transfer of juvenile offenders to Adult Court and youth offenders' profiles and delinquent pathways. In recent years her research interests are in the area of female offenders. Her work currently focuses on life histories and criminal careers of female prisoners, delinquent pathways of girls in the juvenile justice system, gendered pathways to crime and prison, motherhood in prison and Romani girls in the Youth Court.

13

Denmark

Anette Storgaard

From a global perspective Denmark is a rich welfare state with a low crime rate and a low prison rate. Nevertheless criminal policy plays an important role on the contemporary political agenda. Danish criminal policy occurs in a political context and has a good deal in common with other Scandinavian countries. However, the current debates and developments suggest that Denmark may be taking the first significant divert steps from that road.

THE LEGAL STATUS OF JUVENILES

The legal status of juveniles varies across legal spheres in Denmark. Many legal definitions of age are of old origin and are widely seen by the public as "natural" in the sense that they do not generate much public discussion.[1] This is the case for the age limit of 18 as a general age for becoming legally competent, including the ownership of property. The age of 18 is the age at which one can buy real estate, be married to a Danish citizen,[2] and decide for oneself which—if any—religious community one wants to join. Eighteen is also the age at which one may earn a driving license. The age for the right to vote at elections is 18, too. All in all one would say that the age of 18 is the most important age in regard to Danish legislation.[3]

Within the latest decade the issue of age limits in the Danish legal system has received considerable attention. Not all new legal rules have reached the same broad acceptance and recognition as the abovementioned rules. Some of the new age limits have been much debated in public. A 2007 rule declares that children

[1]For a complete presentation of the historical and legal sociological perspective of the original definition of the legal status of juveniles in Denmark see Dalberg-Larsen.

[2]There are other rules when one person in a couple is not a Danish citizen, see immediately below.

[3]The voting right has been lowered gradually. In 1976 it was lowered from 20 to 18.

A. Storgaard (✉)
Department of Law, Business and Social Sciences, University of Aarhus,
Bartholins Alle 16, 8000 Aarhus C, Aarhus, Denmark
e-mail: as@law.au.dk

S.H. Decker, N. Marteache (eds.), *International Handbook of Juvenile Justice*,
DOI 10.1007/978-3-319-45090-2_13

of all ages are to be heard about their wishes about which parent to live with when their parents are divorced (i.e., the question about whether they want to stay mainly with the mother or the father). Before this change only children above the age of 12 were explicitly involved in this matter. This issue received a good deal of debate. The pros argued that children had the right to influence their lives while those opposed criticized this change arguing that the children were placed in a tremendous dilemma and that the professionals were not sufficiently equipped for their part in this.

Another recent age limit which has been much debated is the rule that in order to marry a non-Danish citizen the Dane as well as the foreign partner must be 24 years old. Recall that 18 is the age at which Danish couples can marry. This rule existed because the authorities wanted to prevent marriages that were arranged by parents. The arguments against this rule were that young people travel much more now than years ago and the likeliness that they meet a future partner while travelling is higher now.

Apart from the above these relatively new and hotly debated legal regulation of the status of juveniles in Denmark, there has been a tendency to increase the amount and the scope of legal regulations in matters that before were seen as matters of parental responsibility. In the Danish context it was very unusual in the 1990s and the beginning of the 2000s that national regulations intervened in questions like selling and using tobacco and alcohol. But lately regulations have been implemented that prohibit selling cigarettes to persons below 18 and beer to be sold to persons below 16 in drugstores. This can be seen as part of two tendencies in Danish society, namely (1) the focus on health and (2) a growing tendency for state intervention in what before was seen as private sphere. The main reason for this relatively new regulation is an effort to protect juveniles from their own possible lack of maturity and their parents' possible lack of responsibility. In a Danish political context there is no difference in the attitude toward such questions regardless of whether it is the right wing or left wing parties are in power (Storgaard 2013). However, there are some inconsistencies if we look at the willingness to protect juveniles from state intervention. This will be illustrated below, mainly in part 3, 7, 8, and 9.

AGE OF MAJORITY

From 1866 to 1905 the age of criminal responsibility was 10 years of age. From age 10 to age 15 the level of maturity (the ability to act responsibly) had to be considered in court from case to case. From 1905 to 1933 the age of responsibility was 14. In the criminal law which came into force in 1933 and is still in force—with adjustments—the age of criminal responsibility was fixed at the age of 15 (Greve 2004).

Neither Denmark nor any other Scandinavian Country have (or have ever had) a particular Juvenile Justice system or Juvenile Justice Law and in all the Scandinavian Countries the age of criminal responsibility as well as the age of (sexual) consent is 15. However, this tradition is currently being challenged by Denmark.

The first challenge to this long tradition was in the period between July 2010 and February 2012 where the age of criminal responsibility was lowered to 14. One political party (Danish People's Party) had proposed this several times before but it was always turned down. In 2009 a political situation came up where the government was in the minority and needed votes for the decision of the state budget for 2010. A compromise was made where the People's Party voted for the budget and in return the party gained consensus on the lowering of the age of criminal responsibility. A few other rules in the Criminal Code were changed in a repressive direction at the same time such as a removal of a maximum of 8 years of imprisonment if the offender was below 18 when the offence was committed. After the following election a new government was in power and the age of criminal responsibility was returned back to 15.

The age of consent was not changed and is not included in the renewed debate. In 2014 a new proposal was presented by four political parties in the Parliament. This was not a proposal for a new law but a proposal to instruct the government to bring forward a proposal for a new juvenile court directed at juveniles between 12 and 17 (B 19/2014). Included in a new court system is a new probation service and a new juvenile criminal process. Included in the proposal was an effort to be consistent with the UN Convention on the Rights of the Child that the Government should secure that juveniles could not be imprisoned with persons over the age of 18. At first this proposal was not endorsed by the Parliament. But after an election (June 2015) the new government has announced that the Juvenile Justice system will be renewed in the near future. The rhetoric in the debate for the time being (spring 2016) is concentrated on a focused response to juvenile crime, defeating the "the hard core" offenders, and things like "stopping little brothers' involvement with crime." On the other hand, the Minister of Justice says in public that as far as he is concerned, children should never go to prison. Important questions have still not been answered, including: what age defines the transition from child to juvenile. For the time being it seems likely that later this year Denmark will become the first Scandinavian Country to introduce a Juvenile Justice Law and a Juvenile Justice System.

The age of sexual consent has not been included in the debate and is not likely to be included. It seems most likely that the age of consent will remain 15. Today it is widely believed that there is no criminal response to cases where a 14- and a 15-year-old have sexual intercourse. How a similar situation will be handed in the future if they are both included in a criminal justice system is hard to say.

DENMARK AND THE UN CONVENTION ON THE RIGHTS OF THE CHILD

The UN Convention on the Rights of the Child of 1989 was ratified in Denmark in 1991. However, Denmark made an explicit reservation concerning article 40b(v) which says: "Every child alleged as or accused of having infringed the penal law has at least the following guarantees: ...(V) If considered to have infringed the penal law, to have this decision and any measures imposed in consequence thereof reviewed by a higher competent, independent and impartial authority or judicial body according to law." This article has not been the object of widespread debate but may be challenged on a regular basis. The challenges are not related to the criminal justice system, which respects the basic principles in criminal procedure such as "nulla poena sine lege" and the right to appeal. But the Danish social welfare system is authorized to impose measures on juveniles between 12 and 17 years old as a consequence of suspected crimes without the criminal guilt being tried in court. The most serious measure is that the child is placed in a secure institution under the auspices of the social welfare system without any concent from itself or the parents. This decision is made in the social welfare system but a judge is involved. There is no appeal and the duration of this confinement is not defined beforehand. This measure is to be based on a holistic assessment of the best interest of the child and is not seen as punishment.

Before the Danish ratification of the UN Convention a comprehensive debate took place among politicians and experts about article 37c, saying: "Every child deprived of liberty shall be treated with humanity and respect for the inherent dignity of the human person, and in a manner which takes into account the needs of persons of his or her age. In particular, every child deprived of liberty shall be separated from adults unless it is considered in the child's best interest not to do so and shall have the right to maintain contact with his or her family through correspondence and visits, save in exceptional circumstances"; The main issue of the debate was the guarantee of separation of children from adults. As the Danish age of criminal responsibility was (and remains) 15 and as the Convention counts an individual as a child until the age of 18 and further as Denmark did not have (and still does not have) a specific juvenile justice system there was (and still is) a risk that children between 15 and 17 years old will be imprisoned with adults.

There were two divergent viewpoints in the debate before the ratification. One the one hand there was the view that individuals below 18 and over 18 should be separated when deprived of their liberty. But on the other hand it was seen as overkill to build a new prison for juveniles. Denmark has a total prison population of roughly 4000 people and only one prison with more than 200 inmates. It would be very costly to build one or more new prisons for juveniles and also very likely that if this would be the solution (a) there would only be one new prison and the consequence of this would be longer distance for visitors to travel and therefore perhaps less contact to parents and others during the prison time and (b) as prison places tend to be in use the existence of a juvenile prison might lead to an increase in the number of juvenile prisoners.

No juvenile prison was ever built and over time it was decided (and to a pretty large degree practiced) to place all juveniles who were supposed to serve in high security facilities in one prison and all juvenile prisoners who were supposed to serve in low security regime in another. These prisons still house a majority of adults but the intention was to concentrate the juveniles in one wing and pay special attention to them.

The juveniles in pretrial custody are in the main transferred to a secured juvenile institution under the auspices of the social welfare system).[4] This main rule is defined in an internal instruction for the prosecutors (Instruction 4/2007 with changes of December 2012 from the superior prosecutor Part 3. (Rigsadvokaten)) but not implemented as a codified legal right for the juveniles.

For illustration of the practical scope of the problem: Per year in the period 2005–2010 there was a daily average of between 8 and 15 juveniles aged 15–17 in the Danish custody (pretrial prisons). For practical reasons juveniles are not concentrated in one or two facilities. The number of juveniles in pretrial in custody (rather than secure social institutions) was unchanged between 2005 and 2010 but in the period 2011–2014 the daily average over each year was between 2 and 3. One explanation would be that the decrease in juvenile crime makes it easier to have access to a place in an institution.

Over the years it has been clear to a small number of people that Denmark is challenging the UN Convention on the Rights of the Child regarding article 37c about being housed with adults and 40b(v) about being suspect and imposed with measures for that reason without having ordinary possibility of appeal. But the topic never really became a matter of debate in the political arena.

TRENDS IN JUVENILE CRIME OVER THE PERIOD 2006–2015

Official Danish crime statistics show a larger number of violations of special acts than of the Criminal Law. But very often the violations of special acts are left out of the statistics because this figure is very sensitive to changes in professional practices. Further the response in these cases is mainly fines and the fine-system is very poorly enlightened statistically because fines are imposed by different authorities, not only the courts (Ministry of Justice 2015a). Regarding juveniles it can further be argued that the types of violations juveniles tend to commit are mainly criminal law violations, so by leaving special acts out while debating juvenile crime the picture will be more accurate.

For almost all age groups between 10 and 17 years old there has been a continuous decrease in registered crime charges in the period 2006–2015. In 2006 there were 25,125 suspicions or charges by the police[5] against 10–17 years old persons. In 2015 the number was reduced to 11,556, that is, a decrease of 54% for the whole group. The reduction was 70% among the minors and 46% among the 15–17 years old (Ministry of Justice 2016).

---

[4]Secure social welfare institutions are used for several purposes. More about this see below in part 7 and 8.

[5]The term suspicion is used when the person is too young for a formal police charge (i.e., 10–14 years old).

Over the 10 year period there has been an increase in the number of individuals in the oldest groups and a decrease among the younger. This turns out to be marginally smaller among the youngest and marginally bigger among the eldest. The overall reduction is 54% which is identical with the reduction for the whole group without the correction for changes in size of age groups.

For all the years there are about twice as many suspicions and charges as there are individuals being suspect or charged. The development in the number of suspicions and charges is parallel to the development in number of individuals being suspect or charged. But the reduction in number of suspected individuals is biggest among the youngest (the minors). The age group with the highest number of suspects was the 16 years old in 2006. This has gradually developed to the 19 years old in 2015.

There is not one single crime type which has a larger number of recorded offenses in 2015 compared to 2005. But there are temporary increases such as, for instance, for shoplifting from 2011 to 2014. The decrease in criminal damage is 75% over the period, car theft 73%, burglary 62%, theft 61%, and assault and threats 58%.

The decrease in criminal suspicions and charges is not equally shared among boys and girls. The crimes for which mainly boys are suspect or charged decreased 58% whereas the crimes for which a girl are suspect or charged decreased 36%. Consequently 23% of the children's and juvenile's crime now refers to girls compared to 17% in 2006.

But if we look at the number of individuals the difference is smaller. The number of girls involved with crime went down 45% whereas the number of boys involved with crime went down 58%. This indicates that those girls who are still involved with crime are a little more active. This is confirmed by the fact that the average number of suspicions and charges per year per boy went down from 2.3 to 2.1 from 2006 to 2015 but in the same period the same numbers for girls went up from 1.6 to 1.8. The main crime type for girls is shoplifting, which comprised 64% of the crimes committed by girls in 2015 against only 16% of the crimes committed by boys. Burglary, car theft, and robbery forms a more than five times bigger share of boys' crimes than of girls' crimes.

Generally speaking, there is no doubt that crime among children and juveniles in Denmark is decreasing. The tendency which 5–8 years ago still was described as a phenomenon which might be temporary now seems to be a trend.

CAUSES OF JUVENILE CRIME

Even though juvenile crime has declined, there still is crime among juveniles in Denmark. As there is no single explanation of crime, there is also not one single explanation why crime is decreasing. It is assumed among criminologists that relatively good public schools where there is much focus on integration of vulnerable pupils explains part of the decline. The crime preventive cross-professional cooperation among schools, social welfare and police is working well in many municipalities and receiving much support from the national crime preventive council. This too is credited for part of the decline.

For at least the last decade, there has been increased public attention on education and employment. The necessity of having a clean criminal record—and unlucky situations for persons who did not have this—has been much debated in public. This is also supposed to play a role and supposedly a bigger role in families and among juveniles who are in a relatively strong social position.

Another factor which is assumed to play an important role for the decrease of juvenile crime is changes in social behavior among children and juveniles. Neither children nor juveniles are seen as much in public as before. To a much larger degree they spend time at home accompanied by their computer and communicating in cyberspace. What this development will lead to in a longer perspective is now debated in public and among experts.

The debate about causes for crime has developed in Denmark in the latest decade. The debate has transitioned from a strong focus on causation inspired by the old causation theories to a current focus on risk factors. In 2009 a voluminous White Paper compiled by a highly estimated group of experts was published by the Ministry of Justice (more than 700 pages). The title was "Action against Juvenile Crime" (1508/2009). One of the recommendations in the report was that a tool for systematic research on risk factors should be developed. Soon after the crime preventive council argued for more focus on risk factors and criminologists started to refer to foreign studies, mainly Farrington and Welsh.[6]

This may be seen as the beginning of a new era in the approach to juvenile crime in Denmark. The identification of risks and needs has been strengthened—more or less systematically—in schools, day cares, etc. It is possible that the spread of the new method has strengthened the decline in youth crime that had already started. But the new approach has not removed the well-known societal challenges such as poverty and low parental capacity. They still exist and are now categorized as "contextual risk factors" (see for instance the Directorate for Social Affairs)[7].

Muslim immigrants and descendants are largely depicted in the media as radicalized criminals. There have been a few sad episodes with young Muslims having committed serious crimes and much attention is paid to the religious factor in the public and in the justice sector. It is still a fact, though, that the young Muslims who have committed crimes are also characterized by being socially and economically marginalized as well as having a very poor educational basis. In other words, several risk factors can be present within the same persons.

[6] Farrington, D and Welsh, B: Saving Children from a Life of Crime. NY. Oxford University Press.

[7] http://vidensportal.dk/temaer/udadreagerende-adfaerd/risiko-og-beskyttelsesfaktorer

POLICING AND JUVENILES

The police carry out all criminal investigation. The police are obliged to take seriously all reports from the public in order to determine if a crime has been committed or not. But the police also have limitations regarding their time and resources and therefor prioritizations must be made. The investigation of some crimes such as bike theft is therefore not of the same priority as the investigation of a bank robbery.

While in principle there is only one criminal justice system in Denmark covering all relevant age groups, on the other hand when a minor is suspected of a crime and investigative steps are taken this presentation of the policing is divided into two parts. The first part involves minors whereas the second part involves individuals above 15.

Even if there is no legal possibility of criminal prosecution of children below the age of 15, criminal offences which are supposed to be committed by children are to some degree included in the investigation of crime. This is because persons above the age of criminal responsibility may be involved in the same offence and they should be held responsible. Furthermore, there may be a need to clarify the total scope of the crime which was committed and to secure that items (for instance stolen goods) are returned to the right person.

The Administration of Justice Act contains a short chapter, chapter 75b, regulating basic questions regarding the treatment of cases where minors are suspected of a crime by the police. The chapter states that in order to prevent a child from being exposed to harmful treatment during the investigation, the parents and the social welfare systems are to be notified and at least one of them are expected to be present during interviews and interrogations by the police. Informing parents and/or social welfare may, however, be postponed if it is a minor crime or if postponement of the information is necessary or in the interest of the investigation. The police are always obliged to inform the social welfare system if there is any reason to assume that the child needs support from social welfare.

As a consequence of the fact that the behavior of a child cannot lead to legal conviction, the possibility of instigating legal inquiries against a child are limited compared to ordinary criminal cases. The legal possibility of detaining a child when necessary in order to clear up a criminal case does exist, but a child may under no circumstances be taken into custody (Instruction 4/2007 with changes of December 2012 from the superior prosecutor. Part 2. (Rigsadvokaten)). Regardless of age and criminal guilt The Danish Police Code, § 5 opens the possibility of detaining a person regardless of age for 6 h in order to prevent public order or personal health from being threatened by the person.

If a child is under influence of alcohol or drugs the police may detain the child. But if the child is not yet 12 years old they cannot be placed in detention and if a child between 12 and 15 is placed in the detention it must be seen by a doctor (The Police Code, § 12).

In addition to the 6-h rule in the Police Code there is a general constitutional protection securing the right for everyone who is arrested to see a judge within 24 h. It is not a defined presumption in the Administration of Justice Law, § 755 that a person must have reached the age of criminal responsibility to be arrested. Consequently children below 15 are not excluded from being arrested. When a child below 15 years old is arrested, they must be kept in an office or the like and may never be placed in a jail/pretrial prison or prison cell. Children will be let out before 24 h as there is no legal possibility for the judge to decide to keep them any longer. They may, however, be handed over directly to the social welfare system and taken into a secure institution.

When a child in Denmark is suspect of a serious crime, it will be noted in the national investigative register. This is a file with no public access. The register is functioning as a tool for the police in their investigation of crimes.

There is no legal possibility for Danish courts to try the criminal guilt of a suspected child. It has been argued in the public debate related to specific cases that such a possibility should be defended as it might prove the innocence of the child, who in spite of their innocence has already been "convicted" by public opinion. It has also been argued that mitigating circumstances related to the crime might never come forward if the case was not tried in court (Storgaard 2004).

In Denmark as well as the other Scandinavian countries Victim-Offender-Programs are available. In several cases minors as well as persons above 15 years may attend Victim-Offender Mediation (VOM) either as victims or as offenders. When the participants are below 18 years old the parents' consent is needed. In Denmark the police are responsible for organizing and finding relevant cases for VOM and the attendance in VOM (on the offender side) presupposes a confession meaning an explicit realization of the criminal episode. Minors are not directly included in VOM according to the law on VOM but in § 7 of the Law competences are handed over to the Minister of Justice to give additional rules. The number of cases where minors are involved with VOM is very limited and there are no official statistics on that.

Attention to suspects of a young age is required from the police during the investigation process not only as long as a suspect is below 15. The matter of young age still plays a role regarding suspects who are 15 years old but not yet 18 years.

If it is a matter of violation of the Criminal Code or if the offence which the juvenile is suspected of may lead to imprisonment the police are obligated to inform the social welfare system and if possible to invite them for the questioning. An exception to this main rule can be made if the juvenile is apprehended while or in direct relation to the committing of the offence and questioned immediately after the apprehension and provided that the punishment in the concrete case will be no more than a fine (Instruction 4/2007 with changes of December 2012 from the superior prosecutor. Part 3. (Rigsadvokaten)).

If a juvenile between 15 and 17 is arrested the parents must be informed (Instruction 4/2007 with changes of December 2012 from the superior prosecutor. Part 3. (Rigsadvokaten)).

The only difference in the treatment of juveniles below 18 and adults in regard to pretrial imprisonment and solitary confinement during investigation is the limits on the duration of confinement. The limitation rules are in all cases modifiable due to special conditions. But the main rule is that there is a maximum of 6 months of pretrial imprisonment for adults and a maximum for juveniles of 4 months in cases where the maximum prison sentence is under 6 years. If the maximum prison sentence is 6 years or more the maximum for pretrial imprisonment is 1 year for adults and 8 months for juveniles, Administration of Justice Act, § 768a. Concerning solitary confinement there is a maximum for adults of 14 days as long as the crime cannot lead to a prison sentence of 4 years or more. For adults there is an absolute (though still modifiable for special reasons) limitation of the duration of solitary confinement of 8 weeks. For juveniles under 18 years old the absolute time limit for solitary confinement is 4 weeks unless the crime was directed at the security of the state, the Administration of Justice Act, § 770c.

In 1999[8] the Danish Supreme Court stated that in principle it is not against any Danish law or human rights rules to keep juveniles (15 years old or older) in solitary confinement. It also stated that in juvenile cases there must be extraordinary reasons to use solitary confinement. Pretrial imprisonment as well as solitary confinement is decided in a court by the judge, not by the police, and never for more than 4 weeks at the time. There are relatively strict requirements about strong suspicion and concrete reasons like risk of repeated crime, the Administration of Justice Act, chapter 70.

Roughly 25% or more of all prisoners in Denmark are in pretrial imprisonment. Included in the 25% are adults and those juveniles who actually are in custody and not those juveniles who are technically in pretrial prison but spending the pretrial prison time in a secure social institution. In 2014 (the most recent statistics) 1324 out of 3784 prisoners were in pretrial imprisonment (2014 report from the Prison and Probations Service). As mentioned above juveniles in pretrial prison should as far as possible be transferred to social institutions. There are no available statistics on the use of this alternative to custody.

In the preparation for court the police and the prosecutor, who in Denmark work closely together, are in contact with the probation service if there is any chance that the case will result with a conditional sentence. This contact is established in order to have the probation service prepare a report on the accused for the judge as part of his fundament for decision. In juvenile cases, however, the preparatory reports are compiled by the social welfare authorities (unless Community Service Order is seen an option).

[8] The case is identified "UfR 1999.1415 H." The identification refers to year and page in the weekly journal for lawyers.

Instead of taking a juvenile case to court the prosecutor may in some minor cases decide to withdraw the charges; this option is mentioned in the Administration of Justice Act, chapter 65. For juveniles this is also an option and a condition will most often be that the juvenile will be obliged to follow instructions from the social welfare about how to behave, who to hang out with, when to be home at night, etc. A withdrawal of charges is dependent on a confession and on the judge formally accepting the conditions. No trial in court takes place, so the evidence is not controlled by the judge. If new crime is committed within (normally) 2 years the minor crime for which the charges were withdrawn will be included in the sentencing.

COURTS AND JUVENILES

Minors are not taken to courts if they could have been punished if they were older. However, children who commit acts that were punishable will often be seen as in need of help, support, or directions from an authority which will be the social welfare system. Normally this will be a mentor or a family advisor, extra support for schoolwork or a strict structure for the time after school. But a placement in another family or an institution may also be chosen. It is preferred that those noninstitutional approaches will be accepted by the child and the parents but if this is not possible they may be dictated by the social welfare. This is also true for placements outside the home. In reality almost all placements in families or institutions take place after consent. It is sometimes argued that the parents dare not deny to consent because they fear that this may lead to a total separation from the child.

In the public debate it is sometimes argued that the social welfare system is too reluctant to decide to take a child out of the home and that the child is developing too far in the direction of crime before action is taken. These viewpoints are important but complicated to test.

Juveniles are taken to courts. As there are no juvenile courts in Denmark there are also no specific criminal courts. Apart from the Maritime and Commercial Court the Danish court system has only one system. In the local courts (city courts) civil cases as well as criminal cases are heard by the same judges in the same courtrooms. The same is true for the superior courts of which there are two in Denmark and for the supreme courts of which there is one.

In the next section, the main types of penalties will be described. More attention will be given to a few Danish penalties with a specific juvenile orientation. After this follows an overview of the sentencing, this is also focusing on juveniles.

The courts evaluate the evidence that is found by the police and presented in court by the prosecutor, who evaluates the evidence before trial. Based on the evidence the court decides if the accused is guilty. The case is treated in accordance with the same legal principles and procedural rules as criminal case against adults. But when it comes to sentencing the age of the individual charged plays an important role. Compared to comparable crimes and criminal records both the prosecutor and the judge will tend to more actively look for another solution than ordinary imprisonment as long as the person is under 18 years old.

As a consequence of the tradition of not having a specific juvenile justice system there is also not a penalty system only for juveniles. However a few policies that are solely applicable to youth do exist. Below follows a brief introduction for general penalties and penalties solely for juveniles.

The Criminal Law, § 31 introduces the ordinary penalties as fine and imprisonment. But this also allows for a wide range of different solutions not all of which are within the field of imprisonment. Starting from the mildest end of sanctions/ penalties there is withdrawal of charges. This solution is not part of the Criminal Law but regulated in the Administration of Justice Law, § 722. There are a few more possibilities of using withdrawal of charges for juveniles compared to adults. That is, for instances in cases of theft of a bike which for an adult rather would lead to a fine. There is a specific juvenile variant of withdrawal of charges for cases of a little more seriousness. This is a so-called withdrawal of charges with a Youth Contract which was introduced in 1998. The aim was to introduce a quicker and more adequate reaction to crimes which had not caused personal harm and were committed by juveniles who did not already have a substantial criminal record. By including not only the offender but also the parents and the social authorities in the preparation and signing of a contract before having it approved by the court, it was hoped that all parties (especially the parents) would feel more committed to the conditions of the contract. Like all noncustodial measures the youth contract always contains a standard condition of not re-offending within a certain period of time. Furthermore it puts individual obligations on the juvenile to participate in certain activities. These may include requirements to finish school and go through a social training program. If the juvenile fulfils the period and the obligations of the contract the measure will be deleted from his or her criminal record 1 year after the contract was signed, i.e., practically in the moment it is fulfilled. "Normally" withdrawal of charges are deleted from the general record after 2 years. According to an old evaluation the youth contract did neither speed up the process markedly nor lower recidivism (which was already low after an ordinary withdrawal of charges) (Kyvsgaard 2004).

The prosecutors are instructed to propose a Youth Contract in cases that involve property crime, including burglary, but not in cases where assault or robbery is involved (Instruction 4/2007 with changes of December 2012 from the superior prosecutor. Part 4.2. (Rigsadvokaten)).

A fine is normally seen as a less severe penalty. Fines are not used very often for juvenile offenders compared to adults but when they are used the main rule is that compared to adult convicts the fine for a juvenile should be lower, roughly half of that for an adult. In the case of drunken driving that is resolved with a fine, the fine in such cases cannot be reduced due to young age. Fines are in general an option in cases of shoplifting and other minor property crimes (Instruction

4/2007 with changes of December 2012 from the superior prosecutor. Part 4.1. (Rigsadvokaten)).

Imprisonment may be imposed in a conditional and an unconditional form. Apart from these forms the courts may impose a combination of a conditional and unconditional sentence, which is mainly meant for cases where more than one type of crime is involved and where each would lead to each one variant of a prison sentence. Combinations are not used that often and of no specific relevance here.

A sentence to conditional imprisonment is the most lenient of the more serious penalties and such sentences range from conditional imprisonment to conditional imprisonment with the condition of community service. Between community service and unconditional imprisonment is another specific juvenile oriented punishment, the Youth Sanction and after that follows unconditional imprisonment. Unconditional imprisonment may for juveniles be served under different conditions, as described below.

Conditional imprisonment is used in cases where it is not seen as necessary that the sentence is executed immediately, Criminal Law § 56, and the sentence may be combined with different conditions which are seen as relevant in the specific case. For juveniles the conditions are mainly that the offender follows the instructions from the social welfare about school, job, training, etc. This is not different from the way conditional sentences are applied to adults apart from other conditions being put and the juveniles being supervised by the social welfare system whereas adults are supervised by the probation service.

Community Service was introduced in the beginning of the 1980s. Historically it was not used much with juveniles. But over time this was changed a bit. The reluctance was based on a fear that juveniles were too immature and would not follow the conditions. Community Service is a conditional sentence with a stronger condition than other conditional sentences, namely the duty to work unpaid for a specified number of hours—as many as 300—after a specific schedule agreed upon with the employee. The work is not allowed to be dangerous or to increase profit for private companies and it must be scheduled in accordance with the main duties of the convict such as school or job. Community service is meant to be used in cases which do not lead to an ordinary conditional sentence. It is hard to prove, though, that there is no net widening effect in this penalty. Community service is often used in cases with car theft, where juveniles are sometimes involved. It is also used in cases about drunken driving and in those cases there are very few juveniles involved. The newest statistics show that for 2014 there were 1397 sentences to community service for road traffic offences and 2251 cases of violation of the criminal law (Ministry of Justice 2015b).[9]

[9]This report does not include age groups. Another statistics (Statistics Denmark) comes out with a total of 500 less community service orders. This source, however, breaks down the numbers in age groups. According to this source the number of juveniles receiving sentence to community service (with and without a fine added) in 2013 was 66 and in 2014 there 69 juveniles sentenced to community service. Even if the statistics are obviously not comparable it is hard to imagine that community service is used for juveniles to a large degree.

In all cases (except in case of a fine) where unconditional imprisonment is avoided, that is withdrawal of charges, conditional sentences with or without Community Service Orders and electronic monitoring (see below) the mandatory condition is to lead a law-abiding life for a specified period. In addition, other conditions such as a duty to comply with a number of conditions concerning residence, school, job, leisure-time activities, etc. will often be seen. Supervision which is seen as a combined control and support is normally carried out by social welfare in juvenile cases. The only exception from that is in community service cases where the probation service is the supervising service.

Not to be confused with the Youth Contract (mentioned above), Denmark introduced the Youth Sanction by an amendment to the Criminal Code in 2001, § 74a. Contrary to the Youth Contract the Youth Sanction is meant for juveniles with a more substantial criminal career and a need for pedagogical training. The Youth Sanction is imposed by the courts but carried out by the social authorities. Youth Sanctions include deprivation of liberty without ordinary imprisonment. It does not exclude pretrial imprisonment though.

The implementation of the Youth Sanction was the result of a strong political demand for action against serious offences committed by juveniles who have not reached the age of 18 at the time of the crime. If the juvenile turns 18 in during the 2 year long period of the sanction they will still be eligible for this sentence. The sanction is composed of three phases which altogether last 2 years. The first period must take place in a secure social welfare institution;[10] next is a period in an open residential institution. Both types of institutional accommodations are managed by the social welfare system and not by the prison and probation service. In this context the aim is less to impose a punishment and more to help the juvenile. The total time in secured and open residential institutions may not exceed one and a half year and there is a maximum of 1 year to be spent in secure institution. The last phase, the duration of which must be at least 6 months, is aftercare or supervision not in confinement. As the length of a Youth Sanction is always 2 years, the exact length of the last period of supervision depends on how much time has been spent in institutions (Kyvsgaard 2004; Storgaard 2004).

The Youth Sanction did not receive a warm welcome by practitioners or academic experts. Among other things it was criticized as being out of proportion compared to the alternative sentence, it also ceded wide discretionary powers to the social institutions. Further, there was a concern that the juvenile spent time in pretrial prison. This time is not deducted from the 2 years of the sanction like it will be in the time to be spent in prison after a prison sentence (Clausen and Kyvsgaard 2009; Kyvsgaard 2004; Storgaard 2009; Vestergaard 2004).

Some of the criticisms have been addressed over time. The "main-rule" is now that the period in a secure institution is to be 2 months and that it must be assessed if it is longer. It is also now a specific condition that in case the juvenile did spend a pretrial period in a secure institution as an alternative to custody and if the

[10] The institutions are mentioned above.

institution recommends so the juvenile can go directly to open residential care after the court hearing. Before this change juveniles had been transferred to open care during the pretrial time but were redirected to secure regime to start the formal Youth Sanction in accordance with the legal instruction.

The Youth Sanction is used in relatively serious cases where a juvenile of 15–17 years old committed a crime for which he or she (in spite of their young age) is eligible to 3–12 (18) months of imprisonment and he or she at the same time is in need of pedagogical support. If the crime is not serious enough or too serious and/or there is no need for pedagogical support the Youth Sanction is not indicated (Instruction 4/2007 with changes of December 2012 from the superior prosecutor (Rigsadvokaten)).

Unconditional imprisonment is seen as the last resort for juvenile offenders. Until 2010 there was a specific time limit for prison sentences for juveniles of 8 years. This was removed from the Criminal Law in 2010; hereafter the only codified difference between the time limits is that imprisonment for lifetime is not an option for juveniles (Storgaard 2013).

There are still guidelines for the courts to bear in mind the young age of a convict in the sentencing (Criminal Law § 82). It is not easy to prove what role this plays in sentencing practices. But after court the juveniles who are sentenced to unconditional imprisonment may be transferred to different institutions depending on their crime record, developmental level, needs, etc.

There are no prisons in Denmark only for juveniles but there is one high security and one low security prison each with a juvenile unit. It is not legally prohibited for juveniles to go to a prison other than one of those. But efforts are made to find an appropriate prison. Apart from that there is a legal option that a juvenile (and others) serve the sentence (partly) in an appropriate institution (Code of Execution of Penalties, § 78). For the juveniles the secure social institutions are most obvious. But by the end of the sentence there is also a chance for the juvenile to serve in a so-called pension, which is located near to the place where he is expected to stay after prison. The pensions are a kind of transition places, where prisoners or parolees stay while they attend school or job in the society but are obliged to check in afterwards.

Finally there is an option for the majority of those (including juveniles) who receive an unconditional prison sentence for up to 6 months to apply for electronic monitoring as an alternative to going to prison (Code of Execution of Penalties, § 78 a–f). The decision on this matter is not within the power of the courts but in the hands of the prison and probation service. The monitoring is also called "prison at home" and implies the duty of getting out of the home in the morning for school or job and back in the afternoon. The schedule only leaves appropriate time for transportation. After having returned in the afternoon the person in electronic monitoring is not allowed to leave home except after special allowance from the probation service. If the schedule or conditions (for instance not drinking alcohol) are broken the person is taken in to serve the sentence behind bars immediately.

Danish courts can impose imprisonment for lifetime; this is not an option for juveniles. Another liberty depriving punishment is a sort of preventive imprisonment which is not imposed for a fixed time; this is in practice not used to juveniles below 18.

Between 2005 and 2014 the total number of court decisions concerning juveniles in the age group 15–17 years old decreased from 5526 to 3354, with an exception of 1 year (2009). As for the relative numbers, i.e., court decision concerning juveniles per 1000 inhabitants in the age group the development was constant or decreasing every year from 29 in 2005 to 16 in 2014. The trend is similar for boys and girls. But per 1000 boys aged 15–17 there were 45 sentences in 2005 and 22 in 2014. Concerning girls there were 13 sentences in 2005 per 1000 girls against 9 sentences in 2014.

As for the specific crimes the overall trend is also downwards. The numbers for rape and homicide are too small to talk about a trend. For a few specific crimes the trend is not completely uniform but small—not interrelated—deviations are seen, such as shoplifting increasing in 2014 after 9 years of decrease or robbery increasing in 2009 and 2010 but in 2014 being below the 2005-level (Ministry of Justice 2015a).

Even if the Youth Sanction is now 15 years old it still has some attention in Denmark and the Ministry of Justice follows thoroughly the development in its use compared with the use of the alternative, namely unconditional imprisonment for between 30 days and 18 months.

The newest report on this (Ministry of Justice 2015c) shows a decline in these sentences paralleling the downward trend in reported juvenile crime. Between 2005 and 2010 the trend was one of general declines, but for 2010–2014 it is a steady decline. The Youth Sanction is used more rarely than the alternative prison sentences. Out of the total number of sentences studied, the Youth sanction was used in 13% of the cases in 2011. The following 2 years the share increased a bit but went down to 15% of all the sentences included in the study in 2014. In absolute numbers Youths Sanction was used 43 times in 2014 and the comparable prison sentences were imposed 239 times. The youth sanction is more rarely used in the capital, Copenhagen, than other parts of the country.

The courts tends to use imprisonment instead of Youth Sanction more often if the offender is 17 years old than if the offender is 15 or 16 years old. Sixty-one percent of the juveniles who were sentenced to imprisonment were 17 years old and only 7% of those who had a Youth Sanction had reached that age. Only 5% of the prison sentences were imposed on girls[11] in comparison 14% of the Youth Sanction sentences imposed on girls. Sixty-three percent of the Youth Sanctions and 41% of the prison sentences were imposed on persons of Danish origin.

[11] This is the same share as all sentences to unconditional imprisonment concerning females form out of all sentences to unconditional imprisonment.

Generally speaking, a bigger share of those with a Youth Sanction is convicted for serious crimes (53%) than those who had a prison sentence (38%). But there is no information about the actual lengths of the prison sentences, so a rather big share of them may be very low, i.e., 30 or 40 days.

To conclude the discussion regarding the sentencing options and practice for juveniles, there are many options and variations compared to the number of convicted juveniles. This is a practice that is followed intensively. Among others the research office in the Ministry of Justice is always updated on the newest development.

Efforts are made to keep juveniles out of prisons even if for the time being there is opposition from politicians who clamor for more consequence (meaning tougher on crime) and experts and practitioners on the other side arguing for crime prevention to an amount that reaches the most vulnerable groups.

CUSTODIAL RULES FOR JUVENILES (DETENTION, PRISON, MIXING JUVENILES WITH ADULTS)

There are no real codified rules against mixing juveniles with adults in pretrial prisons and prisons as is prescribed in the UN convention on the Rights of the Child article 37(c) (see above and in the European Prison Rules, article 11.1). Building new institutions for that purpose in Denmark would, however, not be without risks because of concerns about travelling long distances for visitors and the possibility that more juveniles may be locked up.

The requirement of separation is met by transferring juveniles in prison and pretrial confinement to juvenile institutions under the auspices of the social welfare system. This has become more feasible in the latest several years due to the declining youth crime. A very important difference between criminal institutions and social welfare institutions is the compositions of the staff. In the first very few staff members are not prison guards but in the social welfare institutions the staff is purely composed of civilians.

A consequence of the transfer of juveniles from the criminal justice system to social welfare institutions implies the mixing of juveniles being institutionalized for very different reasons in the same institutions. There are two types of institutions, namely the secure institutions, which are of the same physical security level as high security prison,[12] and the open residential institutions which are not surrounded by physical barriers and surveilled by guards. In both types of institutions a variety of youth can be found, including: those who are there by the decision of the social welfare with or without consent; those who are in pretrial prison, those who are sentenced to imprisonment, and those who are imposed with a Youth Sanction. The staff is of course better educated to stimulate and

[12] Perimeter wall, electronic monitoring, closed gate, entrance control, etc.

motivate the juveniles for a constructive life-perspective. But the staff is not at all trained in legal matters which may cause complications in regard to legal rights such as use of force, disciplinary measures, time limits, receiving visits, etc.

ALTERNATIVE SANCTIONS FOR JUVENILES: HOME CONFINEMENT, RESTORATIVE JUSTICE, RESTITUTION, ETC.

In spite of political demands for more punitive consequences it may still be said that the general tradition in Denmark is that pure imprisonment is absolutely a last resort for juveniles.

It has been noted that there exists no such thing in Denmark as a specific juvenile justice system. What the future will bring is hard to say right now. There are strong forces against and for the introduction of a juvenile court and more specific responses to juvenile crime. But there already exists a number of legal ways for the social services to intervene in the development of a juvenile if needed. These interventions include mentors, family support in the form of full-time or part-time foster family or institutional residency without consent. Interventions from the welfare system are not a penalty and the professional focus should not be punitive but supportive and directed at the best interest of the child.

In this sense there is an overlap between social welfare and the penal system. Until the age of 15 the initiative belongs to and rests with the social welfare. After the age of 15 a strong argument for a withdrawal of the charge may be that initiatives by the social welfare system have been exhausted. Exactly the same initiatives that the social welfare system might have taken already may now be conditions for a withdrawal of charges or—if the crime is more serious—a conditional sentence. Home-confinement after 8 p.m. may for instance very well be a condition in a youth contract without ever having been understood as a criminal measure. Very often a withdrawal of charges or a conditional sentence for a juvenile ends up with the words "it is a condition that _____ (name of juvenile) follows the instructions given by the social welfare system."

Before the age of 15 only serious crimes are noted in the register of investigation but after the age of 15 all court decisions are noted as well in the aforementioned as in the criminal record of the individual. Notations in the criminal record are understood as having much negative impact for a young person for instance when applying for a job, thus its use is meant to be restricted.

The only form of Restorative Justice in Denmark is Victim offender mediation, which is organized by the police. As mentioned above minors are not excluded from VOM but the main group is criminally responsible individuals and their victims (Lappi-Seppälä and Storgaard 2015). VOM is not and cannot be used as an instrument for diversion. There will always be a criminal court case (when the offender is criminally liable) either before or after the mediation. If the court case follows after a successful VOM this may be used as argument for a marginally lower sentence (the preparatory works for VOM and Criminal Law, § 82).

DIFFERENCES IN TREATMENT OF BOYS AND GIRLS

Historically boys have been registered for more crime than girls. This is still the case even if the crime levels for boys and girls are getting closer and registered crime level for both is decreasing.

Formally there are no legal rules or guidelines establishing differences in the approach to boys and girls by the criminal justice system. It is sometimes argued that the tolerance for misbehavior by girls is greater meaning that adults around the juveniles are more reluctant to define deviant behavior by girls as criminal than if the same deviancy is seen from a boy. This may historically have been the case, but within the latest 8–10 years so-called "girls gangs" have had much attention in the media, so it is not likely that a possible informal reluctance to define a girl as criminal is the case today.

The fact that the share of girls sentenced to imprisonment is the same as the share of female in the population as a whole does not indicate that girls are sentenced more leniently than boys. The fact that the main girls' crime is a sort of crime which without gender specification is expected to be responded to with a fine does also not indicate leniency towards girls in the sentencing. The share of girls being sentenced to Youth Sanction, which is seen as a serious penalty and an alternative to imprisonment, is much larger than the share of girls receiving a sentence to imprisonment. This is also not an indication of leniency. Of course none of this speculation can be seen as proof of a relatively more repressive attitude to deviant and criminal girls. Conclusive the only firm statement to be made is that there exist no formal or binding instructions or guidelines proposing a different treatment of boys and girls in Denmark.

FINAL REMARKS

It is hard to tell where Danish Juvenile Criminal Policy will go in the future. Empirical evidence shows decreasing juvenile crime and decreasing crime in general. Strong political voices are talking about "consequentialism" meaning a more punitive approach to the so-called hard core juvenile offenders. Based on a long tradition there is a very close correspondence between social welfare means and criminal justice means regarding juvenile offenders and for the most part what the leading politicians claim is already being practiced in the overlap between justice and welfare. Therefore two important questions must be answered in the near future: Will Denmark take the lead in Scandinavia and lower the age of criminal responsibility and in addition establish a specific juvenile justice system? If this will be the case how much will it change in practical juvenile justice?

REFERENCES

Clausen, S., & Kyvsgaard, B. (2009). *Ungdomssanktionen. En effektevaluering*. Denmark: The Ministry of Justice.

Greve, V. (2004). *Det strafferetlige ansvar* (2nd ed.). Denmark: Jurist og økonomforbundets forlag.

Kyvsgaard, B. (2004). Youth justice in Denmark. In *Crime and justice: A review of research* (vol. 31). Chicago: The University of Chicago.

Lappi-Seppälä, T., & Storgaard, A. (2015). Nordic mediation—Comparing Denmark and Finland. *Neue Kriminalpolitik, 27*(2), 136–147.

Ministry of Justice. (2009). *Action against justice*.

Ministry of Justice. (2015a). *Kriminalitet og alder* [Crime and Age].

Ministry of Justice. (2015b). *Udviklingen i antallet af samfundstjenestedomme* [The development in the number of community service orders].

Ministry of Justice. (2015c). *Redegørelse om ungdomssanktioner og ubetingede fængselsstraffe til unge lovovertrædere* [On youth sanctions and unconditional imprisonment for young offenders].

Ministry of Justice. (2016). *Udviklingen i børne—og ungdomskriminalitet 2006–2015* [The development in children's and juvenile's crime 2006–2015].

Storgaard, A. (2004). Juvenile justice in Scandinavia. *Journal of Scandinavian Studies in Criminology and Crime Prevention, 5*(2), 188–204.

Storgaard, A. (2009). The youth sanction—A punishment in disguise. In P. Wahlgren (Ed.), *Scandinavian studies in Law* (Vol. 54, pp. 381–396). Stockholm: The Stockholm University Law Faculty.

Storgaard, A. (2013). Unge lovovertræderes strafansvar, retssikkerhed og lavalder. In K. Nordlöf (Ed.), *Argumentation i nordisk straffrätt*. Norstedts Juridik: Sweden.

Vestergaard, J. (2004). A special youth sanction. *Journal of Scandinavian Studies in Criminology and Crime Prevention, 5*(1), 62–84.

LEGISLATION AND WHITE PAPERS

2014 report from the Prison and Probation Service

Betænkning 1508/2009: Justitsministeriet. Indsatsen mod Ungdomskriminalitet. (White paper on Juvenile Crime)

Betænkning 1545/2014: Straffelovrådets betænkning om samfundstjeneste mv. (White paper on community service)

Code of Execution of Penalties, LBK 1242, 2015

Criminal Law, LBK 873, 2015

The Administration of Justice Act, LBK 1255, 2015 (LBK = Consolidated Act)

The Danish Police Code, LBK 956, 2015

Law on VOM, no 467, 2009

Anette Storgaard has a licentiate degree in Law and works as an Associate Professor in criminal law and criminology at the Department of Law, University of Aarhus, Denmark. Her main research fields and publications are about Juvenile Justice, prisons, release from prison and alternatives to imprisonment as well as Alternative Dispute Resolution with a specific focus on Restorative Justice and drug addiction and crime has been included.

14

England and Wales

Tim Bateman

INTRODUCTION

Shifts in the justice system for children in trouble with the law have, at least, two dimensions, which are related but also enjoy a certain autonomy. Legislative change determines the parameters within which children who offend are processed and impacts on the treatment of children who offend. That impact is however mediated by policy and practice which, while being influenced by statutory provisions, can also operate relatively independently of them. The criminal justice landscape for children in England and Wales has in recent decades been characterized by extensive movement in both of these dimensions and the pace of change is such that analysis of the 'system' requires regular revision.

Less than a decade ago, Graham and Moore (2008) noted that the orthodoxy of the 1980s, predicated on an assumption that children should be diverted from formal criminal justice processes wherever possible, had rapidly given way to the opposite prevailing view, namely, that early intervention was required to 'nip offending in the bud' (Home Office 1997). The latter perception was enshrined in New Labour's Crime and Disorder Act 1998 (CDA) whose restructuring of the youth justice system was sufficiently radical to lead commentators to designate the consequent arrangements as a 'new youth justice' (Goldson 2000).

In fact, the Act tended to reinforce increasingly punitive and interventionist trends that had emerged in the early part of the decade under the previous Conservative administration rather than promoting a sudden disjuncture on implementation (Bateman 2015a). In this instance, legislation effectively caught up with policy and practice. Moreover, the more recent period, from around 2008 onward, has seen a marked reversion to a strong preference for diversion over formal intervention (see for instance, Smith 2014), providing further evidence for

T. Bateman (✉)
Department of Applied Social Studies, University of Bedfordshire,
Park Square, Luton LU1 3JU, UK
e-mail: tim.bateman@beds.ac.uk

S.H. Decker, N. Marteache (eds.), *International Handbook of Juvenile Justice*,
DOI 10.1007/978-3-319-45090-2_14

Bernard's (1992) fruitful insight that juvenile justice tends to develop in cyclical form. But this turnaround was not predicated on any particular legislative amendment. In this instance, policy and practice developed independently of the statutory framework.

The abandonment and subsequent discovery of diversion has taken place against the working out of another profound change in the arrangements for dealing with children in trouble. From the establishment of a separate court for children in 1908 up until 1989, children in conflict with the law and those in need of care and protection had both been processed within the single jurisdiction of the juvenile court. The Children Act of 1989 introduced a legal separation between these two populations so that matters relating to care would be dealt with in a new family proceedings court (now the family court), effectively severing the structural link between welfare and justice (Curtis 2005). The Criminal Justice Act 1991completed the transformation through the abolition of the juvenile court (which had continued to deal with crime) and its replacement by the youth court (Cadman 2005). From this point, talk of 'juvenile justice' was swiftly supplanted by references to 'youth justice,' and the former expression no longer had any currency in the jurisdiction. (The current chapter largely adopts the terminology of 'youth justice' in conformity with common usage.) The rekindling of a diversionary impulse has accordingly emerged in a rather different context from that in which it previously held sway, leading some commentators to reflect that diversion may have different connotations to those that were associated with it during the 1980s (Kelly and Armitage 2015).

The current system in England and Wales is thus constituted by a dynamic interplay between policy and practice and the legislative framework, resulting in considerable fluidity. The coming period is likely to herald further change. In September 2015, the Ministry of Justice announced a review of the youth justice system to report mid-2016 (Gove 2015). At the time of writing, the outcome is unknown, but it will in all probability lead to substantial revision of the legislative provisions and organizational frameworks described in this chapter.

THE LEGAL STATUS OF JUVENILES

The youth justice system deals with children aged 10–17 inclusive alleged to have committed a criminal offense. As described previously, arrangements for dealing with this group have, since 1989, been completely separate from those that pertain to children in need of care and protection. The youth justice system is accordingly in vertical alignment with provisions for adult offenders rather than aligned horizontally to other children's services.

The divorce between justice and care is problematic given the shared characteristics and intertwined histories of disadvantage, victimization, poverty, and complex needs of children who come to the attention of criminal justice agencies and care services (Curtis 2005). Children looked after by the local authority are six times more likely be subject to a formal youth justice disposal than the general 10–17 population (Department for Education 2015); conversely, more than a third of boys in young offender institutions report having been in care (Redmond 2015). But the distinct nature of the arrangements for dealing with each cohort creates a dichotomous dynamic that tends to encourage mainstream services to relinquish responsibility to criminal justice agencies where adolescents display problematic behavior. Equally, the involvement of youth justice agencies tends to reduce the perceived need for mainstream intervention (Centre for Social Justice 2012).

Although vertically aligned to it, youth justice is formally distinct from the adult system, having dedicated institutional arrangements, a specialist workforce, and a discrete range of sanctions (Bateman in press). This distinctive nature of youth justice law is however circumscribed: as described later, children continue to appear in adult courts, specialism does not all extend to all youth justice agencies and the legislative framework is largely derived from that which applies to adults. It has been argued that this close correspondence promotes an ethos in which punishment tends to dominate over other considerations more appropriate to childhood status (Haines and Case 2015).

The piecemeal development of youth justice has led to the accumulation of a range of principles that embody competing rationales, leading to a lack of clarity as to the system's purpose (Fergusson 2007). Section 44 of the Children and Young Persons Act (CYPA) 1933 requires that courts regard the welfare of the child and continues to apply them in criminal proceedings despite deriving from a period when proceedings for care and crime were heard in the same court (Curtis 2005). The sentencing framework introduced by the Criminal Justice Act 1991, on the other hand, is predicated on proportionate punishment so that offense seriousness is the 'starting point' in determining what sanctions are imposed (Sentencing Guidelines Council 2009: 3). More recently, the CDA has established that the principal aim of the youth justice system is the prevention of offending and reoffending by children and young people. Ostensibly introduced as a mechanism for resolving inherent tensions between welfare and justice, it arguably does little in that regard, since it leaves open the question of how children's offending is best prevented and whether the appropriate focus is the short or long term (Nacro 2003). Nearly half of magistrates do not take into account the impact on reoffending when determining sentences (Audit Commission 2004) and three quarters of youth practitioners report that it is 'difficult to find evidence of 'what works' for certain areas of their work' (National Audit Office 2010: 36).

The fluid amalgam of welfare, punishment, and rehabilitation no doubt helps to explain how the treatment of children who break the law alters from one period to another without any necessary corresponding modification in the underlying statutory provisions. It has also allowed an element of divergence between England and Wales, despite the two countries constituting a single jurisdiction: the Welsh government's youth crime strategy promotes a 'children first, offender second' agenda that is not present in any explicit form in England where a more offense-oriented focus has tended to prevail (Haines 2010).

THE AGE OF CRIMINAL MAJORITY

The age of criminal liability in England and Wales is at 10 years, low by international standards, as confirmed by a survey of 90 countries which established that the median minimum age of responsibility (adopted by around a quarter of the sample) was 14 years (Hazel 2008). Other differences notwithstanding, Labour and Conservative administrations have shown a remarkable consistency in their opposition to any reform in this regard (Bateman 2013a). Given that intransigence, it is perhaps not surprising that the terms of reference for the ongoing review of justice preclude consideration of the issue (Ministry of Justice 2015a).

After progressive increases in the first half of the twentieth century, the age of criminal responsibility was set at 10 years in 1963 and has accordingly remained unchanged for well over 50 years. The CYPA 1969 did legislate to preclude the prosecution of any child below the age of 14 years but, as the welfarist underpinnings that had hitherto informed responses to children in trouble began to unravel, the provision was never implemented. After 22 years on the statute book, it was repealed (Bateman 2012a).

The most recent relevant legislative change arguably constituted a practical lowering of the age of criminal liability. Until 1998, children under 14 benefitted from a measure of protection afforded by the common law principle of *doli incapax* which presumed that such children were incapable of crime and proscribed their prosecution unless it could be demonstrated, beyond reasonable doubt, that 'they knew what they were doing was seriously wrong as distinct from naughty or mischievous' (Bandalli 2000: 83). The principle was abolished by the CDA, whose New Labour architects declared it to be 'contrary to common sense' (Home Office 1997). Thereafter, children from the age of 10 were presumed to be 'unequivocally responsible and accountable for choices made and harm caused' (Bandalli 2000: 86–87) and exposed to the full rigor of the criminal law. The impact on children was clear in the data: within a year of implementation, there were was a 29% rise in the number of 10–14-year-olds cautioned or convicted for an indictable offense. The equivalent figures for older children showed a fall (Bateman 2012a).

Critics contend that the age of criminal responsibility in England and Wales is in tension with international standards (see later). It also fails to reflect the latest evidence in relation to children's cognitive development which raises questions as to the legitimacy of holding younger children criminally culpable for their wrongdoings (Lipscombe 2012). Recent advances in neuroscience have established that, by comparison with young adults, teenagers find it harder to adopt the perspectives of others, have a reduced capacity for abstract thought, and an increased propensity for risk taking (The Royal Society 2011). Formal induction at a young age into the formal justice system is also associated with an increased risk of reoffending (Huizinga et al. 2003), indicating that early criminalization may be counterproductive. Such factors are pertinent across all jurisdictions, but within England and Wales, the age of criminal responsibility appears out of kilter with other legislative provisions that offer age-related safeguards or impose limitations on children's behavior. Children are precluded from buying alcohol or tobacco below the age of 18 years; they cannot drive under 17; and below 16 years, they are not allowed to purchase a lottery ticket or buy a pet and are not considered competent to consent to sex. Imputing criminal responsibility to much younger children suggest that different standards are being applied to behavior that transgresses the criminal law (Bateman 2012a).

Young people older than 18 years cannot be processed through the youth justice system: they are considered adults for criminal justice purposes with the exception that there are distinct custodial sentences and a discrete secure estate for those aged 18–20 years. Until recently, 17-year-olds represented something of an anomaly since they did not enjoy the same rights applicable to all other children in police detention and the remand options available to them at court were those associated with adult proceedings. These anomalies have now been remedied and arrangements for this age group have been harmonized with those for younger children.

STANCE TOWARD THE UN COMMITTEE ON THE RIGHTS OF THE CHILD

In common with all but a very small number of State parties, the UK is a signatory to the United Nations Convention on the Rights of the Child (UNCRC), which it ratified in 1991 (Monaghan 2005). There is however an interesting distinction within the single jurisdiction of England and Wales in the two countries' stance toward the Convention.

The Welsh Government adopted the UNCRC as the basis for policy making for children in Wales in 2004. In 2011, the Welsh National Assembly unanimously passed the Rights of Children and Young Persons (Wales) Measure which placed a duty on all Ministers to have regard to the Convention and its optional protocols. The Welsh Government (2014) has further published a Children's Rights Scheme which specifies how this duty is to be discharged and describes accountability arrangements in relation to it. However, unlike other child services, youth justice is not a function devolved to the Welsh Government and the extent to which the commitment to a child rights agenda impacts directly on this policy area is accordingly limited. The Welsh Government's (2013: 60–61) contribution to the most recent UK report to the UN Committee on the Rights of the Child notes three core principles that underpin Welsh youth justice provision:

- 'Early, appropriate and sustained intervention to reduce the flow of children and young people into the criminal justice system
- Promoting resettlement and reducing reoffending after sentence
- Most importantly, treating those involved in offending behavior, or at risk of offending, as children and young people first'.

Only the third is distinctively Welsh: the first two might equally well describe policy in England.

For its part, the English Government has made no attempt to enshrine the UNCRC into domestic law: the obligations which ratification entails are accordingly not directly enforceable. The Human Rights Act (HRA) 1998 does, however, incorporate the European Convention on Human Rights (ECHR) so that redress for any breach of that Convention's articles is available in domestic courts. Moreover, the courts have increasingly shown an appetite for interpreting the provisions of the ECHR in the light of the UNCRC in cases involving children. As Baroness Hale put it in a House of Lord's judgment in 2005 [Regina v Durham Constabulary and another [2005] UKHL 21], the , UNCRC is:

> 'not only binding in international law; it is reflected in the interpretation and application by the ECHR of the rights guaranteed by the European Convention...; to that extent at least, therefore, it must be taken into account in the interpretation and application of those rights in our national law' (paragraph 26).

While an increasing body of case law refers explicitly to the provisions of the UNCRC, such progress may be at risk: the Conservative government elected in May 2015 came to a power with a manifesto commitment to abolish the HRA in favor of a British Bill of Rights to 'restore common sense to the application of human rights in the UK' (Conservative Party 2015: 73). At the time of writing, no details of the legislation that would replace the HRA have emerged, but abolition remains government policy.

In any event, explicit reference to the UNCRC in youth justice policy is rare. For instance, the Youth Crime Action plan (YCAP) published in 2008, the same year that the UN Committee on the Rights of the Child last, at the time of writing, reported on the UK's compliance, does not mention the Convention; the only reference to rights is those that pertain to victims (HM Government 2008). Nor is it apparent that priority is given to implementing the Committee's recommendations. In 2008, the Committee recommended an increase in the minimum age of criminal responsibility echoing a recommendation made 6 years previously: as noted earlier, no progress has been made in this regard in the intervening period. A recommendation in both 2002 and 2008, that no child should be tried in an adult court irrespective of the gravity of the offense has also fallen on deaf ears. The Committee's 2002 concluding observations registered concern at the extensive incarceration of children in England and Wales. The number of children deprived of their liberty remained stubbornly high, leading to a further expression of concern from the Committee in 2008 (UN Committee on the Rights of the Child 2002, 2008). As discussed later the youth custodial population has declined rapidly since but the extent to which this reduction can be attributed to a conscious attempt to address the Committee's anxieties is debatable (Bateman 2012b).

The Committee has also questioned the use of antisocial behavior orders (ASBOs) for children. Provisions in the CDA allowed local authorities, the police, and a range of other agencies to apply for an ASBO where a person over the age of 10 years deemed to have behaved 'in a manner that caused or was likely to cause harassment, alarm or distress to one or more persons not of the same household as himself' (Great Britain 1998: section 1). The effect of the order was to impose restrictions as specified by the court for a minimum of 2 years. Although the ASBO was designed to address behavior that fell short of criminality, and the measure itself was civil, breach of any requirements constituted a criminal offense that could attract custody. The provisions applied to children just as adults, although the maximum period of detention for breach was reduced for the former.

The availability of ASBOs for children attracted considerable criticism: the grounds for making the order were subjective; ASBOs were disproportionately targeted at young people's behavior; the measure was primarily negative and the potential to provide support to change behavior limited; the conditions were overly onerous and unrealistic, frequently requiring teenagers to stay away from designated areas (usually those places where they congregated) and to refrain from associating with named individuals (typically their closest friends) for the duration of the order; breach rates were extremely high so the order provided a net-widening mechanism for criminalizing children and expanding the custodial population; and some young people regarded the ASBO as a 'badge of honor' that could encourage, rather than deter, antisocial behavior (Solanki et al. 2006).

The UN Committee endorsed this critique and, in 2008, recommended an independent review of ASBOs 'with a view to abolishing their application to children' (UN Committee on the Rights of the Child 2008: paragraph 80). The Coalition government, elected in 2010, did abolish ASBOs without any review. However, the orders by which they were replaced (criminal behavior orders and injunctions for the prevention of nuisance and annoyance) bore a striking similarity to their predecessor and were vulnerable to the same criticisms. Indeed in some respects they might be considered more intrusive since they allow the imposition of positive requirements as well as prohibitions on behavior: children can be required to undergo interventions equivalent in many respects to those that would constitute sanctions for offending for noncriminal behavior (Wigzell 2014).

The UN Committee is due to report on the UK again in 2016. Although further criticism of arrangements for dealing with children in conflict with the law appears probable, the extent and nature is not known at the time of writing.

TRENDS IN JUVENILE CRIME OVER THE PERIOD 2004–2014

Figures for detected youth crime show a clear pattern of decline. During 2014, 29,800 children received a substantive disposal for an indictable offense compared with 112,900 in 2004, representing a reduction of almost 74% (Bateman

FIGURE 14.1. Detected youth offending (indictable offenses): 1992–2014 (thousands) (Bateman 2015a).

2015a). There are well-known difficulties of inferring the extent of youth crime from official data for detected offending (see, for instance, Bateman 2015b). Nonetheless, the persistence of the fall, and the consistent evidence derived from police recorded crime, national victimization surveys, and self-report studies, all suggest that the trend demonstrated in the figures represents a genuine reduction (Bateman 2015a).

As indicated in Fig. 14.1, the decline in youth crime started much earlier but has not been uniform over the whole period. The 1990s were characterized by a gradual reduction, but the subsequent decade saw a sharp rise between 2003 and 2007 with the number of substantive youth justice disposals imposed in the latter year 20% higher than 4 years earlier. Conversely, the period since 2008 has witnessed a further drop in youth crime but significantly sharper than that experienced during the 1990s: detected youth offending has fallen by more than three-quarters in just 7 years. Rather than representing abrupt fluctuations in children's criminal activity, these anomalies are best understood as reflecting accommodations by criminal justice agencies to successive government performance indicators.

In 2002, consistent with punitive and interventionist ethos then prevailing, the government introduced a target to increase the number of criminal justice sanctions imposed by a quarter of a million by 2008. The target was met a year early and there is a consensus that it was achieved largely by the police criminalizing minor incidents that would previously have attracted an informal response (Flanagan 2008). Although not explicitly focused on children, this process impacted disproportionately on young people who would previously have been more likely to benefit from police discretion to deal with less serious offending without recourse to a criminal sanction. The scope for altered practice was therefore considerably greater with respect to children. This logic is reflected in the data:

TABLE 14.1. First time entrants to the youth justice system: 2003/04–2013/14

Year	*FTEs*
2003/04	88,454
2004/05	96,199
2005/06	107,695
2006/07	110,826
2007/08	100,393
2008/09	80,329
2009/10	62,555
2010/11	45,910
2011/12	36,677
2012/13	27,848
2013/14	22,393

between 2003 and 2007, the number of adults entering the criminal justice system rose by less than 1%; the equivalent figure for children was 22% (Bateman 2015a).

By 2008, the negative implications of the target were becoming clear (Flanagan 2008). It was abandoned and replaced by an indicator which embodied an opposite dynamic. YCAP committed the government to achieving a reduction in the number of children entering the youth justice system for the first time—so called first time entrants (FTEs)—by 20% by 2020 (HM Government 2008). Although not acknowledged in the document that this represented a policy reversal, the measure encouraged the adoption of informal measures where a child with no antecedent history was apprehended. Like its predecessor, it was met early (Bateman 2015a). As presented in Table 14.1, the number of FTEs rose in accordance with the net-widening impetus of the previous target before declining sharply from 2007/08 onward (Ministry of Justice/Youth Justice Board 2015).

POLICING AND JUVENILES

While most policing of children is undertaken by generic officers, there are specialists who work with young people. Most significantly, the CDA established multiagency youth offending teams (YOTs) as the primary delivery mechanism for community-based youth justice services and required the police to contribute staff and other resources. Each local authority accordingly has at least one police officer seconded to the YOT (Souhami 2007).

Other specialist officers work within educational establishments. The debate following the murder of a head teacher in a London school in 1995 culminated in the deployment of police in some schools, through the establishment of Safer Schools Partnerships (SSPs) from 2002 onward, aimed at improving safety through a police presence. By 2011, there were 450 SSPs in operation (Police

Foundation 2011). An evaluation of SSPs has demonstrated some impact on truancy and, while acknowledging that the data should be treated with caution, suggested that some offending may be have been prevented in participating schools (Bowles et al. 2005).

Some areas also have police staff designated as the link to children's services or who work to joint decision-making panels in relation to children who offend (Haines and Case 2015). More commonly, however, policing is undertaken by generic officers and a recent thematic inspection has suggested that a failure to regard children as potentially vulnerable due to their childhood status is not uncommon among police who focus on offending rather than welfare (HM Inspectorate of Constabulary 2015).

As indicated previously, the adoption of a target to reduce FTEs has impacted significantly on police practice with children: the decline in FTEs is largely attributable to a fall in the number of child arrests of 55% between 2010 and 2015 (Howard League for Penal Reform 2015). The decreased reliance on arrest has been achieved through an increased use of informal measures, such as 'community resolutions' which can be delivered without recourse to arrest and do not constitute a formal youth justice sanction (Bateman 2015a).

Little is known about the use of such measures: there are no national data and considerable variations in local practice (Acton 2015).

The move toward increased informality in the treatment of children has been encouraged by the recent publication of a National Strategy for the Policing of Children and Young People which promotes diversion from the criminal justice system 'unless necessary' and indicates that the circumstances of the child should, where appropriate 'open our eyes to alternative avenues for addressing their behavior' (National Police Chiefs' Council 2015: 7). It has also been facilitated by legislation that increases police discretion to divert children.

The final warning scheme introduced by the CDA was a statutory manifestation of New Labour's then preference for early formal intervention: it proscribed informal measures other than in exceptional circumstances and embodied an 'escalator principle' whereby prosecution was mandated on the third offense at the latest (Holdaway and Desborough 2004). A child who admitted a relatively minor first offense might anticipate receiving a reprimand, a formal verbal warning issued by the police. A second offense, if admitted and not so serious that prosecution was required, would generally attract a final warning, which would result in a referral to the YOT for assessment. Further offending would, usually, lead to prosecution, irrespective of its nature. The Legal Aid and Sentencing of Offenders Act 2012 abolished reprimands and final warnings in favor of youth cautions and conditional youth cautions which can be issued at any point in a child's offending career, provided the offense is admitted, thereby undermining the escalator principle that had promoted the use of courts for children at an early stage (Hart 2014). Both youth cautions and youth conditional cautions constitute a formal record of offending, albeit without a court conviction. The latter disposal differs from the former in that the police can impose conditions on the child, such as paying compensation or a requirement to attend substance misuse counseling. If the conditions are not completed within a specified period, the original decision not to prosecute the child can be reviewed (Ministry of Justice 2013).

Recent trends notwithstanding, large numbers of children continue to be subject to arrest each year: 112,037 in 2014 (Howard League for Penal Reform 2015). At the police station, the treatment of children is governed by the Police and Criminal Evidence Act 1984 and the associated Codes of Practice. Most provisions apply to children as to adults: suspects are entitled to free legal advice, to have someone informed of their arrest, make a free phone call, and to see the Code of Practice that sets out their entitlements. Detention is subject to regular review and, unless they have been charged or further detention is authorized by the court, suspects must be released within 36 h of arrest. Children, like adults, have a circumscribed right to silence since a trial court can draw an adverse inference from a failure to answer questions (Cape 2011).

There are however a number of provisions specific to children. The police are obliged to cooperate with arrangements to safeguard child arrestees and must inform parents/carers and anyone else with a statutory responsibility for the child that they have been arrested. Children must be detained separately from adults: in practice they are held in separate cells within a shared custody area. Most significantly, an appropriate adult (AA) must be present when children are given their rights, during interview and at other key stages of the process (Ashford et al. 2006). In most cases, the child's parents will act as AA, but where these are unwilling or unable to attend, or precluded from the role because of involvement in the alleged offense, there is a statutory obligation on the YOT to co-ordinate the provision of nonfamilial AAs (Nacro 2006). Until April 2013, the entitlement to an AA applied to children aged 10–16 years. It was extended to 17-year-olds following a High Court ruling that excluding them constituted a breach of the ECHR (Bateman 2013b).

The AA's remit is to provide the child advice and support, make representations on their behalf, confirm that any questioning is conducted fairly, and ensure that their treatment accords with that laid down in Codes of Practice. It represents a potentially important safeguard. In practice, however, familial AAs lack understanding of children's rights and may not be confident to challenge the police (Nacro 2006); findings from a thematic inspection, moreover, suggest that nonfamilial AAs tend to focus on satisfying the minimum requirements of process rather than ensuring the child's well-being (Criminal Justice Joint Inspection 2011).

Where a suspect below 18 years of age is refused bail by the police after charge, he or she must, other than in exceptional circumstances, be transferred to local authority accommodation pending their appearance at court rather than detained at the police station. Until recently, this provision—as with the entitlement to an AA—did not apply to 17-year-olds but, in October 2015, it was extended to all children (Just for Kids Law 2015). While this extension is welcome, the available evidence indicates that younger children are routinely detained overnight in breach of the statutory requirements: analysis of six police forces found that of the 636 children refused bail just one was recorded as being transferred to local authority accommodation (HM Inspectorate of Constabulary 2015).

THE COURTS AND JUVENILES

The Children Act 1908 established the juvenile court as the first distinct venue for dealing with offending by children aged 7–16 years. As noted earlier, it also heard proceedings for children in need of care and protection (Arthur 2010). The separation of care and justice, effected through the creation of a discrete court for family proceedings in 1989, was followed shortly by the establishment of the youth court by the Criminal Justice Act 1991 which also extended the upper age range to include 17-year-olds who had previously appeared in the adult court.

Youth court proceedings mirror those in adult magistrates' courts in many ways. They are presided over by three lay magistrates or a single qualified district judge and are adversarial in nature with guilt established beyond all reasonable doubt. There are also distinctive features. Youth courts are not open to public and the media cannot identify child defendants, unless authorized to do so by the court (Ashford et al. 2006). Proceedings are intended to be less formal, although the extent to which this is achieved varies (Carlile 2014).

The sentencing framework is derived from the adult provisions—based on punishment proportionate to the offense—with modifications for youth that include the requirement to take account of the welfare of the child and the prevention of offending (Sentencing Guidelines Council 2009). In operational terms, the statutory provisions establish three sentencing bands with requisite thresholds that must be crossed before disposals become available. Custody cannot be imposed unless the offending is deemed by the court to be 'so serious that neither a fine alone nor a community sentence can be justified.' The court can only pass a youth rehabilitation order (YRO) (effectively statutory supervision with a menu of 18 possible requirements) if the offending is 'serious enough' to warrant it (Great Britain 2003: ss52 and p. 148). If neither threshold is met, the court must impose a first-tier disposal, which include fines, discharges, and referral orders.

The latter accounts for 40% of youth sentences and can be imposed for any offense where there is a guilty plea short of that which requires custody. It must be imposed for a first offense providing the child pleads guilty. The effect of the order is to refer the child to a youth offender panel, comprising two community volunteers and a YOT advisor. Panel meetings are attended by the child, the family, other relevant professionals, and the victim if they so wish. Their purpose is to make a contract with the young person that spells out expectations of them for the duration of the order and effectively constitutes the sentence. Referral orders are intended to be restorative but the extent to which they are fully so is open to debate (Newbury 2011).

While the large majority of cases are heard in the youth court, not all child defendants' benefit from the safeguards associated with that venue. Children with adult co-defendants are routinely 'carried' to the adult court and those alleged to have committed 'grave crimes' are tried in the crown court, a venue designed to deal with serious adult offending. Figures for the number of children appearing in adult courts are not published but, during 2014, 1927 were tried in the crown court (Ministry of Justice 2015b).

CUSTODIAL RULES FOR JUVENILES

Child imprisonment rose rapidly during the 1990s and early part of this century, largely because increasing numbers of children were prosecuted over that period in spite of the falls in youth crime. More recently, in line with the rediscovery of diversion, levels of incarceration have declined: the child custodial population contracted by two-thirds between November 2006 and November 2015 (Ministry of Justice 2015c).

Children refused bail are, by default, remanded to nonsecure local authority accommodation, but can be deprived of their liberty where the additional criteria for 'youth detention accommodation' (YDA) are satisfied. YDA is available where the child is aged 12 years or older, the offense is violent or sexual in nature, and is punishable in the case of an adult with a 14-year term of imprisonment (Hart 2012). The standard custodial sentence in the youth court is the detention and training order, available, for between 4 and 24 months, where the offending is so serious that other penalties cannot be justified. Half of the order is by default served in detention, although there is facility for early or late release, with the sentence completed in the community under compulsory YOT supervision. Where children are tried for 'grave crimes' in the crown court, the maximum penalty is identical to that for adults convicted of equivalent offenses (Bateman 2015a).

Since 2000, children have been imprisoned in a discrete under-18 estate consisting of three types of establishment that vary in size and ethos:

- Young offender institutions (YOIs): large-scale children's prisons, some of which have capacity of more than 300, for boys aged 15–17 years
- Secure training centers (STCs): privately managed custodial establishments with a capacity of up to 80 boys and girls aged 12–17 years
- Secure children's homes (SCHs): smaller child care establishments, the largest of which accommodates 40 children with considerably higher staff-to-child ratios. Such units can also accommodate children deprived of their liberty on welfare grounds.

Placement is determined on the basis of gender, age, vulnerability, proximity to home area, and availability. In practice, cost is also a significant variable: a place for a child in an SCH costs more than three times that in a YOI. It is perhaps unsurprising that almost 70% of imprisoned children are detained in the latter institutions while the former accommodate just 11% (Ministry of Justice 2015c).

There have been considerable concerns over the treatment of children in custody, YOIs in particular, and there have been sharp rises in the level of violence within the secure estate in recent years as the custodial population has contracted (Bateman 2015a). Recent research conducted by the Children's Commissioner for England established that children in YOIs were likely to spend three times as long in isolation as their counterparts in SCHs and have significantly less access to education and other aspects of the standard regime as consequence. The Commissioner has accordingly called for the abolition of YOIs (Children's Commissioner for England 2015). Inspections have confirmed such concerns, noting that, at Feltham YOI, 38 % of detainees were locked up when they should be taking part in core activities (HM Inspectorate of Prisons 2015).

ALTERNATIVE SANCTIONS FOR JUVENILES

Courts have available a range of sanctions for children short of custody. As noted earlier, the most commonly used is the referral order, an ostensibly restorative disposal that constitutes 40 % of youth sentences. The YRO accounts for a further 29 % of disposals but the conditions imposed on children may differ significantly. In 2013/14, the most frequently imposed sanction was supervision which was attached to one-third of orders; curfew requirements, monitored by electronic tags, were also common (Ministry of Justice/Youth Justice Board 2015).

Two conditions of the YRO constitute a statutory alternative to incarceration and where the court considers that the statutory threshold for custody is satisfied, it must indicate why it did not consider such requirements appropriate if it imprisons the child. Intensive supervision and surveillance requires the child to participate in a minimum of 25 h activity per week and be subject to an electronically monitored curfew; intensive fostering involves the child being placed away from home with a specialist in foster care for up to 12 months where the court considers that the child's offending is largely due to home circumstances. After piloting the latter, however, a failure of ongoing dedicated funding from the government meant that intensive fostering is no longer available in practice (Hart 2012).

DIFFERENCES IN TREATMENT OF BOYS AND GIRLS

Imprisoned girls cannot be detained in YOIs but there are otherwise no formal distinctions in their treatment within the youth justice system. Nonetheless, girls have consistently represented a small proportion of the offending and custodial populations: in 2013/15 19 % and 5 %, respectively (Ministry of Justice 2015b). This underrepresentation is partly reflective of the fact that girls commit fewer and less serious offenses, and grow out of crime more successfully and at a lower age.

However, it is also indicative of gendered assumptions that operate in contradictory ways. On the one hand, girls' problematic behavior is more likely to receive a lenient response than that displayed by boys, leading to higher levels of diversion. As a consequence, girls who do come into contact with justice agencies are often significantly more vulnerable than their male counterparts and have particularly complex needs (Bateman and Hazel 2014). Conversely, it has been suggested that, for violent offenses, girls are more likely to be imprisoned than boys because such conduct transgresses gender norms as well as the law, thereby rendering them 'doubly deviant.' Moreover, when incarcerated, girls are at higher risk of restraint and self-harm (Sharpe and Gelsthorpe 2015).

These complex dynamics are exacerbated by the manner in which youth justice assessments operate in England and Wales. Based on the risk-factor paradigm, the assessment process requires practitioners to allocate a 'score' to children which purports to be indicative of their risk of reoffending. This score then determines the intensity of contact for community-based intervention. But since girls in the justice system display higher levels of vulnerability—which are inevitably captured in the scoring—and have a lower propensity to reoffending than boys, the process tends to systematically overpredict the risk of recidivism in girls, leading to more extensive intervention than might be warranted by the seriousness of their offending (Bateman 2012a).

There are other forms of disproportionality evident in the youth justice system. The overrepresentation of children in care has already been noted. Perhaps the most disconcerting trends are those which demonstrate that the already disproportionate involvement of minority ethnic children in the justice system is worsening. Black children constitute 4% of the general 10–17 population but, in 2013/14, accounted for 8% of those receiving a youth justice sanction, a rise from 6.1% in 2009/10, suggesting that such children have not benefited to the same extent as their white counterparts from the decline in FTEs. As interventions become increasingly punitive, so does overrepresentation. For example, of the children serving long-term custodial sentences of more than 2 years, more than a quarter were black (Ministry of Justice/Youth Justice Board 2015).

A variety of explanations are posited for the differential treatment of minority ethnic children, including disproportionate levels of stop and search by the police, and discriminatory decision-making by courts and practitioners within the justice system (May et al. 2010). Black children and those of mixed heritage, who come to the attention of youth justice agencies, also have high higher levels of needs as measured in assessment scores of risk (May et al. 2009), and minority ethnic children are disproportionately likely to have backgrounds of poverty and experience of other indicators of disadvantage (Home Affairs Committee 2007).

CONCLUSION

This chapter opened with an indication of the pace of change within youth justice in England and Wales and the prospect that the current review of youth justice will lead to further reform. Previous shifts in legislation, policy, and practice have addressed some concerns, left others untouched and given rise to new, and unanticipated problems. The extent to which any reforms emanating from the ongoing government review of youth justice will fare better remains to be seen.

REFERENCES

Acton, E. (2015). Restorative justice a postcode lottery?—Availability and quality of service. *Safer Communities, 14*(3), 120–125.
Arthur, R. (2010). *Young offenders and the law*. London: Routledge.
Ashford, M., Chard, A., & Redhouse, N. (2006). *Defending young people in the criminal justice system* (3rd ed.). London: Legal Action Group.
Audit Commission. (2004). *Youth justice 2004: A review of the reformed youth justice system*. London: Audit Commission.
Bandalli, S. (2000). Children, responsibility and the new youth justice. In B. Goldson (Ed.), *The new youth justice* (pp. 81–95). Lyme Regis: Russell House publishing.
Bateman, T. (2012a). *Criminalising children for no good purpose: The age of criminal responsibility in England and Wales*. London: NAYJ.
Bateman, T. (2012b). Who pulled the plug? Towards an explanation of the fall in child imprisonment in England and Wales. *Youth Justice, 12*(1), 36–52.
Bateman, T. (2013a). Keeping up (tough) appearances: The age of criminal responsibility in England and Wales. *Criminal Justice Matters, 92*(1), 28–29.
Bateman, T. (2013b). *Detaining children at the police station: A failure to comply with legislation*. London: NAYJ.
Bateman, T. (2015a). *The state of youth justice 2015*. London: NAYJ.
Bateman, T. (2015b). Trends in detected youth crime and contemporary state responses. In B. Goldson & J. Muncie (Eds.), *Youth crime and justice* (pp. 67–82). London: Sage.
Bateman, T. (in press). Youth justice. In P. Davies, J. Harding, & G. Mair (Eds.), *Criminal justice in England and Wales: An introduction*. London: Sage.
Bateman, T., & Hazel, N. (2014). *Resettlement of girls and young women: Research report*. London: Beyond Youth Custody.
Bernard, T. (1992). *The cycle of juvenile justice*. Oxford: Oxford University Press.
Bowles, R., Garcia Reyes, M., & Pradiptyo, R. (2005). *Safer schools partnerships*. London: Youth Justice Board.
Cadman, S. (2005). Proportionality in the youth justice system. In T. Bateman & J. Pitts (Eds.), *The RHP companion to youth justice* (pp. 59–64). Lyme Regis: Russell House publishing.
Cape, E. (2011). *Defending suspects at police stations* (6th ed.). London: Legal Action Group.
Carlile, L. A. (2014). *Report of independent Parliamentarians' inquiry into the operation and effectiveness of the youth court*. London: Sieff Foundation.
Centre for Social Justice. (2012). *Rules of engagement: Changing the heart of youth justice*. London: CSJ.
Children's Commissioner for England. (2015). *Unlocking potential: A study of the isolation of children in custody in England*. London: Children's Commissioner for England.
Conservative Party. (2015). *Strong leadership; a clear economic plan; a brighter more secure future: Conservative party manifesto 2015*. London: Conservative Party.

Criminal Justice Joint Inspection. (2011). *Who's looking out for the children? A joint inspection of appropriate adult provision and children in detention after charge*. London: CJJI.
Curtis, S. (2005). The welfare principle. In T. Bateman & J. Pitts (Eds.), *The RHP companion to youth justice* (pp. 53–58). Lyme Regis: Russell House publishing.
Department for Education. (2015). *Children looked after in England (including adoption and care leavers) year ending 31 March 2015*. London: DfE.
Fergusson, R. (2007). Making sense of the melting pot: Multiple discourses in youth justice policy. *Youth Justice, 7*(3), 179–194.
Flanagan, R. (2008). *The review of policing: Final report*. London: Home Office.
Goldson, B. (2000). *The new youth justice*. Lyme Regis: Russell House publishing.
Gove, M. (2015). *Announcement of a review into youth justice* (Written statement to Parliament 11 September 2015). London: Ministry of Justice.
Graham, J., & Moore, C. (2008). Beyond welfare versus justice: Juvenile justice in England and Wales. In J. Junger-Tas & S. H. Decker (Eds.), *International handbook of juvenile justice* (pp. 65–92). New York: Springer.
Great Britain. (1998). *Crime and Disorder Act 1998*. Elizabeth II. Chapter 37. London: The Stationery Office.
Great Britain. (2003). *Criminal Justice Act 2003*. Elizabeth II. Chapter 44. London: The Stationery Office.
Haines, K. (2010). The dragonization of youth justice. In W. Taylor, R. Earle, & R. Hester (Eds.), *Youth justice handbook: Theory, policy and practice* (pp. 231–242). Cullompton: Willan.
Haines, K., & Case, S. (2015). *Positive youth justice: Children first, offenders second*. Bristol: Policy Press.
Hart, D. (2012). *Legal Aid Sentencing and Punishment of Offenders Act 2012: Implications for children*. London: NAYJ.
Hart, D. (2014). *Pre-court arrangements for children who offend*. London: NAYJ.
Hazel, N. (2008). *Cross national comparison of youth justice*. London: Youth Justice Board.
HM Government. (2008). *Youth crime action plan 2008*. London: HM Government.
HM Inspectorate of Constabulary. (2015). *The welfare of vulnerable people in police custody*. London: HMIC.
HM Inspectorate of Prisons. (2015). *Report on an unannounced inspection of HMYOI Feltham (children and young people)*. London: HMIP.
Holdaway, S., & Desborough, S. (2004). *The national evaluation of the Youth Justice Board's final warning projects*. London: Youth Justice Board.
Home Affairs Committee. (2007). *Young black people and the criminal justice system*. London: The Stationery Office.
Home Office. (1997). *No more excuses: A new approach to tackling youth crime in England and Wales*. London: Home Office.
Howard League for Penal Reform. (2015). *Child arrests in England and Wales 2014*. Research briefing. London: Howard League.
Huizinga, D., Schumann, K., Ehret, B., & Elliott, A. (2003). *The effect of juvenile justice system processing on subsequent delinquent and criminal behavior: A cross-national study*. Washington: US Department of Justice.
Just for Kids Law. (2015). *17-year olds to be treated as children at police stations*. Legal update, Oct. 23, 2015.
Kelly, L., & Armitage, V. (2015). Diverse diversions: Youth justice reform. Localized practices, and a 'New Interventionist Diversion'? *Youth Justice, 15*(2), 117–133.
Lipscombe, S. (2012). *The age of criminal responsibility in England and Wales*. London: House of Commons Library.
May, T., Gyateng, T., & Bateman, T. (2009). *Exploring the needs of young black and minority ethnic offenders and the provision of targeted interventions*. London: Youth Justice Board.
May, T., Gyateng, T., & Hough, M. (2010). *Differential treatment in the youth justice system*. London: Equality and Human Rights Commission.

Ministry of Justice. (2013). *Code of practice for youth conditional cautions*. London: MoJ.
Ministry of Justice. (2015a). *Youth justice review: Terms of reference*. London: MoJ.
Ministry of Justice. (2015b). *Criminal justice statistics: December 2014*. London: MoJ.
Ministry of Justice. (2015c). *Youth custody data: November 2015*. London: MoJ.
Ministry of Justice/Youth Justice Board. (2015). *Youth justice annual statistics 2013/14*. London: MoJ.
Monaghan, G. (2005). Children's human rights and youth justice. In T. Bateman & J. Pitts (Eds.), *The RHP companion to youth justice* (pp. 46–52). Lyme Regis: Russell House publishing.
Nacro. (2003). *The sentencing framework for children and young people*. London: Nacro.
Nacro. (2006). *Acting as an appropriate adult: A good practice guide*. London: Nacro.
National Audit Office. (2010). *The youth justice system in England and Wales: Reducing offending by young people*. London: NAO.
National Police Chiefs' Council. (2015). *National strategy for the policing of children and young people*. London: National Police Chiefs' Council.
Newbury, A. (2011). "I would have been able to hear what they think": Tensions in achieving restorative outcomes in the English youth justice system. *Youth Justice, 11*(3), 250–265.
Police Foundation. (2011). *Safer school partnerships*. London: Police Foundation.
Redmond, A. (2015). *Children in custody 2014–15: An analysis of 12–18-year-olds' perceptions of their experience in secure training centres and young offender institutions*. London: HM Inspectorate of Prisons.
Royal Society. (2011). *Brain waves 4: Neuroscience and the law*. London: The Royal Society.
Sentencing Guidelines Council. (2009). *Overarching principles: Sentencing youths*. London: SGC.
Sharpe, G., & Gelsthorpe, L. (2015). Girls, crime and justice. In B. Goldson & J. Muncie (Eds.), *Youth crime and justice* (pp. 49–63). London: Sage.
Smith, R. (2014). Reinventing diversion. *Youth Justice, 14*(2), 109–121.
Solanki, A. R., Bateman, T., Boswell, G., & Hill, E. (2006). *Anti-social behaviour orders*. London: Youth Justice Board.
Souhami, A. (2007). *Transforming youth justice: Occupational identity and cultural change*. Cullompton: Willan.
UN Committee on the Rights of the Child. (2002). *Concluding observations: United Kingdom of Great Britain and Northern Ireland*. Geneva: UN.
UN Committee on the Rights of the Child. (2008). *Concluding observations: United Kingdom of Great Britain and Northern Ireland*. Geneva: UN.
Welsh Government. (2013). *The Welsh Government Contribution to the 5th UK state party report for the UN Committee on the Rights of the Child*. Cardiff: Welsh Government.
Welsh Government. (2014). *Children's Rights Scheme 2014: Arrangements for having due regard to the United Nations Convention on the Rights of the Child (UNCRC) when Welsh Ministers exercise any of their functions*. Cardiff: Welsh Government.
Wigzell, A. (2014). Moving beyond the ASBO? A review of the proposed anti-social behaviour measures and their implications for children. *Safer Communities, 13*(2), 73–82.

Tim Bateman is Reader in Youth Justice at the University of Bedfordshire, currently seconded for a period of 2 years as Principal Policy Adviser (Youth Justice) to the Children's Commissioner for England. Prior to moving into academia, Tim had an extensive background as a social worker with children in conflict with the law and in juvenile justice policy. He has written widely on issues pertaining to youth crime and juvenile justice. Tim is co-editor of *Community Safety* journal, contributes the news section to *Youth Justice* journal and is Deputy Chair of the National Association for Youth Justice.

15

Germany

Frieder Dünkel and Wolfgang Heinz

THE LEGAL STATUS OF JUVENILES

The legal status of juveniles is defined by civil and penal law and in certain other laws concerning specific rights and duties. According to § 1 (2) of the German Juvenile Justice Act (*Jugendgerichtsgesetz*, JGG), a juvenile is a person who at the time of committing a criminal offence has reached the age of 14 and not yet the age of 18. The same paragraph also deals with young adults, i.e., the age group of between 18 and under 21 years of age. As will be shown, this age group of young adults is also dealt by the juvenile justice system. In civil law, children under 7 years of age are not responsible for any act, whereas persons at the age of 18 reach the status of full contractual capability. Between 7 and 17 there is a limited contractual capability and children can be responsible for acts of damage if they had the capacity to understand the wrongdoing and to act according to that.

There are other age limits beyond the threshold of 18. Children at the age of 14 can choose their religion, at 16 they can marry, and at 17 they are allowed to make their driver's license.

There is no criminal responsibility for those under 14. In these cases, only Juvenile Welfare and Civil Law can be applied (JWL, called *Sozialgesetzbuch* Vol. VIII, SGB VIII of 1990 and the Civil Code, *Bürgerliches Gesetzbuch*, BGB). The juvenile welfare agencies act on the local level of the communities on the demand of parents; exceptionally measures can be imposed by the Family Court, §§ 1631b, 1666, 1666a BGB (incl. placement in closed residential care).

F. Dünkel (✉) • W. Heinz
Rechts-und Staatswissenschaftliche Fakultät, Department of Criminology, Ernst-Moritz-Arndt-Universität Greifswald, Domstr. 20, 17487 Greifswald, Germany
e-mail: duenkel@uni-greifswald.de; wolfgang.heinz@uni-konstanz.de

S.H. Decker, N. Marteache (eds.), *International Handbook of Juvenile Justice*,
DOI 10.1007/978-3-319-45090-2_15

AGE OF MAJORITY

As has been said criminal responsibility in Germany starts at 14 years of age, but between 14 and 18 the juvenile is only criminally responsible if he/she "according to his/her physical and psychological development is able to recognize the wrongdoing of the criminal act and is able to act according to this cognitive discernment" (§ 3 JJA). Full criminal responsibility is given at the age of 18, but until the young adult reaches the age of 21, the sanctions of the JJA apply if a global examination of the offender's personality and of his social environment indicates that at the time of committing the crime the young adult in his moral and psychological development was like a juvenile or if the motives and the circumstances of the offence are those of a typically juvenile crime (§ 105 I No. 1 et 2 JJA).

Civil majority is given at the age of 18, before that age (from 7 to 17 years of age) juveniles can contract only with the consent of their parents (see sect. 104, 106 Civil Law, *Bürgerliches Gesetzbuch, BGB*). Children between 7 and 17, however, can contract in matters of daily life, e.g., buy things in a bakery or supermarket, if the goods belong to the daily life. Juveniles between 14 and 17 years of age have enlarged rights to dispose of pocket money and earnings without the consent of parents.

THE COUNTRY'S STANCE TOWARDS THE UN COMMITTEE ON THE RIGHTS OF THE CHILD

Germany has ratified the Convention of the Rights of the Child (CRC) in 1992. Since then the Convention is a binding Federal Law, but in its legal status below the Federal Constitution. The Constitutional Court (*Bundesverfassungsgericht*), however, in a recent decision concerning a conflict with the jurisprudence of the European Court on Human Rights (ECtHR) has emphasized that the interpretation of the German Constitution should be in conformity with the Human Rights as enshrined in the European Convention on Human Rights (ECHR). In the respective case, the Court changed its jurisprudence in favor of the ECtHR's view on the nature of preventive detention (see BVerfG [Federal Constitutional Court], decision of 4 May 2011—2 BvR 2365/09—www.bverfg.de/e/rs20110504_2bvr236509.html; see in detail Drenkhahn et al. 2012).

The CRC and the Recommendations of the Committee of the Rights of the child are taken seriously although not all German legislation on juvenile justice and procedure is in line with international human rights standards such as the European Rules for Juvenile Offenders Subject to Sanctions or Measures (ERJOSSM). Some indication is given below (see also Dünkel 2011b).

TRENDS IN JUVENILE CRIME OVER THE LAST DECADES, IN PARTICULAR THE PERIOD 2004–2014

Juvenile delinquency became a major issue in the 1960s and 1970s, when official crime rates increased and a lack of adequate delinquency treatment and prevention became evident. At that time no self-report or victimization surveys existed yet. In the 1980s, called the "golden age" of German juvenile justice, juvenile delinquency declined at the same time as major liberal reforms with expanding diversion new community sentences and restorative justice measures, in particular victim-offender mediation, took place (see Dünkel 2006, 2011a). The early 1990s brought different challenges to the youth justice system, as after the German reunification, the East-German federal states showed a strong increase of the juvenile crime rate and in particular the violent crime rate.

Since the mid-1990s the increase of juvenile crime rates levelled off and since the early 2000s another remarkable decrease of registered as well as self-reported juvenile delinquency could be observed (see Baier et al. 2009; Heinz 2014; Baier and Prätor 2016; for similar results in other European countries, see Junger-Tas et al. 2010). In particular, violent offences and therefore violent victimization particularly decreased (see also Dünkel et al. 2008).

When talking about juvenile delinquency in Germany, one has to consider that due to the German juvenile justice system, which deals with 14–17-years-old juveniles as well as with 18–20-years-old young adults statistics refer always to these age groups. Police statistics also refer to young adults between 21 and 25 years of age. Figure 15.1 shows the development of registered juvenile and young adult delinquency from 1984 until 2013. Young adults (18–20) and juveniles show higher prevalence rates than the other age groups, but the levelling off and decrease in the last 10 years is clearly visible (see Fig. 15.1). This decrease is seen as a result of the widespread crime prevention programs in schools and local communities (see Heinz 2015a).

Female juvenile delinquency is also levelling off according to registered crime statistics, but less than the rates of male juveniles. Self-report studies show that the reporting rate for females increased between 1998 and 2006. The increase of female juvenile delinquency in this period to a major part can be explained by this (see Heinz 2015b: 284). Still the prevalence rates for young females are about half of the ones for males (23.6 versus 43.6, see Baier et al. 2009: 65; Heinz 2015b: 276; with regard to violent offences the ratio is about 1: 3, for shoplifting 1:1).

Patterns of Registered Juvenile Delinquency in Germany

Juvenile delinquency—as in other countries (see Junger-Tas et al. 2010)—in general is characterized by its petty and episodic nature (see Spieß 2012, 2015). The large majority of delinquent acts committed by juveniles are property offences, primarily theft, property damage, vandalism, and minor drug crimes. Spieß (2012) demonstrated that in 2010 69% of all registered crimes of juveniles and 56% of (18–20 years old) young adults comprised shoplifting, vandalism,

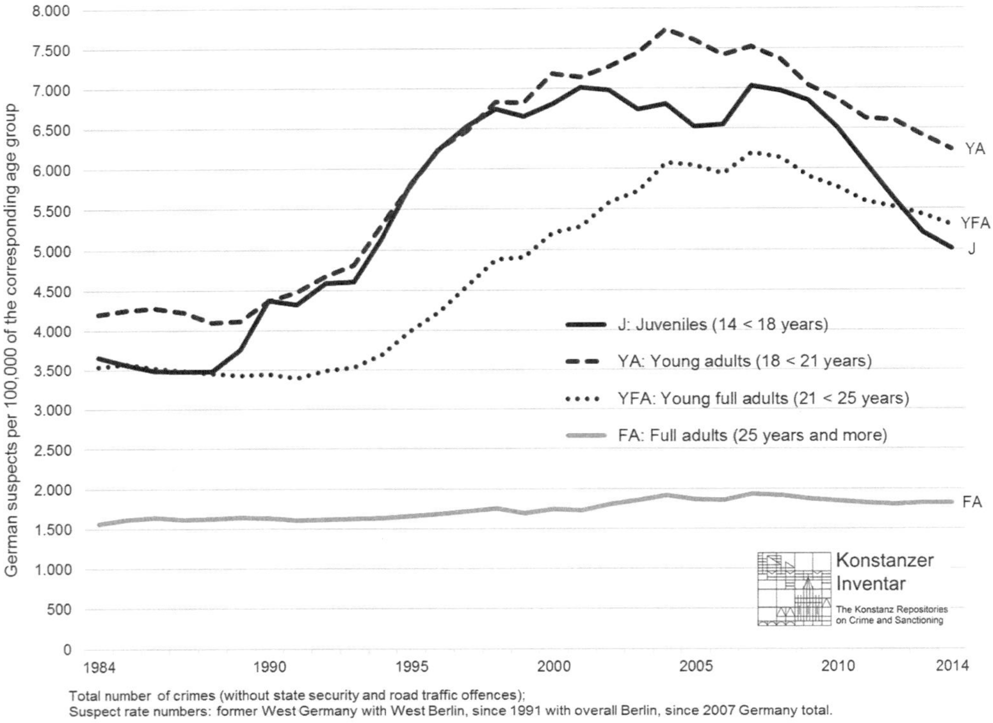

FIGURE 15.1. Police registered suspects of crimes per 100,000 of the population according to different age groups. *Source*: Heinz (2015a).

damage to property, and simple bodily injury. During the 1990s, an increase of violent crimes slightly changed the picture, but not the structure in general. The increase of violence was mainly characterized by bodily injury, often group fights without weapons. Violent acts still counted for only about 10% (2010) of juvenile delinquency (7% simple bodily injury, 3% more serious violent acts; Spieß 2012). 2014, 54% of violent crimes of 14–21-years-old juveniles and young adults were simple bodily injury (without weapons), 35% severe bodily injury, 11% robbery, 1.5% sexual offences (incl. rape and 0.4% (attempted) homicide. The registered prevalence rate for bodily injury decreased very considerably, for severe bodily injury from 2007 to 2014 by 45% (see Heinz 2015a; Spieß 2015). Therefore, juvenile delinquency is not seen as a major problem of the German society. Other age groups such as adults between 21 and 40 between 1998 and 2008 showed a strong increase of registered prevalence rates (+20% and +40%, whereas the rates for juveniles and young adults decreased.

Self-Reported Juvenile Delinquency and Victimization

In the last representative poll with regard ninth grade pupils in Germany in 2007/8 44% of male and 24% of female juveniles report having committed one of the 12 crimes or delinquent acts. However, vandalism, simple bodily injuries

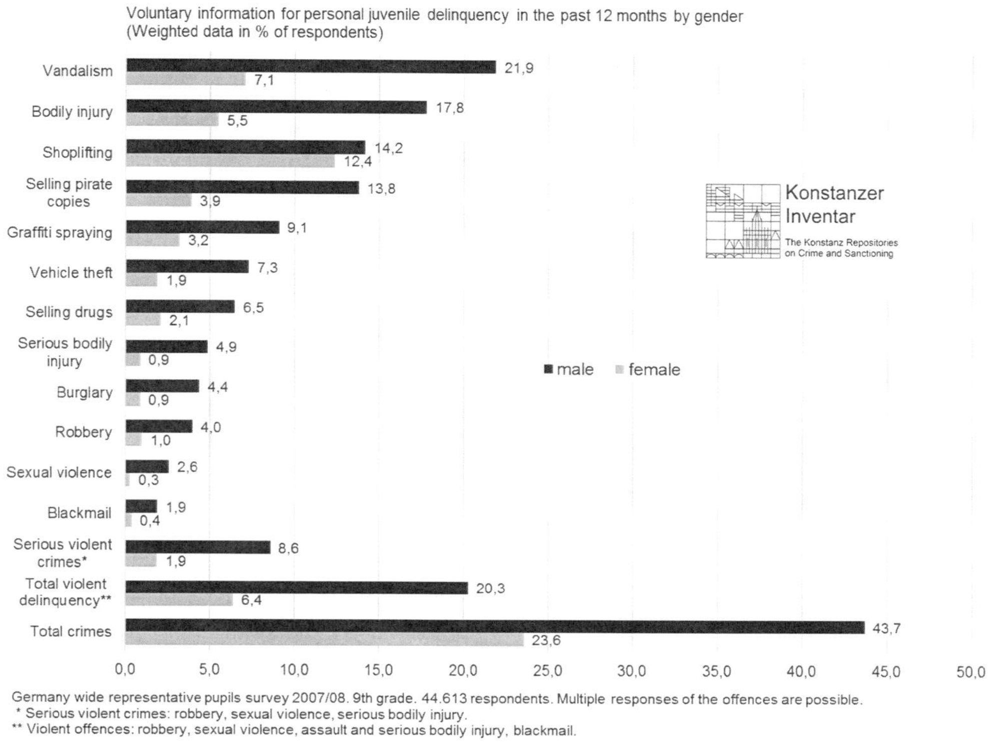

FIGURE 15.2. Self-reported delinquency of ninth grade pupils in Germany, 2007/2008. *Source*: Baier et al. (2009: 69, Figure 5.6); Heinz (2015a).

(without weapons) and shoplifting dominated, whereas serious crimes like robbery or serious bodily injury remained the exception. Young females—with the exception of shoplifting—show significant lower prevalence rates than their male counterparts (see Heinz 2015b: 276 and Fig. 15.2 above; Enzmann 2010: 58 ff).

CAUSES OF JUVENILE CRIME

German criminology is using the same theories for explaining juvenile crime as they have been developed in the Anglo-American literature (Oberwittler 2012). Strong emphasis is given to the notion of juvenile delinquency as a "normal" phenomenon and of its episodic nature. It is because of this and the petty nature of most juvenile crimes that German juvenile justice policy remained moderate by emphasizing diversion, restorative justice, and "constructive" educational measures imposed by the youth court. In the last decades, however, empirical evidence has been found that a small percentage of male juveniles developed carriers of persistent offending. Explanations given are more or less stress and social developmental theories emphasizing a lack of control by the family, a lack of self-control, schooling problems, deficits concerning personality disorders and others (see, e.g., the developmental model of Beelmann and Raabe 2007; see also Lösel and Bliesener 2003). The model can be seen as a modern form of a multi-factorial approach. An accumulation of risk factors does not necessarily lead to a criminal life style, but in most cases is counteracted by protective factors (resilience) and life events, which prevent becoming a persistent offender. Even those who develop a multi-recidivist carrier regularly stop offending during the third decade of life. In a recent panel study on 13- to 18-years-old pupils, the peak age of involvement in violent delinquency was 14 and for property offences 15 (for both females and males, in the case of females on a lower level, see Boers 2008: 346; Oberwittler 2012: 791 f. with further references).

Bio-psycho-social developmental model of antisocial behavior

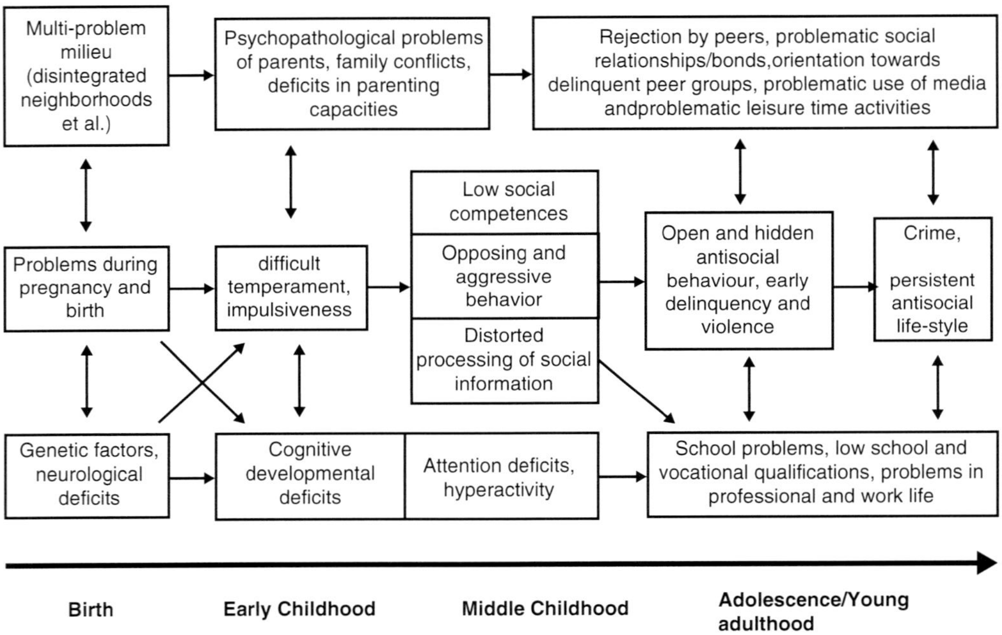

Source : Beelmann & Raabe 2007,modified to Losel & Bender 2003.

A few life course-oriented studies have been conducted (see, e.g., Schumann 2003a, b), which demonstrate the difficulties of problematic juveniles to integrate in adult life, in particular professional life. They also confirm the general German juvenile justice policy to avoid negative stigmatization by diverting young offenders from the justice system as far and as long as possible.

In general, German criminology uses the same theories as the Anglo-American literature to explain juvenile delinquency by referring to anomie and structural theories of crime, learning theories, control theories, and rational choice or routine activity concepts (see Oberwittler 2012: 801 ff., 812 ff.). In the last years, more and more integrated theories such as Wikström's situational action theory (see, e.g., Wikström 2007) are used for explanation with some similarities to the bio-psycho-social model cited above. But also social inequality and disorganization are important theoretical approaches, in particular for explaining violent crimes (see Oberwittler 2012: 830 ff. with further references).

POLICING AND JUVENILES

The German juvenile justice system covers the age groups of juveniles (14–17-years-old) and young adults (18–20-years-old) offenders (see §§ 1, 105 JJA). The relevant legislation is the Juvenile justice Act (JJA), originally passed in 1923, with major amendments in 1943, 1953, 1990, 2008, and 2013 see in Detail Dünkel 2006, 2011a). Both age groups are sentenced by specialized youth courts.

Special juvenile policing in the narrow sense implies that there are specialized police, prosecutors, and youth judges. In the police level in bigger cities, special youth units have been introduced. In some model areas, "Houses of Youth Justice" (*Häuser des Jugendrechts*, see Feuerhelm and Kügler 2003) have been established, where the police, juvenile prosecutors, social workers of the local community, and sometimes mediation schemes work together. The idea behind is to find quick solutions and to avoid detention, due to the efforts of the social work unit, which tries to find alternative solutions to resolving the underlying problems causing the committing of crimes. Juvenile prosecutors and judges must be experienced in questions of education (see § 37 JJA), a legal regulation which sometimes is neglected (see Dünkel 2011a).

The juvenile justice system is strictly based on the idea of education and minimum intervention, in order to avoid stigmatization and negative effects of formal interventions. Therefore, diversion, i.e., the dismissal of cases by the juvenile prosecutor or the youth court has priority (see 5. below). Mediation is given priority in this area of intervention (see § 45(2) JJA), other minor ("informal") diversionary interventions may be community service orders, reparation to the victim, or reprimands (diversion without interventions is given priority to diversion in combination with certain educational measures, which have to be approved by the youth court, see § 45(3) JJA). "Formal" court dispositions are the so-called educational (see § 10 JJA) and disciplinary measures (see § 13 ff. JJA), for example, mediation, reparation to the victim, community service, the so-called social training courses, the supervisory directive (executed by the welfare authorities or the juvenile probation service), etc. "Disciplinary" measures include a week-end detention or detention of up to 4 weeks in a special unit (not prison). Educational and disciplinary sanctions are not classified as punishment and therefore not registered in the records of young offenders.

Youth imprisonment should be used only as a last resort and for the minimum period acceptable (see §§ 17, 18 JJA). However, short-term imprisonment of less than 6 months is not seen as "educationally" appropriate, and therefore the Juvenile Justice Act forbids such penalties. The maximum youth prison sentence is 5 years, in cases of very serious crimes committed by juveniles 10 years

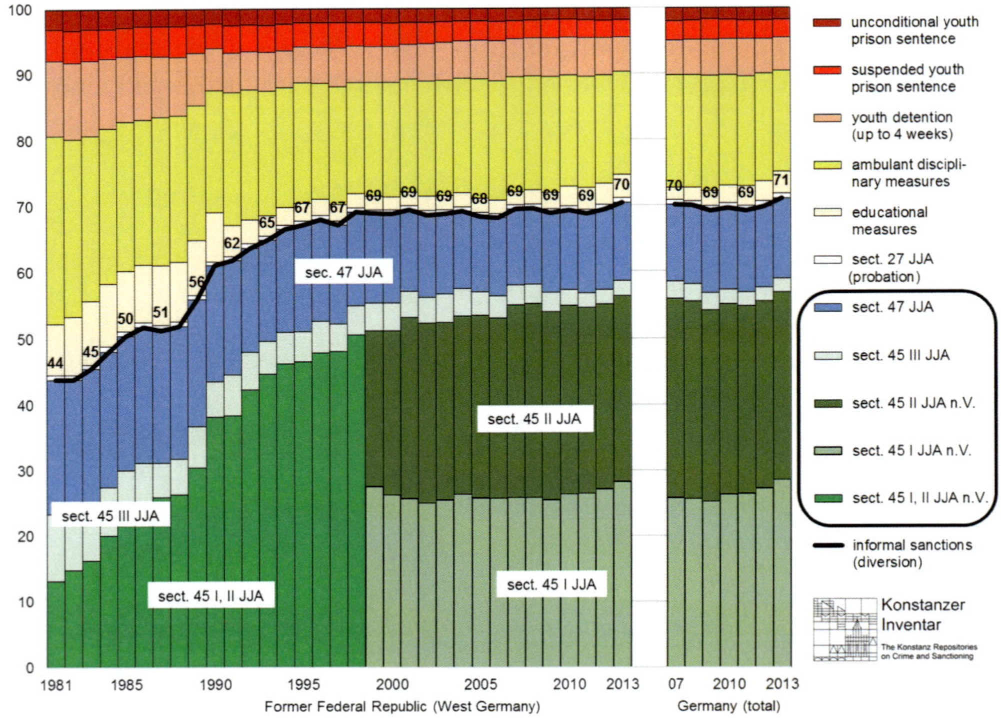

FIGURE 15.3. “Informal” and “formal” (court) sanctions in the German juvenile justice system, 1981–2013. *Source*: Heinz (2015a).

(see § 18 JJA). In the case of young adults, the maximum term in general is 10 years. Since 2013 the maximum penalty may be 15 years for very serious and qualified murder cases.

Youth courts deal with juvenile and young adult offenders. Waiver procedures for serious juvenile offenders are not provided. Young adults, however, according to their maturity, can be sentenced either with sanctions of the general Criminal Law or of the JJA. The practice in two thirds, in serious violent cases even in more than 90% of cases applies the milder juvenile law (in order to avoid higher minimum sentences of the general criminal law, see Dünkel 2006, 2011a; Pruin and Dünkel 2015).

The “penal climate” and the sentencing practice in Germany in general can be characterized as moderate. This is particularly true in the juvenile justice system. As can be seen from Fig. 15.3, 71% of all juveniles and young adults in 2013 were dismissed by the juvenile prosecutor (sect 45 JJA) or the judge (sect. 47 JJA), in most cases because of the pettiness of the offence (sect. 45 I JJA) or because educational measures have been taken by others (parents, school or because mediation, reparation has been agreed).

COURTS AND JUVENILES

The other side of the "medal" showing the "formal" sanctions of the youth court reveals that unconditional youth prison sentences are restricted to the very last resort by counting only for 2% of all juvenile and young adult offenders.

About 85% of youth prison sentences are between 6 months and 2 years, more than 70% of them are suspended, i.e., the juvenile is supported and supervised by the probation service (see Dünkel 2011a; Heinz 2014; Table 15.1 below). The short-term detention order (up to 4 weeks)—although being much criticized and in practice on the decline—still makes for 5% of all offenders sentenced by youth courts. Formal educational and disciplinary measures in the community comprise for 19% (2013). They have partly been replaced by "informal" reactions (dismissal of cases) as described above.

Altogether, one can characterize the German approach to deal with juvenile delinquency as "evidence-based" and moderate (see Dünkel 2011a; Heinz 2014, 2015a). In contrast to other European (see Dünkel et al. 2011; Dünkel 2013, 2015) and non-European countries (see Zimring et al. 2015), a punitive turn in sanctioning juvenile and young adult offenders cannot be seen in Germany. Despite some problems of increasing violent crime rates in the 1990s, Germany kept the moderate way of dealing with these offenders (see Heinz 2009; Dünkel 2012 and Fig. 15.4). Much emphasis was given to further developing crime prevention programs and improving social integrative strategies of state and private youth welfare agencies (see Centre for the Prevention of Youth Crime 2004; Deutsches Jugendinstitut 2015).

TABLE 15.1. Length of youth prison sentences, 1975–2006 (old Federal States) and 2007–2012 (total Germany)

Year	*YI total (abs.)*	*susp. YI (%)*	*6 m.–1 J. (%)*	*6 m.–1 y., susp. (% rel. to col. 4)*	*1–2 y. (%)*	*1–2 y., susp. (% rel. to col. 6)*	*2–3 y. (%)*	*3–5 y. (%)*	*5–10 y. (%)*
1975	15,983	55.9	70.1	74.9	20.4	16.7	5.9	0.6	
1980	17,982	62.2	71.0	79.4	20.1	28.6	4.5	2.1	0.7
1985	17,672	61.9	65.0	79.1	24.6	42.4	5.9	2.6	0.8
1990	12,103	64.3	62.2	79.2	28.0	53.7	6.4	2.4	0.6
1995	13,880	63.9	56.8	78.5	32.4	59.7	7.2	3.0	0.6
2000	17,753	62.1	54.8	78.5	33.8	56.4	7.9	2.9	0.5
2005	16,641	60.7	54.0	77.1	34.4	55.5	8.0	3.1	0.5
2006	16,886	60.5	53.7	77.6	34.0	55.3	8.4	3.3	0.5
2007	20,480	60.7	53.7	77.0	34.6	56.0	8.0	3.2	0.6
2008	19,255	62.3	53.1	80.5	34.5	56.8	8.4	3.3	0.7
2010	17,241	63.0	50.0	82.1	36.6	60.0	9.2	3,7	0,5
2013	13,187	60.2	49.0	80.9	36.5	57.4	9.7	4.3	0.5

Note: *m.* months; *YI* Youth Imprisonment; *susp. YI* Suspended Youth Imprisonment (probation); *y* year(s)
Source: Federal Statistical Office (Ed.): Strafverfolgungsstatistik 1975–2013; own calculations

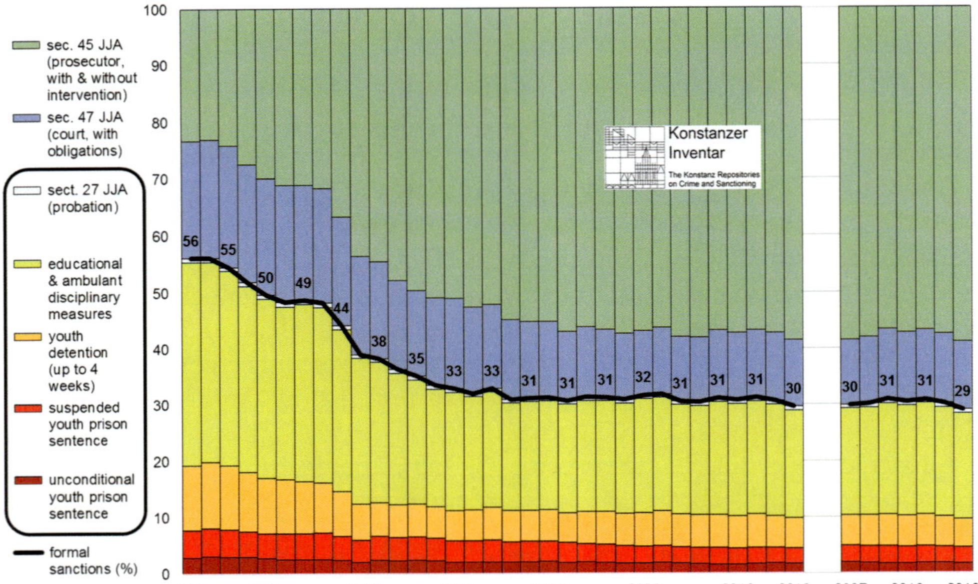

Educational & ambulant disciplinary measures	36	35	32	32	29	28	22	21	20	19	19	20	20	19	20	20	19	19	20	20	19
Youth detention	11	11	10	9	8	6	6	5	6	5	5	6	6	6	6	6	5	5	6	6	5
Youth custody (total)	8	8	7	7	7	7	7	6	6	6	6	5	5	5	5	5	4	5	5	5	5
Deprivation of liberty rate	14	14	13	12	10	8	8	8	8	8	7	8	8	8	8	8	7	7	7	7	7
	Former Federal Republic (West Germany)																	Germany (total)			

FIGURE 15.4. Sanctions of the Youth Court, 1981–2013. *Source*: Heinz (2015a).

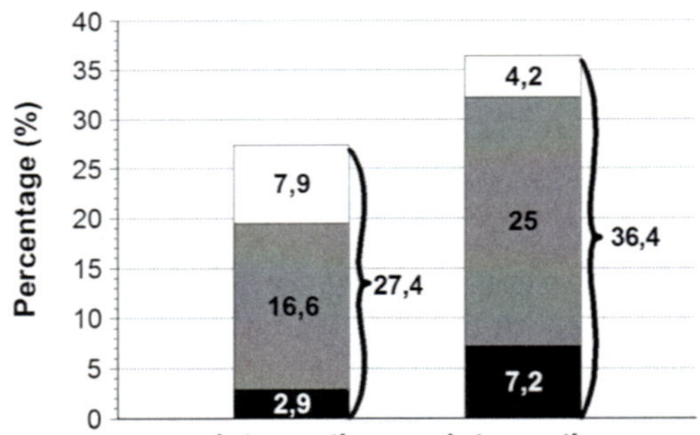

Decisions after reoffending:	1st sanction informal	1st sanction formal
informal only (diversion)	7,9%	4,2%
reconviction without imprisonment	16,6%	25,0%
imprisonment	2,9%	7,2%
total reconviction rate	19,5%	32,2%
total	27,4%	36,4%

FIGURE 15.5. Rates of formal and informal sanctions for reoffending after a first sanction for larceny and a risk period of 3 years (juveniles, 1961 cohort). *Source*: Heinz and Storz (1994).

Recidivism rates after informal sanctions are lower than after formal court sentences (see Heinz 2014 and Fig. 15.5 below) and recidivism rates after being under the supervision of the probation service and after release from youth prisons have declined from 54% to 49% and from 75% to 66% for those released in 2004 compared to 1994 (after a risk period of 3 years, see Jehle et al. 2010: 29; the latest recidivism statistics for those released 2007 indicated stable recidivism rates, see Jehle et al. 2013).

CUSTODIAL RULES FOR JUVENILES (DETENTION, PRISON, MIXING JUVENILES WITH ADULTS)

Youth imprisonment covers the age groups of 14–17-year-old juveniles, 18–20-year-old young adults and adults aged 21–24 who were sentenced by juvenile courts as juveniles or young adults. The German juvenile justice legislator does not follow a clear separation of juveniles and (young) adults as required by the CRC and other international standards. The reason for this is that German juvenile courts deal with 14- to 20-year-old offenders. If they impose a youth prison sentence, it is felt that it would be better to keep the young adult inmates within the juvenile prisons in order to prevent negative effects of prisons for adults. The internal structure of youth prisons in Germany, however, provide for separate living groups in different buildings. Often, special living groups for inmates under 18 are organized.

As mentioned before, the duration of sentences to youth imprisonment ranges from 6 months to 5 years. In serious felony cases or in cases involving young adult offenders, the maximum limit is 10 years. The average sentence to be served is between 1 and 2 years; therefore, the average stay in a youth prison is slightly more than 1 year.

The legal situation for young prisoners changed at the beginning of 2008. Before 2008 only a few general legal provisions existed in the JJA and in the Prison Act for adult prisoners. There had not been a differentiated legal framework covering the legal rights and duties of young prisoners. The Federal Constitutional Court (*Bundesverfassungsgericht*) outlawed this missing primary legislation as being unconstitutional, as in Germany any restriction of fundamental human rights has to be based on regulations in law. Administrative rules are deemed an insufficient basis. The Federal Constitutional Court obliged the legislators of the Federal States to pass primary legislation before the end of 2007. In September 2006, a general reform of the legislative competences came into force, transferring the competences for prison legislation to the Federal States ("*Länder*"). The new State Laws in the Federal States vary to some extent and express different political orientations on what is to be seen as the primary goal and the basic principles of youth imprisonment, and what are viewed as being the most promising concepts of rehabilitation. Nevertheless, there is a strong consensus that the organization of youth prisons, even more than in adult prisons, must be oriented towards rehabilitation and education. Furthermore, the unanimous opinion is that youth prisoners shall be accommodated in small living groups and individual cells during the night. All youth prisons should also provide a variety of school and vocational training programs, special (social) therapeutic units, and a system of progressive preparation for release (including leaves of absence, early release schemes and continuous care and aftercare). Although the competence of youth prison legislation has been transferred to the Federal States, legislation concerning prisoners' complaints rights and procedures are still Federal Law. The reform law of 13 December 2008 brought major improvements, guaranteeing juvenile and young adult inmates an oral hearing as well as regular legal advice when complaining to the court.

The actual situation in German youth prisons can be described as follows: In 2014, there were approximately 5000 young people aged between 14 and 25 in youth custody (31 March 2014: 4910), 181 (or 3.7%) of them female. Further 1908 (of them 51 females) had been sentenced according to the JJA, but were transferred to adult prisons because of reaching the age of 25 or due to better treatment offers in adult prisons after reaching the age of 18 (see § 89b JJA; they are counted as "youth prisoners" in the following Fig. 15.6).

Youth imprisonment rates differ considerably across the Federal States. They are higher in the East, partly because there was more violent crime in the eastern regions. The case of Schleswig-Holstein is interesting in this respect: the imprisonment rate there (2015: 36 per 100,000 of the 14–25 age group) has been reduced to a level less than half of that of many other states; in neighboring Mecklenburg-Western Pomerania, for example, it was 120 per 100,000 (see Fig. 15.6 below). This reflects an explicit criminal policy of opting for different types of sentences and alternatives to custody.

In the last 10 years, a reduction in the rates of youth imprisonment has been observable in almost all Federal States (see Fig. 15.6). With the exception of Berlin an even stronger decrease can be seen for the rates of juveniles and young adults in pretrial detention. The overall pretrial detention rate for 14- to 20-years-old alleged young offenders fell from 47 per 100,000 of the age group in 2000 to 2013 in 2014 (= −51.6%). The youth imprisonment rate altogether decreased by 21% in the last 5 years since 2010, which is to a large extent the result of a strong decline of youth offending rates, in particular violent youth crime.

Strictly speaking, youth custody in Germany does not necessarily imply prison for *juveniles*: very often, it is prison for young adults aged over 18. This reflects the fact that the system of criminal law for juveniles includes young adults aged 18–20 into the jurisdiction of juvenile courts. As a result, youth custody facilities house many young adults aged up to 24, who are serving custodial sentences. Only 9.4% of the total population of 5518 youth prisoners (31 March 2013) were "real juveniles" aged 14 to 18. 90.6% of "youth" prisoners in Germany in 2013 were young adults between 18 and 24 years of age (46.2% aged 18–20, 44.4% 21–24, see also Dünkel 2011a: 600; Ostendorf 2016: 21 f.).

Most young detainees are serving sentences for offences involving violence: in 2013, the figures were 23.6% for bodily harm/assault; 32.4% for robbery; 3.8%

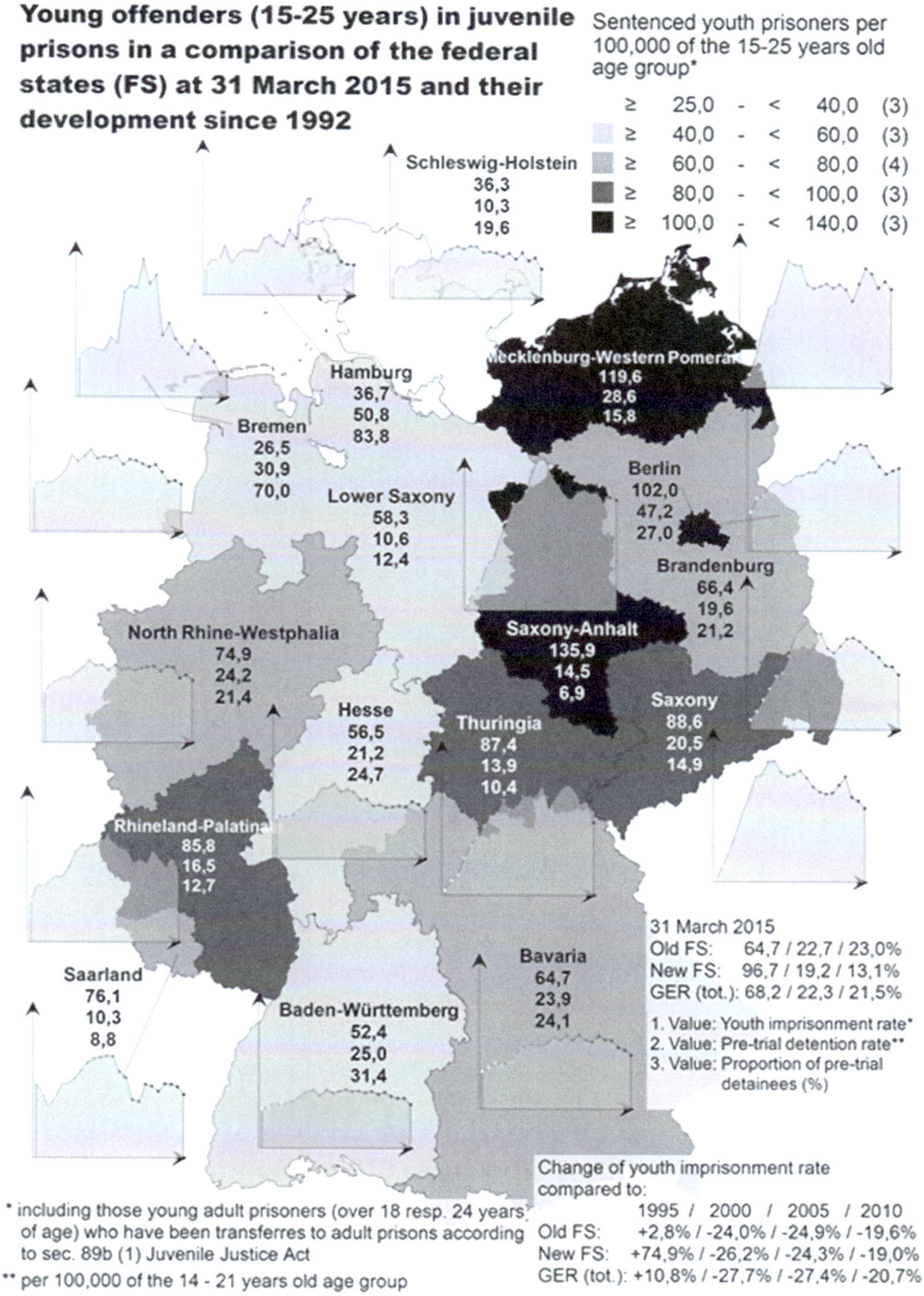

FIGURE 15.6. Young offenders in German juvenile prisons. *Source*: Federal Statistical Office (Ed.): Strafvollzugsstatistik 1992–2015 (own calculations).

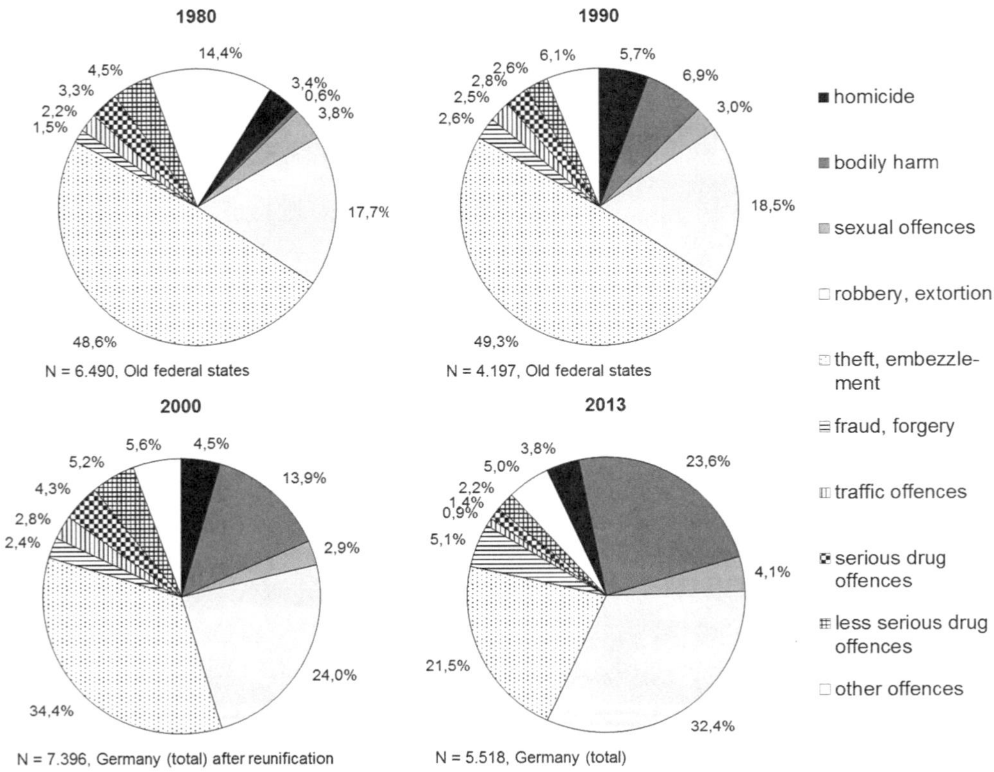

FIGURE 15.7. Youth prison population in Germany, 1980–2013, according to the type of offence. *Source*: Federal Statistical Office (Ed.): Strafvollzugsstatistik 1980–2013 (own calculations).

for homicide; and 4.1% for sexual offences. Drug-related offences including drug trafficking accounted for 3.6%. These figures have changed considerably over the last 25 years (less simple property and more violent offenders, see Fig. 15.7).

ALTERNATIVE SANCTIONS TO JUVENILES: EDUCATIONAL MEASURES, RESTORATIVE JUSTICE, AND RESTITUION

The German juvenile justice system provides for a large variety of community sanctions including restorative justice measures such as reparation, excuse to the victim, community service, and victim-offender mediation. The following graph demonstrates the disposals of the juvenile court. Home confinement or in the European terminology house arrest is not used in Germany, and in particular electronic monitoring is not an issue. Germany does not rely on technical forms of social control, but rather on social pedagogic ways of dealing with juvenile delinquency.

In cases of criminal offences as defined by the general Criminal Law, the interventions of the JJA are characterized by the principle of "subsidiarity" or "minimum intervention" (see the diagram at the end of the article). This means that penal action should only be taken if absolutely necessary. Furthermore, sanctions must be limited by the principle of proportionality. The legislative reform of the JJA in 1990, passed in the same year as that of the JWA, underlines the principle of Juvenile Court sanctions as a last resort ("ultima ratio"). Therefore, priority is given to diversion, and where the Juvenile Courts do impose sanctions, primacy is given to educational or disciplinary measures instead of youth imprisonment.

The most important response to petty offending is the dismissal of the case without any sanction being issued. In this context, one should emphasize that police diversion, like the British form of cautioning or warnings, is not allowed in Germany. The underlying reason for this is of a historical nature, lying more specifically in the possible abuse of police power as it occurred under the Nazi regime. Therefore, all forms of diversion are provided for only at the level of the Juvenile Court prosecutor or the Juvenile Court judge. The police are strictly bound by the principle of legality. All criminal offences have to be referred to the public prosecutor.

The 1990 reform of the Juvenile Justice Act in Germany extended the legal possibilities for diversion considerably. The legislature thus reacted to the reforms that had been developed in practice since the end of the 1970s. The law now emphasizes the discharge of juvenile and young adult offenders on grounds of the petty nature of the crime committed, or because of other social and/or educational interventions that have taken place (see § 45 (1) and (2) JJA). Efforts to make reparation to the victim or to participate in victim-offender reconciliation (mediation) are explicitly put on a par with such educational measures. There is no restriction concerning the nature of offences that are eligible; felony offences ("*Verbrechen*") can also be "diverted" under certain circumstances (e.g., a robbery) if the offender has repaired the damage or made another form of apology (restitution/reparation) to the victim.

We can differentiate four levels of diversion. Diversion without any sanction ("non-intervention") is given priority in cases of petty offences. Diversion with measures taken by other agencies (parents, the school) or in combination with mediation is the second level of diversion ("diversion with education"). The third level is "diversion with intervention." In these cases, the prosecutor proposes that the Juvenile Court judge impose a minor sanction, such as a warning, community service (usually between 10 and 40 h), mediation ("Täter-Opfer-Ausgleich"), participation in a training course for traffic offenders ("Verkehrsunterricht") or certain obligations like reparation/restitution, an apology to the victim, community service or a fine (§ 45 (3) JJA). Once the young offender has fulfilled these obligations, the Juvenile Court prosecutor will dismiss the case in co-operation with the judge. The fourth level is the introduction of levels one to three in the Juvenile Court proceedings after a charge has been filed. In practice, the Juvenile Court judge will fairly often face the situation that the young offender has, in the meantime (after the prosecutor has filed the charge), undergone some form of educational measure like mediation, which would deem a "formal" court sanction unnecessary. Section 47 of the JJA enables the judge to dismiss the case in these instances.

Also formal sanctions of the Juvenile Court are structured according to the principle of minimum intervention ("*Subsidiaritätsgrundsatz*"; see the diagram at the end of the text). Juvenile imprisonment has been restricted to being a sanction of last resort, if educational or disciplinary measures appear to be inappropriate (see §§ 5 and 17 (2) JJA). The reform of the Juvenile Justice Act of 1990 extended the catalogue of juvenile sanctions by introducing new community sanctions like community service, the special care order ("Betreuungsweisung"), the so-called social training course (see in detail Dünkel/Geng/Kirstein 1998) and mediation (see Dünkel 1996, 1999; Dünkel and Păroşanu 2015). The educational measures of the Juvenile Court, furthermore, comprise different forms of directives concerning the everyday life of juvenile offenders in order to educate and to prevent dangerous situations. Thus, the judge can forbid contact with certain persons and prohibit going to certain places ("whereabouts," see § 10 JJA). Disciplinary measures include the formal warning, community service, a fine, and detention for 1 or 2 weekends or for up to 4 weeks in a special juvenile detention center ("*Jugendarrest*").

Youth imprisonment is executed in separate juvenile prisons. Youth prison sentences are only a sanction of last resort ("ultima ratio," see §§ 5 (2), 17 (2) JJA), in line with the view espoused by international rules like the so-called Beijing-Rules of the United Nations of 1985. The minimum length of youth imprisonment is 6 months for 14–17-year-old juveniles, and the maximum limit is set at 5 years. In cases of very serious offences for which adults could be punished with more than 10 years of imprisonment, the maximum length of youth imprisonment is 10 years. In the case of 18–20-year-old young adults sentenced according to the JJA (see Section "Custodial Rules for Juveniles (Detention, Prison, Mixing Juveniles with Adults)" above) the maximum penalty is 10 years, too (see §§ 18, 109 JJA; in case of particularly serious murder 15 years). The preconditions for youth imprisonment are either the "dangerous tendencies" of the offender that are likely to exclude community sanctions as inappropriate, or the "gravity of guilt" concerning particular, serious crimes (such as murder, aggravated robbery etc.; see § 17 (2) JJA).

Youth imprisonment sentences of up to 2 years can be suspended (a similar sanction as probation) in cases of a favorable prognosis; in all cases, the probation service gets involved. The period of probationary supervision is 1 to 2 years, and the period of probation lasts for a total of 2–3 years.

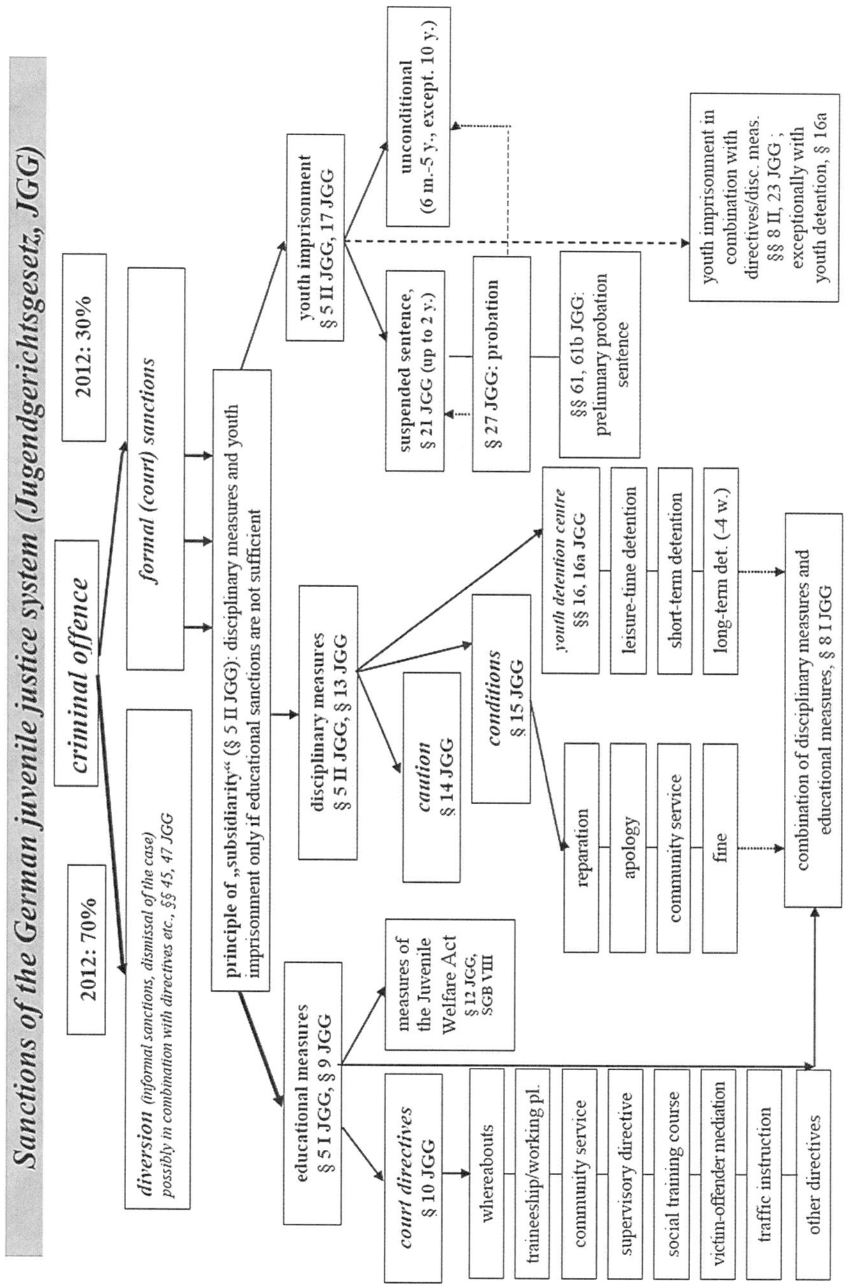
Sanctions of the German juvenile justice system (Jugendgerichtsgesetz, JGG)
2012: 70%
criminal offence
2012: 30%
diversion (informal sanctions, dismissal of the case) possibly in combination with directives etc., §§ 45, 47 JGG
formal (court) sanctions
principle of „subsidiarity" (§ 5 II JGG): disciplinary measures and youth imprisonment only if educational sanctions are not sufficient
educational measures § 5 I JGG, § 9 JGG
disciplinary measures § 5 II JGG, § 13 JGG
youth imprisonment § 5 II JGG, 17 JGG
court directives § 10 JGG
measures of the Juvenile Welfare Act § 12 JGG, SGB VIII
caution § 14 JGG
conditions § 15 JGG
youth detention centre §§ 16, 16a JGG
suspended sentence, § 21 JGG (up to 2 y.)
unconditional (6 m.-5 y., except. 10 y.)
§ 27 JGG: probation
§§ 61, 61b JGG: preliminary probation sentence
youth imprisonment in combination with directives/disc. meas. §§ 8 II, 23 JGG; exceptionally with youth detention, § 16a
whereabouts
traineeship/working pl.
community service
supervisory directive
social training course
victim-offender mediation
traffic instruction
other directives
reparation
apology
community service
fine
leisure-time detention
short-term detention
long-term det. (-4 w.)
combination of disciplinary measures and educational measures, § 8 I JGG

DIFFERENCES IN TREATMENT OF BOYS AND GIRLS

Formally, there are no differences in the treatment of boys and girls by the juvenile justice system. Female juvenile offenders constitute only a small part of the clientele of juvenile courts, as they primarily commit less serious offences which—to a large extent—are dismissed by the juvenile prosecutors. Unfortunately, there are no statistics available on the diversion practice. On the youth court level, we dispose of statistical data, which, however, are of only limited value. In general, we may say that young female offenders (aged 14–20) in only 1.8% of the cases received a youth prison sentence, the proportion of their male counterparts being 7%, i.e., more than three times higher. The proportion of those sentenced to a short-term detention (up to 4 weeks) was 18.1%, for males and 15% for females. All other young female and male offenders were sentenced with community sanctions, amongst them 11% (males) and 4.9% (females to a suspended youth prison sentence (i.e., probation). The at first glance "milder" sanctioning practice for young female offenders may be interpreted in the light of less severe crimes committed by them. Looking only on certain categories of crimes, the differences are less visible or even disappear. The proportion of young offenders sent to youth prisons or youth detention is almost the same in the case of robbery and extortion (see Fig. 15.8). In the case of burglary, the proportion of those sentenced to youth imprisonment in 2014 was 4.3% for females and 14.3% for males, for serious bodily injury 2.7% against 9.7% for males. If females receive a custodial sentence, it will more likely be only a short-term detention of up to 4 weeks than youth imprisonment of at least 6 months.

The interpretation of the data is difficult as the less severe sentencing practice towards female young offenders may be caused by less serious forms of crimes even within the categories of burglary, etc. (see Heinz 2015b: 284). There is the observation that females when committing crimes in groups, they are not the leading persons, but rather supporting their male co-offenders which may result in "milder" sentences.

One of the results of different sentencing practices is that female offenders make only for a small proportion of young offenders in youth prisons. On 31 March 2014, only 181 of the 4910 sentenced offenders in youth prisons were females (3.7%, see Federal Office of Statistics, Ed., Strafvollzugsstatistik 2014: 10). There are problems to accommodate them close to their families or places of future residence and to provide the necessary treatment, schooling and vocational training facilities, as in most Federal States only a few females are in custody. Some youth prison units started to have mixed units with males and females in order to prevent the isolation of young females and to give them the chance to participate in rehabilitation programs (see in detail Haverkamp 2015a, b).

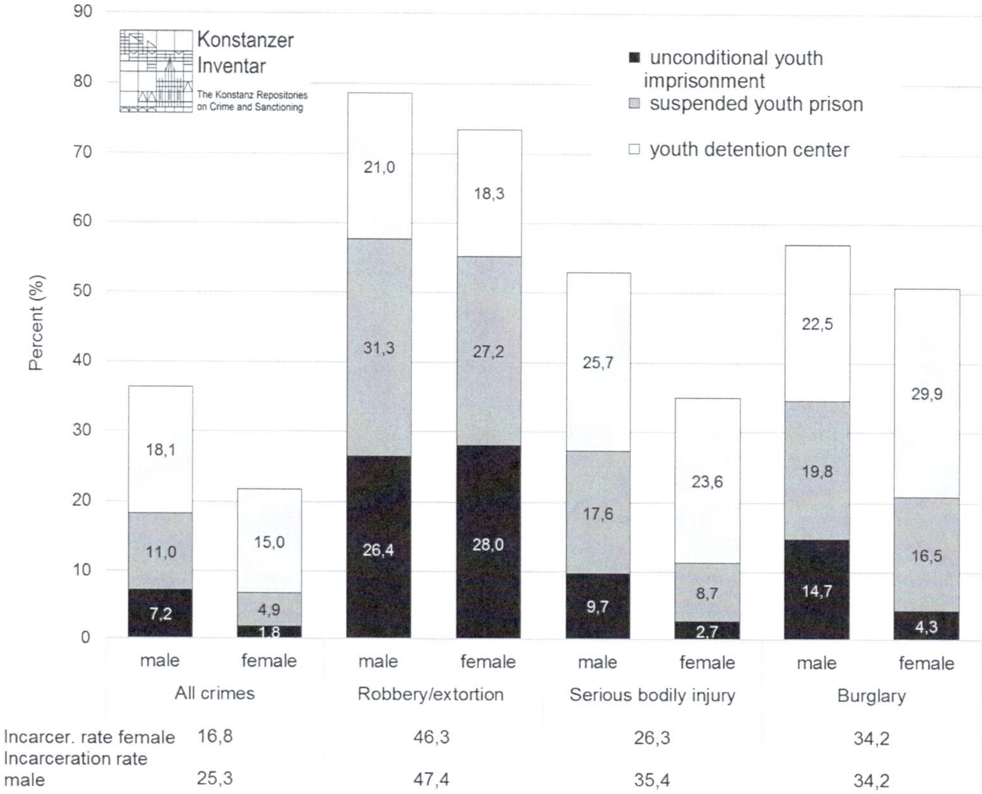

FIGURE 15.8. Sentencing young female and male offenders by youth courts in 2014. *Source*: Federal Office of Statistics (Ed.). Strafverfolgung 2014, author's calculations.

SUMMARY AND OUTLOOK

Juvenile delinquency in Germany is declining in the past 10 years and therefore not a major social problem. There has been empirical research on the increase and causes of juvenile crime in the 1990s, but the recent development is not yet clearly understood. One explanation could be that crime prevention projects have been effective, another, that the economic situation in particular for young people has improved and is rather favorable. The German economy is booming and youth unemployment is not a serious problem. In addition, young people have optimistic views on their future and the social climate in general is positive.

The youth justice system in Germany is strictly based on the idea of education and positive special prevention. The organization of specialized youth prosecution and courts and the sanctions system can be characterized as a mixed justice and welfare model integrating minimum intervention and restorative justice measures. The sentencing practice is moderate and stable over the last decades, more than 70% of all juvenile and young adult offences are diverted, youth imprisonment is the very "last resort."

REFERENCES

Baier, D., & Prätor, S. (2016). Adolescents as victims of violence. In D. Baier & C. Pfeiffer (Eds.), *Representative studies on victimization. Research findings from Germany* (pp. 65–107). Baden-Baden: Nomos.

Baier, D., Pfeiffer, C., Simonson, J., & Rabold, S. (2009). *Jugendliche in Deutschland als Täter und Opfer von Gewalt* (KFN Report No. 107). Hannover: Kriminologisches Forschungsinstitut Niedersachsen.

Beelmann, A., & Raabe, T. (2007). *Dissoziales Verhalten von Kindern und Jugendlichen*. Göttingen: Hogrefe Verlag.

Boers, K. (2008). Kontinuität und Abbruch persistenter Delinquenzverläufe. In: Deutsche Vereinigung für Jugendgerichte und Jugendgerichtshilfen e.V. (DVJJ) (Ed.), *Fördern—Fordern—Fallenlassen. Aktuelle Entwicklungen im Umgang mit Jugenddelinquenz* (pp. 340–376). Mönchengladbach: Forum Verlag Godesberg.

Centre for the Prevention of Youth Crime. (Ed.). (2004). *Prevention of youth crime in Germany. Educational strategies. Trends, experiences, and approaches*. München: Deutsches Jugendinstitut.

Deutsches Jugendinstitut. (Ed.). (2015). *Kriminalitätsprävention im Kindes- und Jugendalter. Perspektiven zentraler Handlungsfelder*. München: Deutsches Jugendinstitut.

Drenkhahn, K., Morgenstern, C., & van Zyl Smit, D. (2012). What is in a name? Preventive Detention in Germany in the Shadow of European Human Rights Law. *Criminal Law Review, 3*, 167–187.

Dünkel, F. (1996). Täter-Opfer-Ausgleich. *German experiences with mediation in a European perspective. European Journal on Criminal Policy and Research, 4*, 44–66.

Dünkel, F. (1999). La justice réparatrice en Allemagne. *Criminologie, 32*, 107–132.

Dünkel, F. (2006). Juvenile justice in Germany: Between welfare and justice. In J. Junger-Tas & S. H. Decker (Eds.), *International handbook of juvenile justice* (pp. 225–262). Berlin, New York: Springer.

Dünkel, F. (2011a). Germany. In F. Dünkel, J. Grzywa, P. Horsfield, & I. Pruin (Eds.), *Juvenile justice systems in Europe. Current situation and reform developments* (2nd ed., pp. 547–622). Mönchengladbach: Forum Verlag Godesberg.

Dünkel, F. (2011b). Die Europäischen Grundsätze für die von Sanktionen oder Maßnahmen betroffenen jugendlichen Straftäter und Straftäterinnen ("European Rules for Juvenile Offenders Subject to Sanctions or Measures", ERJOSSM). *Zeitschrift für Jugendkriminalrecht und Jugendhilfe, 22*, 140–154.

Dünkel, F. (2012). Neue Punitivität im Jugendstrafrecht? Anmerkungen aus europäisch vergleichender Perspektive. In E. Hilgendorf & R. Rengier (Eds.), *Festschrift für Wolfgang Heinz* (pp. 381–397). Baden-Baden: Nomos Verlag.

Dünkel, F. (2013). Youth justice policy in Europe—Between minimum intervention, welfare and new punitiveness. In T. Daems, D. van Zyl Smit, & S. Snacken (Eds.), *European penology?* (pp. 145–170). Oxford, Portland/Oregon: Hart Publishing.

Dünkel, F. (2015). Juvenile justice and crime policy in Europe. In F. E. Zimring, M. Langer, & D. S. Tanenhaus (Eds.), *Juvenile justice in Global Perspective* (pp. 9–62). New York, London: New York University Press.

Dünkel, F., & Păroşanu, A. (2015). Germany. In F. Dünkel, J. Grzywa-Holten, & P. Horsfield (Eds.), *Restorative justice and mediation in penal matters—A stocktaking of legal issues, implementation strategies and outcomes in 36 European countries* (pp. 293–329). Mönchengladbach: Forum Verlag Godesberg.

Dünkel, F., Gebauer, D., & Geng, B. (2008). *Jugendgewalt und Möglichkeiten der Prävention*. Mönchengladbach: Forum Verlag Godesberg.

Dünkel, F., Grzywa, J., Horsfield, P., & Pruin, I. (Eds.). (2011). *Juvenile justice systems in Europe. Current situation and reform developments* (2nd ed.). Mönchengladbach: Forum Verlag Godesberg.

Enzmann, D. (2010). Germany. In J. Junger-Tas et al. (Eds.), *Juvenile delinquency in Europe and beyond* (pp. 47–64). Dordrecht: Springer.
Feuerhelm, W., & Kügler, N. (2003). *Das "Haus des Jugendrechts" in Stuttgart Bad Cannstatt. Ergebnisse einer Evaluation*. Mainz: Institut für Sozialpädagogische Forschung Mainz e.V.
Haverkamp, R. (2015a). Kriminalität junger Frauen und weiblicher Jugendvollzug. *Neue Kriminalpolitik, 27*, 301–318.
Haverkamp, R. (2015b). Mädchen und junge Frauen im Jugendstrafvollzug. In M. Schweder (Ed.), *Handbuch Jugendstrafvollzug* (pp. 392–407). Weinheim/Basel: Juventa.
Heinz, W. (2009). Zunehmende Punitivität in der Praxis des Jugendkriminalrechts? Analysen aufgrund von Daten der Strafrechtspflegestatistiken. In Bundesministerium der Justiz (Ed.), *Das Jugendkriminalrecht vor neuen Herausforderungen? Jenaer Symposium* (pp. 29–80). Mönchengladbach: Forum Verlag Godesberg.
Heinz, W. (2014). *Das strafrechtliche Sanktionensystem und die Sanktionierungspraxis in Deutschland 1882–2012*. Version 1/2014. Retrieved from www.uni-konstanz.de/rtf/kis/Sanktionierungspraxis-in-Deutschland-Stand-2012.pdf
Heinz, W. (2015a). *Jugendkriminalität—Zahlen und Fakten*. Bonn: Bundeszentrale für politische Bildung.
Heinz, W. (2015b). Frauenkriminalität. Immer mehr, immer häufiger, immer brutaler? *Kriminalistik, 70*, 275–285.
Heinz, W., & Storz, R. (Eds.). (1994). *Diversion im Jugendstrafverfahren der Bundesrepublik Deutschland* (3rd ed.). Bonn: Forum Verlag Godesberg.
Jehle, J.-M., et al. (2010). *Legalbewährung nach strafrechtlichen Sanktionen. Eine bundesweite Rückfalluntersuchung 2004 bis 2007*. Berlin: Bundesministerium der Justiz.
Jehle, J.-M., et al. (2013). *Legalbewährung nach strafrechtlichen Sanktionen. Eine bundesweite Rückfalluntersuchung 2007 bis 2010 und 2004 bis 2010*. Berlin: Bundesministerium der Justiz.
Junger-Tas, J., Marshall, I. H., Enzmann, D., Killias, M., Steketee, M., & Gruszczynska, B. (Eds.). (2010). Juvenile delinquency in Europe and beyond. Dordrecht: Springer.
Lösel, F., & Bliesener, T. (2003). *Aggression und Delinquenz unter Jugendlichen*. München, Neuwied: Luchterhand Verlag.
Oberwittler, D. (2012). Kriminalität und Delinquenz als soziales Problem. In G. Albrecht & A. Groenemeyer (Eds.), *Handbuch soziale Probleme* (Vol. 1, 2nd ed., pp. 772–860). Wiesbaden: Springer VS.
Ostendorf, H. (Ed.). (2016). *Jugendstrafvollzugsrecht* (3rd ed.). Baden-Baden: Nomos.
Pruin, I., & Dünkel, F. (2015). *Better in Europe? European responses to young adult offending*. London: Barry Cadbury Trust.
Schumann, K. F. (Ed.). (2003a). *Delinquenz im Lebensverlauf. Bremer Längsschnittstudie zum Übergang von der Schule in den Beruf bei ehemaligen Hauptschülern* (Vols. 1 and 2). München: Juventa.
Schumann, K. F. (2003b). Delinquenz im Lebenslauf–Ergebnisbilanz und Perspektiven. In K. F. Schumann (Ed.), *Delinquenz im Lebensverlauf. Bremer Längsschnittstudie zum Übergang von der Schule in den Beruf bei ehemaligen Hauptschülern* (Vols. 1 and 2, pp. 209–222). München: Juventa.
Spieß, G. (2012). *Jugendkriminalität in Deutschland zwischen Fakten und Dramatisierung. Kriminalstatistische und kriminologische Befunde*. Konstanzer Inventar zur Kriminalitätsentwicklung (KIK). Retrieved from www.uni-konstanz.de/rtf/gs/G.Spiess-Jugendkriminalitaet.htm
Spieß, G. (2015). Das Jugendstrafrecht und die ambulanten Maßnahmen: Vielfalt der Möglichkeiten—Einfalt der Praxis? In: DVJJ (Ed.), *Jugend ohne Rettungsschirm. Herausforderungen annehmen!* (pp. 421–445). Mönchengladbach: Forum Verlag Godesberg.
Wikström, P.-O. H. (2007). The social ecology of crime. The role of the environment in crime causation. In H. J. Schneider (Ed.), *Internationales Handbuch der Kriminologie, Band 1: Grundlagen der Kriminologie* (pp. 333–357). Berlin: de Gruyter.
Zimring, F. E., Langer, M., & Tanenhaus, D. S. (Eds.). (2015). *Juvenile justice in Global Perspective*. New York, London: New York University Press.

Frieder Dünkel is professor emeritus of criminology at the University of Greifswald in Northern Germany. He graduated at the University of Freiburg and worked the Max-Planck-Institute of Foreign and International Penal Law until 1992. Since then he was Head of the Department of Criminology and researched and published widely in the area of international comparative juvenile justice, prisons, and crime policy. Address: University of Greifswald, Domstr. 20, 17489 Greifswald/ Germany.

Wolfgang Heinz is professor emeritus of criminology and penal law at the University of Konstanz in the South of Germany. He graduated at the University of Freiburg and later was Professor at the Universities of Augsburg, Konstanz, Bielefeld, and then since 1981 again in Konstanz. He has widely researched and published on juvenile justice and delinquency as well as on crime and sentencing statistics, furthermore on penal law matters. Address: Holdersteig 13, 78465 Konstanz/ Germany.

16

Ireland

Mairead Seymour

THE LEGAL STATUS OF JUVENILES

Welfare is the primary philosophy that underpins juvenile justice in the Republic of Ireland (Ireland) although the system reflects an international trend in embracing a complex mix of influences ranging from children's rights to justice-based approaches, restorative justice to actuarial justice and from rehabilitation and reintegration to punishment. The Children Act 2001 (hereon in 'the 2001 Act') is the main legislation that underpins the system and provides a contemporary framework for the delivery of responses to children in conflict with the law. The ethos of the legislation is strongly grounded in promoting the diversion of children from the justice system at the earliest possible stage, imposing penalties that have the least restrictive impact on children's legitimate activities and limiting the use of detention as a measure of last resort. The 2001 Act incorporates a number of principles relating to criminal jurisdiction over children across the system. Under the first principle, children charged with offences are entitled to the same rights and freedom before the law as adults, specifically a right to be heard and a right to participate in any court proceedings that affect them. Furthermore, criminal proceedings should not be used solely to provide any assistance or service needed to care for or protect a child. This represents an important departure from previous practice under the 1908 Children Act, where children could be detained for primarily welfare reasons. The second principle states that any penalty imposed on a child for an offence should be the least restrictive and a period of detention should be imposed only as a measure of last resort. Under the third principle, the court may take mitigating factors such as the child's age and level of maturity into consideration when determining the nature of any penalty

M. Seymour (✉)
School of Languages, Law and Social Sciences, Dublin Institute of Technology, Dublin, Ireland
e-mail: mairead.seymour@dit.ie

S.H. Decker, N. Marteache (eds.), *International Handbook of Juvenile Justice*,
DOI 10.1007/978-3-319-45090-2_16

imposed, unless the penalty is fixed by law while the fourth principle posits that the penalty imposed on a child for an offence should be no greater (and may be less) than that which an adult would receive for the same offence. Finally, the fifth principle stipulates that measures for dealing with children's offending should have due regard to the interests of victims.

In addition to the principles, a number of provisions in the legislation also seek to protect children from the negative effects of contact with the juvenile justice system. Reporting, publishing or broadcasting any identifying information about children's involvement in criminal proceedings is forbidden with some exceptions such as if children are unlawfully at large or it is considered in the public interest to do so. Furthermore, children who commit offences under the age of 18 years are eligible to have their criminal record expunged. Conditions include that a 3-year period has lapsed since the finding of guilt and that no other offences have arisen within the 3-year period. Excluded offences are those that must be tried before the Central Criminal Court such as murder, manslaughter, rape and serious sexual assault. The process is automatic and provides an important mechanism in providing children with a clean record as they transition to adulthood and seek out employment, training and other vocational opportunities.

The background to the juvenile justice system in Ireland is characterised by political neglect of juvenile justice matters for most of the twentieth century until the current legislation (2001 Act) replaced the outdated 1908 Children Act (see Seymour 2006). The pace of reform was slow in the aftermath of the 2001 Act in large part because no specific body existed to co-ordinate the implementation of the legislation until the establishment of the Irish Youth Justice Service (IYJS) in 2006. Governance of the juvenile justice system is executed through the Irish Youth Justice Service (IYJS) which is an executive agency located within the Department of Children and Youth Affairs (DCYA) although responsibility for juvenile justice matters is shared with the Department of Justice and Equality (DJE).[1] Previously, responsibility for juvenile justice was divided across three government departments of education, health and justice. The 2001 Act as amended under the Criminal Justice Act 2006 was finally enacted in March 2007. In the years that followed, the economic fortunes of the Irish state reversed dramatically from the prosperous early years of the twenty-first century to a severely depressed economy on the verge of economic collapse. The result was a substantial curtailment on funding to drive forward the changes proposed under the 2001 Act. Most noteworthy was the postponement of plans to construct a modern national detention facility to end the practice of detaining children within the adult prison system. As discussed later in this chapter, it was not until the end of 2013 that construction of this facility commenced as Ireland gradually shifted towards economic recovery.

[1]The DCYA has responsibility for the childcare elements of the Children Act 2001 and for the new National Children Detention Centre. The DJE has responsibility for crime prevention, criminal proceedings and diversionary interventions as well as engagement with key criminal justice agencies such as the police (An Garda Síochána), the Probation Service and the Prison Service.

AGE OF CRIMINAL RESPONSIBILITY

The juvenile justice system incorporates children from 10 to 17 years.[2] The original provisions under the 2001 Act set the age of criminal responsibility at 12 years for all offences and included a rebuttable presumption of *doli incapax* for children up to 14 years. An amendment to the Act contained in the Criminal Justice Act 2006 lowered the age of criminal responsibility to 10 years for children charged with offences of murder, manslaughter, rape and serious sexual assault. The justification provided by the Minister for Justice of the time was that it would not be satisfactory for the victims of serious crimes to have children excluded from the remit of the criminal justice system (Dáil Eireann 2006). The presumption of *doli incapax* was also abolished and replaced with measures which provide some acknowledgement of the reduced competence and culpability of children aged 14 years and under, relative to their older peers and adult contemporaries. For example, the consent of the Director of Public Prosecution (DPP) is required to prosecute children under 14 years. Furthermore, the court has the power to dismiss a case of its own accord, or on the application of any person, if it concludes that the child under 14 years of age did not have a full understanding of what was involved in the commission of the offence. These legislative protections are important safeguards but their implementation is based on the discretion of the prosecutor's office or the courts. The age of criminal responsibility is an important barometer of the extent to which children's age and level of maturity are taken into consideration in responding to their offending behaviour (Seymour 2013). Ireland is similar to its nearest neighbours in Northern Ireland (10 years), Scotland (12 years) and England and Wales (10 years) but digresses from the European norm where the age of criminal responsibility is typically 14 years and over.

IRELAND AND THE UN COMMITTEE ON THE RIGHTS OF THE CHILD

Ireland ratified the UN Convention on the Rights of the Child in 1992. While the convention has not been adopted into domestic law, it has been influential in supporting the development of an apparatus to promote recognition of children's rights. Notable developments include the appointment of the first Ombudsman for Children in 2004 and the establishment of the National Children's Office in 2001 which later evolved into the Office of the Minister for Children and Youth Affairs and subsequently, in 2011, the Department of Children and Youth Affairs headed by a Minister with specific responsibility for coordinating policy on children's issues. More recently in 2015, the 31st Amendment of the Constitution

[2]The 2001 Act refers to persons under 18 years as children and for this reason the terminology of child or children is adopted in this chapter.

(Children) Act 2012 was signed into law further strengthening children's rights. The language and ethos of the Convention is explicitly reflected in the 2001 Act. Key principles recognise the special position and vulnerability of children in conflict with the law arising from their age, level of maturity and circumstances. Provision exists to protect their privacy during criminal proceedings, to inform them about the outcome of proceedings in an accessible manner and to provide alternative dispositions to custodial detention. Despite these developments, the values underpinning the law in theory do not necessarily translate in practice and concern has been raised about the extent to which aspects of the implementation of the Children Act meet international children's rights standards (Kilkelly 2014). Ireland appeared before the UN Committee on the Rights of the Child for the third time in January 2016. In the report that followed, the Committee urged the government to fully align the juvenile justice system with the Convention and other international standards. It further recommended the reinstatement of 'provisions regarding the age of criminal responsibility as established in the Children Act 2001 at 14 years' (Committee on the Rights of the Child 2016:17). The Committee also raised concern about the detention of 17-year-old males under sentence in adult prison.

TRENDS IN JUVENILE CRIME IN IRELAND

The main source of published data on children's offending in Ireland is the 'Annual Reports of the Committee appointed to Monitor the Effectiveness of the Diversion Programme' (An Garda Síochána 2013). These reports detail the total number of referrals (offences) committed by children on an annual basis. These data point to an upward trend in the number of recorded crimes by children between 2003 and 2011 from 19,915 to 27,384 and a considerable decline thereafter to 24,069 and 20,536 in 2012 and 2013, respectively. Analysis of this downward crime trend since 2011 by the Garda Síochána Analysis Service (GSAS) points to a general decline in overall crime nationally and in a number of international jurisdictions. The GSAS also refers to increases in children's participation and/or progression in the primary and secondary educational systems as well as youth self-reported reductions in their use of alcohol, cigarettes and cannabis over the last decade. They also suggest that the increased emphasis on police-led youth crime prevention and diversion initiatives (see Garda Juvenile Diversion Programme) under the 2001 Act may have positively impacted on offending rates, but suggest that further interrogation and analysis of data is required before such conclusions are reached.

Differences in the way crimes are classified in the aforementioned annual reports on children's offending since 2010 means that direct comparisons between crime categories over time is restricted. The available data resonates with international trends demonstrating that the majority of criminal incidents perpetrated by children are not of a serious nature. For example, in 2013, the offence categories that accounted for almost two-thirds of children's offences were: theft and related offences (27%), public order and social code offences (26%), and damage to property and the environment (11%). The pattern of these collective categories is broadly consistent with preceding years. Differences emerge within categories with a decline in public order offences between 2010 and 2013 and a corresponding rise in the proportion of theft offences from 22% in 2010 to 27% in 2013. Notable also are the offences related to young people's behaviour and youthful status. In 2013, over one-fifth (21%) of offences in the category of public order and social code related to public drunkenness and purchasing or consuming alcohol under 18 years, respectively, and 80% of controlled drug offences involved possession of drugs for personal use (An Garda Síochána 2013). As expected, serious offences, particularly of a sexual or violent nature, account for very small proportions of children's crimes. Sexual offences rose slightly from 0.7% in 2010 but remain a small proportion at 1.2% in 2013. Over the 4-year period between 2010 and 2013, an average of four incidents per annum were recorded for homicide offences, incorporating murder, manslaughter, infanticide, and dangerous driving leading to death accounting for less than 0.01% of referrals (offences). The absence of comprehensive victimisation data and self-report data on offending behaviour is a challenge to presenting a more complete picture on the level of crime perpetrated by children in Ireland. This is especially relevant in the context of national statistics demonstrating the level of crime that goes unreported to the police. Results from the 'Crime and Victimisation Quarterly National Household Survey 2010' identify that 37% of thefts without violence were not reported in 2010 with the most common reasons being the perception that the theft was not sufficiently serious or no loss was involved (Central Statistics Office 2010).

CAUSES OF JUVENILE CRIME

It is well established that the causes of juvenile crime are complex and interrelated making explanations unsuited to simplistic analysis. The waters are further muddied in distinguishing between correlates or markers of juvenile crime and actual causation factors; the latter defined as factors that when altered culminate in changed behavioural outcomes. Large-scale systematic investigation into the correlates or causal factors relating to juvenile crime has not been undertaken in Ireland to date. The existing research consists of a number of relatively small-scale studies based on relatively modest sampling frameworks (Carroll and Meehan 2007; Hayes and O'Reilly 2007). Nevertheless, the profile of juvenile offenders presented in these studies broadly resonates with the evidence from international studies in identifying early onset of offending, childhood trauma, behavioural and learning difficulties, problematic family relationships, parenting dynamics, poor educational outcomes, substance misuse, mental health issues, and anti-social peers with involvement in juvenile crime.

Alcohol plays a dominant role in explanations of juvenile crime in Ireland especially when combined with other substances. A national survey of 721 offenders aged 20 years or less on statutory supervision in 2012 found that 87% were considered to have misused drugs (12%), alcohol (12%) or a combination of both (63%) and in over 80% of cases, substance misuse was linked to current offending (Horgan 2013). The level of reported substance misuse was similar for males and females and alcohol was the substance mostly commonly associated with current offending. The relationship between alcohol misuse and juvenile crime cannot be viewed in isolation from a normalised cultural acceptance of excessive alcohol consumption, 'binge-drinking', and public tolerance of drunkenness among the adult population in Ireland (Seymour and Mayock 2009).

The social context of young people's exposure to criminal influences within their respective communities is not inconsequential in explaining pathways to offending behaviour. Previous research reports on young people's access to drugs within impoverished communities, as well as the dangers involved when drug debts accumulate (Seymour and Butler 2008; Seymour 2013). Some are drawn further into criminality in an effort to clear drug-related debts and avoid the wrath of drug dealers. Others are lured by the prospect of financial gain and status in communities, where few legitimate opportunities exist. Vicious struggles for control of drugs markets in some of the main urban centres in Ireland has seen children and young people recruited into criminal gangs and exposed to increasing levels of violence over the last decade and beyond (Hourigan 2012).

Less well documented in the narrative of juvenile crime explanations is the broader systemic issue of inequality including limited access to adequate service provision. This is particularly relevant against the background that more than 11% of children aged 0–17 years live in consistent poverty in Ireland and single adult households with children are recorded with the highest rate of consistent poverty (22.1%) (CSO 2015). A study of the experiences and mental health needs of children and young people in the care and justice systems in Ireland reports an absence of child-centred care, limited focus on early intervention, resourcing problems, and deficiencies and inequities in terms of assessment and interventions (McElvaney et al. 2013). More broadly, a survey of 120 professionals working with young people in the juvenile justice system identified inadequate or unsuitable service provision in key areas including family support, education services, residential care placements, drug and alcohol treatment as well as mental health services (Seymour and Butler 2008). These findings demonstrate the gap that exists between the factors associated with juvenile offending and the absence of holistic approaches to address them.

POLICING AND JUVENILES

The police (An Garda Síochána) play a central role in the juvenile justice system through the delivery of a statutory cautioning programme known as the Garda Juvenile Diversion Programme (GJDP). Although originally established as the Juvenile Liaison Scheme (JLS) in 1963, the Programme was only placed on a statutory footing following the 2001 Act. Eligibility for the programme requires that children are aged between 10 and 17 years, they accept responsibility for their offences and consent to participation. Cases are referred centrally to the Director of the GJDP at the Garda Youth Diversion Office in Dublin who decides the outcome of each referral. The Director may admit the child to the programme which means that an informal caution or a formal caution is executed. Victims' views are considered in the decision to admit a child to the programme but their consent is not a requirement in law. Other outcomes include a decision to take no further action against the child or the child is deemed unsuitable for the programme. A child is considered unsuitable due to the seriousness and/or persistence of offending, where consent to participate is not forthcoming or where the child does not accept responsibility for his/her behaviour. In these situations, cases are referred back to the local police where prosecution is the most likely outcome. There are some exceptions such as the small number of cases (an average of 75 cases per annum between 2010 and 2013) who are resubmitted to the GJDP for review by the Office of the Director of Public Prosecutions. This most commonly occurs where there is a change in circumstances, e.g. a child takes responsibility for the offending behaviour (Mullan 2014).

Specialist police officers known as Juvenile Liaison Officers (JLOs) have responsibility for cautioning and supervising children and engaging directly with their families. These officers are trained in conflict resolution and mediation as required under the 2001 Act. Training is also undertaken in restorative practices. Children who are formally cautioned are supervised for a period up to 12 months and have conditions attached to their supervision. The level of supervision is at the discretion of the JLO subject to a number of guidelines including the seriousness of the offending behaviour, the perceived level of care and control provided by the child's parent(s)/guardian(s), perceived risk of re-offending and/or any direction from the Director of the programme. Legislative provision exists for the victim or victim's representative to attend the formal caution and in these cases the caution becomes a restorative caution. The use of restorative cautions has grown considerably over the last decade from a baseline of 138 in 2004 to 911 in 2013 (An Garda Síochána 2013). There is also scope for a restorative conference to be held as part of the formal caution though in practice these have been used in limited cases since their implementation. These conferences are facilitated by a JLO and attended by the child, the parent/guardian, the victim, agency representatives, and others who are considered positive constituents to the process. An action plan is formulated arising from the conference and may include an apology to the victim; financial reparation; a requirement for the child to attend school, work, or other pro-social activities; restrictions on the child's movements and/or associations; and/or other interventions deemed to reduce re-offending. Participation in restorative cautions and conferences as part of the GJDP is voluntary and contingent on the consent of the child and his/her parent(s)/ guardian(s).

There were 20,536 offences referred to the GJDP in 2013 accounting for 10,420 children. Each offence is counted as a referral and children may also be referred to the GJDP on more than one occasion. These factors account for the differences between the number of referrals and the number of children. Young males accounted for 75% of the children referred. Over half of the referrals involved 16 and 17 year olds, almost one-third related to 14 and 15 year olds and just 12% were for 12 and 13 year olds. This age distribution of children has been relatively consistent over time and demonstrates that the majority of children referred to the programme are between 14 and 17 years (An Garda Síochána 2013). In 2013, just less than three-quarters of children (74%) were accepted on the programme by way of an informal or a formal caution. Of this group, 50% received an informal caution and 24% received a formal caution. In a further 6% of cases, no further action was taken while in 4% of cases a decision on the case was pending. In total, 15% were deemed unsuitable for the programme and of these 88% were male. The outcomes for children referred to the programme in 2013 reflects a general pattern over a 10-year period from 2004 to 2013 demonstrating that the majority of children are diverted from prosecution each year by way of police caution (An Garda Síochána 2013).

Its capacity to divert substantial numbers of children from prosecution and conviction is seen as the key strength of the GJDP. In the narrative of twenty-first century juvenile justice in Ireland, the GJDP is seen to epitomise the diversionary ethos of the 2001 Act. Notwithstanding its prominent position on the juvenile justice landscape, a number of criticisms have been levelled against it. A lack of transparency and accountability in the decision-making processes on the programme and the absence of due process have been raised by a number of commentators (Kilkelly 2011; Walsh 2008). The programme is not independently monitored which is noteworthy in circumstances where the police retain full administrative and management responsibility for it and the Director has complete discretion in decision-making about the outcomes for children referred to the programme. A further concern is that the programme has not been independently evaluated despite being in existence since 1963 and on a statutory footing since 2002. Consequently, there is limited information available on the processes or the outcomes for children referred to the programme.[3] The absence of publicly available data on the programme means that it is not possible to identify changes in patterns of offending behaviour. Neither is it possible to identify if a net-widening effect exists whereby children who previously would have remained outside the juvenile justice system for minor misdemeanours are now brought in by way of a referral to the programme. Finally, an amendment to the 2001 Act means that while children cannot be prosecuted for the offence for which they were cautioned, their admission to the programme can be referenced in circumstances where a court is considering a sentence for offences committed after their admission to the programme.

---

[3]The only available information refers to general criteria used in decision-making such as the seriousness and persistence of children's offending and/or previous involvement in the GJDP. Outcomes are divided into categories of: informal caution, formal caution, no further action, case pending and unsuitable for admission but no further information on the nuances underpinning these outcomes are provided.

Garda Youth Diversion Projects (GYDPs)

In addition to the GJDP, the IYJS in conjunction with An Garda Síochána, fund a network of 110 crime prevention projects known as Garda Youth Diversion Projects (GYDP) across the country. These projects which are delivered by community-based organisations target children aged 10–17 years who are deemed 'at risk' of offending or children who are subject to a caution. The projects aim to divert children from crime through promoting personal development and civic responsibility. In contrast to the discourse underpinning other aspects of the juvenile justice system, the policy documentation for the GYDPs emphasises 'actuarial principles of risk and behavioural management and control: specifically, potential threats posed by children to social order' (Convery and Seymour 2016:252). Government funding to the networks of community-based organisations who deliver the projects is contingent on the completion of annual plans which requires police data on children's offending behaviour in the area, aggregated risk assessment data, and information on the project's 'success' in reducing impulsiveness, improving children's levels of empathy and improving pro-social behaviour (IYJS 2012a, b). These requirements represent a previously unfamiliar approach to the governance of children 'at risk' in the Irish context. They highlight individual explanations for crime without corresponding consideration for the broader social contexts where children live and associate. Furthermore, as Swirak (2015:16) describes 'projects are now positioned as vehicles to enhance surveillance over young people in their respective neighbourhoods'.

COURTS AND JUVENILES

The Children Court has jurisdiction to hear the vast majority of crimes with the exception of murder, manslaughter, rape and/or serious sexual offences which are tried at the Central Criminal Court. Judges have discretion to deal summarily with all other offences in the Children Court or to transfer them to a higher (adult) court. Where a transfer is considered, judges are obliged to take the age and maturity of the child into account. The child's consent is also required to retain the case in the Children Court. According to the Court Service data on outcomes for child defendants, an average of 115 children (accounting for 3–4%) were sent forward for trial to a higher court each year between 2009 and 2013 (Courts Service 2009–2013).

There is one designated Children Court based in Dublin city centre. Outside of the city, the Children Court sits in the local District Court building for each area. A number of provisions exist under the 2001 Act to account for the special status of children appearing before the court. These include that children's cases are held in private, the waiting time for proceedings should be restricted to the minimum required, children should be kept separate from adult defendants and the court should sit at a different time or in a different room or building to other court proceedings. The only personnel permitted to attend children's court proceedings are officers of the court, parents/guardians and adult relatives of the child, bona fide representatives of the press and those admitted at the discretion of the court. Despite these legal protections, the available evidence suggests that disparities exist between the law in theory and its application in practice. Kilkelly's (2008) study of the Children Court found evidence of children waiting for excessive periods before their cases were heard in some courts and privacy provisions being breached where members of the public including adult defendants, and police unrelated to the case, were in attendance at proceedings. Furthermore, it was reported that the physical environment and poor acoustics in some courtrooms negatively impacted on children's opportunities to participate in proceedings (*ibid.*). This was compounded in cases where limited communication took place between children, judges and their legal representatives. Considerable disparity was identified in relation to judicial practice when communicating with children in the courtroom, ranging from high levels of engagement to very limited, if any, interaction (Kilkelly 2005). The length of time to finalise children's cases in the juvenile justice system has been highlighted as a matter that impacts on children's right to an expedient conclusion of proceedings against them. The extent and nature of delays is uncertain in the absence of systematic and up-to-date data however previous research found that 43% of children made their first court appearance more than 6 months after the offence occurred and incurred an average of eight court appearances in respect of each charge (Carroll and Meehan 2007). Mullan (2014) outlines a number of high court and supreme court cases that highlight the issue of delays in prosecuting children's cases and the duty of the prosecutorial apparatus to deal with such cases in a more expedient manner than the 'normal duty of expedition'.[4] The evidence suggests that delays in determining matters for children before the courts have serious repercussions for them. In a study of children on remand in Ireland, Seymour and Butler (2008) found that lengthy delays in processing their cases placed them at greater risk of re-offending, of breaching their bail conditions, and in some cases increased their risk of detention. The time taken to finalise children's cases has been compounded by the absence of bail support and monitoring initiatives for children progressing through the court system. This gap has been partially addressed with the awarding of a contract for the first ever pilot bail supervision scheme in Ireland for children by the IYJS in April 2016. Another intervention which has provided support to children appearing before the courts is the Garda Youth Crime Case Management (YCCM) initiative. Children identified as prolific offenders are matched with a Garda case manager who is responsible for co-ordinating their

[4] DPP v G Judgment of Ms. Justice Iseult O'Malley delivered the 24th January 2014; D v DPP Judgement of the Supreme Court delivered by Ms Justice Dunne on the 30th July, 2014; D v DPP Judgement of the Supreme Court delivered by Ms Justice Dunne on the 30th July, 2014; Sharon Cullen v DPP Judgement of the Supreme Court delivered by Chief Justice Denham on the 16th October, 2014 (Mullan 2014).

charges so that multiple court appearances are avoided. Case managers are also tasked with monitoring children in the community and liaising with families and relevant agencies to provide appropriate interventions (O'Brien 2014).

Family Conferencing

Family conferencing was introduced under the 2001 Act as a mechanism to divert children out of the criminal justice system. Two options are available. A Family Welfare Conference (FWC) is convened where there are substantive concerns about the welfare of a child involved in criminal proceedings. In these circumstances, the conference explores the appropriate care required for the child, including the need for an emergency care or supervision order, and the court may dismiss the charge against the child. The Family Conference is the second option available. The conference is convened by the Probation Service on the direction of the court and involves the young person, the victim, family members and significant others. Conditions of referral include that the child accepts responsibility for their offending and consents to the conference process. The process is based on restorative justice principles and provides an opportunity for each of the parties involved to engage in dialogue about what happened and how to resolve the harm caused. Following the conference, an action plan is drawn up with the child and family members. The action plan which must be approved by the court may include a written apology to the victim, monetary compensation, unpaid work, and/or other such activities deemed to reduce the risk of re-offending. A period of 6 months is provided for the child to complete the action plan before a review takes place in the court. Thereafter, if the child's progress is deemed satisfactory, the court may dismiss the charge and a conviction is not recorded. If the child's compliance with the terms of the action plan is unsatisfactory, the case may be returned to court where standard proceedings commence. Interventions underpinned by restorative justice principles remain on the periphery of the juvenile justice system with an average of 30 referrals per year for family conferencing to the Probation Service over the period 2011–2014 (Probation Service 2014).

Sentencing

Young Persons' Probation (YPP), a division of the Probation Service, has primary statutory responsibility for implementing the courts' directions in relation to the assessment and supervision of children in criminal matters. The procedure for most children convicted before the courts is to have their case adjourned for the purposes of preparing a pre-sanction (pre-sentence) report prior to imposing sentence. The court is obliged in the legislation to order a pre-sanction report except in cases where the penalty for the child's offence is fixed by law or an existing report is deemed adequate. Reports typically include information on the offence, the child's life situation, underlying causes of offending behaviour, motivation to change, risk of re-offending, as well as a statement in relation to the appropriateness of a community sanction. The report has an important function in informing the court about the child against the background of the legislative principle that any penalty imposed should cause the least interference to the child's legitimate activities and maintain and promote the child's development. Probation officers working within YPP complete the pre-sanction report following consultation and assessment with the child, the family and other relevant stakeholders.

CHILDREN AND DETENTION

A snapshot of the population on 13 May 2016 identifies that there was a total of 55 children detained within the juvenile justice system in Ireland. Of those 44 were detained within the Children Detention School system and a further eleven 17 year olds were detained within the prison estate. Ireland currently has a two-tiered approach to the detention of children which differentiates between young males and young females under 18 years. The Children Detention School system operates under the auspices of the DCYA and has a care, educational and rehabilitative ethos. It accommodates all detained females but only some detained males under 18 years. The 2001 Act abolished prison sentences for children but made provision for 16 and 17 year old males to be detained in St. Patrick's Institution, a medium security place of detention within the prison estate. A report by the Inspector of Prisons in 2012 highlighted major concerns about the safety and protection of detainees and provided the catalyst to commence the transfer of most 16- and 17-year-old males out of St. Patrick's Institution from 2013 onwards. While 16-year-old males were transferred to the Children Detention School system, the absence of suitable accommodation culminated in 17-year-old males on remand remaining in St. Patrick's Institution until early 2015 and those under sentence being housed in a separate wing of an adult prison in West Dublin. A new 90-bed facility known as the National Children Detention Centre will replace the existing Children Detention School system and is expected to be fully operational in the latter part of 2016.[5] It will hold all children under 18 years and will finally end the disparity in the treatment of young male and female detainees. Importantly, this will mark the long-awaited implementation of government policy to cease the practice of detaining children under 18 years in adult prison facilities.

As outlined at the beginning of this section, the population of children in the Children Detention School system and the Prison Service has fallen considerably since the implementation of the 2001 Act. However, a concerning and consistent

[5] The detention school estate based in Lusk Co. Dublin consisted of three institutions (Oberstown Boys School, Oberstown Girls School and Trinity House) until 01 June 2016 when the legislation came into effect to amalgamate them into the National Children Detention Centre.

feature has been the disproportionately high numbers of admissions of children on remand, relative to those serving sentences (Convery and Seymour 2016). This is especially notable in the context of research which identifies that many children detained on remand do not subsequently receive a custodial sentence or are necessarily remanded due to the seriousness of their offences or risk of re-offending (Freeman 2008; Seymour and Butler 2008). In these circumstances, it appears that practice is at odds with the legislative principle to use detention as a measure of last resort. A number of legislative provisions exist to protect children from excessive periods of detention. As outlined earlier in this chapter, the 2001 Act stipulates that children should be detained only as a measure of last resort and the period of detention imposed should not exceed the term imposed on an adult for the same offence. In a recent development, the Children (Amendment) Act 2015 introduced provision for children to receive 25% (and up to 33%) remission on their sentences for good behaviour in line with their adult contemporaries.

The detention system is in a period of transition and is likely to experience diverse challenges as legislative, organisational and practical arrangements for the National Children Detention Centre are finalised over 2016. It remains to be seen how the new arrangements for children's detention in the Irish system will unfold in the coming years.

COMMUNITY SANCTIONS

The court has a number of sentencing options at its disposal. These include ordering a child to pay a fine, costs or compensation, imposing a community order, a detention order or a detention and supervision order. Where a court decides to impose a community order it is required to explain its reasons in open court. It must also outline the conditions of the order, the court expectations, and possible consequences of non-compliance in a language appropriate to the child's understanding. The 2001 Act makes provision for a number of community-based supervision orders including a training or activities probation order, an intensive probation order, a residential probation order, a day centre order, a mentor order, a suitable person order, a restriction on movement order, and a dual order (see further Seymour 2012). In practice, orders provided for under the 2001 Act are used in a small number of cases and the standard probation order as adjudicated for under the Probation of Offenders Act 1907 remains the most common community-based supervision order imposed on children before the courts (Seymour 2013).[6] A common judicial practice in Ireland involves a court postponing the decision about the penalty to be imposed and requesting the Probation Service to supervise the offender during the deferral period. The practice known as 'an order for supervision during deferment of penalty' accounted for half of the 740 orders supervised by the Probation Service involving children

[6]The Criminal Justice (Community Sanctions) Bill 2014, when enacted, will replace the Probation Act 1907 and create a modern statutory framework for community sanctions in Ireland.

in 2014 (Probation Service 2014:56).[7] A potential benefit of supervision during deferment of penalty for children is that the court may dismiss the charges and leave them without a criminal conviction following a successful period of supervision. A contrasting argument is that retaining children in the criminal justice system for undefined periods of time compromises their right to have criminal matters finalised in an expedient manner and potentially risks drawing them further into the criminal justice system (Convery and Seymour 2016). Electronic monitoring for children is not used either as a stand-alone measure or as part of the conditions of a community sanction or other measure. A notable feature of practice in the Irish system, relative to other jurisdictions, is that a child cannot be detained in custody for technical violations of community supervision orders. In circumstances where the child does not comply with the conditions of community supervision, the court is required to direct the child to comply or revoke the order and impose an alternative community sanction (for further information on how compliance and enforcement is managed as part of community supervision, see Seymour 2013).

The supervision of children, while varying according to individual need, typically entails one-to-one meetings with probation officers, supported by community-based organisations who deliver programmes and interventions to change behaviour in areas that include vocational and educational training, personal development, substance misuse, and mentoring. Probation officers' professional backgrounds are in the areas of social policy and social work. Their approach to working with children under supervision is framed by their professional training and the welfare, rehabilitation and reintegration ethos of the 2001 Act (Seymour 2013). They have considerable scope to exercise their professional judgement in decision-making about children under their supervision. O'Leary and Halton's (2009) evaluation of the use of risk assessment for children subject to probation supervision in Ireland provides a useful illustration in explaining that probation officers' clinical judgement may supersede the actuarial conclusions from risk assessment exercises where different outcomes arise.[8]

Parental Sanctions

Parents or guardians are obliged to attend court appearances relating to their children's criminal proceedings and to participate if required. The court has the power to adjourn proceedings and issue a warrant for the arrest of the parents or guardian who fails to appear. A number of orders can also be imposed on parents. They can be ordered to pay compensation for offences committed by their children or have a parental supervision order imposed if the court is satisfied that

[7]Probation orders accounted for a further one-third and the remainder consisted of supervision orders under the 2001 Act (13%), community service orders (3%), and full and partially suspended sentences with supervision (2%) *(ibid.)*.

[8]The risk assessment instrument used by the Probation Service in Ireland is the Youth Level of Service/Case Management Inventory (YLS/CMI).

they wilfully neglected to care or to control their child and this contributed to the criminal behaviour. The court may also order parents to enter into a recognisance to exercise proper and adequate control over their children. The recognisance may be forfeited if further offences occur and the court deems that the parents' failure to exercise adequate control over their children was a contributing factor. In practice, parental supervision orders are rarely imposed by the Children Court.

DIFFERENCES IN TREATMENT OF BOYS AND GIRLS

Analysis of outcomes from the GJDP identify that two-thirds (66%) of girls compared to less than half (45%) of boys received an informal caution in 2013 (An Garda Síochána 2013). Boys were more likely to be formally cautioned and more than twice as likely as girls to be sent forward for prosecution. Further analysis of the data is required to explain the differential responses, but a possible explanation is that more girls (81%) than boys (66%) were first-time referrals. Over one-fifth of boys (22%) had 2–3 referrals compared to 14% of girls and 12% of boys, compared to 5% of girls had 4 or more referrals (ibid.). Gender profile data on sentencing outcomes is not provided by the Court Service meaning that no insight can be provided on the courts' treatment of boys' and girls' offending. Probation Service statistics suggest that 8% of the juvenile caseload consists of young females (under 18 years) but no further information exists on how gender manifests within case supervision (Probation Service 2014:55). Girls up to 18 years have been detained within the Children Detention School system since 01 March 2007 unlike their 17-year-old male counterparts, some of whom continue to be detained within the adult prison system (see Children and Detention).

Girls' offending motivation and pathways into crime differs from boys and suggests that differential responses are required (Barry 2006). Despite the evidence, there is no specific gender responsive strategy currently in existence in the juvenile justice system in Ireland to address potential differences in responses to boys' and girls' offending behaviour.

CONCLUSION

The modern juvenile justice system in Ireland has developed slowly since the turn of the century against the backdrop of the 2001 Act which represented the first major legislative reform of juvenile justice since the 1908 Children Act. The absence of a central body to implement legislative change until the establishment of the IYJS in 2006, followed by a prolonged period of economy austerity commencing in 2008, were key impediments to the reform process. Notwithstanding these factors, the system has progressed and common narratives and shared aspirations of diversion, rehabilitation and reintegration exist across the key agencies with responsibility for children in conflict with the law. As outlined in this chapter, challenges exist to ensure that the law in theory and principle is implemented in practice to improve outcomes for children.

The language of the UN Convention on the Rights of the Child is evident in the legislative framework for the juvenile justice system in Ireland and in many of the policies and practices that emanate from it. Key among these is the emphasis on diversion, children's participation, information provision and the use of detention as a measure of last resort. In contrast, the decision to abolish the presumption of *doli incapax* and reduce to 10 years the age of criminal responsibility for children charged with serious criminal matters exposes the contradictions of the system. The juvenile justice system in Ireland is not dissimilar from its international contemporaries in combining a dominant philosophy (welfare) with a hybrid mix of other influences that include restorative justice, actuarial justice, rehabilitation, reintegration and rights-based approaches. A notable feature of the Irish system, and reflecting the dominance of the welfare ethos, is the high levels of discretion afforded to criminal justice managers and practitioners in their decision-making on children's cases. Eadie and Canton (2002) argue that a high level of discretion must be balanced with a corresponding level of accountability to mitigate actual or perceived unfair or discriminatory practices. Their argument resonates in the context of recent research on the juvenile justice systems in Ireland and Northern Ireland which noted that 'increased levels of discretion enjoyed by practitioners ... did not necessarily result in a more "lenient" outcome or experience for the young person' (Hamilton et al. 2016:13–14). It suggests that while discretion plays an important role in decision-making given the differences in children's level of maturity, cognitive understanding, life circumstances and circumstances of their offending, caution is required.

The modest size of the population of detained children is a positive outcome from reform of the juvenile justice system notwithstanding the aforementioned issue of disproportionate numbers of children on remand in the detention system. The legislation is credited with providing the structure from which the principle of using detention as a measure of last resort has been embedded in policy and professional practice. No specific sentencing guidance exists, rather the process has been evolved through what may be described as a shared collective understanding of the values underpinning the 2001 Act. The detention of children is the area of the juvenile justice system that has witnessed the most fundamental change in recent years arising from the amalgamation of existing children detention schools into a single facility and the broadening out of the system to include older and potentially more criminally involved cases. The National Children Detention Centre which is scheduled to be fully operational in 2016 marks a significant milestone in the development of the juvenile justice system in Ireland by finally ending the practice of detaining children in adult facilities almost 15 years after being first outlined in law.

REFERENCES

An Garda Síochána. (2013). *Annual reports of the committee appointed to Monitor the Effectiveness of the Diversion Programme* (Reports from 2003 to 2013). Dublin: Garda Youth Diversion Office.

Barry, M. (2006). *Youth offending in transition: The search for social recognition*. Abingdon: Routledge.

Carroll, J., & Meehan, J. (2007). *The children court: A national study*. Dublin: Association for Criminal Justice Research and Development (ACJRD).

Central Statistics Office. (2010). *Crime and victimisation quarterly national household survey 2010*. Retrieved May 30, 2016, from www.cso.ie

Central Statistics Office (CSO). (2015). *Survey on income and living conditions (SILC) 2014 results (CSO Statistical Release, 26 November 2015)*. Retrieved July 10, 2016, from http://www.cso.ie

Committee on the Rights of the Child. (2016). *Concluding observations on the combined third and fourth periodic reports of Ireland* (CRC/C/IRL/CO/3-4). Retrieved May 30, 2016, from http://www.ohchr.org/

Convery, U., & Seymour, M. (2016). Children, crime and justice. In D. Healy, C. Hamilton, Y. Daly, & M. Butler (Eds.), *The Routledge handbook of Irish Criminology*. Abingdon: Routledge.

Courts Service. (2009–2013). *Annual Reports of the Courts Service 2009–2013*. Dublin: The Courts Service. (Original work published 2009)

Dáil Eireann. (2006). *Dáil Eireann Debate Vol. 624 No. 3 Responses to Q.141 and Q.194, 3 October 2006*. Dublin: Dáil Eireann.

Eadie, T., & Canton, R. (2002). Practising in a context of ambivalence: The challenge for youth justice workers. *Youth Justice, 2*(1), 14–26.

Freeman, S. (2008). Surviving on remand: A study of how young people cope in remand custody in Ireland. Unpublished Ph.D. thesis, Dublin Institute of Technology. Retrieved May 30, 2016, from http://arrow.dit.ie/appadoc/15/

Hamilton, C., Fitzgibbon, W., & Carr, N. (2016). Punishment, youth justice and cultural contingency: Towards a balanced approach. *Youth Justice*. doi:10.1177/1473225415619500.

Hayes, J., & O'Reilly, G. (2007). *Emotional intelligence mental health and juvenile delinquency*. Cork: Juvenile Health Matters.

Horgan, J. (2013). *Drug and alcohol misuse among young offenders on probation supervision in Ireland: Findings from the drugs and alcohol survey 2012* (Probation Service Research Report 3). Dublin: Probation Service.

Hourigan, N. (2012). Juvenile justice, crime and early intervention: Key challenges from the limerick context. *Irish Probation Journal, 9*, 64–74.

Inspector of Prisons. (2012). *Report on an Inspection of St. Patrick's Institution 2012*. Nenagh: Office of the Inspector of Prisons.

Irish Youth Justice Service (IYJS). (2012a). *Garda youth diversion project annual plan for 2013*. Retrieved May 30, 2016, from http://www.iyjs.ie/en/IYJS/Pages/WP09000002

Irish Youth Justice Service (IYJS). (2012b). *Garda youth diversion project annual plan explanatory notes for 2013*. Retrieved May 30, 2016, from http://www.iyjs.ie/en/IYJS/Pages/WP09000002

Kilkelly, U. (2005). *The children court: A children's rights audit*. Cork: Faculty of Law, University College Cork.

Kilkelly, U. (2008). Youth courts and children's rights: The Irish experience. *Youth Justice, 8*(1), 39–56.

Kilkelly, U. (2011). Policing, young people, diversion and accountability. *Crime, Law and Social Change, 55*(2–3), 133–151.

Kilkelly, U. (2014). Diverging or emerging from law? The practice of youth justice in Ireland. *Youth Justice, 14*(3), 212–225.

McElvaney, R., Tatlow-Golden, M., Webb, R., Lawlor, E., & Merriman, B. (2013). *Someone to care: The mental health needs of children and young people with experience of the care and youth justice systems*. Dublin: Children's Mental Health Coalition.
Mullan, P. (2014). Current juvenile justice policy—Impact on DPP. In *Youth Justice Transformation Annual Conference Report of the Association for Criminal Justice Research and Development (ACJRD), 17th October 2014*. Retrieved May 30, 2016, from www.acjrd.ie
O'Brien, J. (2014). *The Garda youth crime case management programme—A Garda perspective on the role and the relationship dynamics involved when managing cases of high-risk young offenders appearing before the children court*. Masters dissertation, Dublin Institute of Technology. Retrieved May 30, 2016, from http://arrow.dit.ie/aaschssldis/94/
O'Leary, P., & Halton, C. (2009). Young persons' probation in the republic of Ireland: An evaluation of risk assessment. *Irish Probation Journal, 6*, 97–112.
Probation Service. (2014). *Annual Reports of the Probation Service* (Reports 2011 to 2014). Dublin: The Probation Service.
Seymour, M. (2006). Transition and reform: Juvenile justice in the republic of Ireland. In J. Junger-Tas & S. Decker (Eds.), *International handbook of juvenile justice*. Dordrecht: Springer.
Seymour, M. (2012). The youth justice system. In C. Hamilton (Ed.), *Social work and social care law*. Dublin: Gill and MacMillan.
Seymour, M. (2013). *Youth justice in context: Community, compliance and young people*. Abingdon: Routledge.
Seymour, M., & Butler, M. (2008). *Young people on remand. The National Children's Strategy Research Series*. Dublin: The Stationery Office.
Seymour, M., & Mayock, P. (2009). Ireland. In P. Hadfield (Ed.), *Nightlife and crime: Social order and governance in international perspective*. New York: Oxford University Press.
Swirak, K. (2015). Problematising advanced liberal youth crime prevention: The impacts of management reforms on Irish Garda youth diversion projects. *Youth Justice*. doi:10.1177/1473225415617859.
Walsh, D. (2008). Balancing due process values with welfare objectives in juvenile justice procedure: Some strengths and weaknesses in the Irish approach. *Youth Studies Ireland, 3*(2), 3–17.

Mairead Seymour is a Senior Lecturer in the School of Languages, Law and Social Sciences at the Dublin Institute of Technology. She is author of the book 'Youth Justice in Context: Community, Compliance and Young People' (Routledge, 2013). Her research interests include juvenile justice, comparative criminal justice, community supervision, offender compliance, procedural justice and prisoner reintegration.

17

Poland

Barbara Stańdo-Kawecka

INTRODUCTION

A juvenile justice system, separate from the adult criminal justice system, was created in Poland in the 1920s and 1930s. At that time, discussions on the need to remove juveniles from the adult criminal justice system were influenced by the Youth Court Movement, which emerged in some European countries at the very beginning of the twentieth century and relied on the North American 'Child-Saver' movement (Albrecht 2013; Stańdo-Kawecka 2015). Polish scientists and practitioners who made efforts aiming at the creation of the juvenile justice system recognized juvenile offenders as different from adults who were still developing. In line with that approach special provisions on juvenile proceedings were introduced in the 1928 Code of Criminal Procedure. This gave the juvenile judge a dominant role in juvenile cases (Taracha 1988). Additionally, the 1932 Criminal Code included a special chapter on criminal responsibility of juvenile offenders.

According to the 1932 Criminal Code, the age of criminal majority was set at 17 years. Juveniles who committed an offense below 13 years of age were treated as not criminally responsible. Only educational measures, such as reprimand, supervision by parents or other trustworthy persons or institutions, or placement in a state or private educational institution, could be imposed on them. The same applied to juveniles who committed an offense after the 13th birthday, but prior to the 17th, and at the time of the offense were lacking discernment (*rozeznanie*). Discernment meant the ability of a juvenile to understand the meaning of his act and control his behaviors. Juveniles aged 13–16 who had committed an offense with discernment as a rule were sentenced to the placement in a correctional institution (*zakład poprawczy*) for an unspecified time and could be institutionalized until the age of 21. In the doctrine of the criminal law, the view prevailed that the placement of a juvenile in a correctional institution was a special penalty

B. Stańdo-Kawecka (✉)
Jagiellonian University in Kraków, Kraków, Poland
e-mail: barbara.stando-kawecka@uj.edu.pl

S.H. Decker, N. Marteache (eds.), *International Handbook of Juvenile Justice*,
DOI 10.1007/978-3-319-45090-2_17

of an educational nature which substituted prison sentences imposed on adult offenders (Makarewicz 1938; Stańdo-Kawecka 1993). Thus, since the very beginning of the creation of a separate juvenile justice system in Poland the legislature aimed at removing juveniles from both criminal courts and criminal penalties provided for adult offenders in order to protect, educate, and resocialize them and facilitate their becoming law-abiding citizens in the future.

The protective and educational approach to juvenile offenders was furthered strengthened in 1982 when a separate Act on proceedings in juvenile cases (further: JA)[1] was enacted. The legislature decided to abolish the criterion of acting with discernment in order to stress that determining the issue of culpability was insignificant to making proper choices of measures to be applied to juveniles. Additionally, the scope of the juvenile justice system was broadened because it covered not only persons who violated criminal law while being under 17 years of age but also minors under 18 years of age who displayed predelinquent, antisocial behaviors not prohibited by the criminal law, referred to by the legislature as 'signs of demoralization.' 'Signs of demoralization' are similar to 'status offenses' known in English-speaking countries and include, among others, violation of social rules, truancy, vagrancy, running away from home, using alcohol or drugs and prostitution. Juvenile proceedings were entrusted to family courts which as a rule applied civil procedure. The use of provisions of criminal procedure in juvenile cases became very limited (Stańdo-Kawecka 2015).

Although in 1989 Poland experienced a change in the political system, the transition from a postcommunist country into the democratic state based on the rule of law did not influence the juvenile justice system much. Reforms undertaken in the 1990s focused mainly on the adult criminal law and aimed at making criminal policy more human, liberal, and rational (Stańdo-Kawecka and Krajewski 2010). The juvenile justice system based on the welfare ideology was not subjected to criticism as opposed to the repressive adult criminal law and criminal policy from the communist era. In the late 1990s, the social and political climate around crime and criminal policy began to change for several reasons, such as the increase in official crime rates, growing fear of crime, and politicization of problems concerning crime control. These changes, however, affected mainly adult criminal law (Stańdo-Kawecka and Krajewski 2010). Family courts turned out resistant to political pressure on tougher reactions to crime. Additionally, strong scientific support for dealing with juveniles according to their needs rather than deeds (Kołakowska-Przełomiec et al. 1994) inhibited reforms aiming at a more severe approach to juvenile offenders. Generally, in the last decades the protective and paternalistic juvenile justice system formed in the 1980s has not experienced fundamental changes.

---

[1] *Ustawa z dnia 26 października 1982 r. o postępowaniu w sprawach nieletnich*, Journal of Laws 1982/35, pos. 228 with subsequent amendments; since its entry into force, the 1982 JA has been amended several times, however, those amendments did not change basic assumptions of the juvenile justice system shaped in the 1980s.

THE LEGAL STATUS OF JUVENILES

In Poland, various fields of law use such terms as 'minor' (*małoletni*), 'child' (*dziecko*), and 'juvenile' (*nieletni*). The term 'minor' is commonly used in civil law. The minimum age of civil majority in Poland is set at 18 years. According to the civil law, persons below 18 are minors (*małoletni*) while those at least 18 are adults (*pełnoletni*). Exceptions include women who marry with the consent of the guardianship court while being at least 16 years of age who are treated as adults under the civil law.[2] Civil law provisions concerning the minimum age of majority are coherent with the Family and Guardianship Code. Pursuant to Article 92 of the latter Code, a child (*dziecko*) remains under parental responsibility until the age of civil majority.[3] The notion 'juvenile' (*nieletni*) is embedded in the criminal law and is used in the juvenile justice system which is separated from the adult criminal law. Additionally, it is commonly used in criminology in the context of juvenile delinquency. Pursuant to Article 10 § 1 of the currently binding Criminal Code of 1997, rules on criminal responsibility determined by the Code apply to perpetrators who committed offenses while being at least 17 years of age. Thus, 17-year-old offenders are 'adults' in the meaning of the Polish criminal law. The 1997 Criminal Code generally does not apply to juveniles, these are persons who have committed an act prohibited by the criminal law below 17 years. Instead, provisions of the JA apply.

In line with fundamental ideas of the protective and educational approach, the JA does not determine rules of criminal responsibility for juveniles but regulates the application of educational, medical, and correctional measures to them. At the same time, the notion of a 'juvenile' has been defined by the JA broadly. According to Article 1 of this Act, this term covers:

(a) Perpetrators of 'punishable acts' committed after having reached 13, but before 17 years of age.
(b) Persons under 18 who show signs of problematic behavior not prohibited by the criminal law, referred to by the legislator as 'signs of demoralization'.
(c) Persons to whom educational or correctional measures are enforced until the person is 18 or 21 years of age; the enforcement of particular measures imposed on juveniles shall cease *ex lege* upon completion by them of 18 or 21 years of age.

'Punishable act' is defined in the JA and means an action or omission defined by the criminal law as an offense, fiscal offense, or selected petty crime. Thus, 'punishable act' means an act or omission which would be an offense or a petty crime if committed by an adult perpetrator. In the JA the legislature did not use

---

[2] See Article 10 of the 1964 Civil Code (*Ustawa z dnia 23 kwietnia 1964 r.—Kodeks cywilny*), Journal of Laws 1964/16, pos. 93 with subsequent amendments.

[3] See Article 92 of the 1964 Family and Guardianship Code (*Ustawa z dnia 25 lutego 1964 r.—Kodeks rodzinny i opiekuńczy*), Journal of Laws 1964/9, pos. 59 with subsequent amendments.

such terms as 'offense' (*przestępstwo*) or 'petty crime' (*wykroczenie*) in order to stress that children below 17 years of age are not mature enough to be criminally responsible for their acts and, additionally, the determination of their culpability is irrelevant for the choice of the most appropriate measure. As for 'demoralization,' the JA has not defined this notion. Article 4 of the JA only enumerates some examples of behavior types or circumstances which are treated as signs of 'demoralization': violation of the principles of community life, commission of a prohibited act, truancy, use of alcohol or drugs, running away from home, prostitution, as well as association with criminal groups.

'Punishable acts' may be committed only by juveniles who are at least 13 years of age. It should be noted that there is no minimum age limit for juveniles showing 'signs of demoralization.' The commission of an act prohibited by the criminal law as an offense or petty crime by a minor less than 13 years of age does not constitute a 'punishable act' under the JA but may be considered as a sign of 'demoralization.' In the science of the juvenile law, 'demoralization' has been defined as a state or process that is characterized by negative attitudes and behaviors by a juvenile, in relation to the fundamental norms and principles of conduct required by the society (Sienkiewicz 1988; Bojarski et al. 2014). Undoubtedly, provisions concerning juveniles who show signs of 'demoralization' are intended to provide family courts with broad discretion in initiating state intervention according to basic assumptions of the paternalistic and protective approach. They allow family courts to impose on children who behave in an unacceptable way but do not infringe the criminal law the same compulsory educational and medical measures as is possible in the case of juveniles breaking the criminal law. The most severe category of measures provided for by the JA are correctional measures. These consist of suspended or unsuspended placement in a correctional institution and can be applied exclusively to juvenile perpetrators of 'punishable acts' prohibited by the criminal law as offenses.

According to views prevailing in the doctrine of the criminal law, the juvenile law is a separate branch of law and the juvenile justice system is distinct from the criminal justice system. However, educational, medical, and correctional measures applied to juveniles are of a compulsory nature, i.e., the imposition of a measure on a juvenile perpetrator of a 'punishable act' or a juvenile showing 'sings of demoralization' does not require the consent of the juvenile and his parents. Some of the imposed measures deprive juveniles of their liberty, as is the case of the placement of a juvenile in a psychiatric hospital, youth educational center, or correctional institution. Compulsory measures applied to juveniles within the system based on welfare and paternalistic ideology raise concerns about the legal status of juveniles and their procedural rights and safeguards.

Juvenile proceedings due to both 'signs of demoralization' and 'punishable acts' are vested in family courts. According to Article 20 of the JA, in juvenile proceedings as a rule civil procedure is applied. The JA enumerates exceptions to this rule when provisions of the Code of Criminal Procedure shall apply. The exceptions refer such matters as the collection and preservation of evidence by the police and the appointment and functions of a defense lawyer. The 'hybrid' mode of regulating the procedure in juvenile cases chosen by the legislator in 1982 has been criticized in publications on the juvenile law for many years as being unclear, nontransparent, and difficult to apply (Korcyl-Wolska 2004). Contrary to criminal procedure, civil procedure does not allow for the effective protection of some procedural rights required by standards of a fair trial, such as the presumption of innocence and the right to a defense (Stańdo-Kawecka and Kusztal 2015). Current empirical research indicates that the legal status of a juvenile suspect in juvenile proceedings is in many respects worse than the status of an adult suspect in criminal proceedings and far from the standards for child-friendly justice (Stańdo-Kawecka and Kusztal 2016). Among reasons contributing to the weaker status of a juvenile the following could be mentioned: the lack of clear and detailed provisions regulating actions taken by the police before referring the juvenile case to the family court, the lack of easy access to a lawyer free of charge, the concentration of both investigative tasks and the function of a trial judge in hands of the same family judge which raises doubts about the impartiality of the family court in juvenile proceedings. The latter problem was pointed out by the European Court of Human Rights in the case of *Adamkiewicz v. Poland.*[4]

AGE OF MAJORITY

The juvenile justice system in Poland does not recognize the concept of the minimum age of specific criminal responsibility for juveniles. Juveniles who violate criminal law while being under the age of criminal majority are recognized as not criminally responsible. Juvenile proceedings in cases concerning both 'signs of demoralization' and 'punishable acts' are treated as noncriminal proceedings. In a manner typical for the protective and educational approach to juvenile offenders, the minimum age of criminal liability as a rule is the same as the age of criminal majority. The latter is 17 years of age at the time of the offense[5] and differs from the age of civil majority which is set at 18 years. Young offenders aged 17 are dealt with by the common criminal court according to the provisions of the Criminal Code and the Code of Criminal Procedure. However, life imprisonment does not apply to offenders who were below 18 at the time of the offense. Additionally, the criminal court shall apply educational, medical, or correctional measures instead of penalties to a perpetrator who committed a nonserious offense (*występek*) while being 17 years of age,[6] but this possibility has seldom been used by courts. While imposing penalties for young adults between the ages of 17 and 21, the criminal court may apply lower levels of

[4] ECtHR, *Adamkiewicz v. Poland*, 2 March 2010.

[5] See Article 10 § 1 of the 1997 Criminal Code.

[6] See Article 10 § 4 of the 1997 Criminal Code.

punishment; extraordinary mitigation of punishment is possible in such cases but not obligatory.

While the rule is that the age of criminal majority is 17 years of age, there are some exceptions provided by the Criminal Code which refer juvenile perpetrators of the most serious crimes committed by 15- or 16-year–olds.[7] Pursuant to the Code, 15- and 16-year-olds suspected of the most serious crimes may be held criminally responsible as adults and tried by the common criminal court. The possibility to transfer the juvenile case to the common criminal court depends not only on the suspect's age at the time of the alleged offense and the seriousness of the offense but also on other preconditions, such as the circumstances of the offense and the offender, the level of his maturity, as well as the ineffectiveness of educational or correctional measures. The Criminal Code provides for rules concerning the mitigation of punishment imposed on those 15- and 16-year-old juveniles tried as adults by criminal courts. Life imprisonment cannot be imposed on them and the maximum penalty is reduced by one-third compared to the maximum penalty available for an adult for the same offense. Additionally, extraordinary mitigation of punishment on account of the juvenile's age is possible.[8]

THE COUNTRY'S STANCE TOWARD THE UN COMMITTEE ON THE RIGHTS OF THE CHILD

Poland ratified the UN Convention on the Rights of the Child (further: Convention) in 1991. The Optional Protocol to the Convention on the sale of children, child prostitution, and child pornography as well as the Optional Protocol on the involvement of children in armed conflict was ratified in 2005. It should be noted that as early as 1978 Poland launched an initiative for adoption of the Convention on the Rights of the Child and presented the draft of such a convention (Łopatka 1993). Undoubtedly, under the communist regime the protection of civil and political rights was contrary to the interests of the state authorities. Those rights were exclusively of a declaratory nature because of lack of mechanisms for their effective enforcement and were widely violated (Stawicki 2011). However, when it came to the rights of children, the Polish government actively participated in the work of the United Nations aiming at the protection of children and strengthening their rights. Such a stance by state authorities resulted from experiences of World War II in which many children lost their lives and were exposed to immense suffering. Traditions and achievements of Polish human sciences were other factors that seemed to contribute to the involvement of Polish authorities in the creation of the international system of protection of children's rights. Since the 1920s and 1930s it had been stressed in the

[7]See Article 10 § 2 of the 1997 Criminal Code.

[8]See Article 10 § 3 of the 1997 Criminal Code.

pedagogical, psychological, and philosophical literature that the child was a person and not a being that would become a person only in the future. It was emphasized that the child was the subject of rights and not the object of protection who had to be respected and whose rights should be taken seriously (Łopatka 1993). Those ideas were reflected, among others, in books published in the interwar period by Janusz Korczak, the physician, teacher, writer, journalist, and social activist who refused to leave the children from the orphanage during the extermination of the Warsaw Ghetto by Nazis in 1942.

The commitment of Polish pedagogues and psychologists to the concept of a child as subject to rights had an effect on discussions about the juvenile justice system in the postwar period and the final shape of the JA enacted in 1982. In the early 1990s, shortly after the ratification of the Convention on the Rights of the Child by Poland, the juvenile justice system based on the 1982 JA was examined by criminologists in order to assess its compliance with the Convention. In the opinion of Kołakowska-Przełomiec and Wójcik (1993), the JA was generally compatible with standards included in the Convention, although they submitted some reservations concerning particular issues, such as the age of criminal majority or the absence of sufficient procedural safeguards (pp. 39–45).

The minimum age of criminal majority is still a source of discrepancy between the Polish juvenile law and the Convention on the Rights of the Child. Article 1 of the Convention states explicitly that a child means every human being below the age of 18 years unless under the law applicable to the child, majority is attained earlier. The Committee on the Rights of the Child in the General Comment No. 10 drew the attention of state parties of the Convention that the upper age limit for the application of the rules of special juvenile justice should apply for all children who at the time of an offense have not reached the age of 18 years (Committee on the Rights of the Child 2007:11–12). In Poland, the age of criminal majority is set at 17 years of age at the time of the alleged offense. Contrary to standards included in the Convention, the rules of special juvenile justice do not apply to 17-year-old perpetrators.

Additionally, in Poland 15- and 16-year-old juveniles under certain circumstances may be tried as adults by the common criminal court according to the adult criminal procedure. They are also subject to penalties provided for adults with the exception of life imprisonment. Provisions of the 1997 Criminal Code concerning juveniles who are exceptionally criminally responsible as adults deviate from recommendations of the Committee on the Rights of the Child. According to the Committee, state parties that allow, by way of exception, that children, i.e., persons below 18 years of age, are treated as adult criminals, should change their laws with a view to applying their juvenile justice rules to all persons under the age of 18 years (Committee on the Rights of the Child 2007:12). This position of the Committee on the Rights of the Child has recently been supported by the European Committee for the Prevention of Torture (CPT) in its report during the last visit to Poland. According to the CPT, the Polish authorities should ensure, without further delay, that all juveniles who are detained by the police benefit from the relevant specific safeguards for juveniles provided by the law. Those safeguards should apply to all persons under 18 years of age (European Committee for the Prevention of Torture 2014:18).

Another matter of concern relates to the proceedings due to 'signs of demoralization.' The Committee on the Rights of the Child is of the opinion that the state parties of the Convention should abolish the provisions on status offenses in order to establish an equal treatment under the law for children and adults. Behavior such as vagrancy, roaming the streets, or runaways according to recommendations of the Committee should be dealt with through the implementation of child protective measures, including effective support for parents and/or other caregivers and measures which address the root causes of this behavior (Committee on the Rights of the Child 2007). Under the JA problematic behaviors referred to as 'signs of demoralization' are not punished with penalties but responded with educational measures. However, juveniles showing such behaviors are included in the juvenile justice system and receive family court dispositions which stigmatize them as 'demoralized' persons. The growing number of juveniles dealt with by family courts, due to 'signs of demoralization' suggest that in practice such proceedings are used as a substitute for an effective system of support for the child and his family encountering problems.

It should also be noted that the Committee on the Rights of the Child in its General Comment No. 10 emphasized the need to recognize procedural rights and safeguards of every child alleged as, accused of, or recognized as having infringed the penal law. In this context the Committee points out to Article 40 of the Convention containing an important list of rights and guarantees aiming to ensure fair treatment and trial for juveniles (Committee on the Rights of the Child 2007). In Poland, juvenile proceedings due to both 'signs of demoralization' and 'punishable acts' are based on provisions of civil procedure which does not provide the same guarantees of fair trial as those required in criminal cases. Undoubtedly, there is some discrepancy between the legal state and practice in Poland and both recommendations of the Committee on the Rights of the Child and standards developed by the European Court of Human Rights on procedural safeguards for juveniles (Stańdo-Kawecka and Kusztal 2015).

TRENDS IN JUVENILE CRIME OVER THE PERIOD 2004–2014

As in many other countries, juvenile crime has been perceived as a serious social problem, in Poland. It was particularly in the 1990s, the first decade after the political and economic transformation, when a growing number of juvenile offenses was proposed by some criminologists to be one of three dangerous phenomenon, the other two being economic crimes and organized crimes. At the same time it was stressed that changes in juvenile delinquency had not been merely quantitative, but also qualitative, because juvenile crime had become increasingly violent (Siemaszko 2000). Such conclusions were based on the analysis of statistical data published by the police. A self-report delinquency study carried out in the school year 2002/2003 on a national random school sample of 13- to 16-year-old youth did not confirm such an alarming picture of juvenile crime. The results suggested that the prevalence of criminal behaviors among youth was significantly lower than publically perceived. Respondents mainly admitted to nonserious behavior, mostly to taking parents' money without their consent, shoplifting, buying, or receiving stolen goods. However, they also frequently admitted to behavior which was typical for youth but of a more serious nature, such as brawl or assault (Kossowska 2007). It should be added that the results of the self-report delinquency study have to be interpreted with caution because only youth attending schools participated in the research which did not cover young people who dropped out of school.

The current picture of juvenile crime is unclear due to the lack of reliable data. After 2002/2003 no further self-report delinquency studies were conducted on a national sample. Therefore, there are no self-reported data which would allow for an assessment of the long-term trends in juvenile offending. Before 2013 the basic source of knowledge about trends in juvenile crime was the official police statistic. In the period from 1990 to 2012, the police recorded the number of both juvenile offenses and juvenile suspects. They recorded offences or fiscal offenses as 'juvenile offenses' when in the course of police actions taken before referring the case to the family court it was confirmed that the offense was committed by a suspect who was at least 13 but under 17 years of age. Undoubtedly, police statistics did not reflect the actual size of youth crime, because they might be affected by many factors, such as the changing social climate around juvenile crime, the concentration of the police work on certain juvenile lawbreakers, or organizational changes in the police forces. The official police data, however, were collected in a consistent manner and could form the basis for cautious estimations of tendencies in juvenile crime.

In 2013 the manner of collecting data on juvenile crime by the police was modified. Juvenile offenses were recorded by the police only after receiving the information from the family court on the institution and completion of juvenile proceedings concerning a 'punishable act' (Komenda Główna Policji 2014). In 2014 police statistics on crimes did not include offenses committed by juveniles, because in accordance with the amended methodology the specification of the number of juveniles who committed 'punishable acts' took place during court proceedings after the referral of the case by the police to the family court (Główny Urząd Statystyczny 2015). Due to modified methodology of collecting data on juvenile offenses and juvenile suspects the data recorded by the police before 2013 cannot be compared with later data.

As can be seen from Fig. 17.1, the numbers of both juvenile offenses and juvenile suspects recorded by the police were relatively stable in the years 2004–2008. In the next years (2008–2011) the number of juvenile offenses went up although at the same time the number of juvenile suspects remained stable or even diminished. In 2012 the upward trend concerning juvenile crime reversed. In 2013 the

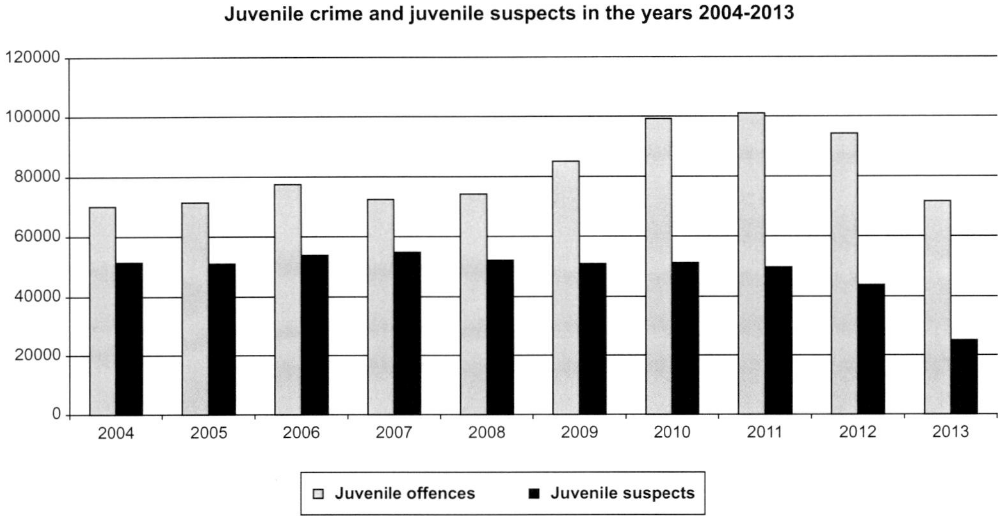

FIGURE 17.1. Number of juvenile crime and juvenile suspects in the years 2004–2013. *Source*: Komeda Główna Policji. (2014). *Przestępczość nieletnich w latach 1990–2013*. Retrieved from http://statystyka.policja.pl/st/wybrane-statystyki/przestepczosc-nieletni/50256,dok.html.

numbers of juvenile offenses as well as juvenile suspects continued to decline, but data coming from that year might be influenced by changes in data collection.

Family court statistics reveal the decline in the number of juveniles adjudicated due to 'punishable acts' in the years 2004–2014 (Fig. 17.2). What is interesting is the fact that in the same period the number of juveniles adjudicated due to 'signs of demoralization' remained at a relatively high level. Generally, under the 1982 JA, which introduced proceedings in juvenile cases concerning 'signs of demoralization,' the number of juveniles adjudicated in such proceedings grew at a much faster rate than the number of juveniles adjudicated due to 'punishable acts' (Stańdo-Kawecka 2015).

CAUSES OF JUVENILE CRIME

Research and discussions on causes of juvenile crime have a long tradition in Poland. As early as the interwar period, social scientists and lawyers devoted much attention to issues related to the etiology of juvenile crime. At that time social factors, such as family breakdown, poverty, unemployment, alcoholism among parents, as well as low moral and ethical levels of parents, were recognized causes of child and youth crime. Additionally, psychological characteristics of children were indicated as conducive to juvenile crime. Generally, the developing Polish criminology field during the interwar period tried to combine exogenous and endogenous factors when explaining the etiology of both the adult and juvenile crime (Rodak 2009).

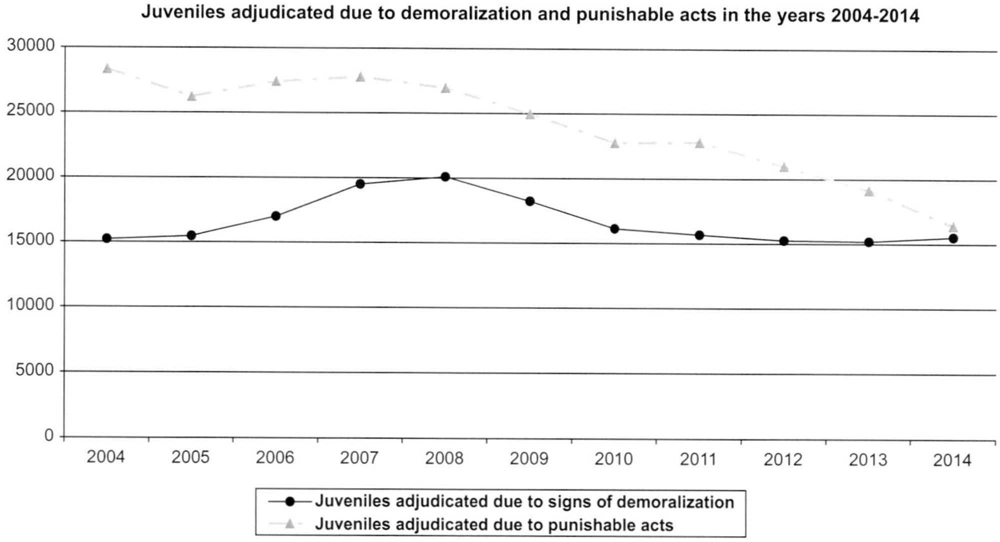

FIGURE 17.2. Number of juveniles adjudicated due to 'punishable acts' and 'signs of demoralization' in the years 2004–2014. Source: Ministerstwo Sprawiedliwości (Ministry of Justice 2015a). Wydział Statystycznej Informacji Zarządczej Departament Strategii i Funduszy Europejskich. *Nieletni—prawomocne orzeczenia w latach 2003–2014*. Retrieved from http://isws.ms.gov.pl/pl/baza-statystyczna/opracowania-wieloletnie/.

Intensive research work focused on causes of juvenile crime that took place in the 1960s and 1970s within the Polish Academy of Sciences. In 1955 in the Institute of State and Law of the Polish Academy of Sciences, the Department of Criminology was established at the initiative of Professor Stanisław Batawia who was the founder of the Polish school of criminology. From the very beginning researchers of the department studied causes of juvenile crime in close connection with problems concerning 'morally neglected' children. In the course of research projects conducted at the department, the latter term was replaced by the concept of socially maladjusted children. The definition of social maladjustment applied to children whose behavior was characterized by a set of signs showing that they repeatedly did not observe some of the fundamental social norms expected of young people of that age (Ostrihanska 1978a). As a result of such a research-oriented approach, the studies conducted covered not only causes of juvenile crime but also causes of juvenile predelinquent behaviors, that is truancy, failure to complete elementary school, loitering in the streets, spending time in the company of demoralized friends, drinking, drug-taking, or promiscuity.

Criminological studies on the etiology of juvenile crime and predelinquent behaviors which were carried out in the 1960s and 1970s paid much attention on family background. The studies revealed that in many cases the families of socially maladjusted or delinquent juveniles had not satisfied the needs of children. Among the most common family factors which contributed to both predelinquent and delinquent behaviors of juveniles were the following: family antagonisms and conflicts, breakup of the family, alcoholism, the absence of sufficient parental care and supervision, inadequate methods used by parents in bringing up their children, criminal or demoralized parents who presented socially undesirable behavior patterns to the child, lack of interest in the child and weakened emotional bonds between the child and his or her parents. Unsatisfied emotional needs led the child to seek compensation outside the home in the company of peers experiencing similar situations, resulting in the formation of youth delinquent groups. Family background was found to be a factor of great importance for both juvenile delinquency and the persistence in violations of criminal law. As noted by Kołakowska-Przełomiec (1977, 1978), those juveniles who persisted in their antisocial and offending behavior were frequently brought up in worse family backgrounds than juveniles who reformed.

Other factors that were found to be correlated with juvenile social maladjustment and delinquency, based on the criminological research conducted in the 1960s and 1970s, were school failure and psychological determinants. Wójcik (1978), for example, emphasized that school failure increased the risk of youth predelinquent and delinquent behaviors, particularly when linked with other factors detrimental to a child's development. The probability of manifestations of social maladjustment and criminal behaviors grew with the agglomeration of a large number of negative factors in the child's living situation that is family background, school progress, or personality. Studies on psychological determinants often dealt with specific issues such as neurotic symptoms or damages of the central nervous system. Generally, the results of such studies indicated that in a group of juvenile offenders, and particularly juvenile recidivists, there was an accumulation of diverse physical–psychological disturbances which coexisted with adverse elements of the family and school situation (Ostrihanska 1978b).

After the political, economic, and social transformations in Poland some researchers stressed the importance of macro-social factors, such as the lack of stable social structures in postmodern societies and the risk of social exclusion of young people because of the changing labor market and growing unemployment (Wysocka-Pleczyk 2009). Most contemporary criminological, pedagogical, and psychological studies on causes of juvenile crime are still dominated by the multifactorial approach. According to this approach, there is no single cause of juvenile crime, but it is rational to search for different factors and variables which affect the functioning of socially maladjusted persons (Gierowski et al. 2009). A detailed analysis of the results of research conducted in this area would require a separate study. Generally, they confirm findings from the 1960s and 1970s according to which the risk of crime and particularly the risk of reoffending increases with the number of accumulated adverse factors connected with the family background, school failure, and individual psychological characteristics (Rzeplińska 2009, 2011).

POLICING AND JUVENILES

Since 1982 family courts have played a dominant role in juvenile proceedings. According to the original wording of the JA, juvenile proceedings consisted of three stages: explanatory proceeding, which was equivalent of preparatory proceeding in adult criminal cases; court proceeding; and enforcement proceeding. The preparatory stage was instituted and conducted by the family judge who after its completion transferred the case to the court stage. In 2013 the JA was amended.[9] As a result of the amendment, juvenile cases due to 'demoralization' as well as 'punishable acts' were dealt with by a family court in a unified court proceeding which did not distinguish the preparatory stage. The scope of activities of the police in juvenile cases was very limited under the original wording of the JA and is still limited after the 2013 amendment.

In terms of Article 32e of JA, the police are competent to collect and preserve evidence of 'signs of demoralization' and 'punishable acts,' including the interrogation of a juvenile suspect, in urgent cases. 'Urgent cases' refer to cases in which it is necessary to collect and preserve traces and evidence of juvenile offences and 'signs of demoralization' against loss or damage, before the formal initiation of proceedings by a family court. The police are obliged to report the case immediately to the family court after performing urgent actions. Empirical research indicates a discrepancy between the normative assumptions of the JA and the practice of dealing with juvenile suspects. In practice, information on juvenile suspects is usually obtained, at first by the police and in many cases the police take several evidence-gathering actions before referring the case to the family court (Czarnecka-Dzialuk et al. 2011; Jasiński and Pietryka 2014; Stańdo-Kawecka and Kusztal 2016). Thus, 'urgent cases' are interpreted broadly. The police have no discretionary powers; on the contrary, they are obliged to report every juvenile case immediately to a family court after having collected and stored the necessary evidence in urgent cases.

The role of the public prosecutor in juvenile proceedings has also been very limited. The JA does not provide for separation of functions of the prosecution and adjudication. A public prosecutor is party to the proceedings in juvenile cases and is entitled to submit requests for the performance of evidence, access files and make copies, attend the family court hearing as well as bring appeals, but does not present accusation nor makes decisions concerning the prosecution of punishable acts. Decisions to initiate formal proceedings in juvenile cases are taken exclusively by family courts.

[9]See *Ustawa z dnia 30 sierpnia 2013 r. o zmianie ustawy o postępowaniu w sprawach nieletnich oraz niektórych innych ustaw*, Journal of Laws 2013, pos. 1165.

COURTS AND JUVENILES

Juvenile cases with a few exceptions are dealt with by family courts. As mentioned earlier, no penalties provided for adults could be imposed on juvenile lawbreakers by family courts. The JA in the current wording[10] enables the family court to impose a penalty exclusively in the course of enforcement proceedings if the juvenile at first was given the disposition of the placement in a correctional institution but he completed 18 years before this judgment started to be enforced and the execution of the correctional measure would be inadvisable in the opinion of the court.[11] In practice, the latter possibility has been used by family courts extremely rarely. In cases concerning 15- and 16-year-old juveniles suspected of most serious crimes, the family court can transfer the case to the public prosecutor in order to bring an accusation to the common criminal court. Juvenile offenders exceptionally tried in common criminal courts may receive penalties provided for adults. The proceedings in such cases are criminal proceedings and sanctions imposed in these proceedings are not included in statistics on family court dispositions in juvenile cases.

Formal judgments issued by the family court in juvenile cases include the imposition of educational, medical, or correctional measures. According to the JA, all educational and medical measures may be applied both to juveniles who have committed 'punishable acts' while between 13 and 16 years of age and to juveniles less than 18 years of age displaying problematic behaviors ('signs of demoralization'). Correctional measures, this is suspended or unsuspended placement of a juvenile in a correctional institution, may be imposed only on juveniles who have committed 'punishable acts' prohibited by the criminal law as offenses or fiscal offenses after the 13th birthday, but prior to the 17th.

While choosing between different measures the family court should take into account the interest of the juvenile concerned, the need to achieve positive changes in his personality and behavior, as well as the need to encourage and support proper fulfillment of duties by the juvenile's parents or guardians. With regard to correctional measures, some additional factors should be pointed out, such as a high degree of the perpetrator's negative antisocial attitudes and behaviors, the circumstances and the nature of the act committed, as well as ineffectiveness of educational measures which have proved unsuccessful in resocializing offenders. The JA does not require the establishment of the culpability of the juvenile in the meaning of his ability to act with discernment at the time of the 'punishable act,' because the legislator considers this to be irrelevant for the

[10] Before the 2013 amendment to the JA it was also possible for the family court to impose a penalty provided for adults on a juvenile perpetrator of a punishable act who at the time of adjudication completed 18 years of age and the family court was of the opinion that the placement in a correctional institution would be inadvisable. In practice, this possibility was used by family courts extremely rarely.

[11] See Article 94 of the 1982 JA.

choice of the most adequate measure. It also does not provide the principle of proportionality in reactions to the seriousness of the 'punishable act.'

The catalog of educational measures has changed since 1982 to a limited extent. Currently, Article 6 of the JA enumerates the following educational measures:

(a) A reprimand
(b) Supervision by parents, a guardian, a youth or other social organization, a workplace, a trustworthy person, or a probation officer
(c) Applying special conditions, such as redressing the damage, making an apology to the victim, performing unpaid work for the benefit of the victim or local community, taking up school education or a job, taking part in educational or therapeutic training, avoiding specific locations, refraining from the use of alcohol and other intoxicants
(d) A ban on driving
(e) Forfeiture of objects gained through the commission of a punishable act
(f) Placing a juvenile in a youth probation center in which he spends a couple of hours daily
(g) Placing a juvenile in a professional foster family
(h) Placing a juvenile in a suitable institution or organization providing education, therapy, or vocational training
(i) Placing a juvenile in a residential youth educational center

The vast majority of educational measures do not change the place of residence of the juvenile who stays with his family during the enforcement of imposed measures. Among measures resulting in the change of residence may be the placement of a juvenile in a professional foster family, in an organization or institution functioning as a boarding school as well as in a youth educational center. Medical measures may be applied to juveniles who are suffering from mental deficiency, mental disease, some kind of mental disorder or from alcohol and drug addiction. These measures imply placing juveniles in a psychiatric hospital, other suitable health care institutions, a social welfare institution, or a suitable youth educational center. Both educational and medical measures are applied for an indeterminate period of time. As a rule these measures terminate when a juvenile reaches the age of 18, but in some cases their duration is extended to his 21st birthday. The family court that executes the measures may change, revise, or repeal them at any time if it is advisable for educational reasons.

The most severe measures provided by the JA are correctional measures. They consist of suspended or unsuspended placement of a juvenile in a correctional institution. Similar to other categories of measures, the correctional ones are also applied for an indeterminate period of time. The juvenile placed in a correctional institution can stay there not longer than up to 21 years of age, although he may be granted conditional release earlier.

In practice, family court dispositions in proceedings concerning 'punishable acts' impose mainly educational measures (Ministerstwo Sprawiedliwości

[Ministry of Justice] 2015b). In the period 2004–2014, the total number of juveniles on whom educational, medical, and correctional measures were imposed due to 'punishable acts' declined from 28,342 in 2004 to 16,388 in 2014 (Table 17.1). The structure of imposed measures remained relatively stable. The most frequently applied measures were educational measures, including reprimand, supervision by a probation officer, supervision by parents, and applying special conditions. As can be seen from the Table 17.1, in the analyzed period about one in three juveniles on whom measures were imposed due to 'punishable acts' received reprimand and also one in three were placed under the supervision of a probation officer. The numbers and percentages of juvenile offenders placed under the supervision of parents were falling while application of special conditions showed an upward trend. Other educational measures that were enumerated in Table 17.1 were imposed on juvenile perpetrators of 'punishable acts' significantly rarely, including the placement of a juvenile in a youth educational center. The latter disposition was received by 811 in 2013 and 728 in 2014.

In comparison with educational measures, the medical ones have been used by family courts very rarely. In 2014 there were 78 juveniles adjudicated due to punishable acts who received medical measures, including 16 juveniles placed in a

Table 17.1. Selected educational measures imposed on juvenile offenders in the years 2004–2014

	Total number of juveniles on whom measures[a] *were imposed*	*Supervision by a probation officer*		*Supervision by parents*		*Application of special conditions*		*Reprimand*	
		N.	*%*	*N.*	*%*	*N.*	*%*	*N.*	*%*
2004	28,342	9445	33.3	4930	17.4	3980	14	10,125	35.7
2005	26,228	8508	32.4	4489	17.1	4514	17.2	9257	35.3
2006	27,419	8914	32.5	4604	16.8	5177	18.9	9695	35.4
2007	27,790	8689	31.3	4633	16.7	6052	21.8	10,034	36.1
2008	26,957	8554	31.7	4244	15.7	5882	21.8	9569	35.5
2009	24,953	7910	31.7	3657	14.7	5835	23.4	8581	34.4
2010	22,758	7615	33.5	3323	14.6	5721	25.1	7338	32.2
2011	22,807	7273	31.9	3022	13.3	5914	25.9	7707	33.8
2012	20,980	6559	31.3	2698	12.9	6032	28.8	6972	33.2
2013	19,135	5782	30.2	2328	12.2	5435	28.4	6374	33.3
2014	16,388	4923	30	1738	10.6	4428	27	5686	34.7

Note: Statistical data in this Table show the most frequently applied educational measures. Family courts imposed on juvenile offenders also other educational measures but less frequently

[a]Data in this column refer to the number of juveniles on whom educational, medical, and correctional measures were imposed and not the number of measures. Educational measures may be combined what means that the family court may impose two or more educational measures on the same juvenile

Source: For the years 2004–2012 Główny Urząd Statystyczny (Central Statistical Office). Rocznik Statystyczny Rzeczypospolitej Polskiej (Statistical Yearbook of the Republic of Poland). Warsaw, yearly publication; for the years 2013–2014 Ministerstwo Sprawiedliwości (Ministry of Justice 2015b). Wydział Statystycznej Informacji Zarządczej Departament Strategii i Funduszy Europejskich. *Nieletni wg orzeczonych środków prawomocne orzeczenia w latach 2008–2014*. Retrieved from http://isws.ms.gov.pl/pl/baza-statystyczna/opracowania-wieloletnie/

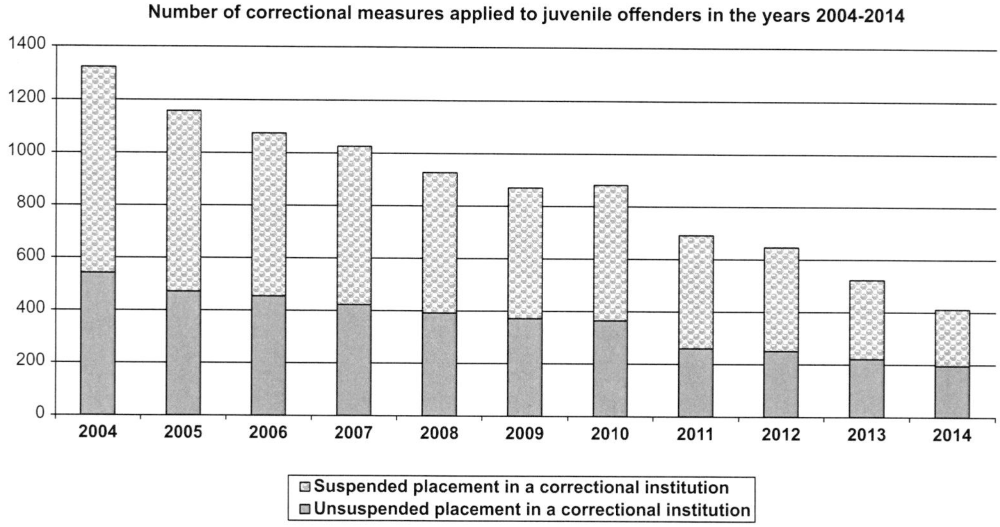

FIGURE 17.3. Number of correctional measures imposed on juvenile offenders in the years 2004–2014. Source: for the years 2004–2012 Główny Urząd Statystyczny (Central Statistical Office). Rocznik Statystyczny Rzeczypospolitej Polskiej (Statistical Yearbook of the Republic of Poland). Warsaw, yearly publication; for the years 2013–2014 Ministerstwo Sprawiedliwości (Ministry of Justice 2015b). Wydział Statystycznej Informacji Zarządczej Departament Strategii i Funduszy Europejskich. *Nieletni wg orzeczonych środków prawomocne orzeczenia w latach 2008–2014*. Retrieved from http://isws.ms.gov.pl/pl/baza-statystyczna/opracowania-wieloletnie/.

psychiatric hospital and 57 in other health care institutions (Ministerstwo Sprawiedliwości [Ministry of Justice] 2015b). The same applies to correctional measures, this is the most severe measure provided by the JA for juvenile offenders. Figure 17.3 shows the clear downward trend in the use of correctional measures. In 2004 such measures were imposed on 1322 juveniles, including 781 juveniles who received a suspended correctional measure, and 541 juveniles placed in a correctional institution without suspension. In 2014 there were only 411 dispositions concerning the placement of a juvenile in a correctional institution, most of which (216) referred to a suspended measure.

It may be added that a steady decline in the use of correctional measures has been a long-term tendency in Poland (Stańdo-Kawecka 2015). Due to the lack of empirical research it is not possible to explain this tendency clearly. It may be assumed that family judges dealing with juvenile offenders are reluctant to place them in correctional institutions because they do not consider it to be in the interest of juveniles. Another possible explanation refers to the assumption that family judges who adjudicate juvenile cases under the civil procedure use cautiously, measures of 'penal' origin as is the case with the correctional institution. The latter hypothesis seems to be particularly substantial after the judgment of the European Court of Human Rights in the case *Adamkiewicz v. Poland*. The

Court found the violation of the European Convention of Human Rights because of the lack of procedural safeguards in juvenile proceeding which resulted in the placement of the juvenile concerned in a correctional institution.

CUSTODIAL RULES FOR JUVENILES (DETENTION, PRISON, MIXING JUVENILES WITH ADULTS)

Juvenile offenders as a rule are not criminally responsible and are not subject to penalties provided for adults. As a result, they are not deprived of their liberty in prisons or remand prisons with the exception of a small number of offenders who committed one of the most serious crimes while being 15 or 16 years of age and were subject to criminal liability in accordance with provisions of the Criminal Code. Prison statistics confirm that both temporary detention in a remand prison and prison sentences apply to juveniles extremely rarely. In December 2014 there was only one juvenile who was aged between 15 and 16 years who was temporarily arrested. At the same time no person below 17 years of age was serving a prison sentence (Ministerstwo Sprawiedliwości [Ministry of Justice] 2015d). Offenders who were 17 years of age at the time of the offense are treated as adults under the criminal law and may be punished with prison sentences. Pursuant to the 1997 Code of Execution of Sentences, all prisoners below 21 years of age serve their prison sentences in prisons for young adults. Such prisons may be organized as a separate penitentiary institution or a separate unit in an institution designed also for other groups of prisoners. Young adult prisoners—with the exception of those punished with short substitute sentences—serve their terms under the therapeutic or programmed treatment system. In both cases an individual sentence plan is prepared for them.

Apart from youth exceptionally criminally responsible under provisions provided for adults, juvenile offenders are dealt with by family courts and receive educational, medical or correctional measures. A vast majority of educational measures applied to juveniles do not deprive them of their liberty, with the exception of placement in a youth educational center. Similarly, correctional measures (unsuspended placement in a correctional institution) as well as some medical measures (placement in a psychiatric hospital, other health care institution) are custodial measures. Institutions in which such measures are enforced are subordinated to different ministries and governed according to different rules (Helsinki Foundation for Human Rights 2014).

Correctional institutions are public institutions subordinated to the Ministry of Justice, but they do not form any part of the prison system. Some basic provisions which relate to granting inmates' rewards, disciplinary penalties, or measures of restraint are included in the JA. Detailed regulations concerning the functioning of correctional institutions are issued by the Minister of Justice.[12] Provisions included in the order issued by the Minister of Justice emphasize the need to prepare an individual treatment plan for each juvenile and provide him or her with a broad range of therapeutic, educational, and vocational activities in order to achieve the goal of resocialization. It should be added that in 2012 the Constitutional Court ruled that several provisions on correctional institutions issued by the Minister of Justice were unconstitutional, because they regulated matters related to the limitation of personal liberty which required the statutory basis. The Prosecutor General while outlining his position before the Constitutional Court stated that the legislator provided adult offenders serving prison sentences with significantly higher standards of protection of their rights and freedoms than juveniles placed in correctional institutions.[13] The judgment of the Constitutional Court resulted in some amendments introduced to the JA in order to provide statutory basis for the imposition of disciplinary penalties and using measures of restraint. However, the enforcement of correctional measures is still underregulated in the sense that there is insufficient statutory basis for some forms of the interference with personal rights of juveniles, such as strip searches or surveillance cameras in rooms.

The lack of sufficient statutory regulations also relates the enforcement of educational measures consisting in the depriving juveniles of their liberty in youth educational centers which may be public or private and are subordinated to the Ministry of Education. Given the complexity of this issue, the detailed analyses of rules governing the enforcement of educational, medical, and correctional measures which deprive juveniles of their liberty would require a separate study.

ALTERNATIVE SANCTIONS FOR JUVENILES

In a broad sense the whole juvenile justice system shaped in the 1980s is meant as a way to divert juvenile offenders from the criminal justice system. It is based on the dominant role of family court judges who at their judgments in juvenile cases are guided by the interest of juveniles and their needs. 'Diversion' in the narrower sense can be understood as efforts aiming at the avoidance of formal court proceedings and/or formal court dispositions. In Poland, the possibility to divert juveniles from formal court proceedings and formal dispositions is limited. First, the JA empowers family courts to diversion with nonintervention. Unlike criminal processes in adult cases which are based on the principles of legality the family court may at any time drop unconditionally the juvenile case on the principle

[12]See *Rozporządzenie Ministra Sprawiedliwości z dnia 17 października 2001 r. w sprawie zakładów poprawczych i schronisk dla nieletnich*, Journal of Laws 2001/124, pos. 1359 with subsequent amendments.

[13]See Wyrok Trybunału Konstytucyjnego z dnia 2 października 2012 r., U 1/12.

of expediency if it is in the opinion of the court that the imposition of educational or correctional measures serve no purpose, in particular when such measures have been imposed on the juvenile in a previous case. Thus, the family court has been equipped by the legislator with discretionary power to discontinue the proceedings.

Second, the family court may at any time refer the case to a mediation program or to the school attended by the juvenile or a social organization to which he belongs, if the court is of the opinion that the educational measures available to the school or organization are sufficient. The transfer of a juvenile case to a school or a social organization is possible only if the juvenile agrees (Article 32j § 1 of the JA). In practice, such a way of diverting juveniles from formal court dispositions does not play a significant role; in 2012–2013, respectively, 27 and 25 juvenile suspects were transferred to schools or social organizations (Główny Urząd Statystyczny 2014).

The legal basis for mediation in juvenile cases is included in Article 3a § 1 of the JA. Pursuant to its provisions the family court may at any time refer the case to mediation by an institution or a trustworthy person. Mediation is voluntary and requires consent of the juvenile suspect and victim. The results of the mediation reported to the family court by the mediator are taken into consideration when deciding the case. The family court may drop the proceedings unconditionally at an early stage as a result of successful mediation. The positive results of mediation, and particularly the performance by the juvenile obligations arising from an agreement reached in mediation, may also be taken into account by the family court while deciding on the measures (educational or correctional) applied to the perpetrator.

Despite long-term efforts made by the Ministry of Justice and nongovernmental organizations in order to promote victim–offender mediation (Stańdo-Kawecka and Deszyńska 2013) the results are less than expected. In the last decade, family courts adjudicated yearly from 28 thousands (in 2004) to 16 thousands (in 2014) of juveniles due to punishable acts. The number of mediations in juvenile cases in the years 2004–2014 oscillated between 198 and 366 (Fig. 17.4). Thus, the ratio of juvenile offenders participating in mediation in comparison to the number of juvenile perpetrators of 'punishable acts' adjudicated by family courts amounted to 1–1.5%.

It seems that the limited use of mediation in juvenile cases to some extent is connected with the paternalistic welfare approach to juvenile offenders included in the JA. This approach is focused on the needs of juvenile offenders who are considered as victims of negative personal, family, and school circumstances and not as moral agents responsible for their behavior. The needs of victims of juvenile crimes are considered less important than the social and educational needs of juvenile offenders. Educational value of victim–offender mediation is appreciated by a few family judges who are personally interested in restorative practices.

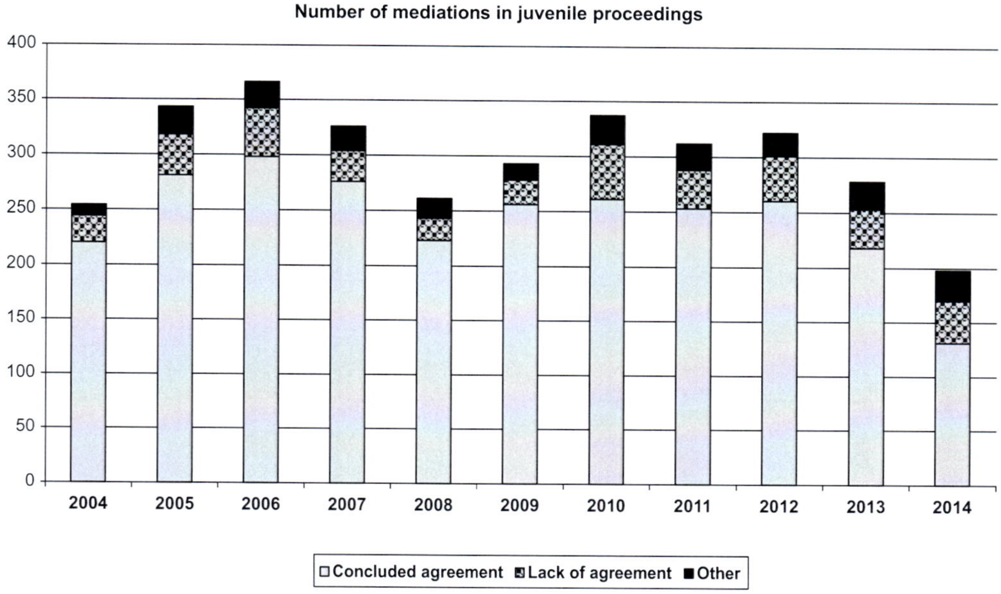

FIGURE 17.4. Number of mediations in juvenile cases according to results of mediation proceedings in the years 2004–2014. Source: Ministerstwo Sprawiedliwości (Ministry of Justice 2015c). *Mediacje w sprawach nieletnich w latach 2004-I p. 2015 r*. Retrieved from http://isws.ms.gov.pl/pl/baza-statystyczna/opracowania-wieloletnie/.

DIFFERENCES IN TREATMENT OF BOYS AND GIRLS

Research on juvenile crime for many years has focused on boys' criminality while delinquent girls were in the background (Rode 2009). Currently, a growing interest in crime committed by girls may be observed although research in this area is still limited.

Family court statistics indicate that in the last decades the number of girls adjudicated due to 'punishable acts' have grown faster than the number of boys. On a basis of those statistics Wieczorek (2006) found that the percentage of girls in the population of adjudicated juveniles increased from 6.2% in 1985 to 8.8% in 1998. He also stated that the trend toward growing proportion of girls in the population of juvenile offenders was confirmed by the analysis of the ratio of adjudicated girls in relation to 10 thousand population of girls which went up at a faster rate than was the case with adjudicated boys (p. 74). In the years 2004–2014 the same tendency was visible in court statistics. Although boys still represent the overwhelming majority of juveniles adjudicated due to 'punishable acts' (Fig. 17.5), the proportion of girls increased from 13% in 2004 to 21% in 2014.

At the same time there has also been a rise in the proportion of girls adjudicated due to 'signs of demoralization.' In 2004, one out of four juveniles adjudicated in such proceedings was a girl and in 2014—one out of three (Ministerstwo Sprawiedliwości [Ministry of Justice] 2015a). The growing participation of girls

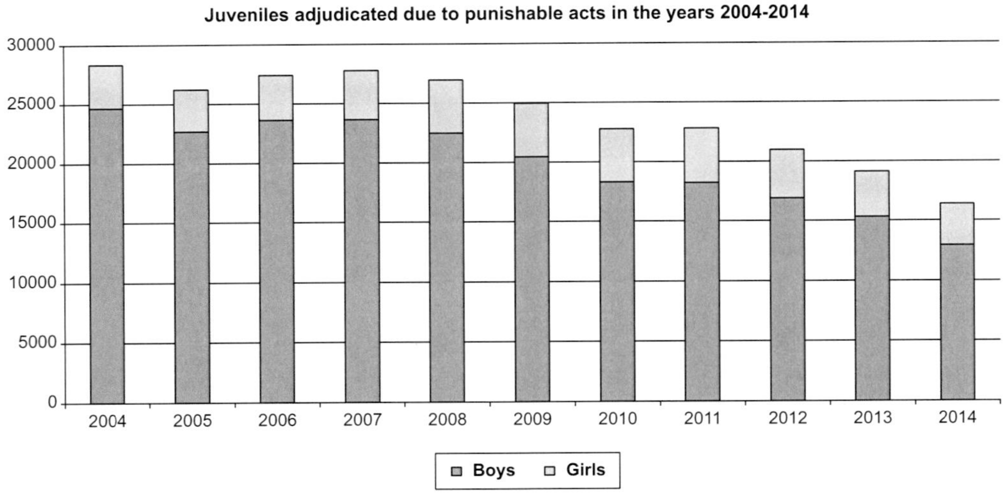

FIGURE 17.5. Number of boys and girls adjudicated due to punishable acts in the years 2004–2014. Source: Ministerstwo Sprawiedliwości (Ministry of Justice 2015a). Wydział Statystycznej Informacji Zarządczej Departament Strategii i Funduszy Europejskich. *Nieletni—prawomocne orzeczenia w latach 2003–2014*. Retrieved from http://isws.ms.gov.pl/pl/baza-statystyczna/opracowania-wieloletnie/.

in the group of juveniles adjudicated by family courts in proceedings concerning both 'punishable acts' and 'signs of demoralization' inspires research on types of crimes committed by girls as well as causes of delinquency among girls (Woźniakowska 2007). So far, the problem of different treatment of delinquent boys and girls has not been the subject of research.

CONCLUSIONS

In Poland, the juvenile justice system is significantly different from the adult criminal justice system. It may be said that the whole system of dealing with juvenile offenders is an alternative to the criminal process and aims at diverting juveniles from criminal proceedings provided for adults. Family courts which were entrusted with juvenile proceedings focus more on the needs of juvenile offenders than the nature and seriousness of acts committed by them. The catalog of measures applied to juveniles differs from penalties provided for adults. According to legal regulations, educational, medical, and correctional measures are imposed on juveniles not in order to punish, but to support, educate, and resocialize them. Family court judgments on the application of measures do not constitute a 'conviction' in the meaning of the criminal law and are registered in a record separate from the criminal record. As a result, the imposition of measures on juveniles has less stigmatizing effects than sentences given by criminal courts.

It does not mean, however, that the juvenile justice system is free from controversial issues. Currently, such matters give cause for concern as the legal status of a juvenile in juvenile proceedings and the growing number of juveniles adjudicated due to 'signs of demoralization.' In the light of international standards concerning rights of children in conflict with the law, the individualized approach to juvenile offenders dealt with by family courts under civil procedure do not seem to be properly balanced with procedural safeguards. A relatively large number of juveniles adjudicated due to 'signs of demoralization' leads to worrying conclusions, that in practice such proceedings may be used as a substitute for effective prevention programs which should be offered to families facing problems and children at risk. Additionally, among problematic issues there are the lack of coordination between different ministries dealing with juveniles and a very limited scope of research on the effectiveness of measures imposed on them.

REFERENCES

Albrecht, H. J. (2013). Juvenile criminal law and justice in Germany—Accounting for trends in the German Juvenile Criminal Law System. In A. Sözüer (Ed.), *3rd International Crime and Punishment Film Festival. Juvenile Justice. Academic Papers* (pp. 643–686), Istanbul.

Bojarski, T., Kruk, E., & Skrętowicz, E. (2014). *Ustawa o postępowaniu w sprawach nieletnich. Komentarz*. Warszawa: LexisNexis.

Committee on the Rights of the Child. (2007). *General Comment No. 10 (2007), Children's rights in juvenile justice*. Retrieved from http://www2.ohchr.org/english/bodies/crc/docs/GC10_en.doc

Czarnecka-Dzialuk, B., Drapała, K., & Więcek-Durańska, A. (2011). *Analiza postępowań karnych oraz przed sądem dla nieletnich o wybrane czyny karalne popełnione przez osoby w wieku 15–17 lat*. Warsaw: Institute of Justice. Retrieved Dec 1, 2015, from http://www.iws.org.pl/pliki/files/badania/raporty/raporty11/AR_Czarnecka-Dzialuk%20,Drapa%C5%82a,%20Wi%C4%99cek-Dura%C5%84ska%20Analiza%20post%C4%99powa%C5%84%20_nieletni_%202011.pdf

European Committee for the Prevention of Torture and Inhuman or Degrading Treatment or Punishment. (2014). *Report to the Polish Government on the visit to Poland carried out by the European Committee for the Prevention of Torture and Inhuman or Degrading Treatment or Punishment (CPT), 5–17 June 2013*, Strasbourg. Retrieved from http://www.cpt.coe.int/documents/pol/2014-21-inf-eng.pdf

Gierowski, J. K., Jaśkiewicz-Obydzińska, T., Szaszkiewicz, M., Wach, E., & Cyboran, M. (2009). Modele przestępczego zachowania nieletnich dziewcząt i chłopców. In B. Gulla & M. Wysocka-Pleczyk (Eds.), *Przestępczość nieletnich. Dziecko jako ofiara i sprawca przemocy* (pp. 51–68). Kraków: Wydawnictwo Uniwersytetu Jagiellońskiego.

Główny Urząd Statystyczny (Central Statistical Office). (2014). *Rocznik Statystyczny Rzeczypospolitej Polskiej (Statistical Yearbook of the republic of Poland)*. Warsaw. Retrieved Nov 28, 2015, from http://stat.gov.pl/obszary-tematyczne/roczniki-statystyczne/roczniki-statystyczne/rocznik-statystyczny-rzeczypospolitej-polskiej-2014,2,9.html

Główny Urząd Statystyczny (Central Statistical Office). (2015). *Mały Rocznik Statystyczny Polski (Concise Statistical Yearbook of Poland)*. Warsaw. Retrieved Nov 28, 2015, from http://stat.gov.pl/obszary-tematyczne/roczniki-statystyczne/roczniki-statystyczne/maly-rocznik-statystyczny-polski-2015,1,16.html

Helsinki Foundation for Human Rights. (2014). *Children's rights behind bars. Human rights of children deprived of liberty: Improving monitoring mechanisms. Poland national report*. Retrieved Dec 19, 2015, from http://www.childrensrightsbehindbars.eu/images/national-reports-2014/POLAND%20FINAL%20REPORT.pdf

Jasiński, W., & Pietryka, A. (2014). Rzetelność postępowania w sprawach nieletnich w świetle badań. In: M. Szwast, K., Wiśniewska, M. Wolny (Eds.), *Rzetelność postępowania w sprawach nieletnich*, Warsaw: Helsińska Fundacja Praw Człowieka. Retrieved Oct 28, 2015, from http://www.hfhr.pl/wp-content/uploads/2014/06/rzetelnosc_postepowania_w_sprawach_nieletnich.pdf

Kołakowska-Przełomiec, H. (1977). *Przestępczość i nieprzystosowanie społeczne nieletnich w genezie przestępczości dorosłych*. Wrocław: Zakład Narodowy im. Ossolińskich.

Kołakowska-Przełomiec, H. (1978). Środowisko rodzinne w świetle badań kryminologicznych. In J. Jasiński (Ed.), *Zagadnienia nieprzystosowania społecznego i przestępczości w Polsce* (pp. 319–343). Wrocław: Zakład Narodowy im. Ossolińskich.

Kołakowska-Przełomiec, H., & Wójcik, D. (1993). Idee Konwencji Praw Dziecka a Ustawa o postępowaniu w sprawach nieletnich. In J. Bińczycka (Ed.), *Prawa dziecka—deklaracje i rzeczywistość* (pp. 33–50). Warsaw: Oficyna Wydawnicza "Impuls".

Kołakowska-Przełomiec, H., Ostrihanska, Z., Kossowska, A., Wójcik, D., Krawczyk, J., Rzeplińska, I., et al. (1994, June 24). Nieletni do więzienia?, Rzeczpospolita 145. Retrieved from http://archiwum.rp.pl/artykul/18630-Nieletni-do-wiezienia.html

Komenda Główna Policji. (2014). *Przestępczość nieletnich w latach 1990–2013*. Retrieved Nov 28, 2015, from http://statystyka.policja.pl/st/wybrane-statystyki/przestepczosc-nieletni/50256,dok.html

Korcyl-Wolska, M. (2004). *Postępowanie w sprawach nieletnich*. Zakamycze: Kantor Wydawniczy Zakamycze.

Kossowska, A. (2007). Przestępczość i zachowania dewiacyjne współczesnej młodzieży polskiej (badania typu self-report). *Archiwum Kryminologii, 28*, 219–226.

Łopatka, A. (1993). Konwencja Praw Dziecka w Polsce. In J. Bińczycka (Ed.), *Prawa dziecka—deklaracje i rzeczywistość* (pp. 15–32). Warszawa: Oficyna Wydawnicza "Impuls".

Makarewicz, J. (1938). *Kodeks karny z komentarzem*. Lwów: Zakład Narodowy im. Ossolińskich.

Ministerstwo Sprawiedliwości (Ministry of Justice). (2015a). Wydział Statystycznej Informacji Zarządczej Departament Strategii i Funduszy Europejskich. *Nieletni—prawomocne orzeczenia w latach 2003–2014*. Retrieved Nov 16, 2015, from http://isws.ms.gov.pl/pl/baza-statystyczna/opracowania-wieloletnie/

Ministerstwo Sprawiedliwości (Ministry of Justice). (2015b). Wydział Statystycznej Informacji Zarządczej Departament Strategii i Funduszy Europejskich. *Nieletni wg orzeczonych środków prawomocne orzeczenia w latach 2008–2014*. Retrieved Nov 16, 2015, from http://isws.ms.gov.pl/pl/baza-statystyczna/opracowania-wieloletnie/

Ministerstwo Sprawiedliwości (Ministry of Justice). (2015c). *Mediacje w sprawach nieletnich w latach 2004-I p. 2015 r*. Retrieved Dec 20, 2015, from http://isws.ms.gov.pl/pl/baza-statystyczna/opracowania-wieloletnie/

Ministerstwo Sprawiedliwości (Ministry of Justice). (2015d). Centralny Zarząd Służby Więziennej. *Roczna informacja statystyczna za rok 2014*. Retrieved Dec 10, 2015, from http://sw.gov.pl/Data/Files/001c169lidz/rok-2014.pdf

Ostrihanska, Z. (1978a). Problem nieprzystosowania społecznego u młodzieży. In J. Jasiński (Ed.), *Zagadnienia nieprzystosowania społecznego i przestępczości w Polsce* (pp. 299–317). Wrocław: Zakład Narodowy im. Ossolińskich.

Ostrihanska, Z. (1978b). Psychologiczne determinanty niedostosowania społecznego i przestępczości. In J. Jasiński (Ed.), *Zagadnienia nieprzystosowania społecznego i przestępczości w Polsce* (pp. 379–408). Wrocław: Zakład Narodowy im. Ossolińskich.

Rodak, M. (2009). Międzywojenna polska debata kryminologiczna—Poszukiwanie społecznych przyczyn przestępczości i sposobów jej zwalczania. *Archiwum Kryminologii, 31*, 101–145.

Rode, M. (2009). Charakterystyka wybranych cech psychicznych nieletnich dziewcząt. In B. Gulla & M. Wysocka-Pleczyk (Eds.), *Przestępczość nieletnich. Dziecko jako ofiara i sprawca przemocy* (pp. 85–99). Kraków: Wydawnictwo Uniwersytetu Jagiellońskiego.
Rzeplińska, I. (2009). Sylwetki społeczne nieletnich—Późniejszych dorosłych sprawców przestępstw. *Archiwum Kryminologii, 29–30*, 409–415.
Rzeplińska, I. (2011). Nieletni w społeczeństwie. Obraz nieletnich sprawców czynów karalnych dawniejszych i współczesnych. In B. Stańdo-Kawecka & K. Krajewski (Eds.), *Problemy penologii i praw człowieka na początku XXI stulecia. Księga poświęcona pamięci Profesora Zbigniewa Hołdy* (pp. 669–680). Warsaw: Wolters Kluwer.
Siemaszko, A. (2000). Crime and criminal policy in Poland: A look back and into the future. In A. Siemaszko (Ed.), *Crime & law enforcement in Poland on the threshold of the 21 century* (pp. 15–25). Warsaw: Oficyna Naukowa.
Sienkiewicz, Z. (1988). Sporne kwestie wokół pojęcia demoralizacji i nieprzystosowania społecznego. In T. Bojarski (Ed.), *Postępowanie z nieletnimi. Orzekanie i wykonywanie środków wychowawczych i poprawczych* (pp. 166–183). Lublin: Uniwersytet Marii-Curie Skłodowskiej.
Stańdo-Kawecka, B. (1993). Charakter prawny zakładu poprawczego w kodeksie karnym z 1932 r. *Przegląd Więziennictwa Polskiego, 4–5*, 3–16.
Stańdo-Kawecka, B. (2015). Juvenile justice in Poland. In F. E. Zimring, M. Langer, & D. S. Tanenhaus (Eds.), *Juvenile justice in global perspective* (pp. 291–326). New York: New York University Press.
Stańdo-Kawecka, B., & Deszyńska, J. (2013). Restorative justice in Poland. In A. Pitsela & E. Symeonidou-Kastanidou (Eds.), *Restorative justice in criminal matters. Comparative research in 11 European countries* (pp. 187–212). Athens-Thessalonica: Sakkoulas.
Stańdo-Kawecka, B., & Krajewski, K. (2010). Polen. In F. Dünkel, T. Lappi-Seppälä, C. Morgenstern, & D. van Zyl Smit (Eds.), *Kriminalität, Kriminalpolitik, strafrechtliche Sanktionspraxis und Gefangenenraten im europäischen Vergleich* (pp. 691–733). Mönchengladbach: Forum Verlag Godesberg.
Stańdo-Kawecka, B., & Kusztal, J. (2015). Procedural complexity within a welfare approach. Country report Poland. In M. Panzavolta, D. de Vocht, M. van Oosterhout, & M. Vanderhallen (Eds.), *Interrogating young suspects: Procedural safeguards from a legal perspective* (pp. 313–368). Cambridge-Antwerp-Portland: Intersentia.
Stańdo-Kawecka, B., & Kusztal, J. (2016). Poland: Empirical findings. In M. Vanderhallen, M. van Oosterhout, M. Panzavolta, & D. de Vocht (Eds), *Interrogating young suspects: Procedural safeguards from an empirical perspective* (pp. 267–304). Cambridge: Intersentia.
Stawicki, R. (2011). *Prawa i wolności obywatelskie w Polsce po 1918 r. w świetle rozwiązań konstytucyjnych—zarys historyczno-prawny*. Kancelaria Senatu, Biuro Analiz i Dokumentacji. Retrieved Nov 18, 2015, from http://www.senat.gov.pl/gfx/senat/pl/senatopracowania/25/plik/ot-607.pdf
Taracha, A. (1988). Udział organów ścigania w postępowaniu w sprawach nieletnich (w postępowaniu przygotowawczym). In T. Bojarski (Ed.), *Postępowanie z nieletnimi. Orzekanie i wykonywanie środków wychowawczych i poprawczych* (pp. 118–129). Lublin: Uniwersytet Marii Curie-Skłodowskiej.
Wieczorek, L. (2006). *Przestępczość i demoralizacja nieletnich w Polsce w okresie transformacji ustrojowej*. Katowice: "Śląsk" Sp. z o.o. Wydawnictwo Naukowe.
Wójcik, D. (1978). Środowisko szkolne a nieprzystosowanie społeczne i przestępczość mlodzieży. In J. Jasiński (Ed.), *Zagadnienia nieprzystosowania społecznego i przestępczości w Polsce* (pp. 345–366). Wrocław: Zakład Narodowy im. Ossolińskich.
Woźniakowska, D. (2007). Przestępczość nieletnich dziewcząt. *Archiwum Kryminologii, 28*, 375–387.
Wysocka-Pleczyk, M. (2009). Wstęp. Oblicza przestępczości nieletnich. In B. Gulla & M. Wysocka-Pleczyk (Eds.), *Przestępczość nieletnich. Dziecko jako ofiara i sprawca przemocy* (pp. 7–8). Kraków: Wydawnictwo Uniwersytetu Jagiellońskiego.

Barbara Stańdo-Kawecka is Professor of Law at the Department of Penal Executive Law in Faculty of Law, Jagiellonian University in Kraków (Poland). She graduated in special pedagogy and law from the Jagiellonian University. At the same institution she obtained her PhD and defended her habilitation thesis. Her main research interests focus on criminal policy, juvenile law, prison systems, and penitentiary policy. She teaches master courses in penal executive law and juvenile law and is author (coauthor) of publications in these fields. Her past publications include chapters on juvenile justice system in Poland (in *Juvenile Justice in Global Perspective*, 2015 and *Interrogating Young Suspects: Procedural Safeguards from a Legal Perspective*, 2015) and long-term prisoners in Poland (in *Long-Term Imprisonment and Human Rights*, 2014). In the last years she took part in several international research projects concerning juvenile justice, restorative justice, and prison systems.

18

Scotland

Michele Burman and Susan McVie

INTRODUCTION

The aim of every juvenile justice system should surely be to get it right for every child? It is poignant then that, after a very turbulent period of juvenile justice policy development in Scotland which threatened to get it wrong for many children, the Scottish system is now predicated on a set of principles enshrined in law that are explicitly known as Getting it Right for Every Child (GIRFEC). This chapter provides a brief history of juvenile justice in Scotland before going on to examine the age of criminal responsibility (which currently stands at 8 years) and how this fits with the country's stance towards the United Nations Convention for the Rights of the Child (UNCRC). It then provides an overview of trends in juvenile crime in Scotland, focusing mainly on the last decade, from a range of sources of information. It examines the role played by various agencies in relation to juveniles, including the police, the courts and the prison system, as well as discussing various alternative sanctions. Finally, it discusses some of the main gender differences in juvenile crime and justice system involvement in the Scottish context.

THE SYSTEM OF JUVENILE JUSTICE IN SCOTLAND

In Scotland, juvenile justice was formally separated from the adult criminal justice system in 1908 following the Children Act, which required some courts to act as juvenile courts on certain days. Court procedures were modified to try to improve children's understanding of what was happening, but the principles of

M. Burman (✉)
University of Glasgow, Glasgow, UK
e-mail: michele.burman@glasgow.ac.uk

S. McVie, O.B.E., F.R.S.E.
University of Edinburgh, Edinburgh, UK
e-mail: smcvie@ed.ac.uk

S.H. Decker, N. Marteache (eds.), *International Handbook of Juvenile Justice*,
DOI 10.1007/978-3-319-45090-2_18

criminal procedure remained the same as those applied in the adult court (Morris and McIsaac 1978). It was not until the passage of the Children and Young Persons (Scotland) Act 1932 that specially constituted juvenile courts were introduced which had specific responsibility for ensuring the welfare of the child. Nevertheless, only four juvenile courts were ever established in Scotland and most juvenile offenders continued to be dealt with in the adult courts.

Welfare Versus Punishment

The development of juvenile justice in Scotland has been characterised by debates around the appropriate treatment of young people who break the law. On the one hand, welfarist imperatives have sought to protect and improve the well-being of the individual young person; while on the other, punitive compulsions have been aimed at protecting and defending broader societal or public interest concerns (McAra and McVie 2014). The 1908 Children Act, for example, restricted the use of imprisonment for young offenders, but retained penal servitude as a means of dealing with those considered "truly depraved and unruly" and whipping was retained as a disposal for children (Gelsthorpe and Morris 1994). Reform of juvenile justice remained piecemeal and torn between welfarism and criminal justice imperatives until the 1960s, until a major review was commissioned by the Secretary of State for Scotland. The resultant Kilbrandon Committee Report (1964) laid the groundwork for an innovative new system of juvenile justice that remains in place today.

Charged with finding solutions to the rise in the rate of juvenile delinquency in post-World War 2 Scotland, the Kilbrandon Committee found that most cases coming before the juvenile courts on offence grounds also had underlying care issues and, moreover, most of their offences were trivial in nature. In a significant departure from the adjudication and punishment model of court-based juvenile justice that prevailed in Scotland (and other parts of the UK) at that time, the Kilbrandon Committee proposed an integrative welfare-oriented approach, and recommended a single system of civil jurisdiction for young people brought before the courts for offending, for those beyond parental control and for those in need of care and protection (Batchelor and Burman 2009). A key message from the Kilbrandon Committee Report was that young people who offend should be seen as no different from those in need of care and protection because both groups of young people are affected by similar problems. It recommended that appropriate interventions should be put in place at an early stage and in a way that supported the young person's general well-being to avoid criminalising and stigmatising young people through unnecessary court-based intervention.

The Introduction of the Children's Hearings System

In response to the Kilbrandon Report, the Social Work (Scotland) Act 1968 established the Scottish Children's Hearings System (CHS), which was formally implemented in 1971 and replaced juvenile courts in Scotland. It assumed powers to make decisions about the social education and welfare supervision of those brought to its attention. The CHS was founded on the key principle that the child's best interests should be paramount in decision-making and the welfare principle must be the key test guiding decisions concerning the necessity and extent of compulsory intervention. The CHS is described in more detail in Box 18.1.

Box 18.1: The Children's Hearings System in Scotland

The CHS can receive referrals from anyone about a child who may be in need to compulsory measures of care. The statutory grounds for referral are diverse and include the neglect and abuse of a child, involvement in offending, being beyond the control of a relevant person and failure to attend school. A young person may be referred on more than one ground and these may include both offence and non-offence grounds.

The CHS deals with children and young people referred on care grounds from birth up to 16 years old (and increasingly up to 18), and on offence grounds from age 8. The central tenets of the System are welfare based (see Burman et al. 2006), that is:

- emphasis is on the 'needs' of the child rather than their 'deeds';
- all decisions of the CHS should be made in the best interests of the child;
- offending is symptomatic of deeper psychological or social malaise;
- the focus should be on early and minimal intervention;
- and the hearing should be an informal meeting which maximises the participation of children and their families in decision-making.

Hearings are lay tribunals comprised of a 'panel' of trained volunteers drawn from the local community.[1] Professional staff (trained in law or social work) are appointed as 'Reporters' to the CHS. When the Reporter receives a referral about a child (from police, health, education or members of the public) he/she initiates an investigation in order to establish whether there is sufficient evidence to support legal grounds for a hearing.

The Reporter must be satisfied that compulsory measures of supervision may be required to help address the needs and/or behaviour of the young person. If grounds are established, the Reporter arranges a hearing. Reporters are also involved in arranging review hearings, warrant hearings and other related matters.

Hearings are held in private and only those who have a legal right to be there or those who are allowed to be there by the Panel chair can be present.

[1] Lay panel members (aged 18–60 years) are recruited from the public, and undergo selection and training processes. They are appointed (or reappointed) for a 3-year period.

(continued)

Box 18.1: (continued)

In addition to the young person, this usually includes at least one parent or guardian, the Reporter, a social worker and, depending on the case, a teacher, police officer or youth worker. The panel can make a number of different decisions, such as:

- decide that formal, compulsory supervision measures are not required and discharge the case;
- request information to assist in decision-making, in which case the hearing is deferred to a later date (if so, panel members can make decisions about what should happen to the child in the meantime);
- decide that compulsory measures of supervision are needed, under the Children's Hearings (Scotland) Act 2011 (section 83) and make a compulsory supervision order. This will usually have conditions attached to it which can include where the child or young person is to live (for example with foster carers or a relative) or who the child should see and when.

A Punitive Phase of Juvenile Justice

The framing of juvenile justice in terms of welfare values remained a relatively stable feature of Scottish policy for over a quarter of a century. The period since the mid-1990s, however, marks arguably the most turbulent phase in Scottish juvenile justice history. This began with the Children (Scotland) Act 1995 which introduced a new statutory framework placing the principle of public protection above that of the best interests of the child in cases where the child presented a significant risk to the public. Responsibility for the CHS was removed from Scottish local authorities and a single Scottish Children's Reporter Administration (SCRA) was created to manage and administer the CHS. However, the Act empowered the court to substitute decisions for that of the CHS in disputed cases, whereas previously it could only make recommendations or discharge a case. These legislative changes impacted significantly on the practical and philosophical principles underpinning juvenile justice in Scotland.

Political change in Scotland was to have an even greater impact on juvenile justice. Following the election of the 'New Labour' UK Government in 1997, public interest discourse penetrated the CHS as issues of juvenile justice became increasingly caught up in a set of social inclusion and crime prevention agendas driven by the government (see McAra and McVie 2014). Following political devolution[2] and the creation of a Scottish Parliament in 1999, Scotland witnessed

[2]The process by which powers on devolved matters were transferred from Westminster to Scottish Ministers. For further information on the process of devolution and its implications on Scottish criminal and juvenile justice, see Scott and Mooney (2015) and McVie (forthcoming).

a steady flow of new policies, legislative changes and initiatives targeted at children and young people. This included an overt political commitment to a more punitive approach to youth offending (McAra 2006). Government policies around social inclusion and crime prevention were driven as much by a community and victim-centred ethos as the child-centred ethos that had characterised the juvenile justice system between 1968 and the mid-1990s. As a result, the primary concern of juvenile justice policy shifted from the social and personal needs of young people to a focus on the nature and frequency of their offences.

In a process that has been referred to as 'de-tartanisation' (McAra 2006), children identified as being at risk of offending became subject to high levels of scrutiny and surveillance and the Scottish system increasingly came to reflect the much more punitive and managerialist juvenile justice systems of England and Wales. There was a strong focus on reducing persistent offending and anti-social behaviour by legislating to enable the use of civil orders to tackle low level crime and disorder, and a new youth court model was reintroduced to Scotland which reflected the government's position that "punishment is a key part of the youth justice process" (Scottish Executive 2005a). Such policies were deeply unpopular amongst juvenile justice practitioners and, as we shall see later, government efforts to tackle the perceived problem of youth crime by creating a set of performance targets for the juvenile justice system was undermined by evidence that it had actually exacerbated the problem (McAra and McVie 2010, 2014).

A Return to Welfare-Based Principles

With a tide of antipathy amongst juvenile justice practitioners towards the government's punitive stance, another review of juvenile justice was conducted in 2004. This led to publication of the policy document, *Getting it Right for Every Child: Proposals for Action* (GIRFEC), (Scottish Executive 2005b) which set out a vision for children's services running counter to the prevailing political rhetoric on youth crime. More aligned with the original principles of the Kilbrandon Committee, GIRFEC places primary emphasis on individual well-being, improving outcomes for vulnerable children and early targeted intervention. GIRFEC was adopted by the incoming SNP Government in 2007 and underpinned a further strategy document, *Preventing Offending by Young People: A Framework for Action* (Scottish Government 2008), which outlined a shared vision of what national and local agencies working with children and young people should do to prevent, divert, manage and change the behaviour of those who offend or are at risk of offending. This paved the way for increased diversion from both the youth and adult justice systems for under 18s. Unlike the prior punitive phase, these new policies were based on strong research evidence that the long-term outcomes for young people involved in offending behaviour could be best served by diverting them away from statutory measures, prosecution and custody, and implementing early intervention and robust community alternatives (McAra and McVie 2007). Research had also shown that persistent serious offending is strongly associated with victimisation and social adversity, such that these problems needed to be addressed alongside offending behaviours (McAra and McVie 2010).

The juvenile justice system underwent further transformation in 2011 with the Scottish Government roll out of a new 'Whole System Approach' (WSA) for young people who engage in offending. The WSA represents a reinvigorated welfare-based system delivered through multi-agency partnership and a renewed commitment to education and skills. The aim is to provide a more streamlined and consistent response to young people that works across all systems and agencies to achieve better outcomes for young people, especially those from the most vulnerable backgrounds and deprived communities. There are three main dimensions to the WSA (see Murray et al. 2015): first, a focus on 'early and effective intervention' (EEI) which aims to divert young people from the CHS through pre-referral screening and respond quickly to early signs of offending by putting in place forms of support with the aim of reducing future offending; second, a commitment to diverting 16 and 17 year olds away from prosecution to keep them out of the adult criminal justice system; and third, to ensure resources are available for all young people under the age of 18 returning to communities from secure care and custody to support their reintegration and reduce the risk of reoffending. Key components of the WSA are outlined in Box 18.2.

Box 18.2: The Whole Systems Approach to Young People Who Offend
The WSA aims to achieve positive outcomes for young people who are involved in offending through the following mechanisms:

- Integrated processes and services across child and adult services;
- Streamlined and consistent planning, assessment and decision-making processes for young people who offend, ensuring they receive the right help at the right time;
- Effective ways of working with high risk young people involved in offending;
- Diversion of young people from statutory measures, prosecution and custody;
- Increased opportunities for community alternatives to secure care and custodial sentences;
- A consistent approach to risk assessment and risk management;
- Improved support for young people attending court;
- Improved services for young people in custody and reintegrating into the community.

Actions that can be taken under EEI include:

- No further action
- Direct police measures
- Single agency support, e.g. through education, health, social work
- Referral for targeted intervention, e.g. restorative justice, substance misuse work
- Referral to the Children's Reporter

A Compassionate System of Juvenile Justice

Despite the introduction of the WSA, the CHS continues to be at the heart of juvenile justice in Scotland. The Children's Hearings (Scotland) Act 2011 replaced much of the 1995 Act and now forms the legislative framework governing the CHS. The 2011 Act specifically sought to strengthen the role of and deliver better protection for children within the CHS. It legislated that offences admitted during Children's Hearings could be classified as alternatives to prosecution rather than convictions and it was agreed that only very high tariff offences could be disclosed as criminal convictions, unlike previously. And, more recently, the Children and Young People (Scotland) Act 2014 has enshrined in law key elements of the GIRFEC approach and imposed further welfare-based measures, such as a named person for all young people. Contemporary transformations have led to Scottish juvenile justice being described as "a positive and inclusive process based on a broader vision of Scotland as a compassionate nation" (McAra and McVie 2014:272).

AGE OF MAJORITY AND STANCE TOWARDS UN CRC

The age of criminal responsibility in Scotland was set at 8 years by the Children and Young Persons (Scotland) Act 1937 and remains in place today. This is very low in comparison to other European jurisdictions. As discussed earlier, most children and young people who offend are referred to the CHS, which largely protects them from prosecution by retaining them within a system which is required to hold their welfare as its paramount consideration (see McDiarmid 2013). Irrespective of the CHS however, Scotland's low age of criminal responsibility has given rise to concern from children's rights proponents and other legal commentators (McDiarmid 2013; UNCRC 2007).

The UN Convention on the Rights of the Child (1989), which states that signatory states shall seek to promote "the establishment of a minimum age below which children shall be presumed not to have the capacity to infringe the penal law", was ratified in the UK in 1991. The UNCRC has stated clearly that the absolute minimum acceptable age of criminal responsibility should be 12 years (UNCRC 2007); and, indeed, have singled out Scotland, England and Wales for criticism over their low age of majority (UNCRC 2008). The approach taken by the CHS, and the inclusion of 16- to 18-year-olds within the ambit of Children's Hearings, was welcomed by the UN Committee monitoring compliance, but it expressed concern that young people aged 16 and 17 could be tried in adult courts.

In 2009, the Scottish Government proposed increasing the age of criminal prosecution to 12 years, although it stopped short of recommending that the age of criminal responsibility be raised from 8 years. The 2011 Children's Hearings (Scotland) Act (s. 25) subsequently restricted the prosecution of children only to those aged 12 or over, unless there were exceptional circumstances, based on the seriousness of the offence or the age of their co-accused, and *only* on the instructions of the Lord Advocate (Scotland most senior prosecutor). In practice, however, this happens very rarely. Immunity from prosecution is not quite the same as decriminalisation, and these arrangements do not mean that the acquisition of criminal responsibility at the age of 8 is without consequences. However, these are somewhat moderated by the requirement that a disposal by a Children's Hearing should not be overtly punitive, and there are restrictions placed on the recording of offences admitted or established through the CHS.[3] At age 16 or 17 years, young offenders who are already on a compulsory supervision order imposed by the CHS (or awaiting the outcome of a referral) may (at the discretion of the Reporter or a court judge) be retained within the juvenile system, but at 18 years, all are dealt with by the adult court system.

With a commitment to GIRFEC principles underpinning juvenile justice, as enshrined in the Children and Young People (Scotland) Act 2014, focus has once again returned to the age of criminal responsibility in Scotland. In response, a recent government policy document, *Preventing Offending: Getting It Right for Children and Young People* (Scottish Government 2015a), made a clear commitment to keeping children out of the criminal justice system and promised to review the age of criminal responsibility again. An expert Advisory Group was set up to consider the issue and approached it not from the perspective of *if* it should happen, but rather *how and when* it should happen. The final report of the Advisory Group recommended that the Scottish Government raise the minimum age of criminal responsibility from 8 to 12 years, and ensure that children under age 12 are only referred to the CHS on non-offence grounds (Marshall 2016). At the time of writing, the Scottish Government has put the matter out to public consultation before making a final decision.

TRENDS IN JUVENILE CRIME 2004–2014

Obtaining meaningful data about the nature and extent of young people's offending behaviour in Scotland is not straightforward. The most recent estimates indicate that there are 835,186 young people aged 8–21 years living in Scotland, accounting for 15.6% of Scotland's total population of 5.35 million (National Records of Scotland 2015). Yet estimating how many offend and establishing the nature of those offences is very difficult because there are no national surveys of offending. Consequently, researchers must rely on official sources such as the routine statistics collated by the police, CHS, courts and prison service (which vary enormously in terms of their focus, structure and content).

[3] Rehabilitation of Offenders Act 1974, ss. 3, 5(3)(b), 5(5)(f).

These administrative datasets all have limitations in the extent to which they provide accurate and reliable information on the extent of crimes and offences committed by young people.

For example, police data represents the youth crimes that come to their attention, but we know from self-report studies that the majority of youth crimes do not (McAra and McVie 2005). Statistics on offence referrals to the CHS provide some indication of trends in juvenile crime, but the majority of offence referrals come from the police and so these data also underestimate actual offending levels. The recent implementation of the WSA in Scotland, described earlier, has led to a significant reduction in offence referrals to the CHS and the complex nature by which young people involved in offending are now dealt with by a variety of organisations is not yet being captured by current statistical reports (see Scottish Government 2016). Similarly, statistics on court proceedings and imprisonment rates show trends in the number of young people dealt with by the adult criminal justice system, but they are influenced by decision-making practices at earlier stages of the criminal justice process, which serve to filter out many cases before they reach the courts (which would include young people diverted away from prosecution). As such, the available statistics can only provide a partial account of the levels and trends of youth crime in Scotland.

Whilst it is generally agreed that young people are responsible for a disproportionately large amount of crime in Scotland, there is evidence of a significant decrease in offending amongst young people in Scotland in recent years, at least according to convictions data (Matthews 2014).

Police Data on Juvenile Offending

Like many other developed countries, rates of recorded crimes and offences[4] in Scotland have shown a sharp decline in recent decades (Scottish Government 2015b). Importantly, there is strong evidence that the crime drop has been driven to a large extent by a fall in youth offending. Police data on juvenile offending have not been published routinely in Scotland. However, according to the most recently available data, the overall **number of detected crimes and offences** involving young people aged 8–17 declined from 78,572 in 2008/09 to 43,117 in 2012/13, a fall of 45%; while the total **number of 8- to 17-year-olds** who were known to have committed detected crimes and offences also declined, from 35,466 in 2009/10 to 23,726 in 2012/13, a 33% decrease (Scottish Government 2013:53). In addition, the number of restorative justice warnings issued by the police to young people declined from 2479 young people in 2008/9 to 216 in 2014/15, a fall of 92% (Scottish Government 2016). It is notable that this apparent fall in youth

[4]In Scotland, recorded crime is separated (mainly for statistical purposes) into "crimes"—which tend to be more serious criminal acts and "offences" which are generally less serious incidents.

[5]Note that although there was a drop in the youth population over the last three decades this does not explain the drop in offence referrals as per capita rates show a similar level of decline (McAra and McVie 2014).

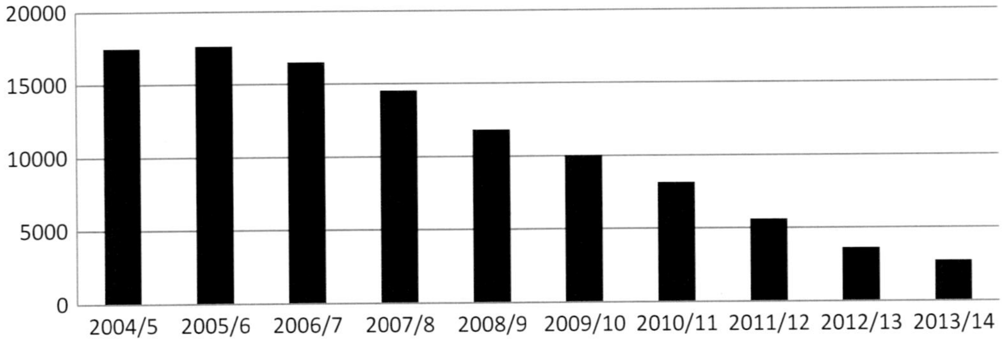

FIGURE 18.1. Number of people aged under 18 referred to the CHS on offence grounds, 2004/5 to 2013/14. *Source*: SCRA Statistical Dashboard (The SCRA Statistical Dashboard is available at http://www.scra.gov.uk/publications/online_statistical_service.cfm)

offending coincides with the period of juvenile justice reform based on the GIRFEC model of welfare, described earlier; although, without reliable data for earlier periods it is not possible to draw definitive conclusions.

Offence Referrals to the CHS

The number of young people referred to the CHS on offence grounds has fallen dramatically over the last decade, as shown in Fig. 18.1. The recent figures mask some earlier fluctuations, however. From the mid-1990s to 2002/3, the number of referrals remained relatively stable at around 14,500 per year; however, between 2002/03 and 2005/6 there was an 18% increase in the number of children referred on offence grounds which accounts for the high levels at the start of Fig. 18.1. This coincided with the punitive phase of Scottish juvenile justice policy, described earlier, where a set of misguided performance targets were introduced, aimed at reducing the number of persistent young offenders by 10%. However, the extent of the police focus on so-called at-risk youths served to drive up the number of offence referrals to the CHS instead (see McAra and McVie 2010).

By 2006/7, the politically-driven targets had been abandoned and the numbers referred to the CHS on offence grounds began to fall, and have continued to do so annually ever since. In fact, there has been an 84% reduction in the number of children referred to the Reporter on offence grounds between 2005/6 and 2013/14.[5]

It seems likely that the dramatic fall in offence referrals to the CHS is largely an artefact of wider changes in the procedures for dealing with juvenile offenders. Following its introduction as a pilot initiative in 2008/9, the number of young people being referred for Early and Effective Intervention (EEI) rose to 650 by 2011/12. Following national implementation in 2011, EEI referrals quadrupled to 2637 by 2013/14 as use of the practice became commonplace (Scottish Government 2016). This increase may, of course, be due to better recording of EEI since its introduction; however, it is certain that it accounts for at least some of the reduction in CHS offence referrals and police restorative warnings. It is worth noting, however, that WSA involves a great many other juvenile justice interventions that are not being accurately measured, so the picture in Scotland is rather unclear at the present time.

The combination of extensive system change and the absence of repeated self-report survey data in Scotland makes it impossible to determine whether there has been any actual fall in offending by young people over the last decade. However, repeated cross-sectional survey data on substance use indicates a large and significant drop in other forms of risky behaviour over this period. For example, recent findings from the Scottish Schools Adolescent Lifestyle and Substance Use Survey (SALSUS) reported significant reductions in smoking, drinking and drug use amongst 13- and 15-year-old boys and girls, bringing levels of all three forms of substance use to their lowest recorded levels (NHS 2014). If substance use is assumed to follow a similar trend to certain forms of offending, this would suggest that there has been a real drop in juvenile crime in the last decade. It is regrettable that data were not collected on juvenile offending over the same period as the SALSUS survey, which began in 1982.

CAUSES OF JUVENILE CRIME

The causes of juvenile crime are, of course, diverse and highly documented (see for example, Muncie 1999) and there is no unified theory as to how these manifest across different groups, contexts and circumstances. Nevertheless, research in Scotland has identified some common themes. One of the most significant studies on youth offending in recent years is the Edinburgh Study of Youth Transitions and Crime (ESYTC), a longitudinal programme of research on pathways into and out of offending for a cohort of around 4300 young people. Drawing on over 10 years of fieldwork from the study, McAra and McVie identified "four key 'facts' about youth crime which any system of youth justice 'ought to fit'" (2010:180).

First, they found compelling evidence that persistent engagement in serious offending was associated with various forms of victimisation, vulnerability and social adversity in young people's lives that could not be controlled away by taking account of other factors associated with a high risk of offending. Second, they stated that the process of 'early identification', which was considered by UK governments as key to intervening in the lives of at-risk children, was a highly fallible process which had a negative impact on the long-term offending outcomes of many disadvantaged young people. Third, they identified the early teenage years as being a critical period during which the nature and effectiveness of interventions imposed on young people could significantly determine whether they had a desisting or rising pattern of convictions during the teenage years. Importantly, they showed that significant contact with the juvenile justice system was likely to greatly increase the risk of entry to the adult criminal justice system.

And, fourth, they presented evidence that the working cultures of juvenile justice agencies led to the creation of a group of 'usual suspects' who were sucked into a repeat cycle of contact with the system with damaging consequences in terms of inhibiting desistance from offending. This led them to recommend diversionary strategies to facilitate the desistence process.

Taken together, McAra and McVie's findings highlighted that a wide variety of risk factors were implicated in the reasoning behind juvenile offending; however, there were two critical factors that needed to be addressed with urgency in order to reduce the problem. First, the profound disadvantage, deprivation and vulnerability experienced by many young people outweighed other risk factors and was at the root of their pathway into a life of serious and persistent offending behaviour *and* their route into the criminal justice system. And, second, the system of juvenile justice itself, while predicated on well-intentioned policies and principles, was failing many young people by increasing their chances of both longer term criminal justice intervention and engagement in offending. The findings from this study underpinned the significant changes to the system of juvenile justice, discussed earlier. Importantly, however, they have also been reflected in a range of other Scottish studies.

Scotland has a rather unenviable reputation for violence and, in particular, knife crime which dates back to the early part of the last century (see Fraser et al. 2010; Fraser 2015; McVie in press). The problem has been particularly pervasive amongst young people, leading to high homicide rates compared to many other jurisdictions. A major study of youth gangs and knife crime found that gang membership and violent behaviour were regarded as a normal part of growing up for some young people, especially those living in more economically deprived parts of Scotland (Bannister et al. 2010). Those who engaged in knife carrying or gang membership tended to have more difficult and chaotic backgrounds than other young people. This included parental separation, poor parental supervision, hanging about the streets, engagement in offending and anti-social behaviour, and getting in trouble with the police. However, they were also more likely to have experienced crime victimisation and to engage in self-harming (McVie 2010). Both reports highlighted a prevailing sense of vulnerability and hardship underlying the behaviours of these young people.

Further work by McAra and McVie (2015) has found evidence of an incremental effect of early poverty on criminal justice and labour market outcomes in early adulthood. Members of the ESYTC cohort from the most deprived backgrounds in childhood were more likely to be not in education, employment or training (NEET), to have been convicted and to have been imprisoned compared to other young people, even when controlling for a wide range of other early risk factors. Furthermore, there is evidence that although crime has fallen in Scotland, the risk of victimisation has not fallen amongst those who are the most likely to be victims of crime and that it is becoming more highly concentrated within socio-economically deprived families and neighbourhoods (McVie et al. 2015). These findings provide a basis for the work of other scholars who argue for the development of a more inclusive social justice agenda in Scotland, which recognises the engrained inequalities in Scottish communities and their impact on the criminal justice outcomes of the most vulnerable people in our society (Scott and Mooney 2015).

POLICING AND JUVENILES

Anyone can make a referral to the CHS, but in reality the police are the key gatekeepers to the juvenile justice system in Scotland. Prior to the introduction of the WSA, any child aged between 8 and 15 who was charged with committing an offence had to be referred to the CHS (although those who committed serious crimes would also be jointly referred to the Scottish prosecution service). Evidence from Scottish studies has consistently shown that between a third and a half of young people aged between 11 and 15 have experienced some form of adversarial police contact (Anderson et al. 1994; Jamieson et al. 1999; McAra and McVie 2005). However, most of this tends to be fairly low level and only a fraction of these are ever formally charged by the police and reported to the CHS. For example, the ESYTC found that at age 15, 46% of young people reported having adversarial police contact during the previous year but only 8.5% believed they had been 'charged' with committing a crime (McAra and McVie 2005). In addition, only 45% of those who believed they had been charged by the police were actually referred to the CHS.

Since the implementation of the WSA, the police have continued to be primary gatekeepers to the juvenile justice system, but practice varies considerably across different local authorities and the actual pathways that individual young people take can be quite diverse (Murray et al. 2015). In most local authorities, the police tend to be the initial decision makers and may indeed deal with a young person who has committed an offence directly; for example, in the form of a warning (formal or informal), a restorative justice warning or a fixed penalty notice. They also retain the power to make a referral to the CHS (and the prosecution system), although as noted in the previous section, such referrals have been declining year on year. Increasingly, the police will refer the child to a multi-agency screening meeting which is attended by various practitioners (including health, social work, education and community safety) and a joint decision will be taken on the most appropriate agency to take the lead. This reflects the welfare-based perspective of the GIRFEC model of juvenile justice which aims to divert young people from formal justice interventions and provide appropriate supports to reduce future reoffending.

There is another aspect to the policing of young people in Scotland that is less in keeping with the GIRFEC model and, until very recently, the police applied it without scrutiny or transparency. Research by Murray (2014) highlighted a marked increase in the use of stop and search in Scotland, particularly directed at children and young people, between 2005 and 2010 (although some of this rise was almost certainly due to better recording practices). By 2012/13, however, the rate of stop and search per capita was seven times greater in Scotland than in England and Wales despite very similar demands on the police and near parity in terms of legal capacity (Lennon and Murray 2016). This difference was largely accounted for by the unrestrained use of non-statutory stop and search in Scotland, i.e. searches that did not require legal suspicion, a practice that was prohibited in England and Wales in 1990. Murray (2014) found that non-statutory stop and search was disproportionately targeted against children and young people, some as young as four and five, and in some parts of Scotland (predominantly the West) there were more searches of young people per capita than there were young people living in the area. She concluded that "the sharp discrepancy between the age distribution of searches and persons charged, together with low detection rates, suggests that young people may be over-policed in some parts of Scotland, that is, subject to excessive levels of stop and search, over and above the probability of offending" (2014: 26).

Murray's findings resonate with a darker side of policing in Scotland that is contra to the WSA principles and is not dissimilar to that of many other jurisdictions. In fact, Scottish police have traditionally enjoyed a high level of discretion in their dealings with young people and this has led to some inequality in terms of their treatment of particular groups. McAra and McVie (2005) found that working practices and rules of suspicion tended to lead to discrimination against certain types of young people, most especially those from low socio-economic status backgrounds and those who were more available for policing by virtue of hanging around the streets. However, the most powerful predictor of a police warning or charge was prior police contact, which highlighted their tendency to concentrate on a population of 'usual suspects' driven by stereotypical notions of suspiciousness. Studies such as these have led to a tightening up on police procedures for dealing with the detention, arrest and prosecution of children and young people. For example, the Lord Advocate has issued guidelines to the police regarding the reporting of offences by children (Mulholland 2014) and a new agreement on 'joint reporting' has set out clearer criteria for and emphasis on the importance of clear communication and information sharing (COPFS 2015). In addition, the Scottish Government has accepted the recommendations of an independent Advisory Group to legislate against the use of non-statutory stop and search and place far greater restrictions on the searching of children and young people (see Scott 2015). However, this aspect of the intersecting role between the police, CHS and the adult criminal justice system is under-researched.

COURTS AND JUVENILES

Cases involving a young person between the age of 12 and 17 can be jointly referred to the CHS and the Procurator Fiscal (Scottish prosecutor) if they are considered serious enough. If the Procurator Fiscal considers that there is

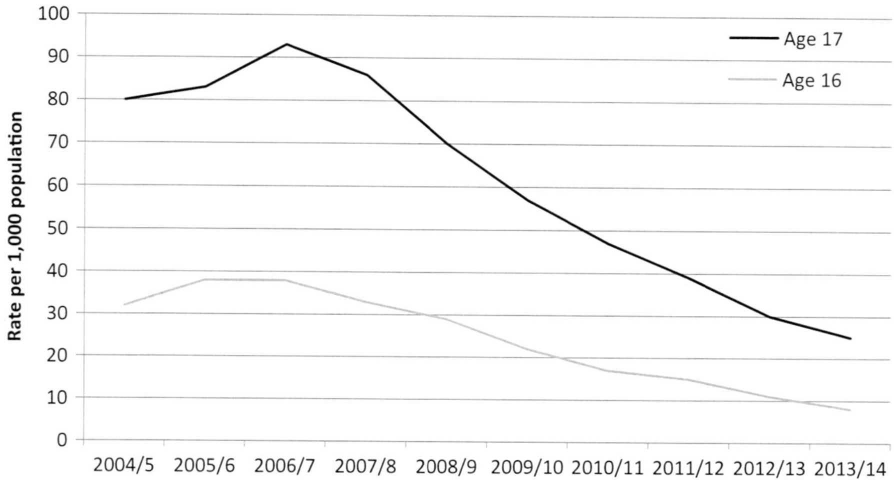

FIGURE 18.2. Number of 16- and 17-year-olds proceeded against in the Scottish courts per 1000 population, 2004/5 to 2013/14. *Source*: Scottish Government 2016:51.

sufficient evidence that a serious offence has been committed, there are several options that may be considered. These include various forms of diversion from prosecution, such as formal warnings, financial penalties or participation in a specialist programme. The latter can be offered if an assessment by a social worker deems this suitable, in which case the young person would undertake work or receive services tailored to their particular needs. Failure to complete the programme could result in the case returning to court.

If it is decided that prosecution is necessary, a young person may be tried in court. As noted earlier, juvenile courts in Scotland were abolished with the introduction of the CHS in 1971. However, in 2003 two pilot youth court projects were created in Scotland to deal with persistent offenders aged 15–17 who would otherwise have been dealt with in an adult court. The referral criterion was three or more police referrals to the Procurator Fiscal in a 6-month period. While a government sponsored evaluation of the courts was largely positive (McIvor et al. 2006), an independent report claimed that the new proceedings undermined children's human rights (Piacentini and Walters 2006). A further review concluded that the youth courts were not cost effective and their outcomes in terms of reconviction and offending rates were no better than adult courts (Scottish Government 2009), following which funding was withdrawn and the courts were phased out.

In reality, very few children aged between 12 and 15 are dealt with by the courts. In 2011/12, only 47 children were convicted in an adult court and, of these, the majority were either remitted back to the CHS for disposal or they received an admonishment or absolute discharge (McAra and McVie 2014). As noted earlier, a key aim of the WSA is to also keep 16- and 17-year-olds out of court and trend data suggests that there has been a decline in convictions amongst this group. Figure 18.2 shows the number of 16- and 17-year-olds proceeded against in the Scottish courts (i.e. convicted) during the last decade as a rate per 1000 of the population, to adjust for changes in population size. Since 2006/7, the conviction rate for both age groups has fallen significantly which appears to match the trend in offence referrals. The decline in convictions amongst 17-year-olds is particularly pronounced. While this was expected as a result of the introduction of the WSA, it could also partially reflect a real underlying decline in youth offending, as noted earlier.

Other significant legislative changes during this period may also have impacted on the number of young people proceeded against in court. For example, the Antisocial Behaviour etc. (Scotland) Act 2004 led to the introduction of police Fixed Penalty Notices in 2007 which were identified as having driven down prosecutions for minor offences including breach of the peace and public order offences (Cavanagh 2009). In addition, the Criminal Proceedings etc. (Reform) (Scotland) Act 2007 increased the use of 'direct measures' for low level offenders in order to keep them out of the courts. It seems likely that the introduction of these types of non-court disposals have had some impact on the trends shown in Fig. 18.2; however, analysis by Matthews (2016) suggests that the introduction of such measures does not fully account for the fall in convictions for those aged under 21. Indeed, the largest change in convictions across all age groups has occurred amongst young men aged under 21, for whom the conviction rate fell by 72% between 1989 and 2012 (Matthews 2014). There has been an unprecedented shift in the age–crime curve in Scotland according to convictions data, with the peak age of conviction increasing from 18 years to 23 years for males and from 18 years to 30 years for females. In comparison, conviction rates for those aged over 25 have remained steady or increased over this period. However, it is important to note that this data is somewhat limited as it is only based on convictions in court and therefore may hide where changes in other parts of the criminal justice system have had an effect.

CUSTODIAL RULES FOR JUVENILES

Children and young people under the age of 16 who are considered to be in need of secure care will typically be placed in secure accommodation that is managed by social work services. Secure accommodation, because it is defined as provision for children and young people who are a risk to themselves as well as others, sits at the complex interface between needs and deeds approaches. Around 250 young people per year are placed in secure care in Scotland (Johnstone and Burman 2009). Two-thirds of these come through the CHS on a supervision order, which must be reviewed every 3 months, and most are placed for welfare reasons rather than offending. The remaining third of secure cases come through the courts and involve young people who have received a custodial sentence. Once they reach 16 years, convicted young people may be transferred to a young offender's institution; however, since the introduction of GIRFEC the Scottish Government has extended the upper age for secure care in these cases up to 18 years of age.

Young Offender Institutions (YOI) house young prisoners (on direct sentence and on remand) up to the age of 21, thereafter they are moved to an adult prison at 21 years. Currently, there is one dedicated YOI and four further YOIs located within adult prisons at various locations across Scotland. Young people may sometimes be housed temporarily in other adult prisons across Scotland, although this practice is contrary to the UN CRC and reviewed by the Scottish Prison Service. The Prisons and Young Offenders Institutions (Scotland) Rules 2011 apply to prisons and YOIs and both are inspected regularly by Her Majesty's Inspectorate of Prisons for Scotland. Outcomes for young people who have been detained in custody tend to be poor. For this reason, the Scottish Prison Service (SPS) has committed to a new *Vision for Young People in Custody* (SPS 2014) and more broadly *Unlocking Potential: Report of the Scottish Prison Service Organisational Review* (SPS 2013) addressing work to address the causes of offending behaviour while young people are in a YOI and on release.

Along with England and Wales, Scotland has one of the highest imprisonment rates in the world. The average daily population in Scottish prisons rose continually from 1950 to 2011/12 and has only declined very slightly in recent years (Scottish Government 2015c). Figure 18.3 presents the average daily prison population for those aged under 21 in Scottish prisons over the last decade. It shows an increasing trend which peaked in 2009/10 before declining quite sharply over the last 4 years. However, if we were to look back over the last two decades the trend in imprisonment for this age group has been largely on the decline since the early 1990s (see McAra and McVie 2014).

The period of increase evident in Fig. 18.3 began during the punitive phase of juvenile justice, described earlier and was relatively short-lived; however, it did continue well into the period when the GIRFEC model was introduced which aimed to reduce the number of young people in the criminal justice system.

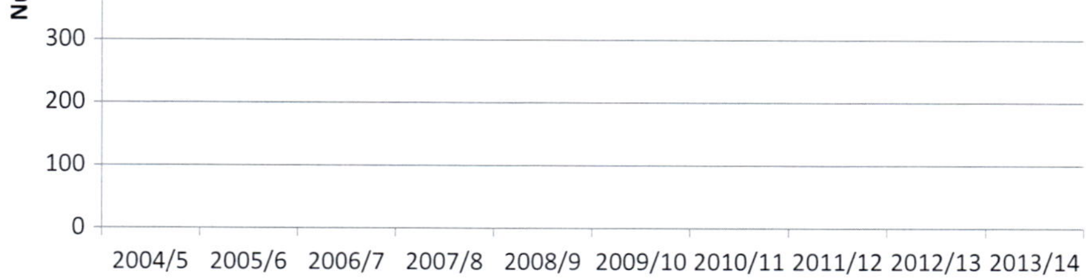

FIGURE 18.3. Average daily prison population of prisoners aged under 21 in Scotland, 2004/5 to 2013/14. *Source*: Scottish Government 2015c;25.

Indeed, there appears to have been a time lag before the trend in imprisonment began to decline in 2010/11. This may indicate that the behaviour of individuals who assign sentences, while moving in the right direction, has been much slower to respond to recent policy shifts than other parts of the juvenile and adult criminal justice system. It could also, of course, reflect a cohort of young people who were 'caught up' in the system during the punitive phase and who became labelled and criminalised, and were therefore over-represented in the prison system during this time (see McAra and McVie 2010, 2012).

ALTERNATIVE SANCTIONS FOR JUVENILES

Community Sentences

A range of community-based sanctions are available to the courts in respect of young people. Formal community-based disposals include Probation Orders, Community Service Orders, Restriction of Liberty Orders and Intensive Supervision Monitoring Services (ISMS) all of which are considered as disposals for the youth justice process in Scotland. These also include structured deferred sentences, imposed for a period of time to allow the young person to engage with interventions that address the causes of their offending behaviour and to demonstrate that he or she has changed their behaviour. If this is achieved, typically the young person will be admonished on return to court within 3–6 months. Drug Treatment and Testing Orders (DTTO) can served on someone over 16 who is 'dependant on or has propensity to misuse drugs, and the dependency or propensity requires and may be susceptible to treatment, and is a suitable person to be subject to an order' (as detailed in ss 89–95 Crime and Disorder Act 1998), and who consents to the order being made. DTTOs are imposed for between 6 months to 3 years and require compliance with an intensive drug treatment and testing programme.

In early 2011, the Community Payback Order (CPO) came into force in Scotland (under the Criminal Justice and Licensing (Scotland) Act 2010 s.14) replacing existing provisions for Community Service Orders, Probation Orders and Supervised Attendance Orders. The CPO can be imposed on those aged 12 years and over, and incorporates a number of requirements from which the court can create an individualised sentence, tailored specifically to each individual based on the nature of the offence as well as the underlying issues that may have facilitated it, and which may need to be addressed in order to prevent future reoffending. This might include a requirement to carry out a specified amount of hours of unpaid work in the community with benefits for the community (those aged 16 and over only), intensive supervision, compensation, alcohol or drug treatment or behavioural programmes, with individual and/or group work. It may also specify a residence requirement (where the young person is to reside or places they may not visit) and an order of conduct specifying they must refrain from certain actions.

Restorative Justice

Scotland has been rather slow in embracing restorative principles in comparison with other jurisdictions. There continues to be some debate as to what constitutes 'restorative' justice and a distinction is made between mediation on the one hand and restorative justice measures on the other. While both have a certain degree of overlap due to their consideration of repairing the harm caused to the victim, mediation places emphasis on the process of negotiating, while others apply a more outcome-oriented definition of restorative efforts of the offender through compensation or reparation.

In the early 1980s, a small number of pilot restorative justice projects were initiated in relation to youth justice, but it was to be another 20 years before the Scottish Government showed interest in further developing restorative measures. Since the early 2000s there has been significant growth of Restorative Justice Services across Scotland, largely as a consequence of Government strategies and policies to prevent, address and reduce behaviour by children and young people that causes harm to individuals and communities. Scotland's *Action Programme to Reduce Youth Crime* (2002) indicated that the confidence of victims in Scotland's youth justice system needs to be restored, and that restorative justice approaches can 'go some way' towards meeting this objective. It outlined plans for the provision of community-based youth justice and, in January 2004, as part of that expansion, 3000 restorative justice places were made available for young people. In 2006, the Scottish Government stated its commitment to provide all young people harmed by youth crime with the opportunity to participate in a restorative process. Local Authorities were provided funding to develop restorative justice services and strategies for young people. Most restorative services are delivered through third sector organisations. In 2008 the Government reaffirmed its commitment to making restorative approaches available to young people in its report on *Preventing Offending by Young People* and produced guidance on implementing standards for the delivery of restorative justice services, and best practice guidelines for restorative justice practitioners. Whilst restorative justice measures are increasingly used in juvenile justice, for adults it remains marginal.

Restorative justice processes are generally taken to mean any process in which all those involved participate together actively to address or repair the harm caused by an offence, generally with the help of one or two facilitators (Johnstone and Burman 2015). Each process aims to enable the participants to explore, in a safe and structured way, (1) the facts—what happened and why, (2) the consequences—how people were affected and (3) the future—what agreements or Action Plan needs to be made to meet the needs of all participants, including the central needs of addressing the harm and preventing the incident from reoccurring.

The police were early adopters of restorative practices. Police restorative warnings were introduced in 2006 replacing an earlier tradition of 'police inspector's warnings' which, more often than not, had little impact. In 2011 the introduction of the WSA and the development of EEI strategies led to a shift from individual police decision making to group/multi-agency decisions on disposals for young people, and hence police restorative warnings have decreased. CHS compulsory supervision orders are arguably restorative, although court-based restorative measures remain rare. Currently, there is very limited detailed data on the use of restorative measures in juvenile justice and this is an area where more research is needed.

DIFFERENCES IN TREATMENT OF BOYS AND GIRLS

Girls are less likely than boys to be referred to a Children's Hearing on offence grounds and are more likely to come to the attention of the CHS as a result of being the victim of an offence, such as neglect or sexual abuse. There are also indications of a differential in the thresholds and reasons for admission to secure care, with girls appearing to be admitted at a lower threshold and for being a risk to themselves as opposed to a risk to others (Burman and Batchelor 2009; Rigby et al. 2011).

There are similarities and differences with regards to court disposals for males and females aged 16–17 (Scottish Government 2016). In 2014/15, a large proportion of 16- to 17-year-olds, around; a third of both males and females, were dealt with by means of a Community Payback Order, a form of community sentence. Other common disposals were an absolute discharge or admonishment with the latter the most common type of disposal for females. Custodial sentences are not commonly used for 16- to 17-year-olds, but males are generally five times more likely than females to receive a custodial disposal at this age, which is likely to reflect the more serious and persistent patterns of offending which male offenders present, rather than being indicative of particular leniency towards females.

Unlike CHS data, criminal proceedings statistics do give information on the nature of offences for which young people have been convicted by gender (although the available data groups together all young people under the age of 21). Table 18.1 shows the types of crimes and offences for which males and females were convicted in 2014/15, broken down by the crime and offence groups used to classify crimes in Scotland. Convictions for serious violent and sexual crimes are rare, with most being convicted of miscellaneous offences (such as breach of the peace or minor assaults) and, to a slightly lesser extent, other crimes (mainly shoplifting) and motor vehicle offences. Therefore, while justice reforms aim to keep more minor crimes and offences out of the courts, the data presented in Table 18.1 indicate that these types of behaviour are still the main driver of conviction for young people in Scotland.

Research evidence regarding girls drawn into juvenile justice systems has developed, particularly over the last 15 years or so. Yet, girls/young women are often marginalised in juvenile justice debates, policies and strategic action plans where the focus is on boys/young men and/or adult women offenders (Burman and Batchelor 2009). In Scotland, some attempts have been made to address this,

TABLE 18.1. Males and females under 21 with a charge proved in 2014/15 by crime and offence type

Crime/offence	*Males %* (*n*=8624)	*Females %* (*n*=1488)
Non-sexual crimes of violence	3	2
Crimes of indecency (inc. crimes relating to prostitution)	a	a
Crimes of dishonesty	12	9
Fire-raising and vandalism etc.	6	4
Other crimes (inc. drugs and crimes against justice)	25	19
Miscellaneous offences (inc. simple assault, breach of the peace)	34	47
Motor vehicle offences	19	19

Source: Scottish Government (2016)
[a]Represents less than 1%

for example, through the setting up of a 'champions group' with those girls/young women with complex needs and seen as 'high risk'. Yet, despite evidence which indicates that girls offending follows a different pathway from that of boys (Burman and Batchelor 2009), until recently, little priority has been given to the development of services and interventions for girls and young women in Scotland.

CONCLUSION

In the years since devolution, Scotland has witnessed some quite remarkable shifts in juvenile justice discourse, policy and practice, segueing between the distinctive Kilbrandon-informed welfarist ethos and public interest concerns. Following a period of intense punitiveness, where the adherence to welfarism was almost entirely eroded, the more recent implementation of GIRFEC and WSA have facilitated diversionary measures, reasserted the values and principles of Kilbrandon, and contributed to getting it right for those children and young people drawn into the juvenile justice system.

REFERENCES

Anderson, S., Kinsey, R., Loader, I., & Smith, C. (1994). *Cautionary tales: Young people, crime and policing in Edinburgh*. Aldershot: Avebury.

Bannister, J., Pickering, J., Batchelor, S., Burman, M., Kintrea, K., & McVie, S. (2010). *Troublesome youth groups, gangs and knife carrying in Scotland*. Edinburgh: Scottish Government Social Research.

Batchelor, S., & Burman, M. (2009). The children's hearing system. In J. Johnstone & M. Burman (Eds.), *Youth justice*. Edinburgh: Dunedin Press.

Burman, M., & Batchelor, S. (2009). Between two stools? Responding to young women who offend. *Youth Justice, 9*(3), 270–285.
Burman, M., Bradshaw, P., Hutton, N., McNeill, F., & Munro, M. (2006). The end of an Era?—Youth justice in Scotland. In J. Junger-Tas & S. Decker (Eds.), *International handbook of juvenile justice* (pp. 439–471). Verlag: Springer.
Cavanagh, B. (2009). *A review of fixed penalty notices for antisocial behaviour*. Edinburgh: Scottish Government.
Crown Office and Procurator Fiscal Service. (2015). *Decision making in cases of children jointly reported to the Procurator Fiscal and Children's Reporter*. Edinburgh: Crown Office and Procurator Fiscal Service.
Fraser, A. (2015). *Urban legends: Gang identity in the post-industrial city. Clarendon series in criminology*. Oxford: Oxford University Press.
Fraser, A., Burman, M., Batchelor, S., & McVie, S. (2010). *Youth violence in Scotland: A literature review*. Edinburgh: Scottish Government. Retrieved from http://www.gov.scot/resource/Doc/326952/0105428.pdf
Gelsthorpe, L., & Morris, A. (1994). Juvenile justice 1954–1992. In R. Maguire, R. Morgan, & R. Reiner (Eds.), *The Oxford handbook of criminology*. Oxford: Oxford University Press.
Jamieson, J., McIvor, G., & Murray, C. (1999). *Understanding offending among young people*. Edinburgh: The Scottish Executive Central Research Unit.
Johnstone, J., & Burman, M. (2009). *Youth justice in Scotland Edinburgh*. Edinburgh: Dunedin Academic Press.
Johnstone, J., & Burman, M. (2015). Scotland. In F. Dunkel, J. Gryzwa-Holten, & P. Horsfeld (Eds.), *Restorative justice and mediation in penal matters*. Monchengladbach: Forum Verlag Godesberg.
Kilbrandon Committee. (1964). *Report on children and young persons, Scotland*. Edinburgh: Her Majesty's Stationery Office.
Lennon, G., & Murray, K. (2016). *Under-regulated and unaccountable? Explaining variation in stop and search rates in Scotland*. England: Policing and Society. http://dx.doi.org/10.1080/10439463.2016.1163359 [published online 29 March 2016].
Marshall, R. (2016). *The report of the Advisory Group on the minimum age of criminal responsibility*. Edinburgh: Scottish Government. Retrieved from http://www.gov.scot/Resource/0049/00497071.pdf
Matthews, B. (2014). *Where have all the young offenders gone?* Edinburgh: AQMeN. Retrieved from https://www.aqmen.ac.uk/sites/default/files/RB4-young-offenders.pdf
Matthews, B. (2016). Comparing trends in convictions and non-court disposals in Scotland. *Scottish Justice Matters, 4*(1), 36–37.
McAra, L. (2006). Welfare in crisis? Youth justice in Scotland. In J. Muncie & B. Goldson (Eds.), *Comparative youth justice* (pp. 127–145). London: Sage.
McAra, L., & McVie, S. (2005). The usual suspects? Street-life, young people and the police. *Criminal Justice, 5*(1), 5–35.
McAra, L., & McVie, S. (2007). Youth justice? The impact of system contact on patterns of desistance from offending. *European Journal of Criminology, 4*(3), 315–345.
McAra, L., & McVie, S. (2010). Youth crime and justice in Scotland. In H. Croall, G. Mooney, & M. Munro (Eds.), *Criminal justice in Scotland*. Oxon: Willan Publishing.
McAra, L., & McVie, S. (2012). Negotiated order: Towards a theory of pathways into and out of offending. *Criminology and Criminal Justice, 12*(4), 347–376.
McAra, L., & McVie, S. (2014). The Scottish juvenile justice system: Policy and practice. In J. A. Winterdyk (Ed.), *Juvenile justice: International perspectives, models and trends* (pp. 263–294). Boca Raton, FL: CRC Press.
McAra, L., & McVie, S. (2015). The reproduction of poverty: Impacts of system contact on the life chances of young people. *Scottish Justice Matters 3*(3).

McDiarmid, C. (2013). An age of complexity: Children and criminal responsibility in law. *Youth Justice, 13*, 145.
McIvor, G., Barnsdale, L., Brown, A., Eley, S., Macrae, R., Malloch, M., et al. (2006). *Evaluation of the Airdrie sheriff youth court pilot*. Edinburgh: Scottish Executive Social Research.
McVie, S. (2010). *Gang membership and knife carrying: Findings from the Edinburgh study of youth transitions and crime*. Edinburgh: Scottish Government Social Research.
McVie, S. (in press). Social order: crime and justice in Scotland. In: D. McCrone (Ed.), *The New Sociology of Scotland.* Edinburgh: Edinburgh University Press.
McVie, S., Norris, P., & Pillinger, R. (2015). Is poverty reflected in changing patterns of victimisation in Scotland? *Scottish Justice Matters 3*(3).
Morris, A., & McIsaac, M. (1978). Juvenile justice? The practice of social welfare. In: *Cambridge studies in criminology*. Cambridge: Heinemann.
Mulholland, F. (2014). *Lord advocate's guidelines to the chief constable on the reporting to procurators fiscal of offences alleged to have been committed by children: Revised categories of offence which require to be jointly reported*. Scotland: COPFS.
Muncie, J. (1999). *Youth and crime: A critical introduction*. London: Sage.
Murray, K. (2014). *Stop and search in Scotland: An evaluation of police practice* (SCCJR Research Report/14). Glasgow: Scottish Centre for Crime and Justice.
Murray, K., McGuinness, P., Burman, M., & McVie, S. (2015). *Evaluation of the whole system approach to young people who offend in Scotland*. Glasgow: SCCJR. Retrieved from http://www.sccjr.ac.uk/wp-content/uploads/2015/06/Evaluation-of-the-WSA-approach.pdf
National Records of Scotland. (2015). *Mid-2014 population estimates Scotland: Population estimates by sex, age and administrative area*. Edinburgh: National Records of Scotland. Retrieved from http://www.nrscotland.gov.uk/files//statistics/population-estimates/midyear-2014/14mid-year-pe-cahb-publication-correction.pdf
NHS. (2014). Scottish Schools Adolescent Lifestyle and Substance Use Survey (SALSUS).
Piacentini, L., & Walters, R. (2006). The politicization of youth justice in Scotland and the rise of the "Burberry Court". *Youth Justice, 6*(1), 43–59.
Rigby, P., Jardine, C., & Whyte, B. (2011). *Girls and young women in the youth justice system—vulnerable or risky?* (Towards Effective Practice Paper 12). Criminal Justice Social Work Development Centre for Scotland.
Scott, J. (2015). *Report of the Independent Advisory Group on Stop and Search*. Edinburgh: The Scottish Government.
Scott, G., & Mooney, G. (2015). Scotland's political and policy landscape: Devolution, social and criminal justice. In H. Croall, G. Mooney, & M. Munro (Eds.), *Crime, justice and society in Scotland*. London: Routledge.
Scottish Executive. (2005a). *Getting it right for every child: Proposals for action*. Edinburgh: The Scottish Government. Retrieved from http://www.gov.scot/resource/doc/54357/0013270.pdf
Scottish Executive. (2005b). *Scotland's first youth court opens*. Press release. Retrieved from http://www.scotland.gov.uk/News/Releases/2005/06/15112358
Scottish Government. (2008). *Preventing offending by young people: A framework for action*. Edinburgh: The Scottish Government. Retrieved from http://www.gov.scot/Resource/Doc/228013/0061713.pdf.
Scottish Government. (2009). *Review of the Hamilton & Airdrie Youth Courts report*. Edinburgh: Scottish Government.
Scottish Government. (2013). *Scottish policing performance framework* (Annual Rep. 2012–13). Edinburgh: The Scottish Government. Retrieved from http://www.gov.scot/Resource/0043/00437520.pdf
Scottish Government. (2015a). *Preventing offending: Getting it right for children and young people*. Edinburgh: The Scottish Government. Retrieved from http://www.gov.scot/Publications/2015/06/2244

Scottish Government. (2015b). *Recorded crime in Scotland, 2014/15*. Edinburgh: The Scottish Government. Retrieved from http://www.gov.scot/Publications/2015/09/5338

Scottish Government. (2015c). *Prison statistics and population projections Scotland: 2013–14*. Edinburgh: The Scottish Government. Retrieved from http://www.gov.scot/Resource/0049/00491398.pdf

Scottish Government. (*2016*). *Criminal proceedings in Scotland, 2014–15*. Edinburgh: The Scottish Government. Retrieved from http://www.gov.scot/Resource/0049/00494474.pdf

Scottish Prison Service. (2013). *Unlocking potential: Report of the Scottish Prison Service Organisational Review*. Edinburgh: SPS.

Scottish Prison Service. (2014). *Vision for young people in custody*. Edinburgh: SPS.

UNCRC. (2007). *Committee on the rights of the child*. Forty-fourth session. General comment No. 10: Children's right in juvenile justice. Retrieved from http://www2.ohchr.org/english/bodies/crc/docs/CRC.C.GC.10.pdf

UNCRC. (2008). *Committee on the rights of the child*. Forty-ninth session. Consideration of reports submitted by states parties under article 44 of the convention. Concluding observations: United Kingdom of Great Britain and Northern Ireland. Retrieved from http://www2.ohchr.org/english/bodies/crc/docs/AdvanceVersions/CRC.C.GBR.CO.4.pdf

Michele Burman is Professor of Criminology and Head of the School of Social and Political Sciences at the University of Glasgow. She is a founding Co-Director of the Scottish Centre for Crime and Justice Research which is a collaborative research and knowledge exchange research centre involving a partnership between four Scottish Universities. She is also co-Editor-in-Chief of the Sage journal Criminology and Criminal Justice.

Michele has long-standing research and teaching interests in gender, crime and justice, with a particular focus on women's imprisonment; criminal justice responses to gender-based violence; and young women and youth justice.

Susan McVie is Chair of Quantitative Criminology in the School of Law at the University of Edinburgh. She is Director of the Applied Quantitative Methods Network (AQMeN), a leading research centre focused on advanced research in the areas of crime, education and urban inequalities. She is also Co-Director of the Edinburgh Study of Youth Transitions and Crime (ESYTC), one of the founder members of the Scottish Centre for Crime and Justice Research (SCCJR) and leader of the Crime and Justice work strand of the Administrative Data Research Centre in Scotland (ADRC-S).

Susan's research interests and published works focus on crime patterns and trends, youth crime and justice, criminal careers and developmental criminology, crime and space, violence and homicide, and gangs and knife crime. She is the author (with Lesley McAra) of a series of influential articles on youth crime and justice which have had a dramatic impact in reforming the Scottish youth justice system and Scottish school exclusion policies. She sits on a number of influential government committees, including the Building Safer Communities Programme Board and the Independent Advisory Group on Stop and Search in Scotland. She is an editor for the *British Journal of Criminology, Youth Justice, and Criminology and Criminal Justice*.

In 2013, Susan was awarded (jointly with Lesley McAra) the Howard League for Penal Reform Research Medal. In 2014, she was elected a Fellow of the Royal Society of Edinburgh. In 2016, she received an OBE for services to social science in the Queen's New Year's Honours List.

19

Slovenia

Katja Filipčič and Mojca M. Plesničar

THE LEGAL STATUS OF JUVENILES

The Constitution of the Republic of Slovenia regulates the rights of children, who enjoy special protection and care in the system. They are endowed with human rights and fundamental freedoms which they can enjoy consistent with their age and maturity, and are guaranteed special protection from economic, social, physical, mental, or other exploitation and abuse.

The best interest of the child is a guiding principle for all legislation regarding children and is well reflected in the criminal justice system as well. In fact, even though punitiveness has been on the rise in Slovenia in the past decades (Flander and Meško 2016), rehabilitation continues to remain at the core of juvenile criminal justice (Filipčič 2006).

Slovenia is a typical continental legal system and at the normative level, in most respects, resembles closely the German or Austrian systems, with which it shares its legal tradition. The criminal system is shaped accordingly, with the Criminal Code and Criminal Procedure Act as the main normative documents in criminal justice.

For an extensive period of time, Slovenia adhered to the uniform structure of substantive criminal law, meaning that all norms related to criminal justice were to be found in the Criminal Code. In 2008, a new Criminal Code was passed that envisioned a separate law for juvenile offenders. However, due to different reasons as explained later on, such a law has not yet been enforced nor has it been passed by the legislature, resulting in the old Criminal Code's continued use with juveniles. The general orientation is still and is supposed to remain highly rehabilitative: juvenile offending is seen mostly as a sign that the juveniles need some sort of help in

K. Filipčič (✉)
Faculty of Law, University of Ljubljana, and Institute of Criminology at the Faculty of Law University of Ljubljana, Ljubljana, Slovenia
e-mail: katja.filipcic@pf.uni-lj.si

M.M. Plesničar
Institute of Criminology at the Faculty of Law University of Ljubljana, Ljubljana, Slovenia
e-mail: mojca.plesnicar@pf.uni-lj.si

S.H. Decker, N. Marteache (eds.), *International Handbook of Juvenile Justice*,
DOI 10.1007/978-3-319-45090-2_19

readjusting their behavior toward a more conforming stance. The tide may be changing on that notion, but so far normative documents as well as professional practice still remains within those limits (Filipčič 2010a).

AGE OF MAJORITY

Generally, in the Slovenian system children reach the age of majority at 18 years of age but are granted partial independence at 15. Once aged 15, the child is allowed to use their own earnings, enter into legal contracts (with parental consent if they may have significant impact on their future), enter into a work contract, dispose of their copyrights, file law suits, or write their own will.

After the age of 15, a child may also get married or attest to the paternity of a child, by which he or she becomes emancipated. In order to do so, the Centre for Social Work (acting as a child protection service) needs to give its approval, conditioned on the child's mental and physical ability to live independently.

Criminal Responsibility of Children

With regard to criminal responsibility there are several categories into which children are divided and according to which their legal status differs.

- Children (under the age of 14): are not criminally responsible, in case a criminal offense is committed, social services (Centre for Social Work) are alerted and get involved with the child and their family
- Younger minors (aged 14–16): are criminally responsible, but may only be sentenced with educational measures
- Older minors (aged 16–18): are criminally responsible and may be sentenced with all sanctions available for juvenile offenders, including juvenile imprisonment and fines
- Young adults II (committed the criminal offense as adults, but have not reached the age of 21 by the end of the trial): criminally responsible and typically sentenced as adults, but given special circumstances the court may decide to sentence them as juveniles and use educational measures

The age of criminal responsibility is set at 14 years of age and has remained unchanged since the mid-twentieth century. The reasoning behind the formal age requirement is that at that age children are able to understand the meaning of their conduct. Children under the age of 14, who commit a criminal offense, may only be dealt with by Centers for Social Work, notwithstanding the severity of the committed offense and notwithstanding their real maturity. Thus, the limitation is determined by the chronological age and the courts may not change it in individual cases (Filipčič 2006).

The analyses of some cases in recent years when children under the age of 14 (allegedly) committed severe criminal offenses brought up the issue of the adequacy of such a regulation. It was found that the procedural protection of children treated by Centers for Social Work are not adequate, which is all the more worrisome, considering that they have the authority to commit children to a juvenile institution, essentially amounting to one of the most severe institutional educational measures that courts may impose after a criminal proceeding. However, these findings did not propel serious propositions for lowering the age of criminal responsibility, but rather reopened consideration about introducing specialized "family courts." Establishing such courts would reduce the competencies of the Centers for Social Work and redefine their role in the system. However, the specific procedure, powers, and systemic placing of such courts have not yet been determined and it is unlikely they will be established in the near future.

On the other end of the spectrum, even though the legal options exist, young adults are not often sentenced with educational measures, making the last of the presented group more of a theoretical possibility than practical option (Filipčič 2010a).

THE COUNTRY'S STANCE TOWARD THE UN COMMITTEE ON THE RIGHTS OF THE CHILD

Generally, the UN Committee on the Rights of the Child is not unfavorable toward the state of the rights of the child in Slovenia. With regard to juvenile justice specifically, there are no intolerable breaches of international documents that would raise concern with the Committee. However, the Committee's last report from 2013 reiterates its distress over the general lack of special provisions for children in the Criminal Code as well as a more specific lack of open educational institutions for children aged 14–16 in conflict with the law (UN Committee on the Rights of the Child 2013). Moreover, the Committee's concern about the rules on juvenile pretrial detention, expressed as far back as 1996, has not yet been addressed.

Generally, juvenile justice is not considered a problematic or pressing issue in Slovenia, which is to an extent understandable given the figures presented later. Accordingly, the Committee's recommendations with regard to juvenile justice have not been addressed immediately (Filipčič and Prelić 2011). However, the Ministry of Justice has been preparing a comprehensive new law regulating juvenile offenders, thus enacting the Committee's first recommendation.

A separate law was envisioned as far back as 2009, when the new Criminal Code came into force. Previously, the Criminal Code had special provisions with regard to sentencing juveniles in its general part, while procedural specifics were included in the Criminal Procedure Act. The new Criminal Code envisioned a separate law regulating all matters regarding juvenile offenders, but the government failed to prepare one immediately. In fact, the intermittent period had to undergo the scrutiny of the Constitutional Court due to a nomotechnic gaffe in the new Criminal Code. While stating that general provisions of the old Criminal Code remain valid until a specific law is enacted, the new Criminal Code failed to expressly state that its special part applies to juveniles nonetheless.[1] After a period of uncertainty, the Constitutional Court, however, held that all relevant provisions, the general ones regarding juveniles from the old Criminal Code and the provisions from the special part of the new Criminal Code are valid.[2]

The Ministry of Justice has assembled a team of experts who have prepared a draft for the new law regulating juvenile offenders in 2010, but the law has since gone through several phases of coordination with main actors (Courts, Prosecutors, Ombudsman, Bar Association, etc.), which have so far yielded no results. According to information from the Ministry and its legislative schedule, however, the law should be passed in 2016.

The passing of such a legislation should also resolve the issue of pretrial detention raised by the Committee on the Rights of the Child. The committee assessed the duration of pretrial detention in Slovenia as excessively long, in fact, when compared to other European systems only Turkey has a longer maximum pretrial detention (Dünkel et al. 2009). In Slovenia juveniles can be detained for a maximum of 3 months prior to the charge being filed (adults for 6 months) and once the charges are filed, detention can last for an additional 2 years (same as for adult offenders). Regardless of the explicit recommendation from the Committee, the legislation has not been amended so far. Partly, this may be due to a rather different practice: statistics show that juveniles spend more than 3 months in detention in just exceptional cases: just 3.6% juveniles (7 juveniles in total) in last 10 years.[3]

Regardless of a more adequate judicial practice, it seems rather inadequate for the government to have ignored the issue at the legislative level for so long. It seems especially problematic when taking into account the numerous amendments in the past years and the fact that such a change would be largely undisputed by the relevant actors in the field as well as by the public (cf. Filipčič and Prelić 2011). The new law regulating juvenile offenders, which will encompass substantive as well as specific procedural rules, is supposed to remedy the situation.

TRENDS IN JUVENILE CRIME OVER THE PERIOD 2004–2014

Slovenia has experienced a steady decline of recorded juvenile crime in the years past its independence in 1991 and the trend has continued in the past 10 years. The number of juveniles involved in registered criminal activities has almost halved from 1912 in 2004 to 1044 in 2014, and the same is true for the number of

[1] The structure of the Slovenian Criminal Code is comparable to those of other continental legal systems. It is divided into a general part regulating general issues such as jurisdiction, culpability, sentencing, etc., and a special part listing incriminations for specific offenses and sentencing ranges. See (Ambrož and Plesničar 2009).

[2] Constitutional Court decision U-I-73/09, 2 July 2009.

[3] More on juvenile detention later on.

Table 19.1. Juvenile crime in Slovenia

	Juvenile offenders		Criminal offenses	
Year	*Number*	*Percentage of all offenders*	*Number*	*Percentage of all criminal offenses*
2004	1912	10.3	3349	3.9
2005	1631	9.3	2847	3.4
2006	1550	8.7	2527	2.8
2007	1508	8.6	2596	2.9
2008	1439	8.4	2352	2.9
2009	1525	8.0	2316	2.6
2010	1440	7.2	2150	2.4
2011	1301	6.9	2007	2.3
2012	1200	6.5	1827	2.0
2013	1083	5.9	2026	2.2
2014	1044	5.7	1909	2.2

(*Source*: Police data)

registered crimes, dropping from 3349 in 2004 to 1909 in 2014. This is not a reflection of an overall drop in crime in Slovenia as the share of crime committed by juveniles has also dropped from 3.9% in 2004 to 2.2% in 2014 (Table 19.1).

The relatively small number of criminal activities committed by the Slovenian youth can, however, be confirmed by a self-report study done by Meško and Bertok (2013). The study found that less than a fifth (18%; 22% for boys and 15% for girls) of the surveyed youth aged 14–16 years old reported committing a criminal offense in the previous year. This puts Slovenian youth at the low end of comparative rankings (Enzmann et al. 2010).

Among experts (e.g., police officer, social workers, and school psychologists) there is no expectation of a radical shifting of the proportions of juvenile crime, in fact they expect the status quo to continue. Police officers, however, have pointed out the drop in the number of recorded crime and have expressed disconcert about the gray field of juvenile criminality, especially with respect to the (ab) uses of modern technologies (Meško and Bertok 2013).

Among the juvenile offenders, most offenses (about 60%) fall into the category of property crimes, a proportion that has been dropping since 2004, but gained momentum after 2012. Drug-related crimes have been on a steady rise, amounting to 7% in 2014, while the proportion as well as the absolute number of violent crimes has been dropping steadily and now amount to about 6% of all juvenile crime (Table 19.2).

A group of criminal offenses rarely prosecuted and hence not included in official statistics, however, arises from the Meško and Bertok's (2013) study. Over 50% of the interviewed youth self-reported perusing modern technologies in order to illegally obtain copyrighted materials, most commonly movies and computer games. These

TABLE 19.2. Types of offenses committed by juveniles

	Violent crimes[a]		*Property crimes*[b]		*Drug related crimes*[c]	
	Number	*Percentage*	*Number*	*Percentage*	*Number*	*Percentage*
2004	229	6.8	2018	60.2	156	4.6
2005	312	11.0	1703	59.8	75	2.6
2006	198	7.8	1516	60.0	84	3.3
2007	228	8.8	1319	50.8	70	2.7
2008	211	9.0	1100	46.8	84	3.6
2009	229	9.9	1187	51.2	104	4.5
2010	195	9.1	1217	56.6	112	5.2
2011	174	8.7	1150	57.3	120	6.0
2012	177	9.7	1035	56.6	98	5.4
2013	131	6.5	1386	68.4	101	5.0
2014	109	5.7	1159	60.7	141	7.4

[a]Violent crimes: homicide, bodily harm, rape, and other forms of sexual violence
[b]Property crimes: theft, robbery, burglary, fraud
[c]Drug related crimes: unlawful manufacture and trade of narcotic drugs (Art. 196 CC), rendering opportunity for consumption of drugs (Art. 197 CC). Possession of drugs for personal use is not a crime—it is a misdemeanor dealt with by the court in a special procedure. According to Slovenian law, misdemeanors are petty offenses, such as traffic offenses or graffiti, penalized under the Code of Misdemeanors with a fine. Some educational measures can also be imposed in the case of misdemeanors
(*Source*: Police data)

are to an extent criminalized in the Slovenian context, but rarely prosecuted and sentenced, and there have been propositions with the view of increasing education on the topic or even amending copyright laws instead of a more stringent criminal response. The relatively lax system is reflected in the views of the youth—they hardly acknowledge these acts as criminal, especially as they are rather nondeviant among their peers, and sometimes have trouble distinguishing between legal and illegal distribution of such materials (Meško and Bertok 2013).

CAUSES OF JUVENILE CRIME

There has been no extensive research into the causes of juvenile crime in Slovenia; however, some limited studies and research might offer some degree of insight into what the causes may be. The sudden rise in the proportion of property crime may be, to an extent, attributed to the upsetting economic downturn after 2008. The rates of child poverty, while still comparatively low, have risen in the past years, causing more and more strain between the perceived necessary goods for youngsters and the ability to obtain them in a law-abiding manner (Leskošek 2015). Child poverty has, moreover, not been properly addressed by the Slovenian government (Stropnik 2013) and many of the actions designed to alleviate the issues of child poverty have not had the wanted results (Strban 2015).

Such friction may be exacerbated by the use of alcohol and occasional drugs as well as peer pressure. Meško and Bertok (2013) in fact describe that within the small group of juveniles who reported committing more than five criminal offenses (2.2% off all youth in the study) all of them also reported using drugs and having friends who committed property offenses. Further, two-thirds reported having friends who committed violent offenses.

This group of youngsters reporting about multiple offenses unsurprisingly also reported on typical predictors of deviant behavior, such as coming from a single-parent family, living in underprivileged neighborhoods, being born in another country. They also reported other deviant behavior, such as school truancy (84.6%), drinking, smoking marihuana, and using drugs (almost 40% reported having been drunk more than two times in the previous month compared to 3.3% among the nonoffending respondents, 32% smoked marihuana in the previous month, over 80% experienced drugs at some point in their lives). Moreover, they expressed lower levels of self-control and a strong identification with the concept of machismo legitimizing violence. Importantly, they also reported being victimized at a higher rate than nonoffending youths. Over half of them were victimized: among them 18% reported that they were battered and 15% were victims of violence due to discriminatory factors (religion, nationality, etc.). Among the nonoffending youth the proportion of victimized children was 33% (Meško and Bertok 2013).

POLICING AND JUVENILES

One of the basic principles of Slovenian criminal procedure is the legality of prosecution (as opposed to the principle of opportunity) (Perrodet 2002). Meaning that officials, be it police officers or prosecutors, who obtain evidence that a criminal offense was committed, are obliged to institute criminal proceedings. Accordingly, there is not much room for any type of police discretion when dealing with juvenile offenders. Police officers are required to report all cases they come in contact with to the prosecution. The prosecution, however, has some opportunity for diversion, as explained later in the chapter (Filipčič 2015).

As there are no empirical studies focused on police practices regarding juvenile offenders, we can only make educated guesses as to what actually happens. Given the declining numbers of juveniles being processed officially by the police, it seems very likely that the police do in fact enact some sort of diversion in the field, only initiating formal proceedings in more serious cases. This is corroborated by individual stories and anecdotes, but, as mentioned earlier, there are no empirical studies to confirm this hypothesis.

COURTS AND JUVENILES

The Courts

There are no separate courts for juvenile offenders in Slovenia. Juvenile offenders are tried at regular first instance Local and District Courts, while Higher Courts and the Supreme Court decide on legal remedies (Plesničar et al. 2006).

However, some level of specialization is achieved by having semispecialized juvenile judges, who preside over adult matters as well, depending on the case load, but are always assigned juvenile cases. At the level of District Courts, who hold jurisdiction over more serious criminal offenses punishable by 3 years imprisonment and more, a panel of judges, composed by one professional and two lay judges typically decides. Lay judges cooperate with a professional judge on equal terms in deciding on the verdict as well as on the sentence. In the case of juvenile offenders, the professional judge is semispecialized as earlier and the lay judges are elected among professors, teachers, educators, and other persons experienced in the education of juveniles (Filipčič 2006).

The Procedure

The criminal procedure for juvenile offenders follows the standard criminal procedure for adult offenders (Šugman Stubbs 2008). The Criminal Procedure Act, however, has special provisions to be used when processing juvenile offenders, aimed at reducing the harmful effects of the procedure on the juvenile.

The proceeding starts with an obligatory preliminary phase, the purpose of which is to establish facts connected to a criminal offense, and, particularly, to evaluate the juvenile offender's maturity, personality, and the circumstances in which the juvenile lives. The judge is obliged to conduct certain acts in order to establish relevant circumstances. In addition to questioning the juvenile, the judge must question the parents or guardians of the juvenile, and other persons who could provide information on these circumstances, who do not have the option to waive testimony on the personality of a juvenile and the conditions in which he/she lives. A report from the Centre for Social Work needs to be obtained as well as expert opinions on the juvenile's health, mental maturity, and psychological characteristics, when the judges deems it necessary.

The judge may order that the juvenile is sent to a diagnostic center, placed under the supervision of the Centre for Social Work, or placed with another family, if his or her home environment is deemed harmful or when help, protection, or accommodation is needed. The duration of the order may last throughout the proceedings but can also be abrogated at any time. A special appeal to the panel for juvenile offenders at the higher court is allowed against the order of any of the stated measures.

Once all relevant data is gathered, the juvenile judge informs the state prosecutor, who may decide to file charges or use other means to divert proceedings as

TABLE 19.3. Juvenile offenders registered by the police and sentenced by the court

Year	*Juvenile offenders registered by the police*	*Juvenile offenders with a court imposed sanction*	
2004	1.912	570	30%
2005	1.631	452	28%
2006	1.550	459	30%
2007	1.508	411	27%
2008	1.439	432	30%
2009	1.525	375	25%
2010	1.440	304	21%
2011	1.301	318	24%
2012	1.200	349	29%
2013	1.083	368	34%
2014	1.044	276	26%

(*Source*: Statistical Office)

explained later on. The charges may be dismissed by the juvenile judge using the opportunity principle, or referred to mediation, or to a panel for juvenile offenders which decides the case.

In practice, generally less than a third of juvenile cases, reported to the police, end up with a court imposed sanction (See Table 19.3). The reason for the stark difference is the options that the prosecutors and juvenile judges have to dismiss the case because of the expediency principle or to refer it to mediation or other forms of diversion (Filipčič 2006).

The proceeding in front of the judicial panel for juvenile offenders reflects regular adult proceedings, with one major exception: in order to safeguard the juvenile offender's identity and future, the public is excluded from all hearings and there is no public record on the proceedings.

Sanctions

One of the more important differences when comparing juvenile to adult proceedings is the notion of sanctions. The primary difference is of a general nature: the purpose of a sanction in cases of juvenile offenders is to ensure that the juvenile receives education, reeducation, and the opportunity for adequate personal development. The purpose is entirely rehabilitative in nature and reflects the view that a criminal offense committed by a juvenile offender is a sign of distress and personality troubles. Moreover, the seriousness and nature of the criminal offense are only relevant in exceptional cases, when juvenile imprisonment is considered as a sanction, and not when deciding on other appropriate sanctions (Filipčič 2006). This differs significantly from the general concept for adult offenders which is also partly rehabilitative, but punitive and preventive as well (Plesničar

2013). The sanction imposed by the court must, therefore, not only provide for assistance and protection, but also for the supervision which the juvenile needs to rehabilitate or reintegrate in society (Filipčič 2006).

Generally, Slovenian penal law acknowledges four types of sanctions: Sentences (e.g., prison and fines), admonitory sanctions (e.g., suspended sentence), safety measures (e.g., compulsory psychiatric treatment), and educational measures. In the case of juvenile offenders the court may only choose among different types of educational measures and, in exceptional circumstances, the sentence of juvenile imprisonment or a fine.

The main criterion in deciding whether to impose an educational measure or a sentence is the age of the juvenile offender. The group of younger minors (aged 14–16) may only be sanctioned with an educational measure, while juvenile imprisonment and a fine may also exceptionally be used for the group of older minors (aged 16–18). When explaining a sentence of juvenile imprisonment the court is required to justify such a measure in great detail and explain why a lesser measure was not applicable.

A fine may only be imposed on a juvenile if the offender has his own financial means and is able to pay it by himself. In the case of a default payment, a fine cannot be substituted by imprisonment but must be converted into nonresidential educational measures. In practice, fines are almost never used as a juvenile sentence.

Data from the Statistical Office shows that in about 98% of all juvenile cases, an educational measure is chosen as the appropriate sanction. It is important to reemphasize that when deciding on educational measure to apply, the only criterion for the court is the juvenile offender's resocialization and in no way the seriousness of the offense.

Educational Measures

There are six educational measures that may be imposed on juvenile offenders:

- A reprimand
- Instructions and prohibitions (with 11 different possibilities)
- Supervision by a social welfare agency (Centre for social work)
- Committal to an educational home
- Committal to a juvenile correctional home
- Committal to an institution for physically or mentally handicapped youth

Three of the six educational measures are carried out in the juvenile's existing home environment (nonresidential), while the last three measures include taking the juvenile out of the environment deemed detrimental toward the youth (residential). Courts are restrictive in using the latter form: in over 85% of cases one of the first three listed measures is applied, meaning the juvenile remains at home (See Table 19.4).

TABLE 19.4. Types of sanctions imposed on juvenile offenders in %

Year	*Total sanctions imposed*	*Nonresidential educational measures %*	*Residential educational measures %*	*Juvenile detention %*	*Fine %*
2000	591	93.0	4.6	1.5	0.8
2001	571	94.8	3.5	0.9	0.9
2002	728	94.3	4.0	0.8	1.0
2003	568	91.9	6.7	0.7	0.7
2004	615	92.6	4.7	1.3	0.8
2005	497	90.8	6.8	1.6	0.6
2006	506	89.9	5.7	2.1	1.7
2007	459	89.6	6.3	2.8	1.3
2008	489	88.4	9.8	1.2	0.6
2009	414	89.7	8.4	0.7	0.2
2010	327	92.1	5.8	0.6	0.6
2011	369	86.2	12.7	0.3	0.3
2012	398	87.7	11.3	1.0	0
2013	434	84.9	13.8	1.1	0.2
2014	314	87.9	11.8	0.3	0

(*Source*: Statistical Office)

Nonresidential Measures

Among the three types of nonresidential educational measures, reprimand has the longest tradition, but its use has been decreasing as (at least seemingly) more effective alternatives have been introduced.

The largest group of measures is hidden under the category "Instructions and prohibitions," which includes 11 different options for the court to choose from. The juvenile offender thus may be required to (1) make a personal apology to the injured party; (2) reach a settlement with the injured party by means of payment, work, or otherwise in order to recover the damages caused in the course of committing the offense; (3) regularly attend school; (4) take up a form of vocational e, ducation or to take up a form of employment suitable to the offender's knowledge, skills, and inclinations; (5) live with a specified family or in a certain institution; (6) perform community service or work for humanitarian organizations; (7) submit oneself to treatment in an appropriate health institution; (8) attend sessions of educational, vocational, psychological, or other consultation; (9) attend a social training course; (10) pass an examination for obtaining a driving license; or may be prohibited to (11) operate a motor vehicle (Art. 77, Par. 2 of the Criminal Code).

While several instructions and prohibitions have become a regular choice of Slovenian courts, there are some issues with their practical implementation. The most problematic seems to be community service, which even after 20 years since its implementation, has not been fully utilized. There have been substantive

Table 19.5. Nonresidential educational measures

Year	*Total nonresidential educational measures*	*Reprimand %*	*Instructions and prohibitions %*	*Supervision by a social welfare agency %*
2000	549	31.7	24.4	43.9
2001	541	30.9	19.2	49.9
2002	686	31.6	15.5	52.9
2003	522	32.8	14.5	52.7
2004	570	25.8	16.7	57.5
2005	452	22.3	19.5	58.2
2006	459	22.2	15.5	62.3
2007	411	19.5	21.2	59.3
2008	432	18.5	28.3	53.2
2009	375	15.7	27.7	56.6
2010	304	21.1	26.3	52.6
2011	318	16.7	29.9	53.4
2012	349	14.3	34.7	51.0
2013	368	20.7	24.1	55.2
2014	276	11.9	15.2	72.9

(*Source*: Statistical Office)

problems in the early stages of implementation, mainly due to nonresolved financial issues, some of which have not been resolved even after two decades (Filipčič 2015).

During the implementation of the imposed measure, the court may decide to replace it with a different measure, should regular reporting from social service agencies indicate that such a change would achieve the purpose of sentencing, i.e., resocializing and reeducating them (Table 19.5).

Residential Measures

There are two types of institutions for residential educational measures: educational and correctional homes. The main differences between them, are the juveniles who can be placed there and the different regimes in place. There are four educational homes for juveniles who are in need of care and help. They can be placed into such an institution by a decision of the Centre for Social Work (e.g., if parents cannot provide proper care to the child, if the child runs away from home often or does not go to school), or by judgment of the court because the juvenile has committed a crime. The total capacity of these institutions is about 500 children and only about 10% are juvenile offenders (Filipčič 2006). In addition, regardless of the reason for being placed in the institution all children are treated in the same way, stemming from the logic that they all need help. All four institutions are organized as small communities with about six juveniles living in a separate apartment together with educators.

Recently, there have been issues placing juvenile offenders in educational homes. Even when judicial panels decide on such a measure, educational homes are not willing to place the juvenile in its care. In some instances they claim that the juvenile has characteristics and needs that require special programs not available at their educational home and thus argue that they are not able to provide the proper care for the youth.

Only one institution specializes in juvenile offenders: a juvenile correctional home center with a capacity for 70 juveniles. The juveniles sanctioned with this educational measure commit more serious offenses and need special help and supervision.

There is no fixed term the child will spend in the educational or correctional home. The minimum length is set at 1 year while the maximum length of time may not exceed 3 years. There are regular 6-month reviews as to whether the measure is still necessary throughout that period. Juvenile judges may stop the execution of the educational measures on the grounds of positive treatment outcomes or they may modify the imposed measure. After the first year the juvenile may be conditionally released, and in that case the court may decide for the supervision of the young person by the social service (Filipčič 2006).

Since 2008 there has been a noticeable increase in the proportion of juveniles being sent away from home as part of their sanction, which may at first glance indicate a more punitive attitude of the courts. However, such a conclusion seems premature, given the lack of empirical research. Other factors could be at play: on the one hand the increase could be linked to an upturn of juveniles with drug or alcohol problems in recent years, who are therefore in need of longer and more intensive treatment (Filipčič 2010a). On the other hand when taking into account that the total number of registered juvenile offenses as well as the total number of sanctioned juveniles have been steadily decreasing, it seems more adequate to assume the changes are due to more serious cases being brought to the sanctioning phase with more official and nonofficial diversion being implemented at earlier stages.

CUSTODIAL RULES FOR JUVENILES (DETENTION, PRISON, MIXING JUVENILES WITH ADULTS)

Imprisonment is extremely rare for juveniles in Slovenia. Among juveniles, less than 2% of offenders are sentenced to juvenile imprisonment—in recent years there has often been just one juvenile offender per year (See Table 19.7) and the total sum of imprisoned juveniles in the last 15 years is just 65, among whom just one was a girl (Prison administration data).

Notwithstanding common generalizations about communist regimes, Slovenia has had a tradition of a lenient penal system through a large part of its communist past (Petrovec and Muršič 2011; Petrovec and Plesničar 2014). Specifically with regard to juveniles, a welfare approach was developed, emphasizing the (re)socializing of youth with a rather nonexistent punitive dimension (Filipčič 2006; Filipčič and Prelić 2011). The approach has been to a large extent continued after the fall of the communist regime, which is in contrast to what has happened with the purposes and practice of sentencing adult offenders (Petrovec and Plesničar 2014).

Detention

As explained early on in the chapter pretrial detention has been a sore spot in Slovenian juvenile justice. Somewhat paradoxically, the practice is less problematic than the normative framework, though the only real problem with it is the allowed length of detention.

Since the purpose of pretrial detention is not punitive, but is parallel to the purpose in adult proceedings, i.e., an unobstructed criminal proceeding, both groups of legally responsible juveniles (aged between 14 and 16 and those aged between 16 and 18) can be placed in pretrial detention (Šugman Stubbs 2008) for reasons of danger of escape or collusion. As explained later on, juvenile prison is only a sentencing option for older juveniles, so it is understandable that more juveniles are in pretrial detention than in prison (Filipčič and Prelić 2011). However, The Criminal Procedure Act explicitly regulates that juvenile offenders may only be detained in exceptional cases (Art. 472).

Additionally, the Criminal Procedure Act regulates for alternatives to pretrial detention, which may be imposed in proceedings against juvenile (and adult) perpetrators of criminal offenses, when conditions to order detention are met, but the judge assesses that a lesser measure could suffice to achieve the same purpose (Art. 192). The alternatives are home detention, the prohibition of being in a certain place or approaching a person, and reporting to the police station (Šugman Stubbs 2008).

Duration is the main problem with the Slovenian system of juvenile detention. Juveniles can be detained for a maximum of 3 months prior to the charges being filed (compared to 6 months for adult suspects). However, once the charges are filed, detention can last for an additional 2 years (the same as for adult offenders). As explained previously this duration is comparatively long and has been subject to repeated criticism from the UN Committee on the Rights of the Child. However, in practice the duration of pretrial detention for juveniles never reaches the extremes. Statistics show that juveniles spend more than 3 months in detention in exceptional cases (just 3.6% juveniles in the last 10 years) and never more than 6 months (see Table 19.1). This indicates that judges understand that the limits set by the Criminal Procedure Act are excessive (Table 19.6).

Moreover, judges seem to follow the norm about pretrial detention being used for juveniles only exceptionally as its frequency is relatively low. Omitting common problems with such comparisons, when compared to other European countries,

TABLE 19.6. Number of juveniles in pretrial detention and length of pretrial detention, 2005–2014

Year	Number of juvenile detainees	Up to 15 days (%)	15–30 days (%)	30–90 days (%)	90–180 days (%)
2005	21	19.0	42.9	38.1	–
2006	32	15.6	25.0	59.4	–
2007	16	–	37.5	62.5	–
2008	14	35.7	28.6	35.7	–
2009	20	5.0	20.0	65.0	–
2010	12	8.4	33.3	58.3	–
2011	14	–	21.4	78.6	–
2012	17	5.9	11.8	64.7	17.6
2013	15	13.4	–	66.8	26.8
2014	6	33.4	–	66.7	–
Sum	197	17.3	24.4	54.7	3.6

(*Source*: Ministry of Justice)

Slovenia is one of the countries with the lowest share of juveniles in pretrial detention in 2007 (Filipčič and Prelić 2011).[4]

Another sore spot of the Slovenian system of pretrial detention for juveniles may be their placement. They are commonly placed in pretrial detention units of adult prisons, which do not have specially determined spaces for juveniles. The Criminal Procedure Code generally requires that juvenile detainees be separated from adults but allows for an exception to this rule: if it is deemed to benefit the juvenile. Such an exception does not generally counter international standards or the Slovenian constitution; however, the Slovenian Constitutional Court has warned against using the exception as a means to resolve overcrowding issues or the authorities' incompetence to provide for a separate unit.[5]

Unfortunately, it seems safe to presume that this is precisely what has been occurring in the past decades. Detaining a juvenile together with an adult is not decided by the prison administration but by the judge for juvenile offenders, an arrangement that should perform as a precaution to ensure that the reason behind the joint placement is not the lack of space in the prison. However, due to

[4]This is true in spite of the peak in pretrial detention for juveniles the Slovenian system in 2006. According to Van Kalmthout et al. (2009) Slovenia shared the third place with Denmark with only 0.7% of detained juveniles, preceded by Belgium and Portugal with 0.2%, Finland 0.3%, and followed by France and Germany with 1%, United Kingdom 2.7%, Ireland 3.2%, Austria 3.4%.

[5]Constitutional Court decision UI 103/95 (24 September 1996).

the overcrowded prisons (and especially their pretrial detention units)[6] the danger that a judge might (at the recommendation of the prison administration) try to solve the lack of space with such a decision seems far from just theoretical (Filipčič and Prelić 2011).

The issue of prison overcrowding has also been brought up by the Slovene ombudsman, who has described the conditions for pretrial prisoners in one of the Slovene prisons as inhumane (Varuh človekovih pravic RS 2008). The Ombudsman has also addressed the issue of placing juveniles in adult pretrial detention units in 1999 when dealing with a specific complaint from a 14-year-old juvenile placed in detention with two adult detainees who was subjected to their abuse and ridicule. After the Ombudsman's intervention the juvenile was separated from the adult detainees (Varuh človekovih pravic RS 2000). Additionally, when the European Committee for the Prevention of Torture and Inhuman or Degrading Treatment or Punishment (CPT) visited Slovenia in 1995 and in 2006, it drew attention to the issue of separated detention. It explicitly emphasized that even in exceptional cases the adults placed with juveniles have to be carefully selected so that they do not exploit the juvenile or have a bad influence upon them in any other way (Committee for the Prevention of Torture (CPT) 2008).

Prison

Juvenile imprisonment is only possible for the older group of juveniles aged between 16 and 18 years old and in special circumstances for young adults aged 18–21. Excluding the younger group of minors from the option of juvenile imprisonment is not a uniquely Slovenian feature (Dünkel et al. 2009), but it is consistent with the overall welfarist approach to juvenile delinquents (Filipčič 2006). A juvenile prison sentence can only be imposed in the case of serious offenses for which a sentence of 5 years or more is prescribed. The Court needs to consider the seriousness of the offense and the level of the juvenile's criminal responsibility as well as the juvenile's maturity and the time necessary for his rehabilitation and vocational training. If a sentence of juvenile imprisonment is imposed, the court has to explain why an educational measure would not be appropriate, which is in line with the stated general purpose of punishment of juveniles, i.e., rehabilitation (Filipčič and Prelić 2011).

A juvenile may be imprisoned for a period not shorter than 6 months and not longer than 5 years. Only in the case of criminal offenses punishable by 30 years imprisonment for adults (e.g., aggravated murder), the maximum for juveniles is set at 10 years. This differs from general rules on imprisonment for adults, which put the general minimum sentence at 30 days and the general maximum at 30

[6] Slovenian prisons face the same overcrowding issues as in most European systems (Plesničar 2012b). In 2013 the average occupancy rate was of 110.6% with some prisons facing as high a rate as 156.1%—the latter number is valid for the Ljubljana prison, which incidentally also houses most juvenile pretrial detainees (UIKS 2014).

years (exceptionally allowing for a life sentence). Similar to other European countries the minimum prison sentence for juveniles is higher than the minimum prison sentence for adults; however, this should not be deemed as a reflection of a more repressive approach to juvenile offenders. A higher threshold aims at mirroring the rehabilitation purpose of the prison sentence and the belief that rehabilitation and treatment programs cannot be successfully carried out within a short period of time (Filipčič and Prelić 2011).

In practice, as seen in Table 19.7, over 70% of juveniles sentenced to imprisonment receive a sentence below 2 years, which is rather consistent with adult sentences. Longer sentences are almost an exception, with less than 14% of juveniles sentenced to more than 3 years and less than 5% sentenced to more than 6 years. There have only been two maximum sentences (10 years) in the past 14 years.

Only a small percentage of juveniles serve the entire prison sentence, as most of them are released before the full sentence runs out. This can occur in two ways—either by being granted conditional release by a special committee set by the Ministry of Justice after a juvenile serves one third of the sentence, or by being granted early release by the Prison Warden. The former is the classical rehabilitative instrument practiced in other systems and may entail a rather substantive proportion of the prison sentence being served outside the prison, while the latter is a sort of reward for good behavior which only allows the warden to shorten the prisoner's stay for a couple of months (Plesničar 2012a). In the last

TABLE 19.7. Length of juvenile imprisonment sentences, 2001–2014

	<1 year	*1–2 years*	*2–3 years*	*3–4 years*	*4–5 years*	*6–10 years*	*10 years*	*Sum*
2000	1	2	2	1		1		7
2001	2	1	2					5
2002		7					1	8
2003	2	3						5
2004		2	1					3
2005	3	3	3	1	1			11
2006		4						4
2007		2	2					4
2008	3	1		1				5
2009	3	1		1				5
2010		1						1
2011							1	1
2012		1						1
2013		3			1			4
2014		1						1
Sum	14	32	10	4	2	1	2	65
	21.50%	49.20%	15.4%	6.2%	3.1%	1.5%	3.1%	

(*Source*: Prison Administration Office)

TABLE 19.8. Release of juveniles from juvenile imprisonment

	Served full sentence	*Conditional release*	*Early release*	*Other*	*Sum*
2005	1	2	1		4
2006	1	7	1	1	10[a]
2007		4			4
2008	1	2	2		5
2009	2	2			4
2010	1				1
2011	1				1
2012	1		3		4
2013		1			1
2014		1			1
Sum	8	19	7	1	35
	22.90%	54.30%	20%	2.80%	

[a]One of the released juveniles was a girl
(*Source*: Prison Administration Office)

10 years (between 2005 and 2014), 35 juveniles were released from juvenile prison; only 23% of them served their entire sentences, 54% were conditionally released on average 6 months before their full sentence, and 20% were released 1 month prior to the full sentence (Table 19.8).

Mixing Juveniles with Adults

The only instance when mixing juveniles with adults seems problematic in Slovenia is the issue of mixing juvenile offenders with adults in the phase of pre-trial detention as explained earlier in greater detail.

In terms of criminal procedure for juveniles, Slovenia follows the tradition of related criminal justice systems such as that of Germany, Austria, and Switzerland, where the transfer of juveniles to adult courts is inadmissible. In the case of juvenile offenders, the court generally cannot apply the procedure for adult offenders and cannot impose the sanctions for adults, notwithstanding the severity of the committed crime (Filipčič and Prelić 2011). Quite the opposite is true in these systems as well as in the Slovenian one, which allows that young adults be tried as juveniles in exceptional cases as explained earlier.[7]

[7]There are two exceptions to applying the adult criminal procedure in cases of juveniles: first, if an offender is tried for offenses committed as juvenile together with offenses committed after coming of age, the procedure for adult offenders is typically used (Criminal Procedure Act, Art. 457). Second, if a juvenile offender commits criminal offenses together with adult offenders, the case is generally tried separately. However, the court may decide for the trials to be held together using the regular procedure, if it deems it absolutely necessary in order to adequately process the case (Criminal Procedure Act, Art. 456).

As the number of juvenile offenders sentenced to imprisonment rarely exceeds 5 per year, there are no separate juvenile prison institutions in Slovenia. The boys' juvenile prison is located within one of the seven adult correctional facilities. However, as opposed to the pretrial detention conditions, the juveniles in prison are completely separated from adult offenders. They are placed in a separate section of the prison and there is no mixing neither at the time of daily meals nor during the time spent outside. There is no separate unit for girls at the only women's prison in Slovenia, but given that there has only been one girl placed in juvenile imprisonment in the last 15 years, that is understandable.

ALTERNATIVE SANCTIONS FOR JUVENILES: HOME CONFINEMENT, RESTORATIVE JUSTICE, RESTITUTION, ETC.

Alternative Sanctions

Alternative sanctions in general do not have a long tradition in Slovenia. The same is true for alternative sanctions for juvenile offenders: they have only been developing in the last two decades after Slovenia's independence and its renewed criminal legislation.

Nevertheless, at least some of them have become a regular and frequent feature of juvenile justice. Among the educational measures described previously, the three nonresidential ones could, to an extent, be considered alternative sanctions. This is less true for reprimands and for orders for supervision by a social welfare agency but is largely valid for the group of measures under the title "Instructions and Prohibitions."

As explained earlier, there are 11 possible measures, among which making a personal apology to the victim, and reaching a settlement with the injured party about ways to remedy damages carry notions of restorative justice. Community service epitomizes the most typical alternative sanction. However, especially with the latter, troubles with practical implementation persist: among the more important ones, lack of adequate demand for such community work combined with an overburdened social service system that is tasked with finding such alternatives are serious issues. Both problems are tied to budgetary issues: there has not yet been a suitable solution for (very limited) expenses incurred due to employing a juvenile offender in community service and social services have not been granted any additional resources or personnel to deal with the new work tasks they are bound to perform with regard to community service (Filipčič 2015).

Diversion

Beside alternative sanctions that would follow the entire procedure other ways of bringing in the "alternative" into juvenile justice have been sought in the past decades. As mentioned earlier, there has been no research into the possible ways police officers divert juveniles from the criminal justice system, though this is likely to have been occurring. On the other hand, there have been extensive normative and practical changes in the role the prosecution plays in diverting juveniles from the formal system.

The state prosecutor may, with the consent of the accused and the injured party, decide to refer the case to one of two forms of alternative diversionary procedures: mediation or the deferment of prosecution. The main criterion for the prosecutor to decide on is the gravity of the offense, yet other factors may be important as well. The only formal limit to the prosecutor's discretion is the nature of the offense: juvenile offenders accused of crimes punishable by more than 5 years of imprisonment cannot be diverted from the regular procedure. Originally the limit was set uniformly for adult and juvenile offenders at offenses punishable by 3 years imprisonment, but prosecutors themselves pushed for normative changes in favor of more discretion with regard to juveniles (Filipčič 2010b).

Data for 2014 show that prosecutors dismissed 54% of all cases, among which 48% for reasons of utility and minor importance of the offense, and 12% for the alternative options of mediation and deferment of prosecution. This is a significant drop from 2002, when the latter group of reasons comprised about 30% of all dismissals (Office of the State Prosecutor General). Again, some of the reasons for such a development may be budget-related. As the prosecution's budged diminished due to the financial crisis, money for alternative procedures, and especially mediation, has become virtually nonexistent thus disabling prosecutors from viably using all the alternative options.

Mediation

A juvenile offender's criminal case may be referred to mediation before or after charges are filed against the juvenile. The prosecutor may refer the case after considering the type of offense, its nature, the circumstances in which it was committed, the offender's personality, and his or her past conduct. The offender's plea has never been a legal requirement for the prosecutor's decision; however, it seems unlikely for the prosecutor to refer a case in which the defendant denies and refuses to accept responsibility, as the probability of success of such mediation would be minimal (Filipčič 2010b). If mediation is deemed successful, which means that the offender comes to and fulfils an agreement made with the victim, the prosecution dismisses the criminal charge.

There are no institutions or agencies specialized in mediation in Slovenia, instead a lay mediator supervises each case. There are currently about 190 specially trained mediators, a quarter of which are mediators qualified to mediate cases involving juvenile offenders (Filipčič 2010b). The mediation agreements may carry different tasks for the juvenile to fulfill, but most often an apology or compensation of damages is sought (see Table 19.9).

Mediation in juvenile cases saw a steep rise after being introduced in 2004 and then plummeted after the financial crisis and budgetary constraints (see

Table 19.9. Tasks determined in mediation agreements, 2011

Tasks	*%*
Apology	51.7
Compensation of damage	36.7
Restitution	6.7
Community service	3.4
Other	1.6

(*Source*: Office of the State Prosecutor General)

Table 19.10. The number of juvenile cases referred to mediation and success rate, 2004–2014

	Referred cases		
Year	*Number*	*% of all cases*	*Success rate (%)*
2004	344	1.16	68
2005	225	6.46	62
2006	191	5.54	63
2007	194	5.95	69
2008	155	4.92	70
2009	100	3.15	61
2010	155	4.72	76
2011	88	2.80	67
2012	52	1.71	52
2013	17	0.58	94
2014	7	0.26	43

(*Source*: Office of the State Prosecutor General)

Table 19.10). It is now almost never used, despite its rather successful use in the past years. When asked for reasons prosecutors explain they are mainly budgetary in nature. Costs for mediation (mediator, processing, etc.) were previously covered by the general budget allotted to the prosecution. Since the austerity measures were put in place in 2011 and formalized in 2012, the prosecution has had to minimize its expenses, and mediation has been one of the "victims" of savings: money is being spent on salaries and indispensable goods, and cannot be used for other purposes.

Deferment of Prosecution

The other option for diversion for prosecutors is that of deferring prosecution under the condition that the suspected juvenile offender performs certain actions to remove the harmful consequences of the criminal offense. These tasks include repairing or compensating for any damage caused, paying a contribution to a public fund, a charity institution or the compensation fund for victims of crimi-

Table 19.11. Number of juvenile cases referred to deferment and success rate, 2005–2014

Year	*Referred cases*		*Success rate (%)*
	Number	*% of all cases*	
2005	360	10.33	60.5
2006	417	12.10	55.9
2007	332	10.19	70.5
2008	317	10.05	72.6
2009	284	8.94	79.2
2010	286	8.71	63.6
2011	264	10.63	67.8
2012	235	7.76	68.9
2013	169	5.76	62.7
2014	186	7.17	69.3

(*Source*: Office of the State Prosecutor General)

nal offenses, or performing community service. If the suspected youth fulfils the obligation undertaken within a period of 6 months, the criminal complaint is dismissed.

The success rate of such procedures has been rather good (see Table 19.11) and the measure has been used more frequently than mediation. Additionally, it is less budget related than mediation, hence it has not seen the same downfall in recent years.

DIFFERENCES IN TREATMENT OF BOYS AND GIRLS

There are no normative differences envisioned, apart for the division between the prison institutions to which girls and boys sentenced to juvenile imprisonment are sent. There is no such distinction with regard to residential educational measures as educational and correctional homes house both genders together.

As common in other systems as well, the proportion of girls among juvenile offenders is significantly smaller than the proportion of boys. A quick look at the data gathered by the Statistical Office shows that among all the criminal complaints against juvenile offenders in 2014 about 20% were girl offenders. The percentage drops at the next stage: among the charges filed against juvenile offenders about 10% are girls and among juvenile offenders sentenced for a criminal offense about 11% are girls. Moreover, in 2014 none of the girls were sentenced to either juvenile imprisonment or any of the residential educational measures, which is also rather common. As previously mentioned, only one girl has been sentenced with juvenile imprisonment in the last 15 years.

There has been no research that would allow us to assess whether such an occurrence is a consequence of preferential treatment for girls or a consequence of actual differences in the criminal offenses boys and girls have committed, but it seems safe to assume it may be a bit of both. The only girl sent to juvenile prison has committed murder and has been sentenced accordingly, but there have been no similar acts from other juvenile girls in recent years (Petrovec and Plesničar 2009).

CONCLUDING THOUGHTS

The Slovenian juvenile justice system has for the most part resisted modern punitive trends in dealing with juvenile offenders. The welfarist tradition remains strong in this specific field of criminal justice, even though dealing with adult offenders has taken a more punitive route.

The rationale behind punishing juveniles is predominantly rehabilitative and educative. This is best reflected by the strong role welfare agencies have in dealing with juvenile offenders as well as the sanctions applied to juvenile offenders: ever since 1959 the predominant role has been given to educational measures, and among those to nonresidential ones. The upsurge in the use of residential educational measures in recent years might, however, be an indicator that the tide may be turning. It is still early to make such claims, especially without detailed analyses of the reasons for such a sentencing stance, but the trend is certainly worth monitoring in the future, from academics and authorities alike. Luckily the trend has not extended to juvenile imprisonment, which remains very scarcely and carefully applied.

The changes in sanctioning juveniles are especially important when put in the context of steadily diminishing numbers of juvenile offenses and offenders, both in numbers and proportions of all offenders in the system. Moreover, there has been no increase in the number or proportion of violent crimes that would warrant a tougher response, quite the opposite: as the number of all juvenile offenses is dropping and the proportion of violent crimes remains the same, there are actually less violent crimes being committed by juveniles every year.

There is no easy explanation for this welcomed trend, but it seems that looking for the reasons and drivers behind it might be worthwhile not only for the Slovenian context, but for a comparative context as well.

REFERENCES

Ambrož, M., & Plesničar, M. M. (2009). Slovenia. In A. Weyembergh & V. Santamaria (Eds.), *The evaluation of European criminal law: The example of the framework decision on combating trafficking in human beings* (pp. 301–313). Brussels: Editions de l'Université de Bruxelles.

Committee for the Prevention of Torture (CPT). (2008). *Report to the Slovenian Government on the visit to Slovenia carried out by the European Committee for the Prevention of Torture and Inhuman or Degrading Treatment or Punishment (CPT)*. Strasbourg. Retrieved from http://www.cpt.coe.int/documents/svn/2008-07-inf-eng.pdf

Dünkel, F., Grzywa, J., & Pruin, I. (Eds.). (2009). *Juvenile justice systems in Europe—Current situation, reform, developments and good practices*. Mönchengladbach: Forum Verlag Godesberg.
Enzmann, D., Marshall, I. H., Killias, M., Junger-Tas, J., Steketee, M., & Gruszczynska, B. (2010). Self-reported youth delinquency in Europe and beyond: First results of the Second International Self-Report Delinquency Study in the context of police and victimization data. *European Journal of Criminology, 7*(2), 159–183. doi:10.1177/1477370809358018.
Filipčič, K. (2006). Welfare versus neo-liberalism: Juvenile justice in Slovenia. In J. Junger-Tas & S. H. Decker (Eds.), *International handbook of juvenile justice* (pp. 397–414). Dordrecht: Springer.
Filipčič, K. (2010a). Slovenia. In F. Dünkel, J. Grzywa, P. Horsfield, & I. Pruin (Eds.), *Juvenile justice systems in Europe: Current situation and reform developments* (pp. 1263–1286). Mönchengladbach: Forum Verlag.
Filipčič, K. (2010b). Slovenia. In F. Bailleau & Y. Cartuyvels (Eds.), *The criminalisation of youth: Juvenile justice in Europe, Turkey and Canada* (pp. 211–229). Brussels: VUBPress.
Filipčič, K. (2015). Slovenia. In F. Dünkel, J. Grzywa-Holten, & P. Horsfield (Eds.), *Restorative justice and mediation in penal matters: A stock-tacking of legal issues, implementation strategies and outcomes in 36 European countries* (Vol. 2, pp. 847–874). Mönchengladbach: Forum Verlag Godesberg.
Filipčič, K., & Prelić, D. (2011). Deprivation of liberty of juvenile offenders in Slovenia. *The Prison Journal, 91*(4), 448–466. doi:10.1177/0032885511424393.
Flander, B., & Meško, G. (2016). Penal and prison policy on the "Sunny Side of the Alps": The swan song of Slovenian exceptionalism? *European Journal on Criminal Policy and Research*, 1–27. doi:10.1007/s10610-015-9299-1
Leskošek, V. (2015). Revščina otrok—izziv za zaščito ekonomskih pravic otrok. In K. Filipčič & A. Šelih (Eds.), *Otrokove pravice v Sloveniji: Sedanje stanje in izzivi za prihodnost*. Ljubljana: Slovenska akademija znanosti in umetnosti.
Meško, G., & Bertok, E. (2013). *Mladoletniška kriminaliteta in mladoletniško nasilje: Ugotovitve evropske študije o prestopništvu in preventivnih dejavnostih: Priporočila za prakso*. Ljubljana: Fakulteta za varnostne vede.
Perrodet, A. (2002). The public prosecutor. In M. Delmas-Marty & J. R. Spencer (Eds.), *European criminal procedures* (pp. 415–458). Cambridge: Cambridge University Press.
Petrovec, D., & Muršič, M. (2011). Science fiction: Opening prison institutions (The Slovenian penological heritage). *The Prison Journal, 91*(4), 425–447. doi:10.1177/0032885511424394.
Petrovec, D., & Plesničar, M. M. (2009). Perception of female criminality through sentencing. In G. Meško & Kury (Eds.), *Crime policy, crime control and crime prevention—Slovenian perspectives*. Ljubljana: Tipografija.
Petrovec, D., & Plesničar, M. M. (2014). The societal impact and role of imprisonment: An example from Slovenia. In E. Carroll & K. Warner (Eds.), *Re-imagining imprisonment in Europe: Effects, failures and the future* (pp. 71–89). Dublin: Liffey Press.
Plesničar, M. M. (2012a). Slovenska ureditev pogojnega odpusta v luči sodobnih razvojnih trendov. *Revija Za Kriminalistiko in Kriminologijo, 63*(2), 136–148.
Plesničar, M. M. (2012b). How to deal with overcrowding? Presented at the Re-imagining Imprisonment in Europe (Scribani conference), Dublin.
Plesničar, M. M. (2013). The individualization of punishment: Sentencing in Slovenia. *European Journal of Criminology, 10*(4), 462–478.
Plesničar, M. M., Tepina, P., & Vrtačnik, U. (2006). The Slovenian judiciary: A guide through Slovenian courts. *Slovenian Law Review, 3*(1/2), 209–239.
Strban, G. (2015). Socialne pravice v dobrobit otroka: Povečanje ali zmanjšanje njihovega obsega v času recesije? In K. Filipčič & A. Šelih (Eds.), *Otrokove pravice v Sloveniji: Sedanje stanje in izzivi za prihodnost*. Ljubljana: Slovenska akademija znanosti in umetnosti.
Stropnik, N. (2013). *Investing in children: Breaking the cycle of disadvantage—A study of national policies: Slovenia*. Brussels: European Commission. Retrieved from http://ec.europa.eu/social/main.jsp?catId=1025&langId=en&newsId=2061&moreDocuments=yes&tableName=news

Šugman Stubbs, K. (2008). Criminal procedure in Slovenia. In R. Vogler & B. Huber (Eds.), *Criminal procedure in Europe* (pp. 483–539). Berlin: Duncker & Humbolt.

UIKS (Prison Administration). (2014). *Letno poročilo 2013*. Ljubljana. Retrieved from http://www.mp.gov.si/fileadmin/mp.gov.si/pageuploads/UIKS/Letna_porocila/140505_Letno_porocilo_2013.pdf

UN Committee on the Rights of the Child. (2013). *Concluding observations on the combined third and fourth periodic reports of Slovenia adopted by the Committee at its sixty-third session (27 May–14 June 2013)*. New York. Retrieved from http://www.un.org/ga/search/view_doc.asp?symbol=CRC/C/SVN/CO/3-4&Lang=E

Van Kalmthout, A. M., Knapen, M. M., & Morgenstern, C. (Eds.). (2009). *Pre-trial detention in the European Union: An analysis of minimum standards in pre-trial detention and the grounds for regular review in the member states of the EU*. Nijmegen: Wolf Legal.

Varuh človekovih pravic RS (Human Rights Ombudsman). (2000). *Letno poročilo varuha človekovih pravic*. Ljubljana. Retrieved from http://www.varuh-rs.si/fileadmin/user_upload/pdf/lp/vcp_lp_1999_slo.pdf

Varuh človekovih pravic RS (Human Rights Ombudsman). (2008). *Letno poročilo varuha človekovih pravic*. Ljubljana. Retrieved from http://www.varuh-rs.si/fileadmin/user_upload/pdf/lp/VCP-LP07-splet.pdf

Katja Filipčič is associate professor for criminology and criminal law at the Faculty of Law, University in Ljubljana and researcher at the Institute of Criminology in Ljubljana. Her fields of interest: juvenile justice, domestic violence, victims, restorative justice, school violence.

Mojca M. Plesničar is research fellow at the Institute of Criminology in Ljubljana and assistant professor at the University of Ljubljana. Her research focuses on sentencing and punishment, but includes issues of gender, nationality, juveniles, and technology in criminal justice. She has authored several articles and chapters in national and international publications.

20

Spain

Esther Fernández-Molina, María José Bernuz Beneitez, and Raquel Bartolomé-Gutiérrez

JUVENILE OFFENDERS, LAWS, AND RIGHTS

The Legal Status of Juveniles

Juvenile Justice in Spain has evolved differently from its equivalents in other European countries. The idiosyncrasy of the Spanish system and the special political situation which dominated Spain during a large part of the twentieth century, produced in this field, as in many others, a peculiar evolution. Although the Juvenile Justice system in Spain emerged at the beginning of the twentieth century, in accordance with the general movement at that moment in the Western world, the impact of the Franco dictatorship (1939–1975) maintained the tutelary approach while things were changing in the rest of the Western world. Nevertheless, the system started to change when Spain became a democratic country, in 1978 (Rechea and Fernández-Molina 2003).

The juvenile justice process in Spain has evolved considerably in this time as a consequence of both the pressure of legislation and legal practice shaped by the democratic rule of law and Spain's ratification of the United Nations Convention on the Rights of the Child in 1990. Such evolution is manifest in the legislative transition from the OL 4/1992, Juvenile Court Reform Act of 1992 (JCRA) to the OL 5/2000 Juvenile Criminal Act of 2000 (JCA). The 1992 act was the legal text which first allowed the implementation of the "model of responsibility" in

E. Fernández-Molina (✉) • R. Bartolomé-Gutiérrez
University of Castilla-La Mancha, Albacete, Spain
e-mail: esther.fdez@uclm.es; raquel.bartolome@uclm.es

M.J. Bernuz Beneitez
University of Zaragoza, Zaragoza, Spain
e-mail: mbernuz@unizar.es

S.H. Decker, N. Marteache (eds.), *International Handbook of Juvenile Justice*,
DOI 10.1007/978-3-319-45090-2_20

Spain, a "dual" framework striving for a balance between education and punishment in juvenile justice, as proposed by the United Nations and in accordance with the new concept of children as subjects of law and progressively responsible for their acts. This legislation also included the culture of rights and guarantees in juvenile justice, replacing the tutelary model, which considered these concepts unnecessary and, instead, relied on the good practice and goodwill of those operating in the field of child intervention. Intervention with unprotected children (children who are in poverty, neglected or abused, or those who are unruly or are at risk of becoming offenders) had previously been the domain of the institutions for the protection of children of each autonomous region. These regions were now to be responsible for adopting protective and educational measures with both children and families. This act was largely criticized since it was provisional and did not change the overall performance of the juvenile justice system in an organized manner. However, such balance was finally achieved due to the efforts of those involved in the implementation of the act, mainly through the work that was done around two courses of action established by this act: "decriminalization" and "deinstitutionalization" (Rechea and Fernández-Molina 2003).

Finally, a new law, the JCA, was passed in 2000. This act compiles all Juvenile Justice Regulation as a single, complete, and constitutional system. According to this law, justice for juveniles is to be administered by a separate system within the general legal system, with its own specific and specialized court. Jurisdiction of the juvenile court is determined by the offender's age and his or her conduct. With respect to that conduct, the system is, exclusively, a penal responsibility system. Juvenile justice is concerned only with those who commit acts that are defined as crimes according to adult Criminal Law. With respect to age, the act applies to young people under the age of 18 and older than 14. Art. 4 of the JCA allowed juveniles between 18 and 21 years, under some circumstances, to be judged by the Juvenile Court, so as to benefit from a more lenient system. However, this article was suspended, by a new law, OL 8/2006, and was finally repealed without ever coming into effect.

A juvenile committing a crime before the age of 14 is referred by the Juvenile Court to the Welfare institutions, once their age has been verified. Their situation is then assessed and, if appropriate, educational measures are proposed. While voices are periodically raised in favor of the need to reduce legal minority to the age of 12, it is also true that these voices are usually silenced by the effective response of the institutions for protection. Indeed, most autonomous communities have created teams and specific measures for intervention with minors who commit crimes, even for those who do not exhibit the most traditional problems of unprotected children.

Within this age range (14–18 years old), the JCA established two differentiated groups of young people with regard to the consequences of their responsibility and the measures to be applied to each group; for juveniles aged 14 and 15 measures would not last more than 2 years, while for those aged 16 and 17 any measure, even custody, could last for 5 years. The JCA intends to give more criminal responsibility to the older juveniles, as a kind of transition in order to avoid the abruptness of becoming fully responsible before an adult criminal court for crimes committed after their 18th birthday.

The Country's Stance Toward the UN Committee on the Rights of the Child

The legislation regulating juvenile justice adapts to the proposals and principles of the Convention on the Rights of the Child (CRCh), especially as per its original version. The amendments to the JCA of 2000 (2002 and 2006, mainly) have introduced stricter measures for older juveniles and those who commit more serious crimes or repeat offenders, ignoring the rationale of juvenile justice as a specialized jurisdiction: that juveniles lack the maturity of adults (Bernuz 2005). Specifically, the JCA has assimilated the principles of diversion, deinstitutionalization, and the respect for the rights and guarantees of individuals in criminal proceedings on behalf of the institutions intervening with juveniles. Nevertheless, the Committee on the Rights of the Child considers it essential to link these principles with the rights also considered as fundamental by the Convention. Specifically, with the right to nondiscrimination (art. 2), the best interest of the child (art. 3), the right to life and development (art. 6), and the right to be heard (art. 12).

Of these rights, the most constant references in the legislation and practice of juvenile justice in Spain are those to the best interest of the child. Despite the vagueness of the term, this principle has a direct relationship with the notion that juveniles have *limited culpability*, as a result of their incomplete physical and psychological development and their special emotional and educational needs. To this end, the Committee on the Rights of the Child considers, broadly speaking, that the best interest of the child shall be applied, when the objectives of rehabilitation and restorative justice take precedence over those of repression and punishment more typical of adult justice. This is taken into account by Spanish legislators when juveniles commit minor or less serious crimes, but is questioned when juveniles commit very serious crimes. In this case, the best interest of the child must be reconciled with the functions of the general prevention of punishment more typical of adult justice.

In accordance with the CRCh, the JCA accepts that juvenile justice is a variation of criminal justice which must recognize and realize the rights and guarantees of criminal proceedings. These are formal and constitutional issues which are more easily assimilated into the legislation and also by judicial operators. This may be because they believe the security of a system of legal responsibility is more favorable to juveniles than a tutelary, protectionist system and because respect for the rights and guarantees forms part of their professional training and is in line with traditional adult justice. For example, the importance of the presumption of innocence is clearly upheld in the process of accountability of juveniles and in their educational process. It is accepted that an intervention by the legal institutions is only educational and meaningful for juveniles when they have been declared guilty and have accepted and understood their responsibility.

However, the effective implementation of the right to be heard is more complex in the context of juvenile justice. According to the Committee on the Rights of the Child, in order to take a decision in the interest of a juvenile, depending on his or her maturity, the juvenile's own opinions must be taken into account. This, however, according to the Committee of Ministers of the Council of Europe, does not mean that the final decision necessarily coincides with the juvenile's wishes (2011, section 28). This difficulty in the implementation of the right to be heard is perhaps due to the continuing existence of the idea that the capacity to decide lies with the State or because the consequences of the Convention stating that the child must be heard as a subject of law, with the right to participate in the decisions which affect him or her is still to be assimilated, even when these decisions occur within the framework of juvenile justice (Bernuz 2015).

It can be said that 25 years after signing the CRCh, the principles and philosophy of the Convention have gradually filtered through into the Spanish legislation and have also transformed the procedures inherited from previous models. International organizations, mainly the United Nations and the Council of Europe, are aware of the need to improve the processes of implementation and effective realization of the rights. To this end, it is fundamental to continue reflecting on what juveniles understand by rights. In this sense, it is especially important to pay attention to a child's right to be heard since this is what really involves juveniles in the decisions affecting them, because they are treated as a true subject of law, because when institutions listen we have the impression they are fairer and because, consequently, we tend to obey decisions coming from institutions we consider legitimate. It could be said that juveniles feel more responsible when faced by a system of justice which is interested in them, which listens to them and explains its decisions. It must be stressed that in the legitimation of juvenile justice, it is not only important to assess whether rights are being realized but also how they are being realized (Bernuz 2014).

JUVENILE DELINQUENCY IN SPAIN

Trends in Juvenile Crime over the Period 2004–2014

In this section, we analyse the evolution of juvenile delinquency in Spain over the last decade. To do so, we will use both official and self-report data. The official data are those supplied each year by the Ministry of Home Affairs. We have used the information provided by the Police as it is commonly accepted these data most closely reflect the commission of crime (Estrada 1999). The results will be shown in the rate per 1000 inhabitants aged 14–17 years, so as to control the possible effects of population changes across the period analyzed.

Spain's participation in the International Self-Report Delinquency Study (IRSD), which collected data at three different points in time, 1992 (ISRD-I), 2006 (ISRD-II), and 2015 (ISRD-III), facilitates the use of information provided

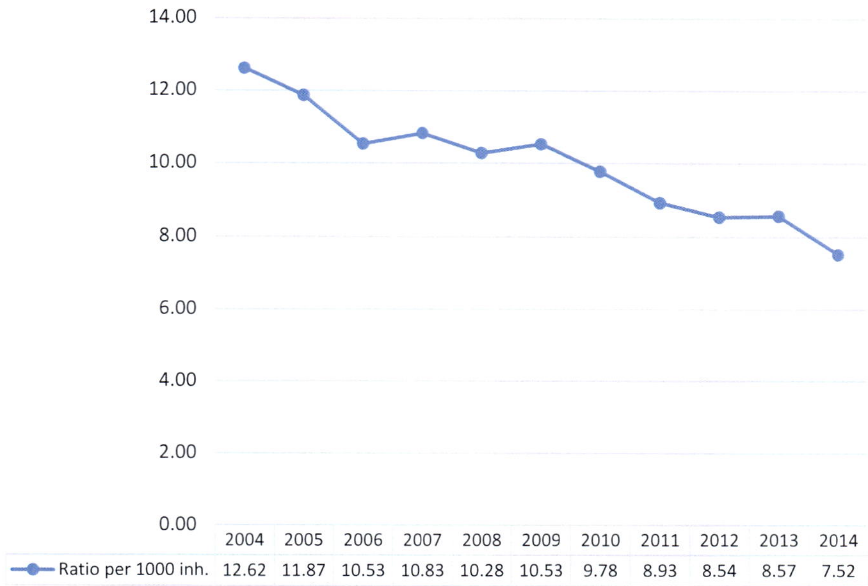

FIGURE 20.1. Police arrests (14–17 years old) Rate/1000 population of this age. *Source*: Ministry of Home Affairs.

by young people themselves. This can then be compared against the data supplied by the formal social control agencies.

Figure 20.1 depicts the evolution of official juvenile delinquency statistics. The graph clearly reflects a descending trend. In fact, delinquency rates have been steadily decreasing over the last 10 years.

Figure 20.2 now puts this evolution into context, as it differentiates between the two major categories of crime: property crime and violent crime. The graph shows how the decrease in juvenile delinquency largely results from the reduction in property crime, while the statistics for violent crime have remained constant over time.

A detailed analysis of the different criminal behaviors in each category (Figs. 20.3 and 20.4) provides more comprehensive information on the behavior of Spanish juveniles over the decade.

Figure 20.3 shows that all property crimes have decreased over the last decade, especially during the last 5 years. The reduction in car theft is especially dramatic. The most common property crime is burglary, followed by theft, which is typically a juvenile crime.

Figure 20.4 depicts the evolution of violent crime. Robbery with violence and intimidation is included in the category of violent crime, since, despite being property crime, it undoubtedly has violent connotations. The graph shows that this behavior is the most common in this category, although in recent years it has undeniably decreased. The other violent behaviors have also decreased except for the category of other crimes against persons, which has steadily increased.

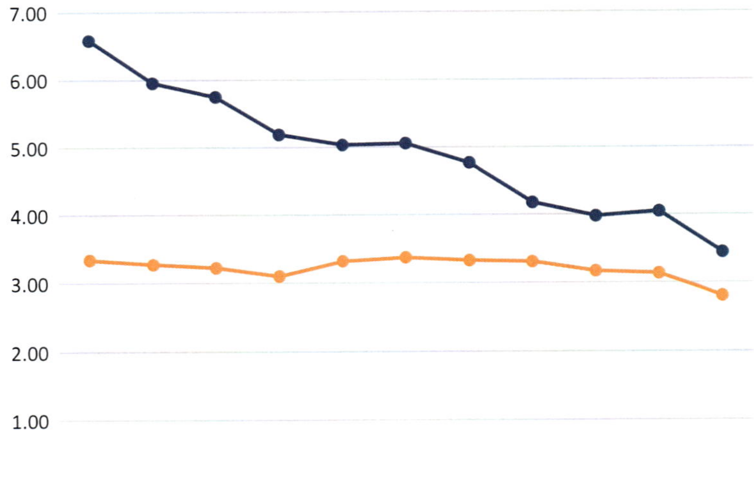

	2,004	2,005	2,006	2,007	2,008	2,009	2,010	2,011	2,012	2,013	2,014
Violent	3.34	3.28	3.23	3.10	3.32	3.37	3.33	3.31	3.17	3.14	2.81
Patrimoniales	6.58	5.95	5.75	5.19	5.03	5.06	4.77	4.18	3.98	4.05	3.45

FIGURE 20.2. Rate of arrests (14–17 years old) for violent and property crimes. *Source*: Ministry for Home Affairs.

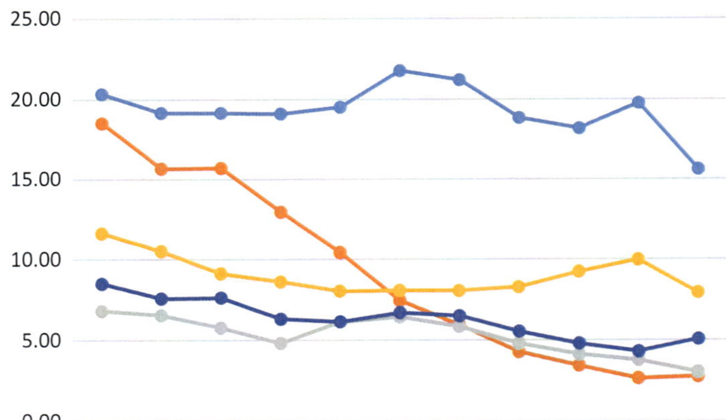

	2,004	2,005	2,006	2,007	2,008	2,009	2,010	2,011	2,012	2,013	2,014
Burglary	20.35	19.15	19.15	19.10	19.52	21.81	21.23	18.84	18.17	19.77	15.61
Car theft	18.51	15.66	15.70	12.95	10.44	7.48	5.97	4.29	3.45	2.66	2.77
Theft from inside cars	6.84	6.57	5.78	4.82	6.15	6.45	5.85	4.81	4.13	3.77	3.04
Theft	11.62	10.52	9.16	8.66	8.07	8.10	8.10	8.32	9.26	10.00	7.97
Other property crimes	8.54	7.61	7.66	6.35	6.16	6.73	6.54	5.55	4.81	4.32	5.09

FIGURE 20.3. Rate of arrests (14–17 years old) for property crimes. *Source*: Ministry for Home Affairs.

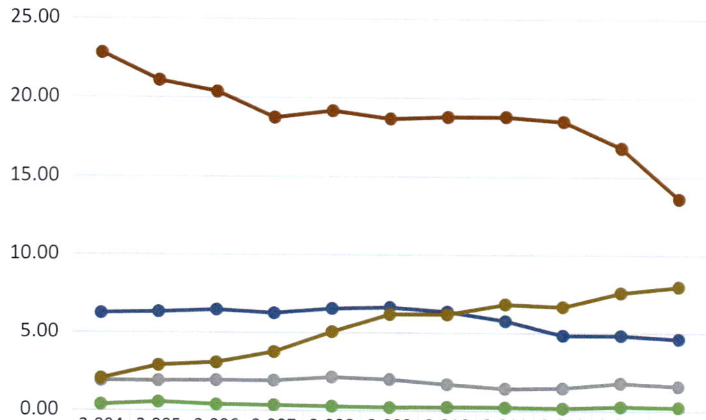

	2,004	2,005	2,006	2,007	2,008	2,009	2,010	2,011	2,012	2,013	2,014
Homicide	0.39	0.55	0.40	0.35	0.29	0.22	0.25	0.24	0.18	0.29	0.24
Assault	6.26	6.34	6.47	6.26	6.56	6.65	6.37	5.79	4.85	4.86	4.64
Robbery	22.83	21.09	20.38	18.74	19.17	18.67	18.80	18.81	18.52	16.86	13.64
Sex crimes	1.91	1.89	1.93	1.92	2.14	2.00	1.69	1.42	1.46	1.78	1.58
Others against persons	2.05	2.90	3.08	3.76	5.06	6.19	6.20	6.85	6.70	7.60	7.99

FIGURE 20.4. Rate of arrests (14–17 years old) for violent crimes. *Source*: Ministry for Home Affairs.

Such is the increase that at the beginning of the decade the rate was 2 arrests per 1000 inhabitants, in the last few years, this rate has increased almost fourfold. Child-to-parent violence is to blame for this dramatic rise. This type of violence is rapidly increasing and has been a focus of attention for researchers, legislators, and legal practitioners, who have had to deal with the emergence of a group which does not necessarily correspond to the typical profile of juvenile offenders (Ibabe and Jaureguizar 2011).

The official data reflect a clear decreasing trend in the criminal behavior of juveniles, which is confirmed by the self-report data shown in Fig. 20.5.

All criminal behaviours, excepted shoplifting and illegal downloads, decreased the national self-report study of 2006 (ISRD-II) and that of 2015 (ISRD-III). A large number of behaviours, such as vandalism, burglary, group fight and assault, have all decreased steadily from the time of the first self-report study of 1992 (ISRD-I) until now. However, shoplifting has increased over the last twenty years, and vehicle theft, stealing from car and robbery have increased too despite descending over the last ten. Finally, illegal downloading, which obviously did not exist in 1992, has been on the increase in recent years. Indeed, as in other countries, new behaviours have emerged, such as cyberbullying, hacking or sexting. However, although the scenario or the means may be new, these are simply manifestations of previously recognised juvenile behaviours. Unfortunately, no data are currently available on juvenile crime trends on the Internet.

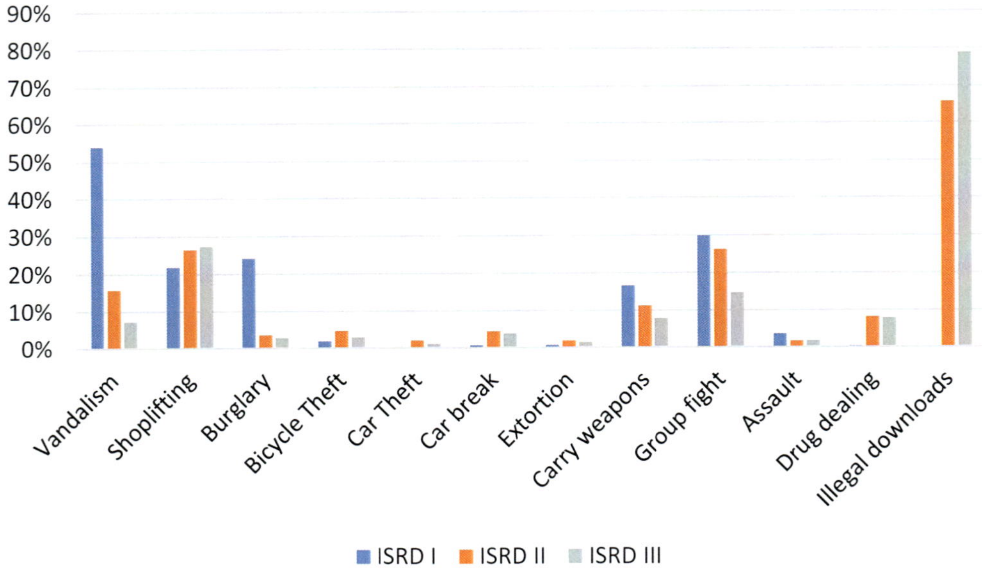

FIGURE 20.5. Antisocial and criminal behavior self-reported. *Source*: ISRD I, II y III.

In conclusion, the results presented earlier describe the transformation in juvenile delinquency over recent years. They show that, broadly speaking, young people in Spain today commit fewer crimes than 10 years ago. Crimes which were especially common in previous decades, such as car theft, are no longer committed. At the same time, behaviors which were unknown to the formal social control agencies have taken on major relevance in recent years. This is true of crimes such as child-to-parent violence, illegal downloading, and a number of other behaviors, which have developed with the spread of the Internet.

Causes of the Decline in Juvenile Crime

There are various explanations for this decline. The development of public policies regarding childhood and social welfare, which began several decades ago, may well be yielding results today (Acosta et al. 2012). It is widely considered that the design of a juvenile crime policy, and specifically, the development of community intervention programs as an integral part of a society with well-structured social services, could be responsible for this decline (Redondo et al. 2012). In the same way, the trend toward the use of diversion measures (reparation, conciliation, community service) for minor crimes or offenses, which otherwise would have remained unredressed; or the creation of specific teams to intervene with minors under 14 years who commit crimes but are not typically unprotected, have also possibly had an effect on the reduction of juvenile delinquency (Bernuz et al. 2006).

New generations have also experienced the effect of greater formal and informal control, which could also explain the decrease in criminal behavior among young people. Greater control limits their opportunities for antisocial behavior and increases the risk of loss which stems from involvement in risk-taking behavior. A comparison of the data from ISRD-I and ISRD-II allows us to see that adolescents spend more time at home and/or with their families, which increases supervision and reduces time spent outside with their peers. We also see that detection of juvenile criminal behavior by adults (police, teachers, parents) was significantly higher in 2006 (Fernández-Molina et al. 2009).

The data from Spain also shows how opportunity has a significant effect on crime. Furthermore, as in other countries (Farrell et al. 2014), the increase in car security systems has led to a dramatic decrease in car theft. However, the emergence of the Internet and the organization of free time around the new technologies as methods of communication and enjoyment is associated with a rise in criminal behaviors in this scenario, such as illegal downloading,[1] which is sometimes not really regarded as "wrong."

Finally, these data illustrate how the hypothesis put forward by some authors to explain the decrease in delinquency as a result of economic well-being (Rosenfeld and Fornango 2007) does not hold up in the case of Spain. The country has been in the grip of a severe economic crisis since 2007 and it is precisely in this setting that juvenile delinquency has decreased. Similarly, the self-report data show that the highest rates of self-reported juvenile delinquency, in contrast to this hypothesis, are those from the time of the greatest economic well-being ever experienced in Spain. The decrease in delinquency when Gross Domestic Product (GDP) falls has sometimes been justified in the case of adults, as a reflection of less formal social control due to a reduction in resources in the fight against delinquency (Brandariz 2015). Nevertheless, there is no evidence in Spain of a significant reduction of the number of police officers during the recession.[2]

CONTROL OF JUVENILE DELINQUENCY

There are a number of institutions and professionals in the Spanish juvenile justice system that intervene at different stages with juvenile offenders in order to respond to criminal behavior. It is mainly police officers, public prosecutors, judges, and lawyers who are responsible for setting in motion the legal procedure aimed at making a juvenile accountable for the offenses committed.

[1] There are still no data available regarding the exact dimensions or the evolution over recent years of other criminal behaviours on the Internet, such as sexting or grooming, which are considered to be increasing among young people.

[2] See Annual Report (2014) Ministry of Home Affairs http://www.interior.gob.es/es/web/archivos-y-documentacion/documentacion-y-publicaciones/anuarios-y-estadisticas, p. 154.

Policing and Juveniles

The Police are one of the first institutions that come in contact with juveniles who have committed a crime. Although the JCA recognizes the need for specialized Police Groups, called GRUME (Juvenile Groups) in urban areas and EMUME (*Guardía Civil* specialized in working with juveniles and women) in rural areas, they have not been assigned many functions. In Spain the police do not act differently with juveniles than with adults, as opposed to what happens in other countries like the Netherlands, the United Kingdom, or Ireland (Junger-Tass and Decker 2006) where they can caution the juvenile or adopt diversionary measures.

The GRUME/EMUME are in charge of arresting the juvenile delinquent and helping the prosecutor clarify the facts. The JCA only mentions the police twice, first, when it rules on the functions of the prosecutor and entrusts them to order the police to verify the facts and the juvenile's participation (art. 6), and second, when it regulates the arrest of juveniles (art. 17).

However, although it is not mentioned in the Act, there is no doubt that the GRUMES/EMUMES' actions are wider. On one hand, because the groups have responsibilities with juvenile delinquents as well as with juvenile victims, their work has undoubtedly preventive potential. In fact, when presented as a figure of authority which respects accordingly the rights and guarantees of children as described by the Committee on the Rights of the Child (2007, 6), it serves to encourage pro-social behavior. On the other hand, in practice, the groups are an important element in the juvenile justice system since they are in permanent contact with all its institutions: Juvenile Courts, Prosecutors, Social Services, etc.

The first action to be taken with juvenile delinquents is to determine their age. If the juvenile is under 14 years old (thus excluded from the actions of the juvenile justice system), the police must restrict their actions to the field of juvenile protection. Once the juvenile's age and identity are determined, the rules of juvenile protection will be applied. The prosecutor will be informed of the known facts and circumstances by sending the police report, referring the juvenile either to his attorney or to the public entity for juvenile protection.

Another main action carried out by the Police is detaining the juvenile. In this case, the action must be most respectful of the juvenile's rights; in particular, they must ensure the juvenile's protection (art. 17).

The Police can also keep juveniles in short-term custody, but only for 24 h before formally accusing them of a crime. During that time, juveniles have the same constitutional rights as adults, as well as some specific rights due to their juvenile status such as:

- Act enforcement officers must use clear and understandable language according to the offender's age,
- Before a statement is taken, a written notice of the time, place, and purpose of the taking of the statement is given to the parents or guardians, the lawyer, and the prosecutor, and
- During these 24 h, the juvenile must be kept in a special room away from adult offenders.

Courts and Juveniles

Once the Police determine that the juvenile has committed an offense, they must inform the juvenile prosecution service. The prosecutor then assesses the case and decides if it is necessary to notify the judge and so set in motion criminal proceedings or whether, in the juvenile's best interest, it is deemed convenient to give him or her a second chance by dismissing the case and informing him or her of the consequences of committing another offense.

The actions of judges and public prosecutors, in line with the CRCh, are guided by two fundamental principles: decriminalization and deinstitutionalization. There now follows a more detailed explanation of the balance of the application of these two strategies.

Alternatives to Avoid Criminalization

The JCA allows the proceedings to be dismissed in the best interest of the juvenile, thus avoiding a formal response either by the prosecutor at his own office or by the judge immediately after initiating proceedings.

- "Decriminalization" carried out by the Public Prosecutor

  The JCA allows the Public Prosecutor to act more freely. The prosecutor may dismiss proceedings without asking the judge, if the offense is minor and committed by a first time offender (art. 18). In this way, the prosecutor carries out an important "filtering" task in the juvenile justice system because first time offenders committing minor offenses will stay out of the system. In any event, the Public Prosecutor refers the case for assessment to the institutions for child protection. If the juvenile is in a social risk situation, the Welfare Services must intervene with an educational measure of protection.
- Decriminalization carried out by the judge

  The other method of preventing trial and punishment is requested by the prosecutor but is decided by the judge. In this case it is possible to drop the charges (art. 19) when the juvenile has carried out any kind of activity guided, in some respect, by the principles of "Restorative Justice" (victim–offender conciliation, reparation of the damage, or an educational task). The prosecutor has the power to request the charges be dropped through this alternative, depending on the seriousness and circumstances of the offense when it is a nonserious offense and when the mere promise of the juvenile to repair the damage or injury caused to the victim seems sufficient. If the mediation process is successfully completed, or is not completed due to causes beyond the control of the juvenile, the prosecutor can request that the judge dismiss the case.

The judge may also dismiss proceedings (art. 27.4) when, although the juvenile is not a first time offender, the *Technical Team* (TT) recommends a second chance in the juvenile's best interest. This is possible provided that the offense is not serious, when the measures carried out have been sufficient to make the juvenile responsible for his acts, or because of the time elapsed since the acts were committed makes any intervention unnecessary.

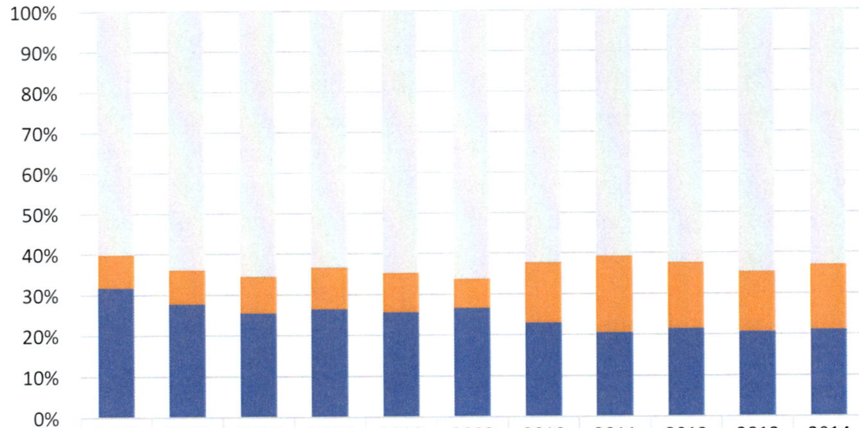

	2004	2005	2006	2007	2008	2009	2010	2011	2012	2013	2014
Open files	29,399	31,713	33,681	31,343	35,353	34,019	30,926	29,614	29,598	29,428	27,472
Des Judge	4,004	4,181	4,630	5,101	5,307	3,680	7,377	9,161	7,705	6,687	6,940
Des Prosecutor	15,568	13,823	13,118	13,113	14,010	13,688	11,414	10,048	10,238	9,450	9,278

FIGURE 20.6. Balance of the decriminalizing strategies. *Source*: Spanish Public Prosecution Service.

Figure 20.6 shows the balance over the last 10 years of this line of action. It can be seen that nearly 40% of the cases are dismissed for one of the reasons previously analyzed. In the early years, it seemed that decriminalization was mainly established by the Prosecutor's Office and was mainly unconditional. However, currently most cases are closed following conciliation with the victim, repairing of damage caused, or because the ET considers the circumstances of the case makes it advisable to terminate proceedings. The detailed data supplied by the Juvenile Prosecutor's Office show that the number of conciliations with victims and agreements to repair the damage caused is growing year by year, which indicates a trend toward restorative justice as a way to respond to the more minor offenses reaching the juvenile justice system.

This may be due to a greater specialization of the teams responsible for mediation proceedings, and the conviction that, if the juvenile is guilty, this type of proceedings results in greater accountability for the damage caused and a possible reduction of recidivism. However, it is also clear that the greater number of interventions with juveniles have also played a role.

Juveniles on Trial

Once the Prosecutor decides not to dismiss the case, the process continues and the formal adjudication process begins. The next phase is the trial, where the 'hearing' takes place informally. The judge must hear everyone including the juvenile, the parents, the prosecutor, the TT, and the defense lawyer and make a decision. In order to make this decision in the juvenile's best interest, the judge must bear in mind the seriousness of the offense, the juvenile's family, and his/her social and educational history.

Indeed, the juvenile's best interest is the underlying premise of the Juvenile Justice System, addressed by the JCA, which is one of the fundamental rights according to the ChRC: in all legal actions concerning those under the age of 18, the 'best interests of the child' shall be a primary consideration (article 3.1). However, sometimes, the age, the kind of crime committed, its seriousness, and recidivism must be taken into consideration, since these are the criteria set out by the legislator to predetermine the court action, which in some cases affects the length of the sentence. Table 20.1 clarifies the rules to be applied, which have been progressively reinforced in the successive amendments to the JCA since it came into effect.

TABLE 20.1. Special rules for the application of sentences for juvenile offenders

Offense/age	*14–15 years*	*16–17 years*
Serious offenses	Sentences may be up to 3 years. A CSO may be up to 150 h and up to 12 weekends in the case of weekend custody	Sentences may be up to 6 years. A CSO may be up to 200 h and up to 16 weekends in the case of weekend custody[a]
Less serious offenses, but involving violence or intimidation against persons or causing serious risk to life or physical integrity	Sentences may be up to 3 years. A CSO may be up to 150 h and up to 12 weekends in the case of weekend custody	Sentences may be up to 6 years. A CSO may be up to 200 h and up to 16 weekends in the case of weekend custody[b]
Crimes committed in groups or in which the juvenile belonged to or acted as part of a gang, criminal organization or association, albeit temporarily, dedicated to such activities	Sentences may be up to 3 years. A CSO may be up to 150 h and up to 12 weekends in the case of weekend custody	Sentences may be up to 6 years. A CSO may be up to 200 h and up to 16 weekends in the case of weekend custody[c]
Murder, homicide, rape, acts of terrorism, and crimes which carry 15 years' imprisonment in the Criminal Code for adults[c]	From 1 to 4 years in a closed custody center + 3 years' probation (the sentence may not be modified until at least half of the custody period has been served)	From 1 to 8 years in a closed custody center + 5 years' probation (the sentence may not be modified until at least half of the custody period has been served)

[a]When the case is extremely serious, the judge should impose a sentence of detention of 1–6 years and 5 years' probation (the sentence may not be modified until after the first year has been served)

[b]When the case is extremely serious, the judge should impose a sentence of detention of 1–6 years and 5 years' probation (the sentence may not be modified until after the first year has been served)

[c]In the case of connected or continuing offenses and at least one is of those included in this clause, the Judge may extend the period of custody up to 5 years in the case of minors of 14 and 15 and up to 10 years when the offender is 16 or 17 years of age

As laid down in article 10 of the JCA, if the offenses are serious crimes or are less serious but involving violence or intimidation against persons or causing serious risk to life or physical integrity or are crimes committed in groups or in which the juvenile is proved to have belonged to or acted as part of a gang, criminal organization or association, the judge may extend the sentence by up to 3 years in the case of minors of 15 or 16, and by up to 6 years if the offender is 16 or 17. Furthermore, in the case of the older juveniles, the judge *must* impose a sentence of custody of between 1 and 6 years and 5 years' probation, without the possibility of the sentence being modified or substituted until after the first year of custody. It must be pointed out that any case of reoffending will be considered an extremely serious offense by the legislator without any need to specify exactly what is understood by reoffending.

Furthermore, if the juvenile has committed a serious crime such as murder, homicide, rape, or acts of terrorism, the judge *must* impose a sentence of 1–5 years' custody and a further period of up to 3 years' probation, if appropriate, if the offender is under 14 or 15 years and 1–8 years' custody and 5 years' probation if the juvenile is 16 or 17. In this case, the sentence may not be modified, suspended, or substituted until at least half of the sentence has been served.

It is important to note that, according to article 40, the judge may suspend the sentence if it is less than 2 years and always on the condition that the juvenile promises to commit no further offenses, to reintegrate into society, to carry out the tasks set out in the probation plan, to perform a series of socioeducational activities, and/or the parents or guardians have given their commitment to participate.

Deinstitutionalization

We have already mentioned that one of the premises of the Convention and also of the JCA is the promotion of deinstitutionalization by recourse to open regime measures. In order to confirm this is being done, it is necessary to verify the open regime measures legally established to avoid custody, and the use being made of the different regimes of custody. The next two sections describe the sentences judges may apply and their application in recent years. To this end, we have differentiated between community sentences and custodial sentences.

Community Sentences

Community or noncustodial sentences realize the principle of deinstitutionalization in that they propose working with juveniles in their familiar environments, with their family, at their educational institutions and with friends. The greater the range of measures established, the greater the options the judge has to decide in accordance with the seriousness of the offense and according to the juvenile's circumstances. The measures provided for in the JCA are as follows:

Probation: Young offenders must be subjected to the supervision and guidance of a 'Probation Officer,' within a time period that has been decided by the judge, usually not exceeding 2 years.

The probation officer's role is of assistance, guidance, and care. These officers must promote the juvenile's education and they work with parents or guardians, using community resources as much as possible. The main aim will be to improve the juvenile's skills, abilities, and attitudes. The probation officer is appointed by the court and may be given instructions by the judge for their activities. They must report on the behavior of the juvenile at intervals specified by the judge, and they must inform the judge of any change in behavior.

While being on probation, the judge can require the juvenile to comply with the following conditions: attend school, participate in a training course (i.e., a social competence training or a professional course, etc.), abstain from going to specific places of public entertainment, obey the rules of the institution where the juvenile lives, as well as other obligations that the judge may impose that do not violate the juvenile's constitutional rights.

Community service: applicable in those cases where young offenders have infringed the rights or well-being of the community. In order to enhance the educational factor, the nature of the activity should be related to the type of crime committed or to the damage inflicted to the community. If possible, the activities will be done during the offender's leisure time and with the consent of the juvenile.

Socioeducative measures: The young offenders must do some educational tasks in order to achieve their rehabilitation. This measure attempts to satisfy some needs which are delaying the juvenile's full development. The measure can be the obligation to attend a community activity that already exists or to create a specific activity for each specific case.

Community therapeutic treatment: Juveniles must periodically attend a center to follow a specific plan to treat their problem, which could be drug related or psychiatric. In this case it is necessary to have the juvenile's consent.

Attendance at a 'Day Center': Young offenders are diverted to community centers to perform activities to improve their social competence. This measure attempts to provide a structured environment for young offenders. The educational activities try to compensate for family deficits. The young offenders continue to live at home.

Living with another person, another family, or educative group: provide the young offender with a positive socialization environment. The person, the family, or the educative group offer him/her the possibility to live in a family-like environment that tries to develop pro-social and affective responses in the juvenile.

Although the JCA has extended the community measures available to the juvenile court judge, as shown in Fig. 20.7, probation continues to be the most frequently adopted measure. Legal and social agents continue to feel that probation offers the greatest possibility of adapting the sentence to the psychosocial circumstances of the juvenile, bearing in mind the options offered by public and private resources in each autonomous community. Community service is the next most frequently applied measure, due to its implied connection with the offense

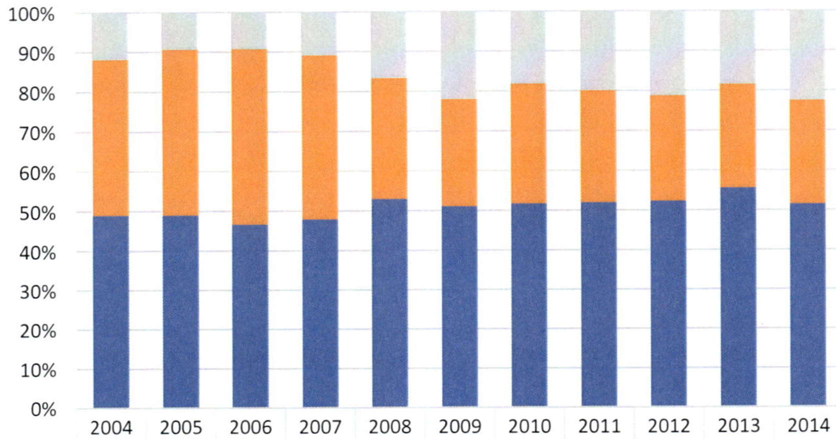

	2004	2005	2006	2007	2008	2009	2010	2011	2012	2013	2014
Others	1,757	1,461	1,510	1,778	2,931	4,425	3,411	4,162	4,151	3,333	3,988
Community service	5,840	6,538	7,195	6,806	5,371	5,441	5,664	5,888	5,206	4,697	4,642
Probation	7,340	7,729	7,655	7,932	9,382	10,346	9,771	10,920	10,289	10,085	9,184

FIGURE 20.7. Community measures. *Source*: Spanish Public Prosecution Service.

committed. However, it is decreasing in importance due to the difficulties in its set-up and supervision. It can also be seen that a group of other measures has also grown as autonomous communities have developed the measures established in law.

Custody for Juveniles

Custody may be imposed by the judge as a precautionary measure, until the trial starts and a definitive measure is imposed. This precautionary measure may only be taken when justified by questions such as the seriousness of the offenses, the personal and social circumstances of the juvenile, a real risk of absconding, or in the case of repeat offenders of the same offense. Custody may also finally be imposed by the judge when other measures are deemed insufficient because of the juvenile's criminal tendencies as demonstrated in the offense, because of the seriousness of the offenses, or because the JCA lays it down as a required measure in certain cases. The main aim of this measure is to provide a good, healthy environment in order to redirect the juvenile's antisocial behavior, even though it might be necessary to restrict the juvenile's freedom. This loss of freedom can vary depending on the kind of restrictions the judge imposes. The judge can only impose custody in a 'closed center' when the juvenile has committed a serious and violent crime. All measures of custody must be followed by a period of probation to encourage the juvenile's progressive deinstitutionalization. There are several types of custody which are implemented in specific centers for juveniles, where they are separated from any adults and where they may remain until the maximum age of 21 years.

In a closed center: the system tries to instill in the juvenile some degree of social competence to encourage later responsible behavior in the community.

In a half-open center: a socio-behavioral plan is implemented in collaboration with community social services. The offenders live in the center.

In an open center: Juveniles are required to perform all activities in the community. However, their residence is in the center.

Therapeutic custody: Juveniles with drug or psychiatric problems need a certain context to implement a therapeutic program, either because his or her environment is not adequate for treatment, or because there are risk factors that require custody in a closed center. This type of custody provides for three regimes: closed, open, or semiopen.

Weekend Custody: Juveniles must stay in their homes or in a Center for juveniles for 36 h over the weekend. They must perform some educational tasks that are imposed by the judge (i.e., road safety education). This measure is usually applied to those juveniles that have committed assault and vandalism offenses during the weekend.

If we analyze more closely the evolution of the different types of custody (see Fig. 20.8), we can see that the closed regime has decreased in favor of the semiopen regime. It seems that judges have accepted the need to restrict this measure to truly serious cases and those in which community sentences have not yielded results. The use of therapeutic custody has also increased, due, perhaps, to an increase in the number of crimes related to mental health problems or substance abuse among juveniles. There has also been an increase in the construction of centers or modules especially designed for juveniles requiring highly specialized attention. There has also been a tendency to reduce weekend custody, which due

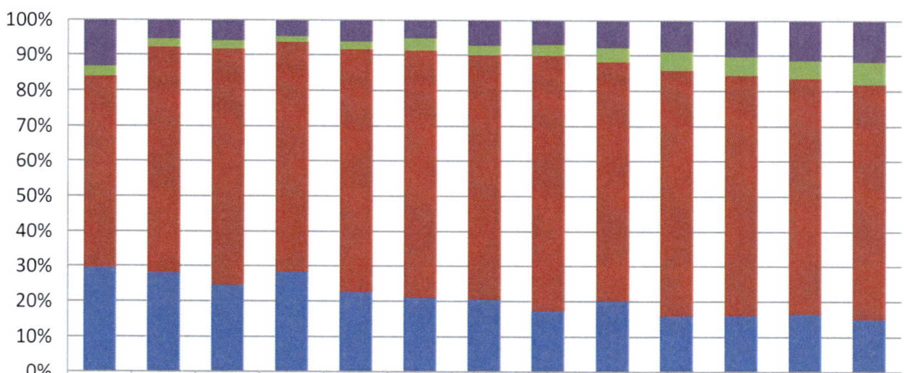

	2002	2003	2004	2005	2006	2007	2008	2009	2010	2011	2012	2013	2014
Therapeutic	482	219	291	251	297	225	299	306	362	443	491	523	495
Open	101	97	115	85	106	156	114	138	190	265	252	231	267
Semi-open	1,989	2,643	3,342	3,528	3,371	3,095	2,891	3225	3,186	3,491	3,265	3079	2818
Closed	1,081	1,160	1,219	1,523	1,099	926	853	771	943	797	766	754	629

FIGURE 20.8. Custodial measures. *Source*: Spanish Public Prosecution Service.

to a general lack of educational support, is seen as a measure of detention and confinement, mainly at home, or alternatively at a center.

Assessment of the Justice Model Applied in Spain

The JCA utilizes a model which aims to educate through punishment and punish through education. To this end, on the basis of the developmental criminology approach, a dual criminal policy is designed to attend to the different realities which the juvenile justice system faces: adolescence-limited and persistent offenders (Moffit 1993). For the first context, the JCA establishes a normalizing policy to give the juvenile a second chance through various strategies (decriminalization, mediation, or low-impact educational measures), and for the second context, it establishes a robust criminal policy which aims to respond to the most serious cases, fundamentally by recourse to custody for periods of time which have gradually been lengthened in the successive amendments to the JCA.

The normalizing policy is the one most commonly employed since most are medium offenses. It is basically structured around diversion mechanisms and low-impact educational measures (fundamentally, socioeducational activities and community service). It is worth remembering that decriminalization is only possible, both by the prosecutor and the juvenile judge, in cases of minor crimes and offenses. In both cases, the law expressly provides that juveniles are taken to court if there has been use of violence or intimidation. Given that violence is a feature of many juvenile behaviors, the possible impact of this decriminalizing policy will not be extensive, as many cases will be taken to court obligatorily. With regards to deinstitutionalization, it must be noted that there has been a fall in custody rates, especially custody in closed centers. Interventions are largely community based. In fact, the measures most commonly adopted are probation and community service. It is worth noting that this normalizing approach is not a soft policy. Indeed, it is relatively interventionist and in most cases, the measures adopted have an effect on the juvenile offender's everyday life.

The criminal policy directed at responding to the "hard-core" delinquents, that is, older delinquents (16 and 17 years of age) who are reoffenders and commit serious crimes, has received the most attention in the media (Bernuz 2005). This is essentially because most of the legislative reforms have referred to tougher measures to manage this serious delinquency, which, however, is less common among juveniles. Nevertheless, despite this process of legal criminalization of serious delinquency, the impact has not been great, since only a relatively small number of juveniles fit this profile and because the judges have preferred, within the limits laid down in the JCA, to opt for shorter measures which aim to contribute to the educational, responsibility-oriented process, which requires a response in the juvenile's best interest (Fernández-Molina 2012).

Treatment of Juvenile Offenders in Spain

When the Judge imposes a measure, the professionals of the Social Welfare system implement the corresponding program. The regional governments in Spain have competence in the social welfare system therefore the services of regional governments are in charge of carrying out the measures adopted by Juvenile Judges. This organization was significant for two reasons: first, because it implied the decentralization of the juvenile criminal enforcement system; and second, because it is in support of an integral child policy, ranging from the protection of juveniles at risk to a judicial response to criminal behavior.

Each region has a different social welfare structure as well as different resources. This difference in resources can make a big difference in the kind of measures the judges can apply to juveniles. Regarding the treatment received by juveniles, there are no standard protocols or common guidelines across the autonomous communities. In consequence, there is a huge variety of programs and interventions, which differ from one region to the other (Redondo et al. 2012) and even within the same region (Uceda and Navarro 2013). In this sense, each institution responsible for attending to and treating the juveniles has its own protocol and intervention programs.

Nonetheless, analysis of the existing protocols and programs confirms that, broadly speaking, they are coherent with current knowledge on antisocial behavior and risk/protective factors (Redondo et al. 2012). Consequently, specific programs exist to work on the juvenile offender's main difficulties in different developmental areas: improvement of training and preparation for employment; psychoeducational programs; psychological treatment for specific substance abuse-related problems, sexual assault, and other mental problems; healthcare programs; leisure and free-time programs. It can also be seen that the pertinent institutions/organizations endeavor to adapt to changes in juvenile behavioral patterns; for example, there has been a gradual increase in the number of specific programs regarding gender violence, internet misuse, or child-to-parent violence. In 2007, most professionals did not feel qualified to approach child-to-parent violence but in 2015, programs or actions have been implemented in all the autonomous communities. This willingness to adapt to emerging problems has also encouraged the development of family-based interventions as opposed to traditional interventions directed specifically at the juvenile.

A review of these protocols/programs allow us to conclude that precedence is given to cognitive behavioral treatments, which have proven to be the most effective tools for reducing recidivism with young delinquents and adults (Garrido et al. 2006). However, a lot of these protocols/programs make almost no reference to rehabilitation theories or models for juvenile offenders.

The specific model for offender rehabilitation more used in Spain has been the cognitive model proposed by Ross and Fabiano (1985); however, the Risk–Need–Responsivity model (Andrews and Bonta 2006) has gradually come to form part of the training of professionals and of the dynamic of the system itself. The

RNR model is clearly a benchmark among Spanish academics and researchers. To the degree that these experts participate in the juvenile justice system, the RNR model and the various approaches to rehabilitation underlying the model, lead the design, implementation, and assessment of the rehabilitation programs. This is clear, for example, in the Community of Madrid (Graña and Rodríguez-Biezma 2010) or in Catalonia (Cano and Andrés-Pueyo 2012), but is difficult to establish in the country as a whole.

As suggested by Redondo et al. (2012), the lack of criminological models as a theoretical reference and the absence of clearly explained specific aims (or criminogenic needs) in most of the protocols/programs, render it impossible, in practice, to assess the actual implementation of this rehabilitation model.

One aspect which characterizes this inconsistent process toward the implementation of the RNR model is the adaptation, validation, and introduction into the system of risk assessment tools. These instruments help to identify static and dynamic risk factors, and the protection factors of each juvenile, which should guide the selection of the measure to be imposed and the objectives of the treatment. Furthermore, they facilitate assessment of the juvenile's progress once the action is implemented.

The use of assessment tools is widespread in the Justice system (Arbach-Lucioni et al. 2015), but there is practically no research in Spain on the applicability of these tools nor the corresponding criminogenic needs of the juveniles. To the best of our knowledge, only one study has analyzed how the introduction of the assessment tools has an impact on the everyday work of professionals with the juveniles; this study concluded there is a mismatch between the information provided by the tools and the proposals for intervention developed by the technicians (Graña et al. 2007). It is worth noting, furthermore, that the tools are not integrated in the protocols. Consequently, within any given resource network, some technicians use them and others don't, and in some cases they even use different tools (Arbach-Lucioni et al. 2015).

Some authors have expressed their concern that the risk assessment tools are seen as a means to "manage the risk posed by a juvenile" rather than a tool to facilitate the application of a needs assessment and the principle of responsivity (Bernuz and Fernández-Molina 2008). This is especially so because the incorporation of these tools has not been accompanied by an adaptation of the available resources. The professionals who attend to and treat the juveniles may also have had this perception, since the implementation of the assessment tools has been met with a considerable amount of resistance. In this line, Bernuz and Fernández-Molina (2008) consider that the discourse of professionals depart from trends toward risk management, which could indeed be found in the successive amendments to the JCA or in criminal policy decisions.

In our opinion, this resistance could reflect both a rejection of the punitive nature of the guidelines they receive regarding the treatment of juvenile offenders (Uceda and Navarro 2013) and the basic training they received, which focuses more on social adaptation and community-based interventions than theories of reoffending (there is still only a small number of criminologists in the Juvenile Justice system). Professionals on correctional treatment usually place more emphasis on improving self-esteem, social adaptation, or empowering the juveniles, than on their impact on recidivism.

Consequently, it could be concluded that we are at a time of transition in the rehabilitation of juvenile offenders in Spain. Starting from highly diverse actions and programs of difficult assessment and with limited grounding in criminology, we are now advancing toward more contemporary models of rehabilitation. Certain resistance voiced by professionals coincides with criticisms made of the RNR model (Ward et al. 2007): insufficient attention to the offender motivation and personal identity, the well-being of juveniles is secondary, and too much emphasis on the risks. Furthermore, the resources available are not consistent with the criminogenic needs evaluated. Spanish professionals appear to prefer a more positive orientation, which focuses more on factors of protection than on risks, and more on desistance than on recidivism (for example, Blasco et al. 2014).

Given the lack of assessment of the programs and interventions, there is little information available on the effectiveness of either the measures applied or the programs/interventions implemented with the juveniles. The data available paint a relatively positive picture (Camps and Cano 2006; Bernuz et al. 2009; Acosta et al. 2012; Martín et al. 2013) despite the doubts and criticisms from the Spanish society. Yet it is still not clear which specific aspects of the system explain the positive results, as has been mentioned previously in this chapter.

With regard to recidivism, there are no national data but there are a number of studies published in some autonomous communities with samples of juveniles under various measures. A review of these works allows us to conclude that the mean rate of recidivism is around 25%, but with significant variations depending on gender, age, and other variables (Redondo et al. 2012; Ortega-Campos et al. 2014). Recidivism is more frequent in younger boys who have committed violent crime, have received heavier judicial measures and present more risk factors; individual factors such as impulsivity, seem to hinder desistance (Blasco et al. 2014). In this sense, Bravo et al. (2009) conclude that interventions with juveniles presenting more risk factors and chronic trajectories seem to be insufficient, both in semiopen and closed regimes. They consider that greater emphasis is required on working with the families of juveniles and in their environment.

Treatment programs for juvenile offenders are designed and applied equally with boys or girls. Although researchers have highlighted the differences in needs between delinquent boys and girls (Morales 2011; Redondo et al. 2012) no specific programs or actions have been designed for girls. There is no evidence, either, that professionals adopt a gender perspective in their work, in contrast to the situation with women in prison.

Generally speaking, the only references to be found in reports on girls' needs are as follows: the number of places available for girls in each center, the living arrangements for girls in mixed-sex centers, and the adaptation of some rooms for young mothers with children under the age of 3. The existence of specific programs for young mothers in centers with places for girls is officially regulated, but no information on these programs has been published. These reports all highlight the fact that, given the limited availability of places for girls (some centers do not have them), it is especially complicated to meet their right to complete the measure in a center near the family home.

Thus, the international debate between the gender-specific approach and neutral approach, which aims for RNR, is not observed in Spain. It is true that the cognitive behavioral programs for recidivism seem to be equally effective for girls and boys (Morales 2011; Gobeil et al. 2016). Although recidivism is lower in girls, there is no evidence that this lower recidivism among girls is the result of correctional interventions.

For those who defend a gender-specific approach is not clear whether needs of girls are met. It is known that girl offenders present more physical and mental health problems and more prior history of abuse (Rodermond et al. 2015). No tool including gender-sensitive assessments has been validated in Spain; nor do protocols include specific actions for girls' needs. The absence of a gender-specific attention for girls could increase their vulnerability, not for crime, but for their own development (and that of their children in the case of mothers). Also, boys could benefit from a gender approach, especially those who show marked masculinity values or sexist attitudes (Carlsson 2013).

Anyway, it is clear that all matters related to juvenile offenders in Spain require further study, especially if they refer to girls offenders.

REFERENCES

Acosta, E., de Bustillo, M., Martín, E., Aragón, N., & Betancort, M. (2012). Evaluation of the effectiveness of minimum intervention measures on young offenders. *The Spanish Journal of Psychology, 15*(2), 702–709.

Andrews, D., & Bonta, J. (2006). *The psychology of criminal conduct* (4th ed.). Cincinnati: Anderson Publishing.

Arbach-Lucioni, K., Desmarais, S. L., Hurducas, C., Condemarin, C., Kimberlie, D., Doyle, M., et al. (2015). La práctica de la evaluación del riesgo de violencia en España. *Revista de la Facultad de Medicina, 63*(3), 357–366.

Bernuz, M. J. (2005). Justicia de menores española y nuevas tendencias penales. La regulación del núcleo duro de la delincuencia. *Revista electrónica de Ciencia Penal y Criminología, 7*, 12.

Bernuz, M. (2014). La legitimidad de la justicia de menores: entre la justicia procedimental y la justicia social. *InDret, 1*, 25.

Bernuz, M. J. (2015). El derecho a ser escuchado: el caso de la infancia en conflicto con la norma. *Derechos y libertades: Revista del Instituto Bartolomé de las Casas, 33*, 67–98.

Bernuz, M. J., & Fernández-Molina, E. (2008). La gestión de la delincuencia juvenil Como riesgo. Indicadores de un Nuevo modelo. *Revista Electrónica de Ciencia Penal y Criminología, 10*, 1–20.

Bernuz, M. J., Fernández-Molina, E., & Pérez, F. (2006). El tratamiento institucional de los menores que cometen delitos antes de los 14 años. *Revista Española de Investigación Criminológica, 4*.

Bernuz, M. J., Fernández, E., & Pérez, F. (2009). La Libertad Vigilada como medida individualizadora en la Justicia de Menores. *Revista Española de Investigación Criminológica, 7*.

Blasco, C., Fuentes-Peláez, N., & Pastor, C. (2014). Aproximación a los factores explicativos del desistimiento en jóvenes infractores. *Educació Social, 58*, 186–203.

Brandariz, J. A. (2015). *Gran Recesión y penalidad: Reflexiones sobre la evolución de la población penitenciaria*. Paper presented at II Simposio de Investigación Criminológica, Albacete, 25 y 26 de junio de 2015.

Bravo, A., Sierra, M. J., & Del Valle, J. (2009). Evaluación de resultados de la ley de responsabilidad penal de menores. *Reincidencia y factores asociados. Psicothema, 21*, 615–621.

Camps, J., & Cano, T. (2006). *Incidència de l'aplicació d'un programa de control de la conducta violenta en joves infractors*. Barcelona: Centro de Estudios Jurídicos y Formación Especializada.

Cano, A., & Andrés-Pueyo, A. (2012). La justicia juvenil en Cataluña: Características generales y funcionamiento. *Edupsykhé, 11*(2), 191–214.

Carlsson, C. (2013). Masculinities, persistence, and desistance. *Criminology, 51*(3), 661–693.

Estrada, F. (1999). Juvenile crime trends in post-war Europe. *European Journal on Criminal Policy and Research, 7*(1), 23–42.

Farrell, G., Tilley, N., & Tseloni, A. (2014). Why the crime drop? *Crime and Justice: Why Crime Rates Fall, and Why They Don't, 43*, 421–490.

Fernández-Molina, E. (2012). El internamiento de menores. Una mirada hacia la realidad de su aplicación en España. *Revista electrónica de Ciencia Penal y Criminología, 14*.

Fernández-Molina, E., Bartolomé, R., Rechea, C., & Megías, A. (2009). Evolución y tendencias de la delincuencia juvenil en España. *Revista Española de Investigación Criminológica, 7*, 1–30.

Garrido, V., Morales, L. A., & Sánchez-Meca, J. (2006). What works for serious juvenile offenders? A systematic review. *Psicothema, 18*(3), 611–619.

Gobeil, R., Blanchette, K., & Stewart, L. (2016). A meta-analytic review of correctional interventions for women offenders: Gender-neutral versus gender-informed approaches. *Criminal Justice and Behavior, 43*, 301–322.

Graña, J. L., & Rodríguez-Biezma, M. J. (2010). *Tratamiento educativo y terapéutico para menores infractores*. Madrid: Agencia de la comunidad de Madrid para la reeducación y reinserción del menor infractor. Disponible en http://www.observatoriodelainfanciadeasturias.es/documentos/f07022012130358.pdf

Graña, J. L., Garrido, V., & González, L. (2007). *Reincidencia delictiva en menores infractores de la comunidad de Madrid: Evaluación, características delictivas y modelos de predicción*. Madrid: Agencia de la Comunidad de Madrid para la Reeducación y Reinserción del menor infractor.

Ibabe, I., & Jaureguizar, J. (2011). El perfil psicológico de los menores denunciados por violencia filio-paternal. *Revista Española de Investigación Criminológica: REIC, 9*.

Junger-Tass, J., & Decker, S. (2006). *Handbook of juvenile justice*. New York: Kluwer/Springer.

Martín, E., García, M. D., & Torbay, A. (2013). Evaluación de la efectividad de las medidas educativas en la ley de responsabilidad penal de menores desde la perspectiva de los infractores. *Cultura y Educación, 25*(3), 389–398.

Moffit, T. (1993). Adolescence-Limited and life-course persistent antisocial behavior: A developmental taxonomy. *Psychological Review, 100*, 674–701.

Morales, L. A. (2011). *Revisión sistemática de la efectividad del tratamiento dirigido a delincuentes juveniles serios institucionalizados*. Tesis Doctoral.

Ortega-Campos, E., García-García, J., & Frías-Armenta, M. (2014). Meta-análisis de la reincidencia criminal en menores: Estudio de la investigación española. *Revista Mexicana de Psicología, 31*(2), 111–123.

Rechea, C., & Fernández-Molina, E. (2003). Juvenile justice in Spain: Past and present. *Journal of Contemporary Criminal Justice, 19*(4), 384–412.

Redondo, S., Martínez-Catena, A., & Andrés-Pueyo, A. (2012). *Factores de éxito asociados a los programas de intervención con menores infractores*. Madrid: Ministerio de Sanidad, Servicios Sociales e Igualdad.

Rodermond, E., Kruttschnitt, C., Slotboom, A. M., & Bijleveld, C. C. (2015). Female desistance: A review of the literature. *European Journal of Criminology, 13*(1), 3–28.

Rosenfeld, R., & Fornango, R. (2007). The impact of economic conditions on robbery and property crime: The role of consumer sentiment. *Criminology, 45*(4), 735.

Ross, R. R., & Fabiano, E. A. (1985). *Time to think: A cognitive model of delinquency prevention and offender rehabilitation*. Johnson City: Institute of Social Sciences and Arts.

Uceda, F. J., & Navarro, J. J. (2013). La política de reeducación en la comunitat valenciana. Un análisis de las prácticas educativas de los centros de justicia juvenil. *Alternativas: Cuadernos de Trabajo Social, 20*, 57–77.

Ward, T., Melser, J., & Yates, P. M. (2007). Reconstructing the risk need responsivity model: A theoretical elaboration and evaluation. *Aggression and Violent Behavior, 12*, 208–228.

Esther Fernández-Molina is Associate Professor in Criminology and Criminal Law at the University of Castilla-La Mancha since 2002 and she is a research member of Criminology Research Centre of this University. She received her doctoral degree in 2004 with the topic "Juvenile justice system in Spanish democracy: between education and punishment." Her research interests have always centered on the juvenile justice system. She has been part of many working groups in Juvenile Justice both national and international. She also developed her research work in other topics related with Criminology: attitudes to punishment, crime and mass media, fear of crime, and trust in legal authorities.

María José Bernuz Beneitez is Ph.D. of Law and Professor of Philosophy of Law and Sociology of Law at the Faculty of Law of the University of Zaragoza (Spain). She has directed and participated in several national and European research projects. Her publications as books, chapters, or articles are related, among other issues, to juvenile justice and juvenile delinquency, the reality of children's rights, human rights and criminal justice, security policies. She is part of the editorial board of some national and international journals on these subjects.

Raquel Bartolomé-Gutiérrez is Ph.D. of Psychology and Associate Professor in Psychology Department of the University of Castilla-La Mancha. She is a research member of Criminology Research Centre of this University since 1994 and she received her doctoral degree in 2001 with the topic "Juvenile delinquency in girls." Dr. Bartolomé's research interests include the antisocial behavior, gender and violence, and lifestyle in youth. She has participated in the International Self-report Delinquency (ISRD) study in Spain.

21

Sweden

Jerzy Sarnecki

INTRODUCTION

In order to understand a country's juvenile justice system, one first needs certain knowledge about that country's juvenile justice system foundations. According to Träskman (1984), the Swedish criminal code of 1864 was based on the views of the classical school of criminal justice, which rested on the two cornerstones of justice and proportionality. Thus, the punishment should proceed from the criminal act and be proportionate to the severity of the act in question. Over time, however, this classical view was abandoned, and sanctions gradually became individualised on the basis of different characteristics of the offender. When determining the severity of sanctions, increasing consideration came to be given to factors such as the offender's anti-social nature, psychological condition, and the danger he or she posed to society. By the end of the 1960s and the beginning of the 1970s, the Swedish justice system was characterised by a treatment focus (Sarnecki 2015). However, this approach came to be questioned in Sweden during the latter part of the 1970s—similar to many other parts of the western world.

The criticism of the treatment ideology was primarily focused on two factors: fairness and its effectiveness. With regard to the issue of fairness, it was argued that reacting to criminal acts on the basis of the offender's perceived need for treatment was unjust (e.g. Brå 1977). Critics noted, for example, that two youths of the same age who together committed the same offense (e.g. breaking into the cellar of an apartment building) could receive completely different sanctions. The second aspect of the criticism related to the effects of treatment and was inspired by contemporary

J. Sarnecki (✉)
Stockholm University, Stockholm, Sweden

Gävle University, Gävle, Sweden
e-mail: Jerzy.Sarnecki@criminology.su.se

S.H. Decker, N. Marteache (eds.), *International Handbook of Juvenile Justice*,
DOI 10.1007/978-3-319-45090-2_21

debates in the USA. In a seminal article on American prison reform and correctional treatment, Martinson (1974) concluded:

> "with few and isolated exceptions, the rehabilitative efforts that have been reported so far have had no appreciable effect on recidivism" (Martinson, 1974:25).

Martinson's conclusion came to be interpreted as "nothing works".

It could be argued that Martinson's (1974) article had a major impact on Sweden (Pratt and Eriksson 2011). The criticism of the treatment ideology had a profound effect on the workings of the Swedish justice system, which has gradually returned to its foundations in the classical school. The final report of the governmental inquiry "Ett reformerat straffsystem" (*A reformed penal system*: SOU 1995:91) proposed that legislation should greatly reduce its focus on the goals of prevention and should, instead, proceed on the basis of a neoclassical perspective, with the courts determining sanctions on the basis of the penal value of a given offence viewed in relation to other crimes. These ideas were largely implemented in Sweden by means of a reform of the Swedish Penal Code, which came into force in 1999. However, the current legislation still includes a range of elements associated with the treatment ideology, especially in regard to young offenders.

THE LEGAL STATUS OF JUVENILES IN SWEDEN

Sweden has special legislation for young offenders and a wide range of institutions that deal with youth who commit offenses. At the same time, and in contrast to other comparable countries, sanctioning decisions for juveniles are made by the same courts that sentence adult offenders. One very clear consequence of this system is that Sweden has no youth courts. Youths are tried in the same courts as adults, and the prosecutors who prosecute youth cases do not work in separation from the public prosecution service in general (although in some places they are special prosecutors who are assigned to deal with youth cases).

Age of Majority

The age of criminal responsibility in Sweden is 15. This is relatively high compared with other countries. In contrast to many other countries (including neighbouring Denmark), the age of criminal responsibility in Sweden is rarely seriously questioned in the national public debate. Nor are there any exceptions to this provision. For example, no criminal offenses committed by persons under the age of 15 can result in a penal sanction.[1] Instead criminal acts committed by those

[1] In certain very special cases, a court case can be held to determine the guilt of a person under the age of 15, in the form of a so-called evidentiary proceeding, in order to establish who committed the act in question without a sanction being imposed. This may be important, for example, in relation to the award of damages. This possibility is in practice almost never utilised however.

under 15 years old are viewed as social problems that are to be dealt with through the municipal social services. In serious cases, however, the social services may apply to an administrative court to take the child into care.

THE RIGHTS OF THE CHILD

Sweden has ratified the UN Convention on the Rights of the Child from 1989 (UNICEF 2015), but this convention has still not been integrated into Swedish law.

In many ways, the Swedish juvenile justice system adapted to meet the special needs of children. It could, therefore, be argued that the system meets many of the Convention's requirements—though not all of these requirements.

While Sweden's legislation makes very clear distinctions between the way the justice system deals with cases involving young offenders versus adult offenders, young offenders are nonetheless processed by the same judicial bodies as their adult counterparts. There have, however, been changes in some areas that represent a move in the required direction. Up until the introduction of the Youth Custody Act LSU, (Lag 1998:603 see later), the few custodial sentences imposed on youths aged 15–17 were served in the same prison institutions as adult offenders. Since Sweden had been subject to criticism for incarcerating youths and adults in the same prisons, the aforementioned reform constituted an, albeit incomplete, adaptation to the Convention on the Rights of the Child. At the same time, since the current legislation still allows for the possibility of sentencing youths aged 15–17 to prison (although this only happens in exceptional cases), there are still youths serving custodial sentences in the same prison institutions as adult offenders.

The most controversial issue in relation to the requirements of the Convention on the Rights of the Child is the way in which Sweden deals with youths who are in pre-trial custody. As previously discussed, youths under the age of 15 cannot be convicted of offenses and thus cannot be held on remand either (although they can, when necessary, be taken into compulsory care). Youths aged 15–17 are, however, permitted to be held in police custody and in remand centres if there is exceptional cause to do so (SFS 2015:446). According to an investigation conducted by the Swedish Ombudsman for Children (2013), a total 3052 youths aged 15–17 were admitted to remand centres/police custody in 2011. Approximately half of these admissions were the result of offending, while the remainder of the admissions were due to drunkenness or other reasons. According to the same report, the number of children admitted to remand centres/police custody has increased somewhat over recent years.

The report of the Ombudsman for Children is highly critical of the Swedish system of holding children in remand centres/police custody. This criticism relates to a number of different factors. The report highlights that there are no official statistics on the number of children held in these forms of custody, the length of time they are held in custody, or the reasons they have been arrested or placed on remand. The Ombudsman for Children report also argues that these forms of custody are used too often in relation to children, and that the periods they spend in custody are too long. Particularly severe criticism is directed towards the conditions under which children are held in remand centres/police custody. In many cases, these conditions are no different from those under which adults are held. These conditions may thus involve severe restrictions on the individual's contacts with the outside world. According to the Ombudsman's report, this can cause serious damage to the children. The Ombudsman argues that these conditions are in conflict with the requirements of Convention on the Rights of the Child, and that they equate to torture.

It is also worth noting that a range of criticisms have also been directed at Sweden's remand regulations in relation to adults. The periods that adults are required to spend on remand are regarded as being very long, and it is relatively easy for prosecutors to obtain the consent of the courts to impose restrictions on remand prisoners' contacts with the outside world. These restrictions may also be in force for very long periods of time. Sweden has also been criticised in this regard by the UN Committee against Torture (United Nations 2014).

TRENDS IN YOUTH CRIME IN SWEDEN

The general trends with regard to traditional crime (primarily theft and violent offending) in Sweden are largely similar to the crime trends of many other western countries. A summary assessment of Swedish crime trends (Sarnecki 2015) shows that crime rates increased substantially from the end of the Second World War until the early 1990s. Since then, crime has been on the decline. Youth crime rates largely mimicked the trends in the general population. In the period in which crime was increasing, crime rates increased most among young people. Over the past 20 years as crime has been decreasing, the decrease has also been most pronounced among young people (ibid). The general trend is that the decline in crime primarily relates to men, whereas crime levels among women appear to be relatively stable (Bäckman et al. 2014).

Figure 21.1 presents the number of convictions[2] among youths aged 15–17.[3]

The figure shows that the number of convictions among youths increased until the mid-1990s, and then gradually declined until the mid-2000s. Since then, conviction rates have been relatively stable, with some indication of a possible upswing in recent years. The trend in convictions for offenses against the person (primarily comprising crimes of violence) differs somewhat, remaining stable following an increase during the first half of the 1990s.

Since 1995, Sweden has conducted national surveys of self-reported offending among a representative sample of youths in their final year of compulsory

[2]The term conviction is used in Sweden to refer to a court conviction, or a sanctioning decision taken by a prosecutor in the form of a summary sanction order or a waiver of prosecution (see later).

[3]As has been noted earlier, the age of criminal responsibility in Sweden is 15. Persons below the age of 15 are therefore not included in the convictions statistics.

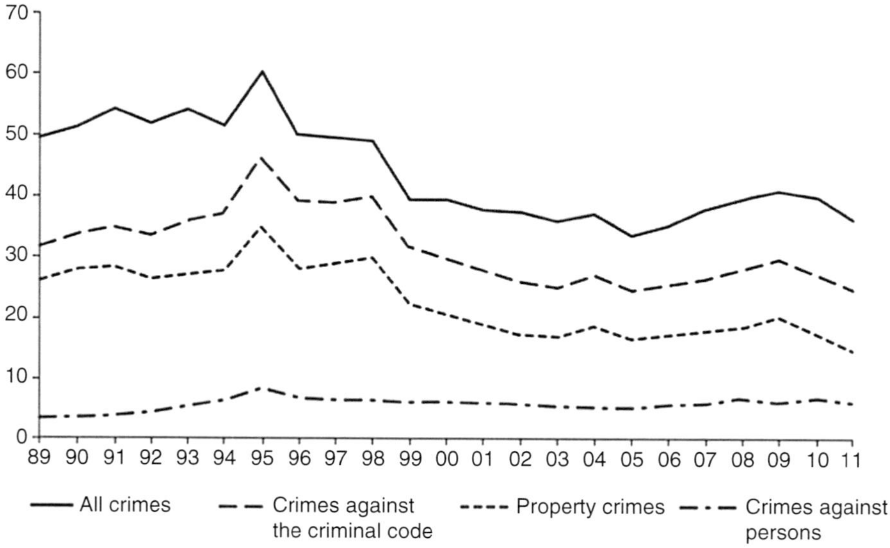

FIGURE 21.1. Convictions among youths age 15–17 per 1000 individuals in this age group in the population, 1989–2011 (Brå 2013a).

education (year 9). The surveys have been conducted every 2 or 3 years. Figure 21.2 presents the results of these surveys for different types of offenses.

The figure shows that levels of self-reported involvement in theft and vandalism have declined considerably during the period examined. Involvement in violent offending has also followed a declining trend, although this primarily relates to having carried a knife in public. Levels of involvement in the "other" category (fare dodging, driving without a license, and the use of a false ID-card) and drug-related offenses (all forms of handling drugs are criminalised in Sweden, including personal consumption) have remained stable over time.

Figure 21.3 shows that the decline in self-reported offending among year 9 youth has been substantial. The group of students who reported no involvement in crime over the course of the year prior to the survey increased in by 56%, and this group now accounts for a majority of the respondents. The figure also shows that the group of youths who report having committed six or more offenses during the past year has also become much smaller. According to these self-reports, offending has declined among both frequent and non-frequent youth offenders.

There are a number of indicators that suggest that youth crime has declined over the past two decades. Figure 21.4 provides us with a basis for drawing some conclusions about the underlying reasons for this decline. This seems a little out of place.

EXPLANATIONS FOR THE CRIME TRENDS AMONG YOUTH

The increase in crime in general and youth offending in particular following the Second World War surprised many Swedish scholars and politicians. Sweden did not participate in the Second World War, and the country started building a

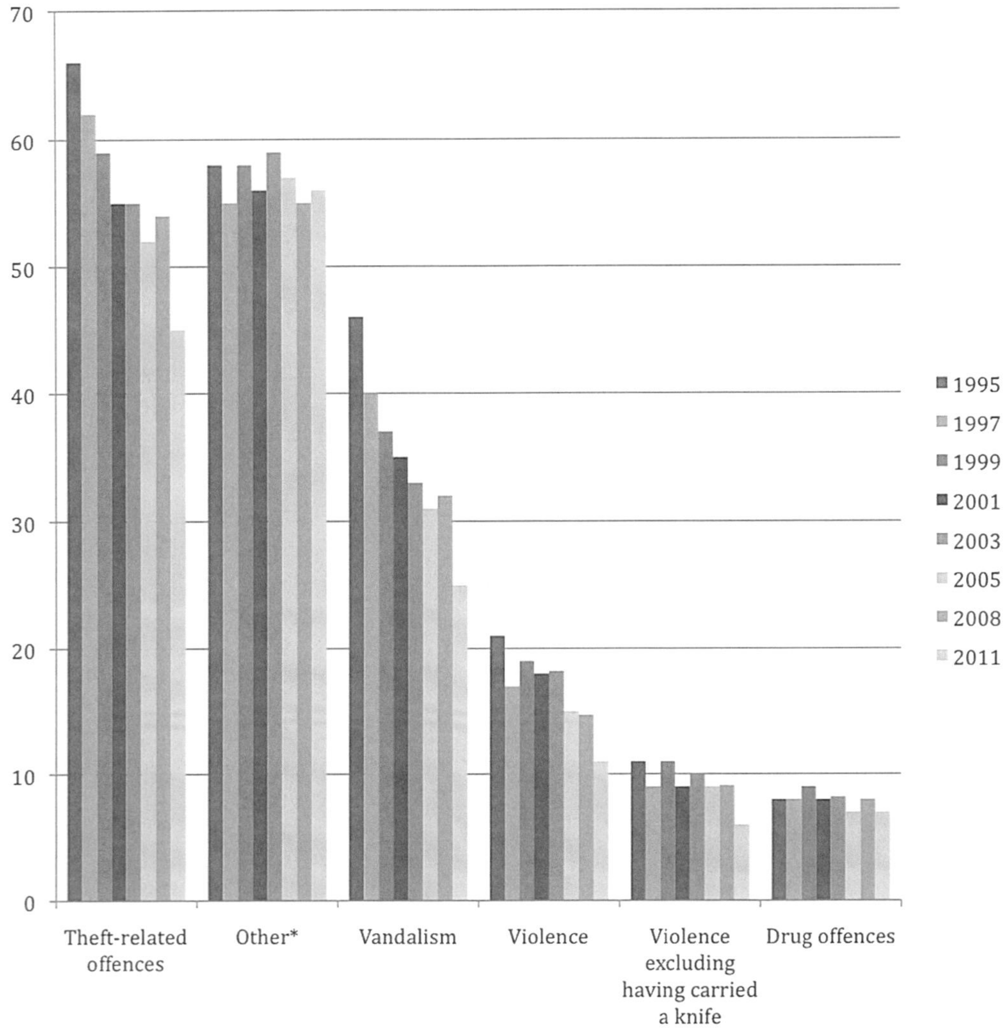

FIGURE 21.2. Self-reported participation by offending types among Swedish students in year 9 (aged 15–16). Percent (Brå 2013a). *Fare dodging, driving without a license, use of false ID-card.

welfare state while large parts of Europe were still recovering from the war's impact. By increasing levels of wealth and reducing social inequality,[4] the goal was to build a society in which all citizens could live well. The expectation was that the development of the welfare state would produce a decline in levels of crime. What actually happened was quite the opposite. Scholars (e.g. von Hofer 2011) have explained this trend as having been a result of the increase in wealth production and thereby an increase in the opportunities for crime. Sarnecki

[4]Levels of social inequality were to be reduced by means of powerful progressive taxation and various types of transfers to the socially and economically disadvantaged groups in Swedish society.

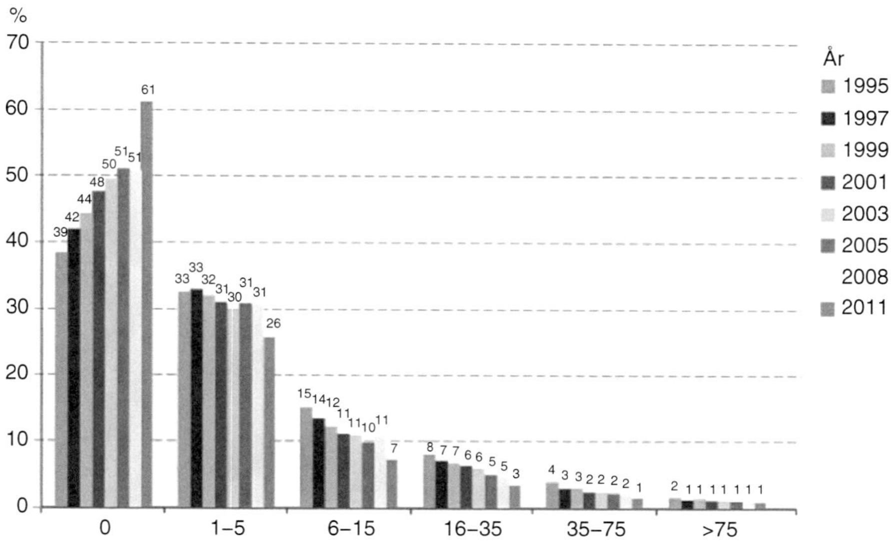

FIGURE 21.3. Numbers of self-reported offenses per year among Swedish students in year 9 (aged 15–16). Percent (Brå 2013b).

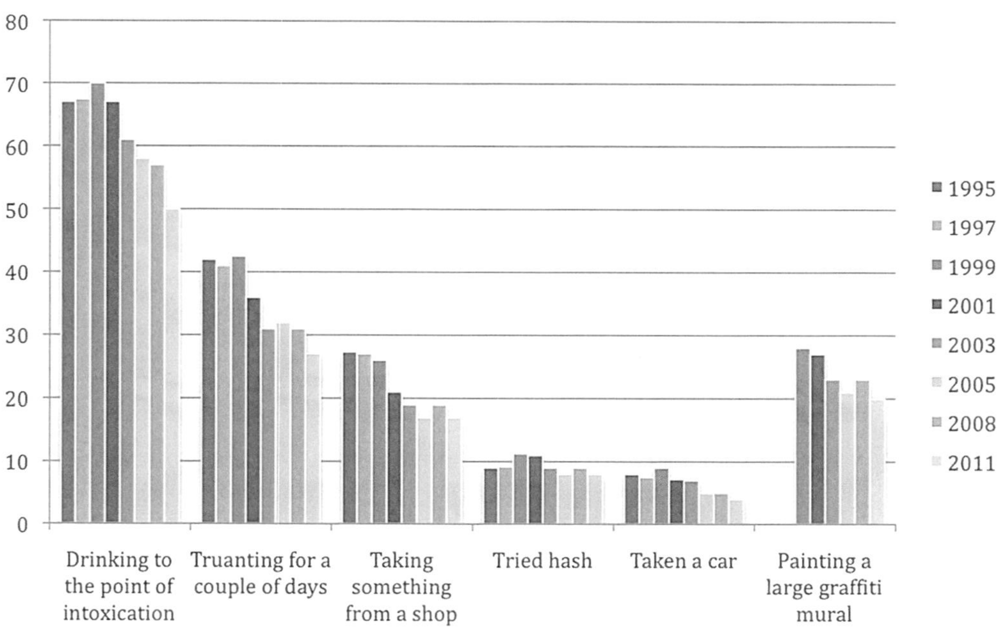

FIGURE 21.4. Proportion of students in year 9 (age 15–16) who believed that their friends would think it was "completely OK" if they themselves engaged in a number of different socially unacceptable behaviours (Brå 2013b).

(2012), who largely agrees with the arguments presented by von Hofer, noted, however, that changes in the opportunity structure alone could not fully explain why crime increased more among young people than adults. In addition, changes in the opportunity structure could not fully account for the decline in crime witnessed in the 1990s. Sarnecki's view is that, in addition to changes in the opportunity structure, developments in the field of social control have also played an important role in explaining changes in crime at the macro level. He argues that levels of social control declined more substantially for young people during the period 1950–1990 than for other groups within the population. According to Sarnecki, the crime decline beginning of the 1990s indicates that levels of social control, particularly among young people, started to increase once again.

Changes in young people's perceptions of their peers' attitudes toward deviant behaviour may be interpreted as an indicator of changes in social control. According to Matza (1964), for example, youths' perceptions of other youths' attitudes to crime may be expected to have a direct effect on their own offending. Figure 21.4 presents data on Swedish youths' perceptions of their peers' attitudes to a range of behaviours. The data are from the above-described self-report surveys conducted among students in year 9.

The figure shows a clear trend in relation to the majority of the deviant behaviours examined. Over the course of the 16-year period, the youths described their peers as having increasingly negative views of involvement in deviant behaviour. The exception is found in relation to "testing hash", where no attitude changes have occurred. As is shown in Fig. 21.2, the level of self-reported drug use has remained stable in contrast to the level of involvement in the other types of offending. The earlier results confirm the hypothesis that levels of social control among young people appear to be increasing, which may constitute one explanation for why youth crime is decreasing, despite the continued increase in economic wealth and subsequent increase in the opportunities for crime.

RESPONSES TO YOUTH CRIME IN SWEDEN

The Criminal Justice System

Sweden has two parallel systems for responding to youth crime: one within the municipal system of social services provision and the other within the criminal justice system. These systems are expected to work in conjunction, which they often do so—although they are sometimes in competition with one another. The following section focuses on the criminal justice system's response to youth crime.

The Police

The age of criminal responsibility being15 years old places restrictions on the ways in which the police deal with the offenses committed by the youngest offenders. The police can, however, initiate investigations into crime, even when the suspect is under the age of 15. This is the case if the penal value of the offense, when similarly committed by an adult, is equivalent to a prison term of 1 year or more and there are no special reasons for not initiating such an investigation (SFS 2015:446). However, the outcomes of such investigations are not presented to the public prosecutor and should focus on the necessary information to provide to social services (see later). At the same time, the police are required to prioritise cases involving young offenders. Investigations of such offenses are required to be conducted promptly. The police officers who investigate offenses committed by young offenders are required to be particularly suited to the task. When offenses committed by persons under the age of 18 are investigated by the police, they should always take place in collaboration with social services and, where possible, with the offender's parents or guardians (SFS 2015:446).

As the age of the suspect increases, so too does the degree of similarity with the investigation of offenses committed by adults. The promptness requirement exists for offenders over the age of 15 as well. The use of special coercive measures, such as pre-trial incarceration, for young suspects is also restricted by law (SFS 2015) although critics feel that these restrictions do not go far enough.

Some argue that the long-term trend in the Swedish legislation is towards an extension of police rights to investigate offenses committed by young people. A statement of opinion from the Swedish Council on Legislation described these trends as involving "a shift in perspective from the social services towards criminal law" (Lagrådet 2010, page 1).

The Youth Custody Act (LSU)

One of few clear consequences for young offenders in the Swedish legislation is found in the introduction of the youth custody sanction (Youth Custody Act—LSU; Lag 1998:603). The objective of this piece of legislation was the introduction of a determinate custodial sanction for youths aged 15–20 who are convicted of more serious offenses. Youth custody was intended to be imposed for offenses that would result in a prison term if the offender were an adult. The length of the sentence can vary between 14 days and 4 years depending on the penal value of the offense. Since the maximum prison term for adults in Sweden for the most serious offenses (murder) is 18 years to life imprisonment, the maximum term for youth custody is considerably lower. In the same way, the length of the custodial sentences imposed on the basis of the youth custody legislation is considerably shorter than the prison sentences that would be imposed on the basis of the legislation that applies to adults. This was also the intention of the legislation. The fundamental principle is that society cannot hold young people accountable for their actions to the same extent as adults. At the same time, the difference in the length of sentences between youth and adults is not as great as might it might appear since all adult prison inmates are released on parole once they have served two-thirds of their sentences, whereas youth custody sentences are served in their entirety.

From the perspective of the philosophy of law, youth custody is a somewhat remarkable sanction. On one hand, its severity is determined in proportion to the penal value of the offenses committed. On the other hand, the sanction's content takes the form of treatment provision at one of the special approved homes (see later). The nature of the treatment provided by special approved homes is largely the same irrespective of whether a given youth has been placed on the basis of the LVU Act (see later) or sentenced to the youth custody sanction by a criminal court. The National Board of Institutional Care, which is the state agency responsible for the special approved homes, has six institutions that receive youths sentenced to youth custody.

Relatively few youths in Sweden are sentenced to youth custody. In 2014, 56 youths served youth custody sentences, of which only two were girls (SiS 2015:10). This number has remained relatively stable in recent years. Over the course of the past 15 years, the number of such sentences has been reduced by half. When the sanction was introduced, it was said to have had a net-widening effect. The original idea was that youth custody would replace prison sentences for youths aged 15–17, but the new sanction was imposed on youths in this age group much more frequently than a prison sentence had been imposed prior to the Youth Custody Act coming into effect.

In 2014, the mean length of youth custody sentences served was 10.7 months. The shortest sentences were between 14 days and 3 months, and the longest sentences of 24 months were very uncommon. The most common offenses that resulted in youth custody sentences were robbery (53 %) and assault (31 %). There are, however, cases where youths are sentenced to youth custody for serious property crime. Two of those sentenced to youth custody in 2014 (6 % of the LSU Lag 1998:603 sentences) were for murder (SIS 2015:10).

Youth Service and Care in Accordance with the Social Services Act

In theory, youths aged 15–17 who have committed serious offenses can still be sentenced to a prison term. In practice, however, this happens very rarely. In 2014, for example, only four individuals below the age of 18 were sentenced to prison. In all of these cases, the youths in question were 17 years of age and had been convicted serious offenses and had extensive criminal histories. Prison sentences are much more common among youths aged 18–20. In 2014, 458 youths in this age group were sentenced to prison and only 12 were sentenced to youth custody (Brå 2015:216). In accordance with Swedish legislation, the prison sentences awarded to youths aged 18–20 are milder than those awarded to persons aged 20 and older for equivalent offenses. Young people cannot be sentenced to life imprisonment. This so-called "youth rebate" has been the subject of debate at the political level. It and might be removed, either in whole or in part, if the nature of the political majority in the Swedish parliament were to change.

Of a total of approximately 110,000 criminal convictions in Sweden in 2014, approximately 9000 were for youths aged 15–17 and approximately 12,000 were for persons aged 18–20. The most common type of conviction among the youngest age group was for a waiver of prosecution (approximately 3100) (Brå 2015:216). A waiver of prosecution is best described as a form of caution, which can be issued by the prosecutor for relatively minor offences following an admission of guilt by the offender. It is not uncommon for prosecutors to make such decisions in the presence of the youths and their parents, having first contacted the social services to ensure that adequate treatment measures are in place. In these cases, no sanction is imposed but the offense is recorded in the convictions register and remains there for a period of 5 years.

The second most common type of conviction among the 15–17 year age group involves the imposition of a fine. According to the Swedish legislation, a fine may be imposed either by means of a court sentence or in the form a prosecutor's decision to issue a summary sanction order. In 2014, approximately 1100 youths aged 15–17 were fined in connection with a court conviction, while 1700 were issued with a summary sanction order. In both cases, the fines take the form of day fines, a system in which the number is determined on the basis of the penal value of the offenses as well as the basis of the individual's income.

Two other types of sanctions worth mentioning in relation to 15–17-year-olds are youth service, which is a form of community service for young people, and youth care, which involves the court stating in its sentencing decision that the youth should be subject to care under the direction of the social services. In 2014, a little over 1300 youths were given youth service sentences and 1200 were sentenced to youth care. The youth service sanction was introduced into the Swedish sanctioning system at the same time as youth custody in 1999 (Prop. 1997/98:96 s. 152 f.). This sanction was initially structured as an additional sanction to be imposed when youths were sentenced to social services care. The responsibility for specifying the contents of the sanction was thus assigned to the social services (Forss 2013), who were already responsible for determining the nature of treatment measures for youths both under and over the age of 15. As will be shown later, these measures may be implemented in relation to young offenders both on the initiative of the social services themselves and (when the youth is over the age of 15) on the basis of a court conviction.

An evaluation conducted by the Swedish National Council for Crime (Brå 2002) showed that the youth service reform had not been implemented to the extent that had been intended. For example, only half of Sweden's municipalities had an organisation in place to implement the sanction. In 2007, the Swedish legislation on young offenders was reformed again (Prop. 2005/06:165 p. 64). Youth service was transformed into an independent sanctioning form, thus removing the requirement that the sanction be linked to a sentence to care on the basis of the Social Services Act. Further, the municipalities were required to have a system in place for implementing the sanction. This reform was clearly appreciated by the courts. In 2008, almost 3000 youths were sentenced to youth service. Since that time, however, the number of such sentences has declined by more than half (Brå 2015:205).

Similar to community service for adults, the youth service sanction involves the offender being required to engage in unpaid work. The sanction can be imposed on individuals aged 15–20. It is, however, much more commonly imposed on youths aged 15–17 than on youths aged 18–20. The number of hours one is sentenced to youth service may vary between 20 and 150. The sanction is only awarded if the defendant consents to participate.

The youth care sanction (which is not the same as youth custody LSU) involves the court sentencing the youth to receive care under the direction of social services. Until the legislative reform of 2007, this sanction, which at the time was formulated slightly differently, was labelled care in accordance with the Social Services Act. In order for this sanction to be imposed, the youth must be regarded as being in need of care, and a care plan must be presented to the court by the local social services administration.

Other Sentences for Young People

In regard to the criminal justice sanctions imposed on youths aged 18–20, the official crime statistics (Brå 2015) show that these sanctions are both greater in number (approximately 11,000 in 2014) and significantly more severe (see Fig. 21.5). In 2014, 458 of these sanctions involved a prison sentence and only 12 were sentenced to youth custody. Almost 900 individuals were sentenced to probation (a very uncommon sanction among 15–17-year-olds).

At the same time, the sanctions imposed on these older youths are also dominated by day-fines in the form of either summary sanction orders (approximately 3900) or court sentences (approximately 2800). Waivers of prosecution are also relatively common (approximately 1500), although considerably less so compared to the 15–17-year-olds. For the younger age group, there are special provisions in the Young Offenders Act (LUL, Lag 1964:167) that allow the prosecutor to issue a waiver of prosecution (i.e. a caution) if there is an expectation that other measures will be put in place, primarily on the initiative of the social services. This same possibility also exists in relation to older youths, but it is very seldom used.

Another common sanction imposed on the 18–20-year-olds was a suspended sentence (approximately 1300 convictions), of which just under one-third were combined with community service.

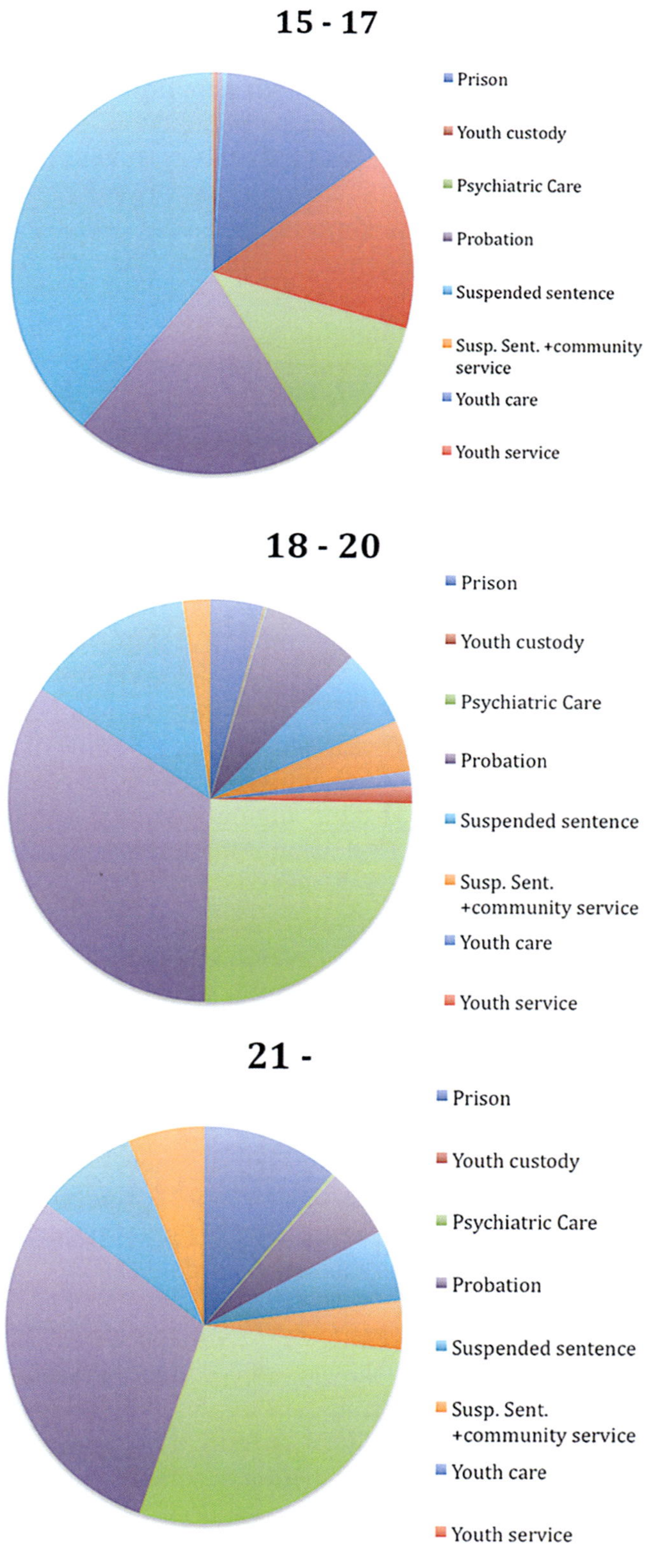

FIGURE 21.5. Distribution of sanctions following a conviction in 2013 for youths aged 15–17 (N=9,124) and 18–20 (N=12,062), and for adults (N=89,509) (Brå 2015).

Comparison with Adults

Figure 21.5 also presents the distribution of criminal justice sanctions among adults, which are considerably more severe. The proportion of custodial sanctions among 15–17-year-olds is 0.04% (including youth custody and forensic psychiatric care) and 0.5% among 18–20-year-olds, while the corresponding proportion of sanctions imposed on adults over the age of 20 is 11%. Day-fines constitute the most common sanction even among adult offenders in Sweden, accounting for a total of 58% of conviction decisions. Among the adults, however, it is more common for these fines to have been imposed by courts rather than on the basis of a summary sanction order.

Changes in the Sanctioning System for Young Offenders

A similar review of the sanctions imposed on young offenders was conducted at the end of the 1980s (Sarnecki 1989) based on conviction data from 1987. It is, therefore, possible to compare changes in the sanctions imposed on young offenders over the course of more than 25 years. The justice system, over the course of this period, has undergone a powerful shift towards the tenets of neoclassicism.

To begin, the total number of sanctions imposed on young people has declined considerably. Among 15–17-year-olds, the number of sanctions has declined by 38%, while for 18–20-year-olds, we see a decline of 41%. Looking at the population as a whole, the number of convictions has declined by 28% over the course of this period. The decline among young people has been greater. At the same time, the size of the Swedish population has increased by approximately 12% to 9.7 million people (Fig. 21.6).

A shift in the type of sanctions imposed can also be observed. With regard to 15–17-year-olds, the use of prison sentences has ceased almost entirely, although prison sentences in this age group were rare even in 1987. In total, however, the proportion of custodial sanctions has increased somewhat as a result of the introduction of youth custody. The use of youth care sentences has increased among 15–17-year-olds. A considerable number—approximately 1300—of the sanctions imposed on youths in this age group in 2013 involve the use of the new youth service sanction. Although summary sanction orders and waivers of prosecution remain the most common forms of conviction decisions among 15–17-year-olds, the proportion of the total number of convictions accounted for by such decisions has declined considerably over the course of the period examined.

In regard to the 18–20-year-olds, the use of prison sentences has declined somewhat, whereas the use of probationary sentences has increased. Fines constitute the largest category of sanctions, although their use has declined to some extent. There has been a dramatic decrease in the number of fines awarded in the form of summary sanction orders. The number of sanctions involving fines

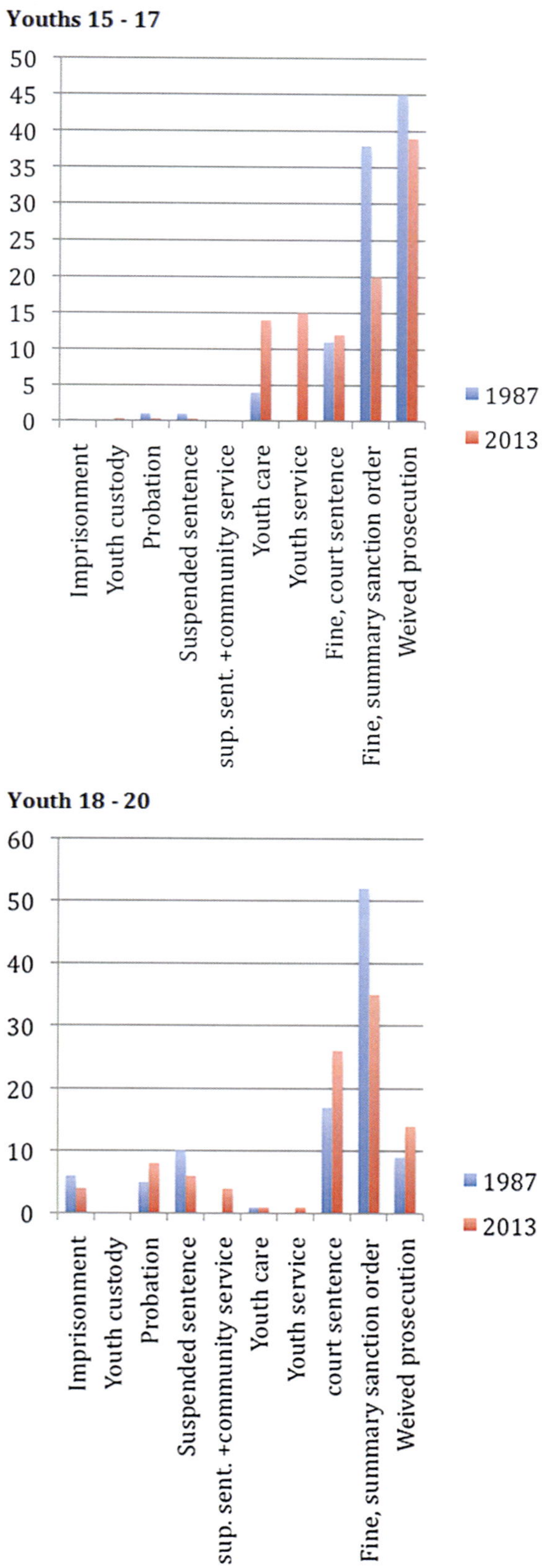

FIGURE 21.6. Comparison of convictions in 1987 and 2014, respectively, for youths aged 15–17 and 18–20. Percent. (*N* 15–17, 1987 = 14,817; *N* 15–17, 2013 = 9,134; *N* 18–20, 1987 = 20,346; *N* 18–20, 2013 = 12,062).

imposed by the courts has increased, but not sufficiently to match the decline in summary sanction orders.

The general impression is that elements of the treatment perspective have retained a prominent position within the Swedish system of youth sanctions. At the same time, the proportion of conviction decisions made by prosecutors has declined, while the proportion of court convictions has increased. Since the total number of convictions for young people has declined considerably over the course of the period examined, however, there has been no increase in the aggregate number of court convictions involving youths.

The Social Services

Measures implemented by or based on decisions made from social services constitute the most dominant form of response to offenses committed by young people in Sweden. The criminal justice system is expected to cooperate with the social services in relation to cases involving young people and able to refer young offenders to the social services. This may take place in different phases of the criminal justice process, such as the initial processing of cases by the police (with the police being required to contact the social services when minors are suspected of offenses), when the prosecutor makes a decision whether to prosecute or issue a waiver of prosecution, and in the final phase of the process when the courts choose to impose certain forms of sanctions (e.g. youth care or youth service). In addition, the social services may implement measures to young offenders on their own initiative.

The section that follows provides a description of the relevant pieces of social services legislation relating to young offenders as well as how this legislation is implemented in practice. Since this legislation views crime as a social problem, it does not distinguish between measures that are taken in response to offending behaviour and measures taken in response to other forms of social problems, which are nonetheless often related to the youths' offending behaviour.

The Social Services Act (SoL)

The fundamental principle underlying the Swedish social services legislation is that measures should be implemented on the basis of consent and that they should proceed from the needs of the individual. This is also the case for social services measures that are initiated in response to offending. Although it is possible to implement coercive measures within the framework of social services, the vast majority of measures employed in relation to young offenders are based on the voluntary participation of the children/youths concerned as well as their legal guardians. Such measures are implemented on the basis of the Social Services Act (Lag 2001:453–SoL) and relate to both youth offenders and young people with other types of social problems. Structured measures[5] of this kind are implemented to almost 56,000 children and youth in Sweden every year. Of these, 55% are boys. The majority of these measures are implemented without the youths being institutionalised. Instead, the youths participate in measures arranged by the social services while living at home. The most common forms employed (approximately two-thirds of the total) involve the appointment of a contact person or contact family. The remaining non-institutional measures commonly involve participation in some form of programme focused on the youths' specific problems, usually with some kind of CBT (cognitive-based therapy?) focus (Socialstyrelsen 2013).

Over the course of 2013, approximately 26,000 Swedish children and youth were placed outside of the family home in accordance with the Social Services Act. These placements can be short, lasting only a few days, but children can sometimes be placed in this way for a number of years. The most common form of placement involves living with a foster family. There are also placements in residential care institutions known as HVB homes. In very rare cases, children can also be placed in special approved homes on a voluntary basis. The number of voluntary placements has increased substantially (by almost 70%) over the past 7 years. However, this is not due to an increase in the number of placements involving young offenders. The increase is instead due to the fact that many unaccompanied child refugees who lack adequate supervision are placed on the basis of the Social Services Act, commonly in the above-mentioned HVB homes (Socialstyrelsen 2013).

The Care of Young People (Special Provisions) Act (LVU)

Young people may be placed into care when they are under the age of criminal responsibility as well as when they are between the ages of 15 and 20. The LVU Act, however, is applied restrictively. It allows the municipal social services to apply to the administrative court for a compulsory care order if the care required by the youth in question cannot be provided (or where there is an assumption that this care cannot be provided) with the consent of the youth (if aged 15 or over) or the youth's guardians (if the youth is below the age of 15).

Young people up to the age of 18 may be taken into care on the basis of Section 2 of the LVU Act, which states that:

> "A decision on care shall be taken if there is a significant risk of harm to the child's health or development as a result of physical or psychological abuse, improper exploitation, neglect or some other aspect of the home environment." Lag (1990:52).

[5] Measures in the form of temporary contacts between the social services and young people who are either suspected of offences or have other types of problems, and their families, are not included in the figures presented here. Contacts of this kind are much more common, but are only registered as and when a decision is taken to implement more structured measures following a social services investigation.

Thus, the principle objective associated with this section of the Act is the protection of the youth in question, and it is often used in relation to young children. In regard to offending behaviour, the use of this section of the LVU Act is therefore focused primarily on the prevention of future offending, rather than providing a response to offenses that have already been committed.

The LVU Act does, however, also provide an opportunity to place young people in compulsory care as a result of their own behaviour. This is specified in Section 3 of the Act:

> "A decision on care shall also be taken if the child places his or her health or development at a significant risk of harm through the abuse of addictive substances, criminal activity or some other form of socially destructive behaviour" Lag (1990:52).

The Act also provides for the compulsory care of young people over the age of 15 following the completion of a youth care sentence imposed by the criminal justice system in accordance with Chapter 32, Section 5 of the Penal Code. It is possible for the local social welfare board (initially often the chairperson of the board) to issue a compulsory care order immediately in an acute situation and to then subsequently to apply to have the care order confirmed by a decision of the administrative court.

In regard to older youths, and particularly those who are taken into care on the basis of Section 3 of the LVU Act, this care is sometimes provided at a category of institutions labelled "special approved homes" (see later), which are administered by a government agency known as the National Board of Institutional Care. It is more common for the care to be provided in foster homes compared to HVB institutions or, in rare cases, in the child's own home. Compulsory care for younger youths is commonly provided in foster homes.

A total of 6893 children and youths were placed in LVU care in Sweden in 2013, of whom 62% were boys. A total of 2530 of these children and youth were subject to immediate care orders (Socialstyrelsen 2013:23). A total of 1.4% of all young people in Sweden aged under 20 were subject to LVU measures over the course of 2013. This proportion has not changed notably since 2005 (Socialstyrelsen 2013:25).

LVU care should be concluded as soon as there is no longer cause for compulsory care measures. Therefore, the length of such measures is not determined in advance. A reassessment of the compulsory care order is conducted every 6 months.

Special Approved Homes

A small group of the young people who are served with compulsory care orders in accordance with the LVU Act, numbering just over 1000 per year, are subject to the most intrusive form of youth care in the form of a placement at a special approved home.[6] These youths are between 15 and 20 years old and 30% of them are girls. There are 24 special approved homes in Sweden, all of which are government-administered institutions, and these are distributed throughout the country with a total of 591 places. The majority of these places (82%) are secure, 12% are non-secure, and the remaining 7% are of mixed form (SiS 2015).

Special approved homes are best described as small institutions located in rural areas with a very high ratio of staff to residents (not uncommonly more than three to one).

The reason for placements at special approved homes is often offending behaviour, commonly in combination with either substance abuse or other socially destructive behaviour (SiS 2015:7).

Care placements at special approved homes are usually relatively short. Half of those admitted are discharged after less than 3 months, while only 7% stay at these institutions for between 1 and 2 years. Less than 2% remain in care placement for over 2 years (SiS 2015:11). Being discharged from a special approved home rarely involves a complete cessation of care provision. In the majority of cases, care provision continues in a more open form. Only a small proportion of those discharged from special approved homes (approximately one-quarter) are discharged to the parental home or, in extremely rare cases, to their own homes. In these cases, there is some form of continued care provision as well. It is more common for youths to be discharged to another type of non-secure institution or to a foster home, with this occurring in over one-half of discharges from special approved homes (SiS 2015:11).

Other Forms of Placement Based on the LVU Act

The vast majority of the youths that are subject to compulsory care placements in accordance with the LVU Act are placed in foster homes or in the non-secure residential institutions known as HVB homes, which also host the majority of youths who have been placed in care on a voluntarily basis. (Certain HVB institutions may also have secure units.) As the age increases, the proportion of youths placed in foster homes declines and the proportion placed in institutions increases.

Restorative Justice

A large proportion of the measures taken for young offenders can be viewed as alternative sanctions that involve youths being diverted away from the criminal justice system and traditional criminal justice sanctions. At the same time, the use of measures based on the restorative justice perspective is limited in Sweden. Mediation is the only form of restorative justice that is employed on a large scale. Since the early 2000s, the use of mediation has been regulated by special legislation

[6] A very small proportion of those placed in special approved homes (approximately 3%) are admitted voluntarily (see above). These are placed on the basis of Chapter 4, Section 1 of the Social Services Act (SoL).

(Lag 2002:445). Mediation also falls under the responsibility of the municipal social services, which is required to cooperate with the criminal justice system. Since 2008, it has been obligatory for all municipalities to have the capacity to offer mediation following offenses where the offender is under the age of 20 (Socialstyrelsen 2009). Municipalities may also offer mediation in cases involving offenders aged 20 or over, but this is not obligatory. There is no lower age limit for mediation, as it can be offered even when a suspect is under the age of 15.

When the social services provide a written opinion to the prosecutor or the courts regarding offenses committed by a suspect under the age of 20, this document is required to state whether the offender has been asked about participating in mediation and whether he/she is willing to participate. The issue of whether the offender is willing to participate in mediation is important to the sanctioning decision. The prosecutor, for example, is required to take the suspect's willingness to participate in mediation into consideration along with the penal value of the offenses, the other information provided in the social services' written opinion, and what the offender has admitted to. The victim's attitude has no significance in this particular context (Ibid.).

It is interesting to note that there remains a certain scepticism towards restorative justice in Sweden. The system was introduced relatively late and its more formal links to the criminal justice process only came to be regulated in 2008. The National Board of Health and Welfare has recommended:

"In connection with certain types of crime, however, mediation may be completely inappropriate. This is first and foremost the case in relation to sexual offences in general, but also violent offences directed at family members or relatives, e.g. violence against women within an intimate relationship. An offer to participate in mediation can in certain cases in and of itself involve a further violation of the crime victim." (Socialstyrelsen 2009:131)

This restrained attitude towards mediation is not in line with findings from the international research literature in this area (Strang and Braithwaite 2002; Sherman and Strang 2007).

Forms of Treatment

Although the treatment perspective continues to enjoy a strong position within the Swedish system of responses to youth crime, the contents of the treatment provided have changed over time. Studies from the 1980s (Sarnecki 1989) show that a substantial majority of these treatment forms provided were based on psychodynamic (psychoanalytical) models. Today, the psychodynamic approach is very uncommon. The most common treatment approach now involves various forms of cognitive behavioural therapy (CBT), which are focused on helping people find solutions to their problems.

The use of methods based on individual deterrence or harsh punishment (e.g. boot camps) does not exist in Sweden. This does not mean that none of the treatments provided to young people involve physical activity and other forms of challenges. There are cases, for example, where the social services offer youths the opportunity to participate in survival courses, such as sailing trips and other activities. These types of activities were more common a couple of decades ago than they are today, primarily due to criticisms voiced by the media and politicians. The critics felt that these activities could be perceived as rewarding, rather than punishing, involvement in unacceptable behaviour. The goal of treating problems rather than imposing punishments for offending is not broadly supported by the general public.

The most common response to less serious offending among young people is that the individual and his or her parents are required to attend the social services to discuss and explore whether there is a need for more extensive measures. In the majority of cases, no further measures are taken. In those cases where additional measures are implemented, these usually take the form of continued counselling contacts with the social services or with a contact person (or contact family) appointed by the social services (Brå 2002). The more structured measures and placements outside of the home that have been previously described are relatively uncommon.

One subject of considerable discussion in Sweden relates to the fact that there are so many different actors involved in the juvenile system. The social services and the criminal justice system constitute the two actors who bear the primary responsibilities. Problems arise because the tasks of these two actors are somewhat different in addition to the issue of confidentiality regulations. Sweden's confidentiality legislation (Lag 2009:400) provides extensive restrictions for information sharing between different agencies. The social services are not permitted to provide information on an individual to the police without the individual's consent. There are also extensive restrictions on the exchange of information between the police, social services, and other important actors involved in prevention work, such as the child psychiatric sector, schools, the substance abuse care sector, the general healthcare sector, the employment service, and those responsible for providing leisure time activities. All these restrictions are viewed as constituting a major obstacle to the chances of improving the effectiveness of crime prevention measures. The majority of these actors have information on a given individual, which regulations prevent from sharing with others.

There are two principles that are in conflict here: the protection of individual integrity and the goal of having effective measures. Both principles are of substantial importance in relation to the perceived legitimacy of the systems involved.

These problems have been a matter of discussion for many decades now (Eriksson and Sarnecki 1979) but a definitive solution has still not been achieved. A few years ago, a governmental inquiry proposed a compromise (SOU 2010:15): that the relevant agencies should cooperate with one another and share information, but only on the condition that the child and the child's parents (if the child was under the age of 15) have provided consent. This has been described by the government and the responsible agencies as a major success (Wollter et al. 2013).

Differences in Measures Focused on Boys and Girls, Respectively

Although the gap in registered crime between boys and girls has declined, it remains very large. This is reflected by the small proportion of girls found among those convicted of serious crimes. Questions remain whether gender differences in the sanctions awarded for crime fully reflect gender differences in offending behaviour. It is not unlikely that women, and perhaps particularly young women, are dealt with somewhat more mildly by the criminal justice system and thus receive somewhat more lenient sanctions (Eriksson 2015). It has also been hypothesised that the extent of this "gender rebate" has declined more recently, which might be one of the reasons for the declining gender gap in registered crime (Estrada et al. 2015; Granath 2009).

Gender differences are smaller, however, in relation to the social services measures directed at young people with various types of social problems. A substantial amount of research has been conducted in Sweden into the differences in both the nature of the problems presented by boys and girls in the context of institutional care provisions and the types of treatment provided. Sarnecki (1996), for example, shows that boys are admitted to secure youth institutions primarily as a result of offending and substance abuse, whereas mental health problems and externalising sexual behaviours dominate among the girls. Boys are almost never taken into care on the basis of sexuality-related issues of this kind.

In a recent study, Axelsson and Sarnecki (2016) show that the post-treatment prognosis for girls admitted to secure youth care is significantly better than for boys in relation to all of the factors examined (offending, substance abuse, mental healthcare, general healthcare, and mortality).

An observational study of secure youth care conducted by Laanemets and Kristiansen (2009) noted substantial differences in the ways in which boys and girls were dealt with by staff at youth institutions. The boys were dealt with in a direct manner: the staff's approach to the boys was confrontational and authoritarian. Units for boys were characterised by a policy of zero tolerance for rule violations and expectations were strongly linked to traditional masculinities. The approach employed for girls was much more personal, and consideration was given to the girls' prior histories of victimisation. The staff was also protective of the girls, and they were eager to avoid the girls experiencing failure. These findings appear to be fairly characteristic of the ways in which youths are dealt with by the social services and the criminal justice system.

Effects of the Measures Employed

Few evaluations are conducted in Sweden regarding the different types of measures employed to prevent offending among young people. Although this situation has improved somewhat over recent years, it remains difficult to find Swedish evaluations that have employed scientifically adequate methods (e.g. randomised control trials). The studies that have been conducted have produced results that largely correspond with the findings of international research. The methods employed, however, do not produce particularly powerful effects (Andreasson 2003; Socialstyrelsen 2015).

The most intrusive social measures, such as placements in special approved homes, have been the subject of considerable debate. A number of follow-up studies of youths admitted to these institutions have shown negative outcomes, such as continued substance abuse, persistent offending and other problems, and high levels of mortality (e.g. Levin 1997). The most recent longitudinal, quasi-experimental follow-up of youths admitted to these institutions during the 1990s (Axelsson and Sarnecki 2015) shows that institutional admissions produce short-term positive effects on crime and mental health problems, but have no effect on drug abuse. Over the longer term, developmental outcomes among the study group do not appear to be any different from those of the control group.

SUMMARY

Following the Second World War, powerful support developed in Sweden for the idea of constructing a welfare society. The causes of crime were viewed as lying in various welfare deficiencies and the work to combat crime became focused on correcting these deficiencies (at both the structural and individual levels). The treatment ideology was well suited to the ideological perspective of this political movement. The treatment perspective that dominated Sweden during the 1960s and 1970s has therefore had a major influence on the Swedish justice system, particularly in relation to young offenders. The system of responses to youth offending that developed against this background was primarily comprised of a range of treatment measures. The social services were given a central role in this system, with the role of the criminal justice system being primarily one of supporting the social services in their work with young offenders.

Criticism focused on the treatment ideology during the 1980s led to a shift in the criminal justice system towards a neoclassicist approach. The focus shifted away from prevention and towards the just desserts perspective. The effects of these changes were considerably less pronounced for young offenders than they were for adult offenders. The development involved the courts being given more influence over the sanctions imposed on young offenders, primarily at the expense of prosecutors, but also to some extent the social services. It became more common for social services measures to be implemented at the instruction of or following the approval of the courts.

The sanctions imposed by the courts in a majority of cases still involve the provision of treatment measures, often within the social services system or similar institutions. The municipal social services also administer sanctions such as mediation and youth service. The Swedish system of responses to young offenders remains relatively mild by comparison with many other countries; the use of punitive measures and custodial sentences remains limited.

This system has been in place without having undergone any dramatic changes during the post-war period that witnessed powerful increases in levels of youth crime as well as more recent periods during which levels of youth crime have been on the decline. The issue of how youth crime trends are linked to changes in the criminal justice system is a complex one. It is difficult to identify direct effects of changes in the justice system on crime levels, either in Sweden or other countries. We cannot, however, exclude the possibility that the political intentions that have led to the reforms described earlier may to some extent be a result of the same changes in the structures of social control that have also produced the noted decline in levels of youth crime.

REFERENCES

Andreasson, T. (2003). *Institutionsbehandling av ungdomar: vad säger forskningen?* [Institutional treatment of youth: what does the research say?]. Stockholm: Gohtia Fortbildning AB.

Axelsson, J., & Sarnecki, J. (2016). *Longitudinal follow-up of adolescents treated in special residential homes in Stockholm County*. Stockholm: Department of Criminology, Stockholm University.

Bäckman, O., Estrada, F., Nilsson, A., & Shannon, D. (2014). The life course of young male and female offenders stability or change between different birth cohorts? *British Journal of Criminology, 54*(3), 393–410. doi:10.1093/bjc/azu007.

Brå. (1977). *Nytt straffsystem: idéer och förslag* [New penal system: Ideas and suggestions]. Stockholm: National Council for Crime Prevention, Sweden.

Brå. (2002). *Vad händer med unga lagöverträdare? Om överlämnande till vård inom socialtjänsten* [What happens to young offenders? If the transfer to care within the social services]. Stockholm: National Council for Crime Prevention, Sweden. Retrieved from https://www.bra.se/bra/publikationer/arkiv/publikationer/2002-10-02-vad-hander-med-unga-lagovertradare.html

Brå. (2013a). *Brott bland elever i årskurs 9. Resultat av skolundersökningen om brott 1995–2011* [Crime among students in grade 9. Results of the school survey on crime from 1995 to 2011]. Stockholm: National Council for Crime Prevention, Sweden. Retrieved from http://www.bra.se/download/18.22a7170813a0d141d21800054454/1371914744194/2013_3_Brott_bland_ungdomar-i_arskurs_nio.pdf

Brå. (2013b). *Handläggningstider i rättskedjan utvecklingen sedan 2008* [Procedural time in the legal process, the development since 2008]. Stockholm: National Council for Crime Prevention, Sweden. Retrieved from http://www.bra.se/download/18.22a7170813a0d141d21800058811/1371914744358/2013_07_Handläggningstider_i_rättskedjan.pdf

Brå. (2015). *Kriminalstatistik 2014* [Crime Statistics 2014]. Stockholm: National Council for Crime Prevention, Sweden. Retrieved from https://www.bra.se/download/18.7571ddb14f448a3848b581c/1443599243637/2015_16_Kriminalstatistik_2014.pdf

Eriksson, E. (2015). *Kvinnorabatt—Enanalys av den rättsliga bedömningen av kvinnliga gärningsmän vid grova våldsbrott* [Women's discount—An analysis of the legal assessment of female offenders for serious crimes of violence]. Lund: Lunds Universitet, Juridiska Institutionen.

Eriksson, U. B., & Sarnecki, J. (1979). Samhället och de unga lagöverträdarna [Society and the young offenders]. Sweden: National Council for Crime Prevention.

Estrada, F., Bäckman, O., & Nilsson, A. (2015). The darker side of equality? The declining gender gap in crime: Historical trends and an enhanced analysis of staggered birth cohorts. *British Journal of Criminology*: adv.access. azv114. Retrieved from http://bjc.oxfordjournals.org/content/early/2015/10/30/bjc.azv114.full.pdf+html

Forss, J. (2013). Förslag till nya ungdomspåföljder En utvärdering av påföljdsutredningens förslag till nya påföljder för unga lagöverträdare (Proposal for a new youth sanctions. An evaluation of the sanction commission's proposed new penalties for young offenders). Uppsala: Juridiska Institutionen, Uppsala University.

Granath, S. (2009). Ökat våld bland unga kvinnor—myt eller fakta? [Increased violence among young women—Myth or facts?]. Apropå. Stockholm: Brottsförebyggande rådet (BRÅ). National Council for Crime Prevention, Sweden. Retrieved from https://www.bra.se/bra/nytt-fran-bra/arkiv/apropa/2009-12-01-okat-vald-bland-unga-kvinnor---myt-eller-fakta.html

Laanemets, L., & Kristiansen, A. (2009). *Kön och behandling inom tvångsvård En studie av hur vården organiseras med avseende på genus* [Sex, and involuntary treatment: A study of how care is organized with respect to the gender]. Stockholm: National Board of Institutional Care (SiS).

Lag. (1964). *Med särskilda bestämmelser om unga lagöverträdare* [Act with the special provisions for care of youths]. Retrieved from http://www.notisum.se/rnp/sls/lag/19900052.htm

Lag. (1998). *om verkställighet av sluten ungdomsvård* (LSU) [Act on the youth custade treatment]. Retrieved from https://www.notisum.se/rnp/sls/lag/19980603.htm

Lag. (2001). *Socialtjänstlagen* [Social services act]. Retrieved from http://www.notisum.se/rnp/sls/lag/20010453.HTM

Lag. (2002). *om medling med anledning av brott* [Act on mediation due to the crime]. Retrieved from http://www.riksdagen.se/sv/Dokument-Lagar/Lagar/Svenskforfattningssamling/Lag-2002445-om-medling-med-_sfs-2002-445/

Lag. (2009). *Offentlighets–och sekretesslag* [Publicity and secrecy act]. Retrieved from www.riksdagen.se/sv/Dokument-Lagar/Lagar/Svenskforfattningssamling/Offentlighets--och-sekretessla_sfs-2009-400/

Lagrådet. (2010). *Barn under 15 år som misstänks för brott. Utdrag ur protokoll vid sammanträde 2010-03-03* [Children under 15 who are suspected of crimes. Excerpts from the minutes of the meeting of the council of justice 2010-03-03]. Retrieved from http://www.lagradet.se/yttranden/Barn%20under%20femton%20ar%20som%20misstanks%20for%20brott.pdf

Levin, C. (1997). *Ungdomar i tvångsvård. Råbyundersökningen 94* [Young people in compulsory care. Råby investigation 94]. Statens Institutionsstyrelse. Stockholm: National Board of Institutional Care (SiS). Retrieved from http://www.stat-inst.se/pagefiles/576/ungdomar-i-tvangsvard-rabyundersokning-94-kapitel-1-5.pdf

Martinson, R. (1974). What works? Questions and answers about prison reform. *The Public Interest, 35*, 22–54.

Matza, D. (1964). *Delinquency and drift*. New York: Wiley.

Pratt, J. D., & Eriksson, A. (2011). In defence of Scandinavian exceptionalism, in nordic prison practice and policy—Exceptional or not? In J. Dullum & T. Ugelvik (Eds.), *Exploring penal exceptionalism in the nordic context* (pp. 235–260). London: Routledge.

Prop. (1997). *Regeringens Proposition till Riksdagen. Vissa reformer av påföljdssystemet* [Governments Bill to the Parliament. Some reforms of the penal system]. Retrieved from http://www.riksdagen.se/sv/Dokument-Lagar/Forslag/Propositioner-och-skrivelser/prop-19979896-Vissa-reformer_GL0396/

Prop. (2005). *Regeringens Proposition till Riksdagen, Ingripanden mot unga lagöverträdare* [Governments Bill to the Parliament, Intervention against young offenders]. Retrieved from http://www.regeringen.se/rattsdokument/proposition/2006/03/prop.-200506165/

Sarnecki, J. (1989), *Juvenile delinquency in Sweden*. Stockholm: Natinal Cauncil for Crime Prevention (Brå), Swdeden.

Sarnecki, J. (1996). Problemprofiler hos ungdomar på särskilda ungdomshem i Stockholms län åren 1990–1994 [Problems profiles of adolescents in special approved homes in Stockholm between 1990–1994]. In: B.-Å. Armelius, S. Bengtzon, P. Rydelius, & J. Sarnecki (Eds.), *och Söderholm-Carpelan* (pp. 111–155). Stockholm: Liber.

Sarnecki, J. (2012). Den ökande socaila kontrollen och brottsutveckling [The increase of social control and crime development]. In: L. Pettersson & T. Pettersson (Eds.), *Kontrollens variationer* [Variations of the control]. Lund: Studentlitteratur.

Sarnecki, J. (2015). *Introduktion till kriminologi volym 2* [Introduction to criminology Volume 2]. Lund: Studentlitteratur.

SFS. (2015). *Svensk Författnings Samling. Lagen om ändringa i lagen om speciella bestämmelser om unga lagöverträdare* [Act with changes in the special provisions for care of youths]. Retrieved from https://lagen.nu/1964
Sherman, L. W., & Strang, H. (2007). *Restorative justice: The evidence*. London: The Smith Institute.
SiS. (2015). *SiS i korthet, en samlind statistiska uppgifter om SiS* [SiS in short, a collection of statistical data on the SiS]. Stockhoum: National Board of Institutional Care (SiS). Retrieved from http://www.stat-inst.se/documents/statistik/rapporter-arlig-statistik/sis-i-korthet-2014.pdf
Socialstyrelsen. (2009). *Barn och unga som begår brott. Handbok för socialtjänsten* [Children and young people who commit crimes. Handbook for social services]. Stockholm: Socialstyrelsen, The National Board of Health and Welfare. Retrieved from https://www.socialstyrelsen.se/Lists/Artikelkatalog/Attachments/8298/2009-101-3_20091013.pdf
Socialstyrelsen. (2013). *Barn och unga—insatser år 2013. Vissa insatser enligt socialtjänstlagen (SoL) och lagen med särskilda bestämmelser om vård av unga [LVU]* [Children and young people—measures in 2013. Some measures under the Social Services Act (SoL) and the Law of special provisions for the care of youth [LVU]]. Stockholm: Socialstyrelsen, The National Board of Health and Welfare.
Socialstyrelsen. (2015). *Utvärderingar av stöd till omsorgssviktande föräldrar. Ökningen av randomiserat kontrollerade utvärderingar mellan 2000–2012*. Stockhoum: Socialstyrelsen, The National Board of Health and Welfare. Retrieved from http://www.socialstyrelsen.se/Lists/Artikelkatalog/Attachments/19905/2015-7-5.pdf
SOU. (1995). *Ett reformerat straffsystem. Betänkande av Straffsystemkommittén* [A reformed penal system. Report by penal Committee for Penal System Reform]. Sweden: Statens Offentliga Utredningar.
SOU. (2010). *Kriminella grupperingar: motverka rekrytering och underlätta, Betänkande av Utredningen mot kriminella grupperingar* [Criminal groups: to counter the recruitment, and facilitation, report of inquiry against criminal groups]. Sweden: Statens Offentliga Utredningar. Retrieved from http://www.regeringen.se/contentassets/b43248191653346fb8ea7a73410f4ec95/kriminella-grupperingar---motverka-rekrytering-och-underlatta-avhopp-sou-201015
Strang, H., & Braithwaite, J. (2002). *Restorative justice and family violence*. Cambridge: Cambridge University Press.
Träskman, P. O. (1984). *Brottspåföljder och brottsmålsförfarande: rättsutvecklingen i Finland och Sverige under femtio år* [Criminal sanctions and criminal proceedings: Legal development in Finland and Sweden *during fifty years*], Svensk Juristtidning, s. 826–840.
UNICEF. (2015). *Convention on the rights of the child*. Retrieved from http://www.unicef.org/crc/index_30160.html
United Nations. (2014). *UN Committee against Torture's Concluding Observations on Sweden, Ukraine, Venezuela, Australia, Burundi, USA, Croatia and Kazakhstan*. United Nations Human Rigs Office of High Commissioner. Retrieved from http://www.ohchr.org/en/NewsEvents/Pages/DisplayNews.aspx?NewsID=15336&LangID=E#sthash.JlcwiXks.dpuf
von Hofer, H. (2011). *Brott och straff i Sverige. Historisk kriminalstatistik 1750–2010 Diagram, tabeller och kommentarer*. Stockholm: Kriminologiska institutionen, Stockholms universitet.
Wollter, F., Kassman, A., & Oscarsson, L. (2013). *Utvärdering av sociala insatsgrupper Individinriktad samverkan kring unga i riskzonen*. Rikspolisstyrelsens utvärderingsfunktion. Retrieved from https://polisen.se/Global/www%20och%20Intrapolis/Rapporter-utredningar/01%20Polisen%20nationellt/Ovriga%20rapporter-utredningar/Utvarderingsrapporter/Utvardering_av_sociala_insatsgrupper_webb.pdf

Jerzy Sarnecki is Professor of Criminology at the Stockholm University and at the Gävle University in Sweden. He is past President of the Scandinavian Research Council for Criminology and past Head of Department of Criminology at Stockholm University. He is the author of numerous books and articles on delinquent networks, life course criminology, juvenile delinquency, police efficiency, violent extremism and textbooks in criminology, etc.

Sarnecki is director of the project "The Stockholm Boys: Life Courses & Crime in the Swedish Welfare State Through Half a Century". He is serving as an expert on several scientific panels and committees in Sweden and internationally. Among others, he is a member of the Scientific Council for the Swedish National Council for Crime Prevention, Expert in the Committee for Evaluation of the Police Reform in Sweden, Member of the Ethics Committee in Stockholm, Member of the Social Services Academy Stockholm, Expert in the National Network Against Violent Extremism in Sweden, Vice President of Ulla Bondeson Foundation and Co-Chairman of the International Jury for the Stockholm Prize in Criminology.

He is also well-known expert on crime in Swedish and International Mass Media.

22

Switzerland

Ineke Pruin, Peter Aebersold, and Jonas Weber

THE LEGAL STATUS OF JUVENILES

The independent legal basis of Swiss juvenile criminal law is composed of the Swiss Juvenile Criminal Procedure Code (*Schweizerische Jugendstrafprozessordnung*, JCPC) of 20 March 2009 (in effect since 1 January 2011) and the Federal Juvenile Criminal Code (JCC) of 20 June 2003 (in effect since 1 January 2007). Thus, there are special legal provisions regarding the procedure as well as the sanctions and measures specifically tailored to juveniles (for changes in the juvenile criminal code vis-à-vis older legal norms, see Riesen-Kupper 2013. The preceding legal system has been described by Zermatten 2006.). The orientation of the Swiss juvenile criminal law system is thus penological in nature. Specific juvenile criminal or status offenses are not included in these laws. Rather, the criminal offenses of the Swiss Criminal Code (*Schweizerisches Strafgesetzbuch, CC*) apply, as do the general provisions on attempts, participation, negligence, and so on. Historically, substantive juvenile criminal law was regulated cantonally, or at the country/territorial subdivision level, until the Swiss Criminal Code came into effect in 1942. Its design differed considerably in terms of age limits and sanctions. Since 1942, substantive juvenile criminal law has been regulated by Art. 82–99 of the Swiss Criminal Code (for further reference see Aebersold 2011; Hebeisen 2011; Urwyler 2011).

The well-being of the juvenile is central to both the old and new rules on juvenile justice. According to Art. 2 JCC, the protection and education of juveniles guide the application of the law, and the development of the personality of the juvenile offender is given special consideration. In addition, Art. 4 JCC emphasizes respect for personal rights and the principle of proportionality in juvenile criminal procedure. The latter is again specified by Art. 5 JCPC and Art. 21 JCC, in which the principle of discretionary prosecution ("Opportunitätsgrundsatz") is outlined: the competent authorities refrain from criminal prosecution or, rather, a penalty, if culpability and damages are minor, if the offender has made amends, or if the offender was sufficiently punished, for example, by his/her parents or by the school.

I. Pruin (✉) • P. Aebersold • J. Weber
Institute for Criminal Law and Criminology, University of Bern, Switzerland
e-mail: ineke.pruin@krim.unibe.ch

S.H. Decker, N. Marteache (eds.), *International Handbook of Juvenile Justice*,
DOI 10.1007/978-3-319-45090-2_22

Specific deterrence ("Spezialprävention") is the overarching aim of the Swiss juvenile justice system (Aebersold 2011). With regard to the provisions, the offender and his personality are at the center of juvenile justice. The aim of sanctions is to alter and prevent undesired behavior. In juvenile criminal procedure, both penalties ("Strafen") and protective measures ("Schutzmassnahmen") can be applied. Whereas penalties require criminal liability in the sense of culpability, protective measures (see Sect. 7 below) can be applied along with or instead of penalties if the juvenile delinquent shows a risk of "delinquent development" ("delinquente Gefährdung," Article 10 JCC; see Aebersold 2011). Similar protective measures can also be ordered by the child protective authority according to the Civil Law Code; those civil measures are sometimes executed in the same institutions as measures ordered by a criminal justice authority (Aebersold 2011). Only juveniles lacking residence status in Switzerland can be exempted from a protective measure although the preconditions set out by Art. 10 paragraph 1 of the JCC are met. Starting on July 1, 2016 protective measures can continue through age 25 compared to before when the maximum age limit was 22. The sanctions catalog of the JCC responds to a culpable criminal act with imprisonment and a fine (monetary penalty), initially the classic tools of criminal punishment. Beyond these, however, as with most European juvenile criminal law systems, the JCC contains a range of alternatives with specific pedagogical objectives and targets (see Chap. 9), in which community service ("persönliche Leistung") is in practice granted particular relevance (as the most applied penalty) and which in Switzerland is regarded as a sanction (and not only or predominantly as a diversion measure as in many other countries).[1]

AGE OF MAJORITY

The age of criminal responsibility is 10 years of age. Before that, no criminal proceeding can be undertaken. However, as in many European countries, an act of an underage minor that satisfies the definition of a statutory offense can be reason for a civil law child protection measure in terms of Art. 307 ff. Civil Law Code. For juveniles under 15 years of age, only a reprimand or community service of up to 10 days can be ordered. According to Art. 24 and 25 JCC, monetary fines, imprisonment, or community service of more than 10 days can only be imposed after the age of 15. Thus, the relatively low age of criminal responsibility has to put into perspective (before the JCC took effect the minimum age of criminal responsibility was 7 years): even when the criminal law system for minors holds them to account at a comparably early age, "typical" penal sanctions in Europe cannot be imposed until age 15. With that age Switzerland is thus in line with the European average in this regard (Pruin 2011).

[1]According to Art. 21 para 1 lit c. community service can however be applied as a diversionary sanction in Switzerland as well.

The application of adult criminal law begins at age 18. Soft transitions, which are currently a topic in several European countries (Pruin & Dünkel 2015), are not recognized by Swiss juvenile criminal law. A draft of Art. 100 of the CC from the 1960s by an expert commission, which intended to regulate the inclusion of 18–20 years old offenders into juvenile criminal law, was not put into force (Stark 1963). Art. 61 of the CC recognizes a special "measure" for young adults aged 18–25, resulting in a placement in a special institution for the age group. This measure for young adults is similar to equivalent youth measures but legally is considered part of the adult criminal law system. Pursuant to Art. 16 para. 3 JCC, an adolescent having reached 17 years of age can be placed in such an institution for young adults. Conversely, pursuant to Art. 61 paragraph 5 CC and by way of exception, young adults can be placed in a youth facility (Aebersold 2011). If sanctions and measures are applied on young adult offenders, the age and maturity of the offender is taken into account (Art. 47 CC).

THE COUNTRY'S STANCE TOWARD THE UN COMMITTEE ON THE RIGHTS OF THE CHILD

Prior to the reform of the juvenile criminal law, the UN Committee on the Rights of the Child (CRC) regularly criticized the age of criminal accountability of 7 years of age as being too low. In its closing statement in the second, third, and fourth state party's periodic report of Switzerland, the UN Committee on the Rights of the Child criticized the new age of criminal accountability of 10 years as being too low as well (United Nations 2015). Furthermore, the committee was concerned that not all underage defendants were granted free legal counsel, and too few attorneys specialize in juvenile criminal law and juvenile criminal law procedure. Above all, children in prison had yet to be separated from the adult inmates. Pursuant to the law, free legal counsel is granted as an "authorized defense" only in cases considered to be "required defense" as stated in Art. 24 JCPC. For this reason there is discrimination vis-à-vis adult defendants with limited financial resources who, according to Art. 132 paragraph 1 of the Criminal Procedure Code (CPC), can already receive a defense counsel at no cost when a defense is merely reasonable but deemed not necessary. Thus, Riedo (2013) suggests an equal treatment with adults in cases when a defense is required.

Regarding the question of shared accommodations, the periodic report of Switzerland asserts that the separation of minors and adult inmates has been introduced with the adoption of the JCPC and JCC (Art. 28 paragraph 1 JCPC and Art. 27 paragraph 2 JCC). The cantons (i.e., country/territorial subdivisions) were granted a 10-year transition period until the end of 2016 for the construction of appropriate juvenile incarceration facilities (Art. 48 JCC, cf. Baechtold/Weber/Hostettler 2016, 62.2). According to the last published progress report of the National Commission for the Prevention of Torture, at a minimum, the separation requirement cannot be consistently met (NKVF 2015). Because of the lack of a transition period, the separation of minors and adult inmates must be observed absolutely if it comes to pretrial detention for juveniles. In practice there are a number of diverse facilities available (Künzli et al. 2015), though according to the report of the Swiss Center of Expertise in Human Rights (SCHR), in isolated cases juveniles are admitted to "normal" prisons. The SCHR also indicated that in exceptional individual cases joint accommodation of children and adults might be permissible from a human rights standpoint in order to prevent serious harm, such as in solitary confinement.

TRENDS IN JUVENILE CRIME OVER THE PERIOD 2004–2014

The official statistics in Switzerland permit—besides general boundaries of the informative value of statistics (Urwyler & Nett 2012)—a few insights into the development of registered juvenile crime. A uniform and consistent collection of data is hindered by Switzerland's federal structure. The official police crime statistics and juvenile sentencing statistics published by the Swiss Federal Statistical Office (Bundesamt für Statistik 2015a) measure different subject matter: "Übertretungen" (violations that are categorized in the level below misdemeanor, from now on translated as petty crimes) are included in some statistics but not others. And whereas some statistics record only criminal offenses included in the CC others include violations of narcotics laws and traffic laws. Considering the fact that the diverse statistics cannot be compared with one another, the statistical information is supplemented with research on the dark figure of crime.

Juvenile Crime in Police Crime Statistics

Figures for juvenile crime in Switzerland are collected within the broader set of police crime statistics. Prior to 2009, the compilation of crimes registered by the police was fractional and the quality of the data and the statistics could not be guaranteed by the Swiss Federal Statistical Office. Therefore, data presented in this report is based on data from 2009 on.

The Police Crime Statistics (PCS) include underage persons who are suspected for perpetrating petty crimes, misdemeanors, or crimes indicted under the CC. Crime rate figures per 100,000 within the same age group are not calculated by the Statistical Office. Table 22.1 clearly shows that since 2009 the number of minor offenders registered by the police has consistently declined in all age groups (see also Urwyler & Nett 2012). The decline in the age group 15–17 until 2014 was 37%, and the decline in the age group 10–14 was even higher at 44%. This strong decrease in number of offenders cannot be explained solely by population changes. Though the absolute number of minors in the resident population also declined between 2004 and 2014, it declined by only 5% (Bundesamt für Statistik 2015b) so that other developments must account for the decreasing number of minor offenders. Empirically driven evidence supporting the assumption that changes in reporting practices or in the investigative practices of the responsible

TABLE 22.1. Number of police registered minors charged with violations against CC by year and age group

Year	*<10 years of age*	*10–14 years of age*	*15–17 years of age*	*All juveniles*
2009	139	5572	9188	14,760
2010	121	5121	8255	13,376
2011	99	3798	6751	10,549
2012	87	3270	6402	9672
2013	70	3065	5971	9036
2014	87	3124	5783	8907

Source: Police Crime Statistics (PCS) 2014 (Bundesamt für Statistik 2015a*)*

TABLE 22.2. Number of convicted minors by year and age group

Year	*<10 years of age*	*10–13 years of age*	*14–15 years of age*	*16–17 years of age*	*All juveniles*
2004	111	1155	2384	3958	7608
2005	102	1076	2346	4056	7580
2006	77	1161	2473	4058	7769
2007	[a]	978	2181	3751	6910
2008	–	897	2157	3921	6975
2009	–	846	2164	3921	6931
2010	–	907	2288	4418	7613
2011	–	664	1645	3118	5427
2012	–	570	1399	3101	5070
2013	–	558	1509	3132	5199
2014	–	572	1493	2784	4849

Source: Bundesamt für Statistik, Juvenile Sentencing Statistics (JUSUS)
[a]*As of 2007, age of criminal responsibility raised to 10 years*

institutions could be responsible for the decline in number is lacking. At issue is whether the decline can be explained by intensified protective measures (Vollmer 2016), changes in migration patterns (Killias et al. 2010), or, alternatively, changing security technologies, such as increasing number of control measures (Killias et al. 2010: 15).

It should be pointed out that the statistics depicted here contain only numbers for offenses against penal laws and not for offenses against narcotics laws or traffic laws. It is important to note that violations of narcotics laws or traffic laws are often counted in determining crime rates in other European countries; therefore, it would be difficult to conduct an international comparison of crime rates. In the case of Switzerland, for example, adding in violations of narcotics laws leads to a much higher number of crimes committed by juveniles: in 201 there was a total of 4982 narcotic law violations among 15–17-year-olds; the number of offenders in the 10–14 age group was 521 (Bundesamt für Statistik 2015a). Furthermore, in the 2014 report the PCS shows that juveniles were predominantly registered by the police for one single offense; serious delinquency constituted an exception. The result that a small number of serious juvenile offenders (*Intensivtätern*) are responsible for a comparatively large number of crimes is true for Switzerland as well (Freihofer 2014).

In the past 15 years, the topic of youth violence has been hotly debated in Switzerland. The Swiss Federal Statistical Office recently published a special report on youth violence (Bundesamt für Statistik 2015b). Whereas analyses of the crime statistics on violent crime showed an increase in numbers over time (Aebersold 2011; Eisner et al. 2009; Kunz 2012; Urwyler & Nett 2012; cf. Lanfranconi 2009; Riedo 2010), the most recent appraisal (Bundesamt für Statistik 2015b) from 2009 on pointed to a clear decline in violent youth criminality. In PCS between 2009 and 2014 the number of violent crimes dropped by 44%; the decline among male offenders is much more pronounced than among female offenders. Furthermore, according to these figures, the crime rates for Swiss as well as for foreign-born male juvenile offenders have declined and over time have drawn closer.

Youth Criminality in Juvenile Sentencing Statistics

Juvenile sentencing statistics include minors who have been convicted of an offense or crime in accordance with the CC. In contrast to the PCS, petty crimes are not included, which prohibits a comparison of the numbers.

The data included in the juvenile sentencing statistics also reveal a clear decline in numbers, such as a drop of 37% between 2004 and 2014. In this category, the percentage of young girls among convicted minors is much lower than among young boys. According to the juvenile sentencing statistics, the most frequent crimes include theft, property damage, and unlawful entry. Crimes of assault, verbal abuse, falsification of identification cards, and pornography are also frequently committed by juveniles. Consistent with reliable international findings on youth criminality, the numbers among juvenile offenders in Switzerland show the absolute primacy of incidents of minor offenses, whereas serious crimes are hardly represented.

The Dark Figure of Crime

Comparative nationwide Swiss research results on the dark figure of juvenile crime were published for the years 1992 and 2006. For these years a decline of crime rates can be ascertained for some crimes and an increase in crime rates for others (Killias et al. 2007; Killias et al. 2010). Beyond that there are studies that focus on specific subjects (Riedo 2013) though they provide conflicting findings: some report an increase of crime rates, specifically violent crimes, while others argue the trend is moving downward (Eisner et al. 2000; Ribeaud & Eisner 2008). At least for the most recent years, most of the studies agree that the statistics reflect an actual decline in youth criminality. This phenomenon is evident in other European countries as well.

CAUSES OF JUVENILE CRIME

In terms of the causes of juvenile crime, Swiss legal doctrine rests on internationally accepted findings that are based on risk and protective factors (Lösel & Bliesener, 2003), specifically for youth criminality (Aebersold 2011; Killias et al. 2011; Riedo 2013; for a special focus on violent youth criminality see Kassis 2003). For example, the family situation and the manner of upbringing, poverty, and parental drug addiction can be significant in the emergence or prevention of juvenile delinquency, though biological and psychological factors can also increase the risk. The consumption of violence vicariously through the media can at best be considered a factor that amplifies existing risk factors.

Furthermore, the Swiss research on the dark figure of crime confirms that youth crime can be viewed as a ubiquitous phenomenon (Killias et al. 2011), so that this form of deviant behavior can, to some extent, be seen as normal within the course of typical adolescent development. The exception here is the aforementioned serious offender.

POLICING AND JUVENILES

In the case of criminally liable behavior in juveniles, the police assume the leading role in criminal investigations. They are routinely the first official public authority that comes in contact with juveniles. Accordingly, the concepts for crime prevention place a strong emphasis on the police (Riedo 2013; Vollmer 2016). Police organization is regulated differently among the cantons (i.e., country/territorial subdivisions). In some cantons there are specialized police units that handle juvenile cases, such as Zurich and Basel-Land. For example, since 2005 the canton Fribourg leads a trained juvenile brigade that focuses heavily on youth crime. The canton Solothurn has created a juvenile police force that has a preventive as well as a repressive mandate. It is tasked not only with following up on cases of youth violence but also preventing violence perpetrated by juveniles and by adults against juveniles. Due to this function, the domestic violence department passes on to the juvenile police unit certain information about families in which domestic violence regularly occurs. The canton Thurgau offers a further example, with numerous means of preventing violence and a network composed of a multiplicity of institutions and projects in the field of juvenile protection (Vollmer 2016).

In contrast to the public prosecutor's office, the investigative authority, or the court, the police do not have the choice of withholding from criminal prosecution for reasons of expediency. Police diversion, which is possible in some other juvenile criminal law systems in Europe (Pruin 2010), is thus nonexistent in Switzerland and, arguably not necessary owing to the multifaceted approach of the investigative authorities, the public prosecutor's office and the courts.

COURTS AND JUVENILES

Swiss juvenile criminal law recognizes a series of alternative disposition options that are mandated not by the juvenile courts, but by the investigative authorities. For one, alternative procedural settlements as defined by the opportunity principle play a large role. For another, summary proceedings without trial ("*Strafbefehlsverfahren*") are accorded a superior position in practice because of its heavy use by the investigative authorities. The organization of the investigative authorities varies from canton to canton (Arn et al. 2011; Urwyler 2011), which is why the JCPC speaks more generally about "investigative authorities" (e.g., Art. 5). The precise form of the administrative structure is set by cantonal introductory laws. In the overwhelmingly French-speaking cantons, juvenile judges conduct the inquisitorial criminal investigation from the very beginning and subsequently preside over the juvenile court or "juvenile judge model" (Jugendrichtermodell) (Zermatten 1990, 2006). In these circumstances, according to Art. 21 JCPC, the canton must provide a juvenile prosecution service, which is responsible for the arraignment in juvenile court and which can take part in the main hearing. Given this, the fact that criminal investigations are not stringently separated from the court proceeding is discussed controversially in Swiss legal practice because it raises the question of the impartiality of juvenile judges (Aebersold 2011; Hebeisen 2010; Murer Mikolasek 2011; Trechsel 2002). Through Art. 9 JCPC, the law strives to accommodate criticism of this model such that the juvenile or his/her legal representative can demand that the juvenile judge leading the investigation does not participate in the main hearing.

In the overwhelmingly German-speaking cantons including Bern and Tessin, the criminal investigation process is conducted by a special investigative authority called Juvenile Council Service ("*Jugendanwaltschaft*") (Art. 6 paragraph 4 JCPC "Juvenile Counsel Model," "*Jugendanwaltmodell*"). In cantons with juvenile counsel models, a Juvenile Prosecution Service is not required since the charge before the juvenile court is represented by the juvenile counsel himself/herself.

Above all, in the practice of juvenile criminal law, it is the investigative authorities that are of particular relevance. Like the juvenile prosecution service or the court, the investigative authorities have (according to Art. 5 JCPC) to halt a criminal proceeding if the prerequisites for a dispensation of penalty set out in Art. 21 JCC ("Strafbefreiung") are satisfied. This means that already in the pretrial phase the case can be diverted for reasons of expediency, if protection measures are not deemed to be necessary (or the civil law authorities have already ordered appropriate measures), and if the juvenile's guilt and the damages are minor; or if there is another reason given such that the court proceedings appear disproportionate or even obsolete—such as if the juvenile has already made amends or has been sufficiently punished by his/her parents or by school authorities or if longer time has elapsed since the offense and the interest of the victim or the public in a prosecution is small.

Furthermore, according to Art. 5 paragraph lit. b, the investigative authorities, the Juvenile Prosecution Service, or the Court have to halt the ongoing criminal prosecution if a compromised settlement or mediation can be successfully concluded.

Because diversion data from the FSO has not been compiled, no dependable assessments regarding the use of diversion options in practice can be made. What can be calculated, however, is the extended use of summary proceedings in juvenile criminal law. Through this the investigative authorities have in fact become the most important decision-making unit in juvenile criminal affairs: in cases that do not fall under the jurisdiction of the juvenile court, they have the authority to waive a summary proceeding. The legal formulation alone shows that the summary proceedings should be the norm: according to Art. 34 JCPC the juvenile court becomes responsible only when criminal actions are disputed for which there is a placement (as a protection measure), a fine of over 1000 Swiss Francs (CHF), or imprisonment of more than 3 months is in question. Thereby all of the relevant alternative sanctions in juvenile proceedings, such as community service and reprimands, and all ambulant protective measures can be mandated by the investigative authorities per a summary proceeding. According to the analysis of Aebersold (2011), at least 98% of judicial convictions are initially issued via summary proceedings. Only the very rare high penalties and placements must be mandated by the juvenile criminal courts. The youth courts are furthermore responsible in the equally rare cases in which an objection to the order of summary punishment is raised. A summary proceeding can be issued without an oral hearing and by its legal nature does not constitute a decision. Instead, to some extent it is viewed from the perspective of Swiss legal doctrine as a proposal for the settlement of a procedure (Aebersold 2011). The summary proceeding becomes a verdict if the accused juvenile or his/her legal representative does not raise an objection. If an objection is raised, then the summary proceeding is not applicable and a judicial action will ensue. In general, the summary proceeding is applied to offenses that are negligible or clearly proven (i.e., when the action has been admitted to) in order to provide relief for the courts and allow them to react appropriately to such offenses. In Swiss juvenile criminal law, the summary proceeding vis-à-vis adult criminal law has been expanded. This might be viewed as somewhat problematic inasmuch as an oral hearing in a summary proceeding is not compulsory and inasmuch as one might inquire whether it is reasonable in terms of educative measures to impose a sanction in a written proceeding (i.e., without direct communication with the juvenile) (Aebersold 2011). Juveniles very rarely raise objections against the summary proceeding.

With summary proceedings, the investigative authorities can determine the following protective measures or penalties:

Protective Measures

- Custody according to Art. 12.
- Personal support services according to Art. 13.
- Ambulant services according to Art. 23.
- Ban on activities ("*Tätigkeitsverbot, Kontakt- und Rayonverbot*") according to Art. 16a (in conjunction with electronic monitoring).

Penalties

- Dispensation of penalty according to Art. 21.
- Reprimand according to Art. 22.
- Community service (“*persönliche Leistung*”) according to Art. 23.
- Fines up to 1000 CHF according to Art. 24.
- Imprisonment between 1 day and up to 3 months according to Art. 25

The charge is lifted by the responsible authorities—or the juvenile prosecution service in the case of the juvenile judges model, and the juvenile counsel in the case of the juvenile counsel model—when: no summary proceedings are issued, the facts of the case and the personal situation of the juvenile have been investigated sufficiently, and a sanction which falls within the jurisdiction of the juvenile court is taken into account.

The juvenile court is responsible for the court proceedings. In the first instance, the court judges those cases that have attained a certain degree of gravity as well when an objection to the summary proceedings exists. The juvenile court is composed of the president and two assessors (Riedo 2013). The JPCP has no guidelines for specialized pedagogical knowledge. But most of the cantons know such requirements in their legislations.

According to Art. 21 JCC, the juvenile court can refrain from issuing a penalty when the conditions outlined in the Article have been complied with, even though the investigative authorities have not dispensed with the criminal prosecution. Apart from that and apart from the sanctions also the investigation authorities can determine, according to juvenile criminal law the juvenile court can mandate:

- The protective measure of placement in housing according to Art. 15.
- A fine of more than 1000 CHF according to Art. 24.
- Imprisonment for more than 3 months.

In Switzerland, judicial practice does not respond to juvenile criminal acts primarily with the classic instruments of criminal law, as presented in Table 22.3. In 2014, nearly 43% of all convicted juveniles were ordered to perform community service (“*persönliche Leistung*”). Only 6.4% were sentenced to prison sentences, and only 2% were sentenced to unconditional imprisonment (Urwyler & Nett 2012). Judicial reprimand (27%) also plays an important role in practice, followed by fines with around 20%. Exemption from punishment (Art. 21 JCC) plays only a subordinate role in the sentencing statistics (3%), which, given the statutory specifications, is to be expected. This is to be expected because according to Art. 5 JCC, the investigative authorities during the presentation of prerequisites set out in Art. 21 must abstain from prosecution. To a large extent juvenile criminal procedures end with a penalty, whereas protective measures are mandated in only a few cases (Urwyler & Nett 2012).

TABLE 22.3. JUSUS: conviction of juveniles by main sanction in 2014[a]

Total[b]		*12.804*
Prison sentences:		818
Of these:	Unconditional prison sentences	268
	Partial prison sentences	54
	Conditional prison sentences	496
Community service:		5.488
Of these:	Unconditional community service	4.247
	Partial community service	569
	Conditional personal service	672
Fines		2.560
Of these:	Unconditional fine	2.153
	Partial fine	135
	Conditional fine	272
Reprimand		3.453
Measures only		34
Of these:	Stationary[c]	12
	Ambulatory[d]	22
Dispensation of penalty		439

[a]The numbers in Table 3 are not comparable to numbers in Tables 1 and 2. The numbers here reflect convictions by main sanction. They refer to all convictions reported to the Bundesamt für Statistik, i.e., convictions for felony, petty offense or misdemeanor charges according to the CC, narcotics laws, foreign residence laws, and convictions of petty offense and felony in traffic laws

[b]For each sentencing a "main sanction" is determined, and only these numbers are disclosed in the table. The sanctions were hierarchized according to severity, and only those with the most severe sanctions were taken into account. The sanction deemed most severe are prison sentences, followed by community service, fines, reprimand, measures, and, finally exemption from punishment

[c]The following are counted as stationary measures: placement in families, educational institutions, or a treatment facilities. The data does only include those stationary measures which have become legally binding until April 27 2015 so that numbers might rise in future

[d]The following are counted as ambulatory measures: supervision, personal support, and ambulatory treatment

Source: FSO 2015: (JUSUS)

CUSTODIAL RULES FOR JUVENILES

In Switzerland, deprivation of liberty as a response to juvenile criminality can be applied in the form of a prison sentence or as a protective measure in the form of a stationary placement. Because of the development of ambulatory alternatives, the number of stationary enforcements declined. Recidivism rates of detention in closed facilities are high in Switzerland as well. In addition, within the framework of criminal proceedings, deprivation of liberty is also possible in the form of pretrial detention.

Execution of Unconditional Prison Sentences

Because of its potentially harmful effects, unconditional imprisonment is a problematic and, in the case of conventional imprisonment, an expensive penalty. Thus, the law endeavors to minimize its scope of application and negative effects via a juvenile-adapted form of imprisonment. From age 15 on, a prison term between 1 day and 1 year can be imposed on juveniles. Petty crimes, e.g., lighter offenses, in accordance with Art. 103 CC, cannot be punished with imprisonment. A sentence of more than 12 months of uninterrupted imprisonment (the so-called qualified imprisonment) is tied to high requirements. It can be ordered only for a juvenile over 16 years of age who has committed a felony or a misdemeanor that under adult criminal law stipulates a period of imprisonment of more than 3 years, such as willful homicide, murder, qualified robbery, qualified kidnapping, qualified sexual coercion, and qualified rape as well as qualified arson. In addition, qualified imprisonment can be applied in particularly unscrupulous commission of the following offenses: grievous bodily harm, gang or dangerous robbery, or qualified unlawful detention or kidnapping.

Until recently, separate juvenile prisons did not exist (for an historical overview see Aebersold 2015). Juveniles serving a prison sentence were sent to either pretrial prisons for adults, resulting in an infraction of the UN-principle of separation between juveniles and adults, or in closed units of welfare institutions—another infraction of the UN-principle of separation between penalties and welfare measures. The JCC requires the existence of independent juvenile prisons, which have to follow high quality standards with a transitional period of 10 years. In the German-speaking Eastern part of Switzerland, a special youth prison unit with 10 places has been established as a part of a center for the execution of protective measures ("Massnahmenzentrum") for young adults in Uitikon (Zürich). Currently, this unit is closed due to staff shortage and the very low number of juvenile prisoners. A further primarily planned project (Arxhof) close to the city of Basel has not been realized. The French-speaking part of Switzerland, where prison sentences are applied more often, has provided three institutions with stronger custodial character for the execution of unconditional prison sentences especially the institution Aux Léchaires in Les Palézieux (Canton Vaud) with 36 places, of which approximately half are actually used. The canton Geneva holds a juvenile prison in La Clairière. A prison for female juveniles has been discussed in the Canton Neuchâtel but has not been planned yet.

Art. 27 JCC sets a few standards for the execution of the prison sentence. Special juvenile prisons have to implement an educative infrastructure that enables them to prepare the juveniles for their social reintegration after release. The juvenile prisons, therefore, have to implement qualified social-pedagogic and/or therapeutic instruments. Vocational trainings and schooling must also be available during imprisonment. A specific juvenile prison law does not exist on a federal level. According to the domestic division of competences between the federal and canton levels, the cantons are authorized to set additional juvenile prison laws. In the house rules of enforcement institutions and at the concordat level, however, additional juvenile criminal law enforcement provisions can be found (Schärer 2014).

In 2014, 322 juveniles were sentenced to unconditional or partial imprisonment (2.5%), and in more than two-thirds of the cases imprisonment of 1 month was pronounced (Bundesamt für Statistik 2015a). In these cases, the punishment often has already been satisfied, with the juvenile having served the sentence while in pretrial custody. For unconditional or partial imprisonment of more than 6 months and up to 1 year, 17 sentences were handed down; only four sentences of more than 1 year were handed down. There has been a continuing decrease of the number of imprisonments over the last 5 years. In one recording date in 2015, a total of 14 juveniles were carrying out a prison sentence (Bundesamt für Statistik 2015a). In general, very few imprisonments are ordered and on average imprisonments are distinctly shorter in duration than in other countries. Qualified imprisonments, for the most part are mandated together with a stationary protective measure since the perpetration of such serious crimes clearly points to the necessity for educational and/or treatment requirements. The enforcement of protective measures then has priority, so that these juveniles do not end up in a prison but in an institution for the execution of protective measures.

Prison sentences of up to 1 year are generally executed in the form of semi-imprisonment. This means that the juvenile spends only nights and weekends in a facility that should not have any evident characteristics of a prison. During the week the juvenile can attend school or go to work. Enforcement in semi-imprisonment is customary, provided that clear reasons, such as risk of absconding, danger of further criminal activity, lack of a daily structure, or insufficient self-discipline, do not argue against it.

Alternatively, imprisonment of up to 1 month can be performed by the day. In doing so, the sentence can be divided into several sections of at least 2 days and served in "installments." These can be shifted to weekends or holidays.

Since 2004 in the canton Basel-Land, electronic monitoring has been applied as an alternative to incarceration. Supporters are of the opinion that electronic monitoring can serve not only defensive goals (such as harm reduction and cost reduction) but can also be pedagogically useful (Jugendanwaltschaft Basel-Landschaft 2015). Several other cantons are planning to introduce electronic monitoring or have actually started such projects such as the canton of Zürich. In addition, there are also contact and travel bans using electric monitoring/GPS (Urwyler & Nett 2012).

A conditional release is possible after half the sentence has been served, provided it is believed that the juvenile would not commit any further crimes or misdemeanors. Hence the exclusion of a negative prognosis should suffice. Through this, as a matter of principle, the legislative authority underlines the desirability of a conditional release so that the authorities in their own motion must examine whether the juvenile can be conditionally released.

In addition to the conditional enforcement as an alternative sanction, incarceration also can be ordered in the form of a partial enforcement. This means that an unconditional part of a sentence is declared as enforceable and thus the sentence is served, while the remainder of the sentence is suspended in combination with a probationary period.

Enforcement of Custodial Protective Measures

Custodial protective measures are normally carried out in an open facility. The placement of a juvenile in the framework of a protective measure in a closed facility is considered absolutely as *ultima ratio* and requires a medical and psychological evaluation. Mindful of the circumstances here, i.e., this restraint is justified for reasons of proportionality. Up to now the measures end when the juvenile reaches his or her 22nd birthday; but according to the last amendment of the law the upper age limit will be raised to the 25th birthday on July 1 2016. The enforcement authorities must examine annually if and when the measure can be lifted.

For the execution of measures, there exists—primarily in German-speaking areas of Switzerland, less so in the French-speaking areas, and not at all in the small Italian-speaking area of Switzerland—a wide and varied range of predominantly open juvenile youth homes (formerly "youth correctional facilities," Cottier 2006). These are monitored and financially supported by the Federal Ministry of Justice. They are principally supported by private beneficent foundations or societies. The youth homes accept juveniles with criminal as well as civil legal status in the same system. The youth homes place juveniles in supervised group homes with family-like environments, often in stand-alone homes and in rural settings. They offer individualized schooling and fully fledged vocational training opportunities with accredited degree programs and have qualified therapy programs if needed. The cost for such a stay ranges from 500 to 1050 CHF per day. In 2014, 75 juvenile offenders were newly placed in such facilities; of that number, 10 juveniles were placed in closed sections (Bundesamt für Statistik 2015a). On one reporting date for Switzerland as a whole, 433[2] juveniles who had committed a criminal act were placed in facilities outside their homes (Bundesamt für Statistik 2015a). Since 2010, the placement of juvenile offenders outside their homes has decreased by half (Bundesamt für Statistik 2015b). The largest closed facility, the youth home Prêles in the canton Bern, will close at the end of 2016.

Alternatives to Incarceration

The drop in the number of admittances to stationary facilities (Bundesamt für Statistik 2015b) is related to a decline in juvenile criminality, high costs, and the expansion of intensive ambulatory and semistationary alternative offerings that

[2] This number is somewhat astonishing in light of the 34 measures mentioned in Table 3. The explanation might be that most juveniles that are placed outside their homes are additionally sanctioned with a criminal sanction that precedes within the counting of JUSUS.

have replaced the stationary measure. Ambulatory outreach approaches, such as the multisystemic therapy developed at the University of South Carolina or the social-pedagogical family support approach (counseling with a certified specialist who participates regularly in family life), are being offered in many cities. Examples for regionally offered programs include ISI-Outreach Family Activity (Thurgau), KOFA-Competence-Oriented Family Activity (Bern), Cognitive-Behavioral Therapy Programme (Geneva and Zürich), ThePas-Treatment Programme for Juvenile Sex Offenders (Zürich), and SUGJ-Social Environment Participation, which is based on the Family Group Conference developed in New Zealand.

Placement in foster families is undertaken as a time-out solution, though only for a short period. Longer term family placement occurs very seldom, mostly in social-pedagogical surrogate families supervised by trained professionals. For juveniles in educational facilities who refuse to be guided by staff, an isolated specialized setting is organized. This setting ensures one-to-one supervision with a specialist in an apartment permanently rented for this purpose. However, because of the very high cost of this measure, which is comparable to closed facilities, such solutions have come under much public criticism. Semistationary proposals stipulate that during the day juveniles must remain in a youth home. There they receive pedagogical support and attend school or successfully complete a vocational training program. The juveniles spend the night at home, where their parents are coached and encouraged to employ their often underused or inhibited instructional skills. Examples of such proposals are the Beo-Sirius in Bollingen (Bern), TAplus in Gfellergut (Zürich), and the Day Clinic in UPK Basel.

Recidivism

According to an investigation ordered by the Zürich government in 2012, 7356 juveniles were convicted of crimes. Within 3 years, 35% of them were convicted again. Admittedly, a small group that was sentenced to unconditional imprisonment drove up the statistical average to a rate of 84%. The recidivism rates for other types of sanctions are 37% for community service and 29% for reprimand (Regierungsratsbeschluss des Kantons Zürich Nr. 930/2012). According to the latest analyses by the FSO, the recidivism rate of convicted juveniles for Switzerland as a whole is 32% (Bundesamt für Statistik 2015a) compared to 41% in Germany (Jehle et al. 2010) and 60% in Austria. The higher rates in these countries can be traced to larger numbers and a longer period of placement in prison.

Pretrial Custody

Pretrial detention can be mandated only in exceptional cases and only after all possible contingency measures have been examined. Compared to cases of adults where a special pretrial sanctions court ("*Zwangsmassnahmengericht*") orders pretrial custody, it is the investigative authorities who are responsible for the pretrial custody order for juveniles. The individual cantons can designate one or several juvenile judges or one or more juvenile counsels as the investigative authorities. The investigative authorities have up to 7 days to provide to the pretrial sanctions court a request for extension. In turn, the sanctions court must decide without delay, at the latest within 48 h after receipt of the request.

The JCPC does not cite any specific provisions regarding the rules of detention, so the reasons for detention that apply to adults are applied to juveniles. The pretrial detention order must take into account the age and level of development of the juvenile. The accepted view is that an absolute minimum age limit of 15 years for the order is required (Queloz 2011). There are provisions for giving instructions and for the rights of appeal, as well as several fundamental maxims relating to the enforcement of a pretrial detention. The enforcement of the pretrial detention is in turn regulated by each canton. There are some cantonal laws or at least regulations at the cantonal level, but in some cantons no regulation of pretrial detention exists (Künzli et al. 2015). Analyses of pretrial detentions by the Swiss Competence Centre for Human Rights (SCHR) reveal large differences in the enforcement of conditions. Whereas certain institutions designate several half-days per week for school instruction, juveniles in other institutions spend up to 23 h in a cell (Künzli et al. 2015). On a given day in 2014, four juveniles were in pretrial detention in Zurich, one in Bern, two in Basel-Stadt, and six in Basel-Land (Künzli et al. 2015).

ALTERNATIVE SANCTIONS FOR JUVENILES

"Alternative sanctions" are understood as noncustodial sentences or measures that can be mandated in an order of summary punishment or in a verdict. In practice the imposition of noncustodial sentences is the rule. The prerequisite for every penalty is the proof of guilt. Relevant for the sentencing, however, is not just the question of guilt but, rather, the need to take educative and, particularly, special preventive considerations and different points of view into account. Both of these criteria can contradict each other. It is essential that the appropriate maximum sentence of guilt must not be exceeded ("Verschulden als Obergrenze"), though it certainly can fall below. In juvenile criminal law, sentencing is far more individualistic than in adult criminal law. According to the highest level of legal jurisprudence, the sentence must be adapted to the age and whole personality of the juvenile so that the sentence does not impede or harm the juvenile's further development but, on the contrary, strives to positively influence it. In matters of educative concerns, the presumed effect of the penalty on the behavior of the juvenile plays a distinct role.

Dispensation of Penalty, Art. 21 JCC

Dispensation of penalty ("Strafbefreiung") is an alternative to sentencing which, if the prerequisites are given, must be adopted by the investigative authorities. The law stipulates six cases of dispensation. On the one hand, the cases reflect factors stipulated in adult criminal law; on the other, they pertain to factors specific to juvenile criminality: minor criminal offenses, compensation, personal impact stemming from the effects of the criminal act, punishment already handed out by the parents or school authorities, length of time since the crime, successful offender–victim reconciliation (mediation), or the success of a protective measure being put at risk through an additional sentence. Most of the time, such decisions fail to show up in the sentencing statistics because the case has been diverted at an earlier stage of the criminal procedure.

Reprimand, Art. 22 JCC

The reprimand is an autonomous punishment within juvenile criminal law and is set within a formal reprobation of the act. It thus appeals to the juvenile's feeling of good will and sense of responsibility. The symbolic character of a limit-setting sanction is in this sense clearly expressed. The reprimand presumes a favorable legal prognosis: it must estimate what is adequate "in order to prevent the juvenile from committing further criminal acts." The application of the reprimand requires that the juvenile is able to respond to such a warning. From the legal formulation it could be deduced that the reprimand is applied independent of the gravity of the offense in all cases in which a favorable prognosis is given. Such an interpretation, however, would be in conflict with the higher principle of guilt. The reprimand thus applies only for minor criminal offenses and as a rule is only considered in the first conviction/offense.

In addition, the reprimand can be tied to a probation period and to instructions directed to the juvenile. If during the probation period the juvenile commits new crimes or the instructions are not obeyed, then the sentencing authorities can impose another sentence for the original offense.

Community Service, Art. 23 JCC

The juvenile can be obliged through personal efforts to work for the benefit of social organizations, the public interest, and handicapped/special needs or impaired individuals. The activity must take the age and abilities of the juvenile into account. They are not compensated for their work. Besides their work performance, other work provisions have recently been made available, particularly the participation in coursework or recreational programs. The community service can be mandated for juveniles up to age 14 for no more than 10 days, and after 15 years of age for up to 3 months. Assignments primarily in public or nonprofit and charitable organizations are particularly worth considering—work in a city nursery, a work site, the fire brigade, museums, sports facilities, or homes for the elderly (though not in the care sector). Moreover, there are assignments at mountain farms or for the maintenance of hiking paths. Contrary to other countries, the nonprofit community service in Switzerland is more often a sentence by Art. 23 JCC than a diversion measure by Art. 21 Paragraph 1 lit. c JCC. It is considered a special pedagogically useful sanction for juveniles because it strives to avoid an experience of passive suffering and instead requires him/her to be actively committed to some good. It is by far the most common type of sentence.

Participation in Coursework or Similar Activities, Art. 23 Paragraph 2 JCC

The coursework can be open to other participants and is not just designated for criminal offenders. Coursework includes social competence training, traffic instruction, healthcare courses or courses related to recreation activities, sex education, and alcohol education and drug education. They can also deal with targeted offender programs, such as social training courses for violent offenders, sexual delinquents, or traffic offenders. The requirement for attendance in such courses can be linked to a fine.

Fines, Art. 24 JCC

Juveniles who at the time of the crime have finished their 15th year can be punished with a monetary fine of no more than 2000 CHF. If the fine is imposed, special consideration is given to the juvenile's personal situation. Not provided for in juvenile criminal law is the envisaged monetary punishment in accordance with a "daily rate system" seen in adult criminal law. Monetary fines play a role particularly in instances of traffic offenses.

Mediation, Art. 17 JCC

Contrary to adult criminal law, the professionally led victim–offender reconciliation (called "mediation" in Switzerland) is specifically regulated: The investigative authorities and the courts can suspend the procedure at any time and order a person or organization from the mediation field to implement a mediation process. If the mediation is successful, the sentencing procedure is halted. If not, the sentencing resumes. Mediation is offered only as a possible option. As a consequence of the "Kann-regulation," the implementation at the canton level is quite varied (Urwyler & Nett 2012). In some cantons no mediation was carried out, though mediation was often applied in Zürich. In 213 cases over a 4-year period, over 95% ended with a settlement. Mediation is relatively more common in the small canton of Fribourg (156 cases in 3 years) and somewhat less common in the cantons of Geneva, Wallis, Aargau, Basel-Land, and Basel-City (Zanolini 2014).

Conditional Enforcement, Art. 35 JCC

Imprisonment for up to 30 months can be conditionally suspended if an unconditional sentence is not considered necessary to prevent the juvenile from committing more crimes (Art. 35, paragraph 1 JCC). The conditional enforcement is used in 60% of the sentences. As in the case of adults, it follows the French practice of "sursis." The sentence is set, but a probation period can be ordered and the enforcement is suspended. If the probation period is passed, the enforcement of the sentence is exempted. Otherwise, the sentence can still be subsequently enforced. In contrast to other countries, in Switzerland other sanctions than prison sentences can also be executed conditionally or partial conditionally. For fines and community service the scope for conditional or partly conditional execution is in principle unrestricted, though the conditional enforcement is seldom applied.

Supervision, Art. 12 JCC

Within a supervision order, the juvenile court can appoint a suitable person or other authority (e.g., family counseling or a psychological service; Aebersold 2011), which can provide the responsible educational authorities with insight and information. In this way the efforts of the often overburdened parents, though still capable and willing to cooperate, can be supported and strengthened (Aebersold 2011).

Personal Care and Assistance, Art. 13 JCC

The order for personal care leans toward the educational guardianship order ("Erziehungsbeistandschaft"). The prerequisite is that as a consequence of serious educational problems, the danger exists that the parents cannot resolve the situation by themselves. A specific person who takes personal responsibility for the juvenile must be appointed (Aebersold 2011).

Ambulatory Treatment, Art. 14 JCC

Ambulatory treatment is applicable when a juvenile is suffering from mental health problems, is impaired in the development of his or her personality, or is suffering from an addiction. The simple presence of danger such as drug use is insufficient (Gürber et al. 2013). What is not necessary is that a committed criminal act has some relationship to this disruption. What is decisive, however, is that at the point at which the pronouncement of a judgment is given, the disruption exists and the condition of the juvenile requires treatment (Gürber et al. 2013).

Work Ban, Contact- and Travel Ban (Rayon Ban), Art. 16a JCC

Under restricted conditions, the court can forbid the juvenile to exercise certain professional or nonprofessional activities if there is a danger that the juvenile might misuse the work visits to inflict sexual criminal acts against particularly vulnerable individuals. If a danger exists that a juvenile will commit a criminal act while in contact with an individual, the court can ban the juvenile from establishing contact with this person or ban the juvenile from staying in particular localities. For enforcement purposes, the investigative authorities can employ electronic monitoring.

DIFFERENCES IN TREATMENTS FOR BOYS AND GIRLS

Assertions regarding the differences in the treatment of boys and girl in juvenile criminal law arise from an investigation by Cottier (2006). The results of her empirical research show that in the canton Basel-Land during the period studied, boys over 10 years of age were more likely to be placed under juvenile criminal law, while girls over 10 years of age were placed under child protection procedures (Cottier 2006). Even with regard to the nationalities of boys and girls diffesrences were evident: while over 89% of girls convicted under juvenile criminal law held Swiss citizenship, 46% of boys convicted under juvenile criminal law were foreign nationals (Cottier 2006). Cottier also discerns in her study that adults appear more likely to evaluate crimes committed by girls as "abnormal" than crimes committed by boys. This is particularly the case with violent crimes. The analysis of the federal sentencing statistics according to gender reveals that girls as a whole comprise one-fifth of convicted juveniles. In comparison to boys they are strongly underrepresented in cases of imprisonment and strongly over-represented in other measures.

Acknowledgments The authors would like to thank Karin L. Johnston, Ph.D. (Washington) for her support with the translation.

REFERENCES

Aebersold, P. (2011). *Schweizerisches Jugendstrafrecht* (2nd ed.). Bern: Stämpfli Verlag AG.

Aebersold, P. (2015). Jugendliche: Wenig Freiheitsentzug. In D. Fink & P. M. Schulthess (Eds.), *Strafrecht, Freiheitsentzug, Gefängnis* (pp. 280–295). Bern: Stämpfli Verlag AG.

Arn, R., Saurer, N., & Kuhn, A. (2011). *Organisation der kantonalen und eidgenössischen Strafbehörden*. Basel: Helbing Lichtenhahn Verlag.

Baechtold, A., Weber, J. P., & Hostettler, U. (2016). *Strafvollzug* (3rd ed.). Bern: Stämpfli Verlag AG.

Bundesamt für Statistik. (2015a). *Polizeiliche Kriminalstatistik, Jahresbericht 2014*. Neuchâtel: Swiss Federal Statistical Office.

Bundesamt für Statistik. (2015b). *Jugendgewalt in der polizeilichen Kriminalstatistik: 2009–2014. Kriminalität und Strafrecht 19*. Neuchâtel: Swiss Federal Statistical Office.

Cottier, M. (2006). *Subjekt oder Objekt? Die Partizipation von Kindern in Jugendstraf- und zivilrechtlichen Kindesschutzverfahren*. Bern: Stämpfli Verlag AG.

Eisner, M., Manzoni, P., & Ribeaud, D. (2000). *Gewalterfahrungen von Jugendlichen*. Aarau: Bildung Sauerländer.

Eisner, M., Ribeaud, D., & Locher, R. (2009). *Prävention von Jugendgewalt, Expertenbericht im Auftrag des Bundesamtes für Sozialversicherungen*. Bern: Bundesamt für Sozialversicherungen.

Freihofer, V. (2014). *Jugendliche Intensiv-, Mehrfach- und Bagatelltäter. Theorie, Empirie und Praxis der Zürcher Jugendstrafrechtspflege*. Zürcher Studien zum Strafrecht (Vol. 74). Zürich: Schulthess.

Gürber, H., Hug, C., & Schläfli, P. (2013). *Vor Art. 1 JStG*. In M. A. Niggli & H. Wiprächtiger (Eds.), *Basler Kommentar. Strafrecht I* (3rd ed., pp. 5–18). Basel: Helbing Lichtenhahn Verlag.

Hebeisen, D. (2010). *Widerspricht das Jugendrichtermodell der EMRK? Schweizerische Zeitschrift für Kriminologie 2010/01* (pp. 41–44). Bern: Stämpfli Verlag AG.

Hebeisen, D. (2011). *Switzerland*. In F. Dünkel, J. Grzywa, P. Horsfield, & I. Pruin (Eds.), *Juvenile justice systems in Europe—Current situation, reform developments and good practices* (2nd ed., pp. 1389–1440). Forum Verlag Godesberg: Mönchengladbach.

Jehle, J.-M., Albrecht, H.-J., Hohmann-Fricke, S., & Tetal, C. (2010). *Legalbewährung nach strafrechtlichen Sanktionen. Eine bundesweite Rückfalluntersuchung 2004 bis 2007*. Berlin: Bundesministerium der Justiz.

Jugendanwaltschaft Basel-Landschaft. (2015). *Electronic Monitoring im Jugendstrafrecht*. Retrieved April 25, 2016, from https://www.baselland.ch/electronic-monitoring-htm.305223.0.html.

Kassis, W. (2003). *Wie kommt die Gewalt in die Jungen?* Bern, Stuttgart, Wien: Haupt Verlag.

Killias, M., Aebi, M. F., Lucia, S., Herrmann, L., & Dilitz, C. (2007). *Self-reported juvenile delinquency in Switzerland in 2006: Overview and explanations*. Retrieved from December 22, 2015, from http://www.rwi.uzh.ch/lehreforschung/alphabetisch/killias/publikationen/ISRD2_SNF-Bericht.pdf.

Killias, M., Haymoz, S., Markwalder, N., Lucia, S., & Biberstein, L. (2010). *Prävention ohne Trendanalyse? Mythen und Trends zur Jugendkriminalität in der Schweiz*. In C. Schwarzenegger & J. Müller (Eds.), *Zweites Zürcher Präventionsforum: Jugendkriminalität und Prävention* (pp. 21–64). Zürich: Schulthess.

Killias, M., Kuhn, A., & Aebi, M. F. (2011). *Grundriss der Kriminologie* (2nd ed.). Bern: Stämpfli Verlag AG.

Kunz, K.-L. (2012): *Jugendgewalt im Blickpunkt von Öffentlichkeit und Jugendstrafrecht*. Schweizerische Zeitschrift für Kriminologie 2012/02 (pp. 17–28). Bern: Stämpfli Verlag AG.

Künzli, J., Frei, N., & Schultheiss, M. (2015). *Untersuchungshaft. Menschenrechtliche Standards und ihre Umsetzung in der Schweiz*. Bern: Schweizerisches Kompetenzzentrum für Menschenrechte (SKMR).

Lanfranconi, B. (2009). *Gewalt unter jungen Menschen*. Luzern: Sammelstelle für die Statistik der Unfallversicherung (SSUV).

Lösel, F., & Bliesener, T. (2003). Aggression und Delinquenz unter Jugendlichen. Neuwied: Luchterhand.

Murer Mikolasek, A. (2011). *Analyse der Schweizerischen Jugendstrafprozessordnung (JStPO). Entspricht sie den Grundsätzen des Jugendstrafrechts?* Zürcher Studien zum Strafrecht (Vol. 60). Zürich: Schulthess.

Nationale Kommission zur Verhütung von Folter (NKVF). (2015). *Tätigkeitsbericht 2014*. Bern: Vertrieb Bundespublikationen.

Pruin, I. (2010). Der Einfluss der Polizei auf Diversionsverfahren im Jugendstrafrecht in einigen europäischen Ländern. *Recht der Jugend und des Bildungswesens, 58*, 353–371.

Pruin, I. (2011). The scope of juvenile justice systems in Europe. In F. Dünkel, J. Grzywa, P. Horsfield, & I. Pruin (Eds.), *Juvenile justice systems in Europe—Current situation, reform developments and good practices* (2nd ed., pp. 1539–1582). Mönchengladbach: Forum Verlag Godesberg.

Pruin, I., & Dünkel, F. (2015). *Young adult offenders in Europe: Interdisciplinary research results and legal practices*. London: Barrow Cadbury Trust.

Queloz, N. (2011). La détention avant jugement des mineurs de moins de 15 ans est absolument illégale en Suisse. *Bulletin DEI, 17*(3), I–II.

Ribeaud, D., & Eisner, M. (2008). Entwicklung von Gewalterfahrungen Jugendlicher im Kanton Zürich. Schlussbericht zuhanden der Bildungsdirektion des Kantons Zürich.
Riedo, C. (2010). *Jugendkriminalität und Jugendstrafrecht im Blickfeld von Öffentlichkeit und Politik*. Schweizerische Zeitschrift für Kriminologie 2010/01 (pp. 21–27). Bern: Stämpfli Verlag AG.
Riedo, C. (2013). *Jugendstrafrecht und Jugendstrafprozessrecht*. Basel: Helbing Lichtenhahn Verlag.
Riesen-Kupper, M. (2013). *Art. 1*. In: Donatsch (Editor): StGB Kommentar Schweizerisches Strafgesetzbuch und weitere einschlägige Erlasse mit Kommentar zu StGB, JStG, den Strafbestimmungen des SVG, BetmG und AuG (19th ed.). Zürich: Orell Füssli.
Schärer, D. (2014). *Minderjährige Inhaftierte*. In B. F. Brägger (Ed.), *Schweizerisches Vollzugslexikon*. Helbing Lichtenhahn Verlag: Basel.
Stark, H. (1963). *Die Behandlung der Heranwachsenden im Strafrecht im Hinblick auf die bevorstehende Teilrevision des schweizerischen Strafgesetzbuches*. Winterthur: Keller.
Trechsel, St. (2002). *Jugendstrafverfahren im Rechtsstaat*, Jusletter vom 7.Januar 2002.
United Nations, Committee on the Rights of the Child. (2015). *Concluding observations on the combined second to fourth periodic reports of Switzerland*. CRC/C/CHE/CO/2-4, 4 February 2015.
Urwyler, C. (2011). *Urteilen und Erziehen. Der Beruf des Jugendrichters*. In C. Honegger (Ed.), *Neue Berner Beiträge zur Soziologie*. Bern: Unversität Bern, Institut für Soziologie.
Urwyler, C., & Nett, J. (2012). *Evaluation der Wirksamkeit des neuen Jugendstrafgesetzes. Schlussbericht zuhanden des Auftraggebers*. Bern: Berner Fachhochschule Soziale Arbeit.
Vollmer, T. (2016). *Prävention statt Repression im Bereich der Jugendkriminalität*. Schweizerische Zeitschrift für Kriminologie 2016/01. Bern: Stämpfli Verlag AG.
Zanolini, V. (2014). *Wiedergutmachung durch Mediation*. Bern: Haupt.
Zermatten, J. (1990). Réflexions sur les rèalités de la justice de mineurs et de la separation de fonctions judiciaires. ZStrR 1990, pp. 367 et seq.
Zermatten, J. (2006). The Swiss Federal Statute on Juvenile Criminal Law. In J. Junger-Tas & S. H. Decker (Eds.), *International handbook of juvenile justice* (pp. 295–307). New York: Springer.

OTHER SOURCES

Regierungsratsbeschluss des Kantons Zürich Nr. 930/2012; KR-Nr. 172/2010.

Ineke Pruin Assistant Professor at the Department for Criminal Law and Criminology at the University of Bern, Switzerland, since 2015. Before she was working at the University of Greifswald in Germany, where she coordinated international Juvenile Justice research together with Frieder Dünkel. Among her main interests are questions about the treatment of young adult offenders in Criminal Law, the reintegration and rehabilitation of (juvenile) offenders, legal guarantees for offenders, and Penal Laws. She is part of the Juvenile Justice Working Group in the European Society of Criminology and regularly counsels the International Juvenile Justice Observatory (Brussels).

Peter Aebersold born 1943, until 2010 Professor for Juvenile Criminal Law, Correctional Law and Criminology at the University of Basel, since 2010 emeritus. Before Judge, Member of the Cantonal Parliament and Counseller in the Public Administration. He still teaches Juvenile Criminal Law at the Universities of Bern and Luzern.

Jonas Weber Assistant Professor with Tenure Track at the Department for Criminal Law and Criminology at the University of Bern, Switzerland, since 2013. In addition, he works as a part-time judge at the criminal court of the canton of Basel-Stadt. Among his main interests are questions about the system of criminal sanctions, alternative sanctions, therapeutic measures, the preventive detention, and probation. He is part of the Swiss specialist group "reform in criminal law."

PART V

Middle East

23

Palestine

Mutaz M. Qafisheh

INTRODUCTION

The State of Palestine became party to the International Convention on the Rights of the Child of 20 November 1989 (CRC)[1] on 2 April 2014.[2] Less than 2 years later, on 4 February 2016, President Mahmoud Abbas enacted Decree-Law No. 4 Concerning Juvenile Protection (hereinafter "Juvenile Protection Law" or "the Law"),[3] which set forth the rights of children in conflict with the law and reformed the entire child justice system.[4] The Law incorporated the international standards relating to children as enshrined in the CRC and other soft law rules. The question remains: would the legal texts, as manifested by the accession to the Convention and by the aforesaid Law, be materialized at the institutional and practical levels?

The number of children in conflict with the law is on the rise.[5] While the number of children who broke the law in the West Bank was 637 in 2005,[6] it increased into 2,457 in 2014.[7] Yet no concrete effort has been undertaken to systematically resolve the issue of such children, despite the progress made at the global level and in cer-

[1] 1577 *United Nations Treaty Series* (UNTS) 3, entered into force 2 September 1990.

[2] Spokesperson for the UN High Commissioner for Human Rights, *Press Briefing Notes on Palestine* (Geneva, 2 May 2014).

[3] Palestine Gazette, No. 118, 28 February 2016, p. 7.

[4] The Law came into force, in accordance with its Article 68, on 29 March 2016.

[5] This study relates to juvenile justice in the Palestinian Authority-controlled territory. It does not cover the violations of children's rights by Israel. Nor does it discuss Palestinian children in East Jerusalem. See Defense for Children International, *Palestinian Child Prisoners* (Ramallah, 2008); and Rinad Abdallah, *Rights of Jerusalem Children* (Ramallah 2010).

[6] These numbers are mainly taken from Ministry of Social Affairs in 2010.

[7] Defense for Children International, *Juvenile Police in Palestine between Practice and International Standards* (Ramallah 2015), p. 61.

M.M. Qafisheh, Ph.D. (✉)
College of Law and Political Science, Hebron University, Hebron, Palestine
e-mail: mutazq@hebron.edu; mmqafisheh@gmail.com

S.H. Decker, N. Marteache (eds.), *International Handbook of Juvenile Justice*,
DOI 10.1007/978-3-319-45090-2_23

tain states in the Middle East,[8] and the significant developments of the Palestinian legal system since the establishment of the Palestinian Authority in 1994.[9] Jordan amended its Juvenile Rehabilitation Law of 1954,[10] which has been applicable in the West Bank until early 2016, just 1 year after its withdrawal from that Palestinian territory during the war with Israel in 1967.[11] Children in Palestine had to wait over 60 years until the new Juvenile Protection Law to be adopted in 2016. The foregoing shows, from the outset, the necessity of reforming the Palestinian juvenile justice system in light of international human rights standards and global developments.[12]

This study has been written after an extensive field research and a series of meetings and interviews that took place in the West Bank for over 5 years (2011–2016). In addition, it builds on the author's experience in supervising a Juvenile Justice Clinic at the College of Law and Political Science of Hebron University which was applied in collaboration with Washington & Lee (W&L) University Law School, USA, in 2013–2015. The Clinic included an academic course on juvenile justice for Hebron and W&L students conducted jointly by two Palestinian and American law professors, study visits to child detention centers and police stations, handling a number of child cases (pro bono advices and representation), hosting several workshops, public awareness campaigns, and organizing joint Palestinian–American moot trials.[13] The author and a team of his students interviewed police officers, prison administrators, prosecutors, judges, probation officers, and representatives of the Ministry of Social Development. The author visited the social rehabilitation institution allocated for male juveniles in the city of Ramallah, the girls juvenile care institution in Bethlehem, the central prison in the city of Tulkarm, and a police station and juvenile detention center in Hebron. In some of these locations, the author and students met children accused to be in conflict with law. They similarly interviewed a number of

[8] Taher Buomidra & Netham Assaf, eds., *Arab Experience on Juvenile Justice* (Amman 2007); Zeinab Aouin, *Juvenile Justice: Comparative Study* (Amman 2009).

[9] There are, however, some initiatives to work on juvenile justice by UN agencies, NGOs, universities, and the Palestinian Authority. But none of these initiatives have been comprehensive. See Suheil Hasanein, *Juvenile Justice in the West Bank and the Gaza Strip* (Birzeit 2003); Abdelkarin Shami, "The Criminal Juvenile Justice in Palestine," in Buomidra & Assaf, *supra* note 8, pp. 52–73.

[10] Jordanian Official Gazette, No. 1182, 16 May 1954, p. 396. See *infra* note 16.

[11] Jordanian Ministry of Social Development, *Juvenile Law No. 24 of 1968 and its Amendments until 2007* (Amman 2008). See Mohammad Tarawneh, "Jordanian Experience on Juvenile Justice," in Buomidra & Assaf, *supra* note 8, pp. 31–37; Christine Fadoul, "Juvenile Justice Reform Project in Jordan: Achievements and Challenges," in *ibid*, pp. 38–51.

[12] For recent developments in nine Arab countries, see Defense for Children International, *Juvenile Police in Palestine … , supra* note 7, pp. 18–25.

[13] Mutaz Qafisheh, "Modern Legal Education in Palestine: The Clinical Programs of Hebron University," in Mutaz Qafisheh & Stephen Rosenbaum, *Experimental Legal Education in a Globalized World: The Middle East & Beyond* (Newcastle 2016), pp. 198–235.

international and Palestinian nongovernmental organizations (NGOs), lawyers, and UN agencies.

The purpose of this chapter is to clarify the legal basis and practical situation relating to children in conflict with law in Palestine with a view to provide a pathway for potential reform, particularly in light of Palestine's obligation pursuant to its recent accession to the CRC. It starts by describing the legal basis that governs the juvenile justice in Palestine. It then explores the formal policy at the level of the Palestinian Ministry of Social Development, its personnel and child care institutions. The study finally analyses the formal juridical cycle: the police, prosecutors, and courts.

LEGISLATIVE FRAMEWORK FOR JUVENILE JUSTICE

The 2016 Juvenile Protection Law: Context

The current law in Palestine, due to the different political regimes that ruled the country since 1917, is mixed of various legal schools. While the Ottoman legislation was based on Islamic Law and Continental Law, law that was adopted by Britain in Palestine until May 1948 came as a reflection of the Common Law. The West Bank and Gaza were once again subjected to the continental-like legal system from 1948 and 1967 when the West Bank was annexed by Jordan; while Egypt administrated the Gaza and retained the British-enacted legislation and issued certain legislation. After its occupation of the West Bank and Gaza in June 1967, Israel did not extend its law to the occupied territory.[14] It ruled the territory largely by the pre-1967 law, proclaiming a series of military orders that amended or replaced existing legislation, mainly in the field of security. The Palestinian Authority, upon its establishment in 1994, retained the previous law, including juvenile justice, and simultaneously started a process of unifying the legislation of the West Bank with that of Gaza.[15]

Before the adoption of the Juvenile Protection Law in 2016, juvenile justice in Palestine had been regulated by two key instruments. In the West Bank, the applicable legislation was the Jordanian Juvenile Rehabilitation Law No. 16 of 29 April 1954;[16] while in Gaza the applicable law was a British-enacted legislation:

---

[14] David Reifen, "The Implications of Laws and Procedures in the Juvenile Court in Israel," 3 *British Journal of Criminology* 130 (1963); Leslie Sebba, "Legalism versus Welfarism in Israeli's Juvenile Justice System," 16 *Israel Law Review* 461 (1981).

[15] Mutaz Qafisheh, "Legislative Drafting in Transitional States: The Case of Palestine," 2 *International Journal for Legislative Drafting and Law Reform* (2014) 7, 26.

[16] Jordan abolished the 1954 Law within 9 months (on 25 March 1968) after the occupation of the West Bank by Israel in June 1967; the Law remained applicable in the West Bank, but not in Jordan. Jordan has amended the 1968 Law a number of times. Jordan is in the process to further reforming its juvenile justice system. See Christine Fadoul, "Draft Law on Reformatory Juvenile Justice System in Jordan: Achievements and Challenges," in Buomidra & Assaf, *supra* note 8, pp. 38–44.

Juvenile Offenders Ordinance No. 2 of 18 February 1937.[17] As these two pieces of legislation are no longer applicable,[18] we will confine the analysis here to the new 2016 Juvenile Protection Law. This Law is revised here, in addition to the CRC, in the light of three United Nations (UN) instruments: (1) the 1985 Standard Minimum Rules for the Administration of Juvenile Justice, commonly known as "Beijing Rules";[19] (2) the 1990 Guidelines for the Prevention of Juvenile Delinquency, or "Riyadh Guidelines";[20] and (3) the 1990 Rules for the Protection of Juveniles Deprived of their Liberty.[21] Although international standards are UN recommendations, or "soft law," some of their content is of customary nature, for instance, the prohibition of torture.[22] They could as such be extended to Palestine as a state, particularly since juvenile justice is primarily under the Palestinian Authority's proper.[23]

Since 1999, there have been several attempts to develop a new juvenile justice law to meet the needs of the Palestinian society. The process has been led by civil society organizations,[24] UNCEF and the UN Office of the High Commissioner for Human Rights.[25] It was thought to include juvenile justice within the Child

[17] Palestine Gazette, No. 667, Supplement 1, 18 February 1937, p. 187. As a background, see W. Fox, "Sentencing the Juvenile Offender," 5 *Western Law Review* 109 (1966); D. Hodges, "Juvenile Offenders," 13 *British Journal of Criminology* 191 (1973). Before this legislation, juvenile justice in Palestine, as in the rest of the Ottoman Empire, was regulated in accordance with the Ottoman Penal Code of 12 July 1858—Aref Ramadan, ed., *Completion of Laws: Ottoman Laws Valid in Arab States Detached from the Ottoman Government* (Beirut: Science Press, 1928), Vol. I, p. 2. Article 40 of this Code, which was amended on 4 June 1911 (*ibid.*), fixed the age of criminal responsibility at 13 years. It provided that no death sentence may be imposed on persons under 18. The article made a distinction between children between 13 and 15 years of age and those above 15 and under 18, providing reduced sentences for each category. It further recognized a number of alternatives to imprisonment, such as signing a commitment by child's parents, fining, or rehabilitation. In certain aspects, these provisions had been more progressive than some rules that had been enacted in Palestine in subsequent periods.

[18] Article 65 of the Juvenile Protection Law of 2016.

[19] General Assembly Resolution 40/33, 29 November 1985.

[20] General Assembly Resolution 45/112, 14 December 1990.

[21] General Assembly Resolution 45/11, 14 December 1990.

[22] F. Sloan, "The Binding Force of a 'Recommendation' of the General Assembly of the United Nations," *British Year Book of International Law* 24 (1948); Yuen-il Liang, "The General Assembly and the Progressive Development and Codification of International Law," 42 *American Journal of International Law* 66 (1948).

[23] Palestine was recognized by the UN as a state in 2012. See Mutaz Qafisheh, *Palestine Membership in the Unites Nations: Legal and Practical Implications* (Newcastle 2013).

[24] E.g. Defence for Children International, Independent Commission for Human Rights, and Al-Haq.

[25] The present writer took part in this process through his previous capacity as Human Rights Officer at the UN Office of the High Commissioner for Human Rights in Ramallah, 2001–2003.

Law, as the case of other Arab countries such as Egypt and Tunisia.[26] However, the drafting yielded the adoption of the Palestinian Child Law No. 7 of 15 August 2004,[27] which excluded children in conflict with the law to have a separate law on that theme. The process of developing a new juvenile law continued and produced a draft in 2006. The draft was far from being consistent with international standards. This led to the slow process in revising the draft. In June 2007, Hamas took over Gaza and Palestine was broken up into two parts: the West Bank led by Fatah, and Gaza by Hamas. Since then, the Palestinian Parliament has not been functioning. And no law has been passed.

In 2010, efforts to have new Palestinian juvenile law were revived. The Ministry of Social Development in Ramallah formed a National Steering Committee to work on a comprehensive policy to reform juvenile justice. The Steering Committee was divided into two task forces, one charged with developing a national plan on juvenile justice reform and the other was mandated to draft a juvenile justice law. As prospects for the Parliament to reconvene in the near future were minimal, it was envisaged that the new law would be submitted to the Palestinian President to enact it as Decree-Law, using the President legislative power vested in him in the absence of the Parliament under Article 43 of the 2003 Amended Palestinian Basic Law.[28] At last this idea has been materialized by the adoption of the 2016 Juvenile Protection Law.

This Law can be considered as a breakthrough in the field of human rights, in general, and the child rights and juvenile justice, in particular. It embodied the most advanced provisions relating to juvenile justice, often exceeding those rules of the CRC. We will here analyze the main positive points of the Law. We will, however, highlight some provisions that have been identified to be a subject of concern.

Positive Aspects of the 2016 Juvenile Law

The Juvenile Protection Law incorporated the entire provisions of CRC relating to children in conflict with the law. It placed "the best interest of the child" as a primary consideration for dealing with juveniles.[29] The Law prohibited subjecting children who breach the law to "torture or other cruel, inhuman or degrading treatment or punishment."[30] It confirmed the nonapplicability of death penalty against children and removed the possibility of life imprisonment against them regardless of the gravity of the offence that the child might have committed.[31]

---

[26] The Egyptians Child Law No. 12 of 1996 (comprehensively amended in 2008), in Buomidra & Assaf, *supra* note 8, p. 655; Tunisia Law No. 92 of 1995 on Child Protection, in *ibid.*, p. 534.

[27] Palestine Gazette, No. 52, 18 January 2005, p. 13.

[28] Palestine Gazette, Special Edition, 19 March 2003, p. 5.

[29] Article 3 of CRC; Article 2 of the Law.

[30] Article 37(a) of CRC; Article 7(1) of the Law.

[31] Article 37(a) of CRC; Article 7(2) of the Law (ban of capital punishment), and Article 46(1) (removing the possibility of imprisonment of the child and rather referring him to a care institution for 9 years if he commits an offence punishable by death, or for 7 years if he commits a crime whose punishment is life imprisonment).

The Law stipulated that detained children should be separated from adults[32] and that the child "shall have the right to maintain contact with his family through correspondence and visits."[33] It also provided basis for deciding the child-related cases promptly,[34] the child's right to benefit from free legal assistance,[35] and his "right to challenge the legality of the deprivation of liberty before a court."[36] Through such provisions, Palestine has not only adhered to Article 37 of the CRC in its legislation, but it also embraced more favored rights than those elaborated by the Convention.

The Law laid down the foundation for a comprehensive specialized juvenile system for children who come in contact with official institutions, separate from that of adults. It established specialized police, prosecution, courts, procedures, and disciplinary measures.[37] A special unit at the Ministry of Social Development relating to "juveniles or children at risk of delinquency" is set up.[38] The Ministry is assigned with the power to establish a "Social Defense Office" to be embedded within the juvenile court to assist judges with sociopsychological information about children.[39] Clearly, the Law regards child's offences as social, rather than criminal, problem.

A notable development in the Juvenile Law stems from its incorporation of a whole range of disposition alternatives to custody[40] which is no longer applicable.[41] Alternatives might be decided based on the circumstances of the child on a case-by-case basis. These dispositions include warning the child not to reoffend[42]; signing the child, one of his parents or guardian a financial commitment that guarantees to bring the child to investigations or court hearings[43]; transferring the child to an alternative family if the parents are unable to take care of the child

---

32 Article 37(c) of CRC; Article 21(1) of the Law.

33 Article 37(c) of CRC; Article 4 of the Law. The latter article added that the child has the right, while under disciplinary measure that deprives him of liberty, to have periodical vacations to visit his family "unless the court decides otherwise based on the child's best interest."

34 Article 37(d) of CRC; Article 8 of the Law.

35 Article 37(d) of CRC; Article 10 of the Law. The latter article made it mandatory to have a lawyer for the child accused of committing felony or misdemeanor. In cases where the child has no lawyer, "the prosecution or the court, as the case might be, shall appoint a lawyer on its own expense."

36 Article 37(d) of CRC; Articles 33 and 34 of the Law.

37 See section III later.

38 Article 64.

39 Article 28.

40 Article 36.

41 Article 20(1).

42 Article 37.

43 Article 20(2–3). See P. Voelcker, "Juvenile Courts: The Parents' Point of View," 1 *British Journal of Criminology* 154 (1961); Jeremy Prichard, "Parents of Young Offenders: Remodelling Restorative Justice," 26 *University of Tasmania Law Review* 101 (2007).

or if they are the reason of his delinquency[44]; referral to a vocational training institution[45]; obliging the child to do certain things, such as attending counseling sessions, banning him from accessing specific locations that endanger the youth,[46] placing the child under judicial examination,[47] subjecting him to social probation by child protection officers,[48] diverting him to any social care institution,[49] or to a hospital.[50] Other dispositions include release on bail in the pretrial phase,[51] posttrial conditional release after spending one-third of the term in a child care institution,[52] and "public community service."[53] These alternatives aim to divert

[44]Article 38. The referral in this case is carried out in accordance with the 2004 Child Law. Article 32 of this law reads as: "A child deprived of his natural family temporarily or permanently has the right to ... a foster (alternative) family to look after him." In 1963, regulations were enacted to organize the alternative family system. The system includes the Ministry of Social Development's supervision over the alternative families, family's characteristics, and allocation of financial compensation for this family payable by the juvenile's family or by the Ministry (Substitute Families Regulations No. 70, 1963; Jordanian Official Gazette, No. 1704, 15 August 1963, p. 1053). In 2012, the alternative family system was included in Article 19(2/a(1)), of the Amended Child Law; it stated that the decision to allocate an alternative family should be held by a judge upon the request of a social protection officer.

[45]Article 39. The Ministry of Labor established certain institutions to provide vocational training for adolescents. The Ministry of Social Development may refer children in conflict with the law to such training facilities. This is consistent with a number of provisions of the Law that provides the possibility of referring children to an institution that can rehabilitate children. *Cf.* H. Parker, "The Juvenile Employment Service," 57 *International Labour Review* 15 (1948).

[46]Article 40.

[47]Article 41.

[48]Article 42. See details on the child protection officers in section II.2 below.

[49]Article 43. See details on the care institutions in section II.3 below.

[50]Article 44.

[51]Article 20(3).

[52]Article 51. Children may benefit from conditional release regardless of the crime's gravity. This option is not conditional to the good conduct of the child deprived of liberty, but it is understood by implication. Once the child is conditionally released, he would be referred to judicial control with the supervision of the child protection officer. It is not possible to bring the child back to complete his term in the care institution if the release has not achieved its objective, but he might be subjected to other disciplinary measures. However, the possibility of exercising the conditional release after passing one-third of the deprivation of liberty's term means that the child might not be released before passing less than three years if he gets a 9-year term under Article 46(1.A). This is a step backward; Article 14(2) of the 1954 Law allows releasing the child after one year of "imprisonment."

[53]This service was inserted as a proviso at the end of Article 46(2): "in case of committing misdemeanor ... the court may ... decide that the juvenile undertakes a public community service according to applicable laws." This is a positive development that did exist in previous laws in Palestine. It goes in line with best practices applied in developed countries. See, e.g., L. Walgrave & H. Geudens, "Restorative Proportionality of Community Service for Juveniles," 4 *European Journal of Crime, Criminal and Law and Criminal Justice* 361 (1996). Community service, as an alternative to incarceration, has never been tested in Palestine. It could be applied, however, by its incorporation to regulations or instructions. It should be flexibly worded to allow courts to select various public locations for juveniles to spend time doing work for the community. The Minister may select a

minors from the state system, particularly the deprivation of liberty.[54] They, in turn, conform to the advanced modern referral mechanisms embraced by the most developed legal and social systems of the world.[55]

Mediation has been elaborated in the Law as a means to resolve cases of juveniles. Article 23 opens the possibility for mediation over misdemeanor and contraventions before initiating a criminal file. Once mediation succeeds, the criminal proceedings would be closed. Successful mediation leads to the case's end. This option can be offered by the prosecutor or be requested by the child, his lawyer, or guardian. Based on mediation, an agreement can be reached. In it, the child should commit to any obligation under the guarantee of his guardian; including reparation of damages, refraining from accessing certain locations, or to undergo a medical treatment. The agreement is monitored by a probation officer and the police, under the supervision of prosecution. If the agreement's fails, the criminal proceedings may reopen.[56]

---

number of locations for such service. The service should not be designed to be a punishment but rather to help the child to develop a sense of responsibility toward the community. The service should meet a number of conditions, including not being humiliating, dangerous, tiring, affecting the health or education of the child. It should also be in line with the local and international labor standards. Such service, which should take in consideration the child's age and abilities, might be required for a couple of hours per week. It could include watering plants in certain public gardens, clean part of classrooms, working in a public library, helping certain disabled people to cross the street or to ride the bus, or working with certain associations in administrative jobs such as photocopying or distributing publications. According to Articles 93–99 of the Palestinian Labor Law No. 7 of 30 April 2000 (Palestine Gazette, No. 39, 25 November 2001, p. 7), children should not work when they are under 15 years of age, should not be employed in dangerous jobs, or work overnight or in remote areas. See International Labor Organization, Convention No. 182 on the Worst Forms of Child Labor (1999), and Convention No. 138 on the Minimum Age for the Admission to Employment or Work (1973). The community service in the Lebanese law offers a model for the Palestinian legislator. See Articles 5(5) and Article 11 of the Lebanese Law relative to Juveniles in Conflict with the Law or those at Risk No. 422, 2 June 2002 (Buomidra & Assaf, *supra* note 8, p. 607).

[54] Article 40(4) of the CRC stated: "A variety of dispositions, such as care, guidance and supervision orders; counselling; probation; foster care; education and vocational training programmes and other alternatives to institutional care shall be available to ensure that children are dealt with in a manner appropriate to their well-being and proportionate both to their circumstances and the offence."

[55] V. Kumar, "The Treatment of Juvenile Offenders in England," 6 *Criminal Law Quarterly* 488 (1964), pp. 491–507; Larry Wilson, "Diversion: The Impact of Juvenile Justice," 18 *Canadian Journal of Criminology and Corrections* 161 (1976); Mark Berlin & Herbert Allard, "Diversion of Children from the Juvenile Courts," 3 *Canadian Journal of Family Law* 439 (1980); Gary Reker, James Cote, & Edward Peacock, "Juvenile Diversion: Conceptual Issues and Program Effectiveness," 22 *Canadian Journal of Criminology* 36 (1980).

[56] Article 16 of the 2001 Criminal Procedures Law states: "Settlements may be reached on contraventions and which are punishable only by a fine. The competent police officer is held … to propose a settlement to the accused in the contravention or to his attorney and to establish same in the minutes. The proposal for a settlement in a misdemeanor shall be made by the Public Prosecution."

The foregoing formulation of "mediation" in such a flexible language may pave the way for Palestine to design a system of restorative justice by a regulation or instructions that complement the Juvenile Law.[57] The key point of restoration is that the crime is personal matter between the offender, the victim, not against the state.[58] Offences can then be resolved by bringing together the victim, the offender, their social networks, and judicial bodies.[59] It could apply for certain offences, not all.[60] Restorative agreements contain reasonable obligations with a view to reintegrate offenders in the society.[61] Restorative justice is a relatively recent alternative in the world; it systematically worked in countries such as Australia,[62] Britain,[63] Canada,[64] New Zealand,[65] and the United States.[66] It exists

[57] Bernd-Dieter Meier, "Restorative Justice: A New Paradigm in Criminal Law," 6 *European Journal of Crime, Criminal Law and Criminal Justice* 125 (1998); Rick Sarre, "Restorative Justice: Translating the Theory into Practice," 1 *University of Notre Dame Australia Law Review* 11 (1999); Jim Consedine, "The Third Millenium: Restorative Justice or More Crime and Prisons," 11 *Sri Lanka Journal of International Law* 1 (1999); John Braithwaite, "Restorative Justice and Social Justice," 63 *Saskatchewan Law Review* 185 (2000); Kent Roach, "Changing Punishment at the Turn of the Century: Restorative Justice on the Rise," 42 *Canadian Journal of Criminology* 249 (2000); Samuel Damren, "Restorative Justice: Prison and the Native Sense of Justice," 47 *Journal of Legal Pluralism and Unofficial Law* 83 (2002); Donald Schmid, "Restorative Justice: A New Paradigm for Criminal Justice Policy," 34 *Victoria University of Wellington Law Review* 91 (2003); George Mousourakis, "Understanding and Implementing Restorative Justice," 11 *Tilburg Foreign Law Review* 626 (2004); Katherine Doolin, "But What Does It Mean? Seeking Definitional Clarity in Restorative Justice," 71 *Journal of Criminal Law* 427 (2007); Barbara Hudson, "Institutionalisation of Restorative Justice: Justice and the Ethics of Discourse," 2007 *Acta Juridica* 56 (2007); Shawn Fields, "Private Crimes and Public Forgiveness: Towards a Refined Restorative Justice Amnesty Regime," 5 *International Journal of Civil Society Law* 7 (2007); Frank Hill, "Restorative Justice: Sketching a New Legal Discourse," 4 *International Journal of Punishment and Sentencing* 51 (2008).

[58] Terre des homes-Lausanne, *Thematic Policy on Juvenile Justice* (Lausanne 2010); Terre des homes-Lausanne, *Lima Declaration of Restorative Juvenile Justice*, 7 November 2009.

[59] Adam Crawford, "Situating Restorative Youth Justice in Crime Control and Prevention," 2007 *Acta Juridica* 1 (2007); Robert Mackay, "Restorative Justice and Children's Hearings: A Proposal," 11 *European Journal of Crime, Criminal Law and Criminal Justice* 1 (2003).

[60] UN Office for Drugs and Crime, *Handbook on Restorative Justice Programmes* (New York 2006).

[61] *Basic principles on the use of restorative justice programmes in criminal matters*; UN Doc. E/2000/INF/2/Add.2 at 35 (2000).

[62] Sharon Hayes & Hennessey Hayes, "Developing Ethical Identities in Young Offenders through Restorative Justice Practice in Australia," 8 *Queensland University of Teaching Law and Justice Journal* 380 (2008).

[63] Georgios Antonopoulos & John Winterdyk, "The British 1998 Crime and Disorder Act: A Restorative Response to Youth Offending," 11 *European Journal of Crime, Criminal Law and Criminal Justice* 386 (2003).

[64] Bruce Archibald & Jennifer Llewellyn, "The Challenges of Institutionalizing Comprehensive Restorative Justice: Theory and Practice in Nova Scotia," 29 *Dalhousie Law Journal* 297 (2006).

[65] Hannah Goodyer, "Rethinking Justice in New Zealand: A Critical Assessment of Restorative Justice," 9 *Canterbury Law Review* 179 (2003).

[66] Joanne Katz & Gene Bonham, Jr., "Restorative Justice in Canada and the United States: A Comparative Analysis," 6 *Journal of the Institute of Justice and International Studies* 187 (2006).

in certain African countries as well.[67] Yet the seeds of this form of justice principles find roots in the Middle East and Islamic traditions,[68] where informal justice is widely practiced to resolve criminal conducts.[69] This justice is even more utilized in Palestine due to the absence of state system under the occupation for half a century.[70] For example, in 2014, out of the 2,457 of juvenile cases received by police in the West Bank, 491 were resolved by conciliation.[71] Much more conflicts were resolved before reaching the police.[72]

Other child-friendly provisions can be found in the new Juvenile Law. The Law rose the age of criminal responsibility to 12 years of age[73] (it was 9 in previously).[74] It preserves the child's privacy by making all juvenile trials confidential,[75] and it criminalizes any person who reveals information that affects the child's honor.[76] Financial penalties against minors are nonapplicable, nor the possibility of filing

---

[67] Boyane Tshehla, "Restorative Justice Bug Bites the South African Criminal Justice System," 17 *South African Journal of Criminal Justice* 1 (2004); Bruce Baker, "He Must Buy What He Stole and Then We Forgive: Restorative Justice in Rwanda and Sierra Leone," 2007 *Acta Juridica* 171 (2007).

[68] Mutaz Qafisheh, "Restorative Justice in Islamic Penal Law: A Contribution to the Global System," 7 *International Journal of Criminal Justice Sciences* 487 (2012).

[69] Mutaz Qafisheh, *Restorative Justice in Palestine and in the Middle East* (presentation delivered at a workshop organized by Terre des hommes-Lausanne in Bethlehem, Palestine, 5 April 2016).

[70] Nadera Shalhoub & Mustafa Abdelbaqi, *Tribal Justice and Its Effect on Formal Justice in Palestine* (Birzeit 2003).

[71] Defense for Children International, *Juvenile Police in Palestine …* , supra note 7, p. 61.

[72] Lisa Traki et al., *Informal Justice System and the Rule of Law and Dispute Settlement in Palestine: The National Report on the Results of the Field Research* (Birzeit 2006).

[73] Article 5.

[74] Article 2 of the 1954 Juvenile Law; and Article 94 of the 1960 Penal Code as amended by Article 2 of Law No. 39 of 25 November 1963 (Jordanian Official Gazette, No. 1727, 16 December 1963, p. 1683). The Jordanian Penal Code No. 16 of 10 April 1960 is still applicable in the West Bank (Jordanian Official Gazette, No. 1487, 1 May 1960, p. 374). See Kamel Said, *Interpretation of the Penal Coode* (Amman 2009); Netham Majali, *Interpretation of the Penal Coode: General Section* (Amman 2010). Criminal responsibility in Gaza was determined by Article 9 of the 1936 Criminal Ordinance: "A person under the age of nine years is not criminally responsible for any act or omission. A person under the age of twelve years is not criminally responsible for an act or omission, unless it is proved that at the time of doing the act or making the omission he had capacity to know that he ought not to do the act or make the omission." On the origin of the 1936 Ordinance, see Norman Bentwich, "The New Criminal Code for Palestine," 20 *Journal of Comparative Legislation and International Law* 71 (1938). Fixing the age of criminal responsibility at 9 years has been unified between the West Bank and Gaza after the adoption of Child Law of 2004 (Article 67). The age was at last fixed at 12 by Article 24 of the Decree-Law No. 19 of 7 December 2012 Concerning the Amendment of the Palestinian Child Law No. 7 of 2004 (Palestine Gazette, No. 101, 20 August 2013, p. 6).

[75] Article 9.

[76] Article 59. Article 11(1) prohibits the reference in any scientific or professional diplomas that such documents were obtained from juvenile care institution.

civil claims before juvenile courts.[77] All juvenile cases are exempted from court fees.[78] The conviction of a child would not be recorded.[79] The Law reduced the applicability of the statute of limitation to the half regarding any case involving children.[80] The child, while deprived of liberty, has the right to complete his primary and secondary education.[81] A separate system is established to enforce juvenile cases with the supervision of the court, prosecution, and child protection officers over the disciplinary measures that affect convicted children.[82]

Concerns

Notwithstanding these remarkable developments in the Juvenile Protection Law, three major issues remain a matter of concern: the absence of executive legislation; vague provisions; and the allocation of human, logistical, and financial resources.[83]

The Law has been adopted without its enforcement secondary legislation (regulations, instructions, and orders). Article 66 empowered the Council of Ministers to enact such executive regulations and delegated the Minister of Social Development to adopt instructions and orders that give effect to the Law. However, past experience shows that, without fixing specific date for enacting executive legislation, laws might face standstill.[84] The Law ought to have been enacted along with its regulations and the necessary instructions to apply many of its non-self-executing provisions. Police officers, prosecutors, judges, and child protection officers would not know how to execute certain stipulations without having specific procedures in place.

[77] Article 63. This is of course without prejudice to the possibility of filing civil claims before other courts according to the general civil obligations, including contacts and torts.

[78] Article 14.

[79] Article 11(2).

[80] Article 12.

[81] Article 13.

[82] Articles 47–55.

[83] Such concerns were expressed, for instance, at a workshop on the Juvenile Protection Law organized by the Independent Commission for Human Rights (Hebron, 28 April 2016). The workshop was attended by a juvenile judge, prosecutors, lawyers, academics, social protection offices, representatives of a number of international and local NGOs, ministries of health and education.

[84] One study revealed that, from 1994 until 2002, out of 60 laws that were adopted by the Palestinian Authority, only 7 regulations were adopted. Maen Idies, *Executive Regulations for the Laws* (Ramallah 2002), p. 26. Even when enacted, regulations were often postponed to longer periods than those required by corresponding laws. Instances include Handicapped Law of 9 August 1999 (regulations passed on 12 April 2004), Traffic Law of 17 September 2000 (regulations adopted on 13 September 2005), and Arbitration Law of 5 April 2000 (regulations enacted on 12 April 2004). Qafisheh, "Legislative Drafting in Transitional States … ," *supra* note 15, p. 32.

Here are some examples. How a convicted child might enjoy "periodical and limited vacation,"[85] and for how long, without an executive legislation? The Law requires that child cases to be decided promptly;[86] yet how long "promptly" might take? Although the basis of legal assistance was set forth in Article 10, the application of assistance's modality remains imprecise. Article 13 on the child's right to education needs executive order to give effect to the juveniles held in social care institutions to complete their schooling. Similarly, how the child protection officers would be able to prepare reports to the prosecution and to courts without having fixed procedures on such report's format, length, content, and timing? What are the mechanisms to enforce the measure of warning for the child to refrain from reoffending,[87] to refer the child to an alternative family,[88] and to conduct judicial examination?[89] The delay in enacting executive legislation may not block the implementation of the Law entirely, but it is expected to create confusion and different procedures in dealing with children from one place of the country to another and from one judge or prosecutor to the next; that might, in turn, infringe the respect of the principles of fairness and equality.[90]

The second problem stems from the vague language of a number of the Law's provisions. Whereas it prohibits torture and ill treatment, Article 7 does not introduce penalties against torturers. Nowhere in Palestinian law can one find explicit penalty against torture perpetrators,[91] notwithstanding its prohibition in the Basic Law and Palestine's accession, on 2 April 2014,[92] to the International Convention against Torture and Other Cruel Inhuman or Degrading Treatment or Punishment of 10 December 1984.[93] Such a vague ban might create impunity for those who torture or mistreat children. It further stipulated that the arrested child should undergo medical check,[94] without saying what would happen if such a measure is not conducted.[95]

---

[85] Article 4.

[86] Article 8.

[87] Article 37. This concern was expressed in a presentation by the Hebron Chief Prosecutor Ashraf Misheal, Commission for Human Rights workshop, *supra* note 83.

[88] Article 38.

[89] Article 41.

[90] That might run counter to Article 40, paragraph 2(a.iv) of the CRC.

[91] Mutaz Qafisheh, "Human Rights Gaps in the Palestinian Criminal System: A United Nations Role?," 16 *International Journal of Human Rights* 358 (2012), pp. 361–363. In fact, the prohibition of torture in the Juvenile Protection Law is not new. The 2004 Palestinian Child Law provided in its Article 68 that "[n]o child shall be subjected to physical or moral torture … ." Yet the main problem, namely the absence of penalty against torture perpetrators, persists.

[92] Spokesperson for the UN High Commissioner for Human Rights, *supra* note 2.

[93] 1465 UNTS 85; entry into force 26 June 1987.

[94] Article 22.

[95] Similar provision can be found in Article 32 of the Law.

Moreover, the Law stipulated that "the juvenile's guardian and lawyer shall be notified of every procedure and decision that the child should be notified of"[96] but there is no answer on who should notify such persons and what the consequences in case of nonnotification. Article 28 authorized the Ministry of Social Development to create "Social Defense Office that incorporates socio-psychological specialists alongside child protection officers" but it did not oblige the Ministry to establish such an office and did not mention the type and number of sociologists or psychologists who may be employed. Lastly, Article 60 did not specify a timetable for creating specialized juvenile courts. It rather opened the possibility of assigning judges to juvenile matters.[97] That means that children will continue to be brought "temporarily" before ordinary judges until such an indefinite time on which separate courts would commence. Such vague stipulations pose the risk of turning the Law into a superfluous document, if no measures are expeditiously undertaken in this respect.

Apparently, the Law has been adopted without allocating the necessary financial, logistical, human, institutional resources, or infrastructure. One district chief prosecutor, for example, explained that he assigned two prosecutors to handle juvenile cases from the already inadequate number of existing prosecutors who are barely able to deal with other cases.[98] The same applies to judges whose number is not enough even to face the already overwhelming caseload.[99] Assigning judges to juvenile cases from existing judges without appointing new ones to exclusively oversee juvenile cases puts extra burden on courts, lawyers, children, and their families.[100]

The Law, likewise, established a series of obligations on child protection officers (below), including accompanying juveniles at police stations, prosecution's investigation, court hearings, preparing reports on the child's family, health, education, psychology, and monitoring him while staying at the social or medical institutions. Ms. Lubna Anani, Head of the Ministry of Social Development's office in the south of the West Bank, complained that "in Yatta [a city with over 170,000 inhabitants] alone, there are over 500 cases of various social issues and

[96] Article 29(1).

[97] Article 60.

[98] Misheal, *supra* note 87.

[99] In this connection, Juvenile Judge Mr. Mohammad Ajlouni said: "In average I oversee 25 felonies per day. After that, I am asked to hear juvenile cases. How can I understand the state of the juvenile and child's best interest afterwards?!" (Commission for Human Rights workshop, *supra* note 83).

[100] One lawyer from the International Legal Foundation, a New York-based criminal defense NGO with field offices in Palestine, explained that in Hebron district, as a case in point, there are 4 magistrate courts (in Hebron city, Halhul city/north, Yatta city/south, and Dura city/west). There is only one judge assigned to juvenile cases. If this judge has a case of one child at each of these four courts, the lawyer might wait for the entire day for one hearing only until the judge has the turn to come to the court in which the lawyer (and the child) will be waiting. The judge might not have the time to come to that particular court and that means the hearing will be postponed. Advocate Imad Salaymeh; Commission for Human Rights workshop, *supra* note 83.

there is only one employee. How that person may work on dozens of juvenile cases with the due care specified in the law on the top of hundreds of cases that she deals with? It is just impossible!"[101] Juvenile care institutions need to be founded to absorb the growing number of children in conflict with the law. Currently, there is only one juvenile institution in the West Bank (Dar Al-Amal in Ramallah). Without opening at least two additional institutions, one in the north and another in the south of the West Bank, it remains hard to imagine how the Law would be properly applied (see later).

Lastly, the Law lacks to preventive measures for juvenile delinquency. Such measures should be formulated as set out through minimum standards in the Riyadh Guidelines. The measures need to be included at the levels of formal procedures, social settings, families, education, and practical and academic research.[102] The Law also does not include clear arrangements for juveniles' reintegration in their communities.[103]

GOVERNMENTAL ADMINISTRATION OF JUVENILE JUSTICE

Ministry of Social Development

The Palestinian juvenile justice is primarily assigned to the "Ministry of Social Development."[104] This implies that the issue of child delinquency is a matter of social concern rather than an issue of security and punishment.[105] There are, however, some limited responsibilities on juvenile aspects to the Ministry of

---

[101] Commission for Human Rights workshop, *supra* note 83.

[102] *Cf.* Eleanor Glueck, "Predicting Juvenile Delinquency," 2 *British Journal of Delinquency* 275 (1952); H. English, "Prevention of Juvenile Crime," 4 *British Journal of Criminology* 68 (1964); Defense for Children International, *Kids Behind Bars—A study on Children in Conflict with the Law: Towards Investing in Prevention, Stopping Incarceration and Meeting International Standards* (Amsterdam 2003).

[103] Najah Hilo & Amneh Abuein, "The Integration and Rehabilitation of Juveniles in the Palestinian Society," in Buomidra & Assaf, *supra* note 8, pp. 74–125.

[104] The name of the Ministry was previously "Ministry of Social Affairs." It was changed on 15 March 2016 into "Ministry of Social Development" by Council of Ministers' Decision No. 94 of 2016. By this change, the name of the Ministry in Palestine has become similar to that of Jordan. However, the Juvenile Protection Law of 2016 still uses the older name as it was drafted a few years ago. We prefer to use the new name ("Ministry of Social Development") in this study.

[105] This is unlike the case in certain countries in the Middle East, such as Egypt, where the juvenile justice system is scattered among four ministries: Ministry of Interior, Ministry of Justice, Ministry of Social Solidarity, and Ministry of Population and Family. See Terre des hommes-Lausanne, *Assessment of Juvenile Justice System in Egypt*, August 2010, pp. 34–37. See also Bishri Shorbaji, "Juvenile Justice in Egypt and its Reform Prospects," in Buomidra & Assaf, *supra* note 8, pp. 126–141; Hani Hilal, "Juvenile Justice Situation in Egypt," in *ibid.*, pp. 142–159.

Justice and Ministry of Interior, as part of their general mandate.[106] While the former is in charge of the technical drafting of legislation, the latter directs the police and manages detention centers and prisons. Besides, the High Judicial Council plays a role with regard to juveniles as it is responsible for courts. The focus in this section is on the Ministry of Social Development and its policies to reform the juvenile justice system.[107]

The mandate of the Ministry of Social Development over juveniles has been explicitly provided in the 2016 Juvenile Protection Law.[108] The Minister is vested with the power to, *inter alia*, enact instructions and orders to execute the Law.[109] Even when certain powers are given to the police, prosecutors, or courts, the Ministry would retain a central role.[110] This role can be concluded from the Ministry's responsibility over child protection officers, as its staff, and its management and supervision of juvenile social rehabilitation or medical treatment institutions, as we will see shortly.

The Ministry runs the affairs of juvenile justice through its Child Protection Unit,[111] which acts as the central administration for child protection officers and manages the juvenile institutions. It coordinates with the police, prosecution, courts and prisons, relevant ministries, and civil society organizations.[112] The Unit took its roots from the Jordanian juvenile system that was applicable in the West Bank between 1948 until 1967. While the Unit has been significantly developed in Jordan after the enactment of the Juvenile Justice Law in 1968,[113] it remained intact under Israeli occupation. Due to the lack of resources and technical capacity, the Unit has been unable to improve its services when Palestinians took control over juvenile justice in 1994. With the adoption of the 2016 Law, it is hoped that the Unit will be strengthened, logistically and by appointing more qualified staff, to carry out its functions.

---

[106] Jessie Clarey, "Juvenile Crime: Its Causes and Treatment," 12 *Police Journal* 286 (1939); Victor Szyrynski, "Sociatric Psychotherapy in Juvenile Delinquency," 6 *Canadian Journal of Corrections* 74 (1964); P. Stephenson, "Myths about Juvenile Delinquency," 15 *Canadian Journal of Criminology and Corrections* 83 (1973); T. Campbell, "Punishment in Juvenile Justice," 4 *British Journal of Law and Society* 77 (1977).

[107] Although under the Ministry of Social Development's mandate, the juvenile care institutions and the role of child protection officers are addressed in two separate sections later for the sake of clarity.

[108] A similar role was given to the Ministry in the 1954 Jordanian Juvenile Law, e.g., Articles 23–25.

[109] Article 66. In the same article, the power to enact regulations was given to the Council of Ministers, as indicated earlier. Even when the Council adopts regulations, normally the Ministry prepares the technical aspects of the draft.

[110] Article 17.

[111] Article 64.

[112] Ministry of Social Affairs, *Procedures of the Social Defense Department* (Ramallah 2010).

[113] The present writer worked in 2009 and 2010 with the Jordanian Social Defense Department of the Ministry of Social Affairs through his former position as the Regional Director of Penal Reform International for the Middle East and North Africa based in Amman, Jordan.

The Ministry has additional role to play. As mentioned previously, the Law gave the Ministry to establish a "Social Defense Department" attached to each juvenile court that incorporates sociopsychological specialists along with child protection offices in order to assist the court in its findings with regard to children brought before it.[114]

We will elaborate on the role of child protection officers and social care institutions as the most significant features of the Ministry's mandate in relation to juvenile justice.

Child Protection Officers

The "Child Protection Officer" is the new name that the 2016 Juvenile Protection Law adopted for the Ministry of Social Development's personnel in charge of dealing with juvenile justice issues. Previous names were "probation officers" and sometimes called "social supervisors." Child protection officers are assigned with a role to perform across all stages of the juvenile justice chain: arrest and detention by the police, investigation and indictment by prosecutors, trial by courts, rehabilitation in social institutions, and aftercare programs.[115] Probation could also mean placing the juvenile under the supervision of a child protection officer instead of incarceration.[116]

The Law attached a great deal of significance to probation, as an alternative to incarceration.[117] The court might order placing the child under the supervision of a child protection officer for a term ranging from 1 to 5 years. The order can stop anytime during this period upon the prosecution's request, the child protection officer, or the juvenile himself or his guardian; and after reviewing the child protection officer's report on the progress that has been achieved. If the child fails to follow the probation's term, the court might consider other dispositions, including deprivation of liberty. If the juvenile commits another offence during the probation period, the probation would come into an end and the child might be retried on the original offence, besides the new one. The Ministry of Social Development, by administrative decisions and capacity building programs, should give a greater attention to the probation as a referral disposition by strengthening the system and its staff.[118]

---

[114] Article 28.

[115] Kenneth Wollan, "Treatment of Juvenile Delinquents," 14 *Police Journal* 305 (1941); Andre Dunant, *Juveniles in Conflict with the Law: The Social Worker at All Stages of the Procedure* (Geneva 2002).

[116] Article 17.

[117] Article 42.

[118] The Amended Palestinian Child Law of 2012 touched upon probation by "placing the child under social control in his natural environment" (Article 19, paragraph 2.b(1)). But this provision is far from establishing probation as a system. *Cf.* Jennifer Babe & Rui Fernandes, "Juvenile Probation in Metropolitan Toronto: An Empirical Study," 2 *Canadian Journal of Family Law* 161 (1979).

Child protection officers work under the direction of the Child Protection Unit, headed by the supervisor at the headquarters of the Ministry of Social Development in the city of Ramallah.[119] Such officers work at the district level under the daily administrative management of the head of Social Directorate of the Ministry of Social Development within each district. As in other countries, the work of these social officers, as they are not supposed to be technically juvenile lawyers, is quite informal.[120] They assist courts and law enforcement officials in determining the personal and social context of the child who violates the law on a case-by-case basis.[121]

The role of child protection officers starts upon the arrest of the child by the police.[122] Once detained and transferred to prosecution, the child officer should continue to monitor the juvenile's case in each interrogation session.[123] At the court hearings, the judge obtains a report from a child officer on the juvenile's personal and social status.[124] The report of the child officer, provided in practice upon formal request from the court,[125] might comprise "general information about the child, his environment, performance in school and his heath."[126] The Ministry has designed a form to be filled out by child protection officers and be used before courts.[127]

Child protection officers in practice provide the required information after interviewing the juvenile and his family. To complete the report, some officers visit the child at home, police station, and in detention.[128] Despite the efforts that some child officers take in its preparation, judges often ignore such a report and

[119] Article 64 of the 2016 Juvenile Protection Law.

[120] N. Adler, "The Work of Juvenile Courts," 7 *Journal of Comparative Legislation and International Law* 217 (1925), pp. 223–224.

[121] Jacob Isaacs, "The Lawyer in the Juvenile Court," 10 *Criminal Law Quarterly* 222 (1968); Greg Johnston, "The Function of Counsel in Juvenile Court," 7 *Osgoode Hall Law Journal* 199 (1970); Roy St. George Stubbs, "The Role of the Lawyer in Juvenile Court," 6 *Manitoba Law Journal* 65 (1975); Inez Dootjes, Patricia Erickson, & Richard Fox, "Defence Counsel in Juvenile Court: A Variety of Roles," 14 *Canadian Journal of Criminology and Corrections* 132 (1972).

[122] Article 18(2).

[123] Article 20.

[124] Article 30(3 and 6).

[125] Letter dated 3 March 2010 from a judge in one West Bank magistrate court to one probation officer requesting information about the social and economic situation of one child in conflict with the law facing a trial on 20 April 2010 (in file with the writer).

[126] Article 11(4) of the 1954 Law (this language does not exist in the 2016 Law, which might be considered is a step backward, unless it is detailed by a regulation or instructions). George Awad & Clive Chamberlain, "The Process of Psychiatric Work with the Juvenile Courts," 1 *Canadian Journal of Family Law* 363 (1978).

[127] A copy of this form in Arabic was handed to the writer by Ms. Khadra Hour, Probation Officer and Director of Social Care, Social Directorate, Yatta city, Hebron district, 18 August 2010, Hebron.

[128] Meeting with Ms. Khadra Hour, *ibid.*

include it to file merely as part of a routine procedure.[129] Most judges do not even bother reading the officer's report. Unfortunately, Article 30 of the 2016 Juvenile Protection Law (on court sessions) uses a language that may imply that the courts only "listen" to, but not under an obligation to build its findings based on the report of the child protection officer. However, the report might have significant weight in the judgment in case of no objection to its content by the parties or the juvenile judge.[130]

Once the court makes a disciplinary measure, particularly if the measure is to place the child in a care institution, the role of child officer will not end. In this connection, Article 48(1) of the Law stated that: "The child protection officer shall supervise the execution of the dispositions set forth in this Law. He shall monitor the convicted child and present recommendations to the juvenile and to those in charge of his education. The officer shall prepare periodical reports to the court and prosecution every three months on the child's situation." The court, based on such reports, might modify or end the measure.[131] In practice, however, a few child officers do visit care institutions or detention centers, mainly on their own personal initiative.[132] The child protection officers have also the power to bring a child prior to the completion of his disciplinary measure to the court to request an extension to that measure.[133] The officers, at the same time, have the right to request the court to release the juvenile after spending one-third of his term at the social care institution.[134]

As noted earlier, child protection officers are overwhelmed with daily work and have no time to work on all cases of children in conflict with the law.[135] With about 10–30 juvenile cases a month in each district, coupled with the lack of transportation to police stations, courts, or rehabilitation institutions, "it is next to impossible for probation officers to perform well in studying all cases of juveniles. The time of the probation officer is barely enough to prepare the report to the court."[136]

---

[129] This is not surprising as courts in other countries often disregard the work of probation officers or social workers. This problem has been characterized as follows: "Psychiatrists have a right to complain that courts do not pay enough attention to their evaluation of the accused. Psychiatric testimony is sometimes ignored by the courts, and sometimes it is opposed by other psychiatric testimony so that the testimony of both sides is nullified." Jonas Robitscher, "The Psychiatrist and the Juvenile Court," 52 *Women Lawyer Journal* 147 (1966).

[130] Article 25(3).

[131] Article 48(2).

[132] Second meeting with Ms. Khadra Al-Hour, 25 August 2010, Hebron.

[133] Article 52.

[134] Article 51.

[135] *Cf.* Herschel Prins, "Psychiatric Services and the Magistrates' and Juvenile Courts: An Analysis of the Views of Probation Officers and Magistrates," 15 *British Journal of Criminology* 315 (1975).

[136] Meeting with Ms. Khadra Hour, *supra* note 127. See the testimony of Ms. Anani, *supra* note 101.

Under such circumstances, child protection officers perform on *ad hoc* basis. Sometimes they respond to phone calls from police stations having cases of children in conflict with the law. It is difficult to respond positively when there are a number of police stations in the district in which the child officer functions. In other instances, child officers coordinate between the family and prosecutor. Such officers cannot attend all juvenile hearings, but rather observe selected court sessions.

In order to advance their efficiency, it is estimated that each district needs minimum three child protection officers. At least one officer should work on full-time basis on juvenile justice issues. Now as the juvenile court can no longer be convened without the presence of the child protection officer (Article 25(2) of the Law), hiring more officers cannot be avoided. The Ministry should make transportation available for the officers to visit children at home, school, police stations, detentions, courts, and social care institutions. The work of these officers does not lack legal basis, but it rather requires executive orders and appointing adequate number of qualified staff.[137]

Juvenile Care Institutions

Juvenile care institutions, known among the public in Palestine as "reformatories," are facilities whereby juveniles spend pretrial detention, terms involving deprivation of liberty, or as a treatment or preventive measure.[138] A general stipulation can be found in Article 19, paragraph 2(b.3), of the 2012 Palestinian Amended Child Law that offers basis for the referral of children to a number of social, educational or health institutions, public or private. The Ministry of Social Development manages a number of institutions that provides social care.[139]

Article 43 of the 2016 Juvenile Protection Law provides basis for the referral of juveniles to social care institutions, besides the institutions in which children would be punished or deprived of liberty. This article is not rigid in terms of the type of the institution in which juveniles may be held. It could be "one of the social care houses affiliated with or recognized by the Ministry [of Social Development]" that the court decides to place the juvenile in. Nothing in the law prevents the Ministry from designating selected associations to host children in conflict with law to stay with other children who have social or economic needs, such as orphanages. Experience in different countries proves that the services,

---

[137] Note made by a child officer at the Commission for Human Rights workshop, *supra* note 83.

[138] *Cf.* Jack Stitt, "Correction Facilities for the Juvenile Offender: a Comparison of Ontario and the U.K.," 2 *Osgoode Hall Law Journal* 356 (1963); John MacDonald, "Juvenile Training Schools and Juvenile Justice Policy in British Columbia," 20 *Canadian Journal of Criminology* 418 (1978).

[139] Amer Junaidi, *The Most Significant Stipulations of the Law-Degree Concerning Juvenile Protection* (Defense Children International, Hebron University Law School, 23 March 2016).

rehabilitation, and educational programs of such charities are often more efficient than official bodies.[140] In such institutions, many of which do exist in Palestine,[141] children can stay all days and nights of the week inside the institution where they study, sleep, and play. Children can go off to spend weekends with their families. In parallel, juveniles who breach the law might need to follow special treatment programs in such institutions.

The first juvenile reformatory in the West Bank, "Dar Al-Amal" (in Arabic means "House of Hope") was established in 1954 in Ramallah.[142] What is surprising is that this care institution is still the only boys' institution in the entire West Bank since that time. The second institution is designed for minor females, the "Girls Care House" in Bethlehem. In Gaza, there is Dar Al-Rabi for boys. In the remaining districts, children who have troubles with the law end up in police detention centers or in prisons, as no social care institutions are available therein. This state poses serious concerns on the equality principle with regard to the treatment of children in different areas.

As Dar Al-Amal is located in the center of the West Bank, it could not logistically absorb children from other districts for three reasons. First, Dar Al-Amal, which can host maximum forty children, cannot accommodate the growing number of juveniles as its space, facilities, and employees are not prepared for that. Second, moving children from other districts to Ramallah is difficult, if not impossible, due to Israeli military checkpoints between districts that do not allow Palestinian police to transfer prisoners or detainees freely. The third reason is that detainees, who form the majority among juveniles, need to attend court hearings from time to time and it is not possible to bring them from Ramallah to courts in the north or the south for every hearing. The police alternatively keep children in jails. Hence, the key solution for resolving children incarceration is to open care institutions in other districts.

Dar Al-Amal was established shortly after the enactment of the 1954 Law and functioned until 1967. Under the occupation, it was closed as Israel kept Palestinian prisoners, including children, in its prisons. The institution was reopened after the creation of the Palestinian Authority in 1994, hosting children aged from 12 to 17 years. Most of them come from Ramallah and Jerusalem areas. The House's staff members are public employees working under the supervision of the Ministry of Social Development and distributed for day and night shifts. Technical staff comprises a manger, deputy, social workers, vocational trainers and teachers, psychologists, and supporting staff. Children in the House

---

[140] *Cf.* Jack Foster, "Juvenile Court Referrals to Voluntary Agencies," 12 *Canadian Journal of Corrections* 129 (1970); Katherine Chiste, "Faith-Based Organizations and the Pursuit of Restorative Justice," 32 *Manitoba Law Journal* 27 (2008).

[141] Independent Commission for Human Rights, *Crackdown on Charitable Associations During the State of Emergency* (Special Report No. 55, Ramallah, 2007).

[142] Based on Article 4 of the 1954 Jordanian Juvenile Law.

cannot leave or attend school. Professional training programs are poor. Yet the situation in the House is much better than detention centers or prisons by every standard.[143]

The Girls Care House in Bethlehem, established in 1958 in the context of the 1954 Juvenile Rehabilitation Law, has the mandate to host girls who might come in conflict with the law. It is the only girls' institution designed for this purpose in Palestine.[144] The House was previously called Juvenile Girls Reform Center and was exclusively in charge of hosting females in conflict with the law. Its name changed upon the creation of the Palestinian Authority and it started to host minor females who might need protection other than those who violate the law, such as threatened girls of attacks on "honor" grounds or those who suffer from domestic violence. The number of juvenile girls in Palestine is low.[145] Most female cases are resolvable through conciliation within families. The House is an open facility. Girls can attend school. A number of educational and training programs exist: hairdressing, computer, and swing.

The Girls House's employees work as teachers, social workers, and psychologists, all officials of the Ministry of Social Development. The House is well equipped, including with computers and internet, furnished and organized. It has the capacity to host up to 22 girls. Statistics of previous years range between 26 and 49 girls. The House conditions are much better than the state of Dar Al-Amal, but its staff members lack the experience in dealing with females in conflict with the law.

As part of its attempt to reform the juvenile system, the Ministry of Social Development looks toward rehabilitation institutions. It has for long plans to open two additional institutions for boys, one in Nablus for the north of the West Bank and one in Hebron for the south. But such proposals have not been materialized yet.

---

[143] *Cf.* J. Kraus, "A Comparison of Corrective Effects of Probation and Detention on Male Juvenile Offenders," 14 *British Journal of Criminology* 49 (1974); Michele Lioy, "Open Residences: An Alternative to Closed Correctional Institutions for Hard-Core Juvenile Delinquents," 20 *Canadian Journal of Criminology* 409 (1978).

[144] This institution used to host girls from both the West Bank and Gaza Strip before the closure of the Strip by Israel in 2000 upon the breakout of the *intifada*. Now all inmate girls are from the West Bank.

[145] No statistics are available regarding girls in conflict with the law in Palestine. *Cf.* Mary Riege, "Parental Affection and Juvenile Delinquency in Girls," 12 *British Journal of Criminology* 55 (1972); Nancy Dowd, "Boys, Masculinities and Juvenile Justice," 8 *Journal of Korean Law* 115 (2009).

THE JUDICIAL ADMINISTRATION OF JUVENILE JUSTICE

Juvenile Police

Children have specialized police units under the 2016 Juvenile Protection Law. Article 15 states that: "The gathering of information with regard to juvenile cases or children under the risk of delinquency is carried out by a specialized police in each district … . Specialized child police would be designated by a decision of the Minister of Interior. It shall comprise female officers." This article legalized the *de facto* existence of specialized police over the past few years. A form of specialized juvenile police was set up by a decision of the Police Commissioner in 2009 in four cities and was extended to the rest of the West Bank in 2011.[146] In 2014, juvenile police was merged with the "Family Protection and Juvenile Police Unit."[147] The adoption of the new Juvenile Law turned the presence of juvenile police into a *de jure* existence.

As in other countries, it is "the police officer who has first contact with the majority of delinquent boys."[148] Such contact starts with the arrest, continues during the investigation period, and lasts throughout detention awaiting trial.[149] Both arrest and pretrial detention are dealt with in Palestine in accordance with the Criminal Procedures Law No. 3 of 12 May 2001.[150] The 2016 Juvenile Law refers to the Criminal Procedures Law with regard to the arrest and detention in an identical way to that of adults. There are, however, a few exceptions by which children are treated differently. Juvenile Law requires that minors to be separated from adults while in detention,[151] at court rooms while awaiting trials, and during the transportation to attend court hearings or from one detention to another, or after concluding court sessions.[152] The Law also underlined the obligation of to provide children, upon arrest, with sociopsychological support. In this connection, Article 18 prescribed that "if the child is arrested by the police in cases of flagrante offence, the child should be immediately transferred to the juvenile police." This police should then "notify the child's guardian and the child protection officer." The juvenile police may retain the child maximum for 24 h before transferring him to the prosecution.

---

[146] Defense for Children International, *Juvenile Police in Palestine … , supra* note 7, p. 36.

[147] *Ibid.*, p. 37.

[148] Masaharu Yanagimoto, "The Juvenile Delinquent in Japan," 13 *British Journal of Criminology* 170 (1973), p. 170.

[149] William Kerr, "How the Police Can Prevent Juvenile Crime," 10 *Police Journal* 306 (1937); Ralph S. Boot, "Police Interest in Juvenile Delinquency," 6 *Canadian Journal of Corrections* 50 (1964); Joseph Simpson, "The Police and Juvenile Delinquency," 8 *British Journal of Criminology* 119 (1968).

[150] Palestine Gazette No. 38, 5 September 2001, p. 94.

[151] Article 23(1).

[152] Article 21(3).

The Criminal Procedures Law deals with arrest in ten articles.[153] It stipulates that "no person may be arrested or imprisoned except by order of the competent authority as designated by law. He must be treated in a manner that will preserve his dignity and may not be physically or morally harmed" (Article 29). It further regulates the arrest in cases of flagrant offence, arrest warrant, resisting arrest, and attempt to escape, etc.

It would be useful to develop specific procedures for the arrest of children. To this effect, a regulation by the Council of Ministers or instructions by the Minister of Interior regarding juvenile police may incorporate procedures on the treatment of children. These procedures need to comprise, *inter alia*, the arrest of children in nonviolent means by special police without uniforms and with the presence of a social worker or a psychologist, use civilian cars, prohibit arrest at night or weekends, and make the arrest subject to judicial decision with minimal exceptions. In August 2014, a manual for the police interaction with children which incorporates most of these procedures was developed.[154] Ideally, and with a view to remove any overlapping, the juvenile police should have been placed under the Ministry of Social Development, as the Ministry of Interior is accustomed to deal with security, rather than social, matters.

Children in pretrial detention are held at police facilities. In certain areas, including one Hebron police station and Dar Al-Amal, children stay in detention facilities designated for juveniles.[155] In the north of the West Bank, children are detained in ordinary prisons,[156] with some reports of mixing children with adults.[157] The Law generally bans child's detention. When it is exceptionally exercised, "the prosecution shall order the juvenile's detention to be in a care institution."[158] However, the Law added that "where care institutions are missing, children shall be held in a place designated for juveniles."[159] In practice, holding children in detentions is virtually the rule and juveniles will continue to be detained until care institutions see light.[160] Until the opening of the care institutions, children should not be left to face their destiny. Better places can be found, for instance, by renting locations on temporary basis. The current child detention centers are generally poor.[161]

---

[153] Articles 29 to 38.

[154] Defense for Children International, *Juvenile Police in Palestine …* , *supra* note 7, pp. 38–39.

[155] *Ibid.*, pp. 49 and 51.

[156] *Ibid.*, pp. 39–51.

[157] *Ibid.*, p. 45: "In Nablus children are detained with adults in the same rooms."

[158] Article 20(1).

[159] Article 20(4).

[160] *Cf.* J. Walker & A. Glasner, "The Process of Juvenile Detention: The Training School Act, the Child Welfare Act," 3 *Osgoode Hall Law Journal* 343 (1965).

[161] Defense for Children International, *Incarceration Places for Children in Conflict with the Law in the West Bank between International Standards and Practice* (Ramallah 2013).

The specialized juvenile police needs institutionalization by sitting up legal basis, for example, by introducing provisions on specialized police in regulations or instructions based on the 2016 Law. Coordination between the Ministry of Social Development and the police might be arrived at by an agreement to be reached between the two sides. Police should receive ongoing training on computerized case management systems and be exposed to models of good practices from other countries.[162] Jordan set up in 2008 juvenile police offices in a number of stations in the capital Amman,[163] so this experience might benefit the promising Palestinian juvenile police.

Juvenile Prosecution

As a general rule, the Palestinian law makes no distinction between children and adults regarding investigation and questioning by the prosecution.[164] In both cases, the applicable legislation is the Criminal Procedures Law of 2001. Reference to the function of the prosecution based on the Criminal Procedures Law was made explicit in the 2016 Juvenile Protection Law.[165] Prosecutors operate under the direction of the Attorney General to investigate and indict suspected offenders.[166] The Law obliges prosecutors to investigate the crime upon its commission.[167] Questioning follows and is carried out to get as much detailed crime-related data as possible.[168]

However, a notable development has been marked by President's signature of the Juvenile Protection Law that created, for the first time in the history of Palestine, a juvenile specialized prosecution.[169] Article 18 of the Law stated: "(1) In accordance with this law, there shall be assigned a prosecution in charge of juvenile and child at risk of delinquency in charge of all matters relating to juveniles … . (2) This prosecution shall investigate based the Criminal Procedures Law, as long as such procedures do not contradict this law. The prosecutor shall instruct the child protection officer to carry out necessary tasks and social research to find the truth and to discover child's personality to advance the appropriate means to rehabilitate and protect him." The specialization of child prosecution in the new law was preceded by an interest from the side of the

---

162 Simha Landau, "Juveniles and the Police—Who is Charged Immediately and who is Referred to the Juvenile Bureau," 21 *British Journal of Criminology* 27 (1981).

163 Terre des hommes-Lausanne, *Assessment of the Juvenile Justice System in Jordan* (Amman 2010).

164 Information in this section is mainly drawn from interviews by the writer with prosecutors, police officers, and experts, including a meeting with Palestinian Attorney General.

165 Article 20(1).

166 Mahmoud Shahin, *Report on the Institution of the Palestinian Public Prosecution* (Ramallah 1999).

167 The investigation process is addressed in Articles 55–63 of the Criminal Procedures Law.

168 Questioning is dealt with in Articles 94–105.

169 Meeting with Palestinian Attorney General, Dr. Ahmad Barak, in Ramallah on 12 May 2016.

Attorney General Office to set up such specialized prosecution.[170] To pave the way for such specialization, there have been a number of training courses provided to prosecutors on juvenile justice issues.[171]

Specialized prosecution came in the context of creating specialized police and judiciary. Awaiting full specialization, one or more prosecutor has been already assigned to deal with juvenile justice matters.[172] Specialized prosecution should be institutionalized. This can be achieved by having detailed procedural basis for juvenile prosecution, assign trained prosecutors to work exclusively on juvenile cases, adopt ongoing training and capacity building programs on juvenile justice for prosecutors, develop simplified manual on the special need of children during the investigation and questioning stages, put in place a computerized case management system, and create coordination mechanisms between prosecutors and other actors in the justice chain: police, judges, probation officers, detention facilities, and prisons.[173]

The new Law added a few other tasks to the prosecution in relation to children cases. It instructed prosecutors to review the report of the child protection officer.[174] Prosecutors cannot interrogate a child in the absence of such an officer.[175] The Law also empowered prosecutors to offer mediation on child cases to end the cases if an agreement between the parties is reached, as discussed previously. Other than these exceptions, the treatment of children before prosecution is similar to adults.

In the first 24 h after referring the accused person to him or her, the prosecutor should undertake the questioning.[176] The prosecutor has the option to detain or release the child. It should be noted that, after the arrest by the police, the detained person should be transferred to prosecutor within 24 h.[177] This means that the accused person, including children, might spend 48 h between the police station and the prosecution before the legal determination whether to keep him in detention or release him.[178] All decisions to extend the pretrial detention after the 48-h periods, which might last up to 6 months, must be issued by the competent court.[179]

[170] Ahmad Barak, "Critical Study of Juvenile Justice in the Initial Investigation Phase according to Juvenile Rehabilitation Law No. 15 of 1954 in the Light of Contemporary Criminal Policy," *Justice and Law Review*, No. 11 (Ramallah, April 2009), pp. 11–23.

[171] Nader Said-Foqahha, *A Study of Juvenile Justice in the Occupied Palestinian Territory* (Ramallah 2010), p. 30.

[172] Misheal, *supra* note 87.

[173] *Cf.* Gwynn Davis, Jacky Boucherat, & David Watson, "Pre-Court Decision-Making in Juvenile Justice," 29 *British Journal of Criminology* 219 (1989).

[174] Article 17.

[175] Article 19.

[176] Criminal Procedures Law, Article 105.

[177] *Ibid.*, Article 107.

[178] *Ibid.*, Article 108.

[179] *Ibid.*, Article 120.

There is a lack of coordination between prosecutors and police on juvenile cases. Police often report that prosecutors transfer children to specific prisons instead of indicating that children should be transferred to social institution or to a "place similar to persons of his case." Thus, police has no choice but to detain children. One chief prosecutor, on the other hand, reported that prosecutors never order the detention of children in prison.[180] As the Palestinian Attorney General pointed out, the detention and imprisonment of children will only end after setting up three modern juvenile care situations in the north, south, and central West Bank (besides Dar Al-Amal).[181]

Juvenile Courts

The first "Juvenile court" at the global level was opened at the end of the nineteenth century.[182] Since then, such courts have become well-established institutions in many developed states, such as Japan, Britain, and Canada. According to Adler, in the United States the first child court was operated in Chicago on 1 July 1899.[183] The basis for specialized juvenile judiciary rested in the 1954 Juvenile Rehabilitation Law. Yet Palestinian children had to wait for over six decades until a provision has been explicitly adopted in the 2016 Juvenile Protection Law (Article 24) toward the establishment of specialized juvenile courts with full-time judges dedicated to the issues of children in conflict with the law.[184] This is indeed a breakthrough.

What distinguish the juvenile court from other courts are the requirements that such a court should meet while dealing with children in conflict with the law. According to the 2016 Juvenile Protection Law, juvenile court's hearings should convene in different location and time than those of adult's sessions.[185] Such a court is obliged to obtain a report from a child protection officer.[186] Before the juvenile court, children should be separated from adults.[187] No one is allowed to attend juvenile court's sessions except the child protection officer, child's parents

---

[180] Misheal, *supra* note 87.

[181] Meeting Attorney General, *supra* note 169.

[182] Christian Herter, "Juvenile Courts Needed," 39 *Women Lawyers Journal* 5 (1953); Graham Parker "Some Historical Observations on the Juvenile Court," 9 *Criminal Law Quarterly* 467 (1967); Graham Parker, "The Juvenile Court Movement," 26 *University of Toronto Law Journal* 140 (1976); Jean Trepanier and Francoise Tulkens, "Juvenile Justice in Belgium and Canada at the Beginning of the Century: Two Models or One," 1 *The International Journal of Children's Rights* 189 (1993); Lawrence Wilson, "Jurisdiction of the Juvenile Court," 19 *Criminal Law Quarterly* 203 (1977).

[183] Adler, *supra* note 120, p. 218.

[184] Eileen Younghusband, "The Juvenile Court and the Child," 7 *British Journal Delinquency* 181 (1957); John MacDonald, "Juvenile Court Jurisdiction," 7 *Criminal Law Quarterly* 426 (1965).

[185] Article 27.

[186] Article 25(3). See earlier, section II.2.

[187] Article 21(3).

or guardian, court's staff, and persons directly related to the case.[188] No one is allowed to release information on child's cases, subject to penalties.[189] Juvenile court should pursue certain procedures that differ from those of adults and impose lighter penalties,[190] including a series of noncustodial dispositions.[191] The Law established a system for enforcing juvenile court decisions that ensures the suitability of each judgment for each child on case-by-case basis,[192] including the option of ending the measure after its execution.[193] Courts overseeing children should decide on their cases promptly.[194]

The current situation of children before courts is alarming. There is no separation between children and adults. Children are often handcuffed. Many children have no lawyer. They wait for long periods, up to 1 or 2 years, before receiving final trial, mostly in detention centers or prisons. Judges treat children as criminals, with disrespect, rather than taking their point of view as the main reason of having child courts. Courts are overcrowded. Children are victimized within the slow process.[195]

The foregoing shows that there is an urgent need to create a specialized juvenile judiciary. There is awareness on the necessity of the juvenile courts in the Palestinian High Judicial Council,[196] as a result of civil society activities on this issue, including training and advocacy. Currently, there are a number of trained judges on juvenile issues. What is needed now is to take a decision, as part of the administrative power assigned to the Judicial Council, to establish fully separate juvenile courts with separate buildings from the other courts, with exclusive mandate over children in conflict with law. At least one judge should be assigned as juvenile, full-time, judge in each district. Special education and training, on national and international juvenile justice law and procedure, should be provided. Manuals and guidelines should be designed for judges' use.[197] The estab-

[188] Articles 8 and 30(1). *Cf.* Carol Van Nijnatten, "Behind Closed Doors: Juvenile Hearings in the Netherlands," 3 *International Journal of Law and the Family* 177 (1989).

[189] Articles 31 and 59.

[190] Article 24–35.

[191] Articles 36–46.

[192] Article 47.

[193] Article 51–55.

[194] Article 8.

[195] Dawoud Dirawi & Jihad Shomali, *Juvenile Judiciary between Practice and Legislation* (Ramallah 2004).

[196] The High Judicial Council is the central body that administrates regular courts of various levels in Palestine. Headed by Chief Justice, the Council is independent of the Executive and the Legislator. See Judicial Authority Law No. 1 of 14 May 2002 (Palestine Gazette No. 40, 18 May 2002, p. 9).

[197] Manuals can be prepared based on existing guides developed globally by actors such as UNICEF and United Nations Office on Drugs and Crime, taking into consideration the local law and practice.

lishment of a juvenile court in March 2016 that embedded within the care institution (Dar Al-Amal) in Ramallah is a step forward.[198]

CONCLUSION

In 2011, I published in an Oxford-based journal a study calling for comprehensive reform of the Palestinian juvenile justice system.[199] The study urged the authorities, while dealing with children in conflict with the law, to adhere to the Convention on the Rights of the Child; to respect the United Nations standards on juvenile justice; to adopt a modern legislation that has the foundations for specialized juvenile courts, prosecution, police, and set up a system for mediation/restorative justice and variety of alternatives to incarceration while dealing with children. Now in 2016, with the enactment of the Juvenile Protection Law, these recommendations have been realized in law. It is indeed a historical development to adopt such an advanced legislation that not only consists with international standards that have been for long neglected, but might be also comparable with many progressive juvenile laws in the world.

However, other recommended actions in the aforementioned study, which are related to policy, institutions, infrastructure, and the allocation of human and financial resources, are still awaiting materialization.[200] The Juvenile Protection Law still needs executive regulations, ministerial instructions, and orders for enforcement. The Ministry of Social Development needs to restructure itself and appoint adequate qualified staff members to form Child Protection Unit, Social Defense Office, and child protection officers. Child care institutions should be opened. Trained judges, prosecutors, and police officers should be designated to juvenile cases, with full organizational structures, and adequate logistical facilities that enable them to carry out the tremendous tasks assigned to them by the law. Without taking such measures, the impact of the Law in practice and on the future of children would remain limited. And, consequently, Palestine's commitments under the CRC remain questionable.

With the recent accession of the State of Palestine to the CRC, time has come to undertake a comprehensive modernization process. Such a process is no longer a matter of choice; it is an obligation of the state toward its inhabitants and the international community as a whole. Palestine is obliged to report its reform actions to the UN Committee on Rights of the Child and it will be held accountable in case of nonaction. The juvenile system, which has been long discussed with limited outcomes, lies in the heart of the required reform. The adoption of

---

198 *Al-Hayat Al-Jadida*, No. 7309, 24 March 2016, p. 1.

199 Mutaz Qafisheh, "Juvenile Justice System in Palestine: Current Situation and Reform Prospects," 25 *International Journal of Law, Policy and the Family* 365 (2011).

200 Meeting with Attorney General, *supra* note 169.

the Juvenile Protection Law is the binging for reforming the child justice system; it is not the end.

Mutaz M. Qafisheh is Dean, College of Law & Political Science, and Associate Professor of Public International Law, Hebron University, Hebron, Palestine. Dr. Qafisheh holds Ph.D. in International Law from the Graduate Institute of International and Development Studies in Geneva. He is a Ph.D. Supervisor at University of Exeter School of Law, UK; Member of the International Law Association's ICC Complementarity Committee, London. He is a former Human Rights Officer at the United Nations in Geneva, Beirut, and Ramallah; Regional Director for the Middle East and North Africa of Penal Reform International, Amman; and Legal Advisor to the Palestinian Parliament. He published 6 books and over 30 refereed articles in Oxford, Cambridge, The Hague, London, Oslo and elsewhere. All translations are done by the writer.

24

Turkey

Neylan Ziyalar and Can Çalıcı

INTRODUCTION

Being that the country is located between Europe and the Middle East, Turkey is important geopolitically. According to the results of an address-based population registration system, Turkey's population is 78,741,053. Ninety-two percent of the country's population lives in cities, with the median age being 31 years. Turkey has a majority youth population, and projections demonstrate that this trend will continue for the next 3 decades (TURKSTAT 2015a, b). The country suffers social problems such as educational-related issues, unemployment, and juvenile delinquency, similar to other countries with youth majorities. Current data shows that the number of children between 12 and 17 years old in prison is 2416, and one in three of them is convicted of theft (Republic of Turkey Ministry of Justice General Directorate of Prisons and Detention Houses 2016).

Turkey has had juvenile laws in place since 1979. However, the country did not see significant reforms in its juvenile justice system until it ratified the Convention on the Rights of Children in 1994. The Child Protection Law came into force in 2005 in order to provide protection for children involved in the justice system as perpetrators, victims, or witnesses at any phase of legal process.

At the same time, a new Criminal Code and the Code of Criminal Procedure, as essential parts of new legal reforms of Turkey, were enforced. Although there has been a radical transformation over the last decade in the Turkish Juvenile Justice System there are still significant inadequacies, especially on alternative sanctions and probation services in practice.

This chapter will discuss the organizational structure and processes of the Turkish Juvenile Justice System. We include statistical information about juveniles involved in crime, the principles of juvenile law and the problems with its

N. Ziyalar (✉) • C. Çalıcı
Division of Social Sciences, Istanbul University Institute of Forensic Sciences, Istanbul, Turkey
e-mail: neylan@istanbul.edu.tr

S.H. Decker, N. Marteache (eds.), *International Handbook of Juvenile Justice*,
DOI 10.1007/978-3-319-45090-2_24

application, juvenile courts, and recent reform efforts. The terminology of this chapter is based on UNICEF'S terminology for the Turkish Juvenile Justice System on UNICEF's web site (UNICEF 2009).

The Legal Status of Juveniles

The Turkish criminal justice system treats juvenile offenders, as well as those who are victims or witnesses of crime, differently from adults. This is in accordance with international standards based on the fact that children possess unique characteristics and thus should be treated distinctively in any process of the criminal justice system such as investigation, prosecution, and execution.

In 2005, the *Child Protection Law (CPL)* was drafted and adopted in response to recommendations made by the Committee on the Rights of the Child to align Turkish laws with the Convention on the Rights of the Child. The Child Protection Law aims "to regulate the procedures and principles with regard to protecting juveniles who are in need of protection (any juvenile whose physical, mental, moral, social or emotional development and personal safety is in danger, who are neglected or abused, or who are victims of crime) or who are juvenile offenders (any juvenile about whom an investigation or prosecution is carried out on the allegation that he/she has committed an act which is defined as a crime in the laws, or any juvenile about whom a security measure has been decided due to an act he/she has committed), and ensuring their rights and well-being."

The CPL reflects an important first step taken by the Turkish government at integrating international standards into the procedures and principles of the Turkish Juvenile Justice System. Empowering the Turkish juvenile justice system is listed as a priority area on the *Ministry of Justice Judicial Reform Strategy 2009* and *2010–2014 Strategic Plan*.

> *Child protection law no. 5395*
> *Purpose*
> *Article 1—(1) The purpose of this law is to regulate the procedures and principles with regard to protecting juveniles who are in need of protection or who are pushed to crime and ensuring their rights and wellbeing.*
> *Scope*
> *Article 2—(1) This law covers the provisions related to the principles and procedures of the measures that will be taken with regard to juveniles who are in need of protection and the safety of measures to be applied with regard to juveniles push to crime, along with the establishment, duties and capacities of juvenile courts.*

Juvenile Justice in Turkey is aimed at integrating juvenile offenders into the community, instead of punishing them. Such an approach is adopted to prevent recidivism among juveniles.

In accordance with Child Protection Law:

> *Article 22—(1) The juvenile, his/her parent, guardian, court assigned social worker, the family that has assumed the care of juvenile, or if the juvenile cared for by the Agency, the representative of the Agency may be present at the hearing,*
> *(2) The court or the judge may allow a social worker to accompany the juvenile during the juvenile's interrogation or during other procedures regarding the juvenile (CPL 2005).*

According to the *Turkish Code of Criminal Procedure* (TCCP) article 236 (3), it is mandatory to provide an attorney during trials involving juvenile victims. There also has to be a defense attorney present during trials of juvenile offenders (TCCP 188 (1)). Further, Article 22 (3) of the Child Protection Law and Article 196 (3) of the Turkish Code of Criminal Procedure allows for any juvenile present at the hearing to be taken outside the courtroom if his/her interests require so. Additionally, a juvenile whose interrogation procedures are completed is not required to be present at the hearing (CPL 2005). Regarding Article 21 of the Turkish Press Code, during a criminal proceeding, the principal statement of a juvenile cannot be presented to the public.

The investigation procedure of a juvenile may begin with an announcement, complaint, or ex officio, similar to an adult criminal justice procedure. Juveniles have the right to petition in cases where they are victims of a crime without needing the permission from their custodians; they may also use this right with their legal representatives (Artuk et al. 2007). Following Supreme Court decisions, custodians are unable to withdraw a complaint by themselves.

Juvenile victims, like juvenile offenders, also have the right to legal aid. This is needed when the victim's statement is taken during the investigation and prosecution stages of a case, when juveniles are often required to tell of his/her victimization more than once. Such experiences are detrimental to the juveniles and cause revictimization. For that reason victims often hesitate to report the crime or to ask for help. Thus, juvenile justice professionals need to be aware that recording a statement from a juvenile victim is a sensitive issue and arrangements need to be made so as to avoid revictimization. When interviewing juvenile victims it is necessary to consider their age, cognitive development, and the effects of the trauma that they may be suffering from (Ziyalar 2006).

According to Article 32 of Child Protection Law, the interviewer who takes the statement of a juvenile victim has to be educated on this subject and must have the skills to prevent secondary victimization. During the interrogation of the juvenile, he/she may be accompanied by a psychology, psychiatry, medical, or pedagogy specialist in order to protect him/her. The Turkish Code of Criminal Procedure Law also mandates that audio and video recording of statements are taken (TCCP Article 52(3), 236 (3)).

During the interrogation the specialists must explain the procedures clearly, in an age-appropriate language that the juvenile is able to understand. This procedure applies both to juvenile offenders and juveniles in need of protection. The main role of the specialist is to prevent secondary victimization of juveniles (İşeri 2006). Therefore, it is essential to provide opportunities for the specialist to communicate with juveniles in a convenient place before the interview.

In accordance to established procedures, the statement of the juvenile should be audio and video recorded. If the need for another interview arises due to insufficient data or defects with the recording, the juvenile is required to appear in court (Centel & Zafer 2008). In principle, trials are open to the public. However, this causes issues for juvenile victims, who must talk about their victimization experience in front of the perpetrator and other people. Whenever deemed necessary for public morality or public security, the court may rule that the main hearing be conducted partly or totally closed to the public (TCCP Article 182).

It is essential to ensure confidentiality of juvenile offenders and juvenile victims at both the investigation and prosecution phases. Based on Article 21 of the Press Law, publishing the identities of perpetrators and victims under the age of 18 years is prohibited. In sexual abuse cases where the victim is a juvenile and the accused is an adult, conducting closed hearings is found to be appropriate.

A witness is defined as a person who has information about a crime based on one or more of his/her five senses. Juveniles can be called as witnesses and asked to testify. In such cases, even though they are witnesses of a crime and not direct victims of crime, they are considered to be juveniles in need of protection (Uluğtekin 2004).

If a juvenile is a relative of the defendant, he/she can refuse to be a witness as this can be traumatic for him/her (TCPP art. 45). In such cases, juveniles need to be informed of their right to refuse to testify. If a juvenile is unable to understand the importance of refraining from testifying, his/her legal representative can do so. The judge can also decide if a juvenile should refuse to give a testimony or not.

In accordance with the Turkish Code of Criminal Procedure Article 52, juveniles under 15 can testify without oath, and their testimony must be audio and video recorded. If testifying in front of the defendant and other people pose a threat to the juvenile witness, the court is required to arrange a safe environment for the hearing to be conducted without others present (Ünver & Hakeri 2012). In those cases the recording is presented to others who have the right to be in court and ask questions. If there is a risk that the juvenile victim will not be able to tell the truth in the presence of the defendant, the court is allowed to exclude the defendant from the courtroom during the interrogation and hearing (TCCP art. 200).

Age of Majority

The United Nations' Convention on the Rights of the Child defines a child as a person under 18 years of age. According to Beijing Rules, "A juvenile is a child or young person who, under the respective legal system, may be dealt with for an offense in a manner which is different from an adult." According to the Turkish Criminal Code 5237 Article 31 and Child Protection Law 5395 Article 3, a juvenile is defined as "any individual that has not yet completed age 18, regardless of whether they have reached full legal age earlier" (UNICEF 2010).

Juvenile offenders who lack "penal liability" are ruled by the Criminal Code and Child Protection Law. From the perspective of criminal responsibility, the minimum age for penal liability is 12 years. The minimum age is set to 15 years for disabled juveniles. If a juvenile under the age of 12 years commits a crime only security measures can be applied. Such children may not be put under the supervision of probation officers, but similar services should be made available by the Social Services and Child Protection Agency (UNICEF 2010). For juvenile offenders who are over the age of 12 years but not yet 15 years old, an evaluation is required to determine if they have criminal responsibility or not. According to Article 63 of the TCPP, this evaluation is undertaken by the judge. However, the judge can consult a specialist and use social inquiry reports to make a decision (UNICEF 2010).

The Country's Stance Toward the UN Committee on the Rights of the Child

There are a number of international guidelines that focus specifically on juvenile justice. In 1985 the *United Nations Standard Minimum Rules for the Administration of Juvenile Justice ("The Beijing Rules")* were approved. Following this, in 1989, the *United Nations Convention on the Rights of the Child (UNCRC)* was declared. Soon after, the *United Nations Guidelines for the Prevention of Juvenile Delinquency (Riyadh Guidelines)* and the *United Nations Rules for the Protection of Juveniles Deprived of their Liberty (Havana Rules)* were ratified in 1990. Finally, the *European Convention on the Exercise of Children's Rights* came into force in 1996 (Gemalmaz 2002).

Turkey is signatory to all of the conventions mentioned earlier. Soon after Turkey ratified the UNCRC in 1994, Turkey's justice system underwent serious changes, and in 1995 the Convention on the Rights of the Child was integrated into the domestic law. Further, as explained in Sect. 1 of this chapter, the last two decades have seen significant legislative changes in the Turkish Juvenile Justice System.

Trends in Juvenile Crime Over the Period 2004–2014

In Turkey, statistics regarding the number of prosecutions, trials, and sentencing of juvenile offenders, juvenile arrestees and prisoners are collected by the Ministry of Justice. The data are published by the Turkish Statistical Institute annually in two volumes: "Judicial Statistics" and "Prison Statistics." Additionally, the Ministry of Justice General Directorate of Prisons and Detention Houses publishes on its official web site the current population of the arrestees and convicts.

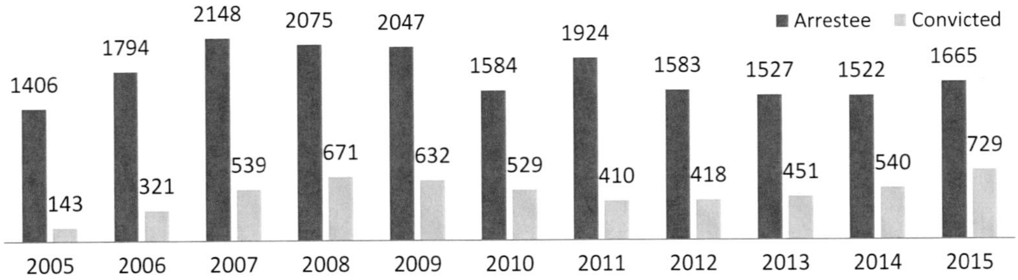

GRAPH 24.1. The juvenile population (12–17 years of age) in prison between the years 2005 and 2015. Source: Republic of Turkey Ministry of Justice General Directorate of Prisons and Detention Houses 2016.

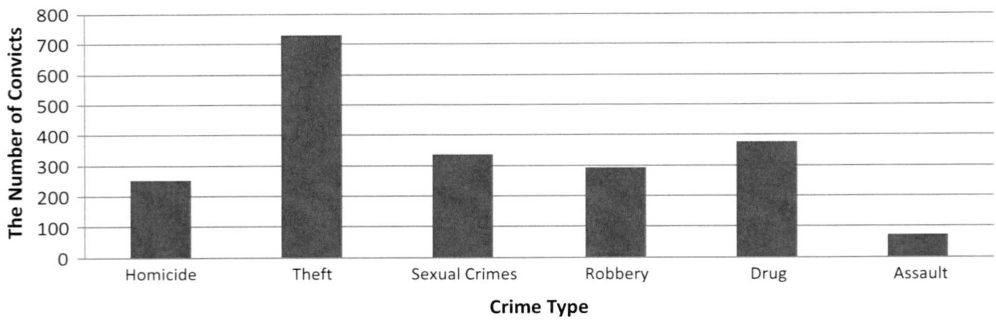

GRAPH 24.2. Juvenile population in prison by crime types by the year 2016. Source: Republic of Turkey Ministry of Justice General Directorate of Prisons and Detention Houses 2016.

According to the Ministry of Justice General Directorate of Prisons and Detention Houses, the number of juvenile arrestees has been undulating during the period 2005–2015, while the number of juvenile convicts has been increasing year by year. The number of juvenile convicts in 2015 is five times higher than in 2005 (see Graph 24.1). The most common crime committed is theft, followed by drug offenses, sex crimes, robbery, homicide, and assault (see Graph 24.2).

The Turkish Statistical Institute's data shows that, in the past 5 years, the percent of juvenile offenders convicted for theft has been increasing, while the percent of juveniles convicted for robbery has been decreasing. Accordingly, between the years 2004 and 2010 the most frequent crime type was robbery, but since 2010 theft has been leading consistently. During this same time period, homicide has been declining, and assault has remained stable. Finally, sex crimes increased considerably from 2012 to 2013 (see Table 24.1).

Causes of Juvenile Crime

It is essential to determine the causes of juvenile crime in order to prevent delinquency. Research in Turkey has shown three main groups of factors influencing juvenile delinquency: demographic, socioeconomic, and familial (Taşkıran &

Table 24.1. Juvenile convicts received into juvenile prison and reformatory by type of crime, 2004–2013 (%)

Type of crime	*2004*	*2005*	*2006*	*2007*	*2008*	*2009*	*2010*	*2011*	*2012*	*2013*
Homicide	13.5	13.9	21.8	8.9	9.1	5.2	4.6	11.7	6.0	6.6
Theft	15.3	14.4	15.4	19.9	28.2	29.8	33.6	36.2	39.0	43.1
Sexual crimes	17.1	16.8	12.8	14.8	8.2	6.4	4.2	2.1	2.7	8.0
Assault	2.1	2.5	3.8	5.9	2.1	2.0	3.6	2.3	2.2	2.6
Robbery	40.1	46.5	35.9	42.4	39.9	41.6	34.0	29.8	38.5	25.9
Other	12.0	5.9	10.3	8.1	12.6	15.0	20.0	17.9	11.5	13.9

Source: Turkish Statistical Institute Prison Statistics, 2014

Ağaoğlu 1943; Şensoy 1947; Gölcüklü 1962; Saran 1968; Yavuzer 1981; Uluğtekin 1991; Avcı 2008).

Young age has been shown to be related with criminal behavior (Yücel 1989; Yenisey 1992). For this reason, one of the major causes of juvenile delinquency in Turkey is the age structure of Turkey's population. According to TURKSTAT's Address Based Registration System, every 1 in 4 Turkish citizens is between ages 0 and 14 (TURKSTAT 2015a, b).

Just like adult delinquency, juvenile delinquency is related to social and individual factors such as behavioral and psychological problems. Juvenile homelessness, drug abuse and addiction, and school dropout are serious risk factors related to juvenile delinquency (Ada 2007; Yıldız 2007).

Juveniles in households where families are fragmented or parents are separated are at a higher risk of committing crime, due to the lack of sufficient family control and the low intrafamily communication generated by that situation (Ada 2007; Avcı & Güçray 2010). Being deprived of efficient parental care as a result of divorce, death, or separation of parents; growing in bad economic conditions; having low educated, drug abuser, or delinquent parents; and being raised in a multichild family are related with abuse and neglect, which are the dominant risk factors of criminal acts during childhood (Yavuzer 1988; Bayındır et al. 2007; Akbaba 2011; Karakuş & Tekin 2012).

On the other hand, some researchers emphasize the social environment and the influence of peers as other important determinants of juvenile delinquency (Acar et al. 2015). Child labor also plays an impressive and negative role on juvenile delinquency: juveniles who are working on the streets or at inappropriate work places for their age have a heightened risk of committing crime (Kuntay 2002; Erbay 2010).

Other factors include rapid societal changes and new social norms due to the country's urbanization and industrialization patterns. In this context it is possible to suggest that rural to urban migration has had a specific effect on Turkish juvenile crime. Due to the level of unemployment and terrorist issues, there has been a dense mobility since the 1950s until today from eastern to western regions, which are more industrialized and urbanized (Erkan & Erdoğdu 2006). According to a Report of the Turkish Grand National Assembly (TGNA), the lack of sufficient education, cultural conflicts caused by internal and external migrations, squatting, economic crisis, fragmented families, and child labor are the main environmental factors associated with migration, which in turn is related to juvenile delinquency (TGNA 2010).

Social and economic inequality also has a direct impact on juvenile delinquency. It has been observed that over the last 2 decades juvenile offenders have mostly been involved in theft crime (Ada 2007; Özbay 2008).

Finally, exposure to violence is another significant component of juvenile crimes. As pointed out in the Report of Turkish Grand National Assembly, juveniles who used to be victims of crime often engage in crime themselves (TGNA 2010).

Policing Juveniles

Law enforcement duties related to juveniles should be carried out by the juvenile units of law enforcement. The personnel in the juvenile units of law enforcement should be provided with training by their own agencies on topics such as juvenile law, prevention of juvenile delinquency, child development and psychology, and social services (CPL 2005).

In cases involving a juvenile offender, the police must notify the child's parents or guardian, the Social Services and Child Protection Agency, and the Bar Association at the beginning of the investigation.

According to Article 65 of the Child Protection Law the investigation of offenses allegedly committed by persons under the age of 18 must be carried out by a prosecutor "assigned to the juvenile bureau." The juvenile bureau is a unit of prosecutors assigned to cases involving juvenile offenders. Such bureaus have been established in big cities in Turkey. In places that lack these juvenile bureaus, the head prosecutor simply assigns one member of the office to cases involving juveniles (UNICEF 2009).

Courts and Juveniles

The Child Protection Law has established procedures and principles for the protection of juveniles who come into contact with the justice system as victims, witnesses, or offenders. The CPL also dictates safety measures applied to juvenile offenders, along with the establishment, duties, and capacities of juvenile courts to ensure their rights and well-being. The protective and supportive measures are taken by the Ministry of Family and Social Policies, the Ministry of National Education, the Ministry of Labour and Social Security, the Ministry of Health, the Ministry of Justice, local municipalities, and state institutions and organizations. This section of the chapter will provide a brief overview of the main actors of the Juvenile Justice System and their missions.

Juvenile judge: The judge of the juvenile court which renders the decisions for the measures that will be taken with regard to juvenile offenders and juveniles that are in need of protection, except for those about whom prosecution procedures have been started.

Juvenile courts: The first juvenile court of law in Turkey was passed in 1979 with the law number 2253 and was valid up until the establishment of CPL in 2005. These courts aim to protect juveniles before and after the commission of an offense by providing sentences of security and/or protective measures in order to integrate juveniles back in their communities. There are two different types of juvenile courts in Turkey. Ordinary courts are moderated by a single judge, and courts for serious crimes, including homicide, sexual assault, and armed robbery, are moderated by a panel of three judges. Both types of juvenile courts may have more than one chamber, if the caseload so requires (UNICEF 2005).

It is preferred to appoint judges specialized in juvenile law who are trained in the fields of child psychology and social services, and who have experience in those fields to juvenile courts. The staff of juvenile courts includes social workers who prepare social inquiry reports (UNICEF 2009).

Juvenile courts have jurisdiction for both criminal and civil cases. Juvenile courts administer the actions filed with regard to juvenile offenders, for crimes falling under the jurisdiction of basic penal courts and penal courts of peace. Courts and juvenile judges have the duty to take the necessary measures specified in Child Protection Law. In addition, juvenile courts are in charge of custody, tutorship, and guardianship (Usta 2012).

Juvenile heavy penal courts: Juvenile heavy penal courts shall have one presiding judge and two members. Juvenile heavy penal courts shall administer suits related to crimes committed by juveniles and falling under the jurisdiction of the heavy penal court (CPL 2005).

Public Prosecutor's juvenile bureau: A juvenile bureau shall be established at the Chief Public Prosecutor's Office. An adequate number of Public prosecutors shall be assigned to this bureau by the Chief Public prosecutor, from among those who have specialized in juvenile law and have a grasp on juvenile psychology (CPL 2005).

Lawyer appointed by the bar association: The right to an attorney is key element of the right to a fair trial. In Turkey, the Bar Association must be advised at the beginning of legal proceedings concerning juveniles suspected or accused of an offense. If the juvenile does not have his/her own attorney, then one will be assigned by the Bar Association (UNICEF 2009).

Article 6 of the European Convention on Human Rights, Article 40 of the Child Protection Law, and Articles 150 and 239 of the Turkish Code of Criminal Procedure regulate the appointment of a legal attorney by the bar association, for those who cannot afford a lawyer. It is mandatory to appoint an attorney for juveniles. However, most of the assigned attorneys are inexperienced, and they are not required to have special training on the relevant laws involving children.

Social workers: Based on articles 33–35 of the CPL, the Ministry of Justice shall appoint an adequate number of social workers to juvenile courts and juvenile heavy penal courts, from among candidates who have completed at least an undergraduate program. Those who have completed graduate programs on child and family problems, juvenile law, and juvenile delinquency shall be given preference. Social workers are required to accompany the juvenile during interrogations. Social workers carry out inquiries about the juvenile assigned to them and are required to submit social inquiry reports for the assigned authorities. Social Inquiry Reports describe the juvenile's individual characteristics and social environment and are taken into account by the court when assessing a juvenile's criminal capacity. They are also taken into consideration by the court when making decisions in the best interest of the juveniles (CPL 2005).

Custodial Rules of Juveniles

The Child Protection Law requires juveniles detained by law enforcement agencies to be kept in special rooms, separate from detained adults. The use of handcuffs on juveniles is prohibited by the law. Juveniles have the right to be visited by family members while they are in detention.

"The Law on The Execution of Penalties and Security Measures (LEPSM)" regulates juvenile execution institutes. These institutions conduct education and training for minors between 12 and 18 years old.

Juveniles serve their sentences in closed juvenile penal execution institutions and reformatories. Juveniles between 12 and 18 years old are sheltered in these institutions and should be separated according to their gender and level of physical development. These institutions must contain classrooms, a library, a separate cafeteria, a kitchen, a laundry room, and therapy rooms (Yücel 2016). In Turkey there are only three closed penal execution institutions for juveniles in Ankara, İzmir, and İstanbul (Yücel 2016).

Reformatories are institutions where convicted minors are educated in order to achieve social integration. These institutions have no barriers against escape; the security of these institutions is provided by internal security personnel. In case of attending an education or training program within or outside the institution minors may be allowed to stay in these facilities after they turn 18, and until they are 21 years of age, so that they may complete their education and training. There are two reformatories in Turkey, one in Ankara and one İzmir. The capacity of these institutions is between 100 and 250 minors (Akyüz 2013). Recently, a UNICEF report stated that neither the number nor the quality of the reformatories is adequate. As a result, some minors are sent to prisons instead of reformatories (Çoban 2016).

Rehabilitation and education programs must be made available to arrested and convicted juveniles. These programs must follow the laws and conventions that regulate the rights of juvenile arrestees and convicts, such as the right to have medical services, education, self-improvement, the right to demand information, communicate with their families, stay separate from adult convicts, etc. However, it is questionable whether in reality juveniles are able to use their rights. For instance, it has been observed that the right to have medical services is not offered properly, and that routine medical services are not always available due to the lack of enough healthcare personnel. Another issue is the implementation of the right to receive an education. Arrested juveniles who are in a closed penal execution institutions are not able to continue their education

Juveniles must be hosted in penal execution institutions according to their age, gender, and level of physical development. However, in some cases when there is no juvenile execution institution available, juveniles may stay in a separate section of an adult execution institution. It has been observed that sometimes adults are sheltered in the same sections as the juveniles and use them to run their own errands (Berktin 2010).

Unfortunately all the concerns mentioned in this section have not been solved yet and it is of the utmost importance to develop new policies focused on the best interest of juveniles.

Alternative Sanctions for Juveniles

In 2007 Turkey created a probation system in order to implement Restorative Justice Practices, just like many other countries around the world. According to the Ministry of Justice General Directorate of Prisons and Detention Houses Department of Probation (2015), The Branch Directorate Responsible for Juvenile and Youth Probation Procedures:

- Follows the execution of probation sentences given to the juvenile.
- Follows the rehabilitation process of juvenile probationers within society.
- Follows the work of juvenile probationers and takes precautions to avoid recidivism of juvenile offenders under probation.
- Helps resocialization of juvenile offenders/probationers.
- Collaborates with all stakeholders, i.e., Ministry of justice, other Ministries, governmental and nongovernmental institutions/organizations, and other professionals in relation to probation of juvenile probationers.

In the Turkish Justice System, the main probation measures for juveniles are Judicial Control, Delaying the pronouncement of the judgment, Suspension of Sentence, and Parole. Probation orders can only be given by the judge. Additionally, the probation system offers alternatives to short-term confinement in order to prevent social exclusion of the juvenile. Alternative sanctions for juveniles are limited and are not regulated in the CPL. These sanctions are available for both adults and juveniles and are regulated in the Turkish Criminal Code (2005) Article 50:

ARTICLE 50 - (1) Short-term imprisonment may be converted to the following punishments according to the personality, social and economic status of the convict, repentance shown by him during the trial period and qualifications of the offense;

a) *Administrative fine.*
b) *Reimbursement of overall loss encountered by the aggrieved party or public, reinstatement or compensation of damages.*
c) *Admittance to an educational institution for a period of at least 2 years to improve professional skills or to learn art by providing shelter.*
d) *Prohibition from traveling to certain places and to conduct certain activities for a period up to half of the imposed punishment.*
e) *In case of commission of an offense by misuse of rights and powers or by failing to take proper care and necessary precautions: seizure of driving license and other license certificates and prohibition from performing certain professions or art for a period from one half up to one fold of the imposed punishment.*
f) *Voluntary employment in a job performed for public interest for a period from one half up to one fold of the imposed punishment (Turkish Criminal Code* 2005*).*

According to statistical data of the Ministry of Justice General Directorate of Prisons and Detention Houses Department of Probation, by 2015 the total number of convicts who had benefited from probation services was 226.970. While 215.633 of these beneficiaries were adults 11.377 of them were juveniles. In other words, for every 100 adults that benefit from probation, there are only five juvenile offenders who benefit from it (Republic of Turkey Ministry of Justice General Directorate of Prisons and Detention Houses Department of Probation 2015).

Differences in Treatment of Boys and Girls

In Turkey, the number of adult female convicts is much lower than the number of male convicts. However, in the past few years this figure has been raising fast: while in 2012 there were 4539 females in penal execution institutions, in 2015 this number reached 6501. Following the same trend, in Turkey most juvenile offenders and the majority of juveniles in prison are boys. Considering the current data of the Turkish Republic Ministry of Justice, there are 21 girls convicts and 57 girls arrestees between the ages 12 and 18 (Giray Sözen 2016).

There are five female closed penal execution institutions and three open penal execution institutions in which convicted and arrestee women and girls are housed in Turkey. "Bozkurt Reformatory" is the only one where is just for convicted girls (ages 12–18) (Giray Sözen 2016).

Its right to emphasize that girls and boys have the same rights and are treated equally during all stages of prosecution and investigation, and in the whole Turkish Juvenile Justice System. The problems and disadvantages of penal execution institutions mentioned earlier are the same for both boys and girls.

REFERENCES

Acar, G., Demir, A., Görmez, D., & Keser, İ. (2015). Aile ve Çocuk Suçluluğu İlişkisi. *Hacettepe University Faculty of Health Sciences Journal, 1*(2), 651–656.

Ada, Ş. (2007). Suçlu Çocukların Türkiye Profili. In A. Solak (Ed.), *Okullarda Şiddet ve Çocuk Suçluluğu Profili* (pp. 297–319). Ankara: Hegem Yayınları.

Akbaba, T. (2011). Kartal-Kadıköy Bölgesi Çocuk Suçluluğu Profili. Doktora tezi. Marmara Üniversitesi.

Akyüz, E. (2013). *Çocuk Hukuku*. Ankara: Pegem Yayınevi.

Artuk, M. E., Gökcen, A., & Yenidünya, A. C. (2007). *Ceza hukuku, Genel Hükümler: Ceza hukukuna giriş, ceza hukuku kurallarının uygulama alanı, suç teorisi, yaptırım hukuku; 5237 sayılı yeni TCK'.ya göre Hazırlanmış*. Ankara: Turhan Yayıncılık.

Avcı, M. (2008). Tutuklu Çocuklar Üzerine Bir Araştırma: Çocukların Suça Yönelmesinde Etkili Olan Toplumsal Nedenler ve Çözüm Önerileri. *Atatürk Üniversitesi Sosyal Bilimler Enstitüsü Dergisi, 11*(1), 67–70.

Avcı, R., & Güçray, S. (2010). Şiddet davranışı gösteren ve göstermeyen ergenlerin ailelerinin aile işlevleri, aile bireylerine ilişkin problemler, öfke ve öfke ifade tarzları açısından incelenmesi. *Kuram ve Uygulamada Eğitim Bilimleri, 10*(1), 45–76.

Bayındır, N., Özel, A., & Köksal, E. (2007). Çocuk Suçluluğu Demografisi: Kütahya Şehri Örneği. *Polis Bilimleri Dergisi, 9*(4), 95–108.

Berktin, H. (2010). Uluslararsı Sözleşmeler ve Türk Hukuk Mevzuatı Açısından Çocuk Cezaevlerinin Hukuki Durumu. In E. Gürsoy (Ed.), *Hapishane Kitabı* (pp. 376–384). İstanbul: Kitabus Yayınevi.

Centel, N., & Zafer, H. (2008). *Ceza Muhakemesi Hukuku*. İstanbul: Beta Yayıncılık.

Çoban, S. (2016). Juvenile justice system in Turkey. *International Journal of Social Science and Humanity, 6*(5), 351.

CPL Child (Juvenile) Protection Law. (2005). Retrieved November 24, 2015, from https://assets.hcch.net/upload/abduct2011cp_tr3.pdf.

Erbay, E. (2010). Çocuk İşçi Olmak. In K. İnan (Ed.), *"Çocuk İşçiliğine Retrospektif Bir Bakış" Türkiye'de Çocuk Emeği*. İstanbul: Ütopya Yayınları.

Erkan, R., & Erdoğdu, M. Y. (2006). Göç ve çocuk suçluluğu. *Sosyal Politika Çalışmaları Dergisi, 9*(9), 79–90.

Gemalmaz, M. S. (2002). *Çocuk ve Genç Haklarına İlişkin Ulusalüstü Belgeler (Bölgesel Sistemler)*. İstanbul: İstanbul Barosu Yayınları.

Giray Sözen, F. (2016). Kadın Suçluluğuna Güncel Bakış. In D. Yücel & B. Gönültaş (Eds.), *Adli Sosyal Hizmet Yaklaşım ve Müdahele* (pp. 155–164). Ankara: Nobel Yayınclık.

Gölcüklü, F. (1962). *Türkiye'de Çocuk Suçluluğu Hakkında Bir Araştırma*. Ankara: Sevinç.

İşeri, E. (2006). *Duygusal İstismar, Çocuk İstismarı ve İhmaline Multidisipliner Yaklaşım*. Ankara: Çocuk İstismarı ve İhmalini Önleme Derneği.

Karakuş, Ö., & Tekin, H. H. (2012). Çocuk Koruma Kanunu Uyarınca Haklarında Danışmanlık Tedbiri Uygulanan Çocukların Özellikleri. *Sosyal Politika Çalışmaları, 7*(29), 29–44.

Kuntay, E. (2002). Family Backgrounds of Teenage Female Sex Workers in Istanbul Metropolitan Area. *Journal of Comparative Family Studies, 33*(3), 345–358.

Özbay, Ö. (2008). Strain, social bonding theories and delinquency. *Cumhuriyet University Journal of Social Sciences, 32*(1), 1–16.

Republic of Turkey Ministry of Justice General Directorate of Prisons and Detention Houses. (2016). *Statistics*. Retrieved April 14, 2016, from http://www.cte.adalet.gov.tr/.

Republic of Turkey Ministry of Justice General Directorate of Prisons and Detention Houses Department of Probation. (2015). *Probation in Turkey*. Retrieved June 12, 2016, from http://cep-probation.org/wp-content/uploads/2015/09/PROBATION-in-TURKEY.pdf.

Republic of Turkey Ministry of Justice General Directorate of Prisons and Detention Houses Department of Probation Statistics. (2015). Retrieved June 08, 2016, from http://www.cte-ds.adalet.gov.tr/istatistik/2015/aralik_2015.pdf.

Saran, N. (1968). *Istanbul Şehrinde Polisle İlgisi Olan On Sekiz Yaşından Küçük Çocukların Sosyo-kültürel Özellikleri Hakkında Bir Araştırma*. İstanbul: Taş Matbaası.
Şensoy, N. (1947). Çocuk Suçluluğunun Aktüel Durumu ve Çocuklar Tarafından İşlenen Suçlar. *İstanbul Üniversitesi Hukuk Fakültesi Mecmuası, 13*(3), 867–892.
Taşkıran, T., & Ağaoğlu, S. (1943). *Suçlu çocuklarımız: Ankara çocuk ıslah evinde bir araştırma*. Ankara: Titaş.
TGNA (Turkish Grand National Assembly). (2010). Retrieved June 06, 2016, from https://www.tbmm.gov.tr/komisyon/insanhaklari/belge/cocuk_ve_genclik.pdf.
Turkish Criminal Code. (2005). Retrieved December 12, 2015, from http://www.legislationline.org/documents/section/criminal-codes.
TURKSTAT. (2014). *Turkish Statistical Institute Prison Statistics*. Retrieved April 16, 2016, from http://www.turkstat.gov.tr/PreTablo.do?alt_id=1070.
TURKSTAT (2015). Retrieved June 04, 2016, from http://www.tuik.gov.tr/PreHaberBultenleri.do?id=21507.
TURKSTAT. (2015). *Address based registration system*. Retreived May, 13, 2016, from http://www.turkstat.gov.tr/PreTablo.do?alt_id=1059#.
Uluğtekin, S. (1991). *Hükümlü çocuk ve yeniden toplumsallaşma*. Ankara: Bizim Büro.
Uluğtekin, S. (2004). *Juvenile Courts and Social Examination Reports*. Ankara: Union of Bars of Turkey Publication.
UNICEF. (2005). Retrieved February 08, 2016, from http://www.unicef.org.tr/mwg-internal/de5f-s23hu73ds/progress?id=0gz4r5eMTm.
UNICEF. (2009). Retrieved December 12, 2015, from http://www.unicef.org/ceecis/UNICEF_JJTurkey08.pdf.
UNICEF. (2010). *Ceza Sorumluluğunun Değerlendirilmesi Rehberi*. Ankara: Dumat Ofset.
Ünver, Y., & Hakeri, H. (2012). *Ceza Muhakemesi Hukuku (Penal Procedure Law)*. İstanbul: Adalet Yayınevi.
Usta, S. (2012). *Çocuk Hakları ve Velayet (Child Rights and Guardianship)*. İstanbul: On İki Levha Yayıncılık.
Yavuzer, H. (1981). *Psiko-Sosyal Açıdan Çocuk Suçluluğu (Juvenile Delinquency From Psycho-Social Point of View)*. Istanbul: Istanbul Üniversitesi Edebiyat Fakültesi Yayınları.
Yavuzer, H. (1988). *Çocuk Psikolojisi*. İstanbul: Remzi Yayınevi.
Yenisey, F. (1992). Juvenile delinquency in Turkey. In H. Messmer & H.-U. Otto (Eds.), *Restorative justice on trial* (pp. 409–415). Springer: Netherlands.
Yıldız, Ö. (2007). Toplumsal Değişme Sürecinde Sokak Çocukları ve Sosyal Dışlanma. *Eğitim Bilim Toplum Dergisi, 5*(20), 56–72.
Yücel, M. (1989). Çocuk Suçluluğu ve Mahkemeler. UNICEF ve Devlet Planlama Teşkilatı (Yayınlayan), Türkiye'de Çocuğun Durumu, 149–175.
Yücel, D. (2016). Ceza İnfaz Kurumları. In D. Yücel & B. Gönültaş (Eds.), *Adli Sosyal Hizmet Yaklaşım ve Müdahele* (pp. 36–58). Ankara: Nobel Yayınclık.
Ziyalar, N. (2006). *Hukukçular İçin İletişim ve Mağdur ile Görüşme Teknikleri*. İstanbul: GOA Yayıncılık.

Index

S.H. Decker, N. Marteache (eds.), *International Handbook of Juvenile Justice*,
DOI 10.1007/978-3-319-45090-2

Kolibri 360 GmbH
Ferdinand-Jühlke-Straße 7
99095 Erfurt, Deutschland
produktsicherheit@kolibri360.de